"This book does a good job of looking at the big picture and the interaction of different cultures that helped form our global world." — Ken Faunce, *University of Idaho*

"Students will not be overwhelmed by a rash of details and will take away a big picture about the history of the world that raises interesting questions about today." — Laura A. Smoller, *University of Arkansas at Little Rock*

"After reading the brief sections, one comes away with a better understanding of these societies than if one had waded through a conventional text." — Barbara A. Moss, *Clark Atlanta University*

"Strayer's text is characterized by a commitment to thematic focus and clarity that should be of great assistance to students as they prepare for essays and analytical questions." — Abel Alves, *Ball State University*

"The class using the Strayer chapters saw an increase of ten points, or an entire grade, when compared to classes of the last twelve years. It was remarkable. I have never been forced to give so many A grades before." — Eric Mayer, *Victor Valley College*

"Unlike most world history texts, it avoids the chronological/geographic formula and instead embraces comparison, connections, and change in a deliberately brief text: quite an achievement." — Timothy J. Coates, *College of Charleston*

"Strayer's engaging book discusses world history not as separate threads that connect and entangle at some points, but as a tapestry where complex events and issues are contextualized in a big-picture approach that emphasizes change, connection, and comparison." — Charles Didier Gondola, *Indiana University–Purdue University Indianapolis*

"An entirely new and engaging approach to the topic. Instead of the traditional chronological slog through various 'civilizations,' the author offers a unique cross-continents examination of world systems of trade and social organization." — Theresa Jordan, *Washington State University*

"The author shows a remarkable agility and flexibility in dealing with cases and examples from all over the planet." — James A. Wood, *North Carolina A&T State University*

Alaska

CANADA

UNITED STATES

Greenland
(Den.)

ICELAND

UNITED
KINGDOM

IRELAND

FRANCE

SPAIN

PORTUGAL

ATLANTIC
OCEAN

Azores
(Port.)

MOROCCO

Canary Is.
(Sp.)

Western Sahara
(Mor.)

Hawaii

MEXICO

BAHAMAS

DOMINICAN
REPUBLIC

HAITI

CUBA

JAMAICA

BELIZE

HONDURAS

GUATEMALA

EL SALVADOR

NICARAGUA

COSTA RICA

PANAMA

Puerto Rico (U.S.)

ST. KITTS AND NEVIS

ANTIGUA AND BARBUDA

DOMINICA

Guadeloupe (Fr.)

Martinique (Fr.)

ST. VINCENT AND THE GRENADINES

ST. LUCIA

BARBADOS

GRENADA

TRINIDAD AND TOBAGO

GUYANA

SURINAME

French Guiana (Fr.)

VENEZUELA

COLOMBIA

CAPE
VERDE

MAURITANIA

SENEGAL

GAMBIA

GUINEA-BISSAU

GUINEA

SIERRA LEONE

LIBERIA

CÔTE D'IVOIRE

BURKINA FASO

GHANA

MALI

PACIFIC OCEAN

Galápagos Is.
(Ec.)

ECUADOR

PERU

BRAZIL

BOLIVIA

PARAGUAY

SAMOA

TONGA

Easter I.
(Chile)

CHILE

URUGUAY

ARGENTINA

ATLANTIC
OCEAN

Falkland Is.
(U.K.)

Abbreviations

ALB.	ALBANIA
AUS.	AUSTRIA
BEL.	BELGIUM
B.H.	BOSNIA AND HERZEGOVINA
CR.	CROATIA
CZ. REP.	CZECH REPUBLIC
DEN.	DENMARK
F.Y.R.O.M.	FORMER YUGOSLAV REPUBLIC OF MACEDONIA
HUNG.	HUNGARY
K.	KOSOVO
LUX.	LUXEMBOURG
M.	MONTENEGRO
NETH.	NETHERLANDS
SLK.	SLOVAKIA
SLN.	SLOVENIA
S.M.	SERBIA AND MONTENEGRO
SWITZ.	SWITZERLAND

0   1,500   3,000 miles

0   1,500   3,000 kilometers

Ways of the World

A Brief Global History

VOLUME I: TO 1500

Ways of the World
A Brief Global History

ROBERT W. STRAYER

California State University, Monterey Bay

Bedford/St. Martin's

Boston • New York

For Bedford/St. Martin's

Publisher for History: Mary Dougherty
Director of Development for History: Jane Knetzger
Developmental Editor: Jim Strandberg
Senior Production Editor: Bridget Leahy
Senior Production Supervisor: Joe Ford
Executive Marketing Manager: Jenna Bookin Barry
Editorial Assistant: Lynn Sternberger
Production Assistant: Lidia MacDonald-Carr
Copyeditor: Linda McLatchie
Text and Cover Design: Joyce Weston
Cover Art: Tomb of Sennedjem (Workmen's Tomb), Deir el-Medina, Tombs of the Nobles, Thebes, Egypt. Detail showing reaping wheat in the mythical fields of Iaru. Werner Forman/Art Resources, NY

Frontispiece: Muslim astronomers. University Library, Istanbul, Turkey/The Bridgeman Art Library
Cartography: Mapping Specialists Limited
Indexer: EdIndex
Composition: Aptara®, Inc.
Printing and Binding: RR Donnelley and Sons

President: Joan E. Feinberg
Editorial Director: Denise B. Wydra
Director of Marketing: Karen R. Soeltz
Director of Editing, Design, and Production: Marcia Cohen
Assistant Director of Editing, Design, and Production: Elise S. Kaiser
Managing Editor: Elizabeth M. Schaaf

Library of Congress Control Number: 2008925891

Manufactured in the United States of America.

1 2 3 4 5 6   12 11 10 09 08

For information, write: Bedford/St. Martin's,
75 Arlington Street, Boston, MA 02116
(617-399-4000)

ISBN-10: 0-312-45287-X ISBN-13: 978-0-312-45287-2 (combined edition)
ISBN-10: 0-312-45288-8 ISBN-13: 978-0-312-45288-9 (Vol. 1)
ISBN-10: 0-312-45289-6 ISBN-13: 978-0-312-45289-6 (Vol. 2)
ISBN-10: 0-312-55728-0 ISBN-13: 978-0-312-55728-7 (high school edition)

Acknowledgments: Acknowledgments and copyrights can be found at the back of the book on page 404, which constitutes an extension of the copyright page.

To Alisa and her generation

Preface

WHEN I ENTERED COLLEGE IN 1960, there was no such thing as a world history course, either in my school or almost anywhere else in the country. When I started teaching at the college level in 1970, the study of world history was just beginning to make itself felt, and the State University of New York College at Brockport, where I taught for many years, was among the first to offer an introductory world history course. By the time I began teaching in California in 2002, world history had become an established and rapidly growing enterprise, in both secondary schools and universities, all across the country. Thus, as a teaching field, world history is a relatively new entry in the course lists of American universities, and as a subject for research and writing, it represents a new agenda within the historical profession.

This flowering of world history has coincided almost precisely with my own career in the academy. Over the course of several decades, I have been able to roam the world with history—as a student, a teacher, a scholar and writer, a traveler, and an active participant in the world history movement. My involvement in the more specialized fields of African and, later, Soviet history has likewise contributed much to the more central focus of my academic life, which is world history.

Like many others who have been attracted to this most exciting field of study, I have become something of a "specialist of the whole" rather than a specialist in one of its parts. No teacher or writer, of course, can be master of the vast array of cultures, themes, and time periods that world history encompasses. However, those of us interested in world history read widely; we look for the big picture processes and changes that have marked the human journey; we are alert to the possibilities of comparison across cultural boundaries; and we pay special attention to the multiple interactions among human communities. Students, the wider public, and professional scholars alike need the larger integrated view of the past that world history provides as well as the more focused and specialized understandings of particular countries, cultures, and peoples that most history courses offer.

On a professional level, world history has afforded me a distinctive and fulfilling career, allowing me to sample a variety of specialized fields, to interact with a remarkable community of scholars and teachers, and to engage thousands of students with the larger trajectory of the human story. More personally, my career in world history has been an immensely fruitful journey, for I have encountered times, places, and peoples that otherwise would have lain well outside my own experience. The writing of *Ways of the World* has provided an opportunity to crystallize the work of my adult life and to share it with others. Doing so has been a rare and rich privilege.

What's in a Title?

The title of a book should evoke something of its character and outlook. *Ways of the World* is intended to suggest at least three dimensions of this text.

The first is **diversity** or **variation**, for the "ways of the world," or the ways of being human in the world, have been many and constantly changing. World history, or global history as it is sometimes called, was conceived in part to counteract a Eurocentric perspective on the human past, deriving from several centuries of Western dominance on the world stage. This book seeks to embrace the experience of humankind in its vast diversity, while noticing the changing location of particular centers of innovation and wider influence.

A second meaning attached to the title *Ways of the World* involves an emphasis on major **panoramas**, **patterns**, or **pathways**, as opposed to highly detailed narratives. This reflects my own observation in the classroom, and that of many world history instructors, that students can easily feel overwhelmed by the sheer quantity of data that a course in global history can require of them. In this book, the larger patterns of world history appear in the foreground on center stage, while the plentiful details, data, and facts occupy the background, serving in supporting roles.

A third implication of the book's title lies in a certain **reflective** or **musing quality** of *Ways of the World*. It is a product of my own growing appreciation that history of any kind, and world history in particular, offers endless raw material for contemplating large questions. And so a final section in each chapter, titled "Reflections," raises questions about the nature of the historical enterprise and of the human processes it explores.

- Chapter 3, for example, about First Civilizations, ponders their ambiguous legacy—great achievements in size, complexity, innovation, and culture and equally great oppression, experienced in massive inequality, patriarchy, slavery, and war.

- Chapter 5, which deals with cultural traditions of the classical era, muses on the tensions or misunderstandings that sometimes arise between historians and the believers of various religious traditions.

- The Reflections section of Chapter 18, on the Industrial Revolution, asks whether we are presenting history as a horse race to the finish line of modernity and unduly celebrating those who arrived there first.

- Chapter 21, about the era of the world wars during the first half of the twentieth century, probes the possibility of deriving specific "lessons" from these conflicts and expresses some skepticism about the familiar notion that "history repeats itself."

Other chapters invite students to reflect on issues such as surprise or unexpectedness in the historical record and contingency or accident as modes of explanation. These Reflections sections seek to engage student readers with the larger and perhaps quasi-philosophical issues with which historians constantly grapple.

Achieving Coherence

The great virtue of world history lies in its inclusiveness, for it allows us to see the world and to see it whole, an obvious necessity given the demands of contemporary life. But that virtue is also the source of world history's greatest difficulty — telling a coherent story. How can we meaningfully present the planet's many and distinct peoples and their intersections with one another in the confines of a single book or a single term? What prevents that telling from bogging down in the endless detail of various civilizations or cultures, from losing the forest for the trees, from implying that history is just "one damned thing after another"?

Less Can Be More

Ways of the World seeks to cope with that fundamental conundrum of world history — the challenge of condensing the history of the world into a single text — in several ways. The first is relative brevity and a corresponding selectivity. This means, of course, leaving some things out or treating them more succinctly than some instructors might expect. The positive side of this brevity is that the textbook need not dominate the pedagogy of the course or overwhelm students with facts. It allows for more professorial creativity in constructing individual world history courses and in mixing and matching various reading materials. And wouldn't it be wonderful if we found students asking for "more," rather than complaining about "too much"?

Brevity also encourages a "themes and cases" rather than a "civilization-by-civilization" approach to the global past. Thus, most chapters in this book focus on a broad theme, explored on a global or transregional scale:

- classical-era empires in Chapter 4
- comparative social structures in Chapter 6
- long-distance commerce in Chapters 8 and 15
- the colonial experience in Chapter 20
- the communist experiment in Chapter 22
- twentieth-century globalization in Chapter 24

Such chapters explore a given theme in general while illustrating it with a few particular cases.

The Three Cs of World History: Change, Comparison, Connection

As a further aid to achieving coherence on a global scale, *Ways of the World* refers repeatedly to what I call the "**three Cs**" of world history. They represent some of

the distinctive perspectives of world history as an academic discipline and are introduced more extensively in the prologue.

The first "C" emphasizes large-scale **changes**, both within and especially across
major regions of the world. Change, of course, is a central theme in all historical
study and serves to challenge "essentialist" descriptions of particular cultures or
peoples. Among the macrochanges highlighted in *Ways of the World* are

- agriculture in Chapter 2
- civilization in Chapter 3
- the rise of universal religions in Chapter 5
- the changing shape of the Islamic world in Chapter 11
- industrialization in Chapter 18
- European global dominance in Chapter 19
- the rise and fall of world communism in Chapter 22

The second "C" involves frequent **comparison**. It is a technique of integration through juxtaposition, of bringing several regions or cultures into our field of
vision at the same time. It encourages reflection both on the common elements of
the human experience and on the many variations in that experience. Such comparisons are a prominent feature of virtually every chapter of the book. We examine the difference, for example,

- between the Agricultural Revolution in the Eastern Hemisphere and that in
  the Western Hemisphere (Chapter 2)
- between early Mesopotamian and Egyptian civilizations (Chapter 3)
- between the beginnings of Buddhism and the early period of Christianity
  (Chapter 5)
- between European and Asian empires of the early modern era (Chapter 14)
- between the Chinese and the Japanese response to European intrusion
  (Chapter 19)
- between Iran and Turkey within the twentieth-century Islamic world
  (Chapter 23)

The final "C" emphasizes **connections**, networks of communication and
exchange that increasingly shaped the character of those societies that participated
in them. For world historians, cross-cultural interaction becomes one of the major
motors of historical change. Such connections are addressed in nearly every chapter.
For example:

- Chapter 3 explores the clash of the Greeks and the Persians during the
  classical era.
- Chapter 8 highlights the long-distance commercial networks that linked the Afro-
  Eurasian world and, less extensively, the Western Hemisphere in premodern times.

- Chapter 11 focuses attention on the transregional world of Islam.
- Chapter 12 turns the spotlight on the multiple interactions of the Mongol era.
- Chapters 14 and 15 explore various facets of the transhemispheric Columbian exchange of the early modern era.
- Chapter 17 probes the linkages among the Atlantic revolutions of the late eighteenth and early nineteenth centuries.
- Chapter 24 concludes the book with an examination of globalization, highlighting its economic, feminist, religious, and environmental dimensions.

Organizing World History: Chronology, Theme, and Region

Organizing a world history textbook is, to put it mildly, a daunting task. How should we divide up the seamless stream of human experience into manageable and accessible pieces, while recognizing always that such divisions are both artificial and to some extent arbitrary? Historians, of course, debate the issue endlessly. In structuring *Ways of the World*, I have drawn on my own sense of "what works" in the classroom, on a personal penchant for organizational clarity, and on established practice in the field. The outcome has been an effort to balance three principles of organization—chronology, theme, and region—in a flexible format that can accommodate a variety of teaching approaches and organizational strategies.

The chronological principle is expressed most clearly in the overall structure of the book, which divides world history into six major periods. Each of these six parts begins with a brief **Big Picture essay** that introduces the general patterns of a particular period and raises questions about the problems historians face in dividing up the human past into meaningful chunks of time.

Part One (to 500 B.C.E.) deals in three separate chapters with beginnings—of human migration and social construction in the Paleolithic era, of agriculture, and of civilization. Each of them pursues an important theme on a global scale and illustrates that theme with regional examples treated comparatively.

Part Two, on the classical era (500 B.C.E. to 500 C.E.), likewise employs the thematic principle in exploring the major civilizations of Eurasia (Chinese, Indian, Persian, and Mediterranean), with separate chapters focusing on their empires (Chapter 4), cultural traditions (Chapter 5), and social organization (Chapter 6). This structure represents a departure from conventional practice, which usually treats the classical era on a civilization-by-civilization basis, but it allows for more effective and pointed comparison. These Eurasian chapters are followed by a single chapter (Chapter 7) that examines regionally the classical era in sub-Saharan Africa and the Americas, while asking whether their histories largely follow Eurasian patterns or depart from them.

Part Three embraces the thousand years between 500 and 1500 C.E., often known simply, and not very helpfully, as the "postclassical" era. The Big Picture essay for Part Three spotlights and seeks to explain a certain vagueness in our descriptions of this period of time, pointing out the various distinctive civilizational patterns of that millennium as well as the accelerating interactions among them. The six chapters of Part Three reflect a mix of thematic and regional principles. Chapter 8 focuses topically on commercial networks, while Chapters 9, 10, and 11 deal regionally with the Chinese, Christian, and Islamic worlds respectively. Chapter 12 treats pastoral societies as a broad theme and the Mongols as the most dramatic illustration of their impact on the larger stage of world history. Chapter 13, which bridges the two volumes of the book, presents an around-the-world tour in the fifteenth century, which serves both to conclude Volume 1 and to open Volume 2.

In considering the early modern era (1450–1750), **Part Four** treats each of its three constituent chapters thematically. Chapter 14 compares European and Asian empires; Chapter 15 lays out the major patterns of global commerce and their consequences (trade in spices, silver, furs, and slaves); and Chapter 16 focuses on cultural patterns, including the globalization of Christianity and the rise of modern science.

Part Five takes up the era of maximum European influence in the world, from 1750 to 1914. Here the Big Picture essay probes how we might avoid Eurocentrism, while describing a period of time in which Europeans were in fact increasingly central to the global story. Part Five, which charts the emergence of a distinctively modern society in Europe, devotes separate chapters to the Atlantic revolutions (Chapter 17) and the Industrial Revolution (Chapter 18). Then it turns to the growing impact of those societies on the rest of humankind—on China, the Ottoman Empire, and Japan, which are treated comparatively in Chapter 19; and on the world of formal colonies in Chapter 20.

The most recent century (1914–2008), which is treated in **Part Six**, is perhaps the most problematic for world historians, given the abundance of data and the absence of time to sort out what is fundamental and what is peripheral. The Big Picture essay that opens Part Six explores this difficulty, asking whether that century deserves the status of a separate period in the human story. Chapters 21, 22, and 23 examine respectively three major regions of the world in that century—the Western or industrial world, the communist world, and the third or developing world—while Chapter 24 explores the multiple processes of globalization, which have both linked and divided the human community in new ways.

Promoting Active Learning: Focus on Features

As all instructors know, students can often "do the assignment" or read the required chapter and yet have nearly no understanding of it when they come to class. The problem, frequently, is passive studying—a quick once-over, perhaps some highlighting of the text—but little sustained involvement with the material. A central pedagogical problem in all teaching at every level is how to encourage more active, engaged styles of learning. How can we push students to articulate in their own words the major ideas of a particular chapter or section of the text? How can we encourage them to recognize arguments, even in a textbook, and to identify and evaluate the evidence on which those arguments are based? Active learning seeks to enable students to manipulate the information of the book, using its ideas and data to answer questions, to make comparisons, to draw conclusions, to criticize assumptions, and to infer implications that are not explicitly disclosed in the book itself. This ability to use and rearrange the material of a text, not simply to recall it, lies at the heart of active college-level learning.

Ways of the World incorporates a number of features or learning aids that are designed to promote active learning, to assist students in reading the text and instructors in teaching it, and to generate more lively classroom exchanges.

- The part-opening **Big Picture essays** preview for students what follows in the subsequent chapters. In doing so, they provide a larger context for those chapters; they enable students to make comparisons with greater ease; they facilitate making connections across several chapters; and they raise questions about periodization.

- Each Big Picture essay is followed by a **Landmarks timeline**, providing a chronological overview of what follows in that particular part of the book. Each of these Landmarks is organized in a series of parallel regional timelines, allowing students to see at a glance significant developments in various regions of the world during the same time.

- A **contemporary vignette** opens each chapter with a story that links the past and the present. Chapter 1, for example, presents Gudo Mahiya, a twenty-first-century member of a gathering and hunting society in Tanzania, who rejects an opportunity to become a settled farmer or herder. Chapter 15, which describes the Atlantic slave trade, opens with a brief account of an African American woman who in 2002 visited what had been a slave port in Ghana. These vignettes seek to show the continuing resonance of the past in the lives of contemporary people.

- To encourage active learning explicitly, a series of **questions in the margins** provides students with "something to look for" as they read particular sections. Those notations also indicate what kind of question is being asked—about change, comparison, or connection, for example. Such questions relate directly to the material that follows. In Chapter 5, for example, beside a discussion of the major schools of thought in classical-era China, a marginal question asks: "Comparison: What different answers to the problem of disorder arose in classical China?" And in Chapter 17, just before a discussion of Latin American independence movements, there appears this marginal question: "Connection: How were the Spanish American revolutions shaped by the American, French, and Haitian revolutions that happened earlier?"

- To further foster active learning, the **Second Thoughts** section at the end of each chapter provides a list of particulars (people, places, events, processes, concepts) under the heading "**What's the Significance?**" inviting students to check their grasp of that chapter's material. The next part of the Second Thoughts section is a set of **Big Picture Questions**. Unlike the marginal questions, which are keyed specifically to the adjacent material, these Big Picture Questions are not directly addressed in the text. Instead, they provide opportunities for integration, comparison, analysis, and sometimes speculation. Such questions might well become the basis for engaging writing assignments, class discussions, or exam items. Finally, a limited **list of suggested readings**—books, articles, and Web sites—invites further exploration of the material in the chapter.

- **Snapshots** appear in every chapter and present succinct glimpses of particular themes, regions, or time periods, adding some trees to the forest of world history. A Snapshot in Chapter 3, for example, compares six different early writing systems, while another in Chapter 11 summarizes key achievements in Islamic science and scholarship. In Chapter 15, a Snapshot briefly summarizes the numerical dimensions of the Atlantic slave trade, and in Chapter 22, yet another Snapshot illustrates with statistical data the accomplishments, limitations, and tragedies of China under Maoist communism.

- As is always true of books published by Bedford/St. Martin's, a **rich program of maps and images** accompanies the narrative. Because history and geography are so closely related, more than 100 maps have been included in the two volumes of the book. They have been carefully chosen to orient the reader to the parts of the world described in the text. About 150 images, most of them contemporary to the times and places they illustrate, provide visual evidence of the ways people understood their worlds and their lives.

Supplements

A comprehensive collection of print and electronic resources for students and instructors accompanies this book. Developed with my collaboration, they are designed to provide a host of practical learning and teaching aids.

For Students

Print Resources

World History Matters: A Student Guide to World History Online. Based on the popular "World History Matters" Web site produced by the Center for History and New Media, this unique resource, written by Kristin Lehner (The Johns Hopkins University), Kelly Schrum (George Mason University), and T. Mills Kelly (George Mason University), combines reviews of 150 of the most useful and reliable world history Web sites, with an introduction that guides students in locating, evaluating, and correctly citing online sources. The Web sites offer opportunities for researching broad themes as well as special topics and regions and feature a range of sources, including primary documents, maps, art, photographs, statistics, and audio and video recordings. This resource is available free when packaged with the text.

Bedford Series in History and Culture.   More than 100 titles in this highly praised series combine first-rate scholarship, historical narrative, and important primary documents for undergraduate courses. Each book is brief, inexpensive, and focused on a specific topic or period. Package discounts are available.

Trade Books.   Titles published by sister companies Farrar, Straus and Giroux; Henry Holt and Company; Hill and Wang; Picador; and St. Martin's Press are available at a 50 percent discount when packaged with Bedford/St. Martin's textbooks. For more information, visit bedfordstmartins.com/tradeup.

New Media Resources

Online Study Guide at bedfordstmartins.com/strayer.   The Online Study Guide helps students synthesize the material covered in *Ways of the World*. For each chapter, it provides a multiple-choice self-test that focuses on important conceptual ideas; an identification quiz that helps students remember key people, places, and events; a flashcard activity that tests students' knowledge of key terms; and two interactive map activities intended to strengthen students' geographic skills. Instructors can monitor students' progress through an online Quiz Gradebook or receive e-mail updates.

Jules Benjamin, **A Student's Online Guide to History Reference Sources at bedfordstmartins.com/strayer.**   This Web site provides links to history-related databases, indexes, and journals, plus contact information for state, provincial, local, and professional history organizations.

The Bedford Bibliographer at bedfordstmartins.com/strayer.   *The Bedford Bibliographer*, a simple but powerful Web-based tool, assists students with the process of collecting sources and generates bibliographies in four commonly used documentation styles.

The Bedford Research Room at bedfordstmartins.com/strayer.   The Research Room, drawn from Mike Palmquist's *The Bedford Researcher*, offers a wealth of resources—including interactive tutorials, research activities, student writing samples, and links to hundreds of other places online—to support students in courses across the disciplines. The site also offers instructors a library of helpful instructional tools.

Diana Hacker's **Research and Documentation Online at bedfordstmartins .com/strayer.**   This Web site provides clear advice on how to integrate primary and secondary sources into research papers, how to cite sources correctly, and how to format in MLA, APA, *Chicago*, or CBE style.

The St. Martin's Tutorial on Avoiding Plagiarism at bedfordstmartins .com/strayer.   This online tutorial reviews the consequences of plagiarism and explains what sources to acknowledge, how to keep good notes, how to organize research, and how to integrate sources appropriately. The tutorial includes exercises to help students practice integrating sources and recognize acceptable summaries.

For Instructors

Print Resources

Instructor's Resource Manual.   This extensive manual by Eric W. Nelson (Missouri State University) and Phyllis G. Jestice (University of Southern Mississippi) offers both experienced and first-time instructors tools for presenting textbook material in exciting and engaging ways—chapter learning objectives; annotated chapter outlines; lecture strategies; tips for helping students with common misconceptions and difficult topics; a list of key terms and definitions; answer guidelines for in-text chapter questions; and suggestions for in-class activities (including using film, video, and literature), ways to start discussions, topics for debate, and analyzing primary sources. Each chapter concludes with a guide to all the chapter-specific supplements available with *Ways of the World*. A guide for first-time teaching assistants, two sample syllabi, a list of useful books for a first-time world history professor, and a list of books that form the basis of a world history reference library are also included.

New Media Resources

Instructor's Resource CD-ROM.   This disc provides instructors with ready-made and customizable PowerPoint multimedia presentations built around chapter outlines, maps, figures, and all images from the textbook, plus jpeg versions of all maps, figures, and images. The disc also contains chapter-related multiple-choice questions that can be used with the i-clicker personal response system.

Computerized Test Bank.   Written by Eric W. Nelson (Missouri State University) and Phyllis G. Jestice (University of Southern Mississippi), the test bank provides more than thirty exercises per chapter, including multiple-choice, fill-in-the-blank, short-answer, and full-length essay questions. Instructors can customize quizzes, add or edit both questions and answers, and export questions and answers to a variety of formats, including WebCT and Blackboard. The disc includes correct answers and essay outlines.

Book Companion Site at bedfordstmartins.com/strayer.   The companion
Web site gathers all the electronic resources for *Ways of the World*, including the
Online Study Guide and related Quiz Gradebook, at a single Web address and provides convenient links to lecture, assignment, and research materials, such as PowerPoint chapter outlines and the digital libraries at Make History.

Make History at bedfordstmartins.com/strayer.   Comprising the content of
Bedford/St. Martin's five acclaimed online libraries—Map Central, the Bedford
History Image Library, DocLinks, HistoryLinks, and PlaceLinks—Make History
provides one-stop access to relevant digital content, including maps, images, documents, and Web links. Students and instructors alike can search this free, easy-to-
use database by keyword, topic, date, or specific chapter of *Ways of the World* and
download the content they find. Instructors can also create collections of content and store them online for later use or post them to the Web to share with
students.

Content for Course Management Systems.   A variety of student and instructor
resources developed for this textbook is ready for use in course management systems
such as Blackboard, WebCT, and other platforms. This e-content includes nearly all
the offerings from the book's Online Study Guide as well as the book's test bank.

Videos and Multimedia.   A wide assortment of videos and multimedia CD-
ROMs on various topics in world history is available to qualified adopters.

"It Takes a Village"

In any enterprise of significance, "it takes a village," as they say. Bringing *Ways of
the World* to life, it seems, has occupied the energies of several villages.

 The largest of these villages consists of those many people who read the manuscript at various stages, and commented on it, sometimes at great length. I continue to be surprised at the power of this kind of collaboration. Frequently, I find
that passages I had regarded as polished to a gleaming perfection benefited greatly
from the collective wisdom and experience of these thoughtful reviewers. Many of
the readers were commissioned by Bedford/St. Martin's and are listed here in
alphabetical order, with my great thanks:

> Hedrick Alixopulos, *Santa Rosa Junior College*
> Abel Alves, *Ball State University*
> Monty Armstrong, *Cerritos High School*
> Eva Baham, *Southern University*
> Cheryl Barkey, *Cabrillo College*
> Eric Bobo, *Hinds Community College*
> Robert W. Brown, *University of North Carolina at Pembroke*

Deborah Buffton, *University of Wisconsin–La Crosse*
Mark W. Chavalas, *University of Wisconsin–La Crosse*
Katherine Clark, *SUNY Brockport*
Timothy J. Coates, *College of Charleston*
John Hillas Cole, *Hawaii Community College*
Melinda S. Courtney, *Saddleback College*
Michael R. Davidson, *Southern Illinois University, Carbondale*
Kyle Eidahl, *Florida A&M University*
Ken Faunce, *University of Idaho*
Nancy Fitch, *California State University, Fullerton*
J. Arch Getty, *University of California, Los Angeles*
Trevor Getz, *San Francisco State University*
Charles Didier Gondola, *Indiana University–Purdue University Indianapolis*
Stephen S. Gosch, *University of Wisconsin–Eau Claire*
Howell H. Gwin Jr., *Lamar University*
John K. Hayden, *Southwestern Oklahoma State University*
Beth Hodges, *Lenoir Community College*
Bryan Jack, *Winston–Salem State University*
Michele G. Scott James, *Mira Costa College*
Theresa Jordan, *Washington State University*
Theodore Kallman, *San Joaquin Delta College*
Carol A. Keller, *San Antonio College*
John Lavalle, *Western New Mexico University*
John Mack, *Labette Community College*
Moira Maguire, *University of Arkansas at Little Rock*
Susan Maneck, *Jackson State University*
Michael Markowski, *Westminster College*
Eric Martin, *Lewis-Clark State College*
Morag Martin, *SUNY Brockport*
Eric Mayer, *Victor Valley College*
Brendan McManus, *Bemidji State University*
Eben Miller, *Southern Maine Community College*
Barbara A. Moss, *Clark Atlanta University*
Andrew Muldoon, *Metropolitan State College of Denver*
Eric Nelson, *Missouri State University*
Leonora Neville, *The Catholic University of America*
Theodore A. Nitz, *Gonzaga University*
Patricia O'Neill, *Central Oregon Community College*
Bill Palmer, *Marshall University*
Stephen Rapp, *Georgia State University*
David Rayson, *Normandale Community College*
Salvador Rivera, *SUNY Cobleskill*
Eric C. Rust, *Baylor University*

David P. Sandgren, *Concordia College*
Daniel Sarefield, *Ohio State University*
Jane Scimeca, *Brookdale Community College*
Kenneth P. Serbin, *University of San Diego*
Robert P. Sherwood, *Georgia Military College*
John M. Simpson, *Pierce College*
Laura A. Smoller, *University of Arkansas at Little Rock*
William Storey, *Millsaps College*
Mark B. Tauger, *West Virginia University*
Donna A. Vinson, *Salem State College*
Frank J. Wetta, *Ocean County College*
James A. Wood, *North Carolina Agricultural and Technical State University*
Eloy Zárate, *Pasadena City College*

Others in the village of reviewers have been friends, family, and colleagues who graciously agreed to read portions of the manuscript and offer helpful counsel: Kabir Helminski, James Horn, Elisabeth Jay, David Northrup, Lynn Parsons, Katherine Poethig, Kevin Reilly, and Julie Shackford-Bradley.

The "Bedford village" has been a second community sustaining this enterprise and the one most directly responsible for the book's appearance in print. Its unofficial chief, at least for this project, has been Jim Strandberg, the development editor assigned to this book. He has read and reread every word, perused every map, and examined every image, all with exegetical care, offering suggestions, encouragement, praise, and useful criticism. As a student and teacher of history himself, Jim has brought to this delicate task the sensitivity of a fine historian as well as the competence of an outstanding editor.

Publisher Mary Dougherty first broached the possibility of this volume and, with a manner as lovely as it is professional, has provided overall editorial leadership and a calming balm to authorial anxieties. Jane Knetzger, director of development, has overseen the project from its beginning, bore my many questions with forbearance, and, even better, provided timely answers. Company president Joan Feinberg has, to my surprise and delight, periodically kept her own experienced hand in this pot, while executive editor Beth Welch, though fully engaged in her own projects, has served as counselor from the sidelines. Photo researcher Carole Frohlich identified and acquired the many images that grace *Ways of the World* and did so with amazing efficiency and courtesy. Senior editor Louise Townsend provided initial guidance as the project got under way, and Denise Wydra, the editorial director, has offered helpful encouragement.

Operating more behind the scenes in the Bedford village, a series of highly competent and always supportive people have shepherded this book along its way. A succession of capable editorial assistants—Holly Dye, Alix Roy, and Lynn Sternberger—provided invaluable assistance in handling the manuscript, contacting reviewers, and keeping on top of the endless details that such an enterprise demands. Bridget Leahy served as project editor during the book's production and, often under considerable pressure, did so with both grace and efficiency. Copy editor Linda McLatchie polished the prose and sorted out my inconsistent usages with a seasoned and perceptive eye.

Jenna Bookin Barry and Sally Constable have overseen the marketing process, while history specialist John Hunger and a cadre of humanities specialists and sales representatives have introduced the book to the academic world. Heidi Hood and Jack Cashman supervised the development of ancillary materials to support the book, and Donna Dennison ably coordinated research for the lovely covers that mark *Ways of the World*.

A final and much smaller community sustained this project and its author. It is that most intimate of villages that we know as a marriage. Here I pay wholly inadequate tribute to its other member, my wife, Suzanne Sturn. She knows how I feel, and no one else needs to.

To all my fellow villagers, I offer deep thanks for perhaps the richest intellectual experience of my professional life. I am grateful beyond measure.

Robert Strayer
La Selva Beach, California

Brief Contents

Contents

PART TWO   The Classical Era in World History, 500 B.C.E.–500 C.E.   *86*

PART THREE   An Age of Accelerating Connections, 500–1500   *208*

8   Commerce and Culture, 500–1500   *217*

Maps

Special Features

Landmarks

Snapshots

Prologue

From Cosmic History to Human History

IN THE BEGINNING, ACCORDING TO THE NAVAHO, the world was created by Holy People, who had long lived underground and were forced to the surface by a great flood, from which they escaped through a hollow reed. First Man and First Woman were later formed from ears of white and yellow corn. To the ancient Greeks, an original Cosmic Egg, floating on a formless mixture of air, water, and matter, gave birth to the deities of Earth and Sky, who then created the earth and all its living creatures, as well as the sun, moon, and stars. For the Hebrews of biblical times, God brought order out of a primordial chaos, creating light and darkness, the earth, and all its living creatures. Pronouncing it good, God then made the first humans, placing them in the Garden of Eden, where they soon encountered temptation and choice in the form of a serpent.

These are among the multitude of stories, or myths of origin, that seek to answer that fundamentally human question: what happened in the beginning? Such stories seek to anchor particular societies in a larger context, providing their people with a sense of place, purpose, and belonging. World historians are among the modern scholars who, like earlier tellers of creation stories, also seek to puzzle out the beginnings of the cosmos, of the earth, of life, and of humankind. Unlike myths of origin, though, modern creation stories rely largely on those fields of study that emerged from the Scientific Revolution of the sixteenth century and later—astronomy, physics, geology, biology. Such accounts claim to be truer and more certain, at least in a literal sense, for they can be checked and verified rather than simply accepted and believed. They are, however, stronger on *how* things began than on *why*. Although they provide a more factually detailed account of beginnings, they may have less to offer about the meaning of it all. Therefore, many people in the modern world have tried hard to reconcile scientifically derived understandings of "in the beginning" with the meaning-based accounts contained in long-standing religious traditions.

The History of the Universe

The very largest of these modern frameworks is sometimes called "big history." It is really the "history of everything" from the big bang to the present, and it extends over the enormous, almost unimaginable timescale of some 13.7 billion years, the current

$\mathcal{S}napshot$ **The History of the Universe as a Cosmic Calendar**[1]

Big bang	January 1	13.7 billion years ago
Stars and galaxies begin to form	End of January/ mid-February	12 billion years ago
Milky Way galaxy forms	March/early April	10 billion years ago
Origin of the solar system	September 9	4.7 billion years ago
Formation of the earth	September 15	4.5 billion years ago
Earliest life on earth	Late September/ early October	4 billion years ago
Oxygen forms on earth	December 1	1.3 billion years ago
First worms	December 16	658 million years ago
First fish, first vertebrates	December 19	534 million years ago
First reptiles, first trees	December 23	370 million years ago
Age of dinosaurs	December 24–28	329–164 million years ago
First humanlike creatures	December 31 (late evening)	2.7 million years ago
First agriculture	December 31: 11:59:35	12,000 years ago
Birth of the Buddha/ Greek civilization	December 31: 11:59:55	2,500 years ago
Birth of Jesus	December 31: 11:59:56	2,000 years ago
Aztec and Inca empires	December 31: 11:59:59	500 years ago

■ Change
What have been the major turning points in the prehuman phases of "big history"?

rough estimate of the age of the universe.[2] Big history provides the largest possible context in which the more familiar story of the human journey might be situated.

To make this vast expanse of time even remotely comprehensible, some scholars have depicted the history of the cosmos as if it were a single calendar year (see the Snapshot). On that cosmic calendar, most of the action took place in the first few milliseconds of January 1. As astronomers, physicists, and chemists tell it, the universe that we know began in an eruption of inconceivable power and heat. Out of that explosion of creation emerged matter, energy, gravity, electromagnetism, and the "strong" and "weak" forces that govern the behavior of atomic nuclei. As gravity pulled the rapidly expanding cosmic gases into increasingly dense masses, stars formed, with the first ones lighting up around 1 to 2 billion years after the big bang, or the end of January to mid-February on the cosmic calendar.

Hundreds of billions of stars followed, each with its own history, though following common patterns. Over eons of time, these stars came together in galaxies, such as our own Milky Way, which probably emerged in March or early April, and in even larger structures called groups, clusters, and superclusters. Within the stars, enormous nuclear reactions gave rise to the elements that are reflected in the periodic table known to all students of chemistry. But stars also collapse and die, and in doing so they sometimes generate supernova, black holes, and pulsars—phenomena at least as fantastic as the most exotic of earlier creation stories. Adding to the strangeness of our picture of the cosmos is the recent and controversial notion that perhaps 90 percent or more of the total mass of the universe is invisible to us, consisting of a mysterious and mathematically predicted substance known to scholars only as "dark matter."

The contemplation of cosmic history has prompted profound religious or philosophical questions about the meaning of human life. For some, it has engendered a sense of great insignificance in the face of cosmic vastness. In disputing the earth- and human-centered view of the Catholic Church, Voltaire, an eighteenth-century French thinker, wrote: "This little globe, nothing more than a point, rolls in space like so many other globes; we are lost in this immensity."[3] Nonetheless, human awareness of the mystery of this immeasurable universe renders us unique and generates for many people feelings of awe and humility that are almost religious. As tiny but knowing observers of this majestic cosmos, we have found ourselves living in a grander home than ever we knew before.

The History of a Planet

For most of us, one star, our own sun, is far more important than all the others, despite its quite ordinary standing among the billions of stars in the universe and its somewhat remote location on the outer edge of the Milky Way galaxy. Circling that star are a series of planets, formed of leftover materials from the sun's birth. One of those planets, the third from the sun and the fifth largest, is home to all of us. Human history—our history—takes place not only on the earth but also as part of the planet's history.

That history began with the emergence of the entire solar system about two-thirds of the way through cosmic history, some 4.7 billion years ago, or early September on the cosmic calendar. Geologists have learned a great deal about the history of the earth—the formation of its rocks and atmosphere, the movement of its continents, the collision of the tectonic plates that make up its crust, and the constantly changing landscape as mountains formed, volcanoes erupted, and erosion transformed the surface of the planet. All of this has been happening for more than 4 billion years and continues still.

The most remarkable feature of the earth's history—and so far as we know unrepeated elsewhere—was the emergence of life from the chemical soup of the early planet. It happened rather quickly, only about 600 million years after the earth itself took shape, or late September on the cosmic calendar. Then for some 3 billion years, life remained at the level of microscopic single-celled organisms. According to biologists, the many species of larger multicelled creatures—all of the flowers, shrubs, and trees as well as all of the animals of land, sea, and air—have evolved in an explosive proliferation of life-forms, punctuated by massive die-offs as well, over the past 600 million years, or since mid-December on the cosmic calendar.

Each of these species also has had a history as it struggled to find resources, cope with changing environments, and deal with competitors. The history of dinosaurs, for example, from their rise to their extinction, occupied about 165 million years, or about five days in late December on the cosmic calendar. Egocentric creatures that we are, however, virtually all of our history books and history courses focus entirely on a single species—our own, *Homo sapiens*, humankind. On the cosmic calendar, *Homo sapiens* is an upstart primate whose entire history occurred in the last few minutes of December 31. Almost all of what we normally study in history courses—agriculture, writing, civilizations, empires, industrialization—took place in the very last minute of that cosmic year.

Yet during that brief time, humankind has had a career more remarkable and arguably more consequential for the planet than any other species. At the heart of human uniqueness lies our amazing capacity for accumulating knowledge and skills. Other animals learn, of course, but they learn the same things over and over again. Twenty-first-century chimpanzees in the wild master the same skills as their ancestors did a million years ago, but the exceptional communication abilities provided by human language allow us to learn from one another, to express that learning in abstract symbols, and then to pass it on, cumulatively, to future generations. Thus we have moved from stone-tipped spears to nuclear weapons, from "talking drums" to the Internet, from ox-drawn carts to the family car.

This extraordinary ability has translated into a human impact on the earth that is unprecedented among all living species.[4] Human populations have multiplied far more extensively and have come to occupy a far greater range of environments than has any other large animal. Through our ingenious technologies, we have appropriated for ourselves, according to recent calculations, some 25 to 40 percent of the solar energy that enters the food chain. We have recently gained access to the stored solar energy of coal, gas, and oil, all of which have been millions of years in the making, and we have the capacity to deplete these resources in a few hundred or a few thousand years. Other forms of life have felt the impact of human activity, as numerous extinct or threatened species testify. Human beings have even affected the atmosphere itself as global warming alters the climate of the planet. Thus human history has been, and remains, of great significance not for ourselves alone, but also for the earth itself and for the many other living creatures with which we share it.

The History of the Human Species … in a Single Paragraph: A Preview

The history of our species has occupied roughly the last 250,000 years, conventionally divided into three major phases, based on the kind of technology that was most widely practiced. The enormously long Paleolithic age, with its gathering and hunting way of life, accounts for 95 percent or more of the time that humans have occupied the planet. People utilizing a Paleolithic technology initially settled every major landmass on the planet and constructed the first human societies (see Chapter 1). Then beginning about 12,000 years ago with the first Agricultural Revolution, the domestication of plants and animals increasingly became the primary means of sustaining human life and societies. In giving rise to farming village societies, to pastoral communities depending on their herds of animals, and to state- and city-based civilizations, this agrarian way of life changed virtually everything and fundamentally shaped the human experience ever since. Finally around 1750, a quite sudden spurt in the rate of technological change, which we know as the Industrial Revolution, took hold. That vast increase in productivity, wealth, and human control over nature once again transformed almost every aspect of human life and gave rise to new kinds of societies that we call "modern."

Here then, in a single paragraph, is the history of humankind—the Paleolithic era, the agricultural era, and, most recently and briefly, the modern industrial era. Clearly this is a world history perspective, encompassing the human species as a whole rather than focusing solely on one or another of its particular and distinctive cultures. That perspective—known variously as planetary, global, or world history—has become increasingly prominent among students of the past. Why should this be so?

Why World History?

Not long ago—in the mid-twentieth century, for example—virtually all college-level history courses were organized in terms of particular civilizations or nations. In the United States, courses such as Western Civilization or some version of American History served to introduce students to the study of the past. Since then, however, a set of profound changes has pushed much of the historical profession in a different direction.

The world wars of the twentieth century, revealing as they did the horrendous consequences of unchecked nationalism, persuaded some historians that a broader view of the past might contribute to a notion of global citizenship. Economic and cultural globalization has highlighted both the interdependence of the world's peoples and their very unequal positions within that world. Moreover, we are aware as never before that our problems—whether they involve economic well-being, environmental deterioration, disease, or terrorism—respect no national boundaries. To many thoughtful people, a global present seemed to call for a global past. Furthermore, as colonial empires shrank and newly defined third world peoples

■ **Change**
Why has world history achieved an increasingly prominent place in American education in recent decades?

asserted themselves on the world stage, these people also insisted that their histories be accorded equivalent treatment with those of Europe. An explosion of new knowledge about the histories of Asia, Africa, and pre-Columbian America erupted from the research of scholars around the world. All of this has generated a "world history movement," reflected in college and high school curricula, in numerous conferences and specialized studies, and in a proliferation of textbooks, of which this is one.

This world history movement has attempted to create a global understanding of the human past that highlights broad patterns cutting across particular civilizations and countries, while acknowledging in an inclusive fashion the distinctive histories of its many peoples. This is, to put it mildly, a tall order. How is it possible to encompass within a single book or course the separate stories of the world's various peoples? Surely it must be something more than just recounting the history of one civilization or culture after another. How can we distill a common history of humankind as a whole from the distinct trajectories of particular peoples? Because no world history book or course can cover everything, what criteria should we use for deciding what to include and what to leave out? Such questions have ensured no end of controversy among students, teachers, and scholars of world history, making it one of the most exciting fields of historical inquiry.

Comparison, Connection, and Change: The Three Cs of World History

Despite much debate and argument, most world historians would probably agree on three major issues or questions that define their field of study. Each of them confronts a particular problem in our understanding of the past.

The first involves constant **comparison**. Whatever else it may be, world history is a comparative discipline, seeking to identify similarities and differences in the experience of the world's peoples. What is the difference between the development of agriculture in the Middle East and in Mesoamerica? Was the experience of women largely the same in all patriarchal societies? What did the Roman Empire and Han dynasty China have in common? Why did the Industrial Revolution and a modern way of life evolve first in Western Europe rather than somewhere else? What distinguished the Russian and Chinese revolutions? What different postures toward modernity emerged within the Islamic world? Describing and, if possible, explaining such similarities and differences are among the major tasks of world history. Comparison, then, is a recurring theme in this book, with expressions in every chapter.

Comparison has proven an effective tool in the struggle against Eurocentrism, the notion that Europeans or people of European descent have long been the primary movers and shakers of the historical process. That notion arose in recent centuries when Europeans were in fact the major source of innovation in the world and did for a time exercise something close to world domination. This temporary preeminence decisively shaped the way Europeans thought and wrote about their own histories and those of other people. In their own eyes, Europeans alone were progressive people, thanks to some cultural or racial superiority. Everyone else was stagnant, backward, savage, or barbarian. The unusual power of Europeans allowed them for a time to act on those beliefs and to impose such ways of thinking on much of the world. World historians have been among the critics of such Eurocentric views, for world history sets European achievements in a comparative and global context, helping us to sort out what was distinctive about its historical development and what similarities it bore to other major regions of the world.

The art of comparison is a learned skill, entailing several steps. It requires, first of all, asking explicitly comparative questions and determining what particular cases will be involved. If you want to compare revolutions, for example, you would need to decide which ones you are considering—American, French, Russian, Chinese, Cuban. Defining categories of comparison is a further step. Precisely which characteristics of these revolutions will you compare—their origins, their ideologies, the social classes involved, their outcomes? Finally, how will you present your comparison? You might choose a case-by-case analysis in which you would describe, say, the American Revolution first, followed by an account of the Cuban Revolution, which makes explicit comparisons with the former. Or you might choose a thematic approach in which you would consider first the origins of both revolutions, followed by a comparison of their ideologies, and so on. You will find examples of both approaches in this book.

A second major theme of world history involves the interaction, encounters, and **connections** among different and often distant peoples. What happened when people of distinct civilizations or cultures met? Focusing on cross-cultural connections represents an effort to counteract a habit of thinking about particular peoples, states, or cultures as self-contained and isolated communities. Despite the historical emergence of separate and distinct societies, none of them developed alone. Each was embedded in a network of relationships with both near and more distant peoples. Moreover, these cross-cultural connections did not begin with the voyages of Columbus. The Chinese, for example, interacted continuously with the nomadic peoples on their northern border; generated technologies that diffused across all of Eurasia; transmitted elements of their culture to Japan, Korea, and Vietnam; and assimilated a foreign religious tradition, Buddhism, which had originated in India. Though clearly distinctive, China was not a self-contained or isolated civilization. The encounter with strangers, or at least with strange ideas and practices, was everywhere one of the most powerful motors of change in human societies. Thus world history pays attention not only to the internal developments of particular civilizations or peoples but also to the networks, webs, and cross-cultural encounters in which they were enmeshed.

Third, historians of every kind are concerned always with what changes, what persists, and why. In world history, it is the "big picture" **changes**—those that impact large segments of humankind—that are of greatest interest. How did the transition from a gathering and hunting economy to one based on agriculture take place? How did cities, empires, and civilizations take shape in various parts of the world? What generated the amazing transformations of the "revolution of modernity" in recent centuries? World historians also pay attention to the changes that occur within and between particular civilizations. How can we explain the dramatic collapse of Maya civilization or the fall of the Roman Empire? How did Buddhism change when it entered China? How was Islam transformed when it encountered West African societies? What lay behind the emergence of a new balance of global power after 1500, one that featured the growing prominence of Europe on the world stage?

Both change and comparison provide an antidote to a persistent tendency of human thinking that historians call "essentialism." A more common term is "stereotyping." It refers to our inclination to define particular groups of people with an unchanging or essential set of characteristics. Women are nurturing; peasants are conservative; Americans are aggressive; Hindus are religious. Serious students of history soon become aware that every significant category of people contains endless divisions and conflicts and that human communities are constantly in flux. Peasants may often accept the status quo, except of course when they rebel, as they frequently have. Americans have experienced periods of isolationism and withdrawal from the world as well as times of aggressive engagement with it. Things change.

But some things persist, even if they also change. We should not allow an emphasis on change to blind us to the continuities of human experience. A recognizably Chinese state has operated for more than 2,000 years. Slavery and patriarchy persisted as human institutions for thousands of years until they were challenged in recent centuries, and in various forms they exist still. The teachings of Buddhism, Christianity, and Islam have endured for centuries, though with endless variations and transformations.

Comparisons, connections, and changes—all of them operating on a global scale—represent three ways of bringing some coherence to the multiple and complex stories of world history. They will recur repeatedly in the pages that follow.

Second Thoughts

To assess your mastery of the material in this prologue, see the **Online Study Guide** at bedfordstmartins.com/strayer.

What's the Significance?

myths of origin	big history	the three Cs
cosmic calendar	comparative history	

Big Picture Questions

1. What is the difference between religiously based myths of origin and creation stories derived from scientific accounts?
2. How do you respond personally to modern notions of the immense size and age of the universe?
3. What examples of comparison, connection, and change in world history would you like to explore further as your course unfolds?

Next Steps: For Further Study

David Christian, *Maps of Time* (2004). A brilliant survey of "big history" by a leading world historian.

Ross Dunn, ed., *The New World History* (2000). A collection of articles dealing with the teaching of world history.

Patrick Manning, *Navigating World History* (2003). An up-to-date overview of the growth of world history, the field's achievements, and the debates within it.

J. R. McNeill and William H. McNeill, *The Human Web* (2003). An approach to world history that emphasizes the changing webs of connection among human communities.

David Northrup, "Globalization and the Great Convergence: Rethinking World History in the Long Term," *Journal of World History* (September 2005). A thoughtful essay identifying broad patterns of human history.

"The Cosmic Time-Line," http://visav.phys.uvic.ca/~babul/AstroCourses/P303/BB-slide.htm. A more detailed cosmic calendar.

"World History for Us All," http://worldhistoryforusall.sdsu.edu/dev/default.htm. A model world history curriculum for high school courses.

For Web sites and documents related to this prologue, see **Make History** at bedfordstmartins.com/strayer.

Ways of the World

A Brief Global History

First Things First

Beginnings in History

TO 500 B.C.E.

Contents

Turning Points in Early World History

Both the ancient sages who developed their societies' creation myths and the grand-parents who still relate the histories of their families have had to decide at what point to begin their stories and what major turning points in those stories to highlight. So too must historians, whether they narrate the tale of a village, a city, a nation, a civilization, or the entire human community. For world historians, concerned with humankind as a whole, four major "beginnings," each of them an extended histor-ical process, have charted the initial stages of the human journey.

The Emergence of Humankind

Ever since Charles Darwin, most scholars have come to view human beginnings in the context of biological change on the planet. In considering this enormous process, we operate on a timescale quite different from the billions of years that mark the history of the universe and of the earth. According to archeologists and anthropologists, the evolutionary line of descent leading to *Homo sapiens* diverged from that leading to chimpanzees, our closest primate relatives, some 5 million to 6 million years ago, and it happened in eastern and southern Africa. There, perhaps twenty or thirty different species emerged, all of them members of the Homininae (or hominid) family of humanlike creatures. What they all shared was bipedalism, the ability to walk upright on two legs. In 1976, the archeologist Mary Leakey uncovered in what is now Tanzania a series of footprints of three such hominid individuals, preserved in cooling volcanic ash about 3.5 million years ago. Two of them walked side by side, apparently holding hands.

Over time, these hominid species changed. Their brains grew larger, as evidenced by the size of their skulls. About 2.3 million years ago, a hominid creature known as *Homo habilis* began to make and use simple stone tools. Others started to eat meat, at least occasionally. By 1 million years ago, some hominid species, especially *Homo erectus*, began to migrate out of Africa, and their remains have been found in various parts of Eurasia. This species is also associated with the first controlled use of fire.

Eventually all of these earlier hominid species died out, except one: *Homo sapi-ens*, ourselves. We too emerged first in Africa and quite recently, probably no more than 250,000 years ago, although there is constant debate among specialists about these matters. For a long time, all of the small number of *Homo sapiens* lived in Africa, but sometime after 100,000 years ago, they too began to migrate out of Africa onto the Eurasian landmass, then to Australia, and ultimately into the Western Hemisphere and the Pacific islands. The great experiment of human history had begun.

The Global Dispersion of Humankind (p. 14)

The Globalization of Humankind

Today, every significant landmass on earth is occupied by human beings, but it was not always so. A mere half million years ago our species did not exist, and only 100,000 years ago that species was limited to Africa and numbered, some scholars believe, fewer than 10,000 individuals. These ancient ancestors of ours were armed with a very limited technology of stone tools with which to confront the dangers of the natural world. How did *Homo sapiens* move from such a modest role in the scheme of things to a worldwide and increasingly dominant presence? What kind of societies, technologies, and understandings of the world accompanied, and perhaps facilitated, this globalization of humankind?

The phase of human history during which these initial migrations took place is known to scholars as the *Paleolithic* era. The term "Paleolithic" literally means the "old stone age," but it refers more generally to a food-collecting or gathering and hunting way of life, before agriculture allowed people to grow food or raise animals deliberately. Lasting until roughly 11,000 years ago, the Paleolithic era represents over 95 percent of the time that human beings have inhabited the earth, although it accounts for only about 12 percent of the total number of people who have lived on the planet.

It was during this time that *Homo sapiens* colonized the world, making themselves at home in every environmental niche, from the frigid Arctic to the rain forests of Central Africa and Brazil, in mountains, deserts, and plains. It was an amazing achievement, accomplished by no other large species. Accompanying this global migration were slow changes in the technological tool kits of early humankind as well as early attempts to impose meaning on the world through art, ritual, and religion. Although often neglected by historians and history textbooks, this long period of the human experience merits greater attention and is the focus of Chapter 1.

The Revolution of Farming and Herding

In early 2008, almost all of the world's 6.6 billion people lived from the food grown on farms and gardens and from domesticated animals raised for their

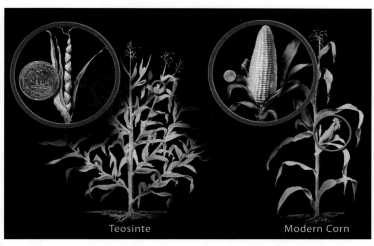

Teosinte

Modern Corn

Teosinte and Maize/Corn
(p. 42)

meat, milk, or eggs, but this was not always so. In fact, before 11,000 years ago, no one survived in this fashion. Then, repeatedly and fairly rapidly, at least in world history terms, human communities in parts of the Middle East, Asia, Africa, and the Americas began the laborious process of domesticating animals and selecting seeds to be planted. This momentous accomplishment represents another "first" in the human story. After countless millennia of relying on the gathering of wild foods and the hunting of wild animals, why and how did human societies begin to practice agriculture and herding? What changes to human life did this new technology bring with it?

This food-producing revolution, considered in Chapter 2, surely marks the single most significant and enduring transformation of the human condition, providing the foundation for virtually everything that followed. The entire period from the beginning of agriculture to the Industrial Revolution around 1750 might be considered a single phase of the human story—the age of agriculture—calculated now on a timescale of millennia or centuries rather than the more extended periods of earlier eras. Although the age of agriculture was far shorter than the immense Paleolithic era that preceded it, farming and herding allowed for a substantial increase in human numbers.

In the various beginnings of food production lay the foundations for some of the most enduring divisions within the larger human community. Much depended on the luck of the draw—on the climate and soils, on the various wild plants and animals that were available for domestication. Many agricultural peoples lived in small settled villages, independent of larger political structures, while drawing their food supply from their own gardens and farms. Some depended on root crops, such as potatoes in the Andes; others relied on tree crops, such as the banana; the most favored areas were those where highly nutritious wild grains such as rice, wheat, or corn could be domesticated. In more arid regions where farming was impossible, some peoples, known as pastoralists, came to depend heavily on their herds of domesticated animals. Because they moved frequently and in regular patterns, in search of pasturelands, they are often referred to as nomads. In terms of animal husbandry, the Americas were at a distinct disadvantage, for there were few large animals that could be tamed—no goats, sheep, pigs, horses, camels, or cattle. In the Afro-Eurasian world, conflicts between settled agricultural peoples and more mobile pastoral peoples represented an enduring pattern of interaction across the region.

The Turning Point of Civilization

The most prominent and powerful human communities to emerge from the Agricultural Revolution were those we often designate as "civilizations," societies that were based in bustling cities and governed by powerful states. Virtually all of the world's people now live in a state with a formal political authority that controls a particular territory, whether it is a tiny country such as The Gambia, a single city such as Singapore, or a huge territory such as Russia. The political, economic, and cultural life of state-based societies everywhere gives prominence to cities. By the early twenty-first century, about half of the world's population lived in urban centers. States and cities have become so common as to seem almost natural.

In world history terms, however, the appearance of states and cities is a rather recent phenomenon. Not until several thousand years *after* the beginning of agriculture did the first cities and states emerge, around 3500 B.C.E. Well after 1000 C.E., substantial numbers of people still lived in communities without any state or urban structures. Nonetheless, people living in state- and city-based societies or civilizations have long constituted the most powerful and innovative human communities on the planet. They gave rise to empires of increasing size, to enduring cultural and religious traditions, to new technologies, to sharp class inequalities, to male domination (patriarchy), and to large-scale warfare.

For all of these reasons, civilizations have featured prominently in accounts of world history, sometimes crowding out the stories of other kinds of human communities. The earliest civilizations, which emerged between 3500 and 500 B.C.E., have long fascinated professional historians and lovers of history everywhere. In at least six separate places—Mesopotamia (present-day Iraq), Egypt, Pakistan and northern India, China, Peru, and Mexico—such state- and city-based societies emerged. What was their relationship to the Agricultural Revolution? What new ways of life did they bring to the experience of humankind? These are the questions that are examined in Chapter 3.

A Note on Dates

Recently it has become standard in the Western world to refer to dates prior to the birth of Christ as B.C.E. (before the Common Era), replacing the earlier B.C. (before Christ) usage. This convention is an effort to become less Christian-centered and

Eurocentric in our use of language, although the chronology remains linked to the birth of Jesus. Similarly the time following the birth of Christ is referred to as C.E. (the Common Era) rather than A.D. (*Anno Domini*, Latin for "year of the Lord"). Dates in the more distant past are designated in this book simply as so many "years ago." Of course, these conventions are only some of the many ways that human societies have reckoned time. The Chinese frequently dated important events in terms of the reign of particular emperors, while Muslims created a new calendar beginning with Year 1, marking Muhammad's emigration to Medina in 622 C.E. As with so much else, the ways that we measure time reflect the cultures in which we have been born and the historical experience of our societies.

Landmarks of Early World History, to 500 B.C.E.

27,000	26,000	25,000	24,000	23,000	22,000	21,000	20,000	19,000	18,000	17,000	16,000	15,000	14,000

Africa

◄ **250,000 years ago**
Emergence of *Homo sapiens*

◄ **100,000 years ago**
Human migration out of Africa into Eurasia

16,000–9000 B.C.E.
Development of distinctive regional cultures

Eurasia

◄ **60,000 years ago**
Human entry into Australia

◄ **40,000 years ago**
Human entry into Europe

■ **15,000 B.C.E.**
Lascaux cave paintings in southern France

The Americas

◄ **30,000–15,000 years ago**
Human entry into the Americas

13,000	12,000	11,000	10,000	9000	8000	7000	6000	5000	4000	3000	2000	1000	900

3000–2000 B.C.E.
Agricultural breakthroughs in sub-Saharan Africa

13,000–11,000 B.C.E.
Harvesting of wild grains in northeastern Africa

9000 B.C.E.
Cattle herding in Sudanic Africa

3100 B.C.E.
Unification of Egypt

1000 B.C.E.
Beginning of ironworking in sub-Saharan Africa

3500 B.C.E.
Emergence of Nubian civilization

2000 B.C.E. Beginnings of Bantu migrations

1650 B.C.E. Hyksos invasion of Egypt

14,000–8000 B.C.E.
End of last Ice Age

9000–7000 B.C.E. First agricultural breakthrough (Fertile Crescent)

4000 B.C.E.
Domestication of horses in Ukraine/southern Russia

2000 B.C.E. Beginnings of Indus Valley and Chinese civilizations

1792–1750 B.C.E.
Reign of Hammurabi in Babylonian Empire

3000–1000 B.C.E.
Indo-European migrations

3500 B.C.E.
Beginning of Mesopotamian civilization

1500–1000 B.C.E.
Beginnings of ironworking in Anatolia

10,000–9000 B.C.E.
Flourishing of Clovis culture

9000 B.C.E.
Extinction of various large mammals in North America

3000–2000 B.C.E.
Cultivation of maize, squash, and beans in Mesoamerica

3000–2000 B.C.E.
Cultivation of potatoes, quinoa, and manioc in the Andes

3000–1800 B.C.E.
Norte Chico ("mother civilization" of the Andes)

1000 B.C.E.
Beginnings of Olmec civilization

900 B.C.E.
Chavín religious cult in Peru

First Peoples

Populating the Planet

TO 10,000 B.C.E.

"We do not want cattle, just wild animals to hunt and water that we can drink."[1] That was the view of Gudo Mahiya, a prominent member of the Hadza people of northern Tanzania, when he was questioned in 1997 about his interest in a settled life of farming and cattle raising. With only about 1,000 total members, the Hadza represent one of the very last peoples on earth to continue a way of life that was universal among humankind until 10,000 to 12,000 years ago. At the beginning of the twenty-first century, several hundred Hadza still made a living by hunting game, collecting honey, digging up roots, and gathering berries and fruit. They lived in quickly assembled grass huts located in small mobile camps averaging eighteen people and moved frequently around their remote region. Almost certainly their way of life is doomed, as farmers, governments, missionaries, and now tourists descend on them. The likely disappearance of their culture parallels the experience of many other such societies, which have been on the defensive against more numerous and powerful neighbors for 10,000 years.

NONETHELESS, THAT WAY OF LIFE SUSTAINED HUMANKIND for more than 95 percent of the time that our species has inhabited the earth. During countless centuries, human beings successfully adapted to a wide variety of environments without benefit of deliberate farming or animal husbandry. Instead, our early ancestors wrested a livelihood by gathering wild foods such as berries, nuts, roots, and grain; by scavenging dead animals; by hunting live animals; and by fishing. Known to scholars as "gathering and hunting" peoples, they were foragers or food collectors

Paleolithic Art: The rock art of gathering and hunting peoples has been found in Africa, Europe, Australia, and elsewhere. This image from the San people of southern Africa represents aspects of their outer life in the form of wild animals and hunters with bows as well as the inner life of their shamans during a trance, reflected in the elongated figures with both human and animal features. (Image courtesy of S.A. Tourism) rather than food producers. Instead of requiring the earth to produce what they wanted, they took—or perhaps borrowed—what nature had to offer. Because they used stone rather than metal tools, they also have been labeled "Paleolithic," or "old stone age," peoples.

History courses and history books often neglect this long phase of the human journey and instead choose to begin the story with the coming of agriculture about 12,000 years ago or with the advent of civilizations about 5,000 years ago. Some historians identify "real history" with writing and so dismiss the Paleolithic era as largely unknowable because its people did not write. Others, impressed with the rapid pace of change in human affairs since the coming of agriculture, assume that nothing much of real significance happened in the Paleolithic era—and no change meant no history.

But does it make sense to ignore the first 200,000 years or more of human experience? Although written records are absent, scholars have learned a great deal about these people through their material remains: stones and bones, fossilized seeds, rock paintings and engravings, and much more. Archeologists, biologists, botanists, demographers, linguists, and anthropologists have contributed much to our growing understanding of gathering and hunting peoples. Furthermore, the achievements of Paleolithic peoples—the initial settlement of the planet, the creation of the earliest human societies, the beginning of reflection on the great questions of life and death—deserve our attention. The changes they wrought, though far more slowly than we are accustomed to, provided the foundation on which all subsequent human history was constructed. Our grasp of the human past is incomplete—massively so—if we choose to disregard them.

Out of Africa to the Ends of the Earth: First Migrations

The first 150,000 years or more of human experience was an exclusively African story. Around 250,000 years ago, in the grasslands of eastern and southern Africa, *Homo sapiens* first emerged, following in the footsteps of many other hominid species before it. Time and climate have erased much of the record of these early people, and Africa has witnessed much less archeological research than have other parts of the world, especially Europe. Nonetheless, scholars have turned up evidence of distinctly human behavior in Africa long before its appearance elsewhere. Africa, almost certainly, was the place where the "human revolution" occurred, where "culture," defined as learned or invented ways of living, became more important than biology in shaping behavior.

What kinds of uniquely human activity show up in the early African record?[2] In the first place, human beings began to inhabit new environments within Africa—forests and deserts—where no hominids had lived before. Accompanying these movements of people were technological innovations of various kinds: stone blades and points fastened to shafts replaced the earlier "hand axes"; tools made from bones appeared, and so did grindstones. Evidence of hunting and fishing, not just the scavenging of dead animals, marks a new phase in human food collection.

Snapshot   **The Long Road to the Global Presence of Humankind**

(all dates approximate)	Years Ago
Earliest bipedal hominids (walking upright on two legs)	7 million to 6 million
Homo habilis (earliest use of stone tools)	2.5 million
Homo erectus (first controlled use of fire and first hominid migrations out of Africa)	1.9 million to 200,000
Earliest *Homo sapiens* in Africa	250,000
Beginnings of human migration out of Africa	100,000
Human entry into eastern Asia	70,000
Human entry into Australia (first use of boats)	60,000–40,000
Human entry into Europe	40,000
Extinction of large mammals in Australia	30,000
Human entry into the Americas	30,000–15,000
Cave art in Europe	25,000
Extinction of Neanderthals	25,000
End of last Ice Age (global warming)	16,000–10,000
Earliest agricultural revolutions	12,000–10,000
Extinction of large mammals in North America	11,000
Austronesian migration to Pacific islands and Madagascar	3,500–1,000
Human entry into New Zealand (last major region to receive human settlers)	1,000

Settlements were planned around the seasonal movement of game and fish. Patterns of exchange over a distance of almost 200 miles indicate larger networks of human communication. The use of body ornaments, beads, and pigments such as ochre as well as possible planned burials suggest the kind of social and symbolic behavior that has characterized human activity ever since. All of this occurred before 100,000 years ago and, based on current evidence, long before such activity surfaced elsewhere in the world.

Then, sometime after 100,000 years ago, human beings began their long trek out of Africa and into Eurasia, Australia, the Americas, and, much later, the islands of the Pacific (see Map 1.1). In occupying the planet, members of our species accomplished

Map 1.1 The Global Dispersion of
Humankind
With origins in Africa perhaps 250,000
years ago, members of our species
(*Homo sapiens*) have migrated to
every environmental niche on the
planet over the past 100,000 years.

GREENLAND

*(30,000–15,000
years ago)*

NORTH
AMERICA

(40,0

ATLANTIC OCEAN

PACIFIC OCEAN

Equator

SOUTH
AMERICA

*Easter
Island*
(1500 years ago)

(by 12,500 years ago)

0		1,000		2,000 miles
0	1,000	2,000 kilometers		

EUROPE
~~ars ago)~~

ASIA

(70,000 years ago)

(100,000 years ago)

AFRICA

PACIFIC OCEAN

Equator

(3500 years ago)

(1500 years ago)

INDIAN OCEAN

(60,000–40,000 years ago)

AUSTRALIA

(1000 years ago)

NEW ZEALAND

Ice sheet (20,000 years ago)
Land bridges (20,000 years ago)
Human expansion (dates for earliest human occupation)

ANTARCTICA

the remarkable feat of learning to live in virtually every environmental niche on earth, something that no other large animal had done; and they did it with only stone tools and a gathering and hunting technology to aid them. Furthermore, much of this long journey occurred during the difficult climatic conditions of the last Ice Age (at its peak around 20,000 years ago), when thick ice sheets covered much of northern Eurasia and North America. The Ice Age did give these outward-bound human beings one advantage, however: the amount of water frozen in northern glaciers lowered sea levels around the planet, creating land bridges among various regions that were separated after the glaciers melted. Britain was then joined to Europe; eastern Siberia was connected to Alaska; and New Guinea, Australia, and Tasmania were all part of a huge supercontinent known as Sahul.

Into Eurasia

■ Change
What was the sequence of human migration across the planet?

Human migration out of Africa led first to the Middle East and from there westward into Europe about 40,000 years ago and eastward into Asia. Among the most carefully researched areas of early human settlement in Eurasia are those in southern France and northern Spain. Colder Ice Age climates around 20,000 years ago apparently pushed more northerly European peoples southward into warmer regions. There they altered their hunting habits, focusing on reindeer and horses, and developed new technologies such as spear throwers and perhaps the bow and arrow as well as many different kinds of stone tools.[3] Most remarkably, they also left a record of their world in hundreds of cave paintings, depicting reindeer, bulls, horses, and other animals, brilliantly portrayed in colors of red, yellow, brown, and black. Images of human beings, impressions of human hands, and various abstract designs, perhaps an early form of writing, often accompanied the cave paintings.

The Lascaux Caves
Discovered by four teenage boys in 1940, the Lascaux caves in southern France contain some 2,000 images, dating to perhaps 17,000 years ago. Many of them depict in quite realistic form the wild animals of the region—oxen, bulls, horses, ibex, and birds. (JM Labat/ Photo Researchers, Inc.)

Scholars have debated endlessly what insights these remarkable images might provide into the mental world of Paleolithic Europeans.[4] Were they examples of "totemic" thinking—the belief that particular groups of people were associated with, or descended from, particular animals? Did they represent a form of "hunting magic" intended to enhance the success of these early hunters? Because many of the paintings were located deep within caves, were they perhaps part of religious or ritual practices or rites of passage? Were they designed to pass on information to future generations? Or did they symbolize, as some recent scholars contend, a coded representation of a Paleolithic worldview divided into male and female realms, both opposed to and balancing each other? We simply do not know. Nonetheless, these images excite our imagination still, 20,000 years or more after they were created. In them we sense a kinship with the humanity of our distant ancestors.

Farther east, archeologists have uncovered still other remarkable Paleolithic adaptations to Ice Age conditions. Across the vast plains of Central Europe, Ukraine, and Russia, new technologies emerged, including bone needles, multilayered clothing, weaving, nets, storage pits, baskets, and pottery. Partially underground dwellings constructed from the bones and tusks of mammoths compensated for the absence of caves and rock shelters. All of this suggests that some of these people settled down in more permanent settlements, at least temporarily abandoning their nomadic journeys. Associated with these Eastern European peoples were numerous female figurines. Carved from stone, antlers, mammoth tusks, or, occasionally, baked clay, these so-called Venus figurines depict the female form, often with exaggerated breasts, buttocks, hips, and stomachs. They were not limited to a single region but have been found all across Europe, from Spain to Russia, suggesting a network of human communication and cultural diffusion over a wide area.

Into Australia

Early human migration to Australia, currently dated to around 60,000 years ago, came from Indonesia and involved another "first" in human affairs—the use of boats. Over time, people settled in most regions of this huge continent, though quite sparsely. Scholars estimate the population of Australia at about 300,000 people in 1788, when the first Europeans arrived. Over tens of thousands of years, these people had developed perhaps 250 languages; collected a wide variety of bulbs, tubers, roots, seeds, and cereal grasses; and hunted large and small animals, as well as birds, fish, and other marine life. A relatively simple technology, appropriate to a gathering and hunting economy, sustained Australia's Aboriginal people into modern times. When outsiders arrived in the late eighteenth century, all of the continent's people still practiced that ancient way of life, despite the presence of agriculture in nearby New Guinea.

Accompanying their technological simplicity and traditionalism was the development of an elaborate and complex outlook on the world, known as the Dreamtime. Expressed in endless stories, in extended ceremonies, and in the evocative rock art of the continent's peoples, the Dreamtime recounted the beginning of things; how ancestral beings crisscrossed the land, creating its rivers, hills, rocks, and waterholes; how various peoples came to inhabit the land; and how they relate to animals and to one another. In this view of the world, everything in the natural order was a vibration, an echo, a footprint of these ancient happenings, which link the current inhabitants intimately to particular places and to timeless events in the past.

The journeys of the Dreamtime's ancestral beings reflect in a general way the networks of migration, communication, and exchange that linked the continent's many Paleolithic peoples. Far from isolated groups, they had long exchanged particular stones, pigments, materials for ropes and baskets, wood for spears, feathers and shells for ornaments, and an addictive psychoactive drug known as *pituri* over distances of hundreds of miles.[5] Songs, dances, stories, and rituals likewise circulated. Precisely how far back in time these networks extend is difficult to pinpoint, but it seems clear that Paleolithic Australia, like ancient Europe, was both many separate worlds and, at the same time, one loosely connected world.

Into the Americas

The earliest settlement of the Western Hemisphere occurred much later than that of Australia, for it took some time for human beings to penetrate the frigid lands of eastern Siberia, which was the jumping-off point for the move into the Americas. Experts continue to argue about precisely when the first migrations occurred (somewhere between 30,000 and 15,000 years ago), about the route of migration (by land across the Bering Strait or by sea down the west coast of North America), about how many separate migrations took place, and about how long it took for people to penetrate to the tip of South America.[6] There is, however, good evidence of human activity in southern Chile by 12,500 years ago.

The first clearly defined and widespread cultural tradition in the Americas is associated with people who made a distinctive projectile point, known to archeologists as a Clovis point. Scattered all over North America, Clovis culture flourished around 12,000 to 11,000 years ago. Scattered bands of Clovis people ranged over huge areas, camping along rivers, springs, and waterholes, where large animals congregated. Although they certainly hunted smaller animals and gathered many wild plants, Clovis people show up in the archeological record most dramatically as hunters of very large mammals, such as mammoths and bison. Killing a single mammoth could provide food for many weeks or, in cold weather, for much of the winter. The wide distribution of Clovis point technology suggests yet again a regional pattern of cultural diffusion and at least indirect communication over a large area.

Then, about 10,900 years ago, all trace of the Clovis people disappears from the archeological record at the same time that many species of large animals, including the mammoth and several species of horses and camels, also became extinct. Did the Clovis people hunt these animals to extinction and then vanish themselves as their source of food disappeared? Or did the drier climate that came with the end of the Ice Age cause this "megafaunal extinction"? Experts disagree, but what happened next was the creation of a much greater diversity of cultures as people adapted to this new situation in various ways. Hunters on the Great Plains continued to pursue bison, which largely avoided the fate of the mammoths. Others learned to live in the desert, taking advantage of seasonal plants and smaller animals, while those who lived near the sea, lakes, or streams drew on indigenous fish and birds. Many peoples retained their gathering and hunting way of life into modern times, while others became farmers and, in a few favored regions, later developed cities and large-scale states.[7]

Into the Pacific

The last phase of the great human migration to the ends of the earth took place in the Pacific Ocean and was distinctive in many ways. In the first place, it occurred quite recently, jumping off only about 3,500 years ago from the Bismarck and Solomon islands near New Guinea as well as from the islands of the Philippines. It was everywhere a waterborne migration, making use of oceangoing canoes and remarkable navigational skills, and it happened very quickly and over a huge area of the planet. Speaking Austronesian languages that trace back to southern China, these oceanic voyagers had settled every habitable piece of land in the Pacific basin within about 2,500 years. Other Austronesians had sailed west from Indonesia across the Indian Ocean to settle the island of Madagascar off the coast of eastern Africa. This extraordinary process of expansion—both rapid and extensive—made the Austronesian family of languages the most widespread in the world. With the occupation of Aotearoa (New Zealand) about 1200 C.E., the initial human settlement of the planet was finally complete (see Map 1.2).

In contrast with all of the other migrations, these Pacific voyages were undertaken by people with an agricultural technology, who carried both domesticated plants and animals in their canoes. Both men and women made these journeys, suggesting a deliberate intention to colonize new lands. Virtually everywhere they went, two developments followed. One was the creation of highly stratified societies or chiefdoms, of which ancient Hawaiian society is a prime example. In Hawaii, an elite class of chiefs with political and military power ruled over a mass of commoners. The other development was the dramatic impact that these migrations had on the environment of previously uninhabited islands. Many species of

■ Comparison
How did Austronesian migrations differ from other early patterns of human movement?

Map 1.2 Migration of Austronesian-Speaking People
People speaking Austronesian languages completed the human settlement of the earth quite recently as they settled the islands of the vast Pacific and penetrated the Indian Ocean to Madagascar, off the coast of southeast Africa.

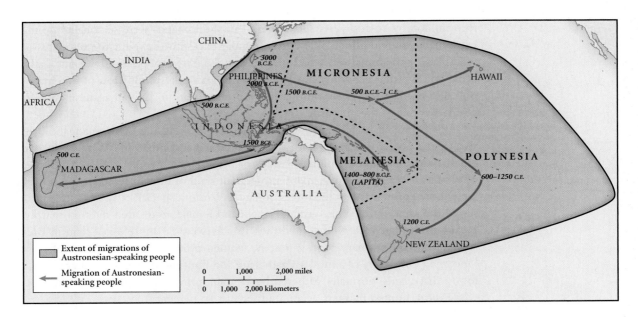

animals quickly became extinct, especially large flightless birds. The destruction of the forests of Rapa Nui (Easter Island) between the fifteenth and seventeenth centuries C.E. brought famine, violent conflict, and a sharp population decline to this small island society, while the absence of large trees ensured that no one could leave the island, for they could no longer build the canoes that had brought them there.[8]

The Ways We Were

During their long journeys across the earth, Paleolithic people created a multitude of separate and distinct societies, each with its own history, culture, language, identity, stories, and rituals, but the limitations of a gathering and hunting technology using stone tools imposed some commonalities on these ancient people. Based on the archeological record and on the example of gathering and hunting societies that still existed in modern times, scholars have sketched out some of the common features of these early societies.

The First Human Societies

■ **Change**
In what ways did a gathering and hunting economy shape other aspects of Paleolithic societies?

Above all else, these Paleolithic societies were small, consisting of bands of twenty-five to fifty people, in which all relationships were intensely personal and thought of normally in terms of kinship. No anonymity or "hiding in the crowd" was possible in a society of relatives. The available technology permitted only a very low population density and ensured an extremely slow rate of population growth. Scholars estimate that world population may have been as low as 10,000 people around 100,000 years ago and grew slowly to 500,000 by 30,000 years ago and then to 6 million by 10,000 years ago.[9] These Paleolithic bands were seasonally mobile or nomadic, moving frequently and in regular patterns to exploit the resources of wild plants and animals on which they depended. The low productivity of a gathering and hunting economy normally did not allow the production of much surplus, and because they were on the move so often, transporting an accumulation of goods was out of the question.

All of this meant highly egalitarian societies, lacking the many inequalities of wealth and power that came with later agricultural and urban life. With no formal chiefs, kings, bureaucrats, soldiers, nobles, or priests, these people were perhaps freer of tyranny and oppression than any subsequent kind of human society, even if they were more constrained by the forces of nature. Without specialists, most people possessed the same set of skills, although male and female tasks often differed sharply. Relationships between women and men usually were far more equal than in later societies. As the primary food gatherers, women provided the bulk of the family "income." One study of a modern gathering and hunting society in southern Africa found that plants, normally gathered by women, provided 70 percent of the diet, while meat, hunted by men, accounted for just 30 percent.[10]

When the British navigator and explorer Captain James Cook first encountered the gathering and hunting peoples of Australia in 1770, he described them, perhaps a little enviously, in this way:

> They live in a Tranquillity which is not disturb'd by the Inequality of Conditions: The Earth and sea of their own accord furnishes them with all things necessary for life, they covet not Magnificent houses, Household-stuff.... In short they seem'd to set no value upon any thing we gave them.... They think themselves provided with all the necessarys of Life.[11]

Native Australians A number of Aboriginal Australians maintained their gathering and hunting way of life well into the twentieth century. Here an older woman shows two young boys how to dig for honey ants, a popular food. (Bill Bachman/Alamy)

The Europeans who settled permanently among such people some twenty years later, however, found a society in which physical competition among men was expressed in frequent one-on-one combat and in formalized but bloody battles. It also meant recurrent, public, and quite brutal beatings of wives by their husbands.[12] Although sometimes romanticized by Europeans, the relative social equality of Paleolithic peoples did not always generate a utopia of social harmony.

Like all human cultures, Paleolithic societies had rules and structures. A gender-based division of labor usually cast men as hunters and women as gatherers. Values emphasizing reciprocal sharing of goods resulted in clearly defined rules about distributing the meat from an animal kill. Rules about incest and adultery governed sexual behavior, while understandings about who could hunt or gather in particular territories regulated economic activity. Leaders arose as needed to organize a task such as a hunt, but without conferring permanent power on individuals.

Economy and the Environment

For a long time, gathering and hunting peoples were viewed as "primitive," impoverished, barely eking out a living from the land. In more recent decades, anthropologists studying contemporary Paleolithic societies—those that survived into the twentieth century—began to paint a different picture. They noted that gathering and hunting people frequently worked fewer hours to meet their material needs than did people in agricultural or industrial societies and so had more "leisure time." One scholar referred to them as "the original affluent society," not because they had so much, but because they wanted or needed so little.[13] Nonetheless, life expectancy was low, probably little more than thirty-five years on average; life in the wild was surely dangerous; and dependency on the vagaries of nature rendered it insecure as well.

Paleolithic people were not always at the mercy of nature; at times, they acted to alter the natural environment substantially. The use of deliberately set fires to encourage the growth of particular plants certainly changed the landscape and in Australia led to the proliferation of fire-resistant eucalyptus trees at the expense of other plant species. In many parts of the world—Australia, North America, Siberia, Madagascar, Pacific islands—the extinction of various large animals followed fairly quickly after the arrival of human beings, leading scholars to suggest that Paleolithic humankind played a major role, coupled perhaps with changing climates, in the disappearance of these animals. Other hominid, or humanlike, species, such as the Neanderthals in Europe or the recently discovered Flores man in Indonesia, also perished after living side by side with *Homo sapiens* for millennia. Whether their disappearance occurred through massacre, interbreeding, or peaceful competition, they were among the casualties of the rise of humankind. Thus the biological environment inhabited by gathering and hunting peoples was not wholly "natural" but was shaped in part by their own hands.

The Realm of the Spirit

The religious or spiritual dimension of Paleolithic culture has been very hard to pin down because bones and stones tell us little about what people thought, art is subject to many interpretations, and the experience of contemporary gathering and hunting peoples may not reflect the more distant past. There is, however, clear evidence for a rich ceremonial life. The presence of rock art deep inside caves and far from living spaces suggests a "ceremonial space" separate from ordinary living. The extended rituals of contemporary Australian Aboriginal people, which sometimes last for weeks, confirm this impression, as do numerous and elaborate burial sites found throughout the world. No full-time religious specialists or priests led these ceremonies, but part-time shamans, people believed to be especially skilled at dealing with the spirit world, emerged as the need arose. Such people often entered an altered state of consciousness or a trance while performing the ceremonies, often with the aid of psychoactive drugs.

Precisely how these people understood the nonmaterial world is hard to reconstruct, and speculation abounds. Evidence from ancient Africa suggests a variety of understandings: some Paleolithic societies were apparently monotheistic; others saw several levels of supernatural beings, including a Creator Deity, various territorial spirits, and the spirits of dead ancestors; still others believed in an impersonal force suffused throughout the natural order that could be accessed by shamans during a trance dance.[14] The prevalence of Venus figurines and other symbols all across Europe has convinced some scholars, but not all, that Paleolithic religious thought had a strongly feminine dimension, embodied in a Great Goddess and concerned with the regeneration and renewal of life.[15] It seems likely that many gathering and hunting peoples developed a cyclical view of time that drew on the changing phases of the moon and on the cycles of female fertility—birth, menstruation, pregnancy,

The Willendorf Venus
Less than four and a half inches in height and dating to about 25,000 years ago, this female figure, which was found near the town of Willendorf in Austria, has become the most famous of the many Venus figurines. Certain features—the absence of both face and feet, the coils of hair around her head, the prominence of her breasts and sexual organs—have prompted much speculation among scholars about the significance of these intriguing carvings. (Naturhistorisches Museum, Vienna, Austria/The Bridgeman Art Library)

Snapshot   **The Paleolithic Era in Perspective**[16]

	Paleolithic Era (from 250,000 to 10,000 years ago)	Agricultural Era (from 10,000 to 200 years ago)	Modern Industrial Era (since 1800)
Duration of each era, as a percentage of 250,000 years	96%	4%	0.08%
Percent of people who lived, out of 80 billion total	12%	68%	20%
Percent of years lived in each era (reflects changing life expectancies)	9%	62%	29%

new birth, and death. Such understandings of the cosmos, which saw endlessly repeated patterns of regeneration and disintegration, were very different than later Western views, which saw time moving in a straight line toward some predetermined goal.[17]

Settling Down: "The Great Transition"

Though glacially slow by contemporary standards, Paleolithic cultures changed over time as people moved into new environments, as populations slowly grew, as climates altered, and as different human groups interacted with one another. For example, all over the Afro-Eurasian world after 25,000 years ago, a tendency toward the miniaturization of stone tools is evident. Known as "micro-blades," these smaller and more refined spear points, arrowheads, knives, and scrapers were carefully struck from larger cores and often mounted in antler, bone, or wooden handles.[18] This ancient and global technological change was similar perhaps to the miniaturization of electronic components in the twentieth century. Another important change in the strategies of Paleolithic people was the collection of wild grains, which represented a major addition to the food supply beyond the use of roots, berries, and nuts. This innovation originated in northeastern Africa around 16,000 years ago.

But the most striking and significant change in the lives of Paleolithic peoples occurred as the last Ice Age came to an end between 16,000 and 10,000 years ago. What followed was a general global warming, though one with periodic fluctuations and cold snaps. Unlike the contemporary global warming, generated by human activity and especially the burning of fossil fuels, this ancient warming phase was a wholly natural phenomenon, part of a long cycle of repeated heating and

■ Change
Why did some Paleolithic peoples abandon earlier, more nomadic ways and begin to live a more settled life?

cooling characteristic of the earth's climatic history. Plants and animals unable to survive in the Ice Age climate now flourished and increased their range, providing a much richer and more diverse environment for many human societies. Under these improved conditions, human populations grew, and some previously nomadic gathering and hunting communities, but not all of them, found it possible to settle down and live in more permanent settlements or villages. These societies were becoming both larger and more complex, and it was less possible to simply move away if trouble struck. Settlement also meant that households could store and accumulate goods to a greater degree than their nomadic ancestors. Because some people were more energetic, talented, or lucky than others, the thin edge of inequality very gradually began to wear away the egalitarianism of Paleolithic communities.

Changes along these lines emerged in many places. Paleolithic societies in Japan, known as Jomon, settled down in villages by the sea, where they greatly expanded the number of animals, both land and marine, that they consumed. They also created some of the world's first pottery, along with dugout canoes, paddles, bows, bowls, and tool handles, all made from wood. A similar pattern of permanent settlement, a broader range of food sources, and specialized technologies is evident in Scandinavia, Southeast Asia, North America, and the Middle East between 12,000 and 4,000 years ago. Bows and arrows seem to have been invented separately in Europe, Africa, and the Middle East during this period and spread later to the Americas. In Labrador, longhouses accommodating 100 people appear in the archeological record. Far more elaborate burial sites in many places testify to the growing complexity of human communities and the kinship systems that bound them together. Separate cemeteries for dogs suggest that humankind's best friend was also our first domesticated animal friend.

This process of settling down among gathering and hunting peoples—and the changes that followed from it—marked a major turn in human history, away from countless millennia of nomadic journeys by very small communities. It also provided the setting within which the next great transition would occur. Growing numbers of people, living in settled communities, placed a much greater demand on the environment than did small bands of wandering people. Therefore, it is perhaps not surprising that among the innovations that emerged in these more complex gathering and hunting societies was yet another way for increasing the food supply—agriculture. That epic transition is the subject of the next chapter.

Comparing Paleolithic Societies

Over the 200,000 years or more of the Paleolithic era, human societies naturally differed from one another—in their tool kits, their adaptation to the environment, their beliefs, their social organization, and much more. Here we examine more carefully two such societies, the San of southern Africa and the Chumash of southern California. What they shared was a gathering and hunting way of life and a continuing existence into modern times. Unlike many other such peoples who succumbed

Jomon Figurines
Female figurines, dating to perhaps 4,000 years ago, have been found among Japan's Paleolithic people, known as the Jomon. Many scholars believe these carvings had a ritual function, associated with fertility. (Tokyo National Museum, Collection of Mrs. Kane Yamazaka)

to the relentless expansion of agricultural or industrial societies, the San and the Chumash maintained their ancient way of life into the eighteenth, nineteenth, and twentieth centuries. Even though modern gathering and hunting societies studied by anthropologists surely differed in many ways from their ancient counterparts, they do allow us to see the human face of a way of life long vanished from most parts of the earth.

The San of Southern Africa

On the northern fringe of the Kalahari Desert, in Angola, Namibia, and Botswana, lies the country of the San people, who numbered 50,000 to 80,000 at the start of the twenty-first century. Linguistically, they are related to one of the great language families of Africa, Khoisan, whose speakers have lived throughout eastern and southern Africa for many millennia. The immediate ancestors of the San have inhabited southern Africa for at least 5,000 years. Economically, Khoisan-speaking peoples practiced a gathering and hunting way of life with a technology of stone tools that was recognizable to their twentieth-century San descendants. Another cultural practice of long standing was the remarkable rock art of southern Africa, depicting people and animals, especially the antelope, in thousands of naturalistic scenes of hunts, battles, and dances. Dating to as early as 26,000 years ago, this tradition persisted into the nineteenth century, making it the "oldest artistic tradition of humankind."[19] Modern scholars suggest that this art reflected the religious experience of trance healers, who were likely the artists who painted these images. When a late-nineteenth-century anthropologist showed some of these rock paintings to an elderly San couple, the woman began to sing and dance, while the man became sad, remembering the old songs.[20] In these and other ways, contemporary San people are linked to an ancient cultural tradition that is deeply rooted in the African past.

Most Khoisan gathering and hunting peoples had long ago been absorbed or displaced by the arrival of Bantu-speaking peoples bearing agriculture, domesticated animals, and iron tools, but the San, who lived in a relatively remote location, endured. Even the colonization of southern Africa by Europeans left the San largely intact until the 1960s and later, but not completely, for they traded with their agricultural neighbors and sometimes worked for them. The San also began to use iron arrowheads, fashioned from metals introduced by the newcomers. Drums, borrowed from their Bantu-speaking neighbors, now supplemented their own stringed instruments and became part of San musical tradition. Despite these borrowings, when anthropologists descended on the San in the 1950s and 1960s and studied every aspect of their culture, they found a people still practicing an ancient way of life. The following account of San life is drawn largely from the work of Richard Lee, an anthropologist who lived with and was adopted by one of the San groups who called themselves the Ju/'hoansi.[21] The term literally

■ **Description**
What are the most prominent features of San life?

The San of Southern Africa

means "real people"; the virgule (slash) and the apostrophe in the name denote "clicks," which are a distinctive sound in the San language.

In the semidesert conditions of the northern Kalahari, the Ju/'hoansi have drawn a livelihood from a harsh land using some twenty-eight tools for gathering, hunting, and preparing food. The most important implements include an all-purpose wooden digging stick, a large leather garment used for carrying things and also as a blanket, a knife, a spear, a bow and arrow tipped with a potent poison, woven ropes, and nets. The Ju/'hoansi have identified and named some 260 species of wild animals, of which the kudu, wildebeest, and gemsbok are the most commonly hunted, entirely by men. More than 100 species of wild plants, including various nuts, berries, roots, fruits, melons, and greens, were collected, largely by women.

What kind of life did they create for themselves with this modest technology? According to Richard Lee, it was a "happy combination of an adequate diet and a short workweek." He calculated that the Jo/'hoansi consumed 2,355 calories on average every day, about 30 percent from meat and 70 percent from vegetables, well balanced with sufficient protein, vitamins, and minerals—and, he concluded, they "[did] not have to work very hard" to achieve this standard of living. An average workweek involved about seventeen hours of labor in getting food and another twenty-five hours in housework and making and fixing tools, with the total work divided quite equally between men and women. This left plenty of leisure time for resting, visiting, endless conversation, and conducting rituals and ceremonies. Still, it was an uncertain and perpetually anxious life, with fluctuating rainfall, periodic droughts, seasonal depletion of plants, and the unpredictable movement of animals.

What made this way of life possible was a particular kind of society, one characterized by mobility, sharing, and equality. The basic unit of social organization was a band or camp of roughly ten to thirty people, who were connected by ties of exchange and kinship with similar camps across a wide area. The membership of a camp fluctuated over time as many people claimed membership in more than one band. Furthermore, the camps themselves, consisting of quickly built grass huts, were moved frequently, with the Jo/'hoansi seldom staying more than a few months in any one place. The flexibility of this arrangement allowed them to adjust rapidly to the changing seasonal patterns of their desert environment.

At one level, Jo/'hoansi society was extremely simple. No formal leaders, chiefs, headmen, priests, or craft specialists existed, and decisions were made by individual families and camps after much discussion. On another level, social relationships were extremely complex, and it took Richard Lee several years to penetrate them. In addition to common kinship relations of marriage and descent, there were "joking" and "avoidance" relationships that determined the degree of familiarity with which people engaged one another. A further element of complexity lay in a unique "naming" system, which created a deep bond among people with the same name, even though they were not biologically related. For example, a man could not marry any woman who bore the same name as his mother or sister.

At the heart of such a small-scale society of intense personal relationships were values of modesty, cooperation, and equality, which the Jo/'hoansi went to great lengths to inculcate and maintain. One technique, known as "insulting the meat," involved highly negative comments about the size or quality of an animal killed by a hunter and the expectation that a successful hunter would disparage his own kill. As one man put it:

> When a young man kills much meat, he comes to think of himself as a chief or a big man, and he thinks of the rest of us as his servants or inferiors. We can't accept this. We refuse one who boasts, for someday his pride will make him kill someone. So we always speak of his meat as worthless. In this way we cool his heart and make him gentle.

Another practice tending toward equality was the principle that the owner of the arrow that killed an animal, not the successful hunter himself, had the right to distribute the meat from that animal. Because arrows were widely shared, and sometimes owned by women, this custom spread the prestige of meat distribution widely within the society and countered any possibility that the hunter might regard the meat as his private property.

Beyond the sharing of food within a camp was a system of unequal gift exchange among members of different camps. For example, I give you something today, and many months later, you may give me a gift that need not be equivalent in value. When Richard Lee appeared puzzled by the inequality of the exchange, he was told: "we don't trade with things; we trade with people." This system of exchange had more to do with establishing social relations than with accumulating goods. One famous and highly respected hunter named Toma "gave away everything that came into his hands. . . . [I]n exchange for his self-imposed poverty, he won the respect and following of all the people."[22] It was an economic system that aimed at leveling wealth, not accumulating it, and that defined success in terms of possessing friends or people with obligations to oneself, rather than possessing goods.

Social equality extended also to relations between women and men. Richard Lee noted "relative equality between the sexes with no-one having the upper hand." Teenagers engaged quite freely in sex play, and the concept of female virginity was apparently unknown, as were rape, wife beating, and the sexual double standard. Although polygamy was permitted, most marriages were in fact monogamous because women strongly resisted sharing a husband with another wife. Frequent divorce among very young couples allowed women to leave unsatisfactory marriages easily. Lee found that longer-term marriages seemed to be generally fulfilling and stable. Both men and women expected a satisfying sexual relationship, and both occasionally took lovers, although discreetly.

But not all was sweetness and light among the Jo/'hoansi. Frequent arguments about the distribution of meat or the laziness or stinginess of particular people generated conflict, as did rivalries among men over women. Lee identified twenty-two murders that had occurred between 1920 and 1955 and several cases in which the community came together to conduct an execution of particularly disruptive individuals. Lesser tensions were handled through talk; more serious disputes might result in separation, with some people leaving to join another camp or to start their own.

In confronting the world beyond material and social life, the Jo/'hoansi reflected beliefs and practices that were arguably tens of thousands of years old. Unlike later peoples with their many gods, goddesses, spirits, and powers, the San populated the spiritual universe in a quite limited way. A Creator God, *Gao Na*, gave rise to the earth, men, women, animals, waterholes, and all other things; but like the Greek gods, this was a capricious deity, who often visited misfortune on humankind, simply because he chose to. A lesser god, *Gauwa*, was even more destructive, spreading disease, conflict, and death, but also on occasion providing assistance to beleaguered humans. The most serious threat to human welfare came from the ghosts of dead ancestors, the *gauwasi,* who were viewed as primarily malevolent. Asked why the ancestral spirits were so destructive, one woman healer replied:

> Longing for the living is what drives the dead to make people sick. . . . They are very very sad. . . . They miss their people on earth. And so they come back to us. They hover near the villages and put sickness into people, saying "Come, come here to me."

The Jo/'hoansi had one powerful resource for counteracting these evil influences from the world of the gods and ancestors. It was *n/um*, a spiritual potency that lies in the stomach and becomes activated during "curing dances," powerful nightlong rituals held frequently, especially during the dry season when several camps converged on the remaining waterholes. Around a fire, an inner circle of women clapped and sang, while men danced in a circle behind them. Then someone went into a trance and, in that altered state of consciousness, sought to share his or her activated *n/um* with everyone in the camp, pulling the evil out of them. Doing so had the power to heal the sick, to bring harmony to the community, to affect the rainfall and the supply of animals, and to protect everyone from the evil designs of the ancestors.[23]

Recent analysis suggests that the rock art of southern Africa represents the visions achieved by ancient trance dancers as they did battle with the supernatural world. If so, the Jo/'hoansi of the twentieth century were participating in the longest and most continuous religious tradition in world history.

The trance dance was in many ways a distinctive tradition. It did not seek communion with the supernatural; no gifts or sacrifices were offered to the gods or the ancestors, and few prayers were made for their assistance. Viewing the gods as the source of disease, conflict, and death, the Jo/'hoansi hurled at them words of reproach, abuse, and rejection, seeking to ward them off, to expel them from society. It was, as one scholar put it, a "war with God."[24] The leaders of this war, the trance dancers, were not possessed by any supernatural being but used the trance state to activate their own internal *n/um*. Nor were they a priestly elite. Men and women alike could become healers, although a fearful and extended process of spiritual preparation awaited them. Almost half of the men and one-third of the women whom Lee encountered had entered the trance state. It was a much-sought-after role, but it conveyed no permanent power or authority. Finally, Jo/'hoansi religious thinking located the source of evil and misfortune outside of the community in the activity of the gods and ancestors rather than within society in the form of sorcerers or witches. The curing dances brought the community together, united against the external and supernatural enemy.

The Chumash of Southern California

If the San Jo/'hoansi people provide a window into the life of at least one nomadic and long-established gathering and hunting society, the Chumash are more representative of those later post–Ice Age Paleolithic peoples who settled in permanent villages and constructed more complex societies. Together the San and the Chumash illustrate the immense variation that was possible within the limits of a gathering and hunting way of life.

Located in southern California in the vicinity of present-day Santa Barbara, the Chumash occupied a richer and more varied environment than did the San. Speaking a series of related dialects, they lived along the coast, in the immediate interior, and on a series of offshore islands. Thus they were able to draw on the resources of the sea as well as those of the land to support a much more densely settled population of perhaps 20,000 people when they encountered the Spanish in the sixteenth century.

Although the area had been sparsely occupied for about 10,000 years, the history of its people comes into sharper focus only in the centuries of the Common Era. The first millennium C.E. witnessed a growing population, the overhunting and depletion of deer herds in the interior, likely food shortages, and consequently increasing levels of violence and warfare among rival groups. Evidence for this violence is found in the large number of skeletons with bashed-in skulls or arrow and spear wounds. Then, in the several centuries after 1150 C.E., the Chumash, according to a noted scholar, "created an entirely new society."[25] Whereas the history of the San is marked by long-term continuities with a distant past, the Chumash experienced an extraordinary transformation.

A major element of that transformation lay in a remarkable technological innovation—the creation of a planked canoe, or *tomol*—an oceangoing vessel some twenty to thirty feet long and with a cargo capacity of two tons. Called "the most technically sophisticated watercraft developed in the New World," this new craft came into general use around 1000 C.E.[26] Its creation brought immense prestige, wealth, and power to those who built and owned these vessels, injecting a new element of inequality into Chumash society. The boatbuilders organized themselves into an elite craft

■ Comparison
In what ways, and why, did Chumash culture differ from that of the San?

The Chumash of Southern California

San Miguel Island
Santa Barbara
Santa Barbara Channel
Santa Rosa Island   Santa Cruz Island
Los Angeles

PACIFIC OCEAN

▭ Area of Chumash settlement

A Chumash Tomol
A technologically sophisticated seagoing canoe, the tomol, shown here in a contemporary drawing, was constructed from redwood or pine planks sewn together and caulked with hard tar and pine pitch. In recent decades, Chumash descendants have built several tomols and paddled them from the California mainland to the Channel Islands, re-creating a voyage that their distant ancestors had made many times. These reenactments were part of an effort to preserve for future generations the culture and traditions of the ancient Chumash. (Gaviota Coast Conservancy/Redrawn by © Elizabeth Leahy)

guild, the Brotherhood of the Tomol, which monopolized canoe production and held the tools, knowledge, and sacred medicine associated with these boats. The tomol stimulated a blossoming of trade along the coast and between the coast and the islands as plant food, animal products, tools, and beads now moved regularly among Chumash communities. The boats also made possible deep-sea fishing, with swordfish, central to Chumash religious practice, being the most highly prized and prestigious catch.

In other ways as well, the material life of the Chumash was far more elaborate than that of the San. They lived in round, permanent, substantial houses, covered by grass or reeds, some of them fifty feet in diameter and able to hold up to seventy people. Every village had its own sweathouse, built partially underground and entered through an opening in the roof. Soapstone bowls, wooden plates, beautifully decorated reed baskets, and a variety of items made from bone or shell reflected a pattern of technological innovation far beyond that of the San.

A resource-rich environment, a growing and settled population, flourishing commerce, and technological innovation combined to produce something that scholars not long ago would have considered impossible—a market economy among a gathering and hunting people. Whereas the economic life of the San was regulated almost entirely by custom and tradition, that of the Chumash involved important elements of a market-based system: individuals acting out of a profit motive; the use of money in the form of stringed beads; regulation of the supply of money to prevent inflation; specialized production of goods such as beads, stone tools, canoes, and baskets; prices attached to various items; payment for services provided by dancers, healers, and buriers; and private ownership of canoes, stores of food, and some tools. This is how an early Spanish observer described the Chumash in 1792:

> All these Indians are fond of traffic and commerce. They trade frequently with those of the mountains, bringing them fish and beadwork which they exchange for seeds and shawls of foxskin and a kind of blanket. . . . When they trade for profit, beads circulate among them as if they were money, being strung on long threads, according to the greater or smaller wealth of each one. . . . These strings of beads . . . are used by the men to adorn their heads and for collars. . . . They all make a show of their wealth which they always wear in sight on their heads, whence it is taken for gambling and trafficking.[27]

How different is all this from the life of the Jo/'hoansi! Permanently settled villages, ranging in size from several hundred to a thousand people, would have struck the San as unsustainably large compared to their own mobile camps of twenty-five to fifty people. The specialized skills of the Chumash probably would have surprised the Jo/'hoansi, because all San people possessed pretty much the same set of skills. The San no doubt would have been appalled by the public display of wealth, the impulse toward private accumulation, and the inequalities of Chumash society. A bearskin cape, worn only by the elite of canoe owners and village chiefs, marked the beginnings of class distinctions, as did burials, which were far more elaborate for the wealthy and their children than for commoners. Members of the Brotherhood of the Tomol often were buried with parts of their canoes.

Perhaps most offensive to the egalitarian and independent Jo/'hoansi would have been the emergence of a permanent and hereditary political elite among the Chumash. High-ranking Chumash chiefs, who inherited their positions through the male line, exercised control over a number of communities, but each village also had its own chief, some of whom were women. These political leaders, all of whom were also canoe owners, led their people in war, presided over religious rituals, and regulated the flourishing trade that followed the invention of the tomol. They also named the dates for periodic feasts, during which donations and collections from the wealthy were used to feed the poor and to set aside something for a rainy day. This effort at redistributing wealth might have earned the approval of the Jo/'hoansi, who continually sought to level any social and economic distinctions among themselves.

Whatever the Jo/'hoansi might have thought, these transformations—technological, economic, social, and political—created a more unified and more peaceful life among the Chumash in the several centuries after 1150. Earlier patterns of violence apparently subsided as specialized crafts and enhanced trade evened out the distribution of food, making various Chumash communities dependent on one another. More formal political leadership enabled the peaceful resolution of disputes, which formerly had been resolved in battle. Frequent celebrations served to bring various Chumash villages together, while a society-wide organization of ritual experts provided yet another integrating mechanism. These transformations represent a remarkable achievement, especially because they introduced in a gathering and hunting society many social elements normally associated only with agricultural peoples. However, the coming of the Europeans, with their guns, diseases, and missionaries, largely destroyed Chumash society in the centuries following that epic encounter. The mobile San, in their remote location, were able to preserve their ways of life far longer than the more settled, and therefore vulnerable, Chumash, who were unable to avoid the powerful newcomers.

Reflections: The Uses of the Paleolithic

Even when it is about a past as distant as the Paleolithic era, the study of history is also about those who tell it in the present. We search the past, always, for our own purposes. For a long time, modern people were inclined to view their Paleolithic ancestors as "primitive," "superstitious," unevolved, unable to exercise control over nature, and ignorant of its workings. Such a view was, of course, a kind of self-congratulation, designed to highlight the "progress" of modern humankind. It was a way of saying, "Look how far we have come."

In more recent decades, growing numbers of people, disillusioned with modernity, have looked to the Paleolithic era for material with which to criticize, rather than celebrate, contemporary life. Feminists have found in gathering and hunting peoples a much more gender-equal society and religious thinking that featured the "divine feminine," qualities that encouragingly suggested that patriarchy was neither inevitable nor eternal. Environmentalists have sometimes identified peoples in the distant past who were uniquely in tune with the natural environment rather than seeking to dominate it. Some nutritionists have advocated a "Paleolithic diet" of wild plants and animals as better adapted to our physiology. Critics of modern materialism and competitive capitalism have been delighted to discover societies in which values of sharing and equality predominated over those of accumulation and hierarchy. Still others have asked, in light of the long Paleolithic era, whether the explosive population and economic growth of recent centuries should be considered "normal" or "natural." Perhaps it should be regarded as extraordinary, possibly even pathological. Finally, research about the Paleolithic era has been extremely important in efforts by contemporary gathering and hunting peoples, or their descendants, to maintain or recover their older identities amid the conflicting currents of modern life. All of these uses of the Paleolithic have been a way of asking, "What have we lost in the mad rush to modernity, and how can we recover it?"

Both those who look with disdain on Paleolithic "backwardness" and those who praise, often quite romantically, its simplicity and equality seek to use these ancient people for their own purposes. In our efforts to puzzle out the past, all of us—historians and students of history very much included—stand somewhere. None of us can be entirely detached and "outside of it all" when we view the past. Nor is this necessarily a matter for regret. What we may lose in objectivity, we gain in passionate involvement with the historical record and the many people who inhabit it. Despite its remoteness in time and manner of living, the Paleolithic era resonates still in the twenty-first century, reminding us of our kinship with these distant people and the significance of that kinship in finding our own way in a very different world.

Second Thoughts

What's the Significance?

To assess your mastery of the material in this chapter, see the **Online Study Guide** at bedfordstmartins.com/strayer.

Paleolithic rock art	Austronesian migrations	Paleolithic "settling down"
Venus figurines	"the original affluent	San culture
Dreamtime	society"	"insulting the meat"
Clovis culture	shamans	Chumash culture
megafaunal extinction	trance dance	Brotherhood of the Tomol

Big Picture Questions

1. What is the significance of the Paleolithic era in world history?
2. In what ways did various Paleolithic societies differ from one another, and how did they change over time?
3. What statements in this chapter seem to be reliable and solidly based on facts, and which ones are more speculative and uncertain?
4. How might our attitudes toward the modern world influence our assessment of Paleolithic societies?

Next Steps: For Further Study

David Christian, *This Fleeting World: A Short History of Humanity* (2008). The first part of this lovely essay by a leading world historian provides a succinct survey of the Paleolithic era.

Brian M. Fagan, *People of the Earth: An Introduction to World Prehistory* (2006). A global account of early human history, written by a leading archeologist.

Clive Gamble, *Timewalkers: The Prehistory of Global Colonization* (2003). A beautifully written account of the initial human settlement of the earth.

Sally McBreatry and Alison S. Brooks, "The Revolution That Wasn't: A New Interpretation of the Origin of Modern Human Behavior," *Journal of Human Evolution* 39 (2000). A long scholarly article laying out the archeological evidence for the emergence of humankind in Africa.

Marjorie Shostak, *Nisa: The Life and Words of an !Kung Woman* (2000). A vivid first-person account of a San woman's life in a twentieth-century gathering and hunting society.

"Prehistoric Art," http://witcombe.sbc.edu/ARTHprehistoric.html#general. An art history Web site with a wealth of links to Paleolithic art around the world.

For Web sites and documents related to this chapter, see **Make History** at bedfordstmartins.com/strayer.

CHAPTER TWO

First Farmers

The Revolutions of Agriculture

10,000 B.C.E. – 3000 B.C.E.

"After me, I suppose there will be nothing here," remarked seventy-two-year-old Elsie Eiler in 2005. At the time, she was the sole remaining resident of the farm town of Monowi, Nebraska. "There is just no employment for people. Farming is hard and all the small farms have had to merge into bigger ones, and the young people just want to go away to college and a city. Few of them come back." Founded in 1902 by Czech immigrants, Monowi in the early twentieth century boasted a post office, two banks, a high school, a church, and rows of well-built homes. By the early twenty-first century, the church was boarded up, many houses had collapsed, deer and wild elk roamed the town's empty spaces, and flocks of birds nested in thick weeds of what had once been Main Street. With the death of her husband in 2004, Mrs. Eiler became the only living soul in Monowi, where she served as the town's mayor and ran its only business, a tavern whose customers came from passing traffic and nearby settlements.[1]

MRS. EILER'S STORY AND THAT OF HER TOWN were part of a much larger global process taking place over the past several centuries of the industrial age—a dramatic decline in the number of people directly earning their living as farmers. The United States represents an extreme case of this worldwide phenomenon: at the beginning of the twenty-first century, only about 5 percent of Americans lived on farms, and many of them were over the age of sixty-five. Despite the small number of American farmers, modern agriculture was so productive

Chinese Neolithic Pottery: Associated everywhere with the Agricultural Revolution was an explosion of pottery making, because settled farmers needed storage capacity to a much greater extent than did nomadic gatherers and hunters. Pottery also provided an outlet for creative expression in the designs and images that decorated many of these early pots. This painted pottery urn, more than 5,000 years old, is from the Yangshao cultural region in northern China, where one of the world's early agricultural breakthroughs occurred. (The National Museum of China, Beijing) that those few people were able to feed the entire country and to export a large amount of food as well. This modern retreat from the farm marked a dramatic reversal of a much more ancient pattern in which growing numbers of people began to farm and agriculture became for the first time the primary occupation for the vast majority of humankind. The beginnings of that epic process represent the central theme of this chapter.

The Agricultural Revolution in World History

The chief feature of the long Paleolithic era—and the first human process to operate on a global scale—was the initial settlement of the earth. Then, beginning around 12,000 years ago, a second global pattern began to unfold—agriculture. Often called the Neolithic or Agricultural Revolution, it referred to the deliberate cultivation of particular plants as well as the taming and breeding of particular animals. Thus a whole new way of life gradually replaced the earlier practices of gathering and hunting in most parts of the world. Although it took place over centuries and millennia, the coming of agriculture represented a genuinely revolutionary transformation of human life all across the planet and provided the foundation for almost everything that followed: growing populations, settled villages, animal-borne diseases, horse-drawn chariot warfare, cities, states, empires, civilizations, writing, literature, and much more.

Among the most revolutionary aspects of the age of agriculture was a new relationship between humankind and other living things, for now men and women were not simply using what they found in nature but were actively changing it as well. They were consciously "directing" the process of evolution. The actions of farmers in the Americas, for example, transformed corn from a plant with a cob of an inch or so to one measuring about six inches by 1500. Later efforts more than doubled that length. Farmers everywhere stamped the landscape with a human imprint in the form of fields with boundaries, terraced hillsides, irrigation ditches, and canals. Animals too were transformed as selective breeding produced sheep that grew more wool, cows that gave more milk, and chickens that laid more eggs than their wild counterparts.

This was "domestication"—the taming, and the changing, of nature for the benefit of humankind—but it created a new kind of mutual dependence. Many domesticated plants and animals could no longer survive in the wild and relied on human action or protection in order to reproduce successfully. Similarly, human beings in the agricultural era lost the skills of their gathering and hunting ancestors, and in any event there were now too many of them to live in that older fashion. As a consequence, farmers and herders became dependent on their domesticated plants and animals. From an outside point of view, it might well seem that corn and cows had tamed human beings, using people to ensure their own survival and growth as a species, as much as the other way around.

A further revolutionary aspect of the Neolithic age is summed up in the term "intensification." It means getting more for less, in this case more food and resources—far more—from a much smaller area of land than was possible with a gathering and hunting technology. More food meant more people. Growing populations in turn required an even greater need for the intensive exploitation of the environment. And so was launched the continuing human effort to "subdue the earth" and to "have dominion over it," as the biblical story in Genesis recorded God's command to Adam and Eve.

Comparing Agricultural Beginnings

Perhaps the most extraordinary feature of the Agricultural or Neolithic Revolution was that it occurred, separately and independently, in many widely scattered parts of the world: the Fertile Crescent of Southwest Asia, several places in sub-Saharan Africa, China, New Guinea, Mesoamerica, the Andes, and eastern North America (see the Snapshot on p. 38 and Map 2.2). Even more remarkably, all of this took place at roughly the same time (at least as measured by the 250,000-year span of human history on the planet)—between 12,000 and 4,000 years ago. These facts have generated many questions with which historians and other scholars have long struggled. Why was the Agricultural Revolution so late in the history of humankind? What was unique about the period after 10,000 B.C.E. that may have triggered or facilitated this vast upheaval? In what different ways did the Agricultural Revolution take shape in its various locations? How did it spread from its several points of origin to the rest of the earth? And what impact did it have on the shaping of human societies?

Common Patterns

It is no accident that the Agricultural Revolution coincided with the end of the last Ice Age, a process of global warming that began some 16,000 years ago. By about 11,000 years ago, the Ice Age was over, and climatic conditions similar to those of our own time generally prevailed. This was but the latest of some twenty-five periods of glaciation and warming that have occurred over the past several million years of the earth's history and which are caused by minor periodic changes in the earth's orbit around the sun. The end of the last Ice Age, however, coincided with the migration of *Homo sapiens* across the planet and created new conditions that made agriculture possible. Combined with active hunting by human societies, climate change in some areas helped to push into extinction various species of large mammals on which Paleolithic people had depended, thus adding to the pressure to find new food sources. The warmer, wetter, and more stable conditions, particularly in the tropical and temperate regions of the earth, also permitted the flourishing of more wild plants, especially cereal grasses, which were the ancestors of many domesticated crops. What climate change took away with one hand, it apparently gave back with the other.

■ Change
What accounts for the emergence of agriculture after countless millennia of human life without it?

$\mathcal{S}$napshot   **Agricultural Breakthroughs**[2]

Location	Dates (B.C.E.)	Plants	Animals
Southwest Asia (Fertile Crescent)	9000–7000	barley, wheat, lentils, figs	goats, sheep, cattle, pigs
China	6500–5000	rice, millet, soybeans	pigs, chickens, water buffalo
Saharan and sub-Saharan Africa	3000–2000	sorghum, millet, yams, teff	cattle (perhaps 8000 B.C.E.)
Highland New Guinea	7000–4000	taro, bananas, yams, sugarcane	—
Andes region	3000–2000	potatoes, quinoa, manioc	llamas, alpaca, guinea pig
Mesoamerica	3000–2000	maize, squash (perhaps 7000 B.C.E.), beans	turkey
Eastern woodlands of North America	2000–1000	sunflower, goosefoot, sumpweed	—

Over their long history, gathering and hunting peoples had already developed a deep knowledge of the natural world and in some cases an ability to manage it actively. They had learned to make use of a large number of plants and to hunt and eat both small and large animals, creating what archeologists call a "broad spectrum diet." In the Middle East, people had developed sickles for cutting newly available wild grain, baskets to carry it, mortars and pestles to remove the husk, and storage pits to preserve it. Peoples of the Amazon and elsewhere had learned to cut back some plants to encourage the growth of their favorites. Native Australians had built elaborate traps in which they could capture, store, and harvest large numbers of eels.

In hindsight, much of this looks like a kind of preparation for agriculture. Because women in particular had long been intimately associated with collecting wild plants, most scholars believe that they were the likely innovators who led the way to deliberate farming, with men perhaps taking the lead in domesticating animals. Clearly the knowledge and technology necessary for agriculture were part of a longer process of more intense human exploitation of the earth. Nowhere was agriculture an overnight invention.

Using such technologies, and benefiting from the global warming at the end of the last Ice Age, gathering and hunting peoples in various places were able to settle down and establish more permanent villages, abandoning their nomadic ways and more intensively exploiting the local area. This was particularly the case in resource-rich areas close to seas, lakes, marshes, and rivers. In settling down, however, they soon lost some of the skills of their ancestors and found themselves now required to support growing populations. Evidence for increasing human numbers around the world during this period of global warming has persuaded some scholars that agriculture was a response to an impending "food crisis."[3] If the number of people outstripped the local resources, or if sudden fluctuations in climate—prolonged drought or a cold snap, for example—diminished those resources, these newly settled communities were in trouble. It was no longer so easy to simply move away. These vagaries surely were strong motives to experiment and to innovate in an effort to increase the food supply. Clearly, many of the breakthroughs to agriculture occurred only *after* gathering and hunting peoples had already grown substantially in numbers and had established a sedentary way of life.

These were some of the common patterns that facilitated the Agricultural Revolution. New opportunities appeared with the improved conditions that came at the end of the Ice Age. New knowledge and technology emerged as human communities explored and exploited that changed environment. The disappearance of many large mammals, growing populations, newly settled ways of life, and fluctuations in the process of global warming—all of these represented pressures or incentives to increase food production and thus to minimize the risks of life in a new era.[4] From some combination of these opportunities and incentives emerged the profoundly transforming process of the Agricultural Revolution.

This new way of life operated everywhere with a simple technology—the digging stick or hoe (the plow was developed only later). But the several transitions to this hoe-based agriculture, commonly known as horticulture, varied considerably, depending on what plants and animals were available locally. For example, potatoes were found in the Andes region, but not in Africa or Asia; wheat and wild pigs existed in the Fertile Crescent, but not in the Americas. Furthermore, of the world's 200,000 plant species, only several hundred have been domesticated, and just five of these—wheat, corn, rice, barley, and sorghum—supply more than half of the calories that sustain human life. Only fourteen species of large mammals have been successfully domesticated, of which sheep, pigs, goats, cattle, and horses have been the most important. Because they are stubborn, nervous, solitary, or finicky, many animals simply cannot be readily domesticated.[5] In short, the kind of Agricultural Revolution that unfolded in particular places depended very much on what happened to be available locally, and that in turn depended on sheer luck.

Variations

Among the most favored areas—and the first to experience a full Agricultural Revolution—was the Fertile Crescent, an area sometimes known as Southwest Asia, consisting of present-day Iraq, Syria, Israel/Palestine, and southern Turkey (see Map 2.1). In this region, an extraordinary variety of wild plants and animals capable of domestication provided a rich array of species on which the now largely settled gathering and hunting people could draw. What triggered the transition to agriculture, it seems, was a cold and dry spell between 11,000 and 9500 B.C.E., a

■ **Comparison**
In what different ways did the Agricultural Revolution take shape in various parts of the world?

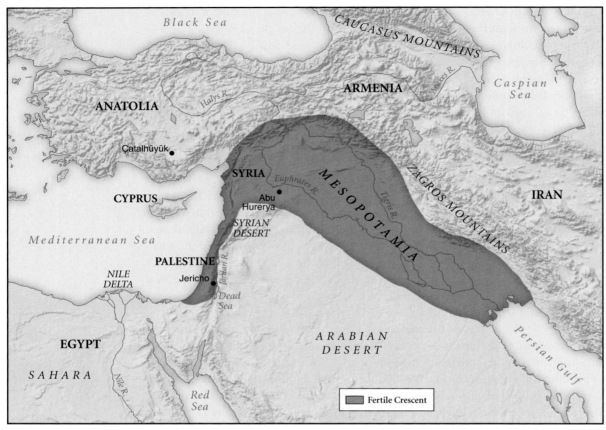

Map 2.1 The Fertile Crescent

Located in what is now called the Middle East, the Fertile Crescent was the site of many significant processes in early world history, including the first breakthrough to agriculture and later the development of some of the First Civilizations.

temporary interruption in the general process of global warming. Larger settled populations were now threatened with the loss of the wild plants and animals on which they had come to depend. Their solution was domestication. In the millennium or so after 9000 B.C.E., figs, wheat, barley, rye, peas, lentils, sheep, goats, pigs, and cattle all came under human control, providing the foundation for the world's first, and most productive, agricultural societies.

Archeological evidence suggests that the transition to a fully agricultural way of life in this region sometimes took place quite quickly, within as few as 500 years. Signs of that transformation included large increases in the size of settlements, which now housed as many as several thousand people. In these agricultural settings, archeologists have found major innovations: the use of sun-dried mud bricks; the appearance of monuments or shrinelike buildings; displays of cattle skulls; more elaborate human burials, including the removal of the skull; and more sophisticated tools, such as sickles, polished axes, and awls.[6] Environmental deterioration in ecologically fragile regions was yet another indication of this new way of life. Numerous settlements in the Jordan River valley and Palestine were abandoned as growing populations of people and goats stripped the area of trees and ground cover, leading to soil erosion and food shortages, which required their human inhabitants to scatter.[7]

At roughly the same time, perhaps a bit later, another process of domestication was unfolding on the African continent in a most unlikely place—the eastern part of what is now the Sahara in present-day Sudan. Between 10,000 and 5,000 years ago, however, "the Saharan desert . . . effectively did not exist," according to scholars, as the region received more rainfall than currently, had extensive grassland vegetation, and was "relatively hospitable to human life."[8] It seems likely that cattle were domesticated in this region about 1,000 years before they were separately brought under human control in the Middle East and India. At about the same time, the donkey also was domesticated in northeastern Africa near the Red Sea and spread from there into Southwest Asia, even as the practice of raising sheep and goats moved in the other direction. In Africa, animal domestication thus preceded the domestication of plants, while elsewhere in the world it was the other way around.

In terms of farming, the African pattern again was somewhat different. Unlike the Fertile Crescent, where a number of plants were domesticated in a small area, sub-Saharan Africa witnessed the emergence of several widely scattered farming practices. Sorghum, which grows well in arid conditions, was the first grain to be "tamed" in the eastern Sahara region. In the highlands of Ethiopia, teff, a tiny, highly nutritious grain, as well as enset, a relative of the banana, came under cultivation. In the forested region of West Africa, yams, oil palm trees, okra, and the kola nut (still used as a flavoring for Coca-Cola and Pepsi) emerged as important crops. The scattered location of these domestications generated a less productive agriculture than in the more favored and compact Fertile Crescent, but a number of the African domesticates—sorghum, castor beans, gourds, millet, the donkey—subsequently spread to enrich the agricultural practices of Eurasian peoples.

Yet another pattern of agricultural development took shape in the Americas. Like the Agricultural Revolution in Africa, the domestication of plants in the Americas occurred separately in a number of locations—in the coastal Andean regions of western South America, in Mesoamerica, in the Mississippi valley, and perhaps in the Amazon basin—but surely its most distinctive feature lay in the absence of animals that could be domesticated. Of the fourteen major species of large mammals that have been brought under human control, only one, the llama/alpaca, existed in the Western Hemisphere. Without goats, sheep, pigs, cattle, or horses, the peoples of the Americas lacked the sources of protein, manure, and power (to draw plows or pull carts, for example) that were widely available to societies in the Afro-Eurasian world. Because they could not depend on domesticated animals for meat, agricultural peoples in the Americas relied more on hunting and fishing than did peoples in the Eastern Hemisphere.

Furthermore, the Americas lacked the rich cereal grains that were widely available in Afro-Eurasia. Instead they had maize or corn, first domesticated in southern Mexico by 4000 to 3000 B.C.E. Unlike the cereal grains of the Fertile Crescent, which closely resemble their wild predecessors, the ancestor of corn, a mountain grass called *teosinte*, looks nothing like what we now know as corn or maize.

Teosinte   Modern Corn

Teosinte and Maize/Corn
The sharp difference in size between the tiny cobs of teosinte, a wild grass, and usable forms of domesticated maize meant that the Agricultural Revolution took place more slowly in Mesoamerica than it had in Mesopotamia. (Nicolle Rager Fuller, National Science Foundation)

Thousands of years of selective adaptation were required to develop a sufficiently large cob and number of kernels to sustain a productive agriculture, an achievement that one geneticist has called "arguably man's first, and perhaps his greatest, feat of genetic engineering."[9] Even then, corn was nutritionally poorer than the protein-rich cereals of the Fertile Crescent. To provide sufficient dietary protein, corn had to be supplemented with squash and beans, which were also domesticated in the Americas. Thus while Middle Eastern societies quite rapidly replaced their gathering and hunting economy with agriculture, that process took 3,500 years in Mesoamerica.

Another difference in the progress of the Agricultural Revolution lay in the north/south orientation of the Americas, which required agricultural practices to move through, and adapt to, quite distinct climatic and vegetation zones if they were to spread. The east/west axis of Eurasia meant that agricultural innovations could spread more rapidly because they were entering roughly similar environments. Thus corn, beans, and squash, which were first domesticated in Mesoamerica, took several thousand years to travel the few hundred miles from their Mexican homeland to the southwestern United States and another thousand years or more to arrive in eastern North America. The llama, guinea pig, and potato, which were domesticated in the Andean highlands, never reached Mesoamerica.[10]

The Globalization of Agriculture

■ Connection
In what ways did agriculture spread? Where and why was it sometimes resisted?

From the various places where it originated, agriculture spread to much of the rest of the earth, although for a long time it coexisted with gathering and hunting ways of life (see Map 2.2). Broadly speaking, this extension of farming occurred in two ways. The first is called *diffusion*, which refers to the gradual spread of agricultural techniques, and perhaps of the plants and animals themselves, but without the extensive movement of agricultural people. Neighboring groups exchanged ideas and products in a "down-the-line" pattern of communication. A second process involved the slow colonization or migration of agricultural peoples as growing populations and pressures to expand pushed them outward. Often this meant the conquest, absorption, or displacement of the earlier gatherers and hunters, along with the spread of the languages and cultures of the migrating farmers. In many places, both processes took place.[11] The spread of corn-based agriculture in the Americas, highlighted in the Snapshot on page 43, illustrates the process.

Snapshot   **The History of Maize/Corn**[12]

The earliest domestication of teosinte—a grass from which modern maize/corn subsequently developed in a process of adaptation and "genetic engineering" over thousands of years—occurs, in southern Mexico. It may have been used for the sugary syrup found in its stalk as well as the nutritional value of its kernels.	9000–8000 B.C.E.
Maize cultivation spreads to South America (Ecuador, Peru).	2300–1000 B.C.E.
Maize cob reaches length of about six centimeters. There is evidence that corn was ground with stone mortars and baked in flat bread.	by 2000 B.C.E.
Maize becomes the staple of Mesoamerican agriculture. Its cultural importance was reflected in its prominence in various myths of origin. Such stories among the Maya, for example, held that humankind was made first of mud, then of wood, and finally, and most successfully, from maize dough.	1500 B.C.E.
Maize spreads to the southwestern United States, along with the migration of farming people	1000 B.C.E.
In Peru, the average size of a maize cob doubles. Maize is used for making maize beer.	500 B.C.E.–1 C.E.
Maize cultivation reaches the eastern woodlands of the Mississippi River valley, largely through diffusion, although people of this region had already domesticated several minor crops, such as sunflowers.	500 C.E.
Maize farming is introduced in New England and is widespread by 1300, about 300 years before the arrival of the Pilgrims.	1000 C.E.
Maize spreads to Europe, Africa, and Asia, following European conquest of the Americas.	16th–18th centuries C.E.

Triumph and Resistance

Some combination of diffusion and migration took the original agricultural package of Southwest Asia and spread it widely into Europe, Central Asia, Egypt, and North Africa between 6500 and 4000 B.C.E. Languages originating in the core region accompanied this movement of people and farming practices. Thus Indo-European languages, which originated probably in Turkey and are widely spoken even today from India to Europe, reflect this movement of culture associated with the spread of agriculture. In a similar process, the Chinese farming system moved into Southeast Asia and elsewhere, and with it a number of related language families developed. India received agricultural influences from the Middle East, Africa, and China alike.

Map 2.2 The Global Spread of Agriculture
From ten or more separate points of origin, agriculture spread to adjacent areas, eventually encompassing almost all of the world's peoples.

Bantu Migrations

Within Africa, the development of agricultural societies in the southern half of the continent is associated with the migration of peoples speaking one or another of the some 400 Bantu languages. Beginning from what is now southern Nigeria or Cameroon around 3000 B.C.E., Bantu-speaking people moved east and south over the next several millennia, taking with them their agricultural, cattle-raising, and, later, ironworking skills, as well as their languages. The Bantus generally absorbed, killed, or drove away the indigenous Paleolithic peoples or exposed them to animal-borne diseases to which they had no immunities. A similar process brought agricultural Austronesian-speaking people, who originated in southern China, to the Philippine and Indonesian islands, with similar consequences for their earlier inhabitants. Later, Austronesian speakers carried agriculture to the uninhabited islands of the Pacific and to Madagascar off the coast of southeastern Africa (see Map 1.2 on p. 19).

The globalization of agriculture was a prolonged process, lasting 10,000 years or more after its first emergence in the Fertile Crescent, but it was not successful everywhere. The Agricultural Revolution in New Guinea, for example, did not spread much beyond its core region. In particular, it did not pass to the nearby peoples of Australia, who remained steadfastly committed to gathering and hunting ways of life. The people of the west coast of North America, arctic regions, and southwestern Africa also maintained their gathering and hunting way of life into the modern era. A very few, such as the Hadza, described at the beginning of Chapter 1, practice it still.

Some of those who resisted the swelling tide of agriculture lived in areas unsuitable to farming, such as harsh desert or arctic environments; others lived in regions of particular natural abundance, like the territory of the Chumash, so they felt little need for agriculture. Such people found it easier to resist agriculture if they were not in the direct line of advance of more powerful agricultural people. But the fact that many of the remaining gathering and hunting peoples knew about agricultural practices from nearby farming neighbors suggests that they quite deliberately chose to resist it, preferring the freer life of their Paleolithic ancestors.

Nonetheless, by the beginning of the Common Era, the global spread of agriculture had reduced gathering and hunting peoples to a small and dwindling minority of humankind. If that process meant "progress" in certain ways, it also claimed many victims as the relentlessly expanding agricultural frontier slowly destroyed gathering and hunting societies. Whether this process occurred through the peaceful diffusion of new technologies, through intermarriage, through disease, or through the violent displacement of earlier peoples, the steady erosion of this ancient way of life has been a persistent thread of the human story over the past 10,000 years. The final chapters of that long story are being written in our own century. After the Agricultural Revolution, the future, almost everywhere, lay with the farmers and herders and with the distinctive societies that they created.

The Culture of Agriculture

■ Change
What was revolutionary
about the Agricultural
Revolution?

What did that future look like? In what ways did societies based on the domestication of plants and animals differ from those rooted in a gathering and hunting economy? In the first place, the Agricultural Revolution led to an increase in human population, as the greater productivity of agriculture was able to support much larger numbers. An early agricultural settlement uncovered near Jericho in present-day Israel probably had 2,000 people, a vast increase in the size of human communities compared to much smaller Paleolithic bands. On a global level, scholars estimate that the world's population was about 6 million around 10,000 years ago, before the Agricultural Revolution got under way, and shot up to some 50 million by 5,000 years ago and 250 million by the beginning of the Common Era. Here was the real beginning of the human dominance over other forms of life on the planet.

But larger communities and more people did not necessarily mean an improved life for ordinary people. Farming involved hard work and more of it than in many earlier gathering and hunting societies. The remains of early agricultural people show some deterioration in health—more tooth decay and anemia, a shorter physical stature, and diminished life expectancy. Living close to animals subjected humans to new diseases—smallpox, flu, measles, chicken pox, malaria, tuberculosis, rabies—while living in larger communities generated epidemics for the first time in human history.[13] Furthermore, relying on a small number of plants or animals rendered early agricultural societies vulnerable to famine, in case of crop failure, drought, or other catastrophes. The advent of agriculture bore costs as well as benefits.

Agriculture also imposed constraints on human communities. Some Paleolithic people had settled in permanent villages, but all agricultural people did so, as farming required a settled life. A good example of an early agricultural settlement comes from northern China, one of the original independent sources of agriculture, where rice, millet, pig, and chicken farming gave rise to settled communities by about 7,000 years ago. In 1953, workers digging the foundation for a factory uncovered the remains of an ancient village, now called Banpo, near the present-day city of Xian. Millet, pigs, and dogs had been domesticated, but diets were supplemented with wild plants, animals, and fish. Some forty-five houses covered with thatch laid over wooden beams provided homes to perhaps 500 people. More than 200 storage pits permitted the accumulation of grain, and six kilns and pottery wheels enabled the production of various pots, vases, and dishes, many decorated with geometric designs and human and animal images. A large central space suggests an area for public religious or political activity, and a trench surrounding the village indicates some common effort to defend the community.

Early agricultural villages such as Banpo reveal another feature of the age of agriculture—an explosion of technological innovation. Mobile Paleolithic peoples had little use for pots, but such vessels were essential for settled societies, and their creation and elaboration accompanied agriculture everywhere, as did the weaving of textiles, made possible by collecting the fibers of domesticated plants (cotton and

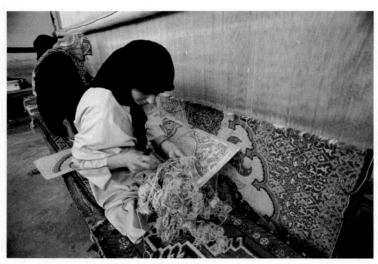

Women and Weaving
During the Paleolithic era and beyond, the weaving of cloth was widely regarded as "women's work." It still is in many places, as this picture from an early twenty-first-century carpet-weaving workshop in Isfahn (Iran) illustrates. (Phil Weymout/Lonely Planet Images/Getty Images)

flax, for example) and animals such as sheep. Evidence for the invention of looms of several kinds dates back to 7,000 years ago, and textiles, some elaborately decorated, show up in Peru, Switzerland, China, and Egypt. Like agriculture itself, weaving clearly seems to be a technology in which women were the primary innovators. It was a task that was compatible with child-rearing responsibilities, which virtually all human societies assigned primarily to women.[14] Another technology associated with the Agricultural Revolution was metallurgy. The working of gold and copper, then bronze, and, later, iron became part of the jewelry-, tool-, and weapon-making skill set of humankind. The long "stone age" of human technological history was coming to an end, and the age of metals was beginning.

A further set of technological changes, beginning around 4000 B.C.E., has been labeled the "secondary products revolution."[15] These technological innovations involved new uses for domesticated animals, beyond their meat and hides. Agricultural people in parts of Europe, Asia, and Africa learned to milk their animals, to harvest their wool, and to enrich the soil with their manure. Even more important, they learned to ride horses and camels and to hitch various animals to plows and carts. Because these types of animals did not exist in the Americas, this revolutionary new source of power and transportation was available only in the Eastern Hemisphere.

A final feature of early agricultural societies lay in their growing impact on the environment, as farming and herding peoples deliberately altered the natural ecosystem by removing the natural ground cover for their fields, by making use of irrigation, and by grazing their now-domesticated animals. In parts of the Middle East within a thousand years after the beginning of settled agricultural life, some villages were abandoned when soil erosion and deforestation led to declining crop yields, which could not support mounting populations.[16] The advent of more intensive agriculture associated with city-based civilizations only heightened this human impact on the landscape (see Chapter 3).

Social Variation in the Age of Agriculture

■ **Comparison**
What different kinds of societies emerged out of the Agricultural Revolution?

The resources generated by the Agricultural Revolution opened up vast new possibilities for the construction of human societies, but they led to no single or common outcome. Differences in the natural environment, the encounter with strangers, and sometimes deliberate choices gave rise to several distinct kinds of societies early on in the age of agriculture, all of which have endured into modern times.

Pastoral Societies

One variation of great significance grew out of the difference between the domestication of plants and the domestication of animals. Many societies made use of both, but in regions where farming was difficult or impossible—arctic tundra, some grasslands, and deserts—some people came to depend far more extensively on their animals, such as sheep, goats, cattle, horses, camels, or reindeer. Animal husbandry was a "distinct form of food-producing economy," relying on the milk, meat, and blood of animals.[17] Known as herders, pastoralists, or nomads, such people emerged in Central Asia, the Arabian Peninsula, the Sahara, and in parts of eastern and southern Africa. What they had in common was mobility, for they moved seasonally as they followed the changing patterns of vegetation necessary as pasture for their animals.

The particular animals central to pastoral economies differed from region to region. The domestication of horses by 4000 B.C.E. and the later mastery of horseback-riding skills enabled the growth of pastoral peoples all across the steppes of Central Asia by the first millennium B.C.E. Although organized primarily in kinship-based clans or tribes, these nomads periodically created powerful military confederations, which played a major role in the history of Eurasia for thousands of years. In the Inner Asian, Arabian, and Saharan deserts, domesticated camels made possible the human occupation of forbidding environments. The grasslands south of the Sahara and in parts of eastern Africa supported cattle-raising pastoralists. The absence of large animals capable of domestication meant that no pastoral societies emerged in the Americas.

The relationship between nomadic herders and their farming neighbors has been one of the enduring themes of Afro-Eurasian history. Frequently, it was a relationship of conflict as pastoral peoples, unable to produce their own agricultural products, were attracted to the wealth and sophistication of agrarian societies and sought access to their richer grazing lands as well as their food crops and manufactured products. The biblical story of the deadly rivalry between two brothers—Cain, a "tiller of the ground," and Abel, a "keeper of sheep"—reflects this ancient conflict, which persisted well into modern times. But not all was conflict between pastoral and agricultural peoples. The more peaceful exchange of technologies, ideas, products, and people across the ecological frontier of pastoral and agricultural societies also served to enrich and to change both sides. In the chapters that follow, and especially in Chapter 12, we will encounter pastoral

The Domestication of Animals Although farming often gets top billing in discussions of the Neolithic Revolution, the raising of animals was equally important, for they provided meat, pulling power, transportation (in the case of horses and camels), and manure. Animal husbandry also made possible pastoral societies, which were largely dependent on their domesticated animals. In this Egyptian carving, dating to about 2380 B.C.E., two workers lead a prime bull to the fields. (G. Dagli Orti/The Art Archive)

societies repeatedly, particularly as they interact with neighboring agricultural and "civilized" peoples.

Agricultural Village Societies

The most characteristic early agricultural societies were those of settled village-based farmers, such as those living in Banpo or Jericho. Such societies retained much of the equality and freedom of gathering and hunting communities, as they continued to do without kings, chiefs, bureaucrats, or aristocracies.

An example of this type of social order can be found at Çatalhüyük, a very early agricultural village in southern Turkey. A careful excavation of the site revealed a population of several thousand people who buried their dead under their houses and then filled the houses with dirt and built new ones on top, layer upon layer. No streets divided the houses, which were constructed adjacent to one another. People moved about the village on adjoining rooftops, from which they entered their homes. Despite the presence of many specialized crafts, few signs of inherited social inequality have surfaced. Nor is there any indication of male or female dominance, although men were more closely associated with hunting wild animals and women with plants and agriculture. "Both men and women," concludes one scholar, "could carry out a series of roles and enjoy a range of positions, from making tools to grinding grain and baking to heading a household."[18]

Çatalhüyük
Since the 1960s, archeologists have uncovered the connected homes of Çatalhüyük, shown here in a photo of the excavation, as well as many artifacts, murals, and sculptures from this early agricultural settlement in southern Turkey. (Courtesy, James Mellaart/ Çatalhöyük Research Project)

Many such village-based agricultural societies flourished well into the modern era, usually organizing themselves in terms of kinship groups or lineages, which incorporated large numbers of people well beyond the immediate or extended family. Such people traced their descent through either the male or the female line to some common ancestor, real or mythical. In many African societies, for example, a lineage system provided the framework within which large numbers of people could make and enforce rules, maintain order, and settle disputes without going to war. In short, the lineage system performed the functions of government, but without the formal apparatus of government, and thus did not require kings

or queens, chiefs, or permanent officials associated with a state organization. The Tiv of central Nigeria organized close to a million people in this fashion at the end of the nineteenth century. Theirs was a system in which power was dispersed throughout the society rather than being concentrated in particular people or institutions. In fact, the Tiv had no word for "politics" as a separate aspect of life, for there was no state that specialized in political matters.

Despite their democratic qualities and the absence of centralized authority, village-based lineage societies sometimes developed modest social and economic inequalities. Elders could exploit the labor of junior members of the community and sought particularly to control women's reproductive powers, which were essential for the growth of the lineage. Among the Igbo of southern Nigeria, "title societies" enabled men and women of wealth and character to earn a series of increasingly prestigious "titles" that set them apart from other members of their community, although these honors could not be inherited. Lineages also sought to expand their numbers, and hence their prestige and power, by incorporating war captives or migrants in subordinate positions, sometimes as slaves.

Many agricultural societies, in Africa and elsewhere, conducted their affairs without formal centralized states or full-time rulers, even when they were aware of these institutions and practices from nearby peoples. Given the frequent oppressiveness of organized political power in human history, such experiments with "stateless" forms of social organization represent an intriguing alternative to states, kingdoms, and empires, so frequently highlighted in the historical record. These agricultural village societies pioneered the human settlement of vast areas; adapted to a variety of environments; created numerous cultural, artistic, and religious traditions; incorporated new crops, institutions, and people into their cultures; and interacted continuously with their neighbors.

Chiefdoms

In other places, agricultural societies gave rise to chiefdoms, in which inherited positions of power and privilege introduced a more distinct element of inequality, but unlike later "kings," chiefs could seldom use force to compel the obedience of their subjects. Instead they relied on their generosity or gift giving, their ritual status, or their personal charisma to persuade their followers. The earliest such chiefdoms seem to have emerged in the Tigris-Euphrates river valley called Mesopotamia (present-day Iraq), sometime after 6000 B.C.E., when temple priests organized irrigation systems and controlled trade with nearby societies.

■ **Comparison**
How did chiefdoms differ from stateless agricultural village societies?

Many chiefdoms followed in all parts of the world, and the more recent ones have been much studied by anthropologists. For example, chiefdoms emerged everywhere in the Pacific islands, which had been colonized by agricultural Polynesian peoples. Chiefs usually derived from a senior lineage, tracing their descent to the first son of an imagined ancestor. With both religious and secular functions, chiefs led important rituals and ceremonies, organized the community for warfare, directed its economic life, and sought to resolve internal conflicts. They collected tribute from commoners in the form of food, manufactured goods, and raw materials. These items in turn were redistributed to warriors, craftsmen, religious specialists, and other subordinates, while the chief kept enough to maintain his prestigious position and his imposing lifestyle.[19] In North America as well, a remarkable series of chiefdoms emerged in the eastern woodlands, where an extensive array of large earthen

Cahokia
Pictured here in an artist's reconstruction, Cahokia (near St. Louis, Missouri) was the center of an important agricultural chiefdom around 1100 C.E. See Chapter 7 for details. (Cahokia Mounds State Historic Site, Illinois. Painting by Lloyd K. Townsend)

mounds testify to the organizational capacity of these early societies. The largest of them, known as Cahokia, flourished around 1100 C.E. In such agricultural chiefdoms—both ancient and more recent—the distinction between elite and commoner, based on birth rather than age or achievement, began to take root. It was a fateful turn in the organization of human societies—one that was replicated, elaborated, and assumed to be natural in all later states and civilizations.

Reflections: The Legacies of Agriculture

Because it is practiced around the world and has achieved virtually universal acceptance, agriculture or "domestication" may seem to be a "natural" or inevitable feature of the human story. In terms of world history, however, it is a recent development, an adaptation to the unique conditions of the latest interglacial period. Who can say how long those conditions will last or whether agriculture would remain a viable way of life in a renewed Ice Age?

No matter how it turns out in the very long run, during the last 10,000 years or so, the Agricultural Revolution has radically transformed both the trajectory of the human journey and the evolution of life on the planet. This epic transformation granted to one species, *Homo sapiens*, a growing power over many other species of plants and animals. Agriculture made possible an increase in human numbers far beyond what a gathering and hunting economy could support, and it enabled human beings to control and manipulate both plants and animals for their own purposes far more than ever before.

But if agriculture provided humankind with the power to dominate nature, it also, increasingly, enabled some people to dominate others. This was not immediately apparent, and for several thousand years, and much longer in some places, agricultural villages retained much of the social equality that had characterized

Paleolithic life. Slowly, though, many of the resources released by the Agricultural Revolution accumulated in the hands of a few. Rich and poor, chiefs and commoners, landowners and dependent peasants, rulers and subjects, dominant men and subordinate women, slaves and free people—these distinctions, so common in the record of world history, took shape most extensively in productive agricultural settings, which generated an economic surplus. The endless elaboration of such distinctions, for better or worse, is a major element in the story of civilization.

Second Thoughts

What's the Significance?

end of the last Ice Age	Bantu migration	pastoral societies
broad spectrum diet	native Australians	Çatalhüyük
Fertile Crescent	Banpo	stateless societies
teosinte	secondary products	chiefdoms
diffusion	revolution	

To assess your mastery of the material in this chapter, see the **Online Study Guide** at bedfordstmartins.com/strayer.

Big Picture Questions

1. The Agricultural Revolution marked a decisive turning point in human history. What evidence might you offer to support this claim, and how might you argue against it?
2. How did early agricultural societies differ from those of the Paleolithic era? How does the example of settled gathering and hunting peoples such as the Chumash complicate this comparison?
3. Was the Agricultural Revolution inevitable? Why did it occur so late in the story of humankind?
4. "The Agricultural Revolution provides evidence for 'progress' in human affairs." Do you agree with this statement?

Next Steps: For Further Study

For Web sites and documents related to this chapter, see **Make History** at bedfordstmartins.com/strayer.

Elizabeth Wayland Barber, *Women's Work: The First 20,000 Years* (1994). Explores the role of women in early technological development, particularly textile making.

Peter Bellwood, *First Farmers* (2005). The most recent and up-to-date account of the Agricultural Revolution, considered on a global basis.

Mark Nathan Cohen, *The Food Crisis in Prehistory* (1977). An older work arguing that mounting human population triggered the breakthrough to agriculture.

Jared Diamond, *Guns, Germs, and Steel* (1998). A provocative and much-publicized explanation for regional economic differences, based on variations among early agricultural revolutions.

Steven Mithen, *After the Ice: A Global Human History, 20,000–5000 B.C.* (2004). An imaginative tour of world archeological sites during the Agricultural Revolution.

Neil Roberts, *The Holocene: An Environmental History* (1998). Explores the role of climate change and human activity in shaping the global environment during the age of agriculture.

"The Agricultural Revolution," http://www.wsu.edu/gened/learn-modules/top_agrev/agrev-index .html. A Web-based tutorial from Washington State University.

CHAPTER THREE

First Civilizations

Cities, States, and Unequal Societies

3500 B.C.E. – 500 B.C.E.

"Over 100 miles of wilderness, deep exploration into pristine lands, the solitude of backcountry camping, 4×4 trails, and ancient American Indian rock art and ruins. You can't find a better way to escape civilization!"[1] So goes an advertisement for a vacation in Utah's Canyonlands National Park, one of thousands of similar attempts to lure apparently constrained, beleaguered, and "civilized" city-dwellers into the spacious freedom of the wild and the imagined simplicity of earlier times. This urge to "escape from civilization" has long been a central feature in modern life. It is a major theme in Mark Twain's famous novel *Huck Finn*, in which the restless and rebellious Huck resists all efforts to "sivilize" him by fleeing to the freedom of life on the river. It is a large part of the "cowboy" image in American culture, and it permeates environmentalist efforts to protect the remaining wilderness areas of the country. Nor has this impulse been limited to modern societies and the Western world. The ancient Chinese teachers of Daoism likewise urged their followers to abandon the structured and demanding world of urban and civilized life and to immerse themselves in the eternal patterns of the natural order. It is a strange paradox that we count the creation of civilization among the major achievements of humankind and yet people within these civilizations have often sought to escape the constraints, artificiality, hierarchies, and other discontents of city living.

WHAT EXACTLY ARE THESE CIVILIZATIONS that have generated such ambivalent responses among their inhabitants? When, where, and how did they first arise in human history? What changes did they bring to

Raherka and Mersankh: Writing was among the defining features of civilizations almost everywhere. In ancient Egyptian civilization, the scribes who possessed this skill enjoyed both social prestige and political influence. This famous statue shows Raherka, the chief of the scribes during Egypt's Fifth Dynasty (about 2350 B.C.E.), in an affectionate pose with his wife, Mersankh. (Réunion des Musées Nationaux/Art Resource, NY) the people who lived within them? Why might some people criticize or seek to escape from them? These are the issues addressed in this chapter.

As historians commonly use the term, civilization represents a new and particular type of human society, made possible by the immense productivity of the Agricultural Revolution. Such societies encompassed far larger populations than any earlier form of human community and for the first time concentrated some of those people in sizable cities, numbering in the many tens of thousands. In these cities, people were organized and controlled by powerful states whose leaders could use force to compel obedience. Profound differences in economic function, skill, wealth, and status sharply divided the people of civilizations, making them far less equal, and subject to much greater oppression, than had been the case in earlier agricultural villages, pastoral societies, and chiefdoms. Pyramids, temples, palaces, elaborate sculptures, written literature, complex calendars, as well as class, slavery, patriarchy, and large-scale warfare—all of these have been among the cultural products of civilization.

Something New: The Emergence of Civilizations

■ **Change**
When and where did the First Civilizations emerge?

Like agriculture, civilization was a global phenomenon, showing up independently in six major locations scattered around the world during the several millennia after 3500 B.C.E. and in a number of other smaller expressions as well (see Map 3.1). At the time, these breakthroughs to a new way of life were small islands of innovation in a sea of people living in much older ways. In the long run of human history, however, civilizations gradually absorbed, overran, or displaced people practicing other ways of living. Over the next 5,000 years, civilization, as a unique kind of human community, gradually encompassed ever-larger numbers of people and extended over ever-larger territories, even as particular civilizations rose, fell, revived, and changed.

Introducing the First Civilizations

The earliest of these civilizations emerged around 3500 B.C.E. to 3000 B.C.E. in three places. One was the "cradle" of Middle Eastern civilization, expressed in the many and competing city-states of Sumer, in southern Mesopotamia (located in present-day Iraq). Much studied by archeologists and historians, Sumerian civilization gave rise to the world's earliest written language, which was used initially by officials to record the goods received by various temples. Almost simultaneously, the Nile River valley in northeastern Africa witnessed the emergence of Egyptian civilization, famous for its pharaohs and pyramids, as well as a separate civilization known as Nubia, farther south along the Nile. Unlike the city-states of Sumer, Egyptian civilization took shape as a unified territorial state in which cities were rather less prominent. Later in this chapter, we will explore these two First Civilizations in greater detail.

Less well known and only recently investigated by scholars was a third early civilization that was developing along the central coast of Peru from roughly 3000 B.C.E. to 1800 B.C.E., at about the same time as the civilizations of Egypt and Sumer. This desert region received very little rainfall, but it was punctuated by dozens of rivers that brought the snowmelt of the adjacent Andes Mountains to the Pacific Ocean. Along a thirty-mile stretch of that coast and in the nearby interior, a series of some twenty-five urban centers emerged in an area known as Norte Chico, the largest of which was Caral, in the Supe River valley. In Norte Chico, archeologists have found monumental architecture in the form of earthen platform mounds, one of them measuring 60 feet tall and 500 feet long, as well as large public ceremonial structures, stone buildings with residential apartments, and other signs of urban life.

Norte Chico was a distinctive civilization in many ways. Its cities were smaller than those of Mesopotamia and show less evidence of economic specialization. The economy was based to an unusual degree on an extremely rich fishing industry in anchovies and sardines along the coast. These items apparently were exchanged for cotton, essential for fishing nets, as well as food crops such as squash, beans, and guava, all of which were grown by inland people in the river valleys using irrigation agriculture. Unlike Egypt and Mesopotamia, Peruvian civilization did not rest upon grain-based farming, the people of Norte Chico did not develop pottery or writing, and few sculptures, carvings, or drawings have been uncovered so far. Archeologists have, however, found a 5,000-year-old *quipu* (a series of knotted cords, later used extensively by the Inca for accounting purposes), which some scholars have suggested may have been an alternative form of writing. Furthermore, the cities of Norte Chico lacked defensive walls, and archeologists have discovered little evidence of warfare, such as burned buildings and mutilated corpses. It was also an unusually self-contained civilization. Whereas Egypt and Mesopotamia had long interacted with each other, the only import from the outside world evident in Norte Chico, or in Andean civilization generally, was maize (corn), which was derived ultimately from Mesoamerica, though without direct contact between the two regions. Norte Chico apparently "lighted a cultural fire" in the Andes and established a pattern for the many Andean civilizations that followed— Chavín, Moche, Nazca, and, much later, the Inca.[2]

Somewhat later, three additional First Civilizations made their appearance. In the Indus and Saraswati river valleys of what is now Pakistan, a remarkable civilization arose during the third millennium B.C.E. By 2000 B.C.E., it embraced a far larger area than Mesopotamia, Egypt, or coastal Peru and was expressed primarily in its elaborately planned cities. All across this huge area, about twice the size of Texas, common patterns prevailed: standardized weights, measures, architectural styles, even the size of bricks. As elsewhere, irrigated agriculture provided the economic foundation for the civilization, and a written language, thus far undeciphered, provides evidence of a literate culture.

Unlike its Middle Eastern counterparts, the Indus Valley civilization apparently generated no palaces, temples, elaborate graves, kings, or warrior classes. In short,

Map 3.1   First Civilizations

Six First Civilizations emerged independently in locations scattered across the planet, all within a few thousand years, from 3500 to 1000 B.C.E.

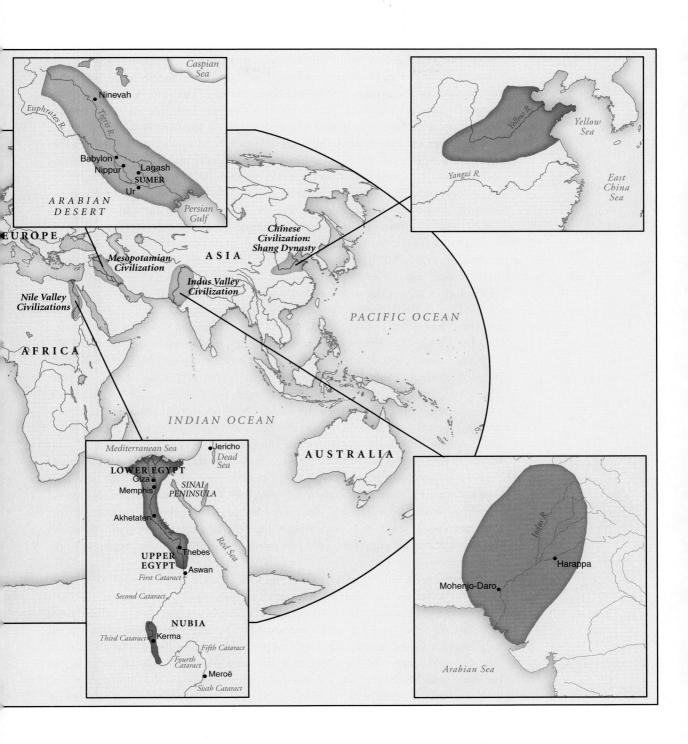

the archeological evidence provides little indication of a political hierarchy or centralized state. This absence of evidence has sent scholars scrambling to provide an explanation for the obvious specialization, coordination, and complexity that the Indus Valley civilization exhibited. A series of small republics, rule by priests, an early form of the caste system—all of these have been suggested as alternative mechanisms of integration in this first South Asian civilization. Although no one knows for sure, the possibility that the Indus Valley may have housed a sophisticated civilization without a corresponding state has excited the imagination of scholars.

Whatever its organization, the local environmental impact of the Indus Valley civilization, as in many others, was heavy and eventually undermined its ecological foundations. Repeated irrigation increased the amount of salt in the soil and lowered crop yields. The making of mud bricks, dried in ovens, required an enormous amount of wood for fuel, generating large-scale deforestation and soil erosion. As a result, these magnificent cities were abandoned by about 1700 B.C.E. and largely forgotten thereafter. Nonetheless, many features of this early civilization—ceremonial bathing, ritual burning, yoga positions, bulls and elephants as religious symbols, styles of clothing and jewelry—continued to nourish the later classical civilization of the Indian subcontinent and in fact persist into the present.[3]

The early civilization of China, dating to perhaps 2200 B.C.E., was very different from that of the Indus Valley. The ideal of a centralized state was evident from the days of the Xia dynasty (2200–1766 B.C.E.), whose legendary monarch Wu organized flood control projects that "mastered the waters and made them to flow in great channels." Subsequent dynasties—the Shang (1766–1122 B.C.E.) and the Zhou (1122–256 B.C.E.)—substantially enlarged the Chinese state, erected lavish tombs for their rulers, and buried thousands of human sacrificial victims to accompany them in the world to come. By the Zhou dynasty, a distinctive Chinese political ideology had emerged, featuring a ruler, known as the Son of Heaven, who served as an intermediary between heaven and earth and ruled by the Mandate of Heaven only so long as he governed with benevolence and maintained social harmony among his people. An early form of written Chinese has been discovered on numerous oracle bones, which were intended to predict the future and to assist China's rulers in the task of governing. Chinese civilization, more than any other, has experienced an impressive cultural continuity from its earliest expression into modern times.

A final First Civilization, known as the Olmec, took shape around 1200 B.C.E. along the coast of the Gulf of Mexico near present-day Veracruz in southern Mexico. Based on an agricultural economy of maize, beans, and squash, Olmec cities arose from a series of competing chiefdoms and became ceremonial centers filled with elaborately decorated temples, altars, pyramids, and tombs of rulers. The most famous artistic legacy of the Olmecs lay in some seventeen colossal basalt heads, weighing twenty tons or more. Recent discoveries suggest that the Olmecs may well have created the first written language in the Americas by about 900 B.C.E. Sometimes regarded as the "mother civilization" of Mesoamerica, Olmec cultural patterns—mound building, artistic styles, urban planning, a game played with a rubber ball, ritual sacrifice, and bloodletting by rulers—spread widely throughout the region and influenced subsequent civilizations, such as the Maya and Teotihuacán.

Beyond these six First Civilizations, other smaller civilizations also flourished. Lying south of Egypt in the Nile Valley, Nubian civilization was clearly distinctive and independent of its northern neighbor, although Nubia was involved in a long and often contentious relationship with Egypt. Likewise in China, a large city known as Sanxingdui, rich in bronze sculptures and much else, arose separately but at the same time as the more well-known Shang

Shang Dynasty Bronze
This bronze tiger, created around 1100 B.C.E., illustrates Chinese skill in working with bronze and the mythological or religious significance of the tiger as a messenger between heaven and the human world. (Jiangxi Provincial Museum, Nanchang/Visual Connection Archive)

dynasty. As a new way of living and a new form of human society, civilization was beginning its long march toward encompassing almost all of humankind by the twentieth century.

The Question of Origins

The first question that historians ask about almost everything is "How did it get started?" Scholars of all kinds—archeologists, anthropologists, sociologists, and historians—have been arguing about the origins of civilization for a very long time, with no end in sight.[4] Amid all the controversy, one thing seems reasonably clear: civilizations had their roots in the Agricultural Revolution. That is the reason they appeared so late in the human story, for only an agricultural technology permitted human communities to produce sufficient surplus to support large populations and the specialized or elite minorities who did not themselves produce food. Furthermore, all of the First Civilizations emerged from earlier and competing chiefdoms, in which some social ranking and economic specialization had already developed. It was a gradual and evolutionary process. However, not all agricultural societies or chiefdoms developed into civilizations, so something else must have been involved. It is the search for this "something else" that has provoked such great debate among scholars.

Some scholars have emphasized the need to organize large-scale irrigation projects as a stimulus for the earliest civilizations, but archeologists have found that the more complex water control systems appeared long after states and civilizations had already been established. Others have suggested that powerful states were

■ **Change**
What accounts for the initial breakthroughs to civilization?

useful in protecting the privileges of favored groups. Warfare and trade have figured in still other explanations for the rise of civilizations. Anthropologist Robert Carneiro combined several of these factors in a thoughtful approach to the question.[5] He argued that a growing density of population, producing more congested and competitive societies, was a fundamental motor of change, and especially in areas where rich agricultural land was limited, either by geography (oceans, deserts, mountains) or by powerful competing societies. Such settings provided incentives for innovations, such as irrigation or plows that could produce more food, because opportunities for territorial expansion were not readily available. But circumscribed environments with dense populations also generated intense competition among rival groups, which led to repeated warfare. A strong and highly organized state was a decided advantage in such competition. Because losers could not easily flee to new lands, they were absorbed into the winner's society as a lower class. Successful leaders of the winning side emerged as an elite with an enlarged base of land, a class of subordinated workers, and a powerful state at their disposal—in short, a civilization.

Although such a process was relatively rapid by world history standards, it took many generations, centuries, or perhaps millennia to evolve. It was, of course, an unconscious undertaking in which the participants had little sense of the long-term outcome as they coped with the practical problems of survival on a day-to-day basis. What is surprising, though, is the rough similarity of the result in many widely separated places from about 3000 B.C.E. to the beginning of the Common Era.

However they got started (and much about this is still guesswork), the First Civilizations, once established, represented a very different kind of human society than anything that came before. All of them were based on highly productive agricultural economies. Various forms of irrigation, drainage, terracing, and flood control enabled these early civilizations to tap the food-producing potential of their regions. In dry lands with good soil, such as northern China and southern Iraq, water made all the difference and vastly increased the agricultural output. In all these civilizations, pottery likewise enhanced the productivity of farming, as did animal-drawn plows and metalworking in Afro-Eurasia. Ritual sacrifice, often of people, usually accompanied the growth of civilization, and the new rulers normally served as high priests or were seen as divine beings, their right to rule legitimated by association with the sacred.

An Urban Revolution

■ Change
What was the role of cities in the early civilizations?

It was these resources from agriculture that made possible one of the most distinctive features of the First Civilizations—cities. What would an agricultural villager have made of Uruk, ancient Mesopotamia's largest city? Uruk had walls more than twenty feet tall and a population around 50,000 in the third millennium B.C.E. The city's center, visible for miles around, was a stepped pyramid, or *ziggurat*, topped with a temple. Inside the city, our village visitor would have found other temples as well, serving as centers of worship and as places for the redistribution of stored food. Numerous craftspeople labored as masons, copper workers, weavers, and many other specialties, while bureaucrats helped administer the city. It was, surely, a "vibrant, noisy, smelly, sometimes bewildering and dangerous, but also exciting place."[6] Here is how the *Epic of Gilgamesh*, Mesopotamia's ancient epic poem, describes the city:

> Come then, Enkidu, to ramparted Uruk,
> Where fellows are resplendent in holiday clothing,
> Where every day is set for celebration,
> Where harps and drums are played.
> And the harlots too, they are fairest of form,
> Rich in beauty, full of delights,
> Even the great gods are kept from sleeping at night.[7]

Equally impressive to a village visitor would have been the city of Mohenjo Daro, which flourished along the banks of the Indus River around 2000 B.C.E. With a population of perhaps 40,000, Mohenjo Daro and its sister city of Harappa featured large, richly built houses of two or three stories, complete with indoor plumbing, luxurious bathrooms, and private wells. Streets were laid out in a gridlike pattern, and beneath the streets ran a complex sewage system. Workers lived in row upon row of standardized two-room houses. Grand public buildings, including what seems to be a huge public bath, graced the city, while an enormous citadel was surrounded by a brick wall some forty-five feet high.

Even larger, though considerably later, was the Mesoamerican city of Teotihuacán, located in the central valley of Mexico. It housed perhaps 200,000 people in the middle of the first millennium C.E. Broad avenues, dozens of temples, two huge pyramids, endless stone carvings and many bright frescoes, small apartments for the ordinary, palatial homes for the wealthy—all of this must have seemed another world for a new visitor from a distant village. In shopping for obsidian blades, how was she to decide among the 350 workshops in the city? In seeking relatives, how could she find her way among many different compounds, each surrounded by a wall and housing a different lineage? And what would she make of a neighborhood composed entirely of Mayan merchants from the distant coastal lowlands?

Cities, then, lay at the heart of all of the First Civilizations. They were political/administrative capitals; they were centers for the production of

Mohenjo Daro
Flourishing around 2000 B.C.E., Mohenjo Daro was by far the largest city of the Indus Valley civilization, covering more than 600 acres. Here is a picture of a small part of that city as it has been uncovered by archeologists during the past century. (Paolo Koch/Photo Researchers, Inc.)

culture, including art, architecture, literature, ritual, and ceremony; they served as marketplaces for both local and long-distance exchange; and they housed most manufacturing activity. Everywhere they generated a unique kind of society, compared to earlier agricultural villages. Urban society was impersonal, for it was no longer possible to know everyone. Relationships of class and occupation were at least as important as those of kinship and village loyalty. Most notably, the degree of specialization and inequality far surpassed that of all preceding human communities.

The Erosion of Equality

Among the most novel features of early urban life, at least to our imaginary village visitor, was the amazing specialization of work. In an amusing Egyptian document from about 1200 B.C.E., a teacher tries to persuade a reluctant student, preparing to be a scribe (a literate public official), to take his lessons seriously by pointing out the disadvantages of the many other occupations that await him. His lazy pupil might wind up as a washerman, potter, maker of boots and shoes, watchman, merchant, crewman on a ship, field worker, peasant, soldier, or unskilled worker, possibly hauling stones for the pyramids. All of these jobs he describes as dirty, demeaning, or laborious and concludes: "If you have any sense, be a scribe."[8] In ancient Mesopotamia, even scribes were subdivided into many categories: junior and senior scribes, temple scribes and royal scribes, scribes for particular administrative or official functions.[9] None of these people, of course, grew their own food; they were supported by the highly productive agriculture of farmers.

Hierarchies of Class

■ **Change**
In what ways was social inequality expressed in early civilizations?

Alongside the occupational specialization of the First Civilizations lay their vast inequalities—in wealth, status, and power. Here we confront a remarkable and persistent feature of the human journey. As ingenuity and technology created more-productive economies, the greater wealth now available to societies was everywhere piled up rather than spread out. Early signs of this erosion of equality were evident in the more settled and complex gathering and hunting societies such as the Chumash and in agricultural chiefdoms such as Cahokia, but the advent of urban-based civilizations multiplied and magnified these inequalities many times over, as the egalitarian values of earlier cultures were everywhere displaced. This transition represents one of the major turning points in the social history of humankind.

As the First Civilizations took shape, inequality and hierarchy soon came to be regarded as normal and natural. Upper classes everywhere enjoyed great wealth in land or salaries, were able to avoid physical labor, had the finest of everything, and occupied the top positions in political, military, and religious life.

Frequently, they were distinguished by the clothing they wore, the houses they lived in, and the manner of their burial. Early Chinese kings bestowed special clothing, banners, chariots, weapons, and ornaments on their regional officials, and all of these items were graded according to the officials' precise location in the hierarchy. In Mesopotamia, the punishments prescribed in the famous Code of Hammurabi depended on social status. A free-born commoner who struck a person of equal rank had to pay a small fine, but if he struck "a man who is his superior, he shall receive 60 strokes with an oxtail whip in public." Clearly, class had consequences.

In all civilizations, free commoners represented the vast majority of the population and included artisans of all kinds, lower-level officials, soldiers and police, servants, and, most numerous of all, farmers. It was their surplus production— appropriated through a variety of taxes, rents, required labor, and tribute payments— that supported the upper classes. At least some of these people were aware of, and resented, these forced extractions and their position in the social hierarchy. Most Chinese peasants, for example, owned little land of their own and worked on plots granted to them by royal or aristocratic landowners. An ancient poem compared the exploiting landlords to rats and expressed the farmers' vision of a better life.

> Large rats! Large rats!
> Do not eat our spring grain!
> Three years have we had to do with you.
> And you have not been willing to think of our toil.
> We will leave you,
> And go to those happy borders.
> Happy borders, happy borders!
> Who will there make us always to groan?[10]

At the bottom of social hierarchies everywhere were slaves. Slavery and civilization, in fact, seem to have emerged together. The Code of Hammurabi, dating to almost 2000 B.C.E., mentions slavery in a casual, accepted, matter-of-fact way. Female slaves, captured in the many wars among rival Mesopotamian cities, were put to work in large-scale semi-industrial weaving enterprises, while males helped to maintain irrigation canals and construct ziggurats. Others worked as domestic servants in the households of their owners. In all of the First Civilizations, slaves— derived from prisoners of war, criminals, and debtors—were available for sale; for work in the fields, mines, homes, and shops of their owner; or on occasion for sacrifice. From the days of the earliest civilizations until the nineteenth century, the practice of "people owning people" has been an enduring feature of state-based societies everywhere.

The practice of slavery in ancient times varied considerably from place to place. Egypt and the Indus Valley civilizations initially had far fewer slaves than did Mesopotamia, which was highly militarized. Later, the Greeks of Athens and the Romans employed slaves far more extensively than did the Chinese or Indians (see Chapter 6). Furthermore, most ancient slavery differed from the type of slavery practiced in the Americas during recent centuries; in the early civilizations, slaves were not a primary agricultural labor force, many children of slaves could become free people, and slavery was not associated primarily with "blackness" or with Africa.

Hierarchies of Gender

■ Change
In what ways have historians tried to explain the origins of patriarchy?

Accompanying the hierarchies of class were those of gender, as civilizations everywhere undermined the earlier and more equal relationships between men and women. Most scholars agree that early horticultural societies, those using a hoe or digging stick, continued the relative gender equality that had characterized Paleolithic peoples. In such societies, women were much involved in agricultural labor, which generated most of the food for the village. Women were also engaged in spinning, weaving, and making pots—activities that were compatible with their role as mothers. Their central economic function, together with their amazing capacity to produce new life, gave women considerable respect and, arguably, a status generally equal to that of men. Some scholars have seen this respect and status reflected, at least in Europe and the Middle East, in a proliferation of figurines, masks, signs, symbols, and myths, all featuring women and feminine themes dealing with birth, growth, death, and regeneration.[11]

But as the First Civilizations took shape, the institutions and values of male dominance, often referred to as patriarchy, gradually emerged. The big question, of course, lies in trying to explain this momentous change. What was it about civilization that seemed to generate patriarchy?

One approach to answering this question highlights the role of a new and more intensive form of agriculture, involving the use of animal-drawn plows and the keeping and milking of large herds of animals. Unlike earlier farming practices that relied on a hoe or digging stick, plow-based agriculture meant heavier work, which men were better able to perform. Taking place at a distance from the village, this new form of agriculture was perhaps less compatible with women's primary responsibility for child rearing. Furthermore, the growing population of civilizations meant that women were more often pregnant and even more deeply involved in child care than before. Thus, in plow-based communities, men took over most of the farming work, and the status of women declined correspondingly, even though their other productive activities—weaving and food preparation, for example—continued. "As women were increasingly relegated to secondary tasks . . . ," writes archeologist Margaret Ehrenberg, "they had fewer personal resources with which to assert their status."[12]

Patriarchy also developed in civilizations untouched by plow agriculture, such as those of Mesoamerica and the Andes. Perhaps something else was at work. Historian David Christian suggests that the declining position of women was connected more generally to the growth of social complexity in civilizations as economic, religious, and political "specialists" became more prominent. Because men were less important in the household, they may have been more available to assume the powerful and prestigious specialist roles. From these positions of authority, men were able to shape the values and practices of their societies in ways that benefited themselves at the expense of women. Here, perhaps, lies the origin of an ancient distinction between the realm of the home, defined as the domain of women, and the world of public life, associated with men.[13]

Women have long been identified not only with the home but also with nature, for they are intimately involved in the fundamental natural process of reproduction. But civilization seemed to highlight culture, or the human mastery of nature, through agriculture, monumental art and architecture, and the creation of large-scale cities and states. Did this mean, as some scholars have suggested, that women were now associated with an inferior dimension of human life (nature), while men assumed responsibility for the higher order of culture?[14]

A further aspect of civilization that may well have contributed to patriarchy was warfare. Large-scale military conflict with professionally led armies was a feature of almost all of the First Civilizations, and female prisoners of war often were the first slaves. With military service largely restricted to men, its growing prominence in the affairs of civilizations served to enhance the power and prestige of a male warrior class. So too, perhaps, did private property and commerce, central elements of the First Civilizations. Without sharp restrictions on women's sexual activity, how could a father be certain that family property would be inherited by his offspring? In addition, the buying and selling associated with commerce was soon applied to male rights over women, as female slaves, concubines, and wives were exchanged among men.

Patriarchy in Practice

Whatever the precise origins of patriarchy, male dominance permeated the First Civilizations, marking a gradual change from the more equal relationships of men and women within agricultural villages or Paleolithic bands. Historian Gerda Lerner documented this transition in ancient Mesopotamian civilization. By the second millennium B.C.E., various written laws codified and sought to enforce a patriarchal family life that offered women a measure of paternalistic protection while insisting on their submission to the unquestioned authority of men. Central to these laws was the regulation of female sexuality. A wife caught sleeping with another man might be drowned at her husband's discretion, whereas he was permitted to enjoy sexual relations with his female servants, though not with another man's wife. Divorce was far easier for a man than for his wife. Rape was a serious offense, but the injured party was primarily the father or the husband of the victim, rather than the violated woman herself. Even elite women, who were often

■ Comparison
How did Mesopotamian and Egyptian patriarchy differ from each other?

allowed to act on behalf of their powerful husbands, saw themselves as dependent. "Let all be well with [my husband]," prayed one such wife, "that I may prosper under his protection."[15]

Furthermore, women in Mesopotamian civilization were sometimes divided into two sharply distinguished categories. Respectable women, those under the protection and sexual control of one man, were required to be veiled when outside the home, whereas nonrespectable women, such as slaves and prostitutes, were forbidden to do so and were subject to severe punishment if they presumed to cover their heads.

Finally, the powerful goddesses of earlier times were gradually relegated to the home and hearth and were replaced by dominant male deities, who now were credited with the power of creation and fertility and viewed as the patrons of wisdom and learning. The culmination of this "demotion of the goddess," argues Gilda Lerner, lies in the Hebrew Scriptures, in which a single male deity, Yahweh, alone undertakes the act of creation without any participation of a female goddess.

Patriarchy was not everywhere the same, however. Egypt, while clearly patriarchal, afforded its women greater opportunities than did most other First Civilizations. In Egypt, women were recognized as legal equals to men, able to own property and slaves, to administer and sell land, to make their own wills, to sign their own marriage contracts, and to initiate divorce. Royal women occasionally exercised significant political power, acting as regents for their young sons or more rarely as queens in their own right. Clearly, though, this was seen as abnormal, for Egypt's most famous queen, Hatshepsut (reigned 1472–1457 B.C.E.), was sometimes portrayed in statues as a man, dressed in male clothing and sporting the traditional false beard of the pharaoh. Moreover, married women in Egypt were not veiled as in Mesopotamia. Statues and paintings often showed men and women in affectionate poses and as equal partners, as can be seen in the photo at the beginning of this chapter. Although marriages were clearly arranged by parents, the love poetry of New Kingdom Egypt (1550–1064 B.C.E.) suggests an element of romance and longing. One lovesick boy lamented the absence of his beloved, referred to as a "sister."

> Seven days since I saw my sister,
> and sickness invaded me; . . .
> The sight of her makes me well . . .
> Her speaking makes me strong;
> Embracing her expels my malady. . . .

And a young woman exults at the sight of her love:

> I passed before his house,
> I found his door ajar;
> My brother stood by his mother; . . .

He looked at me as I passed by, . . .
How my heart exulted in gladness,
My brother, at your sight[16]

The Rise of the State

What, we might reasonably ask, held ancient civilizations together despite the many
tensions and complexities of urban living and the vast inequalities of civilized societies? Why did they not fly apart amid the resentments born of class and gender
hierarchies? The answer, in large part, lay in yet another distinctive feature of the
First Civilizations—states. Organized around particular cities or larger territories,
early states were headed almost everywhere by kings, who employed a variety of
ranked officials, exercised a measure of control over society, and defended it against
external enemies. To modern people, the state is such a familiar reality that we find
it difficult to imagine life without it. Nonetheless, it is a quite recent invention in
human history, with the state replacing, or at least supplementing, kinship as the
basic organizing principle of society and exercising far greater authority than earlier chiefdoms.

Coercion and Consent

Early states in Mesopotamia, Egypt, China, Mesoamerica, and elsewhere drew
their power from various sources, all of which assisted in providing cohesion for
the First Civilizations. One basis of power was the recognition that the complexity of life in cities or densely populated territories required some authority to
coordinate and regulate the community. Someone had to organize the irrigation
systems of river valley civilizations. Someone had to adjudicate conflicts among
the many different peoples, unrelated to one another, who rubbed elbows in the
early cities. Someone had to direct efforts to defend the city or territory against
aggressive outsiders. The state, in short, solved certain widely shared problems and
therefore had a measure of voluntary support among the population. For many
people, it was surely useful.

■ **Change**
What were the sources
of state authority in the
First Civilizations?

The state, however, was more useful for some people than for others, for it also
served to protect the privileges of the upper classes, to require farmers to give up a
portion of their product to support city-dwellers, and to demand work on large
public projects such as pyramids and fortifications. If necessary, state authorities had
the ability, and the willingness, to use force to compel obedience. The Egyptian
teacher mentioned earlier described to his reluctant student what happens to a
peasant unable to pay his tax in grain.

Now the scribe lands on the shore. He surveys the harvest. Attendants are behind
him with staffs, Nubians with clubs. One says [to the peasant], "Give grain." There
is none. He is beaten savagely. He is bound, thrown into a well, submerged head

A Mesopotamian Ziggurat
This massive ziggurat/temple to the Mesopotamian moon god Nanna was built around 2100 B.C.E. in the city of Ur. The solitary figure standing atop the staircase illustrates the size of this huge structure. (Richard Ashworth/Robert Harding World Imagery/Corbis)

down. His wife is bound in his presence. His children are in fetters. His neighbors abandon them and flee.[17]

Such was the power of the state, as rulers accumulated the resources to pay for officials, soldiers, police, and attendants. This capacity for violence and coercion marked off the states of the First Civilizations from earlier chiefdoms, whose leaders had only persuasion, prestige, and gifts to back up their authority.

Force, however, was not always necessary, for the First Civilizations soon generated ideas suggesting that state authority and class and gender inequalities were normal, natural, and ordained by the gods. Kingship everywhere was associated with the sacred. Ancient Chinese kings were known as the Son of Heaven, and they alone could perform the rituals and sacrifices necessary to keep the cosmos in balance. Mesopotamian rulers were thought to be the stewards of their city's patron gods. Their symbols of kingship—crown, throne, scepter, mace—were said to be of divine origin, sent to earth when the gods established monarchy. Egyptians, most of all, invested their pharaohs with divine qualities. Rulers claimed to embody all the major gods of Egypt, and their supernatural power ensured the regular flooding of the Nile and the defeat of the country's enemies.

But if religion served most often to justify unequal power and privilege, it might also on occasion be used to restrain, or even undermine, the established order. Hammurabi claimed that his law code was inspired by Marduk, the chief god of Babylon, and was intended to "bring about the rule of righteousness in the land, to destroy the wicked and the evil-doers; so that the strong should not harm the weak."[18] Another Mesopotamian monarch, Urukagina from the city of Lagash, claimed authority from the city's patron god for reforms aimed at ending the corruption and tyranny of a previous ruler. In China during the Zhou dynasty (1122–256 B.C.E.), emperors ruled by the Mandate of Heaven, but their bad behavior could result in the removal of that mandate and the overthrow of the ruler.

Writing and Accounting

A further support for state authority lay in the remarkable invention of writing. It was a powerful and transforming innovation, regarded almost everywhere as a gift

Snapshot   **Writing in Ancient Civilizations**

Most of the early writing systems were "logophonetic," using symbols to designate both whole words and particular sounds or syllables. Chinese characters, which indicated only words, were an exception. None of them employed alphabets.

Location	Type	Initial Use	Example	Comment
Sumer	Cuneiform: wedge-shaped symbols on clay tablets representing objects, abstract ideas, sounds, and syllables	Records of economic transactions, such as temple payments and taxes	bird	Regarded as the world's first written language; other languages such as Babylonian and Assryian were written with Sumerian script
Egypt	Hieroglyphs ("sacred carvings"): a series of signs that denote words and consonants (but not vowels or syllables)	Business and administrative purposes; later used for religious inscriptions, stories, poetry, hymns, and mathematics	rain, dew, storm	For everyday use, less formal systems of cursive writing (known as "hieratic" and "demotic") were developed
Andean	Quipu: a complex system of knotted cords in which the color, length, type, and location of knots conveyed mostly numerical meaning	Various accounting functions; perhaps also used to express words	numerical data (possibly in codes), words and ideas	Widely used in the Inca Empire; recent discoveries place quipus in Caral some 5,000 years ago
Indus River Valley	Some 400 pictographic symbols representing sounds and words, probably expressing a Dravidian language currently spoken in southern India	Found on thousands of clay seals and pottery; probably used to mark merchandise	6 fish	As yet undeciphered
China	Oracle bone script: pictographs (stylized drawings) with no phonetic meaning	Inscribed on turtle shells or animal bones; used for divination (predicting the future) in the royal court of Shang dynasty rulers	horse	Direct ancestor of contemporary Chinese characters
Olmec	Signs that represent sounds (syllables) and words; numbering system using bars and dots	Used to record the names and deeds of rulers and shamans, as well as battles and astronomical data	jaguar	Structurally similar to later Mayan script; Olmec calendars were highly accurate and the basis for later Mesoamerican calendars

from the gods, while people without writing often saw it as something magical or supernatural. Distinctive forms of writing emerged in all of the First Civilizations except the Andes, although some scholars now regard their knotted strings, or quipus, as a kind of writing.[19]

Writing sustained the First Civilizations and their successors in many ways. Literacy defined elite status and conveyed enormous prestige to those who possessed it. Because it can be learned, writing also provided a means for some commoners to join the charmed circle of the literate. Writing as propaganda, celebrating the great deeds of the kings, featured prominently, especially among the Egyptians and later among the Maya. A hymn to the pharaoh, dating to about 1850 B.C.E., extravagantly praised the ruler.

> He has come unto us . . . and has given peace to the two Riverbanks
> . . . and has made Egypt to live; he hath banished its suffering;
> . . . he has caused the throat of the subjects to breathe
> . . . and has trodden down foreign countries
> . . . he has delivered them that were robbed
> . . . he has come unto us, that we may (nurture up?) our children and bury our aged ones.[20]

In Mesopotamia and elsewhere, writing served an accounting function, recording who had paid their taxes, who owed what to the temple, and how much workers had earned. Thus it immensely strengthened bureaucracy. Complex calendars indicated precisely when certain rituals should be performed. Writing also gave weight and specificity to orders, regulations, and laws. Hammurabi's famous law code, while correcting certain abuses, made crystal clear that fundamental distinctions divided men and women and separated slaves, commoners, and people of higher rank.

Once it had been developed, writing, like religion, proved hard to control and operated as a "wild card" in human affairs. It gave rise to literature and philosophy, to astronomy and mathematics, and, in some places, to history. On occasion, the written word proved threatening, rather than supportive, to rulers. China's so-called First Emperor, Qin Shihuangdi (reigned 221–210 B.C.E.), allegedly buried alive some 460 scholars and burned their books when they challenged his brutal efforts to unify China's many warring states, or so his later critics claimed. Thus writing became a major arena for social and political conflict, and rulers always have sought to control it.

The Grandeur of Kings

Yet another source of state authority derived from the lavish lifestyle of elites, the impressive rituals they arranged, and the imposing structures they created. Everywhere, kings, high officials, and their families lived in luxurious palaces, dressed in splendid clothing, bedecked themselves with the loveliest jewelry, and were attended by endless servants. Their deaths triggered elaborate burials, of which the pyramids of the Egyptian pharaohs were perhaps the most ostentatious. Almost all of the First Civilizations accompanied high-status funerals with the human sacrifice of numerous retainers, who would nourish the souls or serve the needs of their rulers in the afterlife. Monumental palaces, temples, ziggurats, pyramids, and statues conveyed the immense power of the state and its elite rulers. The Olmec civilization of Mesoamerica (1200–400 B.C.E.) erected enormous human heads, more than ten feet tall and weighing at least twenty tons, carved from blocks of basalt and probably representing particular rulers. Somewhat later the Maya Temple of the Giant Jaguar, towering 154 feet tall, was the most impressive among many temples, pyramids, and palaces that graced the city of Tikal. All of this must have seemed overwhelming to common people in the cities and villages of the First Civilizations.

Olmec Head
This colossal statue, some six feet high and five feet wide, is one of seventeen such carvings, dating to the first millennium B.C.E., that were discovered in the territory of the ancient Olmec civilization. Thought to represent individual rulers, each of the statues has a distinct and realistically portrayed face. (Danny Lehman/Corbis)

Comparing Mesopotamia and Egypt

A productive agricultural technology, city living, immense class inequalities, patriarchy, the emerging power of states—all of these were common features of First Civilizations across the world and also of those that followed. Still, these civilizations were not everywhere the same, for differences in political organization, religious beliefs and practices, the role of women, and much more gave rise to distinctive traditions. Nor were they static. Like all human communities, they changed over the centuries. Finally, these civilizations did not exist in isolation, for they participated in networks of interactions with near and sometimes more distant neighbors. In looking more closely at two of these First Civilizations—Mesopotamia and Egypt—we can catch a glimpse of the differences, changes, and connections that characterized early civilizations.

■ **Comparison**
In what ways did Mesopotamian and Egyptian civilizations differ from each other?

Environment and Culture

The civilizations of both Mesopotamia and Egypt grew up in river valleys and depended on their rivers to sustain a productive agriculture in otherwise arid lands. Those rivers, however, had radically different characteristics. At the heart of Egyptian life was the Nile, "that green gash of teeming life," which rose predictably every year to bring the soil and water that nurtured a rich Egyptian agriculture. The

Snapshot   **Key Moments in Mesopotamian History**

Beginning of irrigated agriculture	6000 B.C.E.
Period of independent Sumerian city-states	3200–2350 B.C.E
Earliest cuneiform texts	3000 B.C.E.
First Sumerian law codes	2500 B.C.E.
First Mesopotamian empire: conquest of Sumer by Sargon of Akkad	2350 B.C.E.
Epic of Gilgamesh compiled	after 2000 B.C.E.
Babylonian empire	1900–1500 B.C.E.
Reign of Hammurabi	1792–1750 B.C.E.
Assyrian rule in Mesopotamia	900–612 B.C.E.
Assyrian conquest of Israel	722 B.C.E.
Babylonian conquest of Judah by King Nebuchadnezzar	586 B.C.E.
Mesopotamia incorporated into Persian empire	by 500 B.C.E.

Tigris and Euphrates rivers, which gave life to Mesopotamian civilization, also rose annually, but "unpredictably and fitfully, breaking man's dikes and submerging his crops."[21] (See Map 3.2.) Furthermore, an open environment without serious obstacles to travel made Mesopotamia far more vulnerable to invasion than the much more protected space of Egypt, which was surrounded by deserts, mountains, seas, and cataracts. For long periods of its history, Egypt enjoyed a kind of "free security" from external attack that Mesopotamians could only have envied.

Does the physical environment shape the human cultures that develop within it? Most historians are reluctant to endorse any kind of "determinism," especially one suggesting that "geography is destiny," but in the case of Mesopotamia and Egypt, many scholars have seen at least some relationship between the physical setting and culture.

In at least some of its literature, the Mesopotamian outlook on life, which developed within a precarious, unpredictable, and often violent environment, viewed humankind as caught in an inherently disorderly world, subject to the whims of capricious and quarreling gods, and facing death without much hope of a life beyond. A Mesopotamian poet complained: "I have prayed to the gods and sacrificed, but who can understand the gods in heaven? Who knows what they plan for us? Who has ever been able to understand a god's conduct?"[22] In the *Epic of Gilgamesh*, Mesopotamia's most famous literary work, death is described as a journey "down the road from which there is no turning back." The afterworld is a "house whose people sit in darkness; dust is their food and clay is their meat." In a futile effort to avoid this fate, the hero Gilgamesh sets out on a search for eternal

Map 3.2 **Mesopotamia**
After about 1,000 years of independent and competitive existence, the city-states of Sumer were incorporated into a number of larger imperial states based in Akkad, Babylon, and then Assyria.

life, but after many adventures and false starts, he is told, "[Y]ou will never find that life for which you are looking. When the gods created man, they allotted to him death, but life they retained in their own keeping." Nonetheless, not all is despair.

> As for you, Gilgamesh, fill your belly with good things; day and night, night and day, dance and be merry, feast and rejoice. Let your clothes be fresh, bathe yourself in water, cherish the little child that holds your hand, and make your wife happy in your embrace; for this too is the lot of man.[23]

By contrast, elite literate culture in Egypt, developing in a more stable, predictable, and beneficent environment, produced a rather more cheerful and hopeful outlook on the world. The rebirth of the sun every day and of the river every year seemed to assure Egyptians that life would prevail over death. The amazing pyramids, constructed during Egypt's Old Kingdom (2663–2195 B.C.E.), reflected the firm belief that at least the pharaohs and other high-ranking people could successfully make the journey to eternal life in the Land of the West. Incantations carved in royal burial chambers of the pharaohs describe an afterlife that Gilgamesh could only have envied.

> The gatekeeper comes out to you,
> He grasps your hand,
> Takes you into heaven, to your father, Geb.
> He rejoices at your coming,
> Gives you his hand,
> Kisses you, caresses you,
> Sets before you the spirits, the imperishable stars.
> The hidden ones worship you,
> The great ones surround you,
> The watchers wait on you,
> Barley is threshed for you . . .
> Rise up, O Teti, you shall not die.

Over time, larger groups of people, beyond the pharaoh and his entourage, gained access to the afterlife, if they followed proper procedures. By the New Kingdom (1550–1064 B.C.E.), a moral element had entered the equation for eternal life as claims on immortality were now made on the basis of ethical living. One text used in burial ceremonies required "a negative confession" of those seeking entrance to the afterlife: "I have not done crimes against the people; I have not mistreated cattle . . . ; I have not robbed the poor . . . ; I have not made anyone suffer."[24] Thus Egyptian civilization not only affirmed the possibility of eternal life but also democratized access to it.

If the different environments of Mesopotamia and Egypt shaped their societies and cultures, those civilizations, with their mounting populations and growing demand for resources, likewise had an impact on the environment.[25] In Sumer (southern Mesopotamia), deforestation and soil erosion decreased crop yields by some 65 percent between 2400 and 1700 B.C.E. Also contributing to this disaster was the increasing salinization of the soil, a long-term outcome of intensive irrigation. By 2000 B.C.E., there were reports that "the earth turned white" as salt accumulated in the soil. As a result, wheat was largely replaced by barley, which is far more tolerant of salty conditions. This ecological deterioration clearly weakened Sumerian city-states, facilitated their conquest by foreigners, and shifted the center of Mesopotamian civilization permanently to the north.

Egypt, by contrast, created a more sustainable agricultural system, which lasted for thousands of years and contributed to the remarkable continuity of its civilization. Whereas Sumerian irrigation involved a complex and artificial network of canals and dikes that led to the salinization of the soil, its Egyptian counterpart was much less intrusive, simply regulating the natural flow of the Nile. Such a system avoided the problem of salty soils, allowing Egyptian agriculture to emphasize wheat production, but it depended on the general regularity and relative gentleness of the Nile's annual flooding. On occasion, that pattern was interrupted, with serious consequences for Egyptian society. An extended period of low floods between 2250 and 1950 B.C.E. led to sharply reduced agricultural output, large-scale starvation, the loss of livestock, and, consequently, social upheaval and political disruption. Nonetheless, Egypt's ability to work *with* its more favorable natural environment enabled a degree of stability and continuity that proved impossible in Sumer, where human action intruded more heavily into a less benevolent natural setting.

Cities and States

Politically as well as culturally and environmentally, Mesopotamian and Egyptian civilizations differed sharply. For its first thousand years (3200–2350 B.C.E.), Mesopotamian civilization, located in the southern Tigris-Euphrates region known as Sumer, was organized in a dozen or more separate and independent city-states. Each city-state was ruled by a king, who claimed to represent the city's patron deity and who controlled the affairs of the walled city and surrounding rural area. Quite remarkably, some 80 percent of the population of Sumer lived in one or another of these city-states, making Mesopotamia the most thoroughly urbanized society of ancient times. The chief reason for this massive urbanization, however, lay in the great flaw of this system, for frequent warfare among these Sumerian city-states caused people living in rural areas to flee to the walled cities for protection. With no overarching authority, rivalry over land and water often led to violent conflict. After one such conflict destroyed the city of Ur and desecrated its temple, a poet lamented the city's sad fate.

> After your city had been destroyed, how now can you exist!
> After your house had been destroyed, how has your heart led you on!
> Your city has become a strange city . . .
> Your house has become a house of tears.[26]

These conflicts, together with environmental devastation, eventually left Sumerian cities vulnerable to outside forces, and after about 2350 B.C.E., stronger peoples from northern Mesopotamia conquered Sumer's warring cities, bringing an end to the Sumerian phase of Mesopotamian civilization. First the Akkadians (2350–2000 B.C.E.) and later the Babylonians (1900–1500 B.C.E.) and the Assyrians (900–612 B.C.E.) created larger territorial states or bureaucratic empires that encompassed all or most of Mesopotamia. Periods of political unity now descended upon this First Civilization, but it was unity imposed from outside. Much later, a similar process befell the Greek city-states, whose endemic warfare invited Macedonian invasion and their subsequent incorporation into the empires of Alexander the Great and then of the Romans (see Chapter 4).

Egyptian civilization, by contrast, began its history around 3100 B.C.E., with the merger of several earlier states or chiefdoms into a unified territory that stretched some 1,000 miles along the Nile. For an amazing 3,000 years, Egypt maintained that unity and independence, though with occasional interruptions. A combination

of wind patterns that made it easy to sail south along the Nile and a current flow-
ing north facilitated communication, exchange, unity, and stability within the Nile
Valley. Here was a record of political longevity and continuity that the
Mesopotamians and many other ancient peoples might well have envied.

Cities in Egypt were far less important than in Mesopotamia, although political capitals, market centers, and major burial sites gave it an urban presence as well.
Most people lived in agricultural villages along the river rather than in urban centers, perhaps because Egypt's greater security made it less necessary for people to
gather in fortified towns. The focus of the Egyptian state resided in the pharaoh,
believed to be a god in human form. He alone ensured the daily rising of the sun
and the annual flooding of the Nile. All of the country's many officials served at his
pleasure; the law of the land was simply the pharaoh's edict; and access to the afterlife lay in proximity to him and burial in or near his towering pyramids.

This image of the pharaoh and his role as an enduring symbol of Egyptian civilization persisted over the course of three millennia, but the realities of Egyptian
political life changed over time. By 2400 B.C.E., the power of the pharaoh had
diminished, as local officials and nobles, who had been awarded their own land and

Snapshot   Key Moments in Nile Valley Civilizations

Small-scale states in Sudanic Africa	5000 B.C.E.
Nubian kingdom of Ta-Seti	3400–3200 B.C.E.
Unification of Egypt as a single state	3100 B.C.E.
Frequent warfare between Egypt and Nubian states	3100–2600 B.C.E.
Old Kingdom Egypt (high point of pharaohs' power and pyramid building)	2663–2195 B.C.E.
Nubian kingdom of Kush established	2500 B.C.E.
Egyptian commercial expeditions to Nubia	2300 B.C.E.
Hyksos invasion and rule of Egypt	1650–1550 B.C.E.
New Kingdom Egypt	1550–1064 B.C.E.
Emergence of Egyptian empire	1500 B.C.E.
Queen Hatshepsut launches expeditions to Land of Punt, probably along the East African coast	1473–1458 B.C.E.
Kush conquest of Egypt	760–660 B.C.E.
Assyrian conquest of Egypt	671–651 B.C.E.
Persian rule in Egypt	525–404 B.C.E.
Roman conquest of Egypt	30 B.C.E.

were able to pass their positions on to their sons, assumed greater authority. When changes in the weather resulted in the Nile's repeated failure to flood properly around 2200 B.C.E., the authority of the pharaoh was severely discredited, and Egypt dissolved for several centuries into a series of local principalities.

Even when centralized rule was restored around 2000 B.C.E., the pharaohs never regained their old power and prestige. Kings were now warned that they too would have to account for their actions at the Day of Judgment. Nobles no longer sought to be buried near the pharaoh's pyramid but instead created their own more modest tombs in their own areas. Osiris, the god of the dead, became increasingly prominent, and "all men who were worthy . . . not merely those who had known the pharaoh in life" could aspire to immortality in his realm.[27]

Interaction and Exchange

Although Mesopotamia and Egypt represented separate and distinct civilizations, they interacted frequently with each other and with both near and more distant neighbors. Even in these ancient times, the First Civilizations were embedded in larger networks of commerce, culture, and power. None of them stood alone.

The early beginnings of Egyptian civilization illustrate the point. Its agriculture drew upon wheat and barley, which reached Egypt from Mesopotamia, as well as gourds, watermelon, domesticated donkeys, and cattle, which derived from Sudan. Some scholars argue that Egypt's step pyramids and its system of writing were stimulated by Mesopotamian models. The practice of "divine kingship" seems to have derived from the central or eastern Sudan, where small-scale agricultural communities had long viewed their rulers as sacred and buried them with various servants and officials. From this complex of influences, the Egyptians created something distinct and unique, but that civilization had roots in both Africa and Southwest Asia.[28]

Furthermore, once they were established, both Mesopotamia and Egypt carried on extensive long-distance trade. Sumerian merchants had established seaborne contact with the Indus Valley civilization as early as 2300 B.C.E. Other trade routes connected it to Anatolia (present-day Turkey), Egypt, Iran, and Afghanistan. During Akkadian rule over Mesopotamia, a Sumerian poet described its capital of Agade.

> In those days the dwellings of Agade were filled with gold,
> its bright-shining houses were filled with silver,
> into its granaries were brought copper, tin, slabs of
> lapis lazuli [a blue gemstone], its silos bulged at the sides . . .
> its quay where the boats docked were all bustle. . . .[29]

All of this and more came from far away.

Egyptian trade likewise extended far afield. Beyond its involvement with the Mediterranean and the Middle East, Egyptian trading journeys extended deep into

■ Connection

In what ways were Mesopotamian and Egyptian civilizations shaped by their interactions with near and distant neighbors?

Egypt and Nubia
By the fourteenth century B.C.E., Nubia was a part of an Egyptian empire. This wall painting shows Nubian princes bringing gifts or tribute, including rings and bags of gold, to Huy, the Egyptian viceroy of Nubia. The mural comes from Huy's tomb. (Courtesy of the Trustees of the British Museum)

Africa, including Nubia, south of Egypt in the Nile Valley, and Punt, along the East African coast of Ethiopia and Somalia. One Egyptian official described his return from an expedition to Nubia: "I came down with three hundred donkeys laden with incense, ebony . . . panther skins, elephant tusks, throw sticks, and all sorts of good products." [30] What most intrigued the very young pharaoh who sent him, however, was a dancing dwarf that accompanied the expedition back to Egypt.

Along with trade goods went cultural influence from the civilizations of Mesopotamia and Egypt. Among the smaller societies of the region to feel this influence were the Hebrews, who had migrated from Mesopotamia to Palestine and Egypt early in their history. Their sacred writings, recorded in the Old Testament, showed the influence of Mesopotamia in the "eye for an eye" principle of their legal system and in the story of a flood that destroyed the world. Unique to the Hebrews, however, was their emerging awareness of a merciful and single deity, Yahweh, who demanded an ethical life from his people. This conception subsequently achieved global significance when it was taken over by Christianity and Islam.

The Phoenicians, who were commercially active in the Mediterranean basin from their homeland in present-day Lebanon, also were influenced by Mesopotamian civilization. They adopted the Mesopotamian fertility goddess Ishtar, renaming her Astarte. They also adapted the Sumerian cuneiform method of writing to a much easier alphabetic system, which later became the basis for Greek and Latin writing. Various Indo-European peoples, dispersing probably from north-central Anatolia, also incorporated Sumerian deities into their own religions as well as bronze metallurgy and the wheel into their economies. When their widespread migrations carried them across much of Eurasia, they took these Sumerian cultural artifacts with them.

Egyptian cultural influence likewise spread in several directions. Nubian civilization, located to the south of Egypt in the Nile Valley, not only traded with its more powerful neighbor but also was subject to periodic military intervention and political control from Egypt. Skilled Nubian archers were actively recruited for service as mercenaries in Egyptian armies. They often married Egyptian women and were buried in Egyptian style. All of this led to the diffusion of Egyptian culture in Nubia, expressed in building Egyptian-style pyramids, worshipping Egyptian gods and goddesses, and making use of Egyptian hieroglyphic writing. Despite this cultural borrowing, Nubia remained a distinct civilization, developing its own alphabetic script, retaining many of its own gods, developing a major ironworking industry by 500 B.C.E., and asserting its political independence whenever possible. The Nubian kingdom of Kush, in fact, invaded Egypt in 760 B.C.E. and ruled it for about 100 years.

In the Mediterranean basin, clear Egyptian influence is visible in the art of the Minoan civilization, which emerged on the island of Crete about 2500 B.C.E. More controversial has been the claim by historian Martin Bernal in a much-publicized book, *Black Athena* (1987), that ancient Greek culture—its art, religion, philosophy, and language—drew heavily upon Egyptian as well as Mesopotamian precedents. His book lit up a passionate debate among scholars. To some of his critics, Bernal seemed to undermine the originality of Greek civilization by suggesting that it had an Afro-Asian origin. His supporters accused the critics of Eurocentrism. Whatever its outcome, the academic controversy surrounding Bernal's book served to focus attention on Egypt's relationship to black Africa and to the world of the Mediterranean basin.

Influence was not a one-way street, however, as Egypt and Mesopotamia likewise felt the impact of neighboring peoples. Pastoral peoples, speaking Indo-European languages and living in what is now southern Russia, had domesticated the horse by perhaps 4000 B.C.E. and later learned to tie that powerful animal to wheeled carts and chariots. This new technology provided a fearsome military potential that enabled various chariot-driving peoples to temporarily overwhelm ancient civilizations. Based in Anatolia, the Hittites overran the powerful Babylonian empire of Mesopotamia in 1595 B.C.E. About the same time, another pastoral group with chariots, the Hyksos, invaded Egypt and ruled it for more than a century (1650–1535 B.C.E.). But chariot technology was portable, and soon both the Egyptians and the Mesopotamians incorporated it into their own military forces. In fact, this powerful military innovation, together with the knowledge of bronze metallurgy, spread quickly and widely, reaching China by 1200 B.C.E. There it enabled the creation of a strong Chinese state ruled by the Shang dynasty. All of these developments provide evidence of at least indirect connections across the entire Eurasian landmass in ancient times. Even then, no civilization was wholly isolated from larger patterns of interaction.

In Egypt, the intrusion of the chariot-driving Hyksos shattered the sense of security that this Nile Valley civilization had long enjoyed. It also stimulated the normally complacent Egyptians to adopt a number of technologies pioneered earlier in Asia, including the horse-drawn chariot; new kinds of armor, bows, daggers, and swords; improved methods of spinning and weaving; new musical instruments; and olive and pomegranate trees. Absorbing these foreign innovations, Egyptians expelled the Hyksos and went on to create their own empire, both in Nubia and in the eastern Mediterranean regions of Syria and Palestine. By 1500 B.C.E., the previously self-contained Egypt became for several centuries an imperial state bridging Africa and Asia, ruling over substantial numbers of non-Egyptian peoples (see Map 3.3). It also

Map 3.3   An Egyptian Empire

During the New Kingdom period after 1550 B.C.E., Egypt became for several centuries an empire, extending its political control southward into Nubia and northward into Palestine.

became part of an international political system that included the Babylonian and later Assyrian empires of Mesopotamia as well as many other peoples of the region. Egyptian and Babylonian rulers engaged in regular diplomatic correspondence, referred to one another as "brother," exchanged gifts, and married their daughters into one another's families. One Babylonian king complained to an Egyptian pharaoh that the delegation that had come to take his daughter to Egypt contained only five carriages. What would his courtiers say about the daughter of a great ruler traveling with such a paltry escort?[31]

Reflections: "Civilization": What's in a Word?

In examining the cultures of Mesopotamia and Egypt, we are worlds away from life in agricultural villages or Paleolithic bands. Much the same holds for those of the Indus Valley, China, Mesoamerica, and the Andes. Strangely enough, historians have been somewhat uncertain as to how to refer to these new forms of human community. Following common practice, I have called them "civilizations," but scholars have reservations about the term for two reasons. The first is its implication of superiority. In popular usage, "civilization" suggests refined behavior, a "higher" form of society, something unreservedly positive. The opposite of "civilized"— barbarian, savage, or "uncivilized"—is normally understood as an insult implying inferiority, and that, of course, is precisely how the inhabitants of many civilizations have viewed those outside their own societies, particularly those neighboring peoples living without the alleged benefit of cities and states.

Modern assessments of the First Civilizations reveal a profound ambiguity about these new, larger, and more complex societies. On the one hand, these civilizations have given us inspiring art, profound reflections on the meaning of life, more productive technologies, increased control over nature, and the art of writing— all of which have been cause for celebration. On the other hand, as anthropologist Marvin Harris noted, "[H]uman beings learned for the first time how to bow, grovel, kneel, and kowtow."[32] Massive inequalities, state oppression, slavery, large-scale warfare, the subordination of women, and epidemic disease also accompanied the rise of civilization, generating discontent, rebellion, and sometimes the urge to escape. This ambiguity about the character of civilizations has led some historians to avoid the word, referring to early Egypt, Mesopotamia, and other regions instead as complex societies, urban-based societies, state-organized societies, or some more neutral term.

A second reservation about using the term "civilization" derives from its implication of solidity—the idea that civilizations represent distinct and widely shared identities with clear boundaries that mark them off from other such units. It is unlikely, however, that many people living in Mesopotamia, Norte Chico, or ancient China felt themselves part of a shared culture. Local communities defined by occupation, clan affiliation, village, city, or region were surely more important for most people than those of some larger civilization. At best, members of an educated upper class who shared a common literary tradition may have felt themselves part of some more inclusive civilization, but that left out most of the population. Moreover, unlike modern nations, none of the earlier civilizations had definite borders. Any identification with that civilization surely faded as distance from its core region increased. Finally, the line between civilizations and other kinds of societies is not always clear. Just when does a village or town become a city? At what point does a chiefdom become a state? Scholars continue to argue about these distinctions.

Given these reservations, should historians discard the notion of civilization? Maybe so, but this book continues to use it both because it is so deeply embedded in our way of thinking about the world and because no alternative concept has achieved widespread usage for making distinctions among different kinds of human communities. When the term appears in the text, try to keep in mind two points. First, as used by historians, "civilization" is a purely descriptive term, designating a particular type of human society—one with cities and states—and does not imply any judgment or assessment, any sense of superiority or inferiority. Second, it is used to define broad cultural patterns in particular geographic regions—Mesopotamia, the Peruvian coast, or China, for example—even though many people living in those regions may have been more aware of differences and conflicts than of those commonalities.

Second Thoughts

What's the Significance?

To assess your mastery of the material in this chapter, see the **Online Study Guide** at bedfordstmartins.com/strayer.

Norte Chico/Caral	Mohenjo Daro/Harappa	*Epic of Gilgamesh*
Indus Valley civilization	Code of Hammurabi	Egypt: "the gift of the Nile"
Olmec civilization	patriarchy	Nubia
Uruk	rise of the state	Hyksos

Big Picture Questions

1. What distinguished civilizations from other forms of human community?
2. How does the use of the term "civilization" by historians differ from that of popular usage? How do you use the term?
3. "Civilizations were held together largely by force." Do you agree with this assessment, or were there other mechanisms of integration as well?
4. In the development of the First Civilizations, what was gained for humankind, and what was lost?

Next Steps: For Further Study

Cyril Aldred, *The Egyptians* (1998). A brief and up-to-date account from a widely recognized expert.

Samuel Noah Kramer, *History Begins at Sumer* (1981). A classic account of Sumerian civilization, filled with wonderful stories and anecdotes.

David B. O'Connor, *Ancient Nubia: Egypt's Rival in Africa* (1994). An overview of this ancient African civilization, with lovely illustrations based on a museum exhibit.

Christopher A. Pool, *Olmec Archeology and Early Mesoamerica* (2007). A scholarly and up-to-date account of the earliest civilization in Mesoamerica.

Lauren Ristvet, *In the Beginning* (2007). A sweeping examination of the early phases of world history, from human evolution to the First Civilizations.

"The Ancient Indus Civilization," http://www.harappa.com/har/haro.html. Hundreds of vivid pictures and several brief essays on the Indus Valley civilization.

The British Museum, "Ancient Egypt," http://www.ancientegypt.co.uk/menu.html. An interactive exploration of Egyptian civilization.

For Web sites and documents related to this chapter, see **Make History** at bedfordstmartins.com/strayer.

PART TWO

The Classical Era in World History

500 B.C.E. – 500 C.E.

Contents

After the First Civilizations:
What Changed and What Didn't?

Studying world history has much in common with using the zoom lens of a camera. Sometimes, we pull the lens back in order to get a picture of the broadest possible panorama. At other times, we zoom in a bit for a middle-range shot, or even further for a close-up of some particular feature of the historical landscape. Students of world history soon become comfortable with moving back and forth among these several perspectives.

As we bid farewell to the First Civilizations, we will take the opportunity to pull back the lens and look broadly, and briefly, at the entire age of agricultural civilizations, a period from about 3500 B.C.E., when the earliest of the First Civilizations arose, to about 1750 C.E., when the first Industrial Revolution launched a new and distinctively modern phase of world history. During these more than 5,000 years, the most prominent large-scale trend was the globalization of civilization as this new form of human community increasingly spread across the planet, encompassing more people and larger territories.

The first wave of that process, addressed in Chapter 3, was already global in scope, with expressions in Asia, Africa, and the Americas. Those First Civilizations generated the most impressive and powerful human societies created thus far, but they proved fragile and vulnerable as well. The always-quarreling city-states of ancient Mesopotamia had long ago been absorbed into the larger empires of Babylon and Assyria. During the first millennium B.C.E., Egypt too fell victim to a series of foreign invaders, including the forces of Nubia, Assyria, Alexander the Great, and the Roman Empire. The Indus Valley civilization likewise declined sharply, as deforestation, topsoil erosion, and decreased rainfall led to desertification and political collapse by 1500 B.C.E. Norte Chico civilization seems to have faded away by 1800 B.C.E. The end of Olmec civilization around 400 B.C.E. has long puzzled historians, for it seems that the Olmecs themselves razed and then abandoned their major cities, even as their civilizational style spread to neighboring peoples. About the same time, China's unified political system fragmented into a series of warring states.

Even if particular First Civilizations broke down, there was no going back. Civilization as a form of human community proved durable and resilient as well as periodically fragile. Thus, in the thousand years between 500 B.C.E. and 500 C.E., new or enlarged urban-centered and state-based societies emerged to replace the First Civilizations in the Mediterranean basin, the Middle East, India, China, Mesoamerica, and the Andes. Furthermore, smaller expressions of civilization began to take shape elsewhere—in Ethiopia and West Africa, in Japan and Indonesia, in Vietnam and Cambodia. In short, the development of civilization was becoming a global process.

Many of these "second wave" civilizations likewise perished in time, as the collapse of the Roman Empire, Han dynasty China, and the Mayan cities remind us. They were followed by yet a "third wave" of civilizations (roughly 500 to 1500 C.E.; see Part Three). Some of them represented the persistence or renewal of older patterns (China, Byzantium, the Aztecs, and the Incas, for example). Others, such as those in Western Europe, Russia, Japan, and West Africa, marked new expressions of civilization, all of which borrowed heavily from more-established neighboring civilizations. The largest of these, Islamic civilization, incorporated a number of older centers of civilization, Egypt and Mesopotamia for example, under the umbrella of a new religion. The globalization of civilization continued apace.

The size and prominence of these civilizations sometimes lead historians and history textbooks to ignore those cultures that did not embrace the city- and state-centered characteristic of civilizations. World history, as a field of study, has often been slanted in the direction of civilizations at the expense of other forms of human community. To counteract that tendency, the following chapters will, on occasion, point out the continuing historical development of gathering and hunting peoples, agricultural societies organized around kinship principles and village life, emerging chiefdoms, and pastoral peoples.

Continuities in Civilization

The renewal and expansion of civilization, however, remains the leading story. As this account of the human journey moves into the second and third waves of civilization, the question arises as to how they differed from the first ones. From a panoramic perspective, the answer is "not much." States and empires rose, expanded, and collapsed with a tiresome regularity, requiring history students to remember who was up and who was down at various times. It is arguable, however, that little fundamental change occurred amid these constant fluctuations. Monarchs continued to rule most of the new civilizations; men continued to dominate women; a sharp divide between the elite and everyone else persisted almost everywhere, as did the practice of slavery.[1]

Furthermore, no technological or economic breakthrough occurred to create new kinds of human societies as the Agricultural Revolution had done earlier or as the Industrial Revolution would do in later centuries. Landowning elites had little incentive to innovate, for they benefited enormously from simply expropriating the surplus that peasant farmers produced. Nor would peasants have any reason to invest much effort in creating new forms of production when they knew full well that any gains they might generate would be seized by their social superiors. Merchants, who often were risk takers, might have spawned innovations, but they usually were dominated by powerful states and were viewed with suspicion and condescension by more prestigious social groups.

Many fluctuations, repetitive cycles, and minor changes characterize this long era of agricultural civilization, but no fundamental or revolutionary transformation of social or economic life took place. The major turning points in human history had occurred earlier with the emergence of agriculture and the birth of the First Civilizations and would occur later with the breakthrough of industrialization.

Changes in Civilization

While this panoramic perspective allows us to see the broadest outlines of the human journey, it also obscures much of great importance that took place during the second and third waves of the age of agrarian civilization. If we zoom in a bit more closely, significant changes emerge, even if they did not result in a thorough transformation of human life. Population, for example, grew more rapidly than ever before during this period, as the Snapshot illustrates. Even though the overall trend was up, important fluctuations interrupted the pattern, especially during the first millennium C.E., when no overall growth took place. Moreover, the rate of growth, though rapid in comparison with Paleolithic times, was quite slow if we measure it against the explosive expansion of recent centuries, when human numbers quadrupled in the twentieth century alone. This modest and interrupted pattern of population growth during the age of agrarian civilization reflected the absence of any fundamental economic breakthrough, which could have supported much larger numbers.

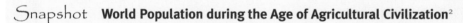

Snapshot   **World Population during the Age of Agricultural Civilization**[2]

The Roman Empire (p. 110)

Another change lies in the growing size of the states or empires that structured civilizations. The Roman, Persian, Indian, and Chinese empires of second-wave civilizations, as well as the Arab, Mongol, and Inca empires of the third wave, all dwarfed the city-states of Mesopotamia and the Egypt of the pharaohs. Each of these empires brought together in a single political system a vast diversity of peoples. Even so, just to keep things in perspective, as late as the seventeenth century C.E., only one-third of the world's landmass was under the control of any state-based system, although these societies now encompassed a considerable majority of the world's people.

The rise and fall of these empires likewise represented very consequential changes to the people who experienced them. In the course of its growth, the Roman Empire utterly destroyed the city of Carthage in North Africa, with the conquerors allegedly sowing the ground with salt so that nothing would ever grow there again. Similar bloodshed and destruction accompanied the creation of other much-celebrated states. Their collapse also had a dramatic impact on the lives of their people. Scholars have estimated that the large population of Mayan civilization shrank by some 85 percent in less than a century as that society dissolved around 840 C.E. It is difficult to imagine the sense of trauma and bewilderment associated with a collapse of this magnitude.

Second- and third-wave civilizations also generated important innovations in many spheres. Those in the cultural realm have been perhaps the most widespread and enduring. Distinctive "wisdom traditions"—the great philosophical/religious systems of Confucianism and Daoism in China, Hinduism and Buddhism in India, Greek rationalism in the Mediterranean, and Judaism, Zoroastrianism, Christianity, and Islam in the Middle East—have provided the moral and spiritual framework within which people have sought to order their lives and define their relationship to the mysteries of life and death. All of these philosophical and religious systems are the product of second- and third-wave civilizations.

Although no technological breakthrough equivalent to the Agricultural or Industrial Revolution took place during the second and third waves of agrarian civilizations, more modest innovations considerably enhanced human potential for manipulating the environment. China was a primary source of such technological change, though by no means the only one. "Chinese inventions and discoveries," wrote one prominent historian, "passed in a continuous flood from East to West for twenty centuries before the scientific revolution."[3] They included piston bellows, the draw-loom, silk-handling machinery, the wheelbarrow, a better harness for draft animals, the crossbow, iron casting, the iron-chain suspension bridge, gunpowder, firearms, the magnetic compass, paper, printing, and porcelain. India pioneered the crystallization of sugar and techniques for the manufacture of cotton textiles. Roman technological achievements were particularly apparent in construction and civil engineering—the building of roads, bridges, aqueducts, and fortifications—and in the art of glassblowing.

A further process of change following the end of the First Civilizations lay in the emergence of far more elaborate, widespread, and dense networks of communication and exchange that connected many of the world's peoples to one another. Many of the technologies mentioned here diffused widely across large areas. Sugar production provides a telling example. The syrup from sugarcane, which was initially domesticated in New Guinea early in the age of agriculture, was first processed into crystallized sugar in India by 500 C.E. During the early centuries of the Islamic era, Arab traders brought this technology from India to the Middle East and the Mediterranean, where Europeans learned about it during the Crusades. Europeans then transferred the practice of making sugar to the Atlantic islands and finally to the Americas, where it played a major role in stimulating a plantation economy and the Atlantic slave trade.[4]

Long-distance trade routes represented another form of transregional interaction. Caravan trade across northern Eurasia, seaborne commerce within the Indian Ocean basin, the exchange of goods across the Sahara, river-based commerce in the eastern woodlands of North America, various trading networks radiating from Mesoamerica—all of these carried goods, and sometimes culture as well. Buddhism, Hinduism, Christianity, and especially Islam spread widely beyond their places of origin, often carried on the camels and ships of merchants, creating ties of culture and religion among distant peoples within the Afro-Eurasian zone. Disease also increasingly linked distant human communities. According to the famous Greek historian Thucydides, a mysterious plague "from parts of Ethiopia above Egypt" descended on Athens in 430 B.C.E. and decimated the city, "inflicting a blow on Athenian society from which it never entirely recovered."[5]

Thus the second and third waves of civilization gave rise to much larger empires, new and distinctive cultural/religious traditions, any number of technological innovations, and novel patterns of interaction among far-flung societies. In these ways, the world became quite different from what it had been in the age of the First Civilizations, even though fundamental economic and social patterns had not substantially changed.

Classical Civilizations

At this point, and in the four chapters that follow, our historical lens zooms in to a middle-range focus on the major second-wave civilizations during the thousand years between 500 B.C.E. and 500 C.E. Historians frequently refer to this period of time as the "classical era" of world history, a term that highlights enduring traditions that have lasted into modern times and persist still in the twenty-first century. Confucianism, Hinduism, Buddhism, Judaism, and Christianity all took shape during this era of second-wave civilizations, and all of them remain very much alive at the dawn of the third millennium C.E. Despite the many and profound transformations of modernity, billions of people in the contemporary world still guide their lives, or at least claim to, according to teachings that first appeared 2,000 or more years ago.

Beyond the practices of individuals, the current identities of entire countries, regions, and civilizations are still linked to the achievements of the classical era. In 1971, a largely Muslim Iran mounted a lavish and much-criticized celebration of the 2,500th anniversary of the ancient Persian Empire. In 2004, a still communist China permitted public celebrations to mark the 2,555th birthday of its ancient sage Confucius. Students in Western schools and universities continue to read the works of Plato and Aristotle, produce the plays of Aeschylus and Sophocles, and admire the accomplishments of Athens. Many Indians still embrace the ancient religious texts called the Vedas and the Upanishads and continue to deal with the realities of caste. These are the continuities and enduring legacies that are reflected in the notion of "classical civilizations."

Designating the millennium between 500 B.C.E. and 500 C.E. as a "classical era" in world history is derived largely from the experience of Eurasian peoples, for it was on the outer rim of that huge continent that the largest and most influential civilizations took shape—in China, India, Persia, and the Mediterranean basin. Furthermore, that continent housed the vast majority of the world's people, some 80 percent or more.[6] Thus the first three chapters of Part Two focus exclusively on these Eurasian civilizations. Chapter 4 introduces them by examining and comparing their political frameworks and especially the empires (great or terrible, depending on your point of view) in which most of them were expressed. Chapter 5 looks at the cultural or religious traditions that each of them generated, while Chapter 6 probes their social organization—class, caste, slavery, and gender. Chapter 7 turns the spotlight on Africa and the Americas, asking whether their histories during the classical era followed Eurasian patterns or explored alternative possibilities.

In recalling the classical era, we will have occasion to compare the experiences of its various peoples, to note their remarkable achievements, to lament the tragedies that befell them and the suffering to which they gave rise, and to ponder their continuing power to fascinate us still.

Landmarks of the Classical Era, 500 B.C.E.–500 C.E.

700 B.C.E.	600 B.C.E.	500 B.C.E.	400 B.C.E.	300 B.C.E.	200 B.C.E.	100 B.C.E.	0

China

551–479 B.C.E. Confucius

221–206 B.C.E. Qin dynasty

6th century B.C.E.(?) Laozi

500–221 B.C.E. Political fragmentation (age of "warring states")

206 B.C.E. –220 C.E. Han dynasty

S. Asia/India

by 750 B.C.E. Urban centers in Ganges valley

563–483 B.C.E. Life of the Buddha

321–185 B.C.E. Mauryan dynasty

327 B.C.E. Invasion of India by Alexander

800–400 B.C.E. Compilation of Upanishads

268–232 B.C.E. Reign of Ashoka

Middle East/Persia

539 B.C.E. Cyrus allows Jews to return from exile

383–323 B.C.E. Seleucid dynasty (Greek)

334 B.C.E. Invasion of Alexander the Great

553–330 B.C.E. Achaemenid dynasty

247 B.C.E.–224 C.E. Parthian dynasty

7th–6th century B.C.E. (?) Life of Zarathustra

Mediterranean Basin

336–323 B.C.E. Reign of Alexander the Great

4 B.C.E.–EARLY 30S C.E. Life of Jesus

800–336 B.C.E. Era of Greek city-states

470–322 B.C.E. Socates, Plato, Aristotle

800–500 B.C.E. Hebrew prophets

500–479 B.C.E. Greco-Persian Wars

509 B.C.E. Founding of Roman Republic

200 B.C.E.–200 C.E. High point of Roman Empire

Africa

760 B.C.E. Kush conquest of Egypt

300 B.C.E.–100 C.E. Nubian kingdom of Meroë

The Americas

9th century B.C.E. Chavín religious cult in Andes

400 B.C.E. Decline of Olmec civilization

200 B.C.E.–500 C.E. Nazca culture

100 C.E.	200 C.E.	300 C.E.	400 C.E.	500 C.E.	600 C.E.

3rd century Spread of Buddhism begins

589–618 C.E. Sui dynasty reunites China

184 C.E. Yellow Turban Rebellion

320–550 C.E. Gupta dynasty

224–651 C.E. Sassanid dynasty

380 C.E. Christianity as official state religion of the Roman Empire

476 C.E. Collapse of western Roman Empire

100 C.E. Rise of Axum

3rd–5th centuries C.E. Early cities/states in West Africa

by 500 C.E. Arrival of banana in Africa

300 C.E. Beginning of trans-Saharan trade

4th century C.E. Introduction of Christianity in Axum

300–700 C.E. Moche civilization (Peru)

300–800 C.E. Mayan civilization

400–600 C.E. High point of Teotihuacán

Eurasian Empires

500 B.C.E. – 500 C.E.

Are We Rome? It was the title of a thoughtful book, published in 2007, asking what had become a familiar question in the early twenty-first century: "Is the United States the new Roman Empire?"[1] With the collapse of the Soviet Union by 1991 and the subsequent U.S. invasions of Afghanistan and Iraq, some commentators began to make the comparison. The United States' enormous multicultural society, its technological achievements, its economically draining and overstretched armed forces, its sense of itself as unique and endowed with a global mission, its concern about foreigners penetrating its borders, its apparent determination to maintain military superiority—all of this invited comparison with the Roman Empire. Supporters of a dominant role for the United States argue that Americans must face up to their responsibilities as "the undisputed master of the world" as the Romans did in their time. Critics warn that the Roman Empire became overextended abroad and corrupt and dictatorial at home and then collapsed, suggesting that a similar fate may await the American empire. Either way, the point of reference was an empire that had passed into history some 1,500 years earlier, a continuing reminder of the relevance of the distant past to our contemporary world. In fact, for at least several centuries, that empire has been a source of metaphors and "lessons" about personal morality, corruption, political life, military expansion, and much more.

Even in a world largely critical of empires, they still excite the imagination of historians and readers of history. The earliest ones show up in the era of the First Civilizations when Akkadian, Babylonian, and Assyrian empires encompassed the city-states of Mesopotamia and established an enduring imperial tradition in the Middle East. Egypt

China's Terra-Cotta Army: Ranking as one of the most spectacular archeological finds of the twentieth century, this collection of terra-cotta soldiers and horses was part of an immense funerary complex of China's "first emperor," Qin Shihuangdi, who died in 210 B.C.E. (Dennis Cox/ChinaStock)

97

became an imperial state when it temporarily ruled Nubia and the lands of the eastern Mediterranean. Following in their wake were many more empires, whose rise and fall have been a central feature of world history for the past 4,000 years.

BUT WHAT EXACTLY IS AN EMPIRE? At one level, empires are simply states, political systems that exercise coercive power. The term, however, is normally reserved for larger and more aggressive states, those that conquer, rule, and extract resources from other states and peoples. Thus empires have generally encompassed a considerable variety of peoples and cultures within a single political system, and they have often been associated with political and cultural oppression. No clear line divides empires and small multiethnic states, and the distinction between them is arbitrary and subjective. Frequently, empires have given political expression to a civilization or culture, as in the Chinese and Persian empires. Civilizations have also flourished without a single all-encompassing state or empire, as in the competing city-states of Mesopotamia, Greece, and the Maya or the many rival states of post-Roman Europe. In such cases, civilizations were expressed in elements of a common culture rather than in a unified political system.

The Eurasian empires of the classical era—those of Persia, Greece under Alexander the Great, Rome, China during the Qin and Han dynasties, India during the Mauryan and Gupta dynasties—shared a set of common problems. Would they seek to impose the culture of the imperial heartland on their varied subjects? Would they rule conquered people directly or through established local authorities? How could they extract the wealth of empire in the form of taxes, tribute, and labor while maintaining order in conquered territories? And, no matter how impressive they were at their peak, they all sooner or later collapsed, providing a useful reminder to their descendants of the fleeting nature of all human creation.

Why have these and other empires been of such lasting fascination to both ancient and modern people? Perhaps in part because they were so big, creating a looming presence in their respective regions. Their armies and their tax collectors were hard to avoid. Maybe also because they were so bloody. Conquest and the violence that accompanies it easily grab our attention, and certainly, all of these empires were founded and sustained at a great cost in human life. The collapse of these once-powerful states is likewise intriguing, for the fall of the mighty seems somehow satisfying, perhaps even a delayed form of justice. The study of empires also sets off by contrast those times and places in which civilizations have prospered without an enduring imperial state.

But empires have also commanded attention simply because they were important. Very large numbers of people—probably the majority of humankind before the twentieth century—have lived out their lives in empires, where they were often governed by rulers culturally different from themselves. These imperial states brought together people of quite different traditions and religions and so stimulated the exchange of ideas, cultures, and values. The Roman Empire, for example, provided the vehicle within which Christianity was transformed from a small Jewish sect into a world religion. Despite their violence, exploitation, and oppression, empires also imposed substantial periods of peace and security, which fostered economic and artistic development, commercial exchange, and cultural mixing.

Empires and Civilizations in Collision: The Persians and the Greeks

The classical era in Eurasia witnessed the flowering of second-wave civilizations in the Mediterranean world, the Middle East, India, and China. For the most part, these distant civilizations did not directly encounter one another, as each established its own political system, cultural values, and ways of organizing society. A great exception to that rule lay in the Mediterranean world and in the Middle East, where the emerging Persian Empire and Greek civilization, physically adjacent to each other, experienced a centuries-long interaction and clash. It was one of the most consequential cultural encounters of the classical world.

The Persian Empire

In 500 B.C.E., the largest and most impressive of the world's empires was that of the Persians, an Indo-European people whose homeland lay on the Iranian plateau just north of the Persian Gulf. Living on the margins of the earlier Mesopotamian civilization, the Persians constructed an imperial system that drew upon previous examples, such as the Babylonian and Assyrian empires, but far surpassed them all in size and splendor. Under the leadership of the famous monarchs Cyrus (reigned 557–530 B.C.E.) and Darius (reigned 522–486 B.C.E.), Persian conquests quickly reached from Egypt to India, encompassing in a single state some 35 million people, an immensely diverse realm containing dozens of peoples, states, languages, and cultural traditions (see Map 4.1).

> ■ **Comparison**
> How did Persian and Greek civilizations differ in their political organization and values?

The Persian Empire centered on an elaborate cult of kingship in which the monarch, secluded in royal magnificence, could be approached only through an elaborate ritual. When the king died, sacred fires all across the land were extinguished, Persians were expected to shave their hair in mourning, and the manes of horses were cut short. Ruling by the will of the great Persian god Ahura Mazda, kings were absolute monarchs, more than willing to crush rebellious regions or officials. Interrupted on one occasion while he was with his wife, Darius ordered the offender, a high-ranking nobleman, killed, along with his entire clan. In the eyes of many, Persian monarchs fully deserved their effusive title—"Great king, King of kings, King of countries containing all kinds of men, King in this great earth far and wide." Darius himself best expressed the authority of the Persian ruler when he observed: "what was said to them by me, night and day, it was done."[2]

Map 4.1   The Persian Empire
At its height, the Persian Empire was the largest in the world. It dominated the lands of the First Civilizations in the Middle East and was commercially connected to neighboring regions.

But more than conquest and royal decree held the empire together. An effective administrative system placed Persian governors, called *satraps*, in each of the empire's twenty-three provinces, while lower-level officials were drawn from local authorities. A system of imperial spies, known as the "eyes and ears of the King," represented a further imperial presence in the far reaches of the empire. A general policy of respect for the empire's many non-Persian cultural traditions also cemented the state's authority. Cyrus won the gratitude of the Jews when in 539 B.C.E. he allowed those exiled in Babylon to return to their homeland and rebuild their temple in Jerusalem. In Egypt and Babylon, Persian kings took care to uphold local religious cults in an effort to gain the support of their followers and officials. The Greek historian Herodotus commented that "there is no nation which so readily adopts foreign customs. They have taken the dress of the Medes and in war they wear the Egyptian breastplate. As soon as they hear of any luxury, they instantly make it their own."[3] For the next 1,000 years or more, Persian imperial bureaucracy and court life, replete with administrators, tax collectors, record keepers, and translators, provided a model for all subsequent regimes in the region, including, later, those of the Islamic world.

The infrastructure of empire included a system of standardized coinage, predictable taxes levied on each province, and a newly dug canal linking the Nile with the Red Sea, which greatly expanded commerce and enriched Egypt. A "royal road," some 1,700 miles in length, facilitated communication and commerce across this vast empire. Caravans of merchants could traverse this highway in three months, but agents of the imperial courier service, using a fresh supply of horses every twenty-five to thirty miles, could carry a message from one end of the road to another in a week or two. Herodotus was impressed. "Neither snow, nor rain, nor heat, nor darkness of night," he wrote, "prevents them from accomplishing the task proposed to them with utmost speed." That description of the imperial Persian postal system was much later adopted as the unofficial motto for its counterpart in the United States Postal Service.

Persepolis
The largest palace in Persepolis, the Persian Empire's ancient capital, was the Audience Hall. The emperor officially greeted visiting dignitaries at this palace, which was constructed around 500 B.C.E. This relief, which shows a lion attacking a bull and Persian guards at attention, adorns a staircase leading to the Audience Hall. (Gianni Dagli Orti/Corbis)

The immense wealth and power of the Persian Empire were reflected in the construction of elaborate imperial centers, particularly Susa and Persepolis. Palaces, audience halls, quarters for the harem, monuments, and carvings made these cities into powerful symbols of imperial authority. Materials and workers alike were drawn from all corners of the empire and beyond. Inscribed in the foundation of Persepolis was Darius's commentary on what he had set in motion: "And Ahuramazda was of such a mind, together with all the other gods, that this fortress (should) be built. And (so) I built it. And I built it secure and beautiful and adequate, just as I was intending to."[4]

The Greeks

It would be hard to imagine a sharper contrast than that between the huge and centralized Persian Empire, governed by an absolute and almost unapproachable monarch, and the small competing city-states of classical Greece, which allowed varying degrees of popular participation in political life. Like the Persians, the Greeks were an Indo-European people whose early history drew on the legacy of the First Civilizations. The classical Greece of historical fame emerged around 750 B.C.E. as a new civilization and flourished for about 400 years before it was incorporated into a succession of foreign empires. During that relatively short period of time, the civilization of Athens and Sparta, of Plato and Aristotle, of Zeus and Apollo took shape and collided with its giant neighbor to the east.

Calling themselves Hellenes, the Greeks created a civilization that was distinctive in many ways, particularly in comparison with the Persians. The total population of

■ **Change**
Why did semidemocratic governments emerge in some of the Greek city-states?

Greece and the Aegean basin was just 2 million to 3 million, a fraction of that of the Persian Empire. Furthermore, Greek civilization took shape on a small peninsula, deeply divided by steep mountains and valleys. Its geography certainly contributed to the political shape of that civilization, which found expression, not in a Persian-style empire, but in hundreds of city-states or small settlements (see Map 4.2). Most were quite modest in size, with between 500 and 5,000 male citizens. Each of these city-states was fiercely independent and in frequent conflict with its neighbors, yet they had much in common, speaking the same language and worshipping the same gods. Every four years they temporarily suspended their persisting rivalries to participate together in the Olympic Games, which had begun in 776 B.C.E. Despite this emerging sense of Greek cultural identity, it did

Map 4.2   Classical Greece The classical civilization of Greece was centered on a small peninsula of southeastern Europe, but Greek settlers spread that civilization along the coasts of the Mediterranean and Black seas.

little to overcome the endemic political rivalries of the larger city-states—Athens, Sparta, Thebes, Corinth, and many others.

Like the Persians, the Greeks were an expansive people, but their expansion took the form of settlement in distant places rather than conquest and empire. Pushed by a growing population, Greek traders in search of iron and impoverished Greek farmers in search of land stimulated a remarkable emigration. Between 750 and 500 B.C.E., Greek settlements were established all around the Mediterranean basin and the rim of the Black Sea. Settlers brought Greek culture, language, and building styles to these new lands, even as they fought, traded, and intermarried with their non-Greek neighbors.

The most distinctive feature of Greek civilization, and the greatest contrast with Persia, lay in the extent of popular participation in political life that occurred within the city-states. It was the idea of "citizenship," of free people running the affairs of state, of equality for all citizens before the law, that was so unique. A foreign king, observing the operation of the public assembly in Athens, was amazed that male citizens as a whole actually voted on matters of policy: "I find it astonishing," he noted, "that here wise men speak on public affairs, while fools decide them."[5] Compared to the rigid hierarchies, inequalities, and absolute monarchies of Persia and other ancient civilizations, the Athenian experiment was remarkable. This is how one modern scholar defined it:

> Among the Greeks the question of who should reign arose in a new way. Previously the most that had been asked was whether one man or another should govern and whether one alone or several together. But now the question was whether all the citizens, including the poor, might govern and whether it would be possible for them to govern as citizens, without specializing in politics. In other words, should the governed themselves actively participate in politics on a regular basis?[6]

The extent of participation and the role of "citizens" varied considerably, both over time and from city to city. Early in Greek history, only the wealthy and well-born had the rights of full citizenship, such as speaking and voting in the assembly, holding public office, and fighting in the army. Gradually, middle- and lower-class men, mostly small-scale farmers, also obtained these rights. At least in part, this broadening of political rights was associated with the growing number of men able to afford the armor and weapons that would allow them to serve as *hoplites*, or infantrymen, in the armies of the city-states. In many places, dictators known as *tyrants* emerged for a time, usually with the support of the poorer classes, to challenge the prerogatives of the wealthy. Sparta—famous for its extreme forms of military discipline and its large population of *helots*, conquered people who lived in slavelike conditions—vested most political authority in its Council of Elders. The council was composed of twenty-eight men over the age of sixty, derived from the wealthier and more influential segment of society, who served for life and provided political leadership for Sparta.

$\mathcal{S}$napshot   **Key Moments in Classical Greek History**

Traditional date for first Olympic Games	776 B.C.E.
Emergence of Greek city-states and overseas colonization	750–700 B.C.E.
Evolution of hoplite military tactics	700–650 B.C.E.
Tyrants rule in many city-states	670–500 B.C.E.
Sparta dominant in Peloponnesus	550 B.C.E.
Cleisthenes' political reforms in Athens	507 B.C.E.
Greco-Persian Wars	490–479 B.C.E.
Golden Age of Athens (building of Parthenon; Athenian democracy, rule of Pericles)	479–429 B.C.E.
Helot rebellion in Sparta	463 B.C.E.
Peloponnesian War	431–404 B.C.E.
Macedonian conquest of Greece	338 B.C.E.
Conquests of Alexander the Great	333–323 B.C.E.
Hellenistic era	323–30 B.C.E.
Greece comes under Roman control	2nd century B.C.E.

It was in Athens that the Greek experiment in political participation achieved its most distinctive expression. Early steps in this direction were the product of intense class conflict, leading almost to civil war. A reforming leader named Solon emerged in 594 B.C.E. to push Athenian politics in a more democratic direction, breaking the hold of a small group of aristocratic families. Debt slavery was abolished, access to public office was opened to a wider group of men, and all citizens were allowed to take part in the Assembly. Later reformers such as Cleisthenes and Pericles extended the rights of citizens even further. By 450 B.C.E., all holders of public office were chosen by lot and were paid, so that even the poorest could serve. The Assembly, where all citizens could participate, became the center of political life.

Athenian democracy, however, was different from modern democracy. It was direct, rather than representative, democracy, and it was distinctly limited. Women, slaves, and foreigners, together far more than half of the population, were wholly excluded from political participation. Nonetheless, political life in Athens was a world away from that of the Persian Empire and even from that of many other Greek cities.

■ Connection
What were the consequences for both sides of the encounter between the Persians and the Greeks?

Collision: The Greco-Persian Wars

If ever there was an unequal conflict between civilizations, surely it was the collision of the Greeks and the Persians. The confrontation between the small and divided Greek cities and Persia, the world's largest empire, grew out of their respective patterns of expansion. A number of Greek settlements on the Anatolian seacoast, known to the Greeks as Ionia, came under Persian control as that empire extended its domination to the west. In 499 B.C.E., some of these Ionian Greek cities revolted against Persian domination and found support from Athens on the Greek mainland. Outraged by this assault from the remote and upstart Greeks, the Persians twice in ten years (490 and 480 B.C.E.) launched major military expeditions to punish the Greeks in general and Athens in particular. Against all odds and all expectations, the Greeks held them off, defeating the Persians on both land and sea.

Though no doubt embarrassing, this defeat on the far western fringes of its empire had little effect on the Persians, but it had a profound impact on the Greeks and especially on Athens, whose forces had led the way to victory. Beating the Persians in battle was a source of enormous pride for Greece. Years later, elderly Athenian men asked one another how old they had been when the Greeks triumphed in the momentous Battle of Marathon in 490 B.C.E. In their view, this victory was the product of Greek freedoms, because those freedoms had motivated men to fight with extraordinary courage for what they valued so highly. It led to a worldview in which Persia represented Asia and despotism, whereas Greece signified Europe and freedom. Thus was born the notion of an East/West divide, which has shaped European thinking about the world into the twentieth century and beyond.

The Greeks' victory also radicalized Athenian democracy, for it had been men of the poorer classes who had rowed their ships to victory, and now they were in a position to insist on full citizenship. The fifty years or so after the Greco-Persian Wars were not only the high point of Athenian democracy but also the Golden Age of Greek culture. During this period, the Parthenon, that marvelous temple to the Greek goddess Athena, was built; Greek theater was born from the work of Aeschylus, Sophocles, and Euripides; and Socrates was beginning his career as a philosopher and an irritant in Athens. The great Athenian statesman Pericles celebrated the uniqueness of Athens in a famous speech.

> It is true that we are called a democracy, for the administration is in the hands of the many and not of the few. But while the law secures equal justice to all alike in their private disputes, the claim of excellence is also recognized.... Neither is poverty a bar, but a man may benefit his country whatever be the obscurity of his condition....We alone regard a man who takes no interest in public affairs, not as a harmless, but as a useless character.[7]

But Athens's Golden Age was also an era of incipient empire. In the Greco-Persian Wars, Athens had led a coalition of more than thirty Greek city-states on the basis of its naval power, but Athenian leadership in the struggle against Persian aggression had spawned an imperialism of its own. After the war, Athenian efforts to solidify its dominant position among the allies led to intense resentment and finally to a bitter civil war (431–404 B.C.E.), with Sparta taking the lead in defending the traditional independence of Greek city-states. In this bloody conflict, known as the Peloponnesian War, Athens was defeated, while the Greeks exhausted themselves and magnified their distrust of one another. Thus the way was open to their eventual takeover by the growing forces of Macedonia, a frontier region on the northern fringes of the Greek world. The glory days of the Greek experiment were over, but the spread of Greek culture was just beginning.

■ Connection
What changes did Alexander's conquests bring in their wake?

Map 4.3 Alexander's Empire and Successor States
Alexander's conquests, though enormous, did not long remain within a single empire, for his generals divided them into three successor states shortly after his death. This was the Hellenistic world within which Greek culture spread.

Collision: Alexander and the Hellenistic Era

The Macedonian conquest of Greece, led by Philip II, finally accomplished by 338 B.C.E. what the Greeks themselves had been unable to achieve—the political unification of Greece, but at the cost of much of the prized independence of its various city-states. It also set in motion a second round in the collision of Greece and Persia as Philip's son, Alexander, prepared to lead a massive Greek expedition against the Persian Empire. Such a project appealed to those who sought vengeance for the earlier Persian assault on Greece, but it also served to unify the fractious Greeks in a war against their common enemy.

The story of this ten-year expedition (333–323 B.C.E.), accomplished while Alexander was still in his twenties, has become the stuff of legend (see Map 4.3). Surely it was among the greatest military feats of the classical world in that it created a Greek empire from Egypt and Anatolia in the west to Afghanistan and India in the east. In the process, the great Persian Empire was thoroughly defeated; its

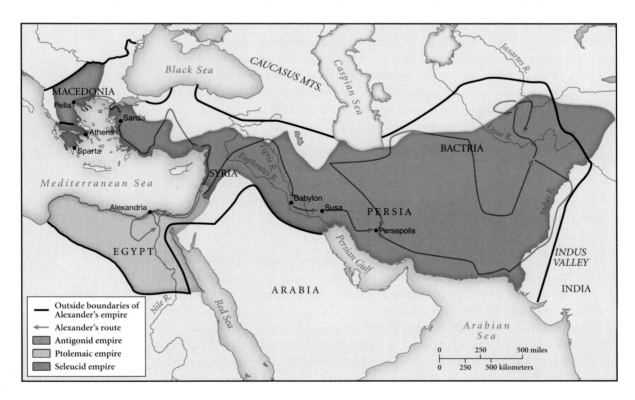

capital, Persepolis, was looted and burned; and Alexander was hailed as the "king of Asia." In Egypt, Alexander, then just twenty-four years old, was celebrated as a liberator from Persian domination, was anointed as pharaoh, and was declared by Egyptian priests to be the "son of the gods." Arrian, a later Greek historian, described Alexander in this way:

> His passion was for glory only, and in that he was insatiable.... Noble indeed was his power of inspiring his men, of filling them with confidence, and in the moment of danger, of sweeping away their fear by the spectacle of his own fearlessness.[8]

Alexander died in 323 B.C.E., without returning to Greece, and his empire was soon divided into three kingdoms, ruled by leading Macedonian generals.

From the viewpoint of world history, the chief significance of Alexander's amazing conquests lay in the widespread dissemination of Greek culture during what historians call the Hellenistic era (323–30 B.C.E.). Elements of that culture, generated in a small and remote Mediterranean peninsula, now penetrated the lands of the First Civilizations—Egypt, Mesopotamia, and India—resulting in one of the great cultural encounters of the classical world.

The major avenue for the spread of Greek culture lay in the many cities that Alexander and later Hellenistic rulers established throughout the empire. Complete with Greek monuments and sculptures, Greek theaters and markets, Greek councils and assemblies, these cities attracted many thousands of Greek settlers serving as state officials, soldiers, or traders. Alexandria in Egypt—the largest of these cities, with half a million people—was an enormous cosmopolitan center where Egyptians, Greeks, Jews, Babylonians, Syrians, Persians, and many others rubbed elbows. A harbor with space for 1,200 ships facilitated long-distance commerce. Greek learning flourished thanks to a library of some 700,000 volumes and the Museum, which sponsored scholars and writers of all kinds.

From cities such as these, Greek culture spread. A simplified form of the Greek language was widely spoken from the Mediterranean to India. The Indian monarch Ashoka published some of his decrees in Greek, while an independent Greek state was established in Bactria in what is now northern Afghanistan. The attraction of many young Jews to Greek culture prompted the Pharisees to develop their own school system, as this highly conservative Jewish sect feared for the very survival of Judaism.

Alexander the Great
This mosaic of Alexander on horseback comes from the Roman city of Pompeii. It depicts the Battle of Issus (333 B.C.E.), in which Greek forces, although considerably outnumbered, defeated the Persian army, led personally by Emperor Darius III. (Scala/Art Resource, NY)

Cities such as Alexandria were very different from the original city-states of Greece, both in their cultural diversity and in the absence of the independence so valued by Athens and Sparta. Now they were part of large conquest states ruled by Greeks: the Ptolemaic empire in Egypt and the Seleucid empire in Persia. These were imperial states, which, in their determination to preserve order, raise taxes, and maintain the authority of the monarch, resembled the much older empires of Mesopotamia, Egypt, Assyria, and Persia. Macedonians and Greeks, representing perhaps 10 percent of the population in these Hellenistic kingdoms, were clearly the elite and sought to keep themselves separate. In Egypt, different legal systems for Greeks and native Egyptians maintained this separation. An Egyptian worker complained that his supervisors despised him and refused to pay him simply because he was an Egyptian.[9] Periodic rebellions expressed the resentment at Greek arrogance, condescension, and exploitation.

But the separation between the Greeks and native populations was by no means complete, and a fair amount of cultural interaction and blending occurred. Alexander himself had taken several Persian princesses as his wives and actively encouraged intermarriage between his troops and Asian women. In both Egypt and Mesopotamia, Greek rulers patronized the building of temples to local gods and actively supported their priests. A growing number of native peoples were able to become Greek citizens by getting a Greek education, speaking the language, dressing appropriately, and assuming a Greek name. In India, Greeks were assimilated into the hierarchy of the caste system as members of the Ksatriya (warrior) caste, while in Bactria a substantial number of Greeks converted to Buddhism, including one of their kings, Menander. A school of Buddhist art that emerged in the early centuries of the Common Era depicted the Buddha in human form for the first time, but in Greek-like garb with a face resembling the god Apollo. Clearly, not all was conflict between the Greeks and the peoples of the East.

In the long run, much of this Greek cultural influence disappeared as the Hellenistic kingdoms that had promoted it weakened and vanished by the first century B.C.E. While it lasted, however, it represented a remarkable cultural encounter, born of the collision of two empires and two classical civilizations. In the western part of that Hellenistic world, Greek rule was replaced by that of the Romans, whose empire, like Alexander's, also served as a vehicle for the continued spread of Greek culture and ideas.

Comparing Empires: Roman and Chinese

While the adjacent civilizations of the Greeks and the Persians collided, two other classical empires were taking shape—the Roman Empire on the far western side of Eurasia and China's imperial state on the far eastern end. They flourished at roughly the same time (200 B.C.E.–200 C.E.); they occupied a similar area (about 1.5 million square miles); and they encompassed populations of a similar size (50 million to 60 million people). They were the giant empires of their time, shaping the lives of close to half of the world's population. Unlike the Greeks and the Persians, the Romans and the Chinese were only dimly aware of each other and had almost no direct contact. Historians, however, have seen them as fascinating variations on an imperial theme and have long explored their similarities and differences.

Rome: From City-State to Empire

How do empires arise? This is one of the perennial questions that historians tackle. Like the Persian Empire, that of the Romans took shape initially on the margins of the civilized world and was an unlikely rags-to-riches story. Rome began as a small and impoverished city-state on the western side of central Italy in the eighth century B.C.E., so weak, according to legend, that Romans were reduced to kidnapping neighboring women in order to reproduce. In a transformation of epic proportions, Rome became an enormous imperial state that encompassed the Mediterranean basin and included parts of continental Europe, Britain, North Africa, and the Middle East.

■ **Change**
How did Rome grow from a single city to the center of a huge empire?

Originally ruled by a king, Roman aristocrats around 509 B.C.E. threw off the monarchy and established a republic in which the wealthy class, known as *patricians*, dominated. Executive authority was exercised by two consuls, who were advised by a patrician assembly, the Senate. Deepening conflict with the poorer classes, called *plebeians*, led to important changes in Roman political life. A written code of law offered plebeians some protection from abuse; a system of public assemblies provided an opportunity for lower classes to shape public policy; and a new office of *tribune*, who represented plebeians, allowed them to block unfavorable legislation. Romans took great pride in this political system, believing that they enjoyed greater freedom than did many of their more autocratic neighbors. The values of the republic—rule of law, the rights of citizens, the absence of pretension, upright moral behavior, keeping one's word—were later idealized as "the way of the ancestors."

With this political system and these values, the Romans launched their empire-building enterprise, a prolonged process that took more than 500 years (see Map 4.4). It began in the 490s B.C.E. with Roman control over its Latin neighbors in central Italy and over the next several hundred years encompassed most of the Italian peninsula. Between 264 and 146 B.C.E., victory in the Punic Wars with Carthage, a powerful empire with its capital in North Africa, extended Roman control over the western Mediterranean and made Rome a naval power. Subsequent expansion in the eastern Mediterranean brought the ancient civilizations of Greece, Egypt, and Mesopotamia under Roman domination. Rome also expanded into territories in Southern and Western Europe, including present-day Spain, France, and Britain. By early in the second century C.E., the Roman Empire had reached its maximum extent.

No overall design or blueprint drove the building of empire, nor were there any precedents to guide the Romans. What they created was something wholly new— an empire that encompassed the entire Mediterranean basin and beyond. It was a

Map 4.4   The Roman Empire
At its height in the second century C.E., the Roman Empire incorporated the entire Mediterranean basin, including the lands of the Carthaginian Empire, the less developed region of Western Europe, the heartland of Greek civilization, and the ancient civilizations of Egypt and Mesopotamia.

piecemeal process, which the Romans invariably saw as defensive. Each addition of territory created new vulnerabilities, which could be assuaged only by more conquests. For some, the growth of empire represented opportunity. Poor soldiers hoped for land, loot, or salaries that might lift their families out of poverty. The well-to-do or well-connected gained great estates, earned promotion, and sometimes achieved public acclaim and high political office. The wealth of long-established societies in the eastern Mediterranean (Greece and Egypt, for example) beckoned, as did the resources and food supplies of the less developed western regions, such as Carthage and Spain. There was no shortage of motivation for the creation of the Roman Empire.

Snapshot   **Key Moments in the History of the Roman Empire**

Traditional date of Rome's founding as a monarchy	753 B.C.E.
Establishment of Roman Republic	509 B.C.E.
Turmoil between patricians and plebeians ("struggle of the orders")	509–287 B.C.E.
Twelve Tables (Rome's first written law code)	450 B.C.E.
Punic Wars	264–146 B.C.E.
Civil war; Julius Caesar appointed dictator and then assassinated	49–44 B.C.E.
Reign of Caesar Augustus	27 B.C.E.–14 C.E.
Great fire in Rome; Emperor Nero blames Christians	64 C.E.
Roman citizenship extended to almost all free subjects	212 C.E.
Constantine converts to Christianity	312 C.E.
Founding of Constantinople as the "New Rome"	324 C.E.
Roman Empire split into eastern and western halves	395 C.E.
"Barbarian" invasions	4th–5th centuries C.E.
Collapse of western Roman Empire	476 C.E.

Although Rome's central location in the Mediterranean basin provided a convenient launching pad for empire, it was the army, "well-trained, well-fed, and well-rewarded," that built the empire.[10] Drawing on the growing population of Italy, that army was often brutal in war. Carthage, for example, was utterly destroyed; the city was razed to the ground, and its inhabitants were either killed or sold into slavery. Nonetheless, Roman authorities could be generous to former enemies. Some were granted Roman citizenship; others were treated as allies and allowed to maintain their local rulers. As the empire grew, so too did political forces in Rome that favored its continued expansion and were willing to commit the necessary manpower and resources.

The relentless expansion of empire raised a profound question for Rome: could republican government and values survive the acquisition of a huge empire? The wealth of empire enriched a few, enabling them to acquire large estates and slaves to work those estates, while pushing growing numbers of free farmers into the cities and poverty. Imperial riches also empowered a small group of military leaders—Marius, Sulla, Pompey, Julius Caesar—who recruited their troops directly from the ranks of the poor and whose fierce rivalries brought civil war to Rome during the first century B.C.E. Traditionalists lamented the apparent decline of republican values—simplicity, service, free farmers as the backbone of the army, the

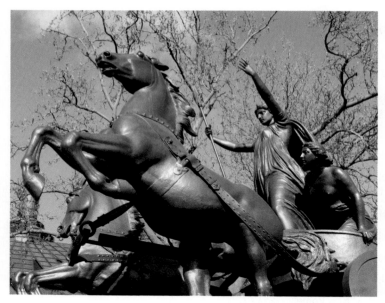

Queen Boudica
This statue in London commemorates the resistance of the Celtic people of eastern Britain against Roman rule during a revolt in 60–61 C.E., led by Queen Boudica. A later Roman historian lamented that "all this ruin was brought upon the Romans by a woman, a fact which in itself caused them the greatest shame." (Daniel Boulet, photographer)

■ **Comparison**
How and why did the making of the Chinese empire differ from that of the Roman Empire?

authority of the Senate—amid the self-seeking ambition of the newly rich and powerful. When the dust settled from the civil war, Rome was clearly changing, for authority was now vested primarily in an emperor, the first of whom was Caesar Augustus (reigned 27 B.C.E.–14 C.E.). The republic was history; Rome was becoming an empire.

But it was an empire with an uneasy conscience, for many felt that in acquiring an empire, Rome had betrayed and abandoned its republican origins. Augustus was careful to maintain the forms of the republic—the Senate, consuls, public assemblies—and referred to himself as "first man" rather than "king" or "emperor." And in a bow to republican values, he spoke of the empire's conquests as reflecting the "power of the Roman people" rather than of the Roman state. Despite this rhetoric, he was emperor in practice, if not in name, for he was able to exercise sole authority, backed up by his command of a professional army. Later emperors were less reluctant to flaunt their imperial prerogatives. During the first two centuries C.E., this empire in disguise provided security, grandeur, and relative prosperity for the Mediterranean world. This was the *pax Romana*, the Roman peace, the era of imperial Rome's greatest extent and greatest authority.

China: From Warring States to Empire

About the same time, on the other side of Eurasia, another huge imperial state was in the making—China. Here, however, the task was understood differently. It was not a matter of creating something new, as in the case of the Roman Empire, but of restoring something old. As one of the First Civilizations, a Chinese state had emerged as early as 2200 B.C.E. and under the Xia, Shang, and Zhou dynasties had grown progressively larger, but by 500 B.C.E. this Chinese state was in shambles. Any earlier unity vanished in an age of warring states, featuring the endless rivalries of seven competing kingdoms.

To many Chinese, this was a wholly unnatural and unacceptable condition, and rulers in various states vied to reunify China. One of them, known to history as Shihuangdi from the state of Qin, succeeded brilliantly. That state had already developed an effective bureaucracy, had subordinated its aristocracy, had equipped its army with iron weapons, and enjoyed rapidly rising agricultural output and a growing population. It also had adopted a political philosophy called Legalism, which advocated clear rules and harsh punishments as a means of enforcing the authority of the state. With these resources, Shihuangdi (ruled 221–210 B.C.E.) launched a military campaign to reunify China and in just ten years soundly defeated the other warring states. Believing that he had created a universal and eternal empire, he grandly named himself Shihuangdi, which means the "first emperor." Unlike Caesar Augustus, he showed little ambivalence about empire. Subsequent conquests extended China's boundaries far to the south into the northern part of Vietnam, to the northeast into Korea, and to the northwest, where the Chinese pushed back the nomadic pastoral people of the steppes. Although the boundaries fluctuated over time, Shihuangdi laid the foundations for a unified Chinese state, which has endured, with periodic interruptions, to the present (see Map 4.5).

Building on earlier precedents, the Chinese process of empire formation was far more compressed than the centuries-long Roman effort, but it was no less dependent on military force and no less brutal. Scholars who opposed Shihuangdi's policies

Map 4.5   Classical China
The brief Qin dynasty brought unity to the heartland of Chinese civilization, and the much longer Han dynasty extended its territorial reach south toward Vietnam, east to Korea, and west into Central Asia. To the north lay the military confederacy of the nomadic Xiongnu.

were executed and their books burned. Aristocrats who might oppose his centraliz-
ing policies were moved physically to the capital. Hundreds of thousands of laborers
were recruited to construct the Great Wall of China, designed to keep out northern
"barbarians," and to erect a monumental mausoleum as the emperor's final resting
place, which included some 7,500 life-size ceramic soldiers (shown in the photo at
the beginning of this chapter). More positively, Shihuangdi imposed a uniform system of weights, measures, and currency and standardized the length of axles for carts
and the written form of the Chinese language.

As in Rome, the creation of the Chinese empire had domestic repercussions,
but they were brief and superficial compared to Rome's transition from republic to
empire. The speed and brutality of Shihuangdi's policies ensured that his own Qin
dynasty did not last long, and it collapsed unmourned in 206 B.C.E. The Han
dynasty that followed (206 B.C.E–220 C.E.) retained the centralized features of
Shihuangdi's creation, although it moderated the harshness of his policies. It was
Han dynasty rulers who consolidated China's imperial state and established the
political patterns that lasted into the twentieth century.

Consolidating the Roman and Chinese Empires

■ Comparison
In comparing the Roman
and Chinese empires,
which do you find more
striking—their similarities
or their differences?

Once established, these two huge imperial systems shared a number of common features. Both, for example, defined themselves in universal terms. The Roman writer
Polybius spoke of bringing "almost the entire world" under the control of Rome,[11]
while the Chinese state was said to encompass "all under heaven." Both of them
invested heavily in public works—roads, bridges, aqueducts, canals, protective
walls—all designed to integrate their respective domains militarily and commercially.

Furthermore, Roman and Chinese authorities both invoked supernatural sanc-
tions to support their rule. By the first century C.E., Romans began to regard their
deceased emperors as gods and established a religious cult to bolster the authority
of living emperors. It was the refusal of early Christians to take part in this cult that
provoked their periodic persecution by Roman authorities.

In China, a much older tradition had long linked events on earth with affairs in
heaven. In this conception, heaven was neither a place nor a supreme being but
rather an impersonal moral force that regulated the universe. Emperors were called
the Son of Heaven and were said to govern by the Mandate of Heaven so long as
they ruled morally and with benevolence. Peasant rebellions, "barbarian" invasions,
or disastrous floods were viewed as signs that the emperor had ruled badly and thus
had lost the Mandate of Heaven. Among the chief duties of the emperor was the
performance of various rituals thought to maintain the appropriate relationship
between heaven and earth. What moral government meant in practice was spelled
out in the writings of Confucius and his followers, which became the official ideology of the empire (see Chapter 5).

Both of these classical civilizations also absorbed a foreign religious tradition—
Christianity in the Roman Empire and Buddhism in China—although the process
unfolded somewhat differently. In the case of Rome, Christianity was born as a

small sect of a small province in a remote corner of the empire. From there, it spread slowly for several centuries, mostly among the poor and lower classes; this process was considerably aided by the *pax Romana* and Roman roads. After suffering intermittent persecution, Christianity in the fourth century C.E. obtained state support from emperors who hoped to shore up a tottering empire with a common religion, and thereafter the religion spread quite rapidly.

In the case of China, by contrast, Buddhism came from India, far beyond the Chinese world. It was introduced to China by Central Asian traders and received little support from Han dynasty rulers. In fact, the religion spread only modestly among Chinese until after the Han dynasty collapsed (220 C.E.), when it appealed to people who felt bewildered by the loss of a predictable and stable society. Not until the Sui dynasty emperor Wendi (581–604 C.E.) reunified China did the new religion gain state support, and then only temporarily. Buddhism thus became one of several religious strands in a complex Chinese mix, while Christianity, though divided internally, ultimately became the dominant religious tradition throughout Europe.

The Roman and Chinese empires also had a different relationship to the societies they governed. Rome's beginnings as a small city-state meant that Romans, and even Italians, were always a distinct minority within the empire. The Chinese empire, by contrast, grew out of a much larger cultural heartland, already ethnically Chinese. Furthermore, as the Chinese state expanded, especially to the south, it actively assimilated the non-Chinese or "barbarian" people. In short, they became Chinese, culturally, linguistically, through intermarriage, and in physical appearance as well. Many Chinese in modern times are in fact descended from people who at one point or another were not Chinese at all.

The Roman Empire also offered a kind of assimilation to its subject peoples. Gradually and somewhat reluctantly, the empire granted Roman citizenship to various individuals, families, or whole communities for their service to the empire or in recognition of their adoption of Roman culture. In 212 C.E., Roman citizenship was bestowed on almost all free people of the empire. Citizenship offered clear advantages—the right to hold public office, to serve in the Roman military units known as legions, to wear a toga, and more—but it conveyed a legal status, rather than cultural assimilation, and certainly did not erase other identities, such as being Greek, Egyptian, or a citizen of a particular city.

Various elements of Roman culture—its public buildings, its religious rituals, its Latin language, its style of city life—were attractive, especially in Western Europe, where urban civilization was something new. In the eastern half of the empire, however, things Greek retained tremendous prestige. Many elite Romans in fact regarded Greek culture—its literature, philosophy, and art—as superior to their own and proudly sent their sons to Athens for a Greek education. To some extent, the two blended into a mixed Greco-Roman tradition, which the empire served to disseminate throughout the realm. Other non-Roman cultural traditions—such as the cult of the Persian god Mithra or the compassionate Egyptian goddess Isis, and, most extensively, the Jewish-derived religion of Christianity—also spread throughout the empire. Nothing similar occurred in Han dynasty China, except for

Buddhism, which established a modest presence, largely among foreigners. Chinese culture, widely recognized as the model to which others should conform, experienced little competition from an older, venerated, or foreign tradition.

Language served these two empires in important but contrasting ways. Latin, an alphabetic language depicting sounds, gave rise to various distinct languages—Spanish, Portuguese, French, Italian, Romanian—whereas Chinese did not. Chinese characters, which represented words or ideas more than sounds, were not easily transferable to other languages, but written Chinese could be understood by all literate people, no matter which spoken dialect of the language they used. Thus Chinese, more than Latin, served as an instrument of elite assimilation. For all of these reasons, the various peoples of the Roman Empire were able to maintain their separate cultural identities far more than was the case in China.

Politically, both empires established effective centralized control over vast regions and huge populations, but the Chinese, far more than the Romans, developed an elaborate bureaucracy to hold the empire together. The Han emperor Wudi (reigned 141–87 B.C.E.) established an imperial academy for training officials for an emerging bureaucracy with a curriculum based on the writings of Confucius. This was the beginning of a civil service system, complete with examinations and selection by merit, which did much to integrate the Chinese empire and lasted into the early twentieth century. Roman administration was a somewhat ramshackle affair, relying more on regional elites and the army to provide cohesion. Unlike the Chinese, however, the Romans developed an elaborate body of law, applicable equally to all people of the realm, dealing with matters of justice, property, commerce, and family life. Chinese and Roman political development thus generated different answers to the question of what made for good government. For those who inherited

Snapshot   **Key Moments in Classical Chinese History**

Political fragmentation ("warring states" period)	500–221 B.C.E.
Unification of China: Shihuangdi and Qin dynasty	221–206 B.C.E.
Beginning of Han dynasty, with Liu Bang as its first emperor	206–195 B.C.E.
Reign of Emperor Wudi, who established Confucian Academy for training imperial bureaucrats	141–87 B.C.E.
Emperor Wang Mang attempts land reform, without success	9–23 C.E.
Yellow Turban peasant revolt	184 C.E.
Collapse of Han dynasty	220 C.E.
Renewed political fragmentation	220–581 C.E.
China's unity is restored (Sui dynasty)	589–618 C.E.
Tang dynasty	618–907 C.E.

the Roman tradition, it was good laws, whereas for those in the Chinese tradition, it was good men.

The Collapse of Empires

Empires rise, and then, with some apparent regularity, they fall, and in doing so, they provide historians with one of their most intriguing questions: What causes the collapse of these once-mighty structures? In China, the Han dynasty empire came to an end in 220 C.E.; the traditional date for the final disintegration of the Roman Empire is 476 C.E., although a process of decline had been under way for several centuries. In the Roman case, however, only the western half of the empire collapsed, while the eastern part, subsequently known as the Byzantine Empire, maintained the tradition of imperial Rome for another thousand years.

Despite this difference, a number of common factors have been associated with the end of these imperial states. At one level, they simply got too big, too overextended, and too expensive to be sustained by the available resources, and no fundamental technological breakthrough was available to enlarge these resources. Furthermore, the growth of large landowning families with huge estates enabled them to avoid paying taxes, turned free peasants into impoverished tenant farmers, and diminished the authority of the central government. In China, such conditions led to a major peasant revolt, known as the Yellow Turban Rebellion, in 184 C.E.

Rivalry among elite factions created instability in both empires and eroded imperial authority. In China, persistent tension between castrated court officials (*eunuchs*) loyal to the emperor and Confucian-educated scholar-bureaucrats weakened the state. In the Roman Empire between 235 and 284 C.E., some twenty-six individuals claimed the title of Roman emperor, only one of whom died of natural causes. In addition, epidemic disease ravaged both societies. The population of the Roman Empire declined by 25 percent in the two centuries following 250 C.E., a demographic disaster that meant diminished production, less revenue for the state, and fewer men available for the defense of the empire's long frontiers.

To these mounting internal problems was added a growing threat from nomadic or semi-agricultural peoples occupying the frontier regions of both empires. The Chinese had long developed various ways of dealing with the Xiongnu and other nomadic people to the north—building the Great Wall to keep them out, offering them trading opportunities at border markets, buying them off with lavish gifts, contracting marriage alliances with nomadic leaders, and conducting periodic military campaigns against them. But as the Han dynasty weakened in the second and third centuries C.E., such peoples more easily breached the frontier defenses and set up a succession of "barbarian states" in north China. Culturally, however, many of these foreign rulers gradually became Chinese, encouraging intermarriage, adopting Chinese dress, and setting up their courts in Chinese fashion.

A weakening Roman Empire likewise faced serious problems from Germanic-speaking peoples living on its northern frontier. Growing numbers of these people

■ **Comparison**
How did the collapse of empire play out differently in the Roman world and in China?

Meeting of Attila and Pope Leo I
Among the "barbarian" invaders of the Roman Empire, none were more feared than the Huns, led by the infamous Attila. In a celebrated meeting in 452 C.E., Pope Leo I persuaded Attila to spare the city of Rome and to withdraw from Italy. This painting from about 1360 C.E. records that remarkable meeting. (National Szechenyi Library, Budapest)

began to enter the empire in the fourth century C.E.—some as mercenaries in Roman armies and others as refugees fleeing the invasions of the ferocious Huns, who were penetrating Europe from Central Asia. Once inside the declining empire, various Germanic groups established their own kingdoms, at first controlling Roman emperors and then displacing them altogether by 476 C.E. Unlike the nomadic groups in China, who largely assimilated Chinese culture, Germanic kingdoms in Europe developed their own ethnic identity—Visigoths, Franks, Anglo-Saxons, and others—even as they drew on Roman law and adopted Roman Christianity. Far more than in China, the fall of the Roman Empire produced a new culture, blending Latin and Germanic elements, which provided the foundation for the hybrid civilization that would arise in Western Europe.

The collapse of empire meant more than the disappearance of centralized government and endemic conflict. In both China and post-Roman Europe, it also meant the decline of urban life, a contracting population, less area under cultivation, diminishing international trade, and vast insecurity for ordinary people. It must have seemed that civilization itself was unraveling.

The most significant difference between the collapse of empire in China and that in the Mediterranean basin lay in what happened next. In China, after about 350 years of disunion, disorder, frequent warfare, and political chaos, a Chinese imperial state, similar to that of the Han dynasty, was reassembled under the Sui (589–618 C.E.), Tang (618–907), and Song (960–1279) dynasties. Once again, a single emperor ruled; a bureaucracy selected by examinations governed; and the ideas of Confucius informed the political system. Such a Chinese empire persisted into the early twentieth century, establishing one of the most continuous political traditions of any civilization in world history.

The story line of European history following the end of the Roman Empire was very different indeed. No large-scale, centralized, imperial authority, encompassing all of Western Europe, has ever been successfully reestablished there for any length of time. The memory of Roman imperial unity certainly persisted, and many subsequently tried unsuccessfully to re-create it. But most of Western Europe dissolved into a highly decentralized political system involving kings with little authority, nobles, knights and vassals, various city-states in Italy, and small territories ruled by princes, bishops, or the pope. From this point on, Europe would be a civilization without an encompassing imperial state.

From a Chinese point of view, Western Europe's post-Roman history must seem an enormous failure. Why were Europeans unable to reconstruct something of the unity of their classical empire, while the Chinese clearly did? Surely the greater cultural homogeneity of Chinese civilization made that task easier than it was amid the vast ethnic and linguistic diversity of Europe. The absence in the Roman legacy of a strong bureaucratic tradition also contributed to European difficulties, whereas in China the bureaucracy provided stability even as dynasties came and went. The Chinese also had in Confucianism a largely secular ideology that placed great value on political matters in the here and now. The Roman Catholic Church in Europe, however, was frequently at odds with state authorities, and its "otherworldliness" did little to support the creation of large-scale empires. Finally, Chinese agriculture was much more productive than that of Europe, and for a long time its metallurgy was more advanced.[12] These conditions gave Chinese state-builders more resources to work with than were available to their European counterparts.

Intermittent Empire: The Case of India

Among the classical civilizations of Eurasia, empire loomed large in Persian, Mediterranean, and Chinese history, but it played a much less prominent role in India. In the Indus River valley flourished the largest of the First Civilizations, embodied in exquisitely planned cities such as Harappa but with little evidence of any central political authority. The demise of this early civilization by 1500 B.C.E. was followed over the next thousand years by the creation of a new civilization based farther east, along the Ganges River on India's northern plain. That process has occasioned considerable scholarly debate, which has focused on the role of the Aryans, a pastoral Indo-European people long thought to have invaded and destroyed the Indus Valley civilization and created the new one along the Ganges. More recent research has called this view into question. Did the Aryans invade suddenly, or did they migrate slowly into the Indus River valley, or were they already there as a part of the Indus Valley population? Was the new civilization largely the work of Aryans, or did it evolve gradually from Indus Valley culture? About all of this, scholars have yet to reach agreement.[13]

However it occurred, by 600 B.C.E. what would become the classic civilization of South Asia had begun to take shape across northern India. Politically, that civilization emerged as a fragmented collection of towns and cities, some small republics governed by public assemblies, and a number of regional states ruled by kings. An astonishing range of ethnic, cultural, and linguistic diversity also characterized this civilization, as an endless variety of peoples migrated into India from Central Asia across the mountain passes in the northwest. These features of Indian civilization—political fragmentation and vast cultural diversity—have informed much of South Asian history throughout many centuries, offering a sharp contrast to the pattern of development in China. What gave Indian civilization a recognizable identity and character was neither an imperial tradition nor ethnolinguistic commonality, but rather a distinctive religious tradition, known later to outsiders as Hinduism, and a unique social organization, the caste system. These features of Indian life are explored further in Chapters 5 and 6.

Nonetheless, empires and emperors were not entirely unknown in India's long history. Northwestern India had been briefly ruled by the Persian Empire and then conquered by Alexander the Great. These Persian and Greek influences helped stimulate

■ **Comparison**
Why were centralized empires so much less prominent in India than in China?

Map 4.6 Empire in South Asia
Large-scale empires in the Indian subcontinent were less frequent and less enduring than in China. Two of the largest efforts were those of the Mauryan and Gupta dynasties.

the first and largest of India's short experiments with a large-scale political system, the Mauryan Empire (326–184 B.C.E.), which encompassed all but the southern tip of the subcontinent (see Map 4.6).

The Mauryan Empire was an impressive political structure, equivalent to the Persian, Chinese, and Roman empires, though not nearly as long-lasting. With a population of perhaps 50 million, the Mauryan Empire boasted a large military force, reported to include 600,000 infantry soldiers, 30,000 cavalry, 8,000 chariots, and 9,000 elephants. A civilian bureaucracy featured various ministries and a large contingent of spies to provide the rulers with local information. The state also operated many industries—spinning, weaving, mining, shipbuilding, and armaments. This complex apparatus was financed by taxes on trade, on herds of animals, and especially on land, from which the monarch claimed a quarter or more of the crop.[14]

Mauryan India is perhaps best known for one of its emperors, Ashoka (reigned 268–232 B.C.E.), who left a record of his activities and his thinking in a series of edicts carved on rocks and pillars throughout the kingdom. Ashoka's reign began in a familiar fashion—ruthless consolidation of his own power and vigorous expansion of the state's frontiers. A particularly bloody battle against the state of Kalinga marked a turning point in Ashoka's reign. Apparently repulsed by the destruction, Ashoka converted to Buddhism and turned his attention to more peaceful ways of governing his huge empire. His carved edicts outlined a philosophy of nonviolence and of toleration for the many sects of the immensely varied religious culture of India. Referring to all Indians as "my children," he urged the "advancement of all sects" and promised to work for "every kind of happiness in this world and the next."

In pursuit of this philosophy, Ashoka abandoned his much-beloved royal hunts, ended animal sacrifices in the capital, eliminated most meat from the royal menu, and was particularly generous in his support of Buddhist monasteries as well as stupas, which housed relics of major Buddhist figures. In addition, he ordered the digging of wells, the planting of shade trees, and the building of rest stops along the empire's major highways—all of which served to integrate the kingdom's economy.

But he did not completely abandon the prerogatives of a ruler, for the edicts reminded people that he retained the power to punish wrongdoing, and the death penalty remained intact. Nonetheless, Ashoka's reign certainly had a different tone than that of China's Shihuangdi or of Alexander the Great, who, according to legend, wept because he had no more worlds to conquer. Of course, Ashoka's policies were good politics as well as good morality. They were an effort to develop an inclusive and integrative moral code for an extremely diverse realm.

Despite their good intentions, these policies ultimately were not very successful. Shortly after Ashoka's death, the Mauryan Empire broke apart into a more common Indian pattern of competing regional states that rose and fell with some regularity. Several other short-lived imperial experiments, such as the Gupta Empire (320–550 C.E.), also marked India's history, but none lasted long. India's political history thus resembled that of Western Europe after the collapse of the Roman Empire far more than that of China or Persia. Neither imperial nor regional states commanded the kind of loyalty or exercised the degree of influence that they did in other classical civilizations. India's unparalleled cultural diversity surely was one reason, as was the frequency of invasions from Central Asia, which repeatedly smashed states that might have provided the nucleus for an all-India empire. Finally, India's social structure, embodied in a caste system linked to occupational groups, made for intensely local loyalties at the expense of wider identities (see Chapter 6).

Nonetheless, a frequently vibrant economy fostered a lively internal commerce and made India the focal point of an extensive network of trade in the Indian Ocean basin. In particular, its cotton textile industry long supplied cloth throughout the Afro-Eurasian world. Strong guilds of merchants and artisans provided political leadership in major towns and cities, and their wealth patronized lavish temples, public buildings, and religious festivals. Great creativity in religious matters generated Hindu and Buddhist traditions that later penetrated much of Asia. Indian mathematics and science, especially astronomy, also were impressive; Indian scientists plotted the movements of stars and planets and recognized quite early that the earth was round. Clearly, the absence of consistent imperial unity did not prevent the evolution of an enduring civilization.

Ashoka of India
This twelfth-century stone relief provides a visual image of the Mauryan dynasty's best-known ruler. (Philip Baird/ www.anthroarcheart.org)

Reflections: Classical Empires and the Twentieth Century

The classical empires discussed in this chapter have long ago passed into history, but we have kept them alive in memory, for they have proven useful, even in the twentieth and early twenty-first centuries. Those empires have provided legitimacy for contemporary states, inspiration for new imperial ventures, and abundant warnings and cautions for those seeking to criticize more recent empires. For example, in bringing communism to China in the twentieth century, the Chinese leader Mao Zedong compared himself to Shihuangdi, the unifier of China and the brutal founder of its Qin dynasty. Reflecting on his campaign against intellectuals in general and Confucianism in particular, Mao declared to a Communist Party conference: "Emperor Qin Shihuang was not that outstanding. He only buried alive 460 Confucian scholars. We buried 460 thousand Confucian scholars....To the charge of being like Emperor Qin, of being a dictator, we plead guilty."[15]

In contrast, modern-day Indians, who have sought to present their country as a model of cultural tolerance and nonviolence, have been quick to link themselves to Ashoka and his policies of inclusiveness. When the country became independent from British colonial rule in 1947, India soon placed an image of Ashoka's Pillar on the new nation's currency.

In the West, it has been the Roman Empire that has provided a template for thinking about political life. Many in Great Britain celebrated their own global empire as a modern version of the Roman Empire. In the early twentieth century, African students in a mission school in British-ruled Kenya were asked on a history exam to list the benefits that Roman occupation brought to Britain. The implication was obvious. If the British had been "civilized" by Roman rule, then surely Africans would benefit from falling under the control of the "superior" British. Likewise, to the Italian fascist dictator Benito Mussolini, his country's territorial expansion during the 1930s and World War II represented the creation of a new Roman Empire. Most recently, of course, America's dominant role in the world has prompted the question: are the Americans the new Romans?

Historians frequently cringe as politicians and students use (and perhaps misuse) historical analogies to make their case for particular points of view in the present. But we have little else to go on except history in making our way through the complexities of contemporary life, and historians themselves seldom agree on the "lessons" of the past. Lively debate about the continuing relevance of classical empires shows that although the past may be gone, it surely is not dead.

Second Thoughts

What's the Significance?

To assess your mastery of the material in this chapter, see the **Online Study Guide** at bedfordstmartins.com/strayer.

Persian Empire	Alexander the Great	Qin Shihuangdi
Athenian democracy	Hellenistic era	Han dynasty
Greco-Persian	Caesar Augustus	Mauryan Empire
Wars	*pax Romana*	Ashoka

Big Picture Questions

1. What common features can you identify in the empires described in this chapter?
2. In what ways did these empires differ from one another? What accounts for those differences?
3. Are you more impressed with the "greatness" of empires or with their destructive and oppressive features? Why?
4. Do you think that the classical empires hold "lessons" for the present, or are contemporary circumstances sufficiently unique as to render the distant past irrelevant?

Next Steps: For Further Study

Norman F. Cantor, *Antiquity* (2003). An overview of ancient and classical civilizations.

Arthur Cotterell, *The First Emperor of China* (1988). A biography of Shihuangdi.

Christopher Kelley, *The Roman Empire: A Very Short Introduction* (2006). A brief, up-to-date, and accessible account of the Roman achievement.

Cullen Murphy, *Are We Rome? The Fall of an Empire and the Fate of America* (2007). A reflection on the usefulness and the dangers of comparing the Roman Empire to the present-day United States.

Sarah Pomeroy et al., *Ancient Greece* (1999). A highly readable survey of Greek history by a team of distinguished scholars.

Romila Thapar, *Ashoka and the Decline of the Mauryas* (1961). A classic study of India's early empire builder.

Illustrated History of the Roman Empire. http://www.roman-empire.net. An interactive Web site with maps, pictures, and much information about the Roman Empire.

For Web sites and documents related to this chapter, see **Make History** at bedfordstmartins.com/strayer.

Eurasian Cultural Traditions

500 B.C.E. – 500 C.E.

In 2004, some 180 married couples in Beijing, China, stood before a picture of their country's ancient sage, Confucius, and took an oath, pledging fidelity to each other and promising never to divorce. This was a small part of a nationwide celebration of the 2,555th anniversary of the birth of Confucius. A public memorial service was held in his hometown of Qufu, while high government officials warmly welcomed delegates attending an international symposium devoted to his teaching. What made this celebration remarkable was that it took place in a country still ruled by the Communist Party, which had long devoted enormous efforts to discrediting Confucius and his teachings. In the view of communist China's revolutionary leader, Mao Zedong, Confucianism was associated with class inequality, patriarchy, feudalism, superstition, and all things old and backward, but the country's ancient teacher and philosopher, apparently, had outlasted its revolutionary hero. High-ranking political leaders, all officially communist, have begun to invoke Confucius and to urge "social harmony," rather than class conflict, as China rapidly modernizes. Many anxious parents offer prayers at Confucian temples when their children are taking the national college entrance exams.

Buddhism also has experienced something of a revival in China, as thousands of temples, destroyed during the heyday of communism, have been repaired and reopened. Christianity too has grown rapidly since the death of Mao in 1976, with professing Christians numbering some 7 percent of China's huge population by the early twenty-first century. Here are reminders, in a Chinese context, of the continuing appeal of cultural traditions forged during the classical era. Those traditions are

---

China's Cultural Traditions: In this idealized painting, attributed to the Chinese artist Wang Shugu (1649–1730), the Chinese teacher Confucius presents a baby Buddha to the Daoist master Laozi. The image illustrates the assimilation of a major Indian religion into China as well as the generally peaceful coexistence of these three traditions. (British Museum/The Art Archive) among the most enduring legacies that second-wave civilizations have bequeathed to the modern world.

IN THE SEVERAL CENTURIES SURROUNDING 500 B.C.E., something quite remarkable happened all across Eurasia. More or less simultaneously, in China, India, the Middle East, and Greece, there emerged cultural traditions that spread widely, have persisted in various forms into the twenty-first century, and have shaped the values and outlooks of most people who have inhabited the planet over the past 2,500 years.

In China, it was the time of Kong Fuzi (Confucius) and Laozi, whose teachings gave rise to Confucianism and Daoism respectively. In India, a series of religious writings known as the *Upanishads* gave expression to the classical philosophy of Hinduism, while a religious reformer, Siddhartha Gautama, set in motion a separate religion known later as Buddhism. In the Middle East, a distinctively monotheistic religious tradition appeared. It was expressed in Zoroastrianism, derived from the teachings of the Persian prophet Zarathustra, and in Judaism, articulated in Israel by a number of Jewish prophets such as Amos, Jeremiah, and Isaiah. Finally, in Greece, a rational and humanistic tradition found expression in the writings of Socrates, Plato, Aristotle, and many others.

These cultural traditions differed greatly. Chinese and Greek thinkers focused more on the affairs of this world and credited human rationality with the power to understand that reality. Indian, Persian, and Jewish intellectuals, who explored the realm of the divine and its relationship to human life, were much more religious. All of these traditions sought an alternative to an earlier polytheism, in which the activities of various gods and spirits explained what happened in this world. These gods and spirits had generally been seen as similar to human beings, though much more powerful. Through ritual and sacrifice, men and women might placate the gods or persuade them to do human bidding. In contrast, the new cultural traditions of the classical era sought to define a single source of order and meaning in the universe, some moral or religious realm, sharply different from and higher than the sphere of human life. The task of humankind, according to these new ways of thinking, was personal moral or spiritual transformation—often expressed as the development of compassion—by aligning ourselves with that higher order.[1] These enormously rich and varied traditions have collectively posed the great questions of human life and society that have haunted and inspired much of humankind ever since. They also defined the distinctive cultures that distinguished the various classical civilizations from one another.

Why did these traditions all emerge at roughly the same time? Here we encounter an enduring issue of historical analysis: What is the relationship between ideas and the circumstances in which they arise? Are ideas generated by particular political, social, and economic conditions? Or are they the product of creative human imagination independent of the material environment? Or do they derive from some combination of the two? In the case of the classical cultural traditions, many historians have

Snapshot   Thinkers and Philosophies of the Classical Era

Person	Date	Location	Religion/Philosophy	Key Ideas
Zoroaster	7th century B.C.E. (?)	Persia (present-day Iran)	Zoroastrianism	Single High God; cosmic conflict of good and evil
Hebrew prophets (Isaiah, Amos, Jeremiah)	9th–6th centuries B.C.E.	Eastern Mediterranean/Palestine/Israel	Judaism	Transcendent High God; covenant with chosen people; social justice
Anonymous writers of Upanishads	800–400 B.C.E.	India	Brahmanism/Hinduism	Brahma (the single impersonal divine reality); karma; rebirth; goal of liberation (moksha)
Confucius	6th century B.C.E.	China	Confucianism	Social harmony through moral example; secular outlook; importance of education; family as model of the state
Mahavira	6th century B.C.E.	India	Jainism	All creatures have souls; purification through nonviolence; opposed to caste
Siddhartha Gautama	6th century B.C.E.	India	Buddhism	Suffering caused by desire/attachment; end of suffering through modest and moral living and meditation practice
Laozi, Zhuangzi	6th–3rd centuries B.C.E.	China	Daoism	Withdrawal from the world into contemplation of nature; simple living; end of striving
Socrates, Plato, Aristotle	5th–4th centuries B.C.E.	Greece	Greek rationalism	Style of persistent questioning; secular explanation of nature and human life
Jesus	early 1st century C.E.	Palestine/Israel	Christianity	Supreme importance of love based on intimate relationship with God; at odds with established authorities
Saint Paul	1st century C.E.	Palestine/Israel/eastern Roman Empire	Christianity	Christianity as a religion for all; salvation through faith in Christ

noted the tumultuous social changes that accompanied the emergence of these new teachings. An iron-age technology, available since roughly 1000 B.C.E., made possible more productive economies and more deadly warfare. Growing cities, increased trade, the prominence of merchant classes, the emergence of new states and empires, new contacts among civilizations—all of these disruptions, occurring in already-literate societies, led thinkers to question older outlooks and to come up with new solutions to fundamental questions: What is the purpose of life? How should human society be ordered? What is the relationship between human life in this world and the moral or spiritual realms that lie beyond? But precisely why various societies developed their own distinctive answers to these questions remains an elusive mystery—a tribute, perhaps, to the unpredictable genius of the human imagination.

China and the Search for Order

As one of the First Civilizations, China had a tradition of state building that historians have traced back to around 2000 B.C.E. or before. By the time the Zhou dynasty took power in 1122 B.C.E., the notion of the Mandate of Heaven had taken root, as had the idea that the normal and appropriate condition of China was one of political unity. By the eighth century B.C.E., the authority of the Zhou dynasty and its royal court had substantially weakened, and by 500 B.C.E. any unity that China had earlier enjoyed was long gone. What followed was a period of chaos, growing violence, and disharmony that became known as the "age of warring states" (403–221 B.C.E.). During these dreadful centuries of disorder and turmoil, a number of Chinese thinkers began to consider how order might be restored, how the apparent tranquillity of an earlier time could be realized again. From their reflections emerged classical cultural traditions of Chinese civilization.

The Legalist Answer

■ **Comparison**

What different answers to the problem of disorder arose in classical China?

One answer to the problem of disorder—though not the first to emerge—was a hardheaded and practical philosophy known as "Legalism." To Legalist thinkers, the solution to China's problems lay in rules or laws, clearly spelled out and strictly enforced through a system of rewards and punishments. "If rewards are high," wrote Han Feizi, one of the most prominent Legalist philosophers, "then what the ruler wants will be quickly effected; if punishments are heavy, what he does not want will be swiftly prevented."[2] Legalists generally entertained a rather pessimistic view of human nature. Most people were stupid and shortsighted. Only the state and its rulers could act in their long-term interests. Doing so meant promoting farmers and soldiers, the only two groups in society who performed essential functions, while suppressing artisans, merchants, aristocrats, scholars, and other classes regarded as useless.

Legalist thinking provided inspiration and methods for the harsh reunification of China under Shihuangdi and the Qin dynasty (221–206 B.C.E.), but the brutality of that short dynasty thoroughly discredited Legalism. Although its techniques and practices played a role in subsequent Chinese statecraft, no philosopher or ruler ever again openly advocated its ideas. The Han and all subsequent dynasties drew instead on the teachings of China's greatest sage—Confucius.

The Confucian Answer

Born to an aristocratic family in the state of Lu in northern China, Confucius (551–479 B.C.E.) was both learned and ambitious. Believing that he had found the key to solving China's problem of disorder, he spent much of his adult life seeking a political position from which he might put his ideas into action. But no such opportunity came his way. Perhaps it was just as well, for it was as a thinker and a teacher that Confucius left a profound imprint on Chinese history and culture and on other East Asian societies, such as Korea and Japan. After his death, his students collected his teachings in a short book called the *Analects*, and later scholars elaborated and commented endlessly on his ideas, creating a body of thought known as Confucianism.

The Confucian answer to the problem of China's disorder was very different from that of the Legalists. Not laws and punishments, but the moral example of superiors was the Confucian key to a restored social harmony. For Confucius, human society consisted primarily of unequal relationships: the father was superior to the son; the husband to the wife; the older brother to the younger brother; and, of course, the ruler to the subject. If the superior party in each of these relationships behaved with sincerity, benevolence, and genuine concern for others, then the inferior party would be motivated to respond with deference and obedience. Harmony then would prevail. As Confucius put it, "The relation between superiors and inferiors is like that between the wind and the grass. The grass must bend when the wind blows across it." Thus, in both family life and in political life, the cultivation of *ren*—translated as human-heartedness, benevolence, goodness, nobility of heart—was the essential ingredient of a tranquil society.

But how are these humane virtues to be nurtured? Believing that people have a capacity for improvement, Confucius emphasized education as the key to moral betterment. He prescribed a broad liberal arts education emphasizing language, literature, history, philosophy, and ethics, all applied to the practical problems of government. Ritual and ceremonies were also important, for they conveyed the rules of appropriate behavior in the many and varying circumstances of life. For the "superior person," or "gentleman" in Confucian

■ **Description**
Why has Confucianism been defined as a "humanistic philosophy" rather than a supernatural religion?

Filial Piety
This Song dynasty painting served as an illustration of an ancient Chinese text in the Confucian tradition called the "Classic of Filial Piety," originally composed sometime around the fourth century B.C.E. and subsequently reissued many times. Here, a son kneels submissively in front of his parents. The long-enduring social order that Confucius advocated began at home with unquestioning obedience and the utmost respect for parents and other senior members of the family. (National Palace Museum, Taipei, Taiwan, Republic of China)

terms, this process of improvement involved serious personal reflection and a willingness to strive continuously to perfect his moral character.

Such ideas left a deep mark on Chinese culture. The discrediting of Legalism during the Qin dynasty opened the door to the adoption of Confucianism as the official ideology of the Chinese state, to such an extent that Confucianism became almost synonymous with Chinese culture. As China's bureaucracy took shape during the Han dynasty and after, Confucianism became the central element of the educational system, which prepared students for the series of examinations required to gain official positions. In those examinations, candidates were required to apply the principles of Confucianism to specific situations that they might encounter once in office. Thus generation after generation of China's male elite was steeped in the ideas and values of Confucianism.

Family life had long been central to Chinese popular culture, expressed in the practice of ancestor veneration, including visiting the graves of the deceased, presenting them with offerings, and erecting commemorative tablets and shrines in their honor. In Confucian thinking, the family became a model for political life, a kind of miniature state. Filial piety, the honoring of one's ancestors and parents, was both an end in itself and a training ground for the reverence due to the emperor and state officials. Confucianism also set the tone for defining the lives of women. A somewhat later woman writer, Ban Zhao (45–116 C.E.), penned a famous work called *Lessons for Women*, which spelled out the implication of Confucian thinking for women.

> Let a woman modestly yield to others. . . . Always let her seem to tremble and to fear. . . . Then she may be said to humble herself before others. . . . To guard carefully her chastity . . . to choose her words with care . . . , to wash and scrub filth away . . . , with whole-hearted devotion to sew and to weave, to love not gossip and silly laughter, in cleanliness and order to prepare the wine and food for serving guests: [These] may be called the characteristics of womanly work.[3]

Ban Zhao called for greater attention to education for young girls, not because they were equal to boys, but so that a young woman might be better prepared to serve her husband.

Confucianism also placed great importance on history, for the ideal good society lay in the past. Confucian ideas were reformist, perhaps even revolutionary, but they were consistently presented as an effort to restore a past golden age. Those ideas also injected a certain democratic element into Chinese elite culture, for the great sage had emphasized that "superior men" and potential government officials were those of outstanding moral character and intellectual achievement, not simply those of aristocratic background. Usually only young men from wealthy families could afford the education necessary for passing examinations, but on occasion villagers could find the resources to sponsor one of their bright sons. Thus the Confucian-based examination system provided a modest element of social mobility in an otherwise hierarchical society. Confucian values clearly justified the many inequalities of Chinese society, but they also established certain expectations for government. Emperors should keep taxes low, administer justice, and provide for the material needs of the people. Those who failed to govern by the moral norms of Confucian values forfeited the Mandate of Heaven and invited upheaval and their replacement by another dynasty.

Finally, Confucianism marked Chinese elite culture by its secular, or nonreligious, character. Confucius did not deny the reality of gods and spirits. In fact, he advised people to participate in family and state rituals "as if the spirits were present," and he believed that the universe had a moral character with which human beings should align themselves. But the thrust of Confucian teaching was distinctly this-worldly and practical, concerned with human relationships, effective government, and social harmony. Asked on one occasion about his view of death and the spirits, Confucius replied that because we do not fully understand this life, we cannot possibly know anything about the life beyond. Although members of the Chinese elite generally acknowledged that magic, the gods, and spirits were perhaps necessary for the lower orders of society, they felt that educated people would find them of little help in striving for moral improvement and in establishing a harmonious society.

The Daoist Answer

No civilization has ever painted its cultural outlook in a single color. As Confucian thinking became generally known in China, a quite different school of thought also took shape. Known as Daoism, it was associated with the legendary figure Laozi, who, according to tradition, was a sixth-century B.C.E. archivist. He is said to have penned a short poetic volume, the *Daodejing* (*The Way and Its Power*), before vanishing in the wilderness to the west of China on his water buffalo. Daoist ideas were later expressed in a more explicit fashion by the philosopher Zhuangzi (369–286 B.C.E.).

In many ways, Daoist thinking ran counter to that of Confucius, who had emphasized the importance of education and earnest striving for moral improvement and good government. The Daoists ridiculed such efforts as artificial and useless, generally making things worse. In the face of China's disorder and chaos, they urged withdrawal into the world of nature and encouraged behavior that was spontaneous, individualistic, and natural. Whereas

Chinese Landscape Paintings
Focused largely on mountains and water, Chinese landscape paintings were much influenced by the Daoist search for harmony with nature. Thus human figures and buildings were usually eclipsed by towering peaks, waterfalls, clouds, and trees. This seventeenth-century painting entitled *Temple on a Mountain Ledge* shows a Buddhist monastery in such a setting, while the poem in the upper right refers to the artist's earlier wanderings, a metaphor for the Buddhist quest for enlightenment. (Mr. and Mrs. John D. Rockefeller 3rd Collection of Asian Art/Asia Society 179.124)

■ **Comparison**
How did the Daoist outlook differ from that of Confucianism?

Confucius focused on the world of human relationships, the Daoists turned the spotlight on the immense realm of nature and its mysterious unfolding patterns. Confucius roams within society, the Chinese have often said; Laozi wanders beyond.

The central concept of Daoist thinking is *dao*, an elusive notion that refers to the way of nature, the underlying and unchanging principle that governs all natural phenomena. According to the *Daodejing*, the dao "moves around and around, but does not on this account suffer. All life comes from it. It wraps everything with its love as in a garment, and yet it claims no honor, for it does not demand to be lord. I do not know its name and so I call it the Dao, the Way, and I rejoice in its power."[4]

Applied to human life, Daoism invited people to withdraw from the world of political and social activism, to disengage from the public life so important to Confucius, and to align themselves with the way of nature. It meant simplicity in living, small self-sufficient communities, limited government, and the abandonment of education and active efforts at self-improvement. "Give up learning," declares the *Daodejing*, "and put an end to your troubles." The flavor of the Daoist approach to life is evident in this passage from the *Daodejing*:

> A small country has few people.
> Though there are machines that can work ten to a hundred times faster
> than man, they are not needed. . . .
> Though they have boats and carriages, no one uses them. . . .
> Men return to the knotting of ropes in place of writing.
> Their food is plain and good, their clothes fine but simple. . . .
> They are happy in their ways.
> Though they live within sight of their neighbors,
> And crowing cocks and barking dogs are heard across the way,
> Yet they leave each other in peace while they grow old and die.[5]

Despite its sharp differences with the ideas of Confucianism, the Daoist perspective was widely regarded by elite Chinese as complementing rather than contradicting Confucian values. Such an outlook was facilitated by the ancient Chinese concept of yin and yang, which expressed a belief in the unity of opposites.

The yin yang symbol

Thus a scholar-official might pursue the Confucian project of "government by goodness" during the day, but upon returning home in the evening or following his retirement, he might well behave in a more Daoist fashion — pursuing the simple life, reading Daoist philosophy, practicing Daoist meditation and breathing exercises, or enjoying landscape paintings in which tiny human figures are dwarfed by the vast peaks and valleys of the natural world. Daoism also shaped the culture of ordinary people as it entered popular religion. This kind of Daoism sought to tap the power of the dao for practical uses and came to include magic, fortune-telling, and the search for immortality. It also on occasion provided an ideology for peasant uprisings, such as the Yellow Turban Rebellion (184–204 C.E.; see Chapter 6), which imagined a utopian society without the oppression of governments and landlords. In its many and varied forms, Daoism, like Confucianism, became an enduring element of Chinese cultural tradition.

Cultural Traditions of Classical India

The cultural development of Indian civilization was far different from that of China. Whereas Confucianism paid little attention to the gods, spirits, and speculation about religious matters, Indian elite culture embraced the divine and all things spiritual with enthusiasm and generated elaborate philosophical visions about the nature of ultimate reality. Still, the Indian religious tradition, known to us as Hinduism, differed from other world religions. Unlike Buddhism, Christianity, or Islam, Hinduism had no historical founder; rather, it grew up over many centuries along with Indian civilization. Although it later spread into Southeast Asia, Hinduism was not a missionary religion seeking converts but was, like Judaism, associated with a particular people and territory.

In fact, "Hinduism" was never a single tradition at all, and the term itself derived from outsiders—Greeks, Muslims, and later the British—who sought to reduce the infinite variety of Indian cultural patterns into a recognizable system. From the inside, however, Hinduism dissolved into a vast diversity of gods, spirits, beliefs, practices, rituals, and philosophies. This endlessly variegated Hinduism served to incorporate into Indian civilization the many diverse peoples who migrated into or invaded the South Asian peninsula over many centuries and several millennia. Its ability to accommodate this diversity gave India's cultural development a distinctive quality.

South Asian Religion: From Ritual Sacrifice to Philosophical Speculation

Despite the fragmentation and variety of Indian cultural and religious patterns, an evolving set of widely recognized sacred texts provided some commonality. The earliest of these texts, known as the *Vedas*, were collections of poems, hymns, prayers, and rituals. Compiled by priests called *Brahmins*, the Vedas were for centuries transmitted orally and were reduced to writing in Sanskrit around 600 B.C.E. In the Vedas, historians have caught fleeting glimpses of classical Indian civilization in its formative centuries (1500–600 B.C.E.). Those sacred writings tell of small competing chiefdoms or kingdoms, of sacred sounds and fires, of numerous gods, rising and falling in importance over the centuries, and of the elaborate ritual sacrifices that they required. Performing these sacrifices and rituals with great precision enabled the Brahmins to acquire enormous power and wealth, sometimes exceeding even that of kings and warriors, but also generated growing criticism, as ritual became mechanical and formal and as Brahmins required heavy fees to perform them.

From this dissatisfaction arose another body of sacred texts, the *Upanishads*. Composed by largely anonymous thinkers between 800 and 400 B.C.E., these were

■ **Change**
In what ways did the religious traditions of South Asia change over the centuries?

Hindu Ascetics
Hinduism called for men in the final stage of life to leave ordinary ways of living and withdraw into the forests to seek spiritual liberation, or moksha. Here, in an illustration from an early thirteenth-century Indian manuscript, a holy man explores a text with three disciples in a secluded rural setting. (Réunion des Musées Nationaux/Art Resource, NY)

mystical and highly philosophical works that sought to probe the inner meaning of the sacrifices prescribed in the Vedas. In the Upanishads, external ritual gave way to introspective thinking, which expressed in many and varied formulations the central concepts of philosophical Hinduism that have persisted into modern times. Chief among them was the idea of *Brahman*, the World Soul, the final and ultimate reality. Beyond the multiplicity of material objects and individual persons and beyond even the various gods themselves lay this primal unitary energy or divine reality infusing all things, similar in some ways to the Chinese notion of the dao. This alone was real; the immense diversity of existence that human beings perceived with their senses was but an illusion.

The fundamental assertion of philosophical Hinduism was that the individual human soul, or *atman*, was in fact a part of Brahman. Beyond the quest for pleasure, wealth, power, and social position, all of which were perfectly normal and quite legitimate, lay the effort to achieve the final goal of humankind—union with Brahman, an end to our illusory perception of a separate existence. This was *moksha*, or liberation, compared sometimes to a bubble in a glass of water breaking through the surface and becoming one with the surrounding atmosphere.

Achieving this exalted state was held to involve many lifetimes, as the notion of *samsara*, or rebirth/reincarnation, became a central feature of Hindu thinking. Human souls migrated from body to body over many lifetimes, depending on one's actions. This was the law of *karma*. Pure actions, appropriate to one's station in life, resulted in rebirth in a higher social position or caste. Thus the caste system of distinct and ranked groups, each with its own duties, became a register of spiritual progress. Birth in a higher caste was evidence of "good karma," based on actions in a previous life, and offered a better chance to achieve moksha, which brought with it an end to the painful cycle of rebirth.

Various ways to this final release, appropriate to people of different temperaments, were spelled out in Hindu teachings. Some might achieve moksha through knowledge or study; others by means of detached action in the world, doing one's work without regard to consequences; still others through passionate devotion to some deity or through extended meditation practice. Such ideas—carried by Brahmin priests and even more by wandering ascetics, who had withdrawn from ordinary life to pursue their spiritual development—became widely known throughout India.

The Buddhist Challenge

About the same time as philosophical Hinduism was taking shape, there emerged another movement that soon became a distinct and separate religious tradition—Buddhism. Unlike Hinduism, this new faith had a historical founder, Siddhartha Gautama (ca. 566–ca. 486 B.C.E.), a prince from a small north Indian state. According to Buddhist tradition, the prince had enjoyed a sheltered and delightful youth but was shocked to his core upon encountering old age, sickness, and death. Leaving family and fortune behind, he then set out on a six-year spiritual quest, finally achieving insight, or "enlightenment," at the age of thirty-five. For the rest of his life, he taught what he had learned and gathered a small but growing community whose members came to see him as the Buddha, the Enlightened One.

"I teach but one thing," the Buddha said, "suffering and the end of suffering." To the Buddha, suffering or sorrow—experiencing life as imperfect, impermanent, and unsatisfactory—was the central and universal feature of human life. Its cause was desire or craving for individual fulfillment and particularly attachment to the notion of a core self or ego that is uniquely and solidly "me." The cure for this "dis-ease" lay in living a modest and moral life combined with meditation practice. Those who followed the Buddhist path most fully could expect to achieve enlightenment or *nirvana*, a virtually indescribable state in which individual identity would be "extinguished" along with all greed, hatred, and delusion. With the pain of unnecessary suffering finally ended, the enlightened person would experience an overwhelming serenity, even in the midst of difficulty, as well as an immense loving-kindness, or compassion, for all beings. It was a simple message, elaborated endlessly and in various forms by those who followed him.

Much of the Buddha's teaching reflected the Hindu traditions from which it sprang. The idea that ordinary life is an illusion, the concepts of karma and rebirth, the goal of overcoming the incessant demands of the ego, the practice of meditation, the hope for final release from the cycle of rebirth—all of these Hindu elements found their way into Buddhist teaching. In this respect, Buddhism was a simplified and more accessible version of Hinduism.

Other elements of Buddhist teaching, however, sharply challenged prevailing Hindu thinking. Rejecting the religious authority of the Brahmins, the Buddha ridiculed their rituals and sacrifices as

■ **Comparison**

In what ways did Buddhism reflect Hindu traditions, and in what ways did it challenge them?

The Mahabodhi Temple Constructed on the traditional site of the Buddha's enlightenment in northern India, the Mahabodhi temple became a major pilgrimage site and was lavishly patronized by local rulers. (Alison Wright/Robert Harding World Imagery/Getty Images)

irrelevant to the hard work of dealing with one's suffering. Nor was he much interested in abstract speculation about the creation of the world or the existence of God, for such questions, he declared, "are not useful in the quest for holiness; they do not lead to peace and to the direct knowledge of *nirvana*." Individuals had to take responsibility for their own spiritual development with no help from human authorities or supernatural beings. "Be a lamp unto yourselves," counseled the dying Buddha. "Work out your own salvation." It was a religion of intense self-effort, based on personal experience. The Buddha also challenged the inequalities of a Hindu-based caste system, arguing that neither caste position nor gender was a barrier to enlightenment. The possibility of "awakening" was available to all.

When it came to establishing a formal organization of the Buddha's most devoted followers, though, the prevailing patriarchy of Indian society made itself felt. Buddhist texts recount that the Buddha's foster mother, Prajapati Gotami, sought to enter the newly created order of monks but was repeatedly refused admission by the Buddha himself. Only after the intervention of the Buddha's attendant, Ananda, did he relent and allow women to join a separate order of nuns. Even then, these nuns were subjected to a series of rules that clearly subordinated them to men. Male monks, for example, could officially admonish the nuns, but the reverse was forbidden.

Nonetheless, thousands of women flocked to join the Buddhist order of nuns, where they found a degree of freedom and independence unavailable elsewhere in Indian society. The classic Hindu text, "The Laws of Manu," had clearly defined the position of women: "In childhood a female must be subject to her father; in youth to her husband; when her lord is dead to her sons; a woman must never be independent." But Buddhist nuns delighted in the relative freedom of their order, where they largely ran their own affairs, were forbidden to do household chores, and devoted themselves wholly to the search for "awakening," which many apparently achieved. A nun named Mutta declared: "I am free from the three crooked things: mortar, pestle, and my crooked husband. I am free from birth and death and all that dragged me back."[6]

Gradually, Buddhist teachings found an audience in India. Its egalitarian message appealed especially to lower-caste groups and to women. The availability of its teaching in the local language of Pali, rather than the classical Sanskrit, made it accessible. Establishing monasteries and stupas containing relics of the Buddha on the site of neighborhood shrines to earth spirits or near a sacred tree linked the new religion to local traditions. The most dedicated followers joined monasteries, devoting their lives to religious practice and spreading the message among nearby people. State support during the reign of Ashoka (268–232 B.C.E.) likewise helped the new religion gain a foothold in India as a distinct tradition separate from Hinduism.

As Buddhism spread, both within and beyond India, differences in understanding soon emerged, particularly as to how nirvana could be achieved or, in a common Buddhist metaphor, how to cross the river to the far shore of enlightenment. The Buddha had taught a rather austere doctrine of intense self-effort, undertaken

■ Comparison
What is the difference between the Theravada and Mahayana expressions of Buddhism?

most actively by monks and nuns who withdrew from society to devote them-selves fully to the quest. This early version of the new religion, known as *Theravada* (the Teaching of the Elders), portrayed the Buddha as an immensely wise teacher and model, but certainly not divine. It was more psychological than religious, a set of practices rather than a set of beliefs. The gods, though never completely denied, played little role in assisting believers in their search for enlightenment. In short, individuals were on their own in crossing the river. Clearly this was not for everyone.

By the early centuries of the Common Era, a modified form of Buddhism called *Mahayana* (Great Vehicle) had taken root in parts of India, proclaiming that help was available for the strenuous voyage. Buddhist thinkers developed the idea of *bodhisattvas*, spiritually developed people who postponed their own entry into nirvana in order to assist those who were still suffering. The Buddha himself became something of a god, and both earlier and future Buddhas were available to offer help. Elaborate descriptions of these supernatural beings, together with vari-ous levels of heavens and hells, transformed Buddhism into a popular religion of salvation. Furthermore, religious merit, leading to salvation, might now be earned by acts of piety and devotion, such as contributing to the support of a monastery, and that merit might be transferred to others. This was the Great Vehicle, allowing far more people to make the voyage across the river.

Hinduism as a Religion of Duty and Devotion

Strangely enough, Buddhism as a distinct religious practice ultimately died out in the land of its birth as it was reincorporated into a broader Hindu tradition, but it spread widely and flourished, particularly in its Mahayana form, in other parts of Asia. Buddhism declined in India perhaps in part because the mounting wealth of monasteries and the economic interests of their leading figures separated them from ordinary people. Competition from Islam after 1000 C.E. also may have played a role. The most important reason for Buddhism's decline in India, however, was the growth during the first millennium C.E. of a new kind of popular Hinduism, which the masses found more accessible than the elaborate sacrifices of the Brahmins or the philosophical speculations of intellectuals. Some scholars have seen this phase of Hinduism as a response to the challenge of Buddhism. Expressed in the widely known epic poems of the *Mahabharata* and the *Ramayana*, this revived Hinduism indicated more clearly that action in the world and the detached performance of caste duties might also provide a path to liberation.

In the much-beloved Hindu text known as the *Bhagavad Gita*, itself an episode within the *Mahabharata*, the troubled warrior-hero Arjuna is in anguish over the necessity of killing his kinsmen as a decisive battle approaches. But he is assured by his charioteer Lord Krishna, an incarnation of the god Vishnu, that performing his duty as a warrior, and doing so selflessly without regard to consequences, is an act of devotion that would lead to "release from the shackles of repeated rebirth."

■ **Change**
What new emphases characterized Hinduism as it responded to the challenge of Buddhism?

This was not an invitation to militarism, but rather an affirmation that ordinary people, not just Brahmins, could also make spiritual progress by selflessly performing the ordinary duties of their lives. "The man who, casting off all desires, lives free from attachments, who is free from egoism, and from the feeling that this or that is mine, obtains tranquility." Withdrawal and asceticism were not the only ways to moksha.

Also becoming increasingly prominent was yet another religious path—the way of devotion to one or another of India's many gods and goddesses. Beginning in south India and moving northward, this *bhakti* (worship) movement involved the intense adoration of and identification with a particular deity through songs, prayers, and rituals associated with the many cults that emerged throughout India. By far the most popular deities were Vishnu, the protector and preserver of creation and associated with mercy and goodness, and Shiva, representing the divine in its destructive aspect, but many others also had their followers. This proliferation of gods and goddesses, and of their *bhakti* cults, occasioned very little friction or serious religious conflict. "Hinduism," writes a leading scholar, "is essentially tolerant, and would rather assimilate than rigidly exclude."[7] This capacity for assimilation extended to an already-declining Buddhism, which for many people had become yet another cult worshipping yet another god. The Buddha in fact was incorporated into the Hindu pantheon as the ninth incarnation of Vishnu. By 1000 C.E., Buddhism had largely disappeared as a separate religious tradition within India.

Thus a constantly evolving and enormously varied South Asian religious tradition had transformed itself from a religion of ritual sacrifice to one of philosophical speculation, to one of devotional worship and detached action in the world. In the process, it had generated Buddhism, which became the first of the great universal religions of world history, and then had absorbed that new religion back into the fold of an emerging popular Hinduism.

Moving toward Monotheism: The Search for God in the Middle East

Paralleling the evolution of Chinese and Indian cultural traditions was the movement toward a distinctive monotheistic religious tradition in the Middle East, which found expression in Persian Zoroastrianism and in Judaism. Neither of these religions themselves spread very widely, but the monotheism that they nurtured became the basis for both Christianity and Islam, which have shaped so much of world history over the past 2,000 years. Amid the proliferation of gods and spirits that had long characterized religious life throughout the ancient world, the idea of a single supreme Deity, the sole source of all creation and goodness, was a radical cultural innovation. That conception created the possibility of a universal religion, open to all of humankind, but it could also mean an exclusive and intolerant faith, committed to the worship of the one true God.

Zoroastrianism

During the glory years of the powerful Persian Empire, a new religion arose to challenge the polytheism of earlier times. Tradition dates its Persian prophet, Zarathustra (Zoroaster to the Greeks), to the sixth or seventh century B.C.E., although some scholars place him hundreds of years earlier. Whenever he actually lived, his ideas took hold in Persia and received a degree of state support during the Achaemenid dynasty (558–330 B.C.E.). Appalled by the endemic violence of recurring cattle raids, Zarathustra recast the traditional Persian polytheism into a vision of a single unique god, Ahura Mazda, who ruled the world and was the source of all truth, light, and goodness. This benevolent deity was engaged in a cosmic struggle with the forces of evil, embodied in an equivalent supernatural figure, Angra Mainyu. Ultimately this struggle would be decided in favor of Ahura Mazda, aided by the arrival of a final Savior who would restore the world to its earlier purity and peace. At a day of judgment, those who had aligned with Ahura Mazda would be granted new resurrected bodies and rewarded with eternal life in Paradise. Those who had sided with evil and the "Lie" were condemned to everlasting punishment. Zoroastrian teaching thus placed great emphasis on the free will of humankind and the necessity for each individual to choose between good and evil.

The Zoroastrian faith achieved widespread support within the Persian heartland, although it also found adherents in other parts of the empire, such as Egypt, Mesopotamia, and Anatolia. Because it never became an active missionary religion, it did not spread widely beyond the region. Alexander the Great's invasion of the Persian Empire and the subsequent Greek-ruled Seleucid dynasty (330–155 B.C.E.) were disastrous for Zoroastrianism, as temples were plundered, priests slaughtered, and sacred writings burned. But the new faith managed to survive this onslaught and flourished again during the Parthian (247 B.C.E.–224 C.E.) and Sassanid (224–651 C.E.) dynasties. It was the arrival of Islam and an Arab empire that occasioned the final decline of Zoroastrianism in Persia, although a few believers fled to India, where they became known as Parsis ("Persians") and continue their faith into present times.

Like Buddhism, the Zoroastrian faith vanished from its place of origin, but unlike Buddhism, it did not spread beyond Persia in a recognizable form. Some parts of the Zoroastrian belief system, however, did become incorporated into other religious traditions. The presence of many Jews in the Persian Empire meant that they surely became aware of Zoroastrian ideas. Many of those ideas—including the conflict of God and an evil counterpart (Satan); the notion of a last judgment and resurrected bodies; and a belief in the final defeat of evil, the arrival of a savior (Messiah), and the remaking of the world at the end of time—found a place in an evolving Judaism. Some of these teachings, especially the concepts of heaven and hell, later became prominent in those enormously

■ **Connection**
What aspects of Zoroastrianism and Judaism subsequently found a place in Christianity and Islam?

Zoroastrian Fire Altar
Representing the energy of the Creator God Ahura Mazda, the fire altar became an important symbol of Zoroastrianism and was often depicted on Persian coins in association with images of Persian rulers. This particular coin dates from the third century C.E. (©AAAC/Topham/The Image Works)

influential successors to Judaism—Christianity and Islam.[8] Thus the Persian tradition of Zoroastrianism continued to echo well beyond its disappearance in the land of its birth.

Judaism

■ Description
What was distinctive about the Jewish religious tradition?

While Zoroastrianism emerged in the greatest empire of its time, Judaism, the Middle East's other ancient monotheistic tradition, was born among one of the region's smaller and, at the time, less significant peoples—the Hebrews. Their traditions, recorded in the Old Testament, tell of an early migration from Mesopotamia to Palestine under the leadership of Abraham. Those same traditions report that a portion of these people later fled to Egypt, where they were first enslaved and then miraculously escaped to rejoin their kinfolk in Palestine. There, around 1000 B.C.E., they established a small state, which soon split into two parts—a northern kingdom called Israel and a southern state of Judah.

In a region politically dominated by the large empires of Assyria, Babylon, and Persia, these tiny Hebrew communities lived a precarious existence. Israel was conquered by Assyria in 722 B.C.E., and many of its inhabitants were deported to distant regions, where they assimilated into the local culture. In 586 B.C.E., the kingdom of Judah likewise came under Babylonian control, and its elite class was shipped off to exile. In Babylon, these people, now calling themselves Jews, retained their cultural identity and later were able to return to their homeland. A large part of that identity lay in their unique religious ideas. It was in creating that religious tradition, rather than in building a powerful empire, that this small people cast a long shadow in world history.

From their unique historical experience of exodus from Egypt and exile in Babylon, the Jews evolved over many centuries a distinctive conception of God. Unlike the peoples of Mesopotamia with their many gods and goddesses, the Jews found in their god, whom they called Yahweh, a powerful and jealous deity, who demanded their exclusive loyalty. "Thou shalt have no other gods before me"—this was the first of the Ten Commandments. It was a difficult requirement, for as the Jews turned from a pastoral life to agriculture, many of them were continually attracted by the fertility gods of neighboring peoples. Their neighbors' goddesses also were attractive, offering a kind of spiritual support that the primarily masculine Yahweh could not. This was not quite monotheism, for the repeated demands of the Hebrew prophets to turn away from other gods show that those deities remained real for many Jews. Over time, however, Yahweh triumphed. The Jews came to understand their relationship to him as a contract or a covenant. In return for their sole devotion and obedience, Yahweh would consider the Jews his chosen people, favoring them in battle, causing them to grow in numbers, and bringing them prosperity and blessing.

Ancient Israel

Unlike the bickering, arbitrary, polytheistic gods of Mesopotamia or ancient Greece, which were associated with the forces of nature and behaved in quite human fashion, Yahweh was increasingly seen as a lofty, transcendent deity of utter holiness and purity, set far above the world of nature, which he had created. But unlike the impersonal conceptions of ultimate reality found in Daoism and Hinduism, Yahweh was encountered as a divine person with whom people could actively communicate. He was also a god who acted within the historical process, bringing the Jews out of Egypt or using foreign empires to punish them for their disobedience.

Furthermore, Yahweh was transformed from a god of war, who ordered his people to "utterly destroy" the original inhabitants of the Promised Land, to a god of social justice and compassion for the poor and the marginalized, especially in the passionate pronouncements of Jewish prophets such as Amos and Isaiah. The prophet Isaiah describes Yahweh as rejecting the empty rituals of his chosen but sinful people: "What to me is the multitude of your sacrifices, says the Lord. . . . Wash yourselves, make yourselves clean . . . cease to do evil, learn to do good . . . ; seek justice; correct oppression; defend the fatherless; plead for the widow."[9]

Here was a distinctive conception of the divine—singular, transcendent, personal, separate from nature, engaged in history, and demanding social justice and moral righteousness above sacrifices and rituals. This set of ideas sustained a separate Jewish identity in both ancient and modern times, and it was this understanding of God that provided the foundation on which both Christianity and Islam were built.

The Cultural Tradition of Classical Greece: The Search for a Rational Order

Unlike the Jews, the Persians, or the civilization of India, Greek thinkers of the classical era generated no lasting religious tradition of world historical importance. The religion of these city-states brought together the unpredictable, quarreling, and lustful gods of Mount Olympus, secret fertility cults, oracles predicting the future, and the ecstatic worship of Dionysus, the god of wine. The distinctive feature of the classical Greek cultural tradition was the willingness of many Greek intellectuals to abandon this mythological framework, to affirm that the world was a physical reality governed by natural laws, and to assert that human rationality could both understand these laws and work out a system of moral and ethical life. In separating science and philosophy from conventional religion, the Greeks developed a way of thinking that bore some similarity to the secularism of Confucian thought in China.

Precisely why Greek thought evolved in this direction is hard to say. Perhaps the diversity and incoherence of Greek religious mythology presented its intellectuals with a challenge to bring some order to their understanding of the world. Greece's geographic position on the margins of the great civilizations of Mesopotamia,

■ Description
What are the distinctive features of the Greek intellectual tradition?

The Death of Socrates
Condemned to death by an Athenian jury, Socrates declined to go into exile, voluntarily drank a cup of poison hemlock, and died in 399 B.C.E. in the presence of his friends. The dramatic scene was famously described by Plato and much later was immortalized on canvas by the French painter Jacques-Louis David in 1787. (Image copyright © The Metropolitan Museum of Art/Art Resource, NY)

Egypt, and Persia certainly provided intellectual stimulation. Furthermore, the growing role of law in the political life of Athens possibly suggested that a similar regularity also underlay the natural order.

The Greek Way of Knowing

The foundations of this distinctive cultural tradition emerged in the three centuries between 600 and 300 B.C.E., coinciding with the flourishing of Greek city-states, especially Athens, and with the growth of its artistic, literary, and theatrical traditions. The enduring significance of Greek thinking lay not so much in the answers it provided to life's great issues, for the Greeks seldom agreed with one another, but rather in its way of asking questions. Its emphasis on argument, logic, and the relentless questioning of received wisdom; its confidence in human reason; its enthusiasm for puzzling out the world without much reference to the gods—these were the defining characteristics of the Greek cultural tradition.

The great exemplar of this approach to knowledge was Socrates (469–399 B.C.E.), an Athenian philosopher who walked about the city engaging others in conversation about the good life. He wrote nothing, and his preferred manner of teaching was not the lecture or exposition of his own ideas but rather a constant questioning of the assumptions and logic of his students' thinking. Concerned always to puncture the pretentious, he challenged conventional ideas about the importance of wealth and power in living well, urging instead the pursuit of wisdom and virtue. He was critical of Athenian democracy and on occasion had positive things to say about Sparta, the great enemy of his own city. Such behavior brought him into conflict with city authorities, who accused him of corrupting the youth of Athens and sentenced him to death. At his trial, he defended himself as the "gadfly" of Athens, stinging its citizens into awareness. To any and all, he declared, "I shall question, and examine and cross-examine him, and if I find that he does not possess virtue, but says he does, I shall rebuke him for scorning the things that are most important and caring more for what is of less worth."[10]

The earliest of the classical Greek thinkers, many of them living on the Ionian coast of Anatolia, applied this rational and questioning way of knowing to the world of nature. For example, Thales, drawing on Babylonian astronomy, predicted an eclipse of the sun and argued that the moon simply reflected the sun's light. He also was one of the first Greeks to ask about the fundamental nature of the universe and came up with the idea that water was the basic stuff from which all else derived, for it existed as solid, liquid, and gas. Others argued in favor of air or fire or some combination. Democritus suggested that atoms, tiny "uncuttable" particles, collided in various configurations to form visible matter. Pythagoras believed that beneath the chaos and complexity of the visible world lay a simple, unchanging mathematical order. What these thinkers had in common was a commitment to a rational and nonreligious explanation for the material world.

Such thinking also served to explain the functioning of the human body and its diseases. Hippocrates and his followers came to believe that the body was composed of four fluids, or "humors," which, when out of proper balance, caused various ailments. He also traced the origins of epilepsy, known to the Greeks as "the sacred disease," to simple heredity: "It seems to me to be no more divine or sacred than other diseases, but has a natural cause from which it originates, like other afflictions."[11] The Hippocratic Oath taken by all new doctors is named for this ancient Greek scientist.

A similar approach informed Greek thinking about the ways of humankind. Herodotus, who wrote about the Greco-Persian Wars, explained his project as an effort to discover "the reason why they fought one another." This assumption that human reasons lay behind the conflict, not simply the whims of the gods, was what made Herodotus a historian in the modern sense of that word. Ethics and government also figured importantly in Greek thinking. Plato (429–348 B.C.E.) famously sketched out in *The Republic* a design for a good society. It would be ruled by a class of highly educated "guardians" led by a "philosopher-king." Such people would be able to penetrate the many illusions of the material world and to grasp the "world of forms," in which ideas such as goodness, beauty, and justice lived a real and unchanging existence. Only such people, he argued, were fit to rule.

Aristotle (384–322 B.C.E.), a student of Plato and a teacher of Alexander the Great, was perhaps the most complete expression of the Greek way of knowing, for he wrote or commented on practically everything. With an emphasis on empirical observation, he cataloged the constitutions of 158 Greek city-states, identified hundreds of species of animals, and wrote about logic, physics, astronomy, the weather, and much else besides. Famous for his reflections on ethics, he argued that "virtue" was a product of rational training and cultivated habit and could be learned. As to government, he urged a mixed system, combining the principles of monarchy, aristocracy, and democracy.

The Greek Legacy

The rationalism of the Greek tradition was clearly not the whole of Greek culture. The gods of Mount Olympus continued to be a reality for many people, and the ecstatic songs and dances that celebrated Dionysus, the god of wine, were anything but rational and reflective. The death of Socrates at the hands of an Athenian jury showed that philosophy could be a threat as well as an engaging pastime. Nonetheless, Greek rationalism, together with Greek art, literature, and theater, persisted long after the glory days of Athens were over. The Roman Empire facilitated the spread of Greek culture within the Mediterranean basin, and not a few leading Roman figures sent their children to be educated in Athens at the Academy that Plato had founded. An emerging Christian theology was expressed in terms of Greek philosophical concepts, especially those of Plato. Even after the western Roman Empire collapsed, classical Greek texts were preserved in the eastern half, known as Byzantium.

In the West, however, direct access to Greek texts was far more difficult in the chaotic conditions of post-Roman Europe, and for centuries classical scholarship was neglected in favor of Christian writers. Much of that legacy was subsequently rediscovered after the twelfth century C.E. as European scholars gained access to classical Greek texts. From that point on, the Greek legacy has been viewed as a central element of an emerging "Western" civilization. It played a role in formulating an updated Christian theology, in fostering Europe's Scientific Revolution, and in providing a point of departure for much of European philosophy.

Long before this European rediscovery, the Greek legacy had also entered Islamic culture. Systematic translations of Greek works of science and philosophy into Arabic, together with Indian and Persian learning, stimulated Muslim thinkers and scientists, especially in the fields of medicine, astronomy, mathematics, geography, and chemistry. It was in fact largely from Arabic translations of Greek writers that Europeans became reacquainted with the legacy of classical Greece, especially during the twelfth and thirteenth centuries. Despite the many centuries that have passed since the flourishing of classical Greek culture, that tradition has remained, especially in the West, an inspiration for those who celebrate the powers of the human mind to probe the mysteries of the universe and to explore the equally challenging domain of human life.

$\mathcal{S}$napshot   **Reflections on Human Love from Mediterranean Civilization**

From the Jews: The Song of Solomon

My beloved speaks and says to me: "Arise my love, my fair one and come away; for lo, the winter is past; the rain is over and gone. The flowers appear on the earth; the time of singing has come, and the voice of the turtle dove is heard in our land. The fig tree puts forth its figs; and the vines are in blossom; they give fragrance. Arise my love, my fair one, and come away."

From the Greeks: Fragments from Sappho of Lesbos

If you will come, I shall put out new pillows for you to rest on.
I was so happy. Believe me, I prayed that that night might be doubled for us.
Now I know why Eros, of all the progeny of Earth and Heaven, has been most dearly loved.

From the Romans: Ovid Giving Advice to a Young Man on the Art of Love

Add gifts of mind to bodily advantage. A frail advantage is beauty, that grows less as time draws on and is devoured by its own years. . . . O handsome youth, will soon come hoary hairs; soon will come furrows to make wrinkles in your body. Now make thee a soul that will abide, and add to it thy beauty; only that endures to the ultimate pyre. Nor let it be a slight care to cultivate your mind in the liberal arts, or to learn the two languages well. Ulysses was not comely, but he was eloquent; yet he fired two goddesses of the sea with love.

From the Christians: Saint Paul on Love: 1 Corinthians 13

Love is patient and kind; love is not jealous or boastful; it is not arrogant or rude. Love does not insist on its own way; it is not irritable or resentful; it does not rejoice at wrong, but rejoices in the right. Love bears all things, believes all things, hopes all things, endures all things. Love never ends. . . . So faith, hope and love abide, these three, but the greatest of these is love.

Comparing Jesus and the Buddha

About 500 years after the time of Confucius, the Buddha, Zarathustra, and Socrates, a young Jewish peasant/carpenter in the remote province of Judaea in the Roman Empire began a brief three-year career of teaching and miracle-working before he got in trouble with local authorities and was executed. In one of history's most unlikely stories, the teachings of that obscure man, barely noted in the historical records of the time, became the basis of the world's second great universal religion. This man, Jesus of Nazareth, and the religion of Christianity, which grew out of his life and teaching, had a dramatic impact on world history, similar to and often compared with that of India's Siddhartha Gautama, the Buddha.

■ **Comparison**
How would you compare the lives and teachings of Jesus and the Buddha? In what different ways did the two religions evolve after the deaths of their founders?

The Lives of the Founders

The family background of the two teachers could hardly have been more different. Gautama was born to royalty and luxury, whereas Jesus was a rural or small-town worker from a distinctly lower-class family. But both became spiritual seekers, mystics in their respective traditions, who claimed to have personally experienced another level of reality. Those powerful religious experiences provided the motivation for their life's work and the personal authenticity that attracted their growing band of followers.

Both were "wisdom teachers," challenging the conventional values of their time, urging the renunciation of wealth, and emphasizing the supreme importance of love or compassion as the basis for a moral life. The Buddha had instructed his followers in the practice of *metta*, or loving-kindness: "Just as a mother would protect her only child at the risk of her own life, even so, let [my followers] cultivate a boundless heart towards all beings."[12] In a similar vein during his famous Sermon on the Mount, Jesus told his followers: "You have heard that it was said 'Love your neighbor and hate your enemy,' but I tell you 'Love your enemies and pray for those who persecute you.'"[13] Both Jesus and the Buddha called for the personal transformation of their followers, through "letting go" of the grasping that causes suffering, in the Buddha's teaching, or "losing one's life in order to save it," in the language of Jesus.[14]

Despite these similarities, there were also some differences in their teachings and their life stories. Jesus inherited from his Jewish tradition an intense devotion to a single personal deity with whom he was on intimate terms, referring to him as *Abba* ("papa" or "daddy"). According to the New Testament, the miracles he performed reflected the power of God available to him as a result of that relationship. The Buddha's original message, by contrast, largely ignored the supernatural, involved no miracles, and taught a path of intense self-effort aimed at ethical living and mindfulness as a means of ending suffering. Furthermore, Jesus' teachings had a sharper social and political edge than did those of the Buddha. Jesus spoke more clearly on behalf of the poor and the oppressed, directly criticized the hypocrisies of the powerful, and deliberately associated with lepers, adulterous women, and tax collectors, all of whom were regarded as "impure." In doing so, Jesus reflected his own lower-class background, the Jewish tradition of social criticism, and the reality of Roman imperial rule over his people, none of which corresponded to the Buddha's experience. Finally, Jesus' public life was very brief, probably less than three years, compared to more than forty years for the Buddha. His teachings had so antagonized both Jewish and Roman authorities that he was crucified as a common criminal. The Buddha's message was apparently less threatening to the politically powerful, and he died a natural death at age eighty.

Establishing New Religions

It seems likely that neither Jesus nor the Buddha had any intention of founding a new religion; rather they sought to reform the traditions from which they had

■ **Change**
In what ways was Christianity transformed in the five centuries following the death of Jesus?

come. Nonetheless, Christianity and Buddhism soon emerged as separate religions, distinct from Judaism and Hinduism, proclaiming their messages to a much wider and more inclusive audience. In the process, both teachers were transformed by their followers into gods. According to many scholars, Jesus never claimed divine status, seeing himself as a teacher or a prophet, whose close relationship to God could be imitated by anyone.[15] The Buddha likewise viewed himself as an enlightened but fully human person, an example of what was possible for anyone who followed the path. But in Mahayana Buddhism, the Buddha became a supernatural being, who could be worshipped and prayed to and was spiritually available to his followers. Jesus too soon became divine in the eyes of his followers, "the Son of God, Very God of Very God," according to one of the creeds of the early Church, while his death and resurrection made possible the forgiveness of sins and the eternal salvation of those who believed.

The transformation of Christianity from a small Jewish sect to a world religion began with Saint Paul (10-65 C.E.), an early convert whose missionary journeys in the eastern Roman Empire led to the founding of small Christian communities that included non-Jews. The Good News of Jesus, Paul argued, was for everyone, and Gentile (non-Jewish) converts need not follow Jewish laws or rituals such as circumcision. In one of his many letters to these new communities, later collected as part of the New Testament, Paul wrote, "There is neither Jew nor Greek . . . neither slave nor free . . . neither male nor female, for you are all one in Christ Jesus."[16] Despite Paul's egalitarian pronouncement, early Christianity, like Buddhism, reflected prevailing patriarchal values, even as they both offered women new opportunities. Although women apparently played leadership roles in the "house churches" of the first century C.E., Paul counseled women to "be subject to your husbands" and declared that "it is shameful for a woman to speak in church."[17]

Nonetheless, the inclusive message of early Christianity was one of the attractions of the new faith as it spread very gradually within the Roman Empire during the several centuries after Jesus' death. The earliest converts were usually lower-stratum people—artisans, traders, and a considerable number of women—mostly from towns and cities, while a scattering of wealthier, more prominent, and better-educated people subsequently joined the ranks of Christians.[18] The spread of the faith often was accompanied by reports of miracles, healings, and the casting out of demons—all of which were impressive to people thoroughly accustomed to seeing the supernatural behind the

Women in the Early Church
This third-century C.E. fresco from a Roman catacomb is called the *Fractio Panis*, "the breaking of the bread" or Holy Communion. Some scholars argue that the figures are those of women, suggesting that women held priestly office in the early Church and were only later excluded from it. (Scala/Art Resource, NY)

events of ordinary life.[19] Christian communities also attracted converts by the way their members cared for one another. In the middle of the third century C.E., the church in Rome supported 154 priests (of whom 52 were exorcists) and some 1,500 widows, orphans, and destitute people.[20] By 300 C.E., perhaps 10 percent of the Roman Empire's population (some 5 million people) identified themselves as Christians.

In the Roman world, the strangest and most offensive feature of the new faith was its exclusive monotheism and its antagonism to all other supernatural powers, particularly the cult of the emperors. Christians' denial of these other gods caused them to be tagged as "atheists" and was one reason behind the empire's intermittent persecution of Christians during the first three centuries of the Common Era. All of that ended with Emperor Constantine's conversion in the early fourth century C.E. and with growing levels of state support for the new religion in the decades that followed.

Roman rulers sought to use an increasingly popular Christianity as glue to hold together a very diverse population in a weakening imperial state. Constantine and his successors thus provided Christians with newfound security and opportunities. The emperor Theodosius (reigned 379–395 C.E.) enforced a ban on all polytheistic ritual sacrifices and ordered their temples closed. Christians by contrast received patronage for their buildings, official approval for their doctrines, suppression of their rivals, prestige from imperial recognition, and, during the late fourth century, the proclamation of Christianity as the official state religion. All of this set in motion a process by which the Roman Empire, and later all of Europe, became overwhelmingly Christian. Beyond the Roman world, the new religion also found a home in various parts of Africa, the Middle East, and Asia (see Map 5.1).

The situation in India was quite different. Even though Ashoka's support gave Buddhism a considerable boost, it was never promoted to the exclusion of other faiths. He sought harmony among India's diverse population through religious tolerance rather than uniformity. The kind of monotheistic intolerance that Christianity exhibited was quite foreign to Indian patterns of religious practice. Although Buddhism subsequently died out in India as it was absorbed into a reviving Hinduism, no renewal of Roman polytheism occurred, and Christianity became an enduring element of European civilization. Nonetheless, Christianity did adopt some elements of religious practice from the Roman world, including perhaps the cult of saints and the dating of the birth of Jesus to the winter solstice. In both cases, however, these new religions spread widely beyond their places of origin. Buddhism provided a network of cultural connections in much of Asia, and Christianity did the same for western Eurasia and parts of Africa (see Map 5.1).

Creating Institutions

As Christianity spread within the Roman Empire and beyond, it developed a hierarchical organization, with patriarchs, bishops, and priests—all men—replacing

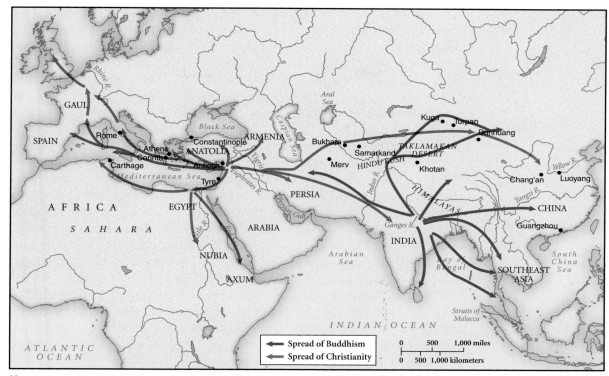

Map 5.1   The Spread of Early Christianity and Buddhism
In the five centuries after the birth of Jesus, Christianity found converts from Spain to northeast Africa, Central Asia, and India. In the Roman Empire, Axum, and Armenia, the new religion enjoyed state support as well. Subsequently Christianity took root solidly in Europe and after 1000 C.E. in Russia as well. Meanwhile, Buddhism was spreading from its South Asian homeland to various parts of Asia, even as it was weakening in India itself.

the house churches of the early years, in which women played a more prominent part. At least in some places, however, women continued to exercise leadership and even priestly roles, prompting Pope Gelasius in 494 to speak out sharply against those who encouraged women "to officiate at the sacred altars, and to take part in all matters imputed to the offices of the male sex, to which they do not belong."[21] In general, though, the exclusion of women from the priesthood established a male-dominated clergy and a patriarchal church, which has lasted into the twenty-first century.

This emerging hierarchical structure of the Church, together with its monotheistic faith, also generated a great concern for unity in matters of doctrine and practice. The bishop of Rome gradually emerged as the dominant leader, or pope, of the Church in the western half of the empire, but this role was not recognized in the east. This division contributed to the later split between Roman Catholic and Eastern Orthodox branches of Christendom, a schism that continues to the present (see Chapter 10). Doctrinal differences also tore at the unity of Christianity and embroiled the Church in frequent controversy about the nature of Jesus (was he human, divine, or both?), his relationship to God (equal or inferior?), and the always-perplexing doctrine of the Trinity (God as Father, Son, and Holy Spirit). A series of church councils—at Nicaea (325 C.E.), Chalcedon (451 C.E.), and Constantinople (553 C.E.), for example—sought to define an "orthodox," or correct, position on these and other issues, declaring those who disagreed as *anathema*, completely expelled from the Church.

Buddhists too clashed over their various interpretations of the Buddha's teachings, and a series of councils failed to prevent the division between Theravada, Mahayana, and other approaches. A considerable proliferation of different sects, practices, teachings, and meditation techniques subsequently emerged within the Buddhist world, but these divisions generally lacked the "clear-cut distinction between 'right' and 'wrong' ideas" that characterized conflicts within the Christian world.[22] Although Buddhist states and warrior classes (such as the famous samurai of Japan) sometimes engaged in warfare, religious differences among Buddhists seldom provided the basis for the kind of bitterness and violence that often accompanied religious conflict within Christendom, such as the Thirty Years' War (1618-1648) between Catholic and Protestant states in Europe. Nor did Buddhists develop the kind of overall church hierarchy that characterized Christianity, although communities of monks and nuns, organized in monasteries, created elaborate rules to govern their internal affairs.

Reflections: Religion and Historians

To put it mildly, religion has always been a sensitive subject, and no less so for historians than for anyone else. For believers or followers of particular traditions, religion partakes of another world—that of the sacred or the divine—which is not accessible to historians or other scholars, who depend on evidence available in this world. This situation has generated various tensions or misunderstandings between historians and religious practitioners.

One of these tensions involves the question of change. Most religions present themselves as timeless, partaking of eternity or at least reflecting ancient practice. In the eyes of historians, however, the religious aspect of human life changes as much as any other. The Hindu tradition changed from a religion of ritual and sacrifice to one of devotion and worship. Buddhism became more conventionally religious, with an emphasis on the supernatural, as it evolved from Theravada to Mahayana forms. A male-dominated hierarchical Christian Church, with its pope, bishops, priests, and state support, was very different from the small house churches, which suffered persecution by imperial authorities in the early Christian centuries. The implication—that religions are at least in part a human phenomenon—has been troublesome to some believers.

Historians, on the other hand, have sometimes been uncomfortable in the face of claims by believers that they have actually experienced a divine reality. Some secular scholars have been inclined to dismiss such claims as unprovable at best. Even the biographical details of the lives of the Buddha and Jesus are difficult to prove by the standards of historians. Certainly, modern historians are in no position to validate or refute the spiritual claims of these teachers, but we need to take them seriously. Although we will never know precisely what happened to the Buddha as he sat in meditation in northern India or what transpired when Jesus spent forty days in the wilderness, clearly those experiences changed the two men and motivated their subsequent actions. Later, Muhammad likewise claimed to have received revelations from God in the caves outside Mecca. Millions of the followers of these religious leaders have also acted on the basis of what they perceived to be an encounter with the divine or other levels of reality. This interior dimension of human experience, though difficult to grasp with any precision, has been a significant mover and shaper of the historical process.

Yet a third problem arises from debates within particular religious traditions about which group most accurately represents the "real" or authentic version of the faith. Historians usually refuse to take sides in such disputes. They simply notice with interest that most human cultural traditions generate conflicting views, some of which become the basis for serious conflict in their societies.

Reconciling personal religious convictions with the perspectives of modern historical scholarship is no easy task. At the very least, all of us can appreciate the immense human effort that has gone into the making of classical religious traditions, and we can acknowledge the enormous significance of these traditions in the unfolding of the human story. They have shaped the meanings that billions of people over thousands of years have attached to the world they inhabit. These religious traditions have justified the vast social inequalities and oppressive states of human civilizations, but they also have enabled human beings to endure those difficulties and on occasion have stimulated reform and rebellion. And they have guided much of humankind in our endless efforts to penetrate the mysteries of the world beyond and of the world within.

Second Thoughts

What's the Significance?

Legalism	Siddhartha Gautama (the	Greek rationalism
Confucianism	Buddha)	Socrates, Plato, Aristotle
Daoism	Theravada/Mahayana	Jesus of Nazareth
Ban Zhao	*Bhagavad Gita*	Saint Paul
Vedas	Zoroastrianism	
Upanishads	Judaism	

To assess your mastery of the material in this chapter, see the **Online Study Guide** at bedfordstmartins.com/strayer.

Big Picture Questions

1. "Religions are fundamentally alike." Does the material in this chapter support or undermine this idea?

2. Is a secular outlook on the world an essentially modern phenomenon, or does it have precedents in the classical era?

3. "Religion is a double-edged sword, both supporting and undermining political authority and social elites." How would you support both sides of this statement?

4. How would you define the appeal of the religious/cultural traditions discussed in this chapter? To what groups were they attractive, and why?

For Web sites and documents related to this chapter, see **Make History** at bedfordstmartins.com/strayer.

Next Steps: For Further Study

Karen Armstrong, *The Great Transformation* (2006). A comparative and historical study of the major classical-era religions by a well-known scholar.

Peter Brown, *The Rise of Western Christendom* (2003). A history of the first 1,000 years of Christianity, cast in a global framework.

Don Johnson and Jean Johnson, *Universal Religions in World History* (2007). A comparative study of the historical development of Buddhism, Christianity, and Islam.

Huston Smith, *An Illustrated World's Religions* (1994). A sympathetic account of major world religions, beautifully illustrated, by a prominent scholar of comparative religion.

Arthur Waley, *Three Ways of Thought in Ancient China* (1983). A classic work, first published more than half a century ago, about the major philosophies of old China.

Jonathan S. Walters, *Finding Buddhists in Global History* (1998). A brief account that situates Buddhism in a world history framework.

"Religions of the World," http://www.mnsu.edu/emuseum/cultural/religion. A succinct and attractively illustrated introduction to six major world religious traditions.

CHAPTER SIX

Eurasian Social Hierarchies

500 B.C.E-500 C.E.

She is a twenty-six-year-old Hindu woman from Goa, on India's west coast. She speaks the Marathi language, has a high school education, is not currently employed, neither smokes nor drinks, but occasionally eats meat. Like millions of other Indians, she is seeking a partner by placing a personal ad in the newspaper or on the Internet. In addition to the personal and professional data found everywhere in such ads, in India they almost always contain another piece of information— the caste of the seeker. The young woman from Goa lists herself as a member of a "scheduled caste" known as Chambar, formerly called "untouchables," the lowest category in the hierarchy of India's ranked society. That personal ads in twenty-first-century India still refer to caste points out how deeply entrenched and enduring ancient patterns of social life can be.

THE MOST RECENT 250 YEARS OF WORLD HISTORY have called into question social structures long assumed to be natural and permanent. The French, Russian, and Chinese revolutions challenged and destroyed ancient monarchies and class hierarchies; the abolitionist movement of the nineteenth century attacked slavery, largely unquestioned for millennia; the women's movement confronted long and deeply held patriarchal assumptions about the proper relationship between women and men; and Mahatma Gandhi, during India's struggle for independence in the twentieth century, sought to raise the status of "untouchables," referring to them as *Harijan*, or "children of God." Nevertheless, caste, class, patriarchy, and even slavery have certainly not vanished from human society, even now. During the era of "second wave" civilizations

---

Indian Society: A fresco from the time of India's Gupta dynasty (320–600 C.E.) shows townspeople in a royal procession. (© Benoy K. Behl)

in Eurasia, these patterns of inequality found expressions and generated social tensions that remain recognizable to the contemporary descendants of these classical societies.

Millions of individual people, inhabiting the classical civilizations of Eurasia, lived within a political framework of states or empires. They occupied as well a world of ideas, religions, and values that derived both from local folkways and from the teaching of the great religious or cultural traditions of their civilizations. They also lived within established societies that defined relationships between rich and poor, powerful and powerless, slaves and free people, and men and women. Those social relationships shaped the daily lives and the life chances of everyone; they provided the foundation for political authority as well as challenges to it; they were both justified and challenged by the religious and cultural traditions of these civilizations.

Like the First Civilizations, those of the classical era were sharply divided along class lines, and they too were patriarchal, with women clearly subordinated to men in most domains of life. In constructing their societies, however, the classical civilizations differed substantially from one another. Chinese, Indian, and Mediterranean civilizations provide numerous illustrations of the many and varied ways in which peoples of the classical era organized their social life. The assumptions, tensions, and conflicts accompanying these social patterns provided much of the distinctive character and texture that distinguished these diverse civilizations from one another.

Society and the State in Classical China

Chinese society was unique in the ancient world in the extent to which it was shaped by the actions of the state. Nowhere was this more apparent than in the political power and immense social prestige of Chinese state officials. For more than 2,000 years, these officials, bureaucrats acting in the name of the emperor both in the capital and in the provinces, represented the cultural and social elite of Chinese civilization. This class had its origins in the efforts of early Chinese rulers to find administrators loyal to the central state rather than to their own families or regions. Philosophers such as Confucius had long advocated selecting such officials on the basis of merit and personal morality rather than birth or wealth. As the Han dynasty established its authority in China around 200 B.C.E., its rulers required each province to send men of promise to the capital, where they were examined and chosen for official positions on the basis of their performance.

An Elite of Officials

■ **Description**
How would you describe the social hierarchy of classical China?

Over time, this system of selecting administrators evolved into the world's first professional civil service. In 124 B.C.E., Emperor Wu Di established an imperial academy where potential officials were trained as scholars and immersed in Chinese classical texts dealing with history, literature, art, and mathematics, with an emphasis on Confucian teachings. By the end of the Han dynasty, it enrolled some 30,000 students, who were by then subjected to a series of written examinations to select officials of various grades. Private schools in the provinces funneled still more aspiring candidates into this examination system, which persisted until the early twentieth century. In theory open to all men, this system in practice favored those whose families were wealthy enough to provide the years of education required to pass even the lower-level exams. Proximity to the capital and family connections to the imperial court also helped in gaining a position in this highest of Chinese elites. Nonetheless, village communities or a local landowner might sponsor the education of a bright young man from a commoner family, enabling him to enter the charmed circle of officialdom. One rags-to-riches story told of a pig farmer who became an adviser to the emperor himself. Thus the examination system provided a modest measure of social mobility in an otherwise quite hierarchical society.

In later dynasties, that system grew to be even more elaborate and became an enduring and distinguishing feature of Chinese civilization. During the Tang dynasty, the famous poet and official Po Chu-I (772-846 C.E.) wrote a poem entitled "After Passing the Examination," which shows something of the fame and fortune that awaited an accomplished student as well as the continuing loyalty to family and home that ideally marked those who succeeded.

> For ten years I never left my books,
> I went up . . . and won unmerited praise.
> My high place I do not much prize;
> The joy of my parents will first make me proud.
> Fellow students, six or seven men,
> See me off as I leave the City gate.
> My covered coach is ready to drive away;
> Flutes and strings blend their parting tune.
> Hopes achieved dull the pains of parting;
> Fumes of wine shorten the long road . . .
> Shod with wings is the horse of him who rides
> On a Spring day the road that leads to home.[1]

Those who made it into the bureaucracy entered a realm of high privilege and enormous prestige. Senior officials moved about in carriages and were bedecked with robes, ribbons, seals, and headdresses appropriate to their rank. Even lower officials who served in the provinces rather than the capital were distinguished by their polished speech, their cultural sophistication, and their urban manners as well as their political authority. Proud of their learning, they were the bearers, and often the makers, of Chinese culture. "Officials are the leaders of the populace," stated an imperial edict of 144 B.C.E., "and it is right and proper that the carriages they ride in and the robes that they wear should correspond to the degrees of their dignity."[2]

The Landlord Class

Most officials came from wealthy families, and in China wealth meant land. When the Qin dynasty unified China by 210 B.C.E., most land was held by small-scale peasant farmers. But by the first century B.C.E., the pressures of population growth, taxation, and indebtedness had generated a class of large landowners as impoverished peasants found it necessary to sell their lands to more prosperous neighbors. This accumulation of land in large estates was a persistent theme in Chinese history, and one that was persistently, though not very successfully, opposed by state authorities. Landlords of large estates often were able to avoid paying taxes, thus decreasing state revenues and increasing the tax burden for the remaining peasants. In some cases, they could also mount their own military forces to challenge the authority of the emperor.

One of the most dramatic state efforts to counteract the growing power of large landowners is associated with Wang Mang, a high court official of the Han dynasty who usurped the emperor's throne in 8 C.E. and immediately launched a series of startling reforms. A firm believer in Confucian good government, Wang Mang saw his reforms as re-creating a golden age of long ago in which small-scale peasant farmers represented the backbone of Chinese society. Accordingly, he ordered the great private estates to be nationalized and divided up among the landless. Government loans to peasant families, limits on the amount of land a family might own, and an end to private slavery were all part of his reform program, but these measures proved impossible to enforce. Opposition from wealthy landowners, nomadic invasions, poor harvests, floods, and famines led to the collapse of Wang Mang's reforms and his assassination in 23 C.E.

Large landowning families, therefore, remained a central feature of Chinese society, although the fate of individual families rose and fell as the wheel of fortune raised them to great prominence or plunged them into poverty and disgrace. As a class, they benefited both from the wealth that their estates generated and from the power and prestige that accompanied membership in the official elite. The term "scholar-gentry" reflected their twin sources of privilege. With homes in both urban and rural areas, members of the scholar-gentry class lived luxuriously. Multistoried houses, the finest of silk clothing, gleaming carriages, private orchestras, high-stakes gambling—all of this was part of the life of China's landlord class.

Peasants

■ **Change**
What class conflicts disrupted Chinese society?

Throughout the history of China's civilization, the vast majority of its population has been peasants, living in households of four to five people, representing two or three generations. Some owned enough land to support their families and perhaps even sell something on the local market. Many others could barely survive. Nature, the state, and landlords combined to make the life of most peasants extremely vulnerable. Famines, floods, droughts, hail, and pests could wreak havoc without warning. State authorities required the payment of taxes, demanded about a month's labor every year on various public projects, and conscripted young men for two years of military service. During the Han dynasty, growing numbers of impoverished and desperate peasants had to sell out to large landlords and work as tenants or sharecroppers on their estates, where rents could run as high as one-half to two-thirds of the crop. Other peasants fled, taking to a life of begging or joining a gang of bandits in a remote area.

An eighth-century C.E. Chinese poem by Li Shen reflects poignantly on the enduring hardships of peasant life.[3]

Chinese Peasants
For many centuries, the normal activities of Chinese peasant farmers included plowing, planting, and threshing grain, as shown in this painting from China's Song dynasty (960–1279 C.E.). (*Farmers at Work*, Northern Song Dynasty, 960–1279 [wall painting]/ Mogao Caves, Dunhuang/The Bridgeman Art Library)

> The cob of corn in springtime sown
> In autumn yields a hundredfold.
> No fields are seen that fallow lie:
> And yet of hunger peasants die.
>
> As at noontide they hoe their crops,
> Sweat on the grain to earth down drops.
> How many tears, how many a groan,
> Each morsel on thy dish did mould!

Such conditions generated periodic peasant rebellions, which punctuated Chinese history over the past 2,000 years. Toward the end of the second century C.E., wandering bands of peasants began to join together as floods along the Yellow River and resulting epidemics compounded the misery of landlessness and poverty. What emerged was a massive peasant uprising known as the Yellow Turban Rebellion because of the yellow scarves the peasants wore around their heads. That movement, which swelled to about 360,000 armed followers by 184 C.E., found leaders, organization, and a unifying ideology in a popular form of Daoism. Featuring supernatural healings, collective trances, and public confessions of sin, the Yellow Turban movement looked forward to the "Great Peace"—a golden age of complete equality, social harmony, and common ownership of property. Although the rebellion was suppressed by the military forces of the Han dynasty, the Yellow Turban and other peasant upheavals devastated the economy, weakened the state, and contributed to the overthrow of the dynasty a few decades later. Repeatedly in Chinese history, such peasant movements, often expressed in religious terms,

Yellow Turban Rebellion

Great Wall
KOREA
Wei R.
Huang He R.
Xian
Yangzi R.
East China Sea
VIETNAM
TAIWAN
South China Sea

Han Empire, c. 100 B.C.E.
Area of Yellow Turban Rebellion

registered the sharp class antagonisms of Chinese society and led to the collapse of more than one ruling dynasty.

Merchants

Peasants were oppressed in China and certainly exploited, but they were also honored and celebrated in the official ideology of the state. In the eyes of the scholar-gentry, peasants were the solid productive backbone of the country, and their hard work and endurance in the face of difficulties were worthy of praise. Merchants, however, did not enjoy such a favorable reputation in the eyes of China's cultural elite. They were widely viewed as unproductive, making a shameful profit from selling the work of others. Stereotyped as greedy, luxury-loving, and materialistic, merchants stood in contrast to the alleged frugality, altruism, and cultured tastes of the scholar-gentry. They were also seen as a social threat, as their ill-gained wealth impoverished others, deprived the state of needed revenues, and fostered resentments.

Such views lay behind periodic efforts by state authorities to rein in merchant activity and to keep them under control. Early in the Han dynasty, merchants were forbidden to wear silk clothing, ride horses, or carry arms. Nor were they permitted to sit for civil service examinations or hold public office. State monopolies on profitable industries such as salt, iron, and alcohol served to limit merchant opportunities. Later dynasties sometimes forced merchants to loan large sums of money to the state. Despite this active discrimination, merchants frequently became quite wealthy. Some tried to achieve a more respectable elite status by purchasing landed estates or educating their sons for the civil service examinations. Many had back-door relationships with state officials and landlords who found them useful and were not averse to profiting from business connections with merchants, despite their unsavory reputation.

Class and Caste in India

India's social organization shared certain broad features with that of China. In both civilizations, birth determined social status for most people; little social mobility was available for the vast majority; sharp distinctions and great inequalities characterized social life; and religious or cultural traditions defined these inequalities as natural, eternal, and ordained by the gods. Despite these similarities, the organization, flavor, and texture of ancient Indian society were distinctive compared to almost all other classical civilizations. These unique aspects of Indian society have long been embodied in what we now call the *caste system*, a term that comes from the Portuguese word *casta*, which means "race" or "purity of blood." That social organization emerged over thousands of years and in some respects has endured into modern times.

Caste as **Varna**

The origins of the caste system are at best hazy. An earlier theory—that caste evolved from a racially defined encounter between light-skinned Aryan invaders

■ Description
What set of ideas underlies India's caste-based society?

and the darker-hued native peoples—has been challenged in recent years, but no clear alternative has emerged. Perhaps the best we can say at this point is that the distinctive social system of classical India grew out of the interaction of many culturally different peoples on the South Asian peninsula together with the development of economic and social differences among these peoples as the inequalities of "civilization" spread in the Ganges River valley and beyond. Notions of race, however, seem less central to the growth of the caste system than those of economic specialization and of culture.

By the beginning of the classical era, around 500 B.C.E., the idea that society was forever divided into four great classes known as *varna* was deeply embedded in Indian thinking. Everyone was born into and remained within one of these classes for life. At the top of this hierarchical system were the Brahmins, priests whose rituals and sacrifices alone could ensure the proper functioning of the world. They were followed by the Ksatriya class, warriors and rulers charged with protecting and governing society. Next was the Vaisya class, originally commoners who cultivated the land. These three classes came to be regarded as pure Aryans and were called the "twice-born," for they experienced not only a physical birth but also formal initiation into their respective varnas and status as people of Aryan descent. Far below these twice-born in the hierarchy of varna groups were the Sudras, native peoples incorporated into the margins of Aryan society in very subordinate positions. Regarded as servants of their social betters, they were not allowed to hear or repeat the Vedas or to take part in Aryan rituals. So little were they valued that a Brahmin who killed a Sudra was penalized as if he had killed a cat or a dog.

According to varna theory, these four classes were formed from the body of the god Purusha and were therefore eternal and changeless. Although these divisions are widely recognized in India even today, historians have noted considerable social flux in ancient Indian history. Members of the Brahmin and Ksatriya groups, for example, were frequently in conflict over which ranked highest in the varna hierarchy, and only slowly did the Brahmins emerge clearly in the top position. Both of them, although theoretically purely Aryan, absorbed various tribal peoples as classical Indian civilization expanded. Tribal medicine men or sorcerers found a place as Brahmins, while warrior groups entered the Ksatriya varna. The Vaisya varna, originally defined as cultivators, evolved into a business class with a prominent place for

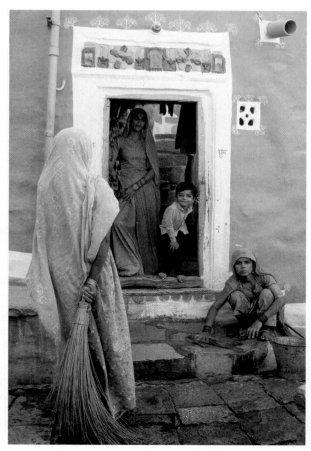

India's Untouchables Although the Indian constitution of 1950 legally abolished "untouchability," active discrimination persists against this lowest group in the caste hierarchy, now known as Dalits, or the oppressed. Sweeping is just one of many Dalit occupations; here several sweepers perform their tasks in front of an upper-caste home. (Lindsay Hebberd/Corbis)

merchants, while the Sudra varna became the domain of peasant farmers. Finally a whole new category, ranking lower even than the Sudras, emerged in the so-called untouchables, people who did the work considered most unclean and polluting, such as cremating corpses, dealing with the skins of dead animals, and serving as executioners.

Snapshot   **Social Life and Duty in Classical India**

Much personal behavior in classical India, at least ideally, was regulated according to caste. Each caste was associated with a particular color, with a part of the body of the god Purusha, and with a set of duties.

Caste (Varna)	Color/Symbolism	Part of Purusha	Duties
Brahmin	white/spirituality	head	priests, teachers
Ksatriya	red/courage	shoulders	warriors, rulers
Vaisya	yellow/wealth	thighs	farmers, merchants, artisans
Sudra	black/ignorance	feet	labor
Untouchables (outside of the varna system; thus no color and not associated with Purusha)	—	—	polluted labor

Beyond caste, behavior was ideally defined in terms of four stages of life, at least for the first three varna groups. Each new stage was marked by a *samskara*, a ritual initiating the person into this new phase of life.

Stage of Life	Duties
Student	Boys live with a teacher (guru); learn Sanskrit, rituals, Vedas; practice obedience, respect, celibacy, nonviolence.
Householder	Marriage and family; men practice caste-based career/occupation; women serve as wives and mothers, perform household rituals and sacrifices, actively support children and elders.
Retirement	Both husband and wife withdraw to the forests following birth of grandchildren; diminished household duties; greater focus on spiritual practice; sex permitted once a month.
Wandering ascetic	Only for men (women return to household); total rejection of ordinary existence; life as wandering hermit without shelter or possessions; caste becomes irrelevant; focus on achieving *moksha* and avoiding future rebirth.

Caste as Jati

As the varna system took shape in India, another set of social distinctions also arose, deriving largely from specific occupations. In India as elsewhere, urban-based civilization gave rise to specialized occupations, many organized in guilds that regulated their own affairs in a particular region. Over time, these occupationally based groups, known as *jatis*, blended with the varna system to create classical India's unique caste-based society.

The many thousands of jatis became the primary cell of India's social life beyond the family or household, but each of them was associated with one of the great classes (varnas). Thus Brahmins were divided into many separate jatis, or sub-castes, as were each of the other varnas as well as the untouchables. In a particular region or village, each jati was ranked in a hierarchy known to all, from the highest of the Brahmins to the lowest of the untouchables. Marriage and eating together were permitted only within an individual's own jati. Each jati was associated with a particular set of duties, rules, and obligations, which defined its members' unique and separate place in the larger society. Brahmins, for example, were forbidden to eat meat, while Ksatriyas were permitted to do so. Upper-caste women, of course, covered their breasts, while some lower-caste women were forbidden to do so as a sign of their lower ranking. "It is better to do one's own duty badly than another's well"—this frequently quoted saying summed up the underlying idea of Indian society.[4]

With its many separate, distinct, and hierarchically ranked social groups, Indian society was quite different from that of China or the Greco-Roman world. It was also unique in the set of ideas that explained and justified that social system. Foremost among them was the notion of ritual purity and pollution applied to caste groups. Brahmins or other high-caste people who came in contact with members of lower castes, especially those who cleaned latrines, handled corpses, or butchered and skinned dead animals, were in great danger of being polluted, or made ritually unclean. Thus untouchables were forbidden to use the same wells or to enter the temples designated for higher-caste people. Sometimes they were required to wear a wooden clapper to warn others of their approach. A great body of Indian religious writing defined various forms of impurity and the ritual means of purification.

A further support for this idea of inherent inequality and permanent difference derived from emerging Hindu notions of *karma, dharma*, and rebirth. Being born into a particular caste was generally regarded as reflecting the good or bad deeds (karma) of a previous life. Thus an individual's own prior actions were responsible for his or her current status. Any hope for rebirth in a higher caste rested on the faithful and selfless performance of one's present caste duties (dharma) in this life. Doing so contributed to spiritual progress by subduing the relentless demands of the ego. Such teachings, like that of permanent impurity, provided powerful ideological support for the inequalities of Indian society. So too did the threat of social

■ **Comparison**

What is the difference between varna and jati as expressions of classical India's caste system?

ostracism, because each jati had the authority to expel members who violated its rules. No greater catastrophe could befall a person than this, for it meant the end of any recognized social life and the loss of all social support.

As caste restrictions tightened, it became increasingly difficult—virtually impossible—for individuals to raise their social status during their lifetimes, but another kind of upward mobility enabled entire jatis, over several generations, to raise their standing in the local hierarchy of caste groups. By acquiring land or wealth, by adopting the behaviors of higher-caste groups, by finding some previously overlooked "ancestor" of a higher caste, a particular jati might slowly be redefined in a higher category. Thus India's caste system was in practice rather more fluid and changing than the theory of caste might suggest.

India's social system thus differed from that of China in several ways. It gave priority to religious status and ritual purity (the Brahmins), whereas China elevated political officials to the highest of elite positions. The caste system divided Indian society into vast numbers of distinct social groups; China had fewer, but broader, categories of society—scholar-gentry, landlords, peasants, merchants. Finally, India's caste society defined these social groups far more rigidly and with even less opportunity for social mobility than in China.

■ Comparison
How did India's caste system differ from China's class system?

The Functions of Caste

A caste-based social structure shaped India's classical civilization in various ways. Because caste (jati) was a very local phenomenon, rooted in particular regions or villages, it focused the loyalties of most people on a quite restricted territory and weakened the appeal or authority of larger all-Indian states. This localization is one reason that India, unlike China, seldom experienced an empire that encompassed the entire subcontinent (see Chapter 4). Caste, together with the shared culture of Hinduism, provided a substitute for the state as an integrative mechanism for Indian civilization. It offered a distinct and socially recognized place for almost everyone. In looking after widows, orphans, and the destitute, jatis provided a modest measure of social security and support. Even the lowest-ranking jatis had the right to certain payments from the social superiors whom they served.

Furthermore, caste represented a means of accommodating the many migrating or invading peoples who entered the subcontinent. The cellular, or honeycomb, structure of caste society allowed various peoples, cultures, and traditions to find a place within a larger Indian civilization while retaining something of their unique identity. The process of assimilation was quite different in China, however; incorporation into Chinese civilization meant becoming Chinese ethnically, linguistically, and culturally. Finally, India's caste system facilitated the exploitation of the poor by the wealthy and powerful. The multitude of separate groups into which it divided the impoverished and oppressed majority of the population made class consciousness and organized resistance across caste lines much more difficult to achieve.

Slavery in the Classical Era: The Case of the Roman Empire

Beyond the inequalities of class and caste lay those of slavery, a social institution with deep roots in human history. One scholar has suggested that the early domestication of animals provided the model for enslaving people.[5] Certainly slave owners have everywhere compared their slaves to tamed animals. Aristotle, for example, observed that the ox is "the poor man's slave." War, patriarchy, and the notion of private property, all of which accompanied the First Civilizations, also contributed to the growth of slavery. Large-scale warfare generated numerous prisoners, and everywhere in the ancient world capture in war meant the possibility of enslavement. Early records suggest that women captives were the first slaves, usually raped and then enslaved as concubines, whereas male captives were killed. Patriarchal societies, in which men sharply controlled and perhaps even "owned" women, may have suggested the possibility of using other people, men as well as women, as slaves. The class inequalities of early civilizations, which were based on great differences in privately owned property, also made it possible to imagine people owning other people.

Slavery and Civilization

Whatever its precise origins, slavery generally meant ownership by a master, the possibility of being sold, working without pay, and the status of an "outsider" at the bottom of the social hierarchy. For most, it was a kind of "social death,"[6] for slaves usually lacked any rights or independent personal identity recognized by the larger society. By the time Hammurabi's law code casually referred to Mesopotamian slavery (around 1750 B.C.E.), it was already a long-established tradition in the region and in all of the First Civilizations. Likewise, virtually all subsequent civilizations—in the Americas, Africa, and Eurasia—practiced some form of slavery.

■ **Comparison**
How did the inequalities of slavery differ from those of caste?

Slave systems throughout history have varied considerably. In some times and places, such as classical Greece and Rome, a fair number of slaves might be emancipated in their own lifetimes, through the generosity or religious convictions of their owners, or to avoid caring for them in old age, or by allowing slaves to purchase their freedom with their own funds. In some societies, the children of slaves inherited the status of their parents, while in others, such as the Aztec Empire, they were considered free people. Slaves likewise varied considerably in the labor they were required to do, with some working for the state in high positions, others performing domestic duties in their owner's household, and still others toiling in fields or mines in large work gangs.

The classical civilizations of Eurasia differed considerably in the prominence and extent of slavery in their societies. In China, it was a minor element, amounting to perhaps 1 percent of the population. Convicted criminals and their families, confiscated by the government and sometimes sold to wealthy private individuals, were among the earliest slaves in Han dynasty China. In desperate circumstances, impoverished or indebted peasants might sell their children into slavery. In southern China, teenage boys of poor families could be purchased by the wealthy, for whom they served as status symbols. Chinese slavery, however, was never very widespread and did not become a major source of labor for agriculture or manufacturing.

In India as well, people could fall into slavery as criminals, debtors, or prisoners of war and served their masters largely in domestic settings, but religious writings and secular law offered, at least in theory, some protection for slaves. Owners were required to provide adequately for their slaves and were forbidden to abandon them in old age. According to one ancient text, "a man may go short himself or stint his

$Snapshot$ **Comparing Greco-Roman and American Slavery**

	Greco-Roman Slavery (500 B.C.E.–500 C.E.)	Slavery in the Americas (1500–1888)
Source of slaves	Majority were prisoners from Roman wars of conquest; victims of pirate kidnapping; obtained through networks of long-distance trade; result of natural reproduction; abandoned children	Derived almost entirely from transatlantic slave trade; many were prisoners of African wars, debtors, or criminals in African societies
Race	Not a major factor	Came to be associated with Africa and "blackness"
Manumission (granting legal freedom to slaves)	Quite common; freed slaves received citizenship in Roman Empire but not in Greece	Much less common, especially in North America; freed slaves were long feared and discriminated against in North America, but less so in Latin America
Roles/Work	No distinction between slave and wage labor; slaves worked at wide variety of jobs, from poets, physicians, scholars, and teachers to field hands and mine laborers	Majority worked as agricultural laborers on plantations producing for export; few held elite occupations
Fate of slavery	Gradual transformation from slavery to serfdom as Roman Empire collapsed; no abolitionist movements; Christianity provided general support for slavery, though some encouragement for manumission	Ended in nineteenth century as a result of slave rebellions, industrialization, and abolitionist movements, some based in Christian teaching; replaced by sharecropping or indentured labor

wife and children, but never his slave who does his dirty work for him."[7] Slaves in India could inherit and own property and earn money in their spare time. A master who raped a slave woman was required to set her free and pay compensation. The law encouraged owners to free their slaves and allowed slaves to buy their freedom. All of this suggests that Indian slavery was more restrained than that of other ancient civilizations. Nor did Indian civilization depend economically on slavery, for most work was performed by lower-caste, though free, people.

The Making of a Slave Society: The Case of Rome

In sharp contrast to other classical civilizations, slavery played an immense role in the Mediterranean, or Western, world. Although slavery was practiced in Chinese, Indian, and Persian civilizations, the Greco-Roman world can be described as a slave society. By a conservative estimate, classical Athens alone was home to perhaps 60,000 slaves, or about one-third of the total population. In Athens, ironically, the growth of democracy and status as a free person were defined and accompanied by the simultaneous growth of slavery on a mass scale. The greatest of the Greek philosophers, Aristotle, developed the notion that some people were "slaves by nature" and should be enslaved for their own good and for that of the larger society.

■ **Comparison**

How did Greco-Roman slavery differ from that of other classical civilizations?

"The ancient Greek attitude toward slavery was simple," writes one modern scholar. "It was a terrible thing to become a slave, but a good thing to own a slave."[8] Even poor households usually had at least one or two female slaves, providing domestic work and sexual services for their owners. Although substantial numbers of Greek slaves were granted freedom by their owners, they usually did not become citizens or gain political rights. Nor could they own land or marry citizens, and particularly in Athens they had to pay a special tax. Their status remained "halfway between slavery and freedom."[9]

Practiced on an even larger scale, slavery was a defining element of Roman society. By the time of Christ, the Italian heartland of the Roman Empire had some 2 to 3 million slaves, representing 33 to 40 percent of the population.[10] Not until the modern slave societies of the Caribbean, Brazil, and the southern United States was slavery practiced again on such an enormous scale. Wealthy Romans could own many hundreds or even thousands of slaves. One woman in the fifth century C.E. freed 8,000 slaves when she withdrew into a life of Christian monastic practice.

Roman Slavery
This Roman mosaic from the third century C.E. shows the slave Myro serving a drink to his master, Fructus. (Bardo Museum Tunis/Gianni Dagli Orti/The Art Archive)

Even people of modest means frequently owned two or three slaves. In doing so, they confirmed their own position as free people, demonstrated their social status, and expressed their ability to exercise power. Slaves and former slaves also might be slave owners. One freedman during the reign of Caesar Augustus owned 4,116 slaves at the time of his death.

The vast majority of Roman slaves had been prisoners captured in the many wars that accompanied the creation of the empire. In 146 B.C.E., following the destruction of the North African city of Carthage, some 55,000 people were enslaved en masse. From all over the Mediterranean basin, such people were funneled into the major slave-owning regions of Italy and Sicily. Pirates also furnished slaves, kidnapping tens of thousands of people and selling them to Roman slave traders on the island of Delos. Roman merchants purchased still other slaves through networks of long-distance commerce extending to the Black Sea, the East African coast, and northwestern Europe. The supply of slaves also occurred through natural reproduction, as the children of slave mothers were regarded as slaves themselves. Such "home-born" slaves had a certain prestige and were thought to be less troublesome than those who had known freedom earlier in their lives. Finally, abandoned or exposed children could legally become the slave of anyone who rescued them.

Unlike New World slavery of later times, Roman slavery was not identified with a particular racial or ethnic group. Egyptians, Syrians, Jews, Greeks, Gauls, North Africans, and many other people found themselves alike enslaved. From within the empire and its adjacent regions, an enormous diversity of people were bought and sold at Roman slave markets.

Like slave owners everywhere, Romans regarded their slaves as "barbarians"— lazy, unreliable, immoral, prone to thieving—and came to think of certain peoples, such as Asiatic Greeks, Syrians, and Jews, as slaves by nature. Nor was there any serious criticism of slavery in principle, although on occasion owners were urged to treat their slaves in a more benevolent way. Even the triumph of Christianity within the Roman Empire did little to undermine slavery, for Christian teaching held that slaves should be "submissive to [their] masters with all fear, not only to the good and gentle, but also to the harsh."[11] In fact, Saint Paul used the metaphor of slavery to describe the relationship of believers to God, styling them as "slaves of Christ," while Saint Augustine described slavery as God's punishment for sin. Thus slavery was deeply embedded in the religious thinking and social outlook of elite Romans.

Similarly, slavery was entrenched throughout the Roman economy. No occupation was off-limits to slaves except military service, and no distinction existed between jobs for slaves and those for free people. Frequently they labored side by side. In rural areas, slaves provided much of the labor force on the huge estates, or *latifundia*, which produced grain, olive oil, and wine, mostly for export, much like the later plantations in the Americas. There they often worked chained together. In the cities, slaves worked in their owners' households, but also as skilled artisans, teachers, doctors, business agents, entertainers, and actors. In the empire's many mines and quarries, slaves and criminals labored under brutal conditions. Slaves in the service of the emperor provided manpower for the state bureaucracy, maintained temples and shrines, and kept Rome's water supply system functioning. Trained in special schools, they also served as gladiators in the violent spectacles of Roman public life. Thus slaves were represented among the highest and most prestigious occupations and in the lowest and most degraded.

Slave owners in the Roman Empire were supposed to provide the necessities of life to their slaves. When this occurred, slaves may have had a more secure life than was available to impoverished free people, who had to fend for themselves, but the price of this security was absolute subjection to the will of the master. Beatings, sexual abuse, and sale to another owner were constant possibilities. Lacking all rights in the law, slaves could not legally marry, although many contracted unofficial unions. Slaves often accumulated money or possessions, but such property legally belonged to their masters and could be seized at any time. If a slave murdered his master, Roman law demanded the lives of all of the victim's slaves. When one Roman official was killed by a slave in 61 C.E., every one of his 400 slaves was condemned to death. For an individual slave, the quality of life depended almost entirely on the character of the master. Brutal owners made it a living hell. Benevolent owners made life tolerable and might even grant favored slaves their freedom or permit them to buy that freedom. As in Greece, manumission of slaves was a widespread practice, and in the Roman Empire, unlike Greece, freedom was accompanied by citizenship.

Resistance and Rebellion

Roman slaves, like their counterparts in other societies, responded to enslavement in many ways. Most, no doubt, did what they had to simply to survive, but there are recorded cases of Roman prisoners of war who chose to commit mass suicide rather than face the horrors of slavery. Others, once enslaved, resorted to the "weapons of the weak"—small-scale theft, sabotage, pretending illness, working poorly, and placing curses on their masters. Fleeing to the anonymous crowds of the city or to remote rural areas prompted owners to post notices in public places, asking for information about their runaways. Catching runaway slaves became an organized private business. Occasional murders of slave owners made masters conscious of the dangers they faced. "Every slave we own is an enemy we harbor" ran one Roman saying.[12]

On several notable occasions, the slaves themselves rose in rebellion. The most famous uprising occurred in 73 B.C.E. when a slave gladiator named Spartacus led seventy other slaves from a school for gladiators in a desperate bid for freedom. The surprising initial success of their revolt attracted a growing following of rebellious slaves, numbering perhaps 120,000 at the height of the uprising. For two years, they set Italy ablaze. In a dramatic reversal of roles, they crucified some captured slave owners and set others to fighting one another in the style of gladiators. Following a series of remarkable military victories, the movement split and eventually succumbed

The Rebellion of Spartacus

to the vastly superior numbers of the Roman legions. A terrible vengeance followed as some 6,000 rebel slaves were nailed to crosses along the Appian Way from Rome to Capua, where the revolt had begun.

Nothing on the scale of the Spartacus rebellion occurred again in the Western world of slavery until the Haitian Revolution of the 1790s. But Haitian rebels sought the creation of a new society free of slavery altogether. None of the Roman slave rebellions, including that of Spartacus, had any such overall plan or goal. They simply wanted to escape Roman slavery themselves. Although rebellions created a perpetual fear in the minds of slave owners, the slave system itself was hardly affected.

Comparing Patriarchies of the Classical Era

No division of human society has had greater significance for the lives of individuals than that between male and female. Every human community has elaborated that basic biological difference into a gender system that sought to define masculinity and femininity and to determine the appropriate roles and positions of men and women in the larger society. At least since the emergence of the First Civilizations, those gender systems have been everywhere patriarchal, featuring the dominance of men over women in the family and in society generally. More widespread than slavery, these inequalities of gender, like those of class or caste, shaped the character of the classical civilizations.

In all of them, men were regarded as superior to women, and sons were generally preferred over daughters. Men had legal and property rights unknown to most women. Public life in general was a male domain, while women's roles—both productive and reproductive—took place mostly in domestic settings. Frequently men could marry more than one woman and claimed the right to regulate the social and sexual lives of the wives, daughters, and sisters in their families. Widely seen as weak and feared as potentially disruptive, women required the protection and control of men.

These common elements of patriarchy have been so widespread and pervasive that historians have been slow to recognize that gender systems evolved, changing over time. New agricultural technologies, the rise or decline of powerful states, the incorporation of world religions, interaction with culturally different peoples—all of these developments and more generated significant change in gender systems. Nor has patriarchy been everywhere the same. Restrictions on women were far sharper in classical civilizations than in those pastoral or agricultural societies that lay beyond the reach of urban centers and powerful empires. The degree and expression of patriarchy also varied from one civilization to another, as the earlier discussion of Mesopotamia and Egypt illustrated (see Chapter 3).

Within particular civilizations, patriarchy interacted with class to generate usually a more restricted life for upper-class women, who were largely limited to the home and the management of servants. In contrast, lower-class women often had a somewhat freer but more burdensome life, for economic necessity required them to work in the fields, to shop in the streets, or to serve in the homes of their social superiors. China provides a fascinating example of how patriarchy changed over time, while the contrasting patriarchies of Athens and Sparta illustrate clear variations even within the limited world of Greek civilization.

A Changing Patriarchy: The Case of China

As Chinese civilization took shape during the Han dynasty, elite thinking about gender issues became more explicitly patriarchal, more clearly defined, and linked to an emerging Confucian ideology. Long-established patterns of thinking in terms of pairs of opposites were now described in gendered and unequal

Chinese Women Musicians
This tenth-century rendering by the painter Gu Hongzhong shows these upper-class women serving as musicians for a high official of a Tang dynasty emperor. It was titled *The Night Revels of Han Xizai*. The painter was apparently sent by the emperor to spy on the suspicious behavior of the minister, who in various tellings was suspected of either rebellion or undignified activity. (Werner Forman/Art Resource, NY)

terms. The superior principle of *yang* was viewed as masculine and related to heaven, rulers, strength, rationality, and light, whereas *yin*, the lower feminine principle, was associated with the earth, subjects, weakness, emotion, and darkness. Thus female inferiority was permanent and embedded in the workings of the universe.

■ **Change**
In what ways did the expression of Chinese patriarchy change over time, and why did it change?

What this meant more practically was spelled out repeatedly over the centuries in various Confucian texts. Two notions in particular summarized the ideal position of women, at least in the eyes of elite male writers. The adage "Men go out, women stay in" emphasized the public and political roles of men in contrast to the domestic and private domain of women. A second idea, known as the "three obediences," emphasized a woman's subordination first to her father, then to her husband, and finally to her son. "Why is it," asked one text, "that according to the rites the man takes his wife, whereas the woman leaves her house [to join her husband's family]? It is because the *yin* is lowly, and should not have the initiative; it proceeds to the *yang* in order to be completed."[13]

The Chinese woman writer and court official Ban Zhou (45–116 C.E.) observed that the ancients had practiced three customs when a baby girl was born. She was placed below the bed to show that she was "lowly and weak," required always to "humble herself before others." Then she was given a piece of broken pottery to play with, signifying that "her primary duty [was] to be industrious." Finally, her birth was announced to the ancestors with an offering to indicate that she was responsible for "the continuation of [ancestor] worship in the home."[14]

Yet such notions of passivity, inferiority, and subordination were not the whole story of women's lives in classical China. A few women, particularly the wives,

Chinese Women at Work
For a long time, the spinning and weaving of cloth were part of women's domestic work in China. So too was fishing, as illustrated by the woman at the bottom right of this Chinese painting. (Palace Museum, Beijing)

concubines, or widows of emperors, were able on occasion to exercise considerable political authority. In doing so, they provoked much antifemale hostility on the part of male officials, who often blamed the collapse of a dynasty or natural disasters on the "unnatural" and "disruptive" influence of women in political affairs. A number of writers, however, praised women of virtue as wise counselors to their fathers, husbands, and rulers and depicted them positively as active agents.[15]

Within her husband's family, a young woman was clearly subordinate as a wife and daughter-in-law, but as a mother of sons, she was accorded considerable honor for her role in producing the next generation of male heirs to carry on her husband's lineage. When her sons married, she was able to exercise the significant authority of a mother-in-law. Furthermore, a woman, at least in the upper classes, often brought with her a considerable dowry, which was regarded as her own property and gave her some leverage within her marriage. Women's roles in the production of textiles, often used to pay taxes or to sell commercially, made her labor quite valuable to the family economy. And a man's wife was sharply distinguished from his concubines, for the wife alone produced the legitimate heirs who could carry on the family tradition. Thus women's lives were more complex and varied than the prescriptions of Confucian orthodoxy might suggest.

Much changed in China following the collapse of the Han dynasty in the third century C.E. Centralized government vanished amid much political fragmentation and conflict. Confucianism, the main ideology of Han China, was discredited, while Daoism and Buddhism attracted a growing following. Pastoral and nomadic people invaded northern China and ruled a number of the small states that had replaced the Han government. These new conditions resulted in some loosening of the strict patriarchy of classical China over the next five or six centuries.

The cultural influence of nomadic peoples, whose women were far less restricted than those of China, was noticed, and criticized, by more Confucian-minded male observers. One of them lamented the sad deterioration of gender roles under the influence of nomadic peoples.

In the north of the Yellow river it is usually the wife who runs the household. She will not dispense with good clothing or expensive jewelry. The husband has to settle for old horses and sickly servants. The traditional niceties between husband and wife are seldom observed, and from time to time he even has to put up with her insults.[16]

Others criticized the adoption of nomadic styles of dress, makeup, and music. By the time of the Tang dynasty (618–907), writers and artists depicted elite women as capable of handling legal and business affairs on their own and on occasion riding horses and playing polo, bareheaded and wearing men's clothing. Tang legal codes even recognized a married daughter's right to inherit property from her family of birth. Such images of women were quite different from those of Han dynasty China.

A further sign of a weakening patriarchy and the cause of great distress to advocates of Confucian orthodoxy lay in the unusual reign of Empress Wu (reigned 690–705 C.E.), a former high-ranking concubine in the imperial court, who came to power amid much palace intrigue and was the only woman ever to rule China with the title of emperor. With the support of China's growing Buddhist establishment, Empress Wu governed despotically, but she also consolidated China's civil service examination system for the selection of public officials and actively patronized scholarship and the arts. Some of her actions seem deliberately designed to elevate the position of women. She commissioned the biographies of famous women, decreed that the mourning period for mothers be made equal to that for fathers, and ordered the creation of a Chinese character for "human being" that suggested the process of birth flowing from one woman without a prominent male role. Her reign was brief and unrepeated.

The growing popularity of Daoism provided new images of the feminine and new roles for women. Daoist texts referred to the *dao* as "mother" and urged the traditionally feminine virtues of yielding and passive acceptance rather than the male-oriented striving of Confucianism. Daoist sects often featured women as priests, nuns, or reclusive meditators, able to receive cosmic truth and to use it for the benefit of others. A variety of female deities from Daoist or Buddhist traditions found a place in Chinese village religion,[17] while growing numbers of women found an alternative to family life in Buddhist monasteries. None of this meant an end to patriarchy, but it does suggest some change in the tone and expression of that patriarchy.

Contrasting Patriarchies in Athens and Sparta

The patriarchies of the classical era not only fluctuated over time but also varied considerably from place to place. Nowhere is this variation more apparent than in the contrasting cases of Athens and Sparta, two of the leading city-states of classical Greek civilization (see Map 4.2). Even within the small area of classical Greece, the opportunities available to women and the restrictions imposed on them differed substantially. Although Athens has been celebrated as a major source of Western democracy and rationalism, its posture toward women was far more negative and restrictive than that of the highly militaristic and much less democratic Sparta.

In the several centuries between about 700 and 400 B.C.E., as the men of Athens moved toward unprecedented freedom and participation in political life, the city's

■ Comparison
How did the patriarchies of Athens and Sparta differ from each other?

Women of Athens
This painting on a seventh-century B.C.E. ceramic vase shows Athenian women gathering water at a fountain. (Museo di Villa Giulia Rome/ Gianni Dagli Orti/The Art Archive)

women experienced growing limitations. They had no role whatsoever in the assembly, the councils, or the juries of Athens, which were increasingly the focus of life for free men. In legal matters, women had to be represented by a guardian, and court proceedings did not even refer to them by name, but only as someone's wife or mother.

Greek thinkers, especially Aristotle, provided a set of ideas that justified women's exclusion from public life and their general subordination to men. According to Aristotle, "a woman is, as it were, an infertile male. She is female in fact on account of a kind of inadequacy." That inadequacy lay in her inability to generate sperm, which contained the "form" or the "soul" of a new human being. Her role in the reproductive process was passive, providing a receptacle for the vital male contribution. Compared often to children or domesticated animals, women were associated with instinct and passion and lacked the rationality to take part in public life. "It is the best for all tame animals to be ruled by human beings," wrote Aristotle. "For this is how they are kept alive. In the same way, the relationship between the male and the female is by nature such that the male is higher, the female lower, that the male rules and the female is ruled."[18]

As in China, proper Greek women were expected to remain inside the home, except perhaps for religious festivals or funerals. Even within the home, women's space was quite separate from that of men. Although poorer women, courtesans, and prostitutes had to leave their homes to earn money, collect water, or shop, ideal behavior for upper-class women assigned these tasks to slaves or to men and involved a radical segregation of male and female space. "What causes women a bad reputation," wrote the Greek playwright Euripides in *The Trojan Women*, "is not remaining inside."

Within the domestic realm, Athenian women were generally married in their mid-teens to men ten to fifteen years older than themselves. Their main function was the management of domestic affairs and the producti on of sons who would become citizens. These sons were expected to become literate, while their sisters were normally limited to learning spinning, weaving, and other household tasks. The Greek writer Menander exclaimed: "Teaching a woman to read and write? What a terrible thing to do! Like feeding a vile snake on more poison." Nor did women have much economic power. Although they could own personal property obtained through dowry, gifts, or inheritance, land was passed through male heirs, with a few exceptions. By law, women were forbidden to buy or sell land and could negotiate contracts only if the sum involved was valued at less than a bushel of barley.

There were exceptions, although rare, to the restricted lives of Athenian women, the most notable of which was Aspasia (ca. 470–400 B.C.E.). She was born in the Greek city of Miletus, on the western coast of Turkey, to a wealthy family that believed in educating its daughters. As a young woman, Aspasia found her way to Athens, where her foreign birth gave her somewhat more freedom than was normally available to the women of that city. She soon attracted the attention of Pericles, Athens's leading political figure. The two lived together as husband and wife until Pericles' death in 429 B.C.E., although they were not officially married. Treated as an equal partner by Pericles, Aspasia proved to be a learned and witty conversationalist who moved freely in the cultured circles of Athens. Her foreign birth and her apparent influence on Pericles provoked critics to suggest that she was a *hetaera,* a professional, educated, high-class entertainer and sexual companion, similar to a Japanese geisha. Although little is known about her, a number of major Athenian writers commented about her, both positively and negatively. She was, by all accounts, a rare and remarkable woman in a city that offered little opportunity for individuality or achievement to its female population.

The evolution of Sparta differed in many ways from that of Athens. Early on, Sparta solved the problem of feeding a growing population, not by creating overseas colonies as did many Greek city-states, but by conquering their neighbors and reducing them to a status of permanent servitude, not far removed from slavery. Called *helots,* these dependents far outnumbered the free citizens of Sparta and represented a permanent threat of rebellion. Solving this problem shaped Spartan society decisively. Sparta's answer was a militaristic regime, constantly ready for war to keep the helots in their place. To maintain such a system, all boys were removed from their families at the age of seven to be trained by the state in military camps, where they learned the ways of war. There they remained until the age of thirty. The ideal Spartan male was a warrior, skilled in battle, able to endure hardship, and willing to die for his city. Mothers are said to have told their sons departing for battle to "come back with your shield . . . or on it." Although economic equality for men was the ideal, it was never completely realized in practice. And unlike Athens, political power was exercised primarily by a small group of wealthy men.

This militaristic and far-from-democratic system had implications for women that, strangely enough, offered them greater freedoms and fewer restrictions. Their central task was reproduction—bearing warrior sons for Sparta. To strengthen their bodies for childbearing, girls were encouraged to take part in sporting events—running, wrestling, throwing the discus and javelin, even driving chariots. At times, they competed in the nude before mixed audiences. Their education, like that of boys, was prescribed by the state, which also insisted that newly married women cut their hair short, unlike adult Greek women elsewhere. Thus Spartan women were not secluded or segregated, as were their Athenian counterparts. Furthermore,

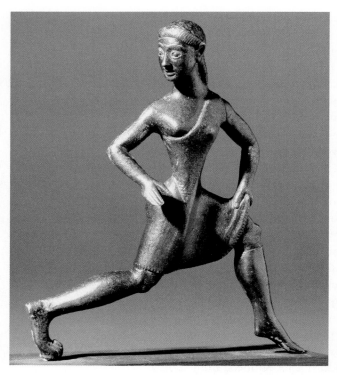

A Girl of Sparta
This figurine portrays a young female Spartan athlete or runner. Compare her clothing with that worn by the Athenian women depicted on the vase (shown on page 174. (National Archaeological Museum, Athens/Archaeological Receipts Fund)

Spartan young women, unlike those of Athens, usually married men of their own age, about eighteen years old, thus putting the new couple on a more equal basis. Marriage often began with a trial period to make sure the new couple could produce children, with divorce and remarriage readily available if they could not. Because men were so often away at war or preparing for it, women exercised much more authority in the household than was the case in Athens.

It is little wonder that the freedom of Spartan women appalled other Greeks, who believed that it undermined good order and state authority. Aristotle complained that the more egalitarian inheritance practices of Spartans led to their women controlling some 40 percent of landed estates. In Sparta, he declared, women "live in every sort of intemperance and luxury" and "the [male] rulers are ruled by women." Plutarch, a Greek writer during the heyday of the Roman Empire, observed critically that "the men of Sparta always obeyed their wives." The clothing worn by Spartan women to give them greater freedom of movement seemed immodest to other Greeks.

Nonetheless, in another way, Sparta may have been more restrictive than Athens and other Greek city-states, particularly in its apparent prohibition of homosexuality. At least this was the assertion of the Athenian writer Xenophon (427–355 B.C.E.), who stated that Sparta's legendary founder Lycurgus "caused lovers to abstain from sexual intercourse with boys."[19] Elsewhere, however, homoerotic relationships were culturally approved and fairly common for both men and women, although this did not prevent their participants from entering heterosexual marriages as well. The ideal homosexual relationship—between an older man and a young adolescent boy—was viewed as limited in time, for it was supposed to end when the boy's beard began to grow. Unlike contemporary Western societies where sexuality is largely seen as an identity, the ancient Greeks viewed sexual choice more casually and as a matter of taste.

Sparta clearly was a patriarchy, with women serving as breeding machines for its military system and lacking any formal role in public life, but it was a lighter patriarchy than that of Athens. The joint efforts of men and women seemed necessary to maintain a huge class of helots in permanent subjugation. Death in childbirth was considered the equivalent of death in battle, for both contributed to the defense of Sparta, and both were honored alike. In Athens, on the other hand, growing freedom and democracy were associated with the strengthening of the male-dominated, property-owning household, and within that household men, the cornerstone of Athenian society, were expected to exercise authority. Doing so required increasingly severe limitations and restrictions on the lives of women. Together, the cases of Athens and Sparta illustrate how the historical record appears different when viewed through the lens of gender. Athens, so celebrated for its democracy and philosophical rationalism, offered little to its women, whereas Sparta, often condemned for its militarism and virtual enslavement of the helots, provided a somewhat wider scope for the free women of the city.

 ## Reflections: Arguing with Solomon and the Buddha

"What has been will be again; what has been done will be done again; there is nothing new under the sun." Recorded in the Old Testament book of Ecclesiastes and generally attributed to King Solomon, this was a despairing view about the essential changelessness and futility of human life. In contrast, central to Buddhist teachings has been the concept of "impermanence"—the notion that "everything changes; nothing remains without change." These observations from classical-era thinkers were intended to point to other levels of reality that lay beyond the dreary constancy or the endless changeability of this world. For students of history, however, these comments from Solomon and the Buddha serve to focus attention on issues of change and continuity in the historical record of classical Eurasian civilizations. What is more impressive—the innovations and changes or the enduring patterns and lasting features of these civilizations?

Clearly there were some new things under the sun, even if they had roots in earlier times. The Greek conquest of the Persian Empire under the leadership of Alexander the Great was both novel and unexpected. The Roman Empire encompassed the entire Mediterranean basin in a single political system for the first time. Buddhism and Christianity emerged as new, distinct, and universal religious traditions, although both bore the marks of their origin in Hindu and Jewish religious thinking respectively. The collapse of dynasties, empires, and civilizations long thought to be solidly entrenched—the Chinese and Roman, for example—must surely have seemed to people of the time as something new under the sun. Historians therefore might take issue with Solomon's dictum, should we seek to apply it to the history of the classical era.

Students of the past might also argue a little with the Buddha and his insistence on the "impermanence" of everything. Much that was created in the classical era—particularly its social and cultural patterns—has demonstrated an impressive continuity over many centuries, even if it also changed in particular ways over time. China's scholar-gentry class retained its prominence throughout the ups and downs of changing dynasties and into the twentieth century. India's caste-based social structure still endures as a way of thinking and behaving for hundreds of millions of people on the South Asian peninsula. Although slavery gave way to serfdom in the post-Roman world, it was massively revived in Europe's American colonies after 1500 and remained an important and largely unquestioned part of all civilizations until the nineteenth century. Patriarchy, with its assumptions of male superiority and dominance, has surely been the most fundamental, long-lasting, and taken-for-granted feature of all civilizations. Not until the twentieth century were those assumptions effectively challenged, but even then patriarchy has continued to shape the lives and the thinking of the vast majority of humankind. And many hundreds of millions of people in the twenty-first century still honor or practice religious and cultural traditions begun during the classical era.

Neither the insight of Solomon nor that of the Buddha, taken alone, offers an effective guide to the study of history, for continuity and change alike have long provided the inextricable warp and woof of historical analysis. Untangling their elusive relationship has figured prominently in the task of historians and has contributed much to the enduring fascination of historical study.

Second Thoughts

What's the Significance?

To assess your mastery of the material in this chapter, see the **Online Study Guide** at bedfordstmartins.com/strayer.

Wang Mang
China's scholar-gentry class
Yellow Turban Rebellion
caste as varna and jati

"ritual purity" in Indian social practice
Greek and Roman slavery
Spartacus

the "three obediences"
Empress Wu
Aspasia and Pericles
helots

Big Picture Questions

1. What is the difference between class and caste?
2. Why was slavery so much more prominent in Greco-Roman civilization than in India or China?
3. What philosophical, religious, or cultural ideas served to legitimate the class and gender inequalities of classical civilizations?
4. "Social inequality was both accepted and resisted in classical civilizations." What evidence might support this statement?
5. What changes in the patterns of social life of the classical era can you identify? What accounts for these changes?
6. "Cultural and social patterns of civilizations seem to endure longer than the political framework of states and empires." Based on Chapters 4, 5, and 6, would you agree with this statement?

Next Steps: For Further Study

For Web sites and documents related to this chapter, see **Make History** at bedfordstmartins.com/strayer.

Jeannine Auboyer, *Daily Life in Ancient India* (2002). A social history of classical India, with a focus on caste, ritual, religion, and art.

Sue Blundell, *Women in Ancient Greece* (1999). A well-written academic study, with occasional humorous stories and anecdotes.

Keith Bradley, *Slavery and Society at Rome* (1994). A scholarly but very readable account of slavery in the Roman Empire.

Michael Lowe, *Everyday Life in Early Imperial China* (1968). A vivid description of social life during the Han dynasty.

Bonnie Smith, ed., *Women's History in Global Perspective*, 3 volumes (2004). A collection of thoughtful essays by major scholars covering world history from ancient times to the twentieth century.

"Women in World History," http://chnm.gmu.edu/wwh/index.html. Documents, reviews, and lesson plans for learning and teaching about women's history in a global context.

CHAPTER SEVEN

Classical Era Variations

Africa and the Americas

500 B.C.E. – 1200 C.E.

"In a [Maya] community called Xolep, there was no paper or pencils where I taught. I started by drawing figures in the dirt. We then taught letters by forming them with sticks. One day students brought flower petals to shape the letters. . . . When we were able to gather enough money for notebooks, we gave them to the students and asked them to report the next day to the tree where we were holding school. . . . They proudly filed under the teaching tree, notebooks tucked under their arms, feeling that they were now officially students."[1]

This incident, reported in 1999 by a participant in an independent schools movement among the Maya of southern Mexico, was a tiny part of an ongoing revival of Maya culture. Despite the collapse of their famous classical civilization more than a thousand years ago, Maya language and folkways have persisted among some 6 million people currently living in Mexico, Belize, Guatemala, and Honduras. And despite five centuries of repression, exploitation, and neglect at the hands of Spanish colonizers and the independent governments that followed, they were now in the midst of what one writer called "a new time of the Maya."[2] They were writing their own histories, celebrating their own culture, creating their own organizations, and teaching their children to read. The most dramatic expression of this recent Maya revival was an armed uprising, begun in early 1994 and led by the Zapatista Army of National Liberation. Growing out of long-term social and economic grievances against local landowners and an unresponsive government, that rebellion stunned Mexico and focused global attention on the poverty and misery of the country's indigenous Maya. Once again, some 1,500 years after the high point of their classical civilization, the Maya were making history.

An Elite Maya Woman: In this painted clay statue, the woman carries an infant under her left arm and a monkey in her right. On the left side of the headdress, a bird is drinking from a flower, indicating a high status. (© Justin and Barbara Kerr)

FOR MANY PEOPLE, THE CLASSICAL ERA EVOKES most vividly the civilizations of Eurasia—especially the Greeks and the Romans, the Persians and the Chinese, and the Indians of South Asia—yet those were not the only classical-era civilizations. During this period, the Mesoamerican Maya and the Peruvian Moche thrived, as did several civilizations in Africa, including Meroë, Axum, and the Niger River valley. Furthermore, those peoples who did not organize themselves around cities or states likewise had histories of note and alternative ways of constructing their societies, although they are often neglected in favor of civilizations. This chapter explores the histories of the varied peoples of Africa and the Americas during the classical era. On occasion, those histories will extend some centuries beyond the chronological boundaries of the classical age in Eurasia, because patterns of historical development around the world did not always coincide precisely.

At the broadest level, however, human cultures evolved in quite similar fashion around the world. All, of course, were part of that grand process of human migration that initially peopled the planet. Beginning in Africa, that vast movement of humankind subsequently encompassed Eurasia, Australia, the Americas, and Oceania. Everywhere except Oceania, gathering and hunting long remained the sole basis for sustaining life and society. Then, in the three major supercontinents—Eurasia, Africa, and the Americas—the momentous turn of the Agricultural Revolution took place independently and in several distinct areas of each landmass. That revolutionary transformation of human life subsequently generated, in particularly rich agricultural environments of all three regions, those more complex societies that we know as civilizations, which featured cities, states, monumental architecture, and great social inequality. In these ways, the historical trajectory of the human journey on the earth has a certain unity and similarity across quite distinct continental regions. At the beginning of the Common Era, that trajectory had generated a total world population of about 250 million people, substantially less than the current population of the United States alone. By contemporary standards, it was still a sparsely populated planet.

The world's human population was distributed very unevenly across the three giant continents, as the Snapshot indicates. If these estimates are even reasonably accurate, then during the classical era Eurasia was home to more than 80 percent of the world's people, Africa about 11 percent, and the Americas between 5 and 7 percent. That unevenness in population distribution is part of the reason that world historians focus more attention on Eurasia than on Africa or the Americas. Here lies one of the major differences among the continents.

There were other differences as well. The absence of most animals capable of domestication meant that no pastoral societies developed in the Americas, and no draft animals were available to pull plows or carts or to carry heavy loads for long distances. Africa lacked wild sheep, goats, chickens, horses, and camels, but its proximity to Eurasia meant that these animals, once domesticated, became widely available to African peoples. Metallurgy in the Americas was likewise far less developed than in the Eastern Hemisphere, where iron tools and weapons played such an

Snapshot   **Continental Population in the Classical Era**[3]

(Note: Population figures for such early times are merely estimates and are often controversial among scholars. Percentages do not always total 100 percent due to rounding.)

	Eurasia	Africa	North America	Central/South America	Australia/ Oceania	Total World
Area (in square miles and as percentage of world total)						
	21,049,000 (41%)	11,608,000 (22%)	9,365,000 (18%)	6,880,000 (13%)	2,968,000 (6%)	51,870,000
Population (in millions and as percentage of world total)						
400 B.C.E.	127 (83%)	17 (11%)	1 (0.7%)	7 (5%)	1 (0.7%)	153
10 C.E.	213 (85%)	26 (10%)	2 (0.8%)	10 (4%)	1 (0.4%)	252
200 C.E.	215 (84%)	30 (12%)	2 (0.8%)	9 (4%)	1 (0.4%)	257
600 C.E.	167 (80%)	24 (12%)	2 (1%)	14 (7%)	1 (0.5%)	208
1000 C.E.	195 (77%)	39 (15%)	2 (0.8%)	16 (6%)	1 (0.4%)	253

important role in economic and military life. In the Americas, writing was limited to the Mesoamerican region and was most highly developed among the Maya, whereas in Africa it was confined to the northern and northeastern parts of the continent during the classical era. In Eurasia, writing emerged elaborately in many regions. Classical-era civilizations in Africa and the Americas were fewer in number and generally smaller than those of Eurasia, and larger numbers of their people lived in communities that did not feature cities and states.

To illustrate the historical developments of the classical era beyond Eurasia, this chapter focuses on three regions in Africa and three in the Americas. To what extent did these histories parallel those of Eurasia? In what ways did they forge new or different paths?

The African Northeast

When historians refer to Africa during the classical era, they are speaking generally of a geographic concept, a continental landmass, and not a cultural identity. Certainly no one living on the continent at that time thought of himself or herself as an African. Like Eurasia or the Americas, Africa hosted numerous separate societies, cultures, and civilizations with vast differences among them as well as some interaction between them.

Many of these differences grew out of the continent's environmental variations. Small regions of Mediterranean climate in the northern and southern extremes, large deserts (the Sahara and the Kalahari), even larger regions of savanna grasslands, tropical rain forest in the continent's center, highlands and mountains in eastern Africa— all of these features, combined with the continent's enormous size, ensured variation and difference among Africa's many peoples. Africa did, however, have one distinctive environmental feature: bisected by the equator, it was the most tropical of the world's three supercontinents. Persistent warm temperatures caused the rapid decomposition of vegetable matter called humus, resulting in poorer and less fertile soils and a less productive agriculture than in the more temperate Eurasia. Those climatic conditions also spawned numerous disease-carrying insects and parasites, which have long created serious health problems in many parts of the continent. It was within these environmental constraints that African peoples made their histories.

A further geographic feature shaped African history—its proximity to Eurasia, which allowed parts of Africa to interact with Eurasian civilizations. During the classical era, North Africa was incorporated into the Roman Empire and used to produce wheat and olives on large estates with slave labor. Christianity spread widely, giving rise to some of the early Church's most famous martyrs and to one of its most important theologians, Saint Augustine (354–430 C.E.). The Christian faith found an even more permanent foothold in the lands now known as Ethiopia.

Arabia was another point of contact with the larger world for African peoples. The arrival of the domesticated camel, probably from Arabia, generated a nomadic pastoral way of life among some of the Berber peoples of the western Sahara during the first three centuries C.E. A little later, camels also made possible trans-Saharan commerce, which linked interior West Africa to the world of Mediterranean civilization. Over many centuries, the East African coast was a port of call for Egyptian, Roman, and Arab merchants, and that region subsequently became an integral part of Indian Ocean trading networks.

Both the external connections and, more important, the internal development of African societies generated various patterns of historical change during the classical era. Three regions—northeastern Africa, the Niger River basin in West Africa, and the vast world of Bantu-speaking Africa south of the equator—serve to illustrate these differences and the many social and cultural experiments spawned by the peoples of this continent.

Meroë: Continuing a Nile Valley Civilization

■ Connection
How did the history of Meroë and Axum reflect interaction with neighboring civilizations?

In the Nile Valley south of Egypt lay the lands of Nubian civilization, almost as old as Egypt itself. Over many centuries, Nubians both traded and fought with Egypt, alternately conquering and being conquered by their northern neighbor. While borrowing heavily from Egypt, Nubia remained a distinct and separate civilization

Map 7.1   Africa in the Classical Era
During the classical era, older African civilizations such as Egypt and Nubia persisted and changed, while new civilizations emerged in Axum and the Niger River valley. South of the equator, Bantu-speaking peoples spread rapidly, creating many new societies and identities.

(see Chapter 3). By the classical era, as Egypt fell under foreign control, Nubian civilization came to center on the southern city of Meroë, where it flourished between 300 B.C.E. and 100 C.E. (see Map 7.1).

Politically, the Kingdom of Meroë was governed by an all-powerful and sacred monarch, a position occasionally conferred on women. Rulers were buried, in

A Bracelet from Meroë
This gold bracelet, dating to about 100 B.C.E., illustrates the skill of Meroë's craftsmen as well as the kingdom's reputation as one of the wealthiest states of the ancient world. (Bracelet with image of Hathor, Nubian, Meroitic Period, about 100 B.C.E. Object Place: Sudan, Nubia, Gebel Barkal, Pyramid 8, Gold, enamel. Museum of Fine Arts, Boston, Harvard University–Boston Museum of Fine Arts Expedition, 20.333. Photograph © 2008 Museum of Fine Arts, Boston)

accordance with ancient traditions, along with a number of human sacrificial victims. The city of Meroë and other urban centers housed a wide variety of economic specialties—merchants, weavers, potters, and masons, as well as servants, laborers, and slaves. The smelting of iron and the manufacture of iron tools and weapons were especially prominent industries. The rural areas surrounding Meroë were populated by peoples who practiced some combination of herding and farming and paid periodic tribute to the ruler. Rainfall-based agriculture was possible in Meroë, and consequently farmers were less dependent on irrigation. This meant that the rural population did not need to concentrate so heavily along the Nile and was less directly controlled from the capital than was the case in Egypt, where state authorities were required to supervise an irrigation system serving a dense population along the river.

The wealth and military power of Meroë derived in part from extensive long-distance trading connections, to the north via the Nile and to the east and west by means of camel caravans. Its iron weapons and cotton cloth, as well as its access to gold, ivory, tortoiseshells, and ostrich feathers, gave Meroë a reputation for great riches in the classical world of northeastern Africa and the Mediterranean. The discovery in Meroë of a statue of the Roman emperor Augustus, probably seized during a raid on Roman Egypt, testifies to contact with the Mediterranean world. Culturally, Meroë seemed to move away from the heavy Egyptian influence of earlier times. A local lion god, Apedemek, grew more prominent than Egyptian deities such as Isis and Osiris, while the use of Egyptian-style writing declined as a new and still undeciphered Meroitic script took its place.

In the centuries following 100 C.E., the Kingdom of Meroë declined, in part because of deforestation caused by the need for wood to make charcoal for smelting iron. The effective end of the Meroë phase of Nubian civilization came with the kingdom's conquest in the 340s C.E. by the neighboring and rising state of Axum. In the centuries that followed, three separate Nubian states emerged, and Coptic (Egyptian) Christianity penetrated the region. For almost a thousand years, Nubia was a Christian civilization, using Greek as a liturgical language and constructing churches in Coptic or Byzantine fashion. After 1300 or so, political division, Arab immigration, and the penetration of Islam eroded this Christian civilization, and Nubia became part of the growing world of Islam.

Axum: The Making of a Christian Kingdom

If Meroë and Nubia represented the continuation of an old African civilization, Axum marked the emergence of a new one. Axum lay in the Horn of Africa, in what is now Eritrea and northern Ethiopia (see Map 7.1). Its economic foundation was a highly productive agriculture that used a plow-based farming system, unlike most of the rest of Africa, which relied on the hoe or digging stick. Axum's agriculture generated substantial amounts of wheat, barley, millet, and teff, a highly nutritious grain unique to that region. By 50 C.E. or so, a substantial state had emerged, stimulated by its participation in Red Sea and Indian Ocean commerce. At Adulis, then the largest port on the East African coast, a wide range of merchants sought the products of the African interior—animal hides, rhinoceros horn, ivory, obsidian, tortoiseshells, and slaves. Taxes on this trade provided a major source of revenue for the Axumite state and the complex society that grew up within it.

The interior capital city, also known as Axum, was a center of monumental building and royal patronage for the arts. The most famous of these were huge stone obelisks, which most likely marked royal graves. Some of them were more than 100 feet tall and at the time were the largest structures in the world hewn from a single piece of rock. The language used at court, in the towns, and for commerce was Geez, written in a script derived from South Arabia. The Axumite state exercised a measure of control over the mostly Agaw-speaking people of the country through a loose administrative structure focusing on the collection of tribute payments. To the Romans, Axum was the third major empire within the world they knew, following their own and the Persian Empire.

The Columns of Axum Dating to the time when Axum first encountered Christianity (300–500 C.E.), this column, measuring some seventy-nine feet tall, probably served as a funeral monument for the kingdom's ancient rulers. (Antonello Langellotto/TIPS Images)

Through its connections to Red Sea trade and the Roman world, particularly Egypt, Axum was introduced to Christianity in the fourth century C.E. Its monarch at the time, King Ezana, adopted the new religion about the same time as Constantine did in the Roman Empire. Christianity took root in Axum, linking that kingdom religiously to Egypt, where a distinctive Christian church known as Coptic was already well established. Although Egypt subsequently became largely Islamic, reducing its Christian community to a small minority, Christianity maintained a dominant position in the mountainous terrain of highland Ethiopia and in the early twenty-first century still represents the faith of perhaps half of the country's population.

During the fourth through the sixth century C.E., Axum mounted a campaign of imperial expansion that took its forces into the Kingdom of Meroë and across the Red Sea into Yemen in South Arabia. By 571, the traditional date for the birth of Muhammad, an Axumite army, including a number of African war elephants, had reached the gates of Mecca, but it was a fairly short-lived

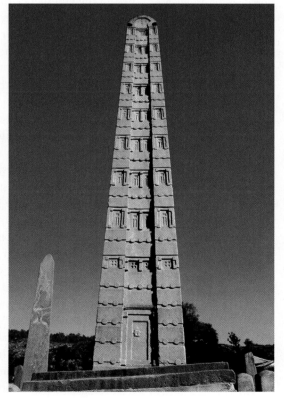

imperial venture. The next several centuries were ones of decline for the Axumite state, owing partly to environmental changes, such as soil exhaustion, erosion, and deforestation, brought about by intensive farming. Equally important was the rise of Islam, which altered trade routes and diminished the revenue available to the Axumite state. Its last coins were struck in the early seventh century. When the state revived several centuries later, it was centered farther south on the Ethiopian plateau. There emerged the Christian church and the state that present-day Ethiopia has inherited, but the link to ancient Axum was long remembered and revered.

With their long-distance trading connections, urban centers, centralized states, complex societies, monumental architecture, written languages, and imperial ambitions, both Meroë and Axum paralleled on a smaller scale the major features of the classical civilizations of Eurasia. Furthermore, both were in direct contact with the world of Mediterranean civilizations. Elsewhere in Africa during the classical era, quite different histories unfolded.

Along the Niger River: Cities without States

■ Description
How does the experience of the Niger Valley challenge conventional notions of "civilization"?

In the middle stretches of the Niger River in West Africa, the classical era witnessed the emergence of a remarkable urbanization (see Map 7.1). A prolonged dry period during the five centuries after 500 B.C.E. brought growing numbers of people from the southern Sahara into the fertile floodplain of the middle Niger in search of more reliable access to water. Accompanying them were their domesticated cattle, sheep, and goats; their agricultural skills; and their ironworking technology. Over the centuries of the classical era and beyond (roughly 300 B.C.E.–900 C.E.), the peoples of this region created a distinctive city-based civilization. The most fully studied of the urban clusters that grew up along the middle Niger was the city of Jenne-jeno, which at its high point probably housed more than 40,000 people.

Among the most distinctive features of these cities was the apparent absence of a corresponding state structure. Unlike the cities of Egypt, China, the Roman Empire, or Axum, these middle Niger urban centers were not encompassed within some larger imperial system. Nor were they like the city-states of ancient Mesopotamia, in which each city had its own centralized political structure, embodied in a monarch and his accompanying bureaucracy. According to a leading historian of the region, they were "cities without citadels," complex urban centers that apparently operated without the coercive authority of a state, for archeologists have found in their remains few signs of despotic power, widespread warfare, or deep social inequalities.[4] In this respect, these urban centers resemble the early cities of the Indus Valley civilization, where likewise little archeological evidence of centralized state structures has been found (see Chapter 3).

In place of such hierarchical organization, Jenne-jeno and other cities of the region emerged as clusters of economically specialized settlements surrounding a larger central town. The earliest and most prestigious of these specialized occupations was iron smithing. Working with fire and earth (ore) to produce this highly useful metal, the smiths of the Niger Valley were both feared and revered. Archeologist Roderick McIntosh, a leading figure in the excavation of Jenne-jeno, argued that "their knowledge of the transforming arts—earth to metal, insubstantial fire to the mass of iron—was the key to a secret, occult realm of immense power and immense danger."[5]

Other specializations followed. Villages of cotton weavers, potters, leather workers, and griots (praise-singers who preserved and recited the oral traditions of their societies) grew up around the central towns. Gradually these urban artisan communities became occupational castes, whose members passed their jobs and skills to their children and could marry only within their own group. In the surrounding rural areas, as in all urban-based civilizations, farmers tilled the soil and raised their animals, but specialization also occurred in farming as various ethnic groups focused on fishing, rice cultivation, or some other agricultural pursuit. At least for a time, these middle Niger cities represented an African alternative to an oppressive state, which in many parts of the world accompanied an increasingly complex urban economy and society. A series of distinct and specialized economic groups shared authority and voluntarily used the services of one another, while maintaining their separate identity through physical separation.

Accompanying this unique urbanization, and no doubt stimulating it, was a growing network of indigenous West African commerce. The middle Niger floodplain supported a rich agriculture and had clay for pottery, but it lacked stone, iron ore, salt, and fuel. This scarcity of resources was the basis for long-distance commerce, which operated by boat along the Niger River and overland by donkey to the north and south. Iron ore from more than 50 miles away, copper from mines 200 miles distant, gold from even more distant sources, stones and salt from the Sahara—all of these items have been found in Jenne-jeno, in return no doubt for grain, fish, smoked meats, iron implements, and other staples. Jenne-jeno itself was an important transshipment point in this commerce, in which goods were transferred from boat to donkey or vice versa. By the 500s C.E., there is evidence of an even wider commerce and at least indirect contact, from Mauritania in the west to present-day Mali and Burkina-Faso in the east.

In the second millennium C.E., new historical patterns developed in West Africa (see Chapter 8). A number of large-scale states or empires emerged in the region— Ghana, Mali, and Songhay, among the most well known. At least partially responsible for this development was the flourishing of a camel-borne trans-Saharan commerce, previously but a trickle across the great desert. As West Africa became more firmly connected to North Africa and the Mediterranean, Islam penetrated the region, marking a gradual but major cultural transformation. All of this awaited West Africa in the postclassical era, submerging, but not completely eliminating, the decentralized city life of the Niger Valley.

South of the Equator: The World of Bantu Africa

In Africa south of the equator, the most significant development of the classical era involved the accelerating movement of Bantu-speaking peoples into this enormous subcontinent. It was a process that had begun many centuries earlier from a homeland region in what is now southeastern Nigeria and the Cameroons. In the long run, that movement of peoples generated some 400 distinct but closely related languages, known collectively as Bantu. By the first century C.E., agricultural peoples speaking Bantu languages had largely occupied the forest regions of equatorial Africa, and at least a few of them had probably reached the East African coast. In the several centuries that followed, they established themselves quite rapidly in most of eastern and southern Africa (see Map 7.1), introducing immense economic and cultural changes to a huge region of the continent.

The spread of Bantu peoples was not a conquest or invasion such as that of Alexander the Great; nor was it a massive and self-conscious migration like that of Europeans to the Americas. Rather it was a slow movement of peoples, perhaps a few extended families at a time, but taken as a whole, it brought to Africa south of the equator a measure of cultural and linguistic commonality, marking it as a distinct region of the continent.

Cultural Encounters

■ Connection

In what ways did the arrival of Bantu-speaking peoples stimulate cross-cultural interaction?

That movement of peoples also generated numerous cross-cultural encounters, as the Bantu-speaking newcomers interacted with already-established societies, changing both of them in the process. Among those encounters, none was more significant than that between the agricultural Bantu and the gathering and hunting peoples who earlier occupied Africa south of the equator. This was part of a long-term global phenomenon in which farmers largely replaced foragers as the dominant people on the planet (see Chapter 2).

In this encounter, Bantu-speaking farmers had various advantages. One was numerical, as agriculture generated a more productive economy, enabling larger numbers to live in a smaller area than was possible with a gathering and hunting way of life. Another advantage was disease, for the farmers brought with them both parasitic and infectious diseases—malaria, for example—to which foraging people had little immunity. A third advantage was iron, so useful for tools and weapons, which Bantu migrants brought to many of their interactions with peoples still operating with stone-age technology. Thus, during the classical era, gathering and hunting peoples were displaced, absorbed, or largely eliminated in most parts of Africa south of the equator—but not everywhere.

In the Kalahari region of southwestern Africa and a few places in East Africa, gathering and hunting peoples such as the San (see Chapter 1) survived into modern times. Furthermore, many of the Bantu languages of southern Africa retain to this day the distinctive "clicks" that they borrowed from the now-vanished gathering and hunting peoples who long preceded them in the region.

In the rain forest region of Central Africa, the foraging Batwa (Pygmy) people, at least some of them, became "forest specialists" who produced honey, wild game, elephant products, animal skins, and medicinal barks and plants, all of which entered regional trading networks in exchange for the agricultural products of their Bantu neighbors. They also adopted Bantu languages, while maintaining a non-agricultural lifestyle and a separate identity. For their part, the Bantu farmers regarded their Batwa neighbors as first-comers to the region and therefore closest to the ancestral and territorial spirits that determined the fertility of the land and people. Thus, as forest-dwelling Bantu peoples grew in numbers and created chiefdoms, those chiefs appropriated the Batwa title of "owners of the land" for themselves, claimed Batwa ancestry, and portrayed the Batwa as the original "civilizers" of the earth.[6]

Khoikhoi of South Africa The Khoikhoi people of South Africa, several of whom are shown here in an 1886 photograph, were originally gatherers and hunters, who adopted cattle and sheep raising from outsiders, perhaps from early Bantu-speaking immigrants to the region, but did not practice agriculture. Living in southern Africa for most of the last two millennia, they illustrate the interaction and selective cultural borrowing that took place among the various peoples of the region. (Hulton-Deutsch Collection/Corbis)

In other ways as well, Bantu cultures changed as they encountered different peoples. In the drier environment of East Africa, the yam-based agriculture of the West African Bantu homeland was unable to support their growing numbers, so Bantu farmers increasingly adopted grains as well as domesticated sheep and cattle from the already-established people of the region. Their agriculture also was enriched by acquiring a variety of food crops from Southeast Asia—coconuts, sugarcane, and especially bananas—which were brought to East Africa by Indonesian sailors and immigrants early in the first millennium C.E. Bantu farmers then spread this agricultural package and their acquired ironworking technology throughout the vast area of eastern and southern Africa, probably reaching present-day South Africa by 400 C.E. They also brought a common set of cultural and social practices, which diffused widely across Bantu Africa. One prominent historian described these practices as encompassing,

> in religion, the centrality of ancestor observances; in philosophy, the problem of evil understood as the consequence of individual malice or of the failure to honor one's ancestors; in music, an emphasis on polyrhythmic performance with drums as the key instrument; in dance, a new form of expression in which a variety of prescribed body movements took preference over footwork; and in agriculture, the pre-eminence of women as the workers and innovators.[7]

All of this became part of the common culture of Bantu Africa.

Society and Religion

In the thousand years or so (500-1500 C.E.) that followed their initial colonization of Africa south of the equator, Bantu-speaking peoples also created a wide variety of quite distinct societies and cultures. Some—in present-day Kenya, for example—organized themselves without any formal political specialists at all. Instead they made decisions, resolved conflicts, and maintained order by using kinship structures or lineage principles supplemented by age grades, which joined men of a particular generation together across various lineages. Elsewhere, lineage heads who acquired a measure of personal wealth or who proved skillful at mediating between the local spirits and the people might evolve into chiefs with a modest political authority. In several areas, such as the region around Lake Victoria or present-day Zimbabwe, larger and more substantial kingdoms evolved. Along the East African coast after 1000 C.E., dozens of rival city-states linked the African interior with the commerce of the Indian Ocean basin (see Chapter 8). The kind of society that developed in any particular area depended on a host of local factors, including population density, trading opportunities, and interaction among culturally different peoples.

In terms of religion, Bantu practice in general placed less emphasis on a High or Creator God, who was viewed as remote and largely uninvolved in ordinary life, and focused instead on ancestral or nature spirits. The power of dead ancestors might be accessed through rituals of sacrifice, especially that of cattle. Supernatural power deriving from ancient heroes, ancestors, or nature spirits also resided in charms, which could be activated by proper rituals and used to control the rains, defend the village, achieve success in hunting, or identify witches. Belief in witches was widespread, reflecting the idea that evil or misfortune was the work of malicious people. Diviners, skilled in penetrating the world of the supernatural, used dreams, visions, charms, or trances to identify the source of misfortune and to prescribe remedies. Was a particular illness the product of broken taboos, a dishonored ancestor, an unhappy nature spirit, or a witch? Was a remedy to be found in a cleansing ceremony, a sacrifice to an ancestor, the activation of a charm, or the elimination of a witch?[8] Such issues constantly confronted the people of Bantu Africa.

Unlike the major monotheistic religions, with their "once and for all" revelations from God through the Christian Bible or the Muslim Quran, Bantu religious practice was predicated on the notion of "continuous revelation"—the possibility of constantly receiving new messages from the world beyond. Moreover, unlike Buddhism, Christianity, or Islam, Bantu religions were geographically confined, intended to explain, predict, and control local affairs, with no missionary impulse or inclination toward universality.

Civilizations of Mesoamerica

Although geography permitted interaction between African and Eurasian peoples, the Atlantic and Pacific oceans ensured that the cultures and societies of the Western Hemisphere had long operated in a world apart from their Afro-Eurasian counterparts.

Nor were the cultures of the Americas stimulated by the kind of fruitful interaction among their own civilizations that played such an important role in the Eastern Hemisphere. Nothing similar to the contact between Egypt and Mesopotamia, or Persia and the Greeks, or the extensive communication along the Silk Road trading network enriched the two major centers of civilization in the Americas—Mesoamerica and the Andes—which had little if any direct contact with each other. Furthermore, the achievements of early American civilizations and cultures occurred without the large domesticated animals or ironworking technologies that were so important throughout the Eastern Hemisphere.

Accounts of pre-Columbian American societies often focus primarily on the Aztec and Inca empires (see Chapter 13), yet these impressive creations, flourishing in the fifteenth and early sixteenth centuries, were but the latest in a long line of civilizations that preceded them in Mesoamerica and the Andes respectively. Although these two regions housed the vast majority of the population of the Americas, the peoples of North America, the Amazon River basin, and elsewhere were the centers of their own worlds and made their own histories. It is the period preceding the Aztecs and Incas that represents the classical era in the history of the Americas.

Stretching from central Mexico to northern Central America, the area known as Mesoamerica was, geographically speaking, one of "extraordinary diversity compressed into a relatively small space."[9] That environment ranged from steamy lowland rain forests to cold and windy highland plateaus, cut by numerous mountains and valleys and generating many microclimates. Such conditions contributed to substantial linguistic and ethnic diversity and to many distinct and competing cities, chiefdoms, and states.

Despite this diversity, Mesoamerica, like Bantu Africa, was also a distinct region, bound together by elements of a common culture. Its many peoples shared an intensive agricultural technology devoted to raising maize, beans, chili peppers, and squash; they prepared maize in a distinctive and highly nutritious fashion; they based their economies on market exchange; they practiced religions featuring a similar pantheon of deities, belief in a cosmic cycle of creation and destruction, human sacrifice, and monumental ceremonial centers; they employed a common ritual calendar of 260 days and hieroglyphic writing; and they interacted frequently among themselves. During the first millennium B.C.E., for example, the various small states and chiefdoms of the region, particularly the Olmec, exchanged a number of luxury goods used to display social status and for ritual purposes—jade, serpentine, obsidian tools, ceramic pottery, shell ornaments, stingray spines, and turtle shells. As a result, aspects of Olmec culture, such as artistic styles, temple pyramids, the calendar system, and rituals involving human sacrifice, spread widely throughout Mesoamerica and influenced many of the civilizations that followed.

Classical Civilizations of Mesoamerica

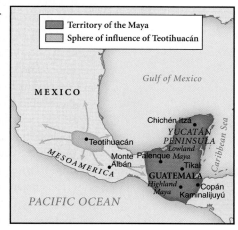

The Maya: Writing and Warfare

■ Comparison
With what Eurasian civilizations might the Maya be compared?

Among the Mesoamerican civilizations, none has attracted more attention than that of the Maya, the major classical civilization of Mesoamerica. Scholars have traced the beginnings of the Maya people to ceremonial centers constructed as early as 2000 B.C.E. in present-day Guatemala and the Yucatán region of Mexico, but it was during the classical phase of Maya civilization, between 250 and 900 C.E., that their most notable cultural achievements emerged. Their intellectuals, probably priests, developed a mathematical system that included the concept of zero and place notation and was capable of complex calculations. They combined this mathematical ability with careful observation of the night skies to plot the cycles of planets, to predict eclipses of the sun and the moon, to construct elaborate calendars, and to calculate accurately the length of the solar year.

Accompanying these intellectual achievements was the creation of the most elaborate writing system in the Americas, which used both pictographs and phonetic or syllabic elements. Carved on stone and written on bark paper or deerskin books, Mayan writing recorded historical events, masses of astronomical data, and religious or mythological texts. Temples, pyramids, palaces, and public plazas abounded, graced with painted murals and endless stone carving. It is not surprising that early scholars viewed Maya civilization as a peaceful society led by gentle stargazing priest-kings devoted to temple building and intellectual pursuits.

The economic foundations for these cultural achievements were also impressive. By 600 C.E., the Maya lived in an "almost totally engineered landscape."[10] They drained swamps, terraced hillsides, flattened ridge tops, and constructed an elaborate water management system. Much of this was in support of a flourishing agriculture, which supported a very rapidly growing and dense population by 750 C.E. This agriculture sustained substantial elite classes of nobles, priests, merchants, architects, and sculptors, as well as specialized artisans producing pottery, tools, and cotton textiles. And it was sufficiently productive to free a large labor force for work on the many public structures that continue to amaze contemporary visitors.

We now know that these many achievements took place within a highly fragmented political system of city-states, local lords, and regional kingdoms with no central authority, with frequent warfare, and with the extensive capture and sacrifice of prisoners. The larger political units of Maya civilization were densely populated urban and ceremonial centers, ruled by powerful kings, who were divine rulers or "state shamans" able to mediate between humankind and the supernatural. One of these cities, Tikal, contained perhaps 50,000 people, with another 50,000 or so in the surrounding countryside, by 750 C.E.[11] Some of these city-states were clearly imperialistic, but none succeeded in creating a unified Maya empire. Various centers of Maya civilization rose and fell; fluctuating alliances among them alternated with periods of sporadic warfare; ruling families intermarried; the elite classes sought luxury goods from far away—jade, gold, shells, feathers from exotic birds, cacao—to bolster their authority and status. In its political dimensions, classical Maya civilization more closely resembled the competing city-states of ancient Mesopotamia or classical Greece than the imperial structures of Rome, Persia, or China.

But that imposing civilization collapsed with a completeness and rapidity rare in world history. In less than a century following the onset of a long-term drought in 840, the population of the low-lying southern heartland of the Maya dropped by 85 percent or more as famine, epidemic, and fratricidal warfare reaped a horrific toll. It was a catastrophe from which there was no recovery. Elements of Maya culture survived in scattered settlements, but the great cities were deserted, and large-scale construction and artistic work ceased. The last date inscribed in stone corresponds to 909 C.E. As a complex civilization, the Maya had passed into history.

Explaining this remarkable demise has long kept scholars guessing. It seems clear that neither foreign invasion nor internal rebellion played a major role, as they had in the collapse of the Roman and Chinese empires. One recent account focuses on ecological and political factors.[12] Extremely rapid population growth after 600 C.E. pushed total Maya numbers to perhaps 5 million or more and soon outstripped available resources, resulting in deforestation and the erosion of hillsides. Under such conditions, climate change in the form of prolonged droughts in the 800s may well have triggered the collapse, while political disunity and endemic rivalries prevented a coordinated and effective response to the emerging catastrophe. Maya warfare in fact became more frequent as competition for increasingly scarce land for cultivation became sharper. Whatever the precise explanation, the Maya collapse, like that of the Romans and others, illustrates the fragility of civilizations, whether they are embodied in large empires or organized in a more decentralized fashion.

Teotihuacán: America's Greatest City

At roughly the same time as the Maya flourished in the southern regions of Mesoamerica, the giant city of Teotihuacán, to the north in the Valley of Mexico, was also thriving. Begun around 150 B.C.E. and apparently built to a plan rather than evolving haphazardly, the city came to occupy about eight square miles and by 550 C.E. had a population variously estimated between 100,000 and 200,000. It was by far the largest urban complex in the Americas at the time and one of the six largest in the world. Beyond this, much about Teotihuacán is unknown, such as its original name, the language of its people, the kind of government that ordered its life, and the precise function of its many deities.

■ Connection

In what ways did Teotihuacán shape the history of Mesoamerica?

Physically, the city was enormously impressive, replete with broad avenues, spacious plazas, huge marketplaces, temples, palaces, apartment complexes, slums, waterways, reservoirs, drainage systems, and colorful murals. Along the main north/south boulevard, now known as the Street of the Dead, were the grand homes of the elite, the headquarters of state authorities, many temples, and two giant pyramids. One of them, the Pyramid of the Sun, had been constructed over an ancient tunnel leading to a cave and may well have been regarded as the site of creation itself, the birthplace of the sun and the moon. At the Temple of the Feathered Serpent, archeologists have found the remains of some 200 people, their hands and arms tied behind them; they were the apparently unwilling sacrificial victims meant to accompany into the afterlife the high-ranking persons buried there.

Off the main avenues in a gridlike pattern of streets lay thousands of residential apartment compounds, home to the city's commoners, each with its own kitchen area, sleeping quarters, courtyards, and shrines. In these compounds, perhaps in groups of related families or lineages, lived many of the farmers who tilled the lands outside the city. Thousands of Maya specialists—masons, leather workers, potters, construction laborers, merchants, civil servants—also made their homes in these apartments. So too did skilled makers of obsidian blades, who plied their trade in hundreds of separate workshops, generating products that were in great demand throughout Mesoamerica. At least two small sections of the city were reserved exclusively for foreigners.

Buildings, both public and private, were decorated with mural paintings, sculptures, and carvings. Many of these works of art display abstract geometric and stylized images. Others depict gods and goddesses, arrayed in various forms—feathered serpents, starfish, jaguars, flowers, and warriors. One set of murals shows happy people cavorting in a paradise of irrigated fields, playing games, singing, and chasing butterflies, which were thought to represent the souls of the dead. Another portrays dancing warriors carrying elaborate curved knives, to which were attached bleeding human hearts.

The art of Teotihuacán, unlike that of the Maya, has revealed few images of self-glorifying rulers or individuals. Nor did the city have a tradition of written public inscriptions as the Maya did, although a number of glyphs or characters suggest at least a limited form of writing. One scholar has suggested that "the rulers of Teotihuacán might have intentionally avoided the personality cult of the dynastic art and writing" so characteristic of the Maya.[13] Some have argued that those rulers may have constituted an oligarchy or council of high-ranking elites rather than a single monarch.

However it was governed, Teotihuacán cast a huge shadow over Mesoamerica, particularly from 300 to 600 C.E., although scholars disagree as to precisely how its power and influence were exercised. A core region of perhaps 10,000 square miles was administered directly from the city itself, while tribute was no doubt exacted from other areas within its broader sphere of influence. At a greater distance, the power of

A Mural of Teotihuacán
The paradise of the god of the rain, portrayed in this mural, was available only to those who died through drowning, storms, or lightning. The deity in the center presides over the waters, and rain springs from his hands, while at the sides, priests make their offerings. The dating of such murals is uncertain, but most were apparently created between 450 and 650 C.E. (Enrique Franco-Torrijos)

Teotihuacán's armies gave it a presence in the Maya heartland more than 600 miles to the east. At least one Maya city, Kaminalijuyu in the southern highlands, was completely taken over by the Teotihuacán military and organized as a colony. In Tikal, a major lowland Maya city, in the year 378 C.E., agents of Teotihuacán apparently engineered a coup that placed a collaborator on the throne and turned the city for a time into an ally or a satellite. Elsewhere—in the Zapotec capital of Monte Alban, for example—murals show unarmed persons from Teotihuacán engaged in what seems to be more equal diplomatic relationships.

At least some of this political and military activity was no doubt designed to obtain, either by trade or by tribute, valued commodities from afar—food products, cacao beans, tropical bird feathers, honey, salt, medicinal herbs. The presence in Teotihuacán of foreigners, perhaps merchants, from the Gulf Coast and Maya lowlands, as well as much pottery from those regions, provides further evidence of long-distance trade. Furthermore, the sheer size and prestige of Teotihuacán surely persuaded many, all across Mesoamerica, to imitate the architectural and artistic styles of the city. Thus, according to a leading scholar, "Teotihuacan meant something of surpassing importance far beyond its core area."[14] Almost a thousand years after its still-mysterious collapse around 650 C.E., the peoples of the Aztec Empire dubbed the great metropolis as Teotihuacán, the "city of the gods."

Civilizations of the Andes

Yet another center of civilization in the Americas lay in the dramatic landscape of the Andes. Bleak deserts along the coast supported human habitation only because they were cut by dozens of rivers flowing down from the mountains, offering the possibility of irrigation and cultivation. The offshore waters of the Pacific Ocean also provided an enormously rich marine environment with an endless supply of seabirds and fish. The Andes themselves, a towering mountain chain with many highland valleys, afforded numerous distinct ecological niches, depending on altitude. On its steep slopes, people carved out huge staircase terrace systems, which remain impressive in the twenty-first century.

The most well known of the civilizations to take shape in this environment was that of the Incas, which encompassed practically the entire region, some 2,500 miles in length, in the fifteenth century. Yet the Incas represented only the most recent and the largest in a long history of civilizations in the area.

The coastal region of central Peru had in fact generated one of the world's First Civilizations, known as Norte Chico, dating back to around 3000 B.C.E. (see Chapter 3). The classical era in Andean civilization, roughly 1000 B.C.E. to 1000 C.E., provides an opportunity to look briefly at several of the cultures that followed Norte Chico and preceded the Inca civilization. Because none of them had developed writing, historians are largely dependent on archeology for an understanding of these civilizations.

Classical Civilizations of the Andes

Chavín: A Pan-Andean Religious Movement

■ Connection
What kind of influence did Chavín exert in the Andes region?

In both the coastal and highland regions of Peru, archeologists have uncovered numerous local ceremonial centers or temple complexes, dating to between 2000 and 1000 B.C.E. Often constructed in a characteristic U shape, they were associated with small-scale irrigation projects and suggest the growing authority of religious leaders. Human trophy heads indicate raiding, warfare, and violence among these local centers. Then around 900 B.C.E., one of them, located in the Andean highlands at a village called Chavín de Huántar, became the focus of a religious movement that soon swept through both coastal and highland Peru.

Chavín de Huántar enjoyed a strategic location, high in the Andes and situated on trade routes to both the coastal region to the west and the Amazon rain forest to the east. By perhaps 750 B.C.E., it had become a small town of 2,000 to 3,000 people, with clear distinctions between an elite class, who lived in stone houses, and ordinary people, with adobe dwellings. An elaborate temple complex included numerous galleries, hidden passageways, staircases, ventilation shafts, drainage canals, and distinctive carvings. Little is known about the rituals or beliefs that animated Chavín's religious practice, but the artwork suggests that it drew on ideas from both the desert coastal region and the rain forests. Major deities were represented as jaguars, crocodiles, and snakes, all of them native to the Amazon basin. Shamans or priests likely made use of the San Pedro cactus and its hallucinogenic properties to penetrate the supernatural world. Some of the fantastic artwork of this civilization—its jaguar-human images, for example—may well reflect the visions of these religious leaders.

Over the next several centuries, this blended religious movement proved attractive across much of Peru and beyond, as Chavín-style architecture, sculpture, pottery, religious images, and painted textiles were widely imitated within the region. Chavín itself became a pilgrimage site and perhaps a training center for initiates from distant centers. At locations three weeks or more away by llama caravan, temples were remodeled to resemble that of Chavín, although in many cases with locally inspired variations.[15] Much of the spread of Chavín religious imagery and practice paralleled the trade routes that linked highland and coastal Peru. Although there is some evidence for violence and warfare, no Chavín "empire" emerged. Instead, a widespread religious cult, traveling on the back of a trading network, provided for the first time and for several centuries a measure of economic and cultural integration to much of the Peruvian Andes.

Moche: A Regional Andean Civilization

■ Description
What supports scholars' contention that Moche represented a regional civilization in the Andes?

By 200 B.C.E., the pan-Andes Chavín cult had faded, replaced by a number of regional civilizations. Among them, the Moche civilization clearly stands out. Dominating a 250-mile stretch of Peru's northern coast and incorporating thirteen river valleys, the Moche flourished between about 100 and 800 C.E. Their economy was rooted in a complex irrigation system, requiring constant maintenance, which funneled runoff from the Andes into fields of maize, beans, and squash and acres of cotton, all fertilized by rich bird droppings called guano. Moche fishermen also harvested millions of anchovies from the bountiful Pacific.

Politically, Moche was governed by warrior-priests, some of whom lived atop huge pyramids. The largest of these structures, dubbed the Pyramid of the Sun, had been constructed from 143 million sun-dried bricks. There shaman-rulers, often under the influence of hallucinogenic drugs, conducted ancient rituals that mediated between the world of humankind and that of the gods, and they also presided over the ritual sacrifice of human victims, drawn from their many prisoners of war, which became central to the politico-religious life of the Moche. Images on Moche pottery show a ruler attired in a magnificent feather headdress and seated on a pyramid, while a parade of naked prisoners marches past him. Other scenes of decapitation and dismemberment indicate the fate that awaited those destined for sacrifice. For these rulers, the Moche world was apparently one of war, ritual, and diplomacy.

The immense wealth of this warrior-priest elite and the exquisite artistry of Moche craftsmen are reflected in the elaborate burials accorded the rulers. At one site, Peruvian archeologists uncovered the final resting place of three such individuals, whom they named the Lords of Sipan. Laid in adobe burial chambers, one above the other, each was decked out in his ceremonial regalia—elaborate gold masks, necklaces, and headdresses; turquoise and gold bead bracelets; cotton tunics covered with copper plates; a gold rattle showing a Moche warrior smashing a prisoner with his war club; and a copper knife. In 2005, in another remarkable discovery dating to about 450 C.E., archeologists found the burial place of a very high-status woman, who was in her late twenties and heavily tattooed. She had been laid to rest with hundreds of funeral objects, including gold sewing needles; weaving tools; much gold, silver, and copper jewelry; and a female sacrificial victim lying beside her. Even more suggestive were two elaborate war clubs and twenty-three spear throwers. Was she perhaps a warrior, a priest, or a ruler?

The most accessible aspect of Moche life and much of what scholars know about the Moche world derive from the superb skill of their craftspeople, such as metalworkers, potters, weavers, and painters. Face masks, figures of animals, small earrings, and other jewelry, many plated in gold, display amazing technical abilities and artistic sensibility. On their ceramic pottery are naturalistic portraits of noble lords and rulers and images from the life of common people, including the blind and the sick. Battle scenes show warriors confronting their enemies with raised clubs. Erotic encounters between men and women and gods making love to humans likewise represent common themes, as do grotesque images of their many gods and goddesses. Much of this, of course, reflects the culture of the Moche elite. Scholars know much less about the daily life of the farmers, fishermen, weavers, traders, construction workers, and servants whose labor made that elite culture possible.

These cultural achievements, however, rested on fragile environmental foundations, for the region was subject to periodic drought, earthquakes, and occasional

The Lord of Sipan
The Moche ruler in the center of the grave, dating to about 290 C.E., was about forty years old when he died and, at five feet five inches, was quite tall for the time. Except for early signs of arthritis, he was in good health and seems to have performed little physical labor during his life. Accompanying him in death were the four individuals shown here, plus three young women, a priest, a guard, a dog, and considerable food and drink. (Kevin Schafter/Corbis)

torrential rains associated with El Niño episodes. Scholars believe that during the sixth century C.E. some combination of these forces caused extended ecological disruption, which seriously undermined Moche civilization. In these circumstances, the Moche were vulnerable to aggressive neighbors and possibly to internal social tensions as well. By the end of the eighth century C.E., that civilization had passed into history.[16]

The Chavín and Moche civilizations were but two of the many that grew up in the Andes region before the Incas consolidated the entire area into a single empire. The Nazca, for example, on the arid southern coast of Peru, have become famous for their underground irrigation canals, polychrome pottery, and textiles, but especially for their gigantic and mysterious lines in the desert in the form of monkeys, birds, spiders, whales, and various abstract designs. In the interior, a series of larger states emerged. One of them was centered on Tiwanaku, a city of monumental buildings and perhaps 40,000 to 50,000 people that flourished during much of the first millennium C.E. The Huari and Chimu kingdoms were further examples of this Andean civilization, to which the Incas gave a final and spectacular expression before all of the Americas was swallowed up in European empires from across the sea.

North America in the Classical Era: From Chaco to Cahokia

The peoples of the Americas in the pre-Columbian era might be divided into three large groupings. The most prominent and well known are those of the Mesoamerican and Andean regions, where cities, states, and dense populations created civilizations broadly similar to those of classical Eurasia. Elsewhere, gathering and hunting peoples carried on that most ancient of human adaptations to the environment. Arctic and subarctic cultures; the bison hunters of the Great Plains; the complex and settled communities of the Pacific coast, such as the Chumash (see Chapter 1); nomadic bands living in the arid regions of southern South America—all of these represent the persistence of gathering and hunting peoples in substantial regions of the Americas.

North America in the Classical Era

Even larger areas—the eastern woodlands of the United States, Central America, the Amazon basin, the Caribbean islands—were populated by peoples sometimes defined as "semi-sedentary."[17] These were agricultural societies, although less intensive and productive than those of Mesoamerica or the Andes and supporting usually much smaller populations. Nor did they generate large urban centers or inclusive empires.

These peoples who lived beyond the direct reach of the major civilizations also made their own histories, changing in response to their unique environments, their interactions with outsiders, and their own visions of the world. The Anasazi of the southwestern United States, now called the Ancestral Pueblo, and the mound-building cultures of the eastern woodlands provide two illustrations from North America during the classical era.

Pit Houses and Great Houses: The Ancestral Pueblo

The southwestern region of North America, an arid land cut by mountain ranges and large basins, first acquired maize from its place of origin in Mesoamerica during the second millennium B.C.E., but it took roughly 2,000 years for that crop, later supplemented by beans and squash, to become the basis of a settled agricultural way of living. In a desert region, farming was risky, and maize had to be gradually adapted to the local environment. Not until around 600 to 800 C.E. did permanent village life take hold widely. People then lived in pit houses with floors sunk several feet below ground level. Some settlements had only a few such homes, whereas others contained twenty-five or more. By 900 C.E., many of these villages also included kivas, much larger pit structures used for ceremonial purposes, which symbolized the widespread belief that humankind emerged into this world from another world below. Individual settlements were linked to one another in local trading networks and sometimes in wider webs of exchange that brought them buffalo hides, copper, turquoise, seashells, macaw feathers, and coiled baskets from quite distant locations.

■ **Comparison**

In what ways were the histories of the Ancestral Pueblo and the Mound Builders similar to each other, and how did they differ?

Pueblo Bonito
Called Pueblo Bonito ("pretty village") by the Spanish, this great house of the Ancestral Pueblo people was at its high point in the eleventh century C.E. The circular structures, known as kivas, were probably ceremonial sites. Their prominence, and the absence of major trash collections, have persuaded some scholars that Pueblo Bonito was more of a ritual center than a residential town. (Courtesy, Chaco Canyon National Historic Park)

These processes of change—growing dependence on agriculture, increasing population, more intensive patterns of exchange—gave rise to larger settlements and adjacent aboveground structures known as pueblos. The most spectacular of these took shape in Chaco canyon in what is now northwestern New Mexico. There, between 860 and 1130 C.E., five major pueblos emerged. This Chaco Phenomenon encompassed 25,000 square miles and linked some seventy outlying settlements to the main centers. The population was not large, perhaps as few as 5,000 people, although experts continue to debate the issue. The largest of these towns or "great houses," Pueblo Bonito, stood five stories high and contained more than 600 rooms and many kivas. Hundreds of miles of roads, up to forty feet wide, radiated out from Chaco, likewise prompting much debate among scholars. Without wheeled carts or large domesticated animals, such an elaborate road system seems unnecessary for ordinary trade or travel. Did the roads represent, as some scholars speculate, a "sacred landscape which gave order to the world," joining its outlying communities to a Middle Place, an entrance perhaps to the underworld?[18]

Among the Chaco elite were highly skilled astronomers, who constructed an observatory of three large rock slabs situated so as to throw a beam of light across a spiral rock carving behind it at the summer solstice. By the eleventh century, Chaco also had become a dominant center for the production of turquoise ornaments, which became a major item of regional commerce. Not all was sweetness and light, however. Warfare, internal conflict, and occasional cannibalism (a matter of much controversy among scholars) apparently increased in frequency as an extended period of drought in the half century following 1130 brought this flourishing culture to a rather abrupt end. By 1200, the great houses had been abandoned, and their inhabitants became scattered in small communities that later became the Pueblo peoples of more recent times.

The Mound Builders of the Eastern Woodlands

Unlike the Chaco region in the southwest, the eastern woodlands of North America and especially the Mississippi River valley hosted an independent Agricultural Revolution. By 2000 B.C.E., many of its peoples had domesticated local plant species, including sunflowers, sumpweed, goosefoot, some gourds and squashes, and a form of artichoke. These few plants, however, were not sufficient to support a fully settled agricultural village life; rather they supplemented diets derived from gathering and hunting without fundamentally changing that ancient way of life. Such peoples created societies distinguished by arrays of large earthen mounds, found all over the United States east of the Mississippi, prompting archeologists to dub them the Mound Builders.[19] The earliest of them date to around 2000 B.C.E., but the most elaborate and widespread of these mound-building cultures took shape between 200 B.C.E. and 400 C.E. and is known to scholars as the Hopewell culture, after an archeological site in Ohio.

Several features of the Hopewell culture have intrigued archeologists. Particularly significant are the striking burial mounds and geometric earthworks, sometimes covering areas equivalent to several city blocks, and the wide variety of artifacts found within them—smoking pipes, human figurines, mica mirrors, flint blades, fabrics, and jewelry of all kinds. The mounds themselves were no doubt the focus of elaborate burial rituals, but some of them were aligned with the moon with such precision as to allow the prediction of lunar eclipses. Developed most elaborately in the Ohio River valley, Hopewell-style earthworks, artifacts, and ceremonial pottery have also been found throughout the eastern woodlands region of North America. Hopewell centers in Ohio contained mica from the Appalachian mountains, volcanic glass from Yellowstone, conch shells and sharks' teeth from the Gulf of Mexico, and copper from the Great Lakes. All of this suggests an enormous "Hopewell Interaction Sphere," linking this huge region in a loose network of exchange, as well as a measure of cultural borrowing of religious ideas and practices within this immense area.[20]

The next and most spectacular phase in the history of these mound-building peoples took shape as corn-based agriculture, derived ultimately but indirectly from

Mexico, gained ground in the Mississippi valley after 800 C.E., allowing larger populations and more complex societies to emerge. The dominant center was Cahokia, near present-day St. Louis, Missouri, which flourished from about 900 to 1250 C.E. Its central mound, a terraced pyramid of four levels, measured 1,000 feet long by 700 feet wide, rose more than 100 feet above the ground, and occupied fifteen acres. It was the largest structure north of Mexico, the focal point of a community numbering 10,000 or more people, and the center of a widespread trading network (see an artist's reconstruction of Cahokia on p. 52).

Cahokia emerged and flourished at about the same time as did the great houses of Chaco canyon, but its urban presence was far larger than that of its southwestern counterpart. Both were made possible by the arrival of corn-based agriculture, originating in Mesoamerica, though direct contact with Mexico is much more apparent in Chaco. Finally, Cahokia emerged as the climax of a long history of mound-building cultures in the eastern woodlands, whereas Chaco was more of a "start-up" culture, emerging quite quickly "with a relatively shallow history."[21]

Evidence from burials and from later Spanish observers suggests that Cahokia and other centers of this Mississippi culture were stratified societies with a clear elite and with rulers able to mobilize the labor required to build such enormous structures. One high-status male was buried on a platform of 20,000 shell beads, accompanied by 800 arrowheads, sheets of copper and mica, and a number of sacrificed men and women nearby.[22] Well after Cahokia had declined and was abandoned, sixteenth-century Spanish and French explorers encountered another such chiefdom among the Natchez people, located in southwestern Mississippi. Paramount chiefs, known as Great Suns, dressed in knee-length fur coats and lived luxuriously in deerskin-covered homes. An elite class of "principal men" or "honored peoples" clearly occupied a different status from commoners, sometimes referred to as "stinkards." These sharp class distinctions were blunted by the requirement that upper-class people, including the Great Suns, had to marry "stinkards."

The military capacity of these Mississippi chiefdoms greatly impressed European observers, as this Spanish account indicates:

> The next day the cacique [paramount chief] arrived with 200 canoes filled with men, having weapons . . . the warriors standing erect from bow to stern, holding bows and arrows. . . . [F]rom under the canopy where the chief man was, the course was directed and orders issued to the rest. . . . [W]hat with the awnings, the plumes, the shields, the pennons, and the number of people in the fleet, it appeared like a famous armada of galleys.[23]

Here then in the eastern woodlands of North America were peoples who independently generated a modest Agricultural Revolution, assimilated corn and beans from distant sources, developed increasingly complex societies, and created monumental structures, new technologies, and artistic traditions. In doing so, they gave rise to a regional cultural complex that enveloped much of the United

States east of the Mississippi in a network of ceremonial, economic, and cultural exchange.

Reflections: Deciding What's Important: Balance in World History

Among the perennial problems that teachers and writers of world history confront is sorting through the vast record of times past and choosing what to include and what to leave out. A related issue involves the extent to which particular peoples or civilizations will be treated. Should the Persians get as much space as the Greeks? Does Africa merit equal treatment with Eurasia? Where do the Americas fit in the larger human story? What, in short, are the criteria for deciding what is important in telling the story of the human venture?

One standard might be duration. Should ways of living that have endured for longer periods of time receive greater attention than those of lesser length? If only this criterion was followed, then the Paleolithic era of gathering and hunting should occupy 90 percent or more of any world history text. On the other hand, perhaps change is more important than continuity. If so, then something new merits more space than something old. Thus we pay attention to both agriculture and civilizations because they represent significant turning points in human experience. Population provides yet another principle for determining inclusion. That, of course, is the reason that Eurasia, with about 80 percent of the world's population during the classical era, is addressed in three chapters, whereas Africa and the Americas together receive only one chapter. There is also the related issue of influence. Buddhism, Christianity, and Islam spread more widely and shaped the lives of more people than did the religions of the Maya or the Bantu-speaking peoples of Africa. Do they therefore deserve more extended treatment?

A final possible criterion involves the location of the historian and his or her audience. The recent development of world history as a field of study has sought vigorously to counteract a Eurocentric telling of the human story. Still, is there anything inherently wrong with an account of world history that is centered on one's own people? When I taught history in an Ethiopian high school in the mid-1960s, I was guided by an Afrocentric curriculum, which focused first on Ethiopian history, then on Africa as a whole, and finally on the larger world. Might a world historian from the Middle East, for example, legitimately strike a somewhat different balance in the treatment of various civilizations than someone writing for a largely Western audience or for Chinese readers?

Any account of the world's past will mix and match these criteria in various and contested ways. Among scholars, there exists neither a consensus about this question nor any formula to ensure a "proper" balance. You may want to consider whether the balance struck in this chapter, this section, and the book as a whole is appropriate or somehow out of line.

Second Thoughts

What's the Significance?

To assess your mastery of the material in this chapter, see the **Online Study Guide** at bedfordstmartins.com/strayer.

Meroë	Maya civilization	Chaco Phenomenon
Axum	Teotihuacán	Cahokia
Niger Valley civilization	Chavín	
Bantu expansion	Moche	

Big Picture Questions

1. "The histories of Africa and the Americas during the classical era largely resemble those of Eurasia." Do you agree with this statement? Explain why or why not.
2. "The particular cultures and societies of Africa and of the Americas discussed in this chapter developed largely in isolation from one another." What evidence would support this statement, and what might challenge it?
3. What generated change in the histories of Africa and the Americas during the classical era?

Next Steps: For Further Study

For Web sites and documents related to this chapter, see **Make History** at bedfordstmartins.com/strayer.

Richard E. W. Adams, *Ancient Civilizations of the New World* (1997). A broad survey based on current scholarship of the Americas before Columbus.

Christopher Ehret, *The Civilizations of Africa* (2002). A recent overview of African history before 1800 by a prominent scholar.

Brian M. Fagan, *Ancient North America* (2005). A prominent archeologist's account of North American history.

Eric Gilbert and Jonathan T. Reynolds, *Africa in World History* (2004). An accessible account of African history set in a global context.

Guy Gugliotta, "The Maya: Glory and Ruin," *National Geographic* (August 2007). A beautifully illustrated account of the rise and fall of Maya civilization.

Kairn A. Klieman, *"The Pygmies Were Our Compass"* (2003). A scholarly examination of the Pygmies (Batwa) of the Congo River basin and their interaction with Bantu-speaking peoples.

Charles Mann, *1491* (2005). A thoughtful journalist's account, delightfully written, of the controversies surrounding the history of the Americas before 1492.

"Ancient Africa's Black Kingdoms," http://www.homestead.com/wysinger/ancientafrica.html. A Web site exploring the history of Nubia.

"Maya Adventures," http://www.smm.org/sln/ma. A collection of text and pictures about the Maya, past and present.

PART THREE
An Age
of Accelerating
Connections
500–1500

Contents

Defining a Millennium

History seldom turns sharp corners, and historians often have difficulty deciding just when one phase of the human story ends and another begins. Between roughly 200 and 850 C.E., many of the classical states and civilizations of the world (Han dynasty China, the Roman Empire, Gupta India, Meroë, Axum, Maya, Teotihuacán, Moche) experienced severe disruption, decline, or collapse. For many historians, this marks the end of the classical era and the start of some new period of world history. Furthermore, almost everyone agrees that the transatlantic voyages of Columbus around 1500 represent yet another new departure in world history. This coupling of the Eastern and Western hemispheres set in motion historical processes that transformed most of the world and signaled the beginning of the modern era.

How are we to understand the thousand years (roughly 500 to 1500) between the end of the classical era and the beginning of modern world history? Historians, frankly, have had some difficulty in defining a distinct identity for this millennium, and this problem is reflected in the vague terms used to describe it. Many textbooks, including this one on occasion, refer to this 1,000-year period simply as the "postclassical" age, but that, of course, merely indicates that it came after the classical era. Others have termed it "medieval," a middle or intermediate age, something in between the classical and modern eras. Many historians feel uncomfortable with this term because it derives specifically from European history and thus runs the risk of appearing Eurocentric. It also seems to suggest that this millennium was merely a run-up to modernity, rather than something of significance in its own right. This book sometimes uses the concept of "third-wave civilizations," distinguishing, at least chronologically, those that emerged after 500 C.E. from both the First Civilizations and those of the classical era (the second-wave civilizations). At best, these terms indicate where this period falls in the larger time frame of world history, but none of them are very descriptive.

Third-Wave Civilizations: Something New, Something Old, Something Blended

A large part of the problem lies in the rather different trajectories of various regions of the world during this postclassical era. It is not easy to identify clearly defined features that encompass all the major civilizations during this period and distinguish them from what went before, but we can point to several distinct patterns of development among these third-wave societies of the postclassical era.

In some areas, for example, wholly new but smaller civilizations arose where none had existed before. Along the East African coast, Swahili civilization emerged in a string of thirty or more city-states, very much engaged in the commercial life of the Indian Ocean basin. In the area now encompassed by Ukraine and western Russia, another new civilization, known as Kievan Rus, likewise took shape with a good deal of cultural borrowing from Mediterranean civilization. East and Southeast Asia also witnessed new centers of civilization. Those in Japan, Korea, and Vietnam were strongly influenced by China, while Srivijaya on the Indonesian island of Sumatra and later the Angkor kingdom, centered in present-day Cambodia, drew on the Hindu and Buddhist traditions of India.

All of these represent a continuation of a well-established pattern in world history—the globalization of civilization. It began with the First Civilizations of Mesopotamia, Egypt, and elsewhere about 3000 B.C.E. and then took new and larger forms in the classical era (500 B.C.E.–500 C.E.), when Greco-Roman, Persian, Indian, and Chinese civilizations flourished across Eurasia. Each of the new third-wave civilizations was, of course, culturally unique, but like their predecessors, they too featured states, cities, specialized economic roles, sharp class and gender inequalities, and other elements of "civilized" life. They were certainly distinctive, but not fundamentally different from earlier civilizations. As newcomers to the growing number of civilizations, all of them borrowed heavily from larger or more established centers.

The largest, most expansive, and most widely influential of the new third-wave civilizations was surely that of Islam. It began in Arabia in the seventh century C.E., projecting the Arab peoples into a prominent role as builders of an enormous empire while offering a new, vigorous, and attractive religion. Viewed as a new civilization defined by its religion, the world of Islam came to encompass many other centers of civilization, including Egypt, Mesopotamia, Persia, India, the interior of West Africa and the coast of East Africa, Spain, southeastern Europe, and more. Here was a uniquely cosmopolitan or "umbrella" civilization that, according to one leading scholar, "came closer than any had ever come to uniting all mankind under its ideals."[1]

Yet another, and quite different, historical pattern during the postclassical millennium involved older or classical civilizations that persisted or were reconstructed. The Byzantine Empire, embracing the eastern half of the old Roman Empire, continued the patterns of Mediterranean Christian civilization and persisted until 1453, when it was overrun by the Ottoman Turks. In China, following almost four centuries of fragmentation, the Sui, Tang, and Song dynasties (589–1279) restored China's imperial unity and reasserted its Confucian tradition. Indian civilization retained its ancient patterns of caste and Hinduism amid vast cultural diversity, even as parts of India fell under the control of Muslim rulers. The West African savanna kingdoms of Ghana, Mali, and Songhay, stimulated and sustained by long-distance trade across the Sahara, built upon the earlier Niger Valley civilization.

Variations on this theme of continuing or renewing older traditions took shape in the Western Hemisphere, where two centers of civilization—in Mesoamerica and in the Andes—had been long established. In Mesoamerica, the collapse of classical Maya civilization and of the great city-state of Teotihuacán by about 900 C.E. opened the way for other peoples to give new shape to this ancient civilization. The most well known of these efforts was associated with the Mexica or Aztec people, who created a powerful and impressive state in the fifteenth century. About the same time, on the western rim of South America, a Quechua-speaking people, now known as the Inca, incorporated various centers of Andean civilization into a huge bureaucratic empire. Both the Aztecs and the Incas gave a new political expression to much older patterns of civilized life.

A final pattern took shape in Western Europe following the collapse of the Roman Empire. There would-be kings and church leaders alike sought to maintain links with the older Greco-Roman-Christian traditions of classical Mediterranean civilization. In the absence of empire, though, new and far more decentralized societies emerged, led now by Germanic peoples and centered in Northern and Western Europe, considerably removed from the older centers of Rome and Athens. It was a hybrid civilization, combining old and new, classical and Germanic elements, in a unique blending. For five centuries or more, this region was a relative backwater, compared to the more vibrant, prosperous, and powerful civilizations of the Islamic world and of China. During the centuries after 1000 C.E., however, Western European civilization emerged as a rapidly growing and expansive set of competitive states, willing, like other new civilizations, to borrow quite extensively from their more developed neighbors.

The Ties That Bind: Transregional Interaction in the Postclassical Era

These quite different patterns of development within particular civilizations of the postclassical millennium have made it difficult to define that era in a single, all-encompassing fashion. In another way, though, a common theme emerges, for during this time, the world's various regions, cultures, and peoples interacted with one another far more extensively than before. More than ever, change in human societies was the product of contact with strangers, or at least with their ideas, armies, goods, or diseases. In a variety of places—island Southeast Asia, coastal East Africa, Central Asian cities, parts of Western Europe, the Islamic Middle East, and the Inca Empire—local cosmopolitan regions emerged in which trade, migration, or empire had brought peoples of different cultures together in a restricted space. These "miniglobalizations," both larger and more common than in the classical era, became a distinctive feature of third-wave civilizations.

"No man is an island, entire of itself," wrote the seventeenth-century English poet John Donne. "Every man is a piece of the continent, a part of the main." Much the same might be said of every civilization, culture, or region. None of them were wholly isolated or separate from their neighbors, although the range and intensity of cross-cultural interaction certainly varied over time. In limited ways, that was the case for the First Civilizations as well as their classical successors. Both Egyptian and Mesopotamian cultural influence spread well beyond the core regions of those civilizations. Horseback-riding skills and chariot technology diffused widely across Eurasia. The encounter of the Greeks and Persians changed both of those classical civilizations. Cross-cultural mixing in northern India gave rise to the caste system, while the Silk Road trading networks across Eurasia provided some contact among the distant empires of Rome, China, and India.

The scale and pace of such interaction accelerated considerably during the era of third-wave, or postclassical, civilizations. Much of Part Three highlights these intersections and spells out their many and varied consequences. Three major mechanisms of cross-cultural interaction, which we will meet in the chapters that follow, were of particular significance for transforming the lives and societies of those who took part in them.

One such mechanism was trade. The exchange of goods has been everywhere one of the primary means of cross-cultural interaction, and virtually every human society has engaged in it at some level. Although most trade in the premodern world occurred locally among nearby communities, world historians have focused attention especially on long-distance trade, commercial relationships that linked distant human communities. This kind of commerce grew considerably during the postclassical era — along the Silk Roads of Eurasia, within the Indian Ocean basin, across the Sahara, and along the Mississippi and other rivers. Everywhere it acted as an agent of change for all of its participants. In places where long-distance trade was practiced extensively, it required that more people devote their energies to producing for a distant market rather than for the consumption of their own communities. Those who controlled this kind of trade often became extremely wealthy, exciting envy or outrage among those less fortunate. Many societies learned about new products via these trade routes. Europe's knowledge of pepper and other spices, for example, derived from Roman seaborne trade with India beginning in the first century C.E. Many centuries later, Europeans' desire for Asian spices played a part in propelling Western commercial and military expansion into the Indian Ocean.

Such trade also had political consequences as many new states or empires were established on the basis of resources derived from long-distance commerce. The West African kingdoms of Ghana and Mali, the Swahili cities of the East African coast, the early eastern Slavic state known as Rus, and the Indonesian state of Srivijaya are four such examples. Furthermore, far more than goods traveled the trade routes that linked various third-wave civilizations with one another. Religious ideas, technologies, and germs also made their ways along those paths of commerce, bringing significant change to their participants.

Yet another mechanism of cross-cultural interaction lay in large empires. Not only did they incorporate many distinct cultures within a single political system, but their size and stability also provided the security that encouraged travelers and traders to journey long distances from their homelands. Empires, of course, were nothing new in world history, but many of those associated with third-wave civilizations were distinctive. In the first place, they were larger. The Arab Empire, which accompanied the initial spread of Islam, stretched from Spain to India. Even more extensive was the Mongol Empire of the thirteenth and fourteenth centuries. In the Western Hemisphere, the Inca Empire encompassed dozens of distinct peoples in a huge state that ran some 2,500 miles along the spine of the Andes Mountains.

Furthermore, the largest of these empires were the creation of nomadic or pastoral peoples. Classical empires in the Mediterranean basin, China, India, and Persia had been the work of settled farming societies. But now, in the thousand years between 500 and 1500, peoples with a recent history of a nomadic or herding way of life entered the stage of world history as empire builders—Arabs, Turks, Mongols, Aztecs—ruling over agricultural peoples and established civilizations. These empires changed those who created them as well as those who were forcibly incorporated within them. They also did much to foster cross-cultural interaction. Marco Polo, for example, made his way from Italy to China and back in the thirteenth century, thanks largely to the security provided by the Mongol Empire.

Together, large-scale empires and long-distance trade facilitated the spread of ideas, technologies, food crops, and germs far beyond their points of origin. Buddhism spread from India to much of Asia; Christianity encompassed Europe and took root in distant Russia as well as in northeastern Africa, southern India, and western China. Hinduism attracted followers in Southeast Asia; and more than any of the other world religions, Islam became an Afro-Eurasian phenomenon with an enormous reach. Beyond the connections born of commerce and conquest, those of culture and religion generated lasting ties among many peoples of the Eastern Hemisphere.

Technologies, too, were diffused widely. Until the sixth century C.E., China maintained a monopoly on the manufacture of raw silk. Then this technology spread beyond East Asia, allowing the development of a silk industry in the eastern Mediterranean and later in Italy. India too contributed much to the larger world— crystallized sugar, a system of numerals and the concept of zero, techniques for making cotton textiles, and many food crops. Arabs, who were responsible for spreading many of these Indian innovations, found India a "place of marvels."[2] In the Americas, corn gradually diffused from Mesoamerica, where it was initially domesticated, to North America, where it stimulated population growth and the development of more complex societies. Disease also linked distant communities. The plague, or Black Death, decimated many parts of Eurasia and North Africa as it made its deadly way from east to west in the fourteenth century.

A focus on these accelerating connections across cultural boundaries puts the historical spotlight on merchants, travelers, missionaries, migrants, soldiers, and administrators—people who traveled abroad rather than those who stayed at home. Frequently, they stimulated cultural change in the lands they visited, and of course they themselves often were changed by the experience. More than a few of the Christian Crusaders who invaded the Middle East to rescue the holy places from Islamic control wound up as Muslims themselves.

This cross-cultural emphasis in world history also raises provocative questions about what happens when cultures interact or when strangers meet. How did external stimuli operate to produce change within particular societies? How did individuals or societies decide what to accept and what to reject when confronted with new ideas or practices? Were they free to decide such questions, or were they acting under pressure or constraints that limited the possibilities of real choice? In what ways did they alter foreign customs or traditions to better meet their own needs and correspond to their own values? These are some of the questions that will arise as we consider the accelerating connections associated with third-wave civilizations.

Landmarks in the Era of Accelerating Connections, 500–1500

500	600	700	800	900

East Asia

589–618
Sui dynasty;
reunification of China

604
Seventeen Article
Constitution
in Japan

688
Withdrawal of
Chinese military
forces from Korea

845
Suppression
of Buddhism
in China

868
First printed
book in China

939
Vietnam establishes
independence
from China

Islamic World

570–632
Life of
Muhammad

650s
Quran compiled

656
Emergence of
Shia Islam

750–900 High point of Abbasid dynasty

800–1000 Emergence of Sufism

The World of Christendom

476
End of western
Roman Empire

527–565
Justinian rules
Byzantine Empire

726–843 Iconoclasm in Byzantium

800
Charlemagne crowned as
new "Roman emperor"

912–961 Reign of
Abd al-Rahman III

988
Conversion
of Kievan
Rus to
Christianity

Africa

300–500
Beginnings of
trans-Saharan trade

7th–8th centuries Introduction of Islam and
Arab culture in North Africa

869–883
African slave
rebellion
in Iraq

900s Kings of Ghana
convert to Islam

The Americas

500 Flourishing
of Teotihuacán

600–1150 Anasazi culture, Ancestral Pueblo

850 Collapse of
Maya civilization

900–1250 Cahokia

950–1150
Flourishing
of Toltec
civilization

| | 1000 | 1100 | 1200 | 1300 | 1400 | 1500 | |

960–1279 Song dynasty China

■ **1000**
Gunpowder invented in China

■ **1000**
Tale of Genji (Japan)

1279–1368
Mongol rule
in China

1405–1433
Ming dynasty maritime
expeditions in the Indian Ocean

1467–1568
Civil war in Japan

■ **1099**
Crusaders seize
Jerusalem

■ **1206**
Delhi Sultanate
in India

■ **1325–1352**
Ibn Battuta's travels

■ **1453** Ottoman Empire
conquers Constantinople

■ **1258**
Mongols sack
Baghdad

■ **1526**
Mughal Empire
established in
India

1000–1200
New monarchies in Western Europe

■ **1266** Marco
Polo goes to
China

■ **1346–1350**
Black Death in
Europe

■ **1453** Turks capture
Constantinople

■ **1095**
Launching of
First Crusade

15th century Portuguese voyages
along West African coast

■ **1492**
Columbus crosses
the Atlantic

■ **1000**
Completion of
Bantu migrations

1250–1350 Kingdom of Zimbabwe

1450–1591 Songhay Empire

14th century Kingdom of Kongo

1000–1500 Flourishing of Swahili civilization

■ **1324–25** Mansa Musa makes pilgrimage to Mecca

12th–16th centuries Christian kingdom of Ethiopia

■ **1400**
Aztec Empire
established

■ **1492** Arrival
of Columbus in
the Caribbean

■ **1450** Inca Empire
established

■ **1142 (?)** Iroquois
confederation established

1520–1530s
Spanish conquest
of Aztecs and
Incas

1100–1350 Chucuito and Chimu kingdoms in the Andes

Commerce and Culture

500–1500

"Forget compass readings, camel caravans, and disorienting, potentially deadly Jeep journeys through the world's most fabled and forbidding desert. Soon it will be possible to take a leisurely drive along a paved two-lane highway from the spot where Europe kisses the tip of this continent into the heart of sub-Saharan Africa. That's the idea, anyway."[1] So wrote a journalist for the *New York Times* in late 2003, describing international plans for a modern highway across the Sahara, linking Europe and North Africa with the vast interior of West Africa. Such a road, its advocates hoped, would not only promote tourism, trade, and economic growth but also provide an alternative route for West African Muslims making the pilgrimage to Mecca. At the same time, in early 2004, some twenty-three nations signed an agreement to build a network of highways all across Asia, ultimately linking Tokyo with Istanbul and enabling a number of landlocked countries of Central Asia to participate more fully in the world economy.

THESE TWO AMBITIOUS PROJECTS OF THE EARLY TWENTY-FIRST CENTURY were part of the accumulating infrastructure of contemporary globalization. But they also evoked much older patterns of global commerce, the famous Silk Road network across Eurasia and the trans-Saharan trade routes, both of which flourished in the postclassical era. Here is a reminder, from the viewpoint of world history, that exchange among distant peoples is not altogether new and that the roots of economic globalization lie deep in the past.

The exchange of goods among communities occupying different ecological zones has long been a prominent feature of human history.

Travels on the Silk Road: This Chinese ceramic figurine from the Tang dynasty (618–907 C.E.) shows a group of musicians riding on a camel along the famous Silk Road commercial network that long linked the civilizations of western and eastern Eurasia. (©Asian Art & Archaeology, Inc./Corbis)

Coastlands and highlands, steppes and farmlands, islands and mainlands, valleys and mountains, deserts and forests—each generates different products desired by others. Furthermore, some societies have been able to monopolize, at least temporarily, the production of particular products, such as silk in China or certain spices in Southeast Asia, that others have found valuable. This uneven distribution of goods and resources, whether natural or resulting from human activity, has long motivated exchange, not only within particular civilizations or regions but among them as well. In the world of 500–1500, long-distance trade became more important than ever before in linking and shaping distant societies and peoples. For the most part, it was indirect, a chain of separate transactions in which goods traveled farther than individual merchants. Nonetheless, a network of exchange and communication extending all across the Afro-Eurasian world, and separately in parts of the Americas as well, slowly came into being.

In what ways was trade significant? How did it generate change within the societies that it connected? Economically speaking, it often altered consumption, enabling West Africans, for example, to import scarce salt, necessary for human diets and useful for seasoning and preserving food, from distant mines in the Sahara in exchange for the gold of their region. Trade also affected the day-to-day working lives of many people, encouraging them to specialize in producing particular products for sale in distant markets rather than for use in their own communities. Trade, in short, diminished the economic self-sufficiency of local societies.

Trade shaped the structure of those societies as well. Traders often became a distinct social group, viewed with suspicion by others because of their impulse to accumulate wealth without actually producing anything themselves. In some societies, trade became a means of social mobility, as Chinese merchants, for example, were able to purchase landed estates and establish themselves within the gentry class. Long-distance trade also enabled elite groups in society to distinguish themselves from commoners by acquiring prestigious goods from a distance—silk, tortoiseshells, rhinoceros horn, or particular feathers, for example. The association with faraway or powerful societies, signaled by the possession of their luxury goods, often conveyed status in communities more remote from major civilizations.

Political life also was sometimes transformed by trade. The wealth available from controlling and taxing trade motivated the creation of states in various parts of the world and sustained those states once they had been constructed. Furthermore, commerce posed a set of problems to governments everywhere. Should trade be left in private hands, as in the Aztec Empire, or should it be controlled by the state, as in the Inca Empire? How should state authorities deal with men of commerce, who were both economically useful and potentially disruptive?

Moreover, the saddlebags of camel caravans or the cargo holds of merchant vessels carried more than goods. Trade became the vehicle for the spread of religious ideas, technological innovations, disease-bearing germs, and plants and animals to regions far from their places of origin. In just this fashion, Buddhism made its way from India to Central and East Asia, and Islam crossed the Sahara into West Africa. So did the pathogens that devastated much of Eurasia during the Black Death. These immense cultural and biological transformations were among the most significant outcomes of the increasingly dense network of long-distance commerce during the era of third-wave civilizations.

Silk Roads: Exchange across Eurasia

The Eurasian landmass has long been home to the majority of humankind as well as to the world's most productive agriculture, largest civilizations, and greatest concentration of pastoral peoples. Beyond its many separate societies and cultures, Eurasia also gave rise to one of the world's most extensive and sustained networks of exchange among its diverse peoples. Known to scholars as the Silk Roads, a reference to its most famous product, these land-based trade routes linked pastoral and agricultural peoples as well as the large civilizations on the continent's outer rim (see Map 8.1). None of its numerous participants knew the full extent of this network's reach, for it was largely a "relay trade" in which goods were passed down the line, changing hands many times before reaching their final destination. Nonetheless, the Silk Roads provide a certain unity and coherence to Eurasian history alongside the distinct stories of its separate civilizations and peoples (see Map 8.1).

Map 8.1 The Silk Roads
For 2,000 years, goods, ideas, technologies, and diseases made their way across Eurasia on the several routes of the Silk Roads.

The Growth of the Silk Roads

■ Change
What lay behind the emergence of Silk Road commerce, and what kept it going for so many centuries?

The beginnings of the Silk Roads lay in both geography and history. As a geographic unit, Eurasia is often divided into inner and outer zones that represent quite different environments. Outer Eurasia consists of relatively warm, well-watered areas, suitable for agriculture, which provided the setting for the great civilizations of China, India, the Middle East, and the Mediterranean. Inner Eurasia, the lands of eastern Russia and Central Asia, lies farther north and has a harsher and drier climate, much of it not conducive to agriculture. Long inhabited by pastoral peoples herding their animals from horseback, the people of this region had for centuries traded with and raided their agricultural neighbors to the south. Products of the forest and of semi-arid northern grasslands known as the steppes—such as hides, furs, livestock, wool, and amber—were exchanged for the agricultural products and manufactured goods of adjacent civilizations. The movement of pastoral peoples for thousands of years also served to diffuse Indo-European languages, bronze metallurgy, horse-based technologies, and more all across Eurasia.

The construction of the classical civilizations and their imperial states during the last five centuries B.C.E. added another element to these earlier Eurasian connections. From the south, the Persian Empire invaded the territory of pastoral peoples in present-day Turkmenistan and Uzbekistan. From the west, Alexander the Great's empire stretched well into Central Asia. From the east, China's Han dynasty extended its authority westward, seeking to control the nomadic Xiongnu and to gain access to the powerful "heavenly horses" that were so important to Chinese military forces. By the early centuries of the Common Era, indirect trading connections, often brokered by pastoral peoples, linked the classical civilizations in a network of transcontinental exchange.

Silk Road trading networks prospered most when large and powerful states provided security for merchants and travelers. Such conditions prevailed during the classical era when the Roman and Chinese empires anchored long-distance commerce at the western and eastern ends of Eurasia. Silk Road trade flourished again during the seventh and eighth centuries C.E. as the Byzantine Empire, the Muslim Abbasid dynasty, and Tang dynasty China created an almost continuous belt of strong states across Eurasia. In the thirteenth and fourteenth centuries, the Mongol Empire briefly encompassed almost the entire route of the Silk Roads in a single state, giving a renewed vitality to long-distance trade.

Goods in Transit

During such times especially, a vast array of goods (detailed in the following Snapshot) made their way across the Silk Roads, often carried in large camel caravans that traversed the harsh and dangerous steppes, deserts, and oases of Central Asia. In high demand and hard to find, most of these goods were luxury products, destined for an elite and wealthy market, rather than staple goods, for only readily moved

Snapshot	Economic Exchange along the Silk Roads	
Region	**Products Contributed to Silk Road Commerce**	
China	silk, bamboo, mirrors, gunpowder, paper, rhubarb, ginger, lacquerware, chrysanthemums	
Forest lands of Siberia and grasslands of Central Asia	furs, walrus tusks, amber, livestock, horses, falcons, hides, copper vessels, tents, saddles, slaves	
India	cotton, herbal medicine, precious stones, spices	
Middle East	dates, nuts, almonds, dried fruit, dyes, lapis lazuli, swords	
Mediterranean basin	gold coins, glassware, glazes, grapevines, jewelry, artworks, perfume, wool and linen textiles, olive oil	

commodities of great value could compensate for the high costs of transportation across such long and forbidding distances.

Of all these luxury goods, it was silk that came to symbolize this Eurasian exchange system. When China held a monopoly on silk-producing technology, this precious fabric moved generally from east to west. The demand for silk as well as cotton textiles from India was so great in the Roman Empire that various Roman writers were appalled at the drain of resources that it represented. They also were outraged at the moral impact of wearing revealing silk garments. "I can see clothes of silk," lamented Seneca the Younger in the first century C.E., "if materials that do not hide the body, nor even one's decency, can be called clothes.…Wretched flocks of maids labour so that the adulteress may be visible through her thin dress, so that her husband has no more acquaintance than any outsider or foreigner with his wife's body."[2] By the sixth century C.E., however, the knowledge and technology for producing raw silk had spread beyond China. An old Chinese story attributes it to a Chinese princess who smuggled out silkworms in her turban when she was married off to a Central Asian ruler. In a European version of the tale, Christian monks living in China did the deed by hiding some silkworms in a bamboo cane, an act of industrial espionage that allowed an independent silk-producing and silk-weaving industry to take hold in the Byzantine Empire. However it happened, Koreans, Japanese, Indians, and Persians likewise learned how to produce this precious fabric.

As the supply of silk increased, its many varieties circulated even more extensively across Eurasian trade routes. In Central Asia, silk was used as currency and as a means of accumulating wealth. In both China and the Byzantine Empire, silk became a symbol of high status, and governments passed laws that restricted silk clothing to members of the elite. Furthermore, silk became associated with the sacred in the expanding world religions of Buddhism and Christianity. Chinese Buddhist pilgrims who made their way to India seeking religious texts and relics took with them large quantities of silk as gifts to the monasteries they visited.

■ Significance
What made silk such a highly desired commodity across Eurasia?

Buddhist monks in China received purple silk robes from Tang dynasty emperors as a sign of high honor. In the world of Christendom, silk wall hangings, altar covers, and vestments became highly prestigious signs of devotion and piety. Because no independent silk industry developed in Western Europe until the twelfth century C.E., a considerable market developed for silks imported from the Islamic world. Ironically, the splendor of Christian churches depended in part on Islamic trading networks and on silks manufactured in the Muslim world. Some of those silks were even inscribed with passages in Arabic from the Quran, unbeknownst to their European buyers.[3]

■ **Connection**
What were the major economic, social, and cultural consequences of Silk Road commerce?

Compared to contemporary global commerce, the volume of trade on the Silk Roads was small, and its focus on luxury goods limited its direct impact on most people. Nonetheless, it had important economic and social consequences. Peasants in the Yangzi River delta of southern China sometimes gave up the cultivation of food crops, choosing to focus instead on producing silk, paper, porcelain, lacquerware, or iron tools, much of which was destined for the markets of the Silk Roads. In this way, the impact of long-distance trade trickled down to affect the lives of ordinary farmers. Furthermore, favorably placed individuals could benefit immensely from long-distance trade. The twelfth-century Persian merchant Ramisht made a personal fortune from his long-distance trading business and with his profits purchased an enormously expensive silk covering for the Kaaba, the central shrine of Islam in Mecca.[4]

Cultures in Transit

■ **Change**
What accounted for the spread of Buddhism along the Silk Roads?

More important even than the economic impact of the Silk Roads was their role as a conduit of culture. Buddhism in particular, a cultural product of Indian civilization, spread widely throughout Central and East Asia, owing much to the activities of merchants along the Silk Roads. From its beginnings in India during the sixth century B.C.E., Buddhism had appealed to merchants, who preferred its universal message to that of a Brahmin-dominated Hinduism that privileged the higher castes. Indian traders and Buddhist monks, sometimes supported by rulers such as Ashoka, brought the new religion to the trans-Eurasian trade routes. To the west, Persian Zoroastrianism largely blocked the spread of Buddhism, but in the oasis cities of Central Asia, such as Merv, Samarkand, Khotan, and Dunhuang, Buddhism quickly took hold. By the first century B.C.E., many of the inhabitants of these towns had converted to Buddhism, and foreign merchant communities soon introduced it to northern China as well.[5]

Conversion to Buddhism in the oasis cities was a voluntary process, without the pressure of conquest or foreign rule. Dependent on long-distance trade, the inhabitants and rulers of those sophisticated and prosperous cities found in Buddhism a link to the larger, wealthy, and prestigious civilization of India. Well-to-do Buddhist merchants could earn religious merit by building monasteries and supporting monks. The monasteries in turn provided convenient and culturally familiar places of rest and resupply for merchants making the long and arduous trek across Central Asia. Many of these cities became cosmopolitan centers of learning and commerce. Scholars have found thousands of Buddhist texts in the city of Dunhuang, where several branches of the Silk Roads joined to enter western China, together with hundreds of cave temples, lavishly decorated with murals and statues.

Outside of the oasis communities, Buddhism progressed only slowly among pastoral peoples of Central Asia. The absence of a written language was an obstacle to the penetration of a highly literate religion, and their nomadic ways made the founding of monasteries, so important to Buddhism, quite difficult. But as pastoralists became involved in long-distance trade or came to rule settled agricultural peoples, Buddhism seemed more attractive. The nomadic Jie people, who controlled much of northern China after the collapse of the Han dynasty, are a case in point. Their ruler in the early fourth century C.E., Shi Le, became acquainted with a Buddhist monk called Fotudeng, who had traveled widely on the Silk Roads. The monk's reputation as a miracle worker, a rainmaker, and a fortune-teller and his skills as a military strategist cemented a personal relationship with Shi Le and led to the conversions of thousands and the construction of hundreds of Buddhist temples. In China itself, Buddhism remained for many centuries a religion of foreign merchants or foreign rulers. Only slowly did it become popular among the Chinese themselves, a process examined more closely in Chapter 9.

As Buddhism spread across the Silk Roads from India to Central Asia, China, and beyond, it also changed. The original faith had shunned the material world, but Buddhist monasteries in the rich oasis towns of the Silk Roads found themselves very much involved in secular affairs. Some of them became quite wealthy, receiving gifts from well-to-do merchants, artisans, and local rulers. The begging bowls of the monks became a symbol rather than a daily activity. Sculptures and murals in the monasteries depicted musicians and acrobats, women applying makeup, and even drinking parties.[6]

Doctrines changed as well. It was the more devotional Mahayana form of Buddhism (see Chapter 5)—featuring the Buddha as a deity, numerous bodhisattvas, an emphasis on compassion, and the possibility of earning merit—that flourished on the Silk Roads, rather than the more austere psychological teachings of the original Buddha. Moreover, Buddhism picked up elements of other cultures

Dunhuang
Located in western China at a critical junction of the Silk Road trading network, Dunhuang was also a center of Buddhist learning, painting, and sculpture as that religion made its way from India to China and beyond. In some 492 caves, a remarkable gallery of Buddhist art has been preserved. These images of Buddhist deities and heavenly beings date from the sixth century C.E. (© Benoy K. Behl)

while in transit on the Silk Roads. In the area northwest of India that had been influenced by the invasions of Alexander the Great, statues of the Buddha reveal distinctly Greek influences. The Greco-Roman mythological figure of Herakles, the son of Zeus and associated with great strength, courage, masculinity, and sexual prowess, was used to represent Vajrapani, one of the divine protectors of the Buddha. In a similar way, the gods of many peoples along the Silk Roads were incorporated into Buddhist practice as bodhisattvas.

Disease in Transit

■ Connection
What was the impact of disease along the Silk Roads?

Beyond goods and cultures, diseases too traveled the trade routes of Eurasia, and with devastating consequences.[7] Each of the major population centers of the Afro-Eurasian world had developed characteristic disease patterns, mechanisms for dealing with them, and in some cases immunity to them. But when contact among human communities occurred, people were exposed to unfamiliar diseases for which they had little immunity or few effective methods of coping. An early example involved Athens, which in 430–429 B.C.E. was suddenly afflicted by a new and still unidentified infectious disease that had entered Greece via seaborne trade from Egypt, killing perhaps 25 percent of its army and permanently weakening the city-state.

Even more widespread diseases affected the Roman Empire and Han dynasty China during the classical era as the Silk Roads promoted contact all across Eurasia. Smallpox and measles devastated the populations of both empires, contributing to their political collapse. Paradoxically, these disasters may well have strengthened the appeal of Christianity in Europe and Buddhism in China, for both of them offered compassion in the face of immense suffering.

Again in the period between 534 and 750 C.E., intermittent outbreaks of bubonic plague ravaged the coastal areas of the Mediterranean Sea as the black rats that carried the disease arrived via the seaborne trade with India, where they originally lived. What followed was catastrophic. Constantinople, the capital city of the Byzantine Empire, lost some 10,000 people per day during a forty-day period in 534 C.E., according to a contemporary historian. Disease played an important role in preventing Byzantium from reintegrating Italy into its version of a renewed Roman Empire encompassing the Mediterranean basin. The repeated recurrence of the disease over the next several centuries also weakened the ability of Christendom to resist the Muslim armies that poured out of Arabia in the seventh century C.E.

The most well-known dissemination of disease was associated with the Mongol Empire, which briefly unified much of the Eurasian landmass during the thirteenth and fourteenth centuries C.E. (see Chapter 12). That era of intensified interaction facilitated the spread of the Black Death—identified variously with the bubonic plague, anthrax, or a package of epidemic diseases—from China to Europe. Its consequences were enormous. Between 1346 and 1350, about one-third of the population of Europe perished from the plague. "A dead man," wrote the Italian writer Boccaccio, "was then of no more account than a dead goat."[8] Despite the terrible human toll, some among the living benefited. Tenant farmers and urban workers, now in short supply, could demand higher wages or better terms. Some landowning nobles, on the other hand, were badly hurt as the price of their grains dropped and the demands of their dependents grew.

A similar death toll afflicted China and parts of the Islamic world. The Central Asian steppes, home to many nomadic peoples including the Mongols, also suffered terribly, undermining Mongol rule and permanently altering the balance between pastoral and agricultural peoples to the advantage of settled farmers. In these and many other ways, disease carried by long-distance trade shaped the lives of millions and altered their historical development.

In the long run of world history, the exchange of diseases gave Europeans a certain advantage when they confronted the peoples of the Western Hemisphere after 1500. Exposure over time had provided them with some degree of immunity to Eurasian diseases. In the Americas, however, the absence of domesticated animals, the less intense interaction among major centers of population, and their isolation from the Eastern Hemisphere ensured that native peoples had little defense against the diseases of Europe and Africa. Thus, when their societies were suddenly invaded by Europeans from across the Atlantic, they perished in appalling numbers. Such was the long-term outcome of the very different histories of the two hemispheres.

Sea Roads: Exchange across the Indian Ocean

If the Silk Roads linked Eurasian societies by land, sea-based trade routes likewise connected distant peoples all across the Eastern Hemisphere. Since the days of the Phoenicians, Greeks, and Romans, the Mediterranean Sea had been an avenue of maritime commerce throughout the region, a pattern that continued during the postclassical era. The Italian city of Venice, for example, emerged by 1000 C.E. as a major center of commerce, with its ships and merchants active in the Mediterranean and Black seas as well as on the Atlantic coast. Much of its wealth derived from control of expensive and profitable imported goods from Asia, many of which came up the Red Sea through the Egyptian port of Alexandria. There Venetian merchants picked up those goods and resold them throughout the Mediterranean basin. This type of transregional exchange linked the maritime commerce of the Mediterranean Sea to the much larger and more extensive network of seaborne trade in the Indian Ocean basin.

Until the creation of a genuinely global oceanic system of trade after 1500, the Indian Ocean represented the world's largest sea-based system of communication and exchange, stretching from southern China to eastern Africa (see Map 8.2). Like the Silk Roads, oceanic trade also grew out of the vast environmental and cultural diversities of the region. The desire for various goods not available at home—such as porcelain from China, spices from the islands of Southeast Asia, cotton goods and pepper from India, ivory and gold from the African coast—provided the incentive for Indian Ocean commerce. Transportation costs were lower on the Sea Roads

■ **Comparison**
How did the operation of the Indian Ocean trading network differ from that of the Silk Roads?

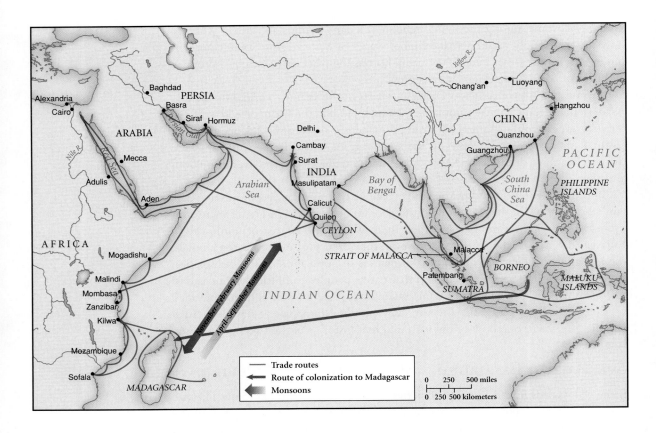

Map 8.2 The Sea Roads
Paralleling the Silk Road trading network, a sea-based commerce in the Indian Ocean basin connected the many peoples between China and East Africa.

than on the Silk Roads, because ships could accommodate larger and heavier cargoes than camels. This meant that the Sea Roads could eventually carry more bulk goods and products destined for a mass market—textiles, pepper, timber, rice, sugar, wheat—whereas the Silk Roads were limited largely to luxury goods for the few.

What made Indian Ocean commerce possible were the *monsoons*, alternating wind currents that blew predictably eastward during the summer months and westward during the winter. An understanding of monsoons and a gradually accumulating technology of shipbuilding and oceanic navigation drew on the ingenuity of many peoples—Chinese, Malays, Indians, Arabs, Swahilis, and others. Collectively they made "an interlocked human world joined by the common highway of the Indian Ocean."[9]

But this world of Indian Ocean commerce did not occur between entire regions and certainly not between "countries," even though historians sometimes write about India, Indonesia, Southeast Asia, or East Africa as a matter of shorthand or convenience. It operated rather across an "archipelago of towns" whose merchants often had more in common with one another than with the people of their own hinterlands.[10] It was these urban centers, strung out around the entire Indian Ocean basin, that provided the nodes of this widespread commercial network.

Weaving the Web of an Indian Ocean World

The world of Indian Ocean commerce was long in the making, dating back to the time of the First Civilizations. Seaborne trade via the Persian Gulf between ancient Mesopotamia and the Indus Valley civilization is reflected in archeological finds in both places. Some scholars believe that the still-undeciphered Indian writing system may have been stimulated by Sumerian cuneiform. The ancient Egyptians, and later the Phoenicians, likewise traded down the Red Sea, exchanging their manufactured goods for gold, ivory, frankincense, and slaves from the coasts of Ethiopia, Somalia, and southern Arabia. These ventures mostly hugged the coast and took place over short distances. An exception was Malay sailors; speaking Austronesian languages, they jumped off from the islands of present-day Indonesia during the first millennium B.C.E. and made their way in double-outrigger canoes across thousands of miles of open ocean to the East African island of Madagascar. There they introduced their language and their crops. Those food crops—bananas, coconuts, and cocoyams—soon spread to the mainland, where they greatly enriched the diets of African peoples. Also spread to the mainland was a Malayo-Polynesian xylophone, which is still played in parts of Africa today.

The tempo of Indian Ocean commerce picked up in the era of classical civilizations during the early centuries of the Common Era, as mariners learned how to ride the monsoons. Merchants from the Roman Empire, mostly Greeks, Syrians, and Jews, established settlements in southern India and along the East African coast. The introduction of Christianity into both Ethiopia and Kerala (in southern India) testifies to the long-term cultural impact of that trade. In the eastern Indian Ocean and the South China Sea, Chinese and Southeast Asian merchants likewise generated a growing commerce, and by 100 C.E. Chinese traders had reached India.

The fulcrum of this growing commercial network lay in India itself. Its ports bulged with goods from both west and east, as illustrated in the Snapshot. Its merchants were in touch with Southeast Asia by the first century C.E., and settled communities of Indian traders appeared throughout the Indian Ocean basin and as far away as

Snapshot	**Economic Exchange in the Indian Ocean Basin**
Region	**Products Contributed to Indian Ocean Commerce**
Mediterranean basin	ceramics, glassware, wine, gold, olive oil
East Africa	ivory, gold, iron goods, slaves, tortoiseshells, quartz, leopard skins
Arabia	frankincense, myrrh, perfumes
India	grain, ivory, precious stones, cotton textiles, spices, timber, tortoiseshells
Southeast Asia	tin, sandlewood, cloves, nutmeg, mace
China	silks, porcelain, tea

Alexandria in Egypt. Indian cultural practices, such as Hinduism and Buddhism, as well as South Asian political ideas began to take root in Southeast Asia.

■ Change
What lay behind the flourishing of Indian Ocean commerce in the postclassical millennium?

In the era of third-wave civilizations between 500 and 1500, two major processes changed the landscape of the Afro-Eurasian world and wove the web of Indian Ocean exchange even more densely than before. One was the economic and political revival of China, some four centuries after the collapse of the Han dynasty. Especially during the Tang and Song dynasties (618–1279), China reestablished an effective and unified state, which actively encouraged maritime trade. Furthermore, the impressive growth of the Chinese economy sent Chinese products pouring into the circuits of Indian Ocean commerce, while providing a vast and attractive market for Indian and Southeast Asian goods. Chinese technological innovations, such as larger ships and the magnetic compass, likewise added to the momentum of commercial growth.

A second transformation in the world of Indian Ocean commerce involved the sudden rise of Islam in the seventh century C.E. and its subsequent spread across much of the Afro-Eurasian world (see Chapter 11). Unlike Confucian culture, which was quite suspicious of merchants, Islam was friendly to commercial life; the Prophet Muhammad himself had been a trader. The creation of an Arab Empire, stretching from the Atlantic Ocean through the Mediterranean basin and all the way to India, brought together in a single political system an immense range of economies and cultural traditions and provided a vast arena for the energies of Muslim traders.

Those energies greatly intensified commercial activity in the Indian Ocean basin in many ways. Middle Eastern gold and silver flowed into southern India to purchase pepper, pearls, textiles, and gemstones. Muslim merchants and sailors, as well as Jews and Christians living within the Islamic world, established communities of traders from East Africa to the southern China coast. Efforts to reclaim wasteland in Mesopotamia to produce sugar and dates for export stimulated a slave trade from East Africa, which landed thousands of Africans in southern Iraq to work on plantations and in salt mines under horrendous conditions. A massive fifteen-year revolt (868–883) among these slaves badly disrupted the Islamic Abbasid Empire before it was brutally crushed.[11]

Beyond these specific outcomes, the expansion of Islam gave rise to an international maritime culture by 1000, shared by individuals living in the widely separated port cities around the Indian Ocean. The immense prestige, power, and prosperity of the Islamic world stimulated widespread conversion, which in turn facilitated commercial transactions. Even those who did not convert to Islam, such as Buddhist rulers in Burma, nonetheless regarded it as commercially useful to assume Muslim names.[12] Thus was created "a maritime Silk Road ... a commercial and informational network of unparalleled proportions."[13] After 1000, the culture of this network was increasingly Islamic.

Sea Roads as a Catalyst for Change: Southeast Asia and Srivijaya

■ Connection
What is the relationship between the rise of Srivijaya and the world of Indian Ocean commerce?

Oceanic commerce transformed all of its participants in one way or another, but nowhere more so than in Southeast Asia and East Africa, at opposite ends of the

Indian Ocean network. In both regions, trade stimulated political change as ambitious or aspiring rulers used the wealth derived from commerce to construct larger and more centrally governed states or cities. Both areas likewise experienced cultural change as local people were attracted to foreign religious ideas from Hindu, Buddhist, or Islamic sources. As on the Silk Roads, trade was a conduit for culture.

Located between the major civilizations of China and India, Southeast Asia was situated by geography to play an important role in the evolving world of Indian Ocean commerce. When Malay sailors, long active in the waters around Southeast Asia, opened an all-sea route between India and China through the Straits of Malacca around 350 C.E., the many small ports along the Malay Peninsula and the coast of Sumatra began to compete intensely to attract the growing number of traders and travelers making their way through the straits. From this competition emerged the Malay kingdom of Srivijaya, which dominated this critical choke point of Indian Ocean trade from 670 to 1025. A number of factors—Srivijaya's plentiful supply of gold; its access to the source of highly sought-after spices, such as cloves, nutmeg, and mace; and the taxes levied on passing ships—provided resources to attract supporters, to fund an embryonic bureaucracy, and to create the military and naval forces that brought some security to the area.

Srivijaya monarchs drew upon local beliefs that chiefs possessed magical powers and were responsible for the prosperity of their people, but they also made use of imported Indian political ideas and Buddhist religious concepts, which had been brought to the area by a multitude of Indian merchants and teachers. Some Indians were employed as advisers, clerks, or officials to Srivijaya rulers, who began to assign Sanskrit titles to their subordinates. The capital city of Palembang was a cosmopolitan place, where even the parrots were said to speak four languages. Buddhism in particular provided a "higher level of magic" for rulers as well as the prestige of association with Indian civilization.[14] These rulers sponsored the creation of images of the Buddha and various bodhisattvas whose faces resembled those of deceased kings and were inscribed with traditional curses against anyone who would destroy them. Srivijaya grew into a major center of Buddhist observance and teaching, attracting thousands of monks and students from throughout the Buddhist world. The seventh-century Chinese monk Yi Jing was so impressed that he advised Buddhist monks headed for India to study first in Srivijaya for several years.[15]

Srivijaya was not the only part of Southeast Asia to be influenced by Indian culture. The Sailendra kingdom in central Java, an agriculturally rich region closely allied with Srivijaya, mounted a massive building program between the eighth and tenth centuries featuring Hindu temples and Buddhist monuments. The most famous, known as Borobudur, is an enormous mountain-shaped structure of ten levels, with a three-mile walkway and elaborate carvings illustrating the spiritual journey from ignorance and illusion to full enlightenment. The largest Buddhist monument anywhere in the world, it is nonetheless a distinctly Javanese creation, whose carved figures have Javanese features and whose scenes are clearly set in Java, not India. Its

Southeast Asia ca. 1200 C.E.

Borobudur
This huge Buddhist monument, constructed probably in the ninth century C.E., was subsequently abandoned and covered with layers of volcanic ash and vegetation as Java came under Islamic influence. It was rediscovered by British colonial authorities in the early nineteenth century and has undergone several restorations over the past two centuries. Although Indonesia is a largely Muslim country, its Buddhist minority (about 1 percent of the country's population) still celebrates the Buddha's birthday at Borobudur. (Robert Harding World Imagery/Alamy)

shape resonated with an ancient Southeast Asian veneration of mountains as sacred places and the abode of ancestral spirits. Borobudur represents the process of Buddhism becoming culturally grounded in a new place.

Temple complexes such as Borobudur and others constructed in Burma, in the Khmer state of Angkor, and elsewhere illustrate vividly the penetration of Indian culture—in both Hindu and Buddhist forms—throughout mainland and island Southeast Asia. Some scholars have spoken of the "Indianization" of the region, similar perhaps to the earlier spread of Greek culture within the empires of Alexander the Great and Rome. In the case of Southeast Asia, however, no imperial control accompanied Indian cultural influence. It was a matter of voluntary borrowing by independent societies that found Hindu or Buddhist ideas useful and were free to adapt those ideas to their own needs and cultures. Somewhat later, but in much the same way, Islam too began to penetrate Southeast Asia, as the world of Indian Ocean commerce brought yet another religious tradition to the region.

■ **Connection**
What was the role of Swahili civilization in the world of Indian Ocean commerce?

Sea Roads as a Catalyst for Change: East Africa and Swahili Civilization

On the other side of the Indian Ocean, the transformative processes of long-distance trade were likewise at work, giving rise to an East African civilization known as

Swahili. Emerging in the eighth century C.E., this civilization took shape as a set of commercial city-states stretching all along the East African coast, from present-day Somalia to Mozambique.

The earlier ancestors of the Swahili lived in small farming and fishing communities, spoke Bantu languages, and traded with the Arabian, Greek, and Roman merchants who occasionally visited the coast during the classical era. But what stimulated the growth of Swahili cities was the far more extensive commercial life of the western Indian Ocean following the rise of Islam. As in Southeast Asia, local people and aspiring rulers found opportunity for wealth and power in the growing demand for East African products associated with an expanding Indian Ocean commerce. Gold, ivory, quartz, leopard skins, and sometimes slaves acquired from interior societies, as well as iron and processed timber manufactured along the coast, found a ready market in Arabia, Persia, India, and beyond. In response to such opportunities, an African merchant class developed, villages turned into sizable towns, and clan chiefs became kings. A new civilization was in the making.

Between 1000 and 1500, that civilization flourished along the coast, and it was a very different kind of society than the farming and pastoral cultures of the East African interior. It was thoroughly urban, centered in cities of 15,000 to 18,000 people, such as Lamu, Mombasa, Kilwa, Sofala, and many others. Like the city-states of ancient Greece, each Swahili city was politically independent, generally governed by its own king, and in sharp competition with other cities. No imperial system or larger territorial states unified the world of Swahili civilization. Nor did any of them control a critical choke point of trade, as Srivijaya did for the Straits of Malacca. Swahili cities were commercial centers that accumulated goods from the interior and exchanged them for the products of distant civilizations, such as Chinese porcelain and silk, Persian rugs, and Indian cottons. While the transoceanic journeys occurred largely in Arab vessels, Swahili craft navigated the coastal waterways, concentrating goods for shipment abroad. Swahili cities were class-stratified societies with sharp distinctions between a mercantile elite and commoners.

Culturally as well as economically, Swahili civilization participated in the larger Indian Ocean world. Arab, Indian, and perhaps Persian merchants were welcome visitors, and some settled permanently. Many ruling families of Swahili cities claimed Arab or Persian origins as a way of bolstering their prestige, even while they dined off Chinese porcelain and dressed in Indian cottons. The Swahili language, widely spoken in East Africa today, was grammatically an African tongue within the larger Bantu family of languages, but it was written in Arabic script and contained a number of Arabic loan words. A small bronze lion found in the Swahili city of Shanga and dating to about 1100 illustrates the distinctly cosmopolitan character of Swahili culture. It depicted a clearly African lion, but it was created in a distinctly Indian artistic style and was made from melted-down Chinese copper coins.[16]

Most important, however, Swahili civilization rapidly became Islamic. Introduced by Arab traders, Islam was voluntarily and widely adopted

The Swahili Coast of East Africa

within the Swahili world. Like Buddhism in Southeast Asia, Islam linked Swahili cities to the larger Indian Ocean world. These East African cities were soon dotted with substantial mosques. When Ibn Battuta, a widely traveled Arab scholar, merchant, and public official, visited the Swahili coast in the early fourteenth century, he found altogether Muslim societies in which religious leaders often spoke Arabic, and all were eager to welcome a learned visitor from the heartland of Islam. But these were African Muslims, not colonies of transplanted Arabs. "The rulers, scholars, officials, and big merchants as well as the port workers, farmers, craftsmen, and slaves, were dark-skinned people speaking African tongues in everyday life."[17]

Islam sharply divided the Swahili cities from their African neighbors to the west, for neither the new religion nor Swahili culture penetrated much beyond the coast until the nineteenth century. Economically, however, the coastal cities acted as intermediaries between the interior producers of valued goods and the Arab merchants who carried them to distant markets. Particularly in the southern reaches of the Swahili world, this relationship extended the impact of Indian Ocean trade well into the African interior. Hundreds of miles inland, between the Zambezi and Limpopo rivers, lay rich sources of gold, much in demand on the Swahili coast. The emergence of a powerful state, known as Great Zimbabwe, seems clearly connected to the growing trade in gold to the coast as well as to the wealth embodied in its large herds of cattle. At its peak between 1250 and 1350, Great Zimbabwe had the resources and the labor power to construct huge stone enclosures entirely without mortar, with walls sixteen feet thick and thirty-two feet tall. "[It] must have been an astonishing sight," writes a recent scholar, "for the subordinate chiefs and kings who would have come there to seek favors at court."[18] Here in the interior of southeastern Africa lay yet another example of the reach and transforming power of Indian Ocean commerce.

Sand Roads: Exchange across the Sahara

In addition to the Silk Roads and the Sea Roads, another important pattern of long-distance trade — this one across the vast reaches of the Sahara — linked North Africa and the Mediterranean world with the land and peoples of interior West Africa. Like the others, these Sand Road commercial networks had a transforming impact, stimulating and enriching West African civilization and connecting it to larger patterns of world history during the postclassical era.

Commercial Beginnings in West Africa

Trans-African trade, like the commerce of the Silk Roads and the Sea Roads, was rooted in environmental variation. The North African coastal regions, long part of Roman or later Arab empires, generated cloth, glassware, weapons, books, and other manufactured goods. The great Sahara held deposits of copper and especially salt, while its oases produced sweet and nutritious dates. Although the sparse populations of the desert were largely pastoral and nomadic, farther south lived agricultural peoples who grew a variety of crops, produced their own textiles and metal products, and mined a considerable amount of gold. The agricultural regions of sub-Saharan Africa are normally divided into two ecological zones: the savanna grasslands immediately south of the Sahara, which produced grain crops such as millet and sorghum; and the forest areas farther south, where root and tree crops such as yams and kola nuts predominated. These quite varied environments provided the economic incentive for the exchange of goods.

The earliest long-distance trade within this huge region was not across the Sahara at all, but largely among the agricultural peoples themselves in the area later known to Arabs as the Sudan, or "the land of black people." During the first millennium B.C.E., the peoples of Sudanic West Africa began to exchange metal goods, cotton textiles, gold, and various food products across considerable distances using boats along the Niger River and donkeys overland. On the basis of this trade, a number of independent urban clusters emerged by the early centuries of the Common Era. The most well known was Jenne-jeno, which was located at a crucial point on the Niger River where goods were transshipped from boat to donkey or vice versa.[19] This was the Niger Valley civilization, described in Chapter 7.

Gold, Salt, and Slaves: Trade and Empire in West Africa

A major turning point in African commercial life occurred with the introduction of the camel to North Africa and the Sahara in the early centuries of the Common Era. This remarkable animal, which could go for ten days without water, finally made possible the long trek across the Sahara. It was camel-owning dwellers of desert oases who initiated regular trans-Saharan commerce by 300 to 400 C.E. Several centuries later, North African Arabs, now bearing the new religion of Islam, also organized caravans across the desert.

■ Connections
What changes did trans-Saharan trade bring to West Africa?

What they sought, above all else, was gold, which was found in some abundance in the border areas straddling the grasslands and the forests of West Africa. From its source, it was transported by donkey to transshipment points on the southern edge of the Sahara and then transferred to camels for the long journey north across the desert. African ivory, kola nuts, and slaves were likewise in considerable demand in the desert, the Mediterranean basin, and beyond. In return, the peoples of the Sudan received horses, cloth, dates, various manufactured goods, and especially salt from the rich deposits in the Sahara.

Thus the Sahara was no longer simply a barrier to commerce and cross-cultural interaction; it quickly became a major international trade route that fostered new relationships among distant peoples. The caravans that made the desert crossing could be huge, with as many as 5,000 camels and hundreds of people. Traveling mostly at night to avoid the daytime heat, the journey might take up to seventy days, covering fifteen to twenty-five miles per day. For well over 1,000 years, such caravans traversed the desert, linking the interior of West Africa with lands and people far to the north.

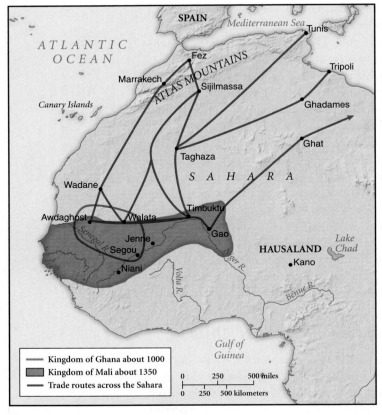

Map 8.3 The Sand Roads

For a thousand years or more, the Sahara was an ocean of sand that linked the interior of West Africa with the world of North Africa and the Mediterranean but separated them as well.

As in Southeast Asia and East Africa, long-distance trade across the Sahara provided both incentive and resources for the construction of new and larger political structures. It was the peoples of the western and central Sudan, living between the forests and the desert, who were in the best position to take advantage of these new opportunities. Between roughly 500 and 1600, they constructed a series of states, empires, and city-states that reached from the Atlantic coast to Lake Chad, including Ghana, Mali, Songhay, Kanem, and the city-states of the Hausa people (see Map 8.3).

All of them were monarchies with elaborate court life and varying degrees of administrative complexity and military forces at their disposal. All drew upon the wealth of trans-Saharan trade, taxing the merchants who conducted it. In the wider world, these states soon acquired a reputation for great riches. An Arab traveler in the tenth century C.E. described the ruler of Ghana as "the wealthiest king on the face of the earth because of his treasures and stocks of gold."[20] At its high point in the fourteenth century, Mali's rulers monopolized the import of strategic goods such as horses and metals; levied duties on salt, copper, and other merchandise; and reserved large nuggets of gold for themselves while permitting the free export of gold dust.

As in all civilizations, slavery found a place in West Africa. Early on, most slaves had been women, working as domestic servants and concubines. As West African civilization crystallized, however, male slaves were put to work as state officials, porters, craftsmen, miners harvesting salt from desert deposits, and especially agricultural laborers producing for the royal granaries on large estates or plantations. Most came from non-Islamic and stateless societies farther south, which were raided during the dry season by cavalry-based forces of West African states, though some white slave women from the eastern Mediterranean also made an appearance in Mali. A song in honor of one eleventh-century ruler of Kanem boasted of his slave-raiding achievements.

> The best you took (and sent home) as the first fruits of battle. The children crying on their mothers you snatched away from their mothers. You took the slave wife from a slave, and set them in lands far removed from one another.[21]

Most of these slaves were used within this emerging West African civilization, but a trade in slaves also developed across the Sahara. Between 1100 and 1400, perhaps 5,500 slaves per year made the perilous trek across the desert. When the famous Muslim traveler Ibn Battuta visited Mali in the fourteenth century, he returned home to Morocco with a caravan that included 600 female slaves, who walked across the burning desert, while he rode a camel. Most such slaves were put to work in the homes of the wealthy in Islamic North Africa, but a small number were sold in Europe. Those who arrived in Ireland, for example, were termed "blue men." Far more significant in Europe were slaves from the Slavic-speaking regions along the northern coast of the Black Sea. They were so numerous that the word "slave" in many European languages derives from the term "Slav." Not until the Atlantic slave trade developed after the 1440s did Africans become the major source of slaves for Europeans.

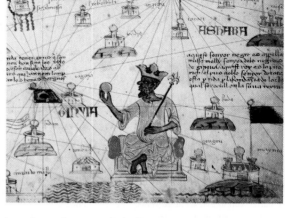

The Gold of Mali
This detail from the *Catalan Atlas*, a series of maps issued in Spain in 1375, illustrates Mali's reputation in Europe for its great wealth in gold. This reputation later propelled Portuguese voyages down the west coast of Africa in search of direct access to that wealth. (Bibliothèque nationale de France)

These states of Sudanic Africa developed substantial urban and commercial centers—such as Koumbi-Saleh, Jenne, Timbuktu, Gao, Gobir, and Kano—where traders congregated and goods were exchanged. Some of these cities also became centers of manufacturing, creating finely wrought beads, iron tools, or cotton textiles, some of which entered the circuits of commerce. Visitors described them as cosmopolitan places where court officials, artisans, scholars, students, and local and foreign merchants all rubbed elbows. As in East Africa, Islam accompanied trade and became an important element in the urban culture of West Africa. The growth of long-distance trade had stimulated the development of an African civilization, which was linked to the wider networks of exchange in the Eastern Hemisphere.

An American Network: Commerce and Connection in the Western Hemisphere

Before the voyages of Columbus, the world of the Americas developed quite separately from that of the Eastern Hemisphere. Despite intriguing hints of occasional contacts, no sustained interaction between the peoples of these two great landmasses took place.[22] But if the Silk, Sea, and Sand Roads linked the diverse peoples of the Afro-Eurasian world, did a similar network of interaction join and transform the various societies of the Western Hemisphere?

Clearly, direct connections among the various civilizations and cultures of the Americas were less densely woven than in the Afro-Eurasian region. The llama and the potato, both domesticated in the Andes, never reached Mesoamerica; nor did the writing system of the Maya diffuse to Andean civilizations. The Aztecs and the

■ Comparison
In what ways did networks of interaction in the Western Hemisphere differ from those in the Eastern Hemisphere?

Incas, contemporary civilizations in the fifteenth century, had little if any direct contact with each other. The limits of these interactions owed something to the absence of horses, donkeys, camels, wheeled vehicles, and large oceangoing vessels, all of which facilitated long-distance trade and travel in Afro-Eurasia.

Geographic or environmental differences added further obstacles. The narrow bottleneck of Panama, largely covered by dense rain forests, surely inhibited contact between South and North America. Furthermore, the north/south orientation of the Americas—which required agricultural practices to move through, and adapt to, quite distinct climatic and vegetation zones—slowed the spread of agricultural products. By contrast, the east/west axis of Eurasia meant that agricultural innovations could diffuse more rapidly because they were entering roughly similar environments. Thus nothing equivalent to the long-distance trade of the Silk, Sea, or Sand Roads of the Eastern Hemisphere arose in the Americas, even though local and regional commerce flourished in many places. Nor did distinct cultural traditions such as Buddhism, Christianity, and Islam spread so widely to integrate distant peoples.

Nonetheless, scholars have discerned "a loosely interactive web stretching from the North American Great Lakes and upper Mississippi south to the Andes."[23] (See Map 8.4.) Partly, it was a matter of slowly spreading cultural elements, such as the gradual diffusion of maize from its Mesoamerican place of origin to the southwestern United States and then on to much of eastern North America as well as to much of South America in the other direction. A game played with rubber balls on an outdoor court has left traces in the Caribbean, Mexico, and northern South America. The spread of particular pottery styles and architectural conventions likewise suggests at least indirect contact over wide distances.

Commerce too played an important role in the making of this "American web." A major North American chiefdom at Cahokia, near

Map 8.4 The American Web
Transcontinental interactions within the American web were more modest than those of the Afro-Eurasian hemisphere. The most intense areas of exchange and communication occurred within the Mississippi valley, Mesoamerican, and Andean regions.

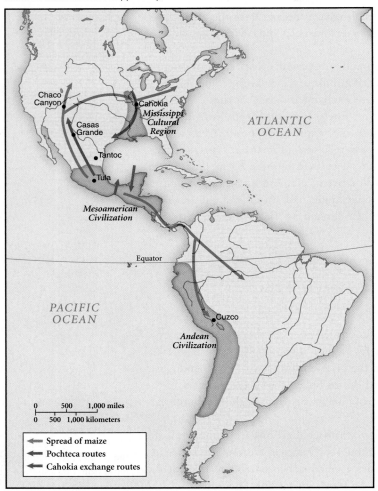

present-day St. Louis, flourished from about 900 to 1250 at the confluence of the Mississippi, Illinois, and Missouri rivers (see Chapter 7). Cahokia lay at the center of a widespread trading network that brought it shells from the Atlantic coast, copper from the Lake Superior region, buffalo hides from the Great Plains, obsidian from the Rocky Mountains, and mica from the southern Appalachian Mountains. Sturdy dugout canoes plied the rivers of the eastern woodlands, connecting their diverse but related societies. Construction in the Tantoc region of northeastern Mexico resembled the earlier building styles of Cahokia, suggesting the possibility of some interaction between the two regions.[24] Many items from Mesoamerica—copper bells, macaw feathers, tons of shells—have been found in the Chaco region of the southwestern United States, while turquoise flowed in the other direction.

Early European explorers and travelers along the Amazon and Orinoco rivers of South America reported active networks of exchange that may well have operated for many centuries. Caribbean peoples using large oceangoing canoes had long conducted an interisland trade, and the Chincha people undertook ocean-based exchange in copper, beads, and shells along the Pacific coast of Peru and Ecuador on large seagoing rafts.[25] But the most active and dense networks of communication and exchange in the Americas lay within, rather than between, the regions that housed the two great civilizations of the Western Hemisphere—Mesoamerica and the Andes.

During the classical era of Mesoamerican civilization (200–900 C.E.), both the Maya cities in the Yucatán area of Mexico and Guatemala and the huge city-state of Teotihuacán in central Mexico maintained commercial relationships with one another and throughout the region. In addition to this land-based trade, the Maya conducted a seaborne commerce, using large dugout canoes holding forty to fifty people, along both the Atlantic and Pacific coasts.[26] Although most of this trade was in luxury goods rather than basic necessities, it was critical to upholding the position and privileges of royal and noble families. Items such as cotton clothing, precious jewels, and feathers from particular birds marked the status of elite groups and served to attract followers. Controlling access to such high-prestige goods was an important motive for war among Mesoamerican states.[27] Among the Aztecs of the fifteenth century, professional merchants, known as *pochteca,* undertook large-scale trading expeditions both within and well beyond the borders of their empire, sometimes as agents for the

Inca Roads
Used for transporting goods by pack animal or sending messages by foot, the Inca road network included some 2,000 inns where travelers might find food and shelter. Messengers, operating in relay, could cover as many as 150 miles a day. Here a modern-day citizen of Peru walks along an old Inca trail road. (Loren McIntyre/lorenmcintyre.com)

state or for members of the nobility, but more often acting on their own as private businessmen.

Unlike the Aztec Empire, in which private traders largely handled the distribution of goods, economic exchange in the Andean Inca Empire during the fifteenth century was a state-run operation, and no merchant group similar to the Aztec *pochteca* emerged there. Instead, great state storehouses bulged with immense quantities of food, clothing, military supplies, blankets, construction materials, and more, all carefully recorded on *quipus* (knotted cords used to record numerical data) by a highly trained class of accountants. From these state centers, goods were transported as needed by caravans of human porters and llamas across the numerous roads and bridges of the empire. Totaling some 20,000 miles, Inca roads traversed the coastal plain and the high Andes in a north/south direction, while lateral roads linked these diverse environments and extended into the eastern rain forests and plains as well. Despite the general absence of private trade, local exchange took place at highland fairs and along the borders of the empire with groups outside the Inca state.

Reflections: Economic Globalization— Ancient and Modern

The densely connected world of the modern era, linked by ties of commerce and culture around the planet, certainly has roots in much earlier patterns. Particularly in the era of third-wave civilizations from 500 to 1500, the Silk, Sea, and Sand roads of the Afro-Eurasian world and the looser networks of the American web linked distant peoples both economically and culturally, prompted the emergence of new states, and sustained elite privileges in many ancient civilizations. In those ways, they resembled the globalized world of modern times.

In other respects, though, the networks and webs of the premodern millennium differed sharply from those of more recent centuries. By and large, most people still produced largely for their own consumption rather than for the market, and a much smaller range of goods was exchanged in the marketplaces of the world. Far fewer people then were required to sell their own labor for wages, an almost universal practice in modern economies. Because of transportation costs and technological limitations, most trade was in luxury goods rather than in necessities. In addition, the circuits of commerce were rather more limited than the truly global patterns of exchange that emerged after 1500.

Furthermore, the world economy of the modern era increasingly had a single center—industrialized Western European countries—which came to dominate much of the world both economically and politically during the nineteenth century. Though never completely equal, the economic relationships of earlier times occurred among much more equivalent units. For example, no one region dominated the complex pattern of Indian Ocean exchange, although India and China generally offered manufactured goods, while Southeast Asia and East Africa contributed agricultural products or raw materials. And with the exception of the brief Mongol control of the Silk Roads and the Inca domination of the Andes for a century, no single power exercised political control over the other major networks of world commerce.

The world of third-wave civilizations, in short, was a more balanced, multicentered world than that of the modern era. Although massive inequalities occurred within particular regions or societies, relationships among the major civilizations operated on a rather more equal basis than in the globalized world of the past several centuries. With the rise of China and India as major players in the world economy of the twenty-first century, are we perhaps returning to that earlier pattern?

Second Thoughts

What's the Significance?

Silk Roads	Srivijaya	Sand Roads
Black Death	Borobudur	Ghana, Mali, Songhay
Indian Ocean trading network	Swahili civilization	trans-Saharan slave trade
	Great Zimbabwe	American web

To assess your mastery of the material in this chapter, see the **Online Study Guide** at bedfordstmartins.com/strayer.

Big Picture Questions

1. What motivated and sustained the long-distance commerce of the Silk Roads, Sea Roads, and Sand Roads?
2. Why did the Eastern Hemisphere develop long-distance trade more extensively than did the societies of the Western Hemisphere?
3. In what ways did commercial exchange foster other changes?
4. In what ways was Afro-Eurasia a single interacting zone, and in what respects was it a vast region of separate cultures and civilizations?

Next Steps: For Further Study

Jerry Bentley, *Old World Encounters* (1993). A wonderfully succinct and engaging history of cross-cultural interaction all across Afro-Eurasia before 1500.

E. W. Bovill, *The Golden Trade of the Moors* (1970). A classic account of the trans-Saharan trade.

Rainer Buschmann, *Oceans in World History* (2007). A brief study of communication and exchange across the world's oceans.

K. N. Chaudhuri, *Trade and Civilization in the Indian Ocean* (1985). A well-regarded study that treats the Indian Ocean basin as a single region linked by both commerce and culture during the postclassical era.

Philip Curtin, *Cross-Cultural Trade in World History* (1984). Explores long-distance trade as a generator of social change on a global level.

Liu Xinru and Lynda Shaffer, *Connections across Eurasia* (2007). A brief, accessible, and up-to-date account by two major scholars of the Silk Road trading network.

Bridging World History, http://www.learner.org/channel/courses/worldhistory. Units 9 and 10 of this Web-based guide to world history provide an illustrated examination of global trade in the postclassical millennium.

For Web sites and documents related to this chapter, see **Make History** at bedfordstmartins.com/strayer.

CHAPTER NINE

China and the World

East Asian Connections

500–1300

"China will be the next superpower."[1] That was the frank assertion of an article in the British newspaper *The Guardian* in June 2006. Nor was it alone in that assessment. As the new millennium dawned, headlines with this message appeared with increasing frequency in public lectures, in newspaper and magazine articles, and in book titles all across the world. China's huge population, its booming economy, its massive trade surplus with the United States, its entry into world oil markets, its military potential, and its growing presence in global political affairs—all of this suggested that China was headed for a major role, perhaps even a dominant role, in the world of the twenty-first century. Few of these analyses, however, paused to recall that China's prominence on the world stage was hardly something new or that its nineteenth- and twentieth-century position as a "backward," weak, or dependent country was distinctly out of keeping with its long history. Is China perhaps poised to resume in the twenty-first century a much older and more powerful role in world affairs?

IN THE WORLD OF THIRD-WAVE CIVILIZATIONS, even more than during the classical era that preceded it, China cast a long shadow. Its massive and powerful civilization, widely imitated by adjacent peoples, gave rise to a China-centered "world order" encompassing most of eastern Asia.[2] China extended its borders deep into Central Asia, while its wealthy and cosmopolitan culture attracted visitors from all over Eurasia. None of its many neighbors—whether nomadic peoples to the

Chinese Astronomy: During classical and postclassical times, the impressive achievements of Chinese astronomy included the observation of sunspots, supernovae, and solar and lunar eclipses as well as the construction of elaborate star maps and astronomical devices. Since the time of the Han dynasty, armillary spheres, such as the one depicted in this seventeenth-century painting, assisted Chinese scholars in representing the position and motion of the earth, sun, moon, planets, and stars. (Courtesy of the Trustees of the British Museum) north and west or smaller peripheral states such as Tibet, Korea, Japan, and Vietnam—could escape its gravitational pull. All of them had to deal with China. Far beyond these near neighbors, China's booming economy and many technological innovations had ripple effects all across Eurasia.

Even as China so often influenced the world, it too was changed by its many interactions with non-Chinese peoples. Northern nomads—"barbarians" to the Chinese—frequently posed a military threat and on occasion even conquered and ruled parts of China. The country's growing involvement in international trade stimulated important social, cultural, and economic changes within China itself. Buddhism, a religion of Indian origin, took root in China, and, to a lesser extent, so did Christianity and Islam. In short, China's engagement with the wider world became a very significant element in a global era of accelerating connections.

The Reemergence of a Unified China

The collapse of the Han dynasty around 220 C.E. ushered in more than three centuries of political fragmentation in China and signaled the rise of powerful and locally entrenched aristocratic families. It also meant the incursion of northern nomads, many of whom learned Chinese, dressed like Chinese, married into Chinese families, and governed northern regions of the country in a Chinese fashion. Such conditions of disunity, unnatural in the eyes of many thoughtful Chinese, discredited Confucianism and opened the door to a greater acceptance of Buddhism and Daoism among the elite.

Those centuries also witnessed the beginning of Chinese migration southward toward the Yangzi River valley, a movement of people that gave southern China some 60 percent of the country's population by 1000. That movement of Chinese people, accompanied by their intensive agriculture, set in motion a vast environmental transformation, marked by the destruction of the old-growth forests that once covered much of the country and the retreat of the elephants that had inhabited those lands. Around 800 C.E., the Chinese official and writer Liu Zongyuan lamented what was happening.

> A tumbled confusion of lumber as flames on the hillside crackle
> Not even the last remaining shrubs are safeguarded from destruction
> Where once mountain torrents leapt—nothing but rutted gullies.[3]

A "Golden Age" of Chinese Achievement

■ **Change**
Why are the centuries of the Tang and Song dynasties in China sometimes referred to as a "golden age"?

Unlike the fall of the western Roman Empire, where political fragmentation proved to be a permanent condition, China regained its unity under the Sui dynasty (589–618). Its emperors solidified that unity by a vast extension of the country's canal system, stretching some 1,200 miles in length and described by one scholar as "an engineering feat without parallel in the world of its time."[4] Those canals linked northern and southern China economically and contributed much to the prosperity that followed. But the ruthlessness of Sui emperors and a futile military campaign to conquer Korea exhausted the state's resources, alienated many people, and prompted the overthrow of the dynasty.

This dynastic collapse, however, witnessed no prolonged disintegration of the Chinese state. The two dynasties that followed—the Tang (618–907) and the Song (960–1279)—built on the Sui foundations of renewed unity (see Map 9.1). Together they established patterns of Chinese life that endured into the twentieth century, despite a fifty-year period of disunity between the two dynasties.

Map 9.1 Tang and Song Dynasty China

During the postclassical millennium, China interacted extensively with its neighbors. The Tang dynasty extended Chinese control deep into Central Asia, while the Song dynasty witnessed incursions by the nomadic Jurchen people, who created the Jin Empire, which ruled parts of northern China.

Culturally, this era has long been regarded as a "golden age" of arts and literature, setting standards of excellence in poetry, landscape painting, and ceramics. Particularly during the Song dynasty, an explosion of scholarship gave rise to Neo-Confucianism, an effort to revive Confucian thinking while incorporating into it some of the insights of Buddhism and Daoism.

Politically, the Tang and Song dynasties built a state structure that endured for a thousand years. Six major ministries—personnel, finance, rites, army, justice, and public works—were accompanied by the Censorate, an agency that exercised surveillance over the rest of the government, checking on the character and competence of public officials. To staff this bureaucracy, the examination system was revived and made more elaborate, encouraged by the ability to print books for the first time in world history. Efforts to prevent cheating on the exams included searching candidates entering the examination hall and placing numbers rather than names on their papers. Schools and colleges proliferated to prepare candidates for the rigorous exams, which became a central feature of upper-class life. A leading world historian has described Tang dynasty China as "the best ordered state in the world."[5]

Selecting officials on the basis of merit represented a challenge to established aristocratic families' hold on public office. Still, a substantial percentage of official positions went to the sons of the privileged, even if they had not passed the exams. Moreover, because education and the examination system grew far more rapidly than the number of official positions, many who passed lower-level exams could not be accommodated with a bureaucratic appointment. Often, however, they were able to combine landowning and success in the examination system to maintain an immense cultural prestige and prominence in their local areas. Despite the state's periodic efforts to redistribute land in favor of the peasantry, the great families of large landowners continued to encroach on peasant plots. This has been a recurring pattern in rural China from classical times to the present.

Underlying these cultural and political achievements was an "economic revolution" that made Song dynasty China "by far the richest, most skilled, and most populous country on earth."[6] The most obvious sign of China's prosperity was its rapid growth in population, which jumped from about 50 million or 60 million during the Tang dynasty to 120 million by 1200. Behind this doubling of the population were remarkable achievements in agricultural production, particularly the adoption of a fast-ripening and drought-resistant strain of rice from Vietnam.

Many people found their way to the cities, making China the most urbanized country in the world. Dozens of Chinese cities numbered over 100,000, while the Song dynasty capital of Hangzhou was home to more than a million people. A Chinese observer in 1235 provided a vivid description of that city.[7] Specialized markets abounded for meat, herbs, vegetables, books, rice, and much

Kaifeng
This detail comes from a huge watercolor scroll, titled *Upper River during Qing Ming Festival*, origi-
nally painted during the Song dynasty. It illustrates the urban sophistication of Kaifeng and other
Chinese cities at that time and has been imitated and copied many times since then. (Palace Museum,
Beijing)

more, with troupes of actors performing for the crowds. Restaurants advertised
their unique offerings—sweet bean soup, pickled dates, juicy lungs, meat pies,
pigs' feet—and some offered vegetarian fare for religious banquets. Inns of various kinds appealed to different groups. Those that served only wine, a practice
known as "hitting the cup," were regarded as "unfit for polite company."
"Luxuriant inns," marked by red lanterns, featured prostitutes, and "the wine
chambers [were] equipped with beds." Specialized agencies managed elaborate
dinner parties for the wealthy, complete with a Perfume and Medicine Office to
"help sober up the guests." Schools for musicians offered thirteen different
courses. Numerous clubs provided companionship for poets, fishermen,
Buddhists, physical fitness enthusiasts, antiques collectors, horse lovers, and many
other groups. No wonder that the Italian visitor Marco Polo described Hangzhou
later in the thirteenth century as "beyond dispute the finest and noblest [city] in
the world."[8]

Supplying these cities with food was made possible by an immense network of
internal waterways—canals, rivers, and lakes—stretching perhaps 30,000 miles.
They provided a cheap transportation system that bound the country together
economically and created the "world's most populous trading area."[9]

Industrial production likewise soared. In both large-scale enterprises employing hundreds of workers and in smaller backyard furnaces, China's iron industry
increased its output dramatically. By the eleventh century, it was providing the
government with 32,000 suits of armor and 16 million iron arrowheads annually,
in addition to supplying metal for coins, tools, construction, and bells in Buddhist
monasteries. Technological innovation in other fields also flourished. Inventions in
printing, both woodblock and movable type, generated the world's first printed

books, and by 1000 relatively cheap books on religious, agricultural, mathematical, and medical topics became widely available in China. Its navigational and ship-building technologies led the world. The Chinese invention of gunpowder created within a few centuries a revolution in military affairs that had global dimensions.

Most remarkably, perhaps, all of this occurred within the world's most highly commercialized society, in which producing for the market, rather than for local consumption, became a very widespread phenomenon. Cheap transportation allowed peasants to grow specialized crops for sale, while they bought rice or other staples on the market. In addition, government demands for taxes paid in cash rather than in kind required peasants to sell something in order to meet their obligations. The growing use of paper money as well as financial instruments such as letters of credit and promissory notes further contributed to the commercialization of Chinese society. Two prominent scholars have described the outcome: "Output increased, population grew, skills multiplied, and a burst of inventiveness made Song China far wealthier than ever before—or than any of its contemporaries."[10]

Women in the Song Dynasty

■ **Change**
In what ways did women's lives change during the Tang and Song dynasties?

The "golden age" of Song dynasty China was perhaps less than "golden" for many of the country's women, for that era marked yet another turning point in the history of Chinese patriarchy. Under the influence of steppe nomads, whose women led less restricted lives, elite Chinese women of the Tang dynasty era, at least in the north, had participated in social life with greater freedom than in classical times. Paintings and statues from that time show aristocratic women riding horses, while the Queen Mother of the West, a Daoist deity, was widely worshipped by female Daoist priests and practitioners (see Chapter 6). By the Song dynasty, however, a reviving Confucianism and rapid economic growth seemed to tighten patriarchal restrictions on women and to restore some of the earlier Han dynasty images of female submission and passivity.

Once again Confucian writers highlighted the subordination of women to men and the need to keep males and females separate in every domain of life. The Song dynasty historian and scholar Sima Guang (1019–1086) summed up the prevailing view: "The boy leads the girl, the girl follows the boy; the duty of husbands to be resolute and wives to be docile begins with this."[11] Women were also frequently viewed as a distraction to men's pursuit of a contemplative and introspective life. The remarriage of widows, though legally permissible, was increasingly condemned, for "to walk through two courtyards is a source of shame for a woman."[12]

The most compelling expression of a tightening patriarchy lay in foot binding. Beginning apparently among dancers and courtesans in the tenth or eleventh century C.E., this practice involved the tight wrapping of young girls' feet, usually breaking the bones of the foot and causing intense pain. During the Tang dynasty, foot binding spread widely among elite families and later became even more wide-spread in Chinese society. It was associated with new images of female beauty and eroticism that emphasized small size, delicacy, and reticence, all of which were necessarily produced by foot binding. It certainly served to keep women restricted to the "inner quarters," where Confucian tradition asserted that they belonged. Many mothers imposed this painful procedure on their daughters, perhaps to assist them in competing with concubines for the attention of their husbands.[13]

A rapidly commercializing economy undermined the position of women in the textile industry. Urban workshops and state factories, run by men, increasingly took over the skilled tasks of weaving textiles, especially silk, which

Foot Binding
The two young women pictured in this late-nineteenth-century photograph have bound feet, while the boy standing between them does not. A girl of a similar age would likely have begun this painful process already. The practice, dating back to around 1000 C.E., lasted into the twentieth century, when it was largely eliminated by reformist and Communist governments. (Photograph courtesy Peabody Essex Museum; image #A9392)

had previously been the work of rural women. But as their economic role in textile production declined, other opportunities emerged in an increasingly prosperous Song China. In the cities, women operated restaurants, sold fish and vegetables, and worked as maids, cooks, and dressmakers. The growing prosperity of elite families funneled increasing numbers of women into roles as concubines, entertainers, courtesans, and prostitutes. Their ready availability surely reduced the ability of wives to negotiate as equals with their husbands. It set women against one another and created endless household jealousies.

In other ways, the Song dynasty witnessed more positive trends in the lives of women. Their property rights expanded, in terms of both controlling their own dowries and inheriting property from their families. "Neither in earlier nor in later periods," writes one scholar, "did as much property pass through women's hands" as during the Song dynasty.[14] Furthermore, lower-ranking but ambitious officials strongly urged the education of women, so that they might more effectively raise their sons and increase the family's fortune. Song dynasty China, in short, offered a mixture of tightening restrictions and new opportunities to its women.

China and the Northern Nomads: A Chinese World Order in the Making

Chinese history has been subjected to two enduring misconceptions, in popular thinking, if not in scholarly writing. First, it was often viewed as the story of an impressive but largely static civilization. In fact, however, China changed substantially over the centuries as its state structures evolved, as its various cultural traditions mixed and blended, as its economy expanded, as its population grew and migrated to the south, and as its patriarchy altered in tone and emphasis. A second

$\mathcal{S}$napshot   **Key Moments in the History of Postclassical China**

Collapse of Han dynasty; end of classical era	220
Political fragmentation of China; incursion of nomads in the north; Buddhism takes root	220–581
Sui dynasty; reunification of China	589–618
Reign of Emperor Wendi; state support for Buddhism	581–604
Tang dynasty; golden age of Chinese culture; expansion into Central Asia; high point of Chinese influence in Japan	618–907
Withdrawal of Chinese military forces from Korea	688
Reign of Empress Wu, China's only female emperor	690–705
State action against Buddhism	9th century
Political breakdown between dynasties	907–960
Vietnam establishes independence from China	939
Song dynasty; China's economic revolution; northern China ruled by peoples of nomadic background (Khitan, Jurchen)	960–1279
Yuan dynasty; Mongol rule of China	1271–1368
Ming dynasty; Chinese rule resumed	1368–1644
Maritime expeditions in the Indian Ocean	1405–1433

misconception has portrayed China as a self-contained civilization. The balance of this chapter challenges this impression by showing how China's many interactions with a larger Eurasian world shaped both China's own development and that of classical and postclassical world history more generally.

From early times to the nineteenth century, China's most enduring and intense interaction with foreigners lay to the north, involving the many nomadic pastoral or semi-agricultural peoples of the steppes. Living in areas unable to sustain Chinese-style farming, the northern nomads had long focused their economies around the raising of livestock (sheep, cattle, goats) and the mastery of horse riding. Organized locally in small, mobile, kinship-based groups, sometimes called tribes, these peoples also periodically created much larger and powerful states or confederations that could draw upon the impressive horsemanship and military skills of virtually the entire male population of their societies. Such specialized pastoral societies needed grain and other agricultural products from China, and their leaders developed a taste for Chinese manufactured and luxury goods—wine and silk, for example—with which they could attract and reward followers. Thus the nomads were drawn like a magnet toward China, trading, raiding, and extorting in order to obtain the resources so vital to their way of life. For 2,000 years or more, pressure

■ **Connection**
How did the Chinese and their nomadic neighbors to the north view each other?

from the steppes and the intrusion of nomadic peoples were constant factors in China's historical development.

From the nomads' point of view, the threat often came from the Chinese, who periodically directed their own military forces deep into the steppes, built the Great Wall to keep the nomads out, and often proved unwilling to allow pastoral peoples easy access to trading opportunities within China.[15] And yet the Chinese needed the nomads. Their lands were the source of horses, so essential for the Chinese military. Other products of the steppes and the forests beyond, such as skins, furs, hides, and amber, were also of value in China. Furthermore, pastoral nomads controlled much of the Silk Road trading network, which funneled goods from the West into China. The continuing interaction between China and the northern nomads brought together peoples occupying different environments, practicing different economies, governing themselves with different institutions, and thinking about the world in quite different ways.

The Tribute System in Theory

An enduring outcome of this cross-cultural encounter was that the Chinese developed a particular view of themselves, fully articulated by the time of the Han dynasty (200 B.C.E.–200 C.E.) and lasting for more than two millennia. That understanding cast China as the "middle kingdom," the center of the world, infinitely superior to the "barbarian" peoples beyond its borders. With its long history, great cities, refined tastes, sophisticated intellectual and artistic achievements, bureaucratic state, literate elite, and prosperous economy, China represented "civilization." All of this, in Chinese thinking, was in sharp contrast to the rude cultures and primitive life of the northern nomads, who continually moved about "like beasts and birds," lived in tents, ate mostly meat and milk, and practically lived on their horses, while making war on everyone within reach. Educated Chinese saw their own society as self-sufficient, requiring little from the outside world, while barbarians, quite understandably, sought access to China's wealth and wisdom. Furthermore, China was willing to permit that access under controlled conditions, for its sense of superiority did not preclude the possibility that barbarians could become civilized Chinese. China was a "radiating civilization," graciously shedding its light most fully to nearby barbarians and with diminished intensity to those farther away.[16]

Such was the general understanding of literate Chinese about their own civilization in relation to northern nomads and other non-Chinese peoples. That worldview also took shape as a practical system for managing China's relationship with these people. Known to us as the "tribute system," it was a set of practices that required non-Chinese authorities to acknowledge Chinese superiority and their own subordinate place in a Chinese-centered world order. Foreigners seeking access to China had to send a delegation to the Chinese court, where they would perform the kowtow, a series of ritual bowings and prostrations, and present their tribute — produce of value from their countries — to the Chinese emperor. In return for these

■ **Connection**
What assumptions underlay the tribute system?

The Tribute System
This Qing dynasty painting shows an idealized Chinese version of the tribute system. The Chinese emperor receives barbarian envoys, who perform rituals of subordination and present tribute in the form of a horse. (Réunion des Musées Nationaux/Art Resource, NY)

expressions of submission, he would grant permission for foreigners to trade in China's rich markets and would provide them with gifts or "bestowals," often worth far more than the tribute they had offered. This was the mechanism by which successive Chinese dynasties attempted to regulate their relationships with northern nomads; with neighboring states such as Korea, Vietnam, Tibet, and Japan; and, after 1500, with those European barbarians from across the sea.

Often, this system seemed to work. Over the centuries, countless foreign delegations proved willing to present their tribute, say the required words, and perform the necessary rituals in order to gain access to the material goods of China. Aspiring non-Chinese rulers also gained prestige as they basked in the reflected glory of even this subordinate association with the great Chinese civilization. The official titles, seals of office, and ceremonial robes they received from China proved useful in their local struggles for power.

The Tribute System in Practice

■ **Connection**
How did the tribute system in practice differ from the ideal Chinese understanding of its operation?

But the tribute system also disguised some realities that contradicted its assumptions. Frequently, China was confronting not separate and small-scale barbarian societies, but large and powerful nomadic empires able to deal with China on at least equal terms. An early nomadic confederacy was that of the Xiongnu, established about the same time as the Han dynasty and eventually reaching from Manchuria to Central Asia. Devastating Xiongnu raids into northern China persuaded the Chinese emperor to negotiate an arrangement that recognized the nomadic state as a political equal, promised its leader a princess in marriage, and, most important, agreed to supply him annually with large quantities of grain, wine, and silk. Although these goods were officially termed "gifts," granted in accord with the tribute system, they were in fact tribute in reverse or even protection money. In return for these goods, so critical for the functioning of the nomadic state, the Xiongnu agreed to refrain from military incursions into China. The basic realities of the situation were summed up in this warning to the Han dynasty in the first century B.C.E.:

> Just make sure that the silks and grain stuffs you bring the Xiongnu are the right measure and quality, that's all. What's the need for talking? If the goods you

deliver are up to measure and good quality, all right. But if there is any defi-
ciency or the quality is no good, then when the autumn harvest comes, we will
take our horses and trample all over your crops.[17]

Something similar occurred during the Tang dynasty as a series of Turkic
empires arose in Mongolia. Like the Xiongnu, they too extorted large "gifts" from
the Chinese. One of these peoples, the Uighurs, actually rescued the Tang dynasty
from a serious internal revolt in the 750s. In return, the Uighur leader gained one
of the Chinese emperor's daughters as a wife and arranged a highly favorable
exchange of poor-quality horses for high-quality silk that brought half a million
rolls of the precious fabric annually into the Uighur lands. Despite the rhetoric of
the tribute system, the Chinese were clearly not always able to dictate the terms of
their relationship with the northern nomads.

Steppe nomads were generally not much interested in actually conquering and
ruling China. It was easier and more profitable to extort goods from a functioning
Chinese state. On occasion, though, that state broke down, and various nomadic
groups moved in to "pick up the pieces," conquering and governing parts of China.
Such a process took place following the fall of the Han dynasty and again after the
collapse of the Tang dynasty, when the Khitan (907–1125) and then the Jurchen
(1115–1234) peoples established states that encompassed parts of northern China as
well as major areas of the steppes to the north. Both of them required the Chinese
Song dynasty, located farther south, to deliver annually huge quantities of silk, silver, and tea, some of which found its way into the Silk Road trading network. The
practice of "bestowing gifts on barbarians," long a part of the tribute system,
allowed the proud Chinese to imagine that they were still in control of the situation even as they were paying heavily for protection from nomadic incursion. Those
gifts, in turn, provided vital economic resources to nomadic states.

Cultural Influence across an Ecological Frontier

When nomadic peoples actually ruled parts of China, some of them adopted
Chinese ways, employing Chinese advisers, governing according to Chinese practice, and, at least for the elite, immersing themselves in Chinese culture and learning. This process of "becoming Chinese" went furthest among the Jurchen, many
of whom lived in northern China and learned to speak Chinese, wore Chinese
clothing, married Chinese husbands and wives, and practiced Buddhism or
Daoism. On the whole, however, Chinese culture had only a modest impact on the
nomadic people of the northern steppes. Unlike the native peoples of southern
China, who were gradually absorbed into Chinese culture, the pastoral societies
north of the Great Wall generally retained their own cultural patterns. Few of them
were incorporated, at least not for long, within a Chinese state, and most lived in
areas where Chinese-style agriculture was simply impossible. Under these conditions, there were few incentives for adopting Chinese culture wholesale. But various modes of interaction—peaceful trade, military conflict, political negotiations,

■ **Connection**
In what ways did China
and the nomads influence
each other?

economic extortion, some cultural influence—continued across the ecological frontier that divided two quite distinct and separate ways of life. Each was necessary for the other.

On the Chinese side, elements of steppe culture had some influence in those parts of northern China that were periodically conquered and ruled by nomadic peoples. The founders of the Sui and Tang dynasties were in fact of mixed nomad and Chinese ancestry and came from the borderland region where a blended Chinese/Turkic culture had evolved. High-ranking members of the imperial family personally led their troops in battle in the style of Turkic warriors. Furthermore, Tang dynasty China was awash with foreign visitors from all over Asia—delegations bearing tribute, merchants carrying exotic goods, bands of clerics or religious pilgrims bringing new religions such as Christianity, Islam, Buddhism, and Manichaeism. For a time in the Tang dynasty, almost anything associated with "western barbarians"—Central Asians, Persians, Indians, Arabs—had great appeal among northern Chinese elites. Their music, dancing, clothing, foods, games, and artistic styles found favor among the upper classes. The more traditional southern Chinese, feeling themselves heir to the legacy of the Han dynasty, were sharply critical of their northern counterparts for allowing women too much freedom, for drinking yogurt rather than tea, for listening to "western" music, all of which they attributed to barbarian influence. Around 800 C.E., the poet Yuan Chen gave voice to a growing backlash against this too easy acceptance of things "western":

> Ever since the Western horsemen began raising smut and dust,
> Fur and fleece, rank and rancid, have filled Hsien and Lo.
> Women make themselves Western matrons by the study of Western makeup.
> Entertainers present Western tunes, in their devotion to Western music.[18]

Coping with China: Comparing Korea, Vietnam, and Japan

Also involved in tributary relationships with China during the postclassical era were the newly emerging states and civilizations of Korea, Vietnam, and Japan. Unlike the northern nomads, these societies were thoroughly agricultural and sedentary. During the first millennium C.E., they were part of a larger process—the globalization of civilization—which produced new city- and state-based societies in various parts of the world. Proximity to their giant Chinese neighbor decisively shaped the histories of these new East Asian civilizations, for all of them borrowed major elements of Chinese culture. But unlike the native peoples of southern China, who largely became Chinese, the peoples of Korea, Vietnam, and Japan did not. They retained distinctive identities, which have lasted into modern times. While resisting Chinese political domination, they also appreciated Chinese culture and sought the source of Chinese wealth and power. In such ways, these smaller East Asian civilizations anticipated the "developing" Afro-Asian societies of the twentieth century, which embraced "modernity" and elements of Western culture, while trying to maintain their political and cultural independence from the European and American centers of that modern way of life. Korea, Vietnam, and Japan, however, encountered China and responded to it in quite different ways.

■ Comparison
In what different ways did Korea, Vietnam, and Japan experience and respond to Chinese influence?

Korea and China

Immediately adjacent to northeastern China, the Korean peninsula and its people have long lived in the shadow of their imposing neighbor. Temporary Chinese conquest of northern Korea during the Han dynasty and some colonization by Chinese settlers provided an initial channel for Chinese cultural influence, particularly in the form of Buddhism. Early Korean states, which emerged in the fourth through seventh centuries C.E., all referred to their rulers with the Chinese term *wang* (king). Bitter rivals with one another, these states strenuously resisted Chinese political control, except when they found it advantageous to join with China against a local enemy. In the seventh century, one of these states—the Silla kingdom—allied with Tang dynasty China to bring some political unity to the peninsula for the first time. But Chinese efforts to set up puppet regimes and to assimilate Koreans to Chinese culture provoked sharp military resistance, persuading the Chinese to withdraw their military forces in 688 and to establish a tributary relationship with a largely independent Korea.

Under a succession of dynasties—the Silla (688–900), Koryo (918–1392), and Yi (1392–1910)—Korea generally maintained its political independence while participating in China's tribute system. Its leaders actively embraced the connection with China and, especially during the Silla dynasty, sought to turn their small state into a miniature version of Tang China.

Tribute missions to China provided legitimacy for Korean rulers and knowledge of Chinese court life and administrative techniques, which they sought to replicate back home. A new capital city of Kumsong was modeled directly on the Chinese capital of Chang'an. Tribute missions also enabled both official and private trade, mostly in luxury goods such as ceremonial clothing, silks, fancy teas, Confucian and Buddhist texts, and artwork—all of which enriched the lives of a Korean aristocracy that was becoming increasingly Chinese in culture. Thousands of Korean students were sent to China, where they studied primarily Confucianism but also natural sciences and the arts. Buddhist monks visited centers of learning and pilgrimage in China and brought back popular forms of Chinese Buddhism, which quickly took root in Korea. Schools for the study of Confucianism, using texts in the Chinese language, were established in Korea. In these ways, Korea became a part of the expanding world of Chinese culture, and refugees from the peninsula's many wars carried Chinese culture to Japan as well.

These efforts to plant Confucian values and Chinese culture in Korea had what one scholar has called an "overwhelmingly negative" impact on

Korean Kingdoms about 500 C.E.

Korean women, particularly after 1300.[19] Early Chinese observers noticed, and strongly disapproved of, "free choice" marriages in Korea as well as the practice of women singing and dancing together late at night. With the support of the Korean court, Chinese models of family life and female behavior, especially among the elite, gradually replaced the more flexible Korean patterns. Earlier a Korean woman had generally given birth and raised her young children in her parents' home, where she was often joined by her husband. This was now strongly discouraged, for it was deeply offensive to Confucian orthodoxy, which held that a married woman belonged to her husband's family. Some Korean customs—funeral rites in which a husband was buried in the sacred plot of his wife's family, the remarriage of widowed or divorced women, and female inheritance of property—eroded under the pressure of Confucian orthodoxy. So too did the practice of plural marriages for men. In 1413, a legal distinction between primary and secondary wives required men to identify one of their wives as primary. Because she and her children now had special privileges and status, sharp new tensions emerged within families. Korean restrictions on elite women, especially widows, came to exceed even those in China itself.

Still, Korea remained Korean. After 688, the country's political independence, though periodically threatened, was largely intact. Chinese cultural influence, except for Buddhism, had little impact beyond the aristocracy and certainly did not penetrate the lives of Korea's serflike peasants or its large slave population. A Chinese-style examination system to recruit government officials, though encouraged by some Korean rulers, never assumed the prominence that it gained in Tang and Song dynasty China. Korea's aristocratic class was able to maintain an even stronger monopoly on bureaucratic office than their Chinese counterparts. And in the 1400s, Korea moved toward greater cultural independence by developing a phonetic alphabet, known as *hangul*, for writing the Korean language. Although resisted by male conservative elites, who were long accustomed to using the more prestigious Chinese characters to write Korean, this new form of writing gradually took hold, especially in private correspondence, in popular fiction, and among women. Clearly part of the Chinese world order, Korea nonetheless retained a distinctive culture as well as a separate political existence.

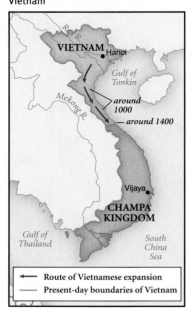

Vietnam

Route of Vietnamese expansion
Present-day boundaries of Vietnam

Vietnam and China

At the southern fringe of the Chinese cultural world, the people who eventually came to be called Vietnamese had a broadly similar historical encounter with China. As in Korea, the elite culture of Vietnam borrowed heavily from China—adopting Confucianism, Daoism, Buddhism, administrative techniques, the examination system, artistic and literary styles—even as its popular culture remained distinctive. And, like Korea, Vietnam achieved political independence, while participating fully in the tribute system as a vassal state.

But there were differences as well. The cultural heartland of Vietnam in the Red River valley was fully incorporated into the Chinese state for more than a thousand years (111 B.C.E.–939 C.E.), far longer than corresponding parts of Korea. Regarded by the Chinese as "southern barbarians," the Vietnamese were ruled by Chinese officials who expected to fully assimilate this rich rice-growing region into China culturally as well as administratively. To these officials, it was simply a further extension of the southward expansion of Chinese civilization. Thus Chinese-style irrigated agriculture was introduced; Vietnamese elites were brought into the local bureaucracy and educated in Confucian-based schools; Chinese replaced the local language in official business; Chinese clothing and hairstyles became mandatory; and large numbers of Chinese, some fleeing internal conflicts at home, flooded into the relative security of what they referred to as "the pacified south," while often despising the local people.[20]

The heavy pressure of the Chinese presence generated not only a Vietnamese elite thoroughly schooled in Chinese culture but also periodic rebellions. In 39 C.E., a short-lived but long-remembered uprising was launched by two sisters, daughters of a local leader deposed by the Chinese. One of them, Trung Trac, whose husband had been executed, famously addressed some 30,000 soldiers, while dressed in full military regalia.

> Foremost I will avenge my country.
> Second I will restore the Hung lineage.
> Third I will avenge the death of my husband.
> Lastly I vow that these goals will be accomplished.[21]

When the rebellion was crushed several years later, the Trung sisters committed suicide rather than surrender to the Chinese, but in literature, monuments, and public memory, they long remained power-ful symbols of Vietnamese resistance to Chinese aggression.

The weakening of the Tang dynasty in the early tenth century C.E. finally enabled a particularly large rebellion to establish Vietnam as a separate state, though one that carefully maintained its tributary role, sending repeated missions to do homage at the Chinese court. Nonetheless, successive Vietnamese dynasties found the Chinese approach to government useful, styling their rulers as emperors, claiming the Mandate of Heaven, and making use of Chinese court rituals, while expanding their state

The Trung Sisters
Although it occurred nearly 2,000 years ago, the revolt of the Trung sisters against Chinese occupation remains a national symbol of Vietnam's independence, as illustrated by this modern Vietnamese painting of the two women, astride war ele-phants, leading their follow-ers into battle against the Chinese invaders. (From William J. Duiker, *Sacred War: Nationalism and Revolution in a Divided Vietnam* [New York: The McGraw-Hill Companies, 1995])

steadily southward. More so than in Korea, a Chinese-based examination system in Vietnam functioned to undermine an established aristocracy, to provide some measure of social mobility for commoners, and to create a merit-based scholar-gentry class to staff the bureaucracy. Furthermore, the Vietnamese elite class remained deeply committed to Chinese culture, viewing their own country less as a separate nation than as a southern extension of a universal civilization, the only one they knew.[22]

Beyond the elite, however, there remained much that was uniquely Vietnamese, such as a distinctive language, a fondness for cockfighting, chewing betel nuts, and a greater role for women in social and economic life. Female nature deities and even a "female Buddha" continued to be part of Vietnamese popular religion, even as Confucian-based ideas took root among the elite. These features of Vietnamese life reflected larger patterns of Southeast Asian culture that distinguished it from China. And like Korea, the Vietnamese developed a variation of Chinese writing called *chu nom* ("southern script"), which provided the basis for an independent national literature.

Japan and China

Unlike Korea and Vietnam, the Japanese islands were physically separated from China by 100 miles or more of ocean and were never successfully invaded or conquered by their giant mainland neighbor. Thus Japan's very extensive borrowing from Chinese civilization was wholly voluntary, rather than occurring under conditions of direct military threat or outright occupation. The high point of that borrowing took place during the seventh to the ninth centuries C.E., as the first more or less unified Japanese state began to emerge from dozens of small clan-based aristocratic chiefdoms. That state found much that was useful in Tang dynasty China and set out, deliberately and systematically, to transform Japan into a centralized bureaucratic state on the Chinese model.

Japan

The initial leader of this effort was Shotoku Taishi (572–622), a prominent aristocrat from one of the major clans. He launched a series of large-scale missions to China, which took hundreds of Japanese monks, scholars, artists, and students to the mainland, and when they returned, they put into practice what they had learned. He issued the Seventeen Article Constitution, proclaiming the Japanese ruler as a Chinese-style emperor and encouraging both Buddhism and Confucianism. In good Confucian fashion, that document emphasized the moral quality of rulers as a foundation for social harmony.

When wise men are entrusted with office, the sound of praise arises. If unprincipled men hold office, disasters and tumults are multiplied. In this world few men are born with knowledge: wisdom is the product of earnest meditation. In all things, great or small, find the right man and they will surely be well managed.[23]

In the decades that followed, court rituals and a system of court rankings for officials also were based on Chinese models, and the Chinese calendar was adopted. Subsequently, Chinese-style taxation systems, law codes, government ministries, and provincial administration were established, at least on paper. Two capital cities, first Nara and then Heian (Kyoto), arose, both modeled on the Chinese capital of Chang'an.

Chinese culture, no less than its political practices, also found favor in Japan. Various schools of Chinese Buddhism took root, first among the educated and literate classes and later more broadly in Japanese society, affecting, according to one scholar, "nearly every aspect of Japanese life." Art, architecture, education, medicine, views of the afterlife, attitudes toward suffering and the impermanence of life—all of this and more reflected the influence of Buddhist culture in Japan.[24] The Chinese writing system—and with it an interest in historical writing, calligraphy, and poetry—likewise proved attractive among the elite.

The absence of any compelling threat from China made it possible for the Japanese to be selective in their borrowing. By the tenth century, deliberate efforts to absorb additional elements of Chinese culture diminished, and formal tribute missions to China stopped, although private traders and Buddhist monks continued to make the difficult journey to the mainland. Over many centuries, the Japanese combined what they had assimilated from China with elements of their own tradition into a distinctive Japanese civilization, which differed from Chinese culture in many ways.

In the political realm, for example, the Japanese never succeeded in creating an effective centralized and bureaucratic state to match that of China. Although the court and the emperor retained an important ceremonial and cultural role, their real political authority over the country gradually diminished in favor of competing aristocratic families, both at court and in the provinces. A Chinese-style university trained officials, but rather than serving as a mechanism for recruiting talented commoners into the political elite, it enrolled students who were largely the sons of court aristocrats.

As political power became increasingly decentralized, local authorities developed their own military forces, the famous *samurai* warrior class of Japanese society. With their exquisite curved swords, the samurai developed a distinctive set of values featuring great skill in martial arts, bravery, loyalty, endurance, honor, and a preference for death over surrender. This was *bushido*, the way of the warrior. Japan's celebration of the samurai and of military virtues contrasted sharply with China's emphasis on intellectual achievements and political officeholding, which were accorded higher prestige than bearing arms. "The educated men of the land," wrote a Chinese minister in the eleventh century, "regard the carrying of arms as a disgrace."[25] The Japanese, clearly, did not agree.

Religiously as well, Japan remained distinctive. Although Buddhism in many forms took hold in the country, it never completely replaced the native beliefs and practices, which focused attention on numerous *kami*, sacred spirits associated with

The Samurai of Japan
This twelfth-century painting depicts the famous naval battle of Dan-no-ura (1185), in which the samurai warriors of two rival clans fought to the death. Many of the defeated Taira warriors, along with some of their women, plunged into the sea rather than surrender to their Minamoto rivals. The prominence of martial values in Japanese culture was one of the ways in which Japan differed from its Chinese neighbor, despite much borrowing. (Tokyo National Museum. Image: TNM Images Archives. Source: http://TnmArchives.jp/)

■ Comparison
In what different ways did Japanese and Korean women experience the pressures of Confucian orthodoxy?

human ancestors and various natural phenomena. Much later referred to as Shinto, this tradition provided legitimacy to the imperial family, based on claims of descent from the sun goddess. Because veneration of the kami lacked an elaborate philosophy or ritual, it conflicted very little with Buddhism. In fact, numerous kami were assimilated into Japanese Buddhism as local expressions of Buddhist deities or principles.

Japanese literary and artistic culture likewise evolved in distinctive ways, despite much borrowing from China. As in Korea and Vietnam, there emerged a unique writing system that combined Chinese characters with a series of phonetic symbols. A highly stylized Japanese poetic form, known as *tanka*, developed early and has remained a favored means of expression ever since. Particularly during the Heian period of Japanese history (794–1192), a highly refined esthetic culture found expression at the imperial court, even as the court's real political authority melted away. Court aristocrats and their ladies lived in splendor, composed poems, arranged flowers, and conducted their love affairs. "What counted," wrote one scholar, "was the proper costume, the right ceremonial act, the successful turn of phrase in a poem, and the appropriate expression of refined taste."[26] Much of our knowledge of this courtly culture comes from the work of women writers, who composed their diaries and novels in the vernacular Japanese script, rather than in the classical Chinese used by elite men. *The Tale of Genji*, a Japanese novel written by the woman author Murasaki Shikibu around 1000, provides an intimate picture of the intrigues and romances of court life.

At this level of society, Japan's women, unlike those in Korea, largely escaped the more oppressive features of Chinese Confucian culture, such as the prohibition of remarriage for widows, seclusion within the home, and foot binding. Perhaps this is because the most powerful Chinese influence on Japan occurred during the Tang dynasty, when Chinese elite women enjoyed considerable freedom. Japanese women continued to inherit property; Japanese married couples often lived apart or with the wife's family; and marriages were made and broken easily. None of this corresponded to Confucian values. When Japanese women did begin to lose status in the twelfth century and later, it had less to do with Confucian pressures than with the rise of a warrior culture. As the personal relationships of samurai warriors to their lords replaced marriage alliances as a political strategy, the influence of women in political life was reduced, but this was an internal Japanese phenomenon, not a reflection of Chinese influence.

Japan's ability to borrow extensively from China while developing its own distinctive civilization perhaps provided a model for its encounter with the West in the nineteenth century. Then, as before, Japan borrowed selectively from a foreign culture without losing either its political independence or its cultural uniqueness.

China and the Eurasian World Economy

Beyond China's central role in East Asia was its economic interaction with the wider world of Eurasia generally. On the one hand, China's remarkable economic growth, taking place during the Tang and Song dynasties, could hardly be contained within China's borders and clearly had a major impact throughout Eurasia. On the other hand, China was recipient as well as donor in the economic interactions of the postclassical era, and its own economic achievements owed something to the stimulus of contact with the larger world.

Spillovers: China's Impact on Eurasia

One of the outcomes of China's economic revolution lay in the diffusion of its many technological innovations to peoples and places far from East Asia as the movements of traders, soldiers, slaves, and pilgrims conveyed Chinese achievements abroad. Chinese techniques for producing salt by solar evaporation spread to the Islamic world and later to Christian Europe. Papermaking, known in China since the Han dynasty, spread to Korea and Vietnam by the fourth century C.E., to Japan and India by the seventh, to the Islamic world by the eighth, to Muslim Spain by 1150, to France and Germany in the 1300s, and to England in the 1490s. Printing, likewise a Chinese invention, rapidly reached Korea, where movable type became a highly developed technique, and Japan as well. Both technologies were heavily influenced by Buddhism, which accorded religious merit to the act of reproducing sacred texts. The Islamic world, however, valued handwritten calligraphy highly and generally resisted printing as impious until the nineteenth century. The adoption of printing in Europe was likewise delayed because of the absence of paper until the fourteenth century. Then movable type was reinvented by Johannes Gutenberg in the fifteenth century, although it is unclear whether he

■ **Connection**
In what ways did China participate in the world of Eurasian commerce and exchange, and with what outcomes?

was aware of Chinese and Korean precedents. With implications for mass literacy, bureaucracy, scholarship, the spread of religion, and the exchange of information, papermaking and printing were Chinese innovations of revolutionary and global dimensions.

Chinese technologies were seldom simply transferred from one place to another. More often a particular Chinese technique or product stimulated innovations in more distant lands in accordance with local needs.[27] For example, as the Chinese recipe for gunpowder, invented around 1000, became available in Europe, together with some early and simple firearms, these innovations triggered the development of cannons in the early fourteenth century. Soon cannons appeared in the Islamic world and by 1356 in China itself, which first used cast iron rather than bronze in their construction. But the highly competitive European state system drove the "gunpowder revolution" much further and more rapidly than in China's imperial state. Chinese textile, metallurgical, and naval technologies likewise stimulated imitation and innovation all across Eurasia. An example is the magnetic compass, a Chinese invention eagerly embraced by mariners of many cultural backgrounds as they traversed the Indian Ocean.

In addition to its technological influence, China's prosperity during the Song dynasty greatly stimulated commercial life and market-based behavior all across the Eurasian trading world. China's products—silk, porcelain, lacquerware—found eager buyers from Japan to East Africa, and everywhere in between. The immense size and wealth of China's domestic economy also provided a ready market for hundreds of commodities from afar. For example, the lives of many thousands of people in the spice-producing islands of what is now Indonesia were transformed as they came to depend on Chinese consumers' demand for their products. "[O]ne hundred million [Chinese] people," wrote historian William McNeill, "increasingly caught up within a commercial network, buying and selling to supplement every day's livelihood, made a significant difference to the way other human beings made their livings throughout a large part of the civilized world."[28] Such was the ripple effect of China's economic revolution.

On the Receiving End: China as Economic Beneficiary

Chinese economic growth and technological achievements significantly shaped the Eurasian world of the postclassical era, but that pattern of interaction was surely not a one-way street, for China too was changed by its engagement with a wider world. During this period, for example, China had learned about the cultivation and processing of both cotton and sugar from India. From Vietnam, around 1000, China gained access to the new, fast-ripening, and drought-resistant strains of rice that made a highly productive rice-based agriculture possible in the drier and more rugged regions of southern China. This marked a major turning point in Chinese history as the frontier region south of the Yangzi River grew rapidly in population, overtaking the traditional centers of Chinese civilization in the north.

Technologically as well, China's extraordinary burst of creativity owed something to the stimulus of cross-cultural contact. Awareness of Persian windmills, for example, spurred the development of a distinct but related device in China. Printing arose from China's growing involvement with the world of Buddhism, which put a spiritual premium on the reproduction of the Buddha's image and of short religious texts that were carried as charms. It was in Buddhist monasteries during the Tang dynasty that the long-established practice of printing with seals was elaborated by Chinese monks into woodblock printing. The first printed book, in 868 C.E., was a famous Buddhist text, the Diamond Sutra. Gunpowder too seems to have had an Indian and Buddhist connection. An Indian Buddhist monk traveling in China in 644 C.E. identified soils that contained saltpeter and showed that they produced a purple flame when put into a fire. This was the beginning of Chinese experiments, which finally led to a reliable recipe for gunpowder.

A further transforming impact of China's involvement with a wider world derived from its growing participation in Indian Ocean trade. By the Tang dynasty, thousands of ships annually visited the ports of southern China, and settled communities of foreign merchants—Arabs, Persians, Indians, Southeast Asians—turned some of these cities into cosmopolitan centers. Buddhist temples, Muslim mosques and cemeteries, and Hindu phallic sculptures graced the skyline of Quanzhou, a coastal city in southern China. Occasionally the tensions of cultural diversity erupted in violence, such as the massacre of tens of thousands of foreigners in Canton during the 870s when Chinese rebel forces sacked the city. Indian Ocean commerce also contributed much to the transformation of southern China from a subsistence economy to one more heavily based on producing for export. In the process, merchants achieved a degree of social acceptance not known before, including their frequent appointment to high-ranking bureaucratic positions. Finally, much-beloved stories of the monkey god, widely popular even in contemporary China, derived from Indian sources transmitted by Indian Ocean commerce.[29]

China and Buddhism

By far the most important gift that China received from India was neither cotton, nor sugar, nor the knowledge of saltpeter, but a religion, Buddhism. The gradual assimilation of this South Asian religious tradition into Chinese culture illustrates the process of cultural encounter and adaptation and invites comparison with the spread of Christianity into Europe. Until the adoption of Marxism in the twentieth century, Buddhism was the only large-scale cultural borrowing in Chinese history. It also made China into a launching pad for Buddhism's dispersion to Korea and from there to Japan as well. Thus, as Buddhism faded in the land of its birth, it became solidly rooted in much of East Asia, providing an element of cultural commonality for a vast region (see Map 9.2).

Map 9.2   The World of Asian Buddhism
Born in India, Buddhism later spread widely throughout much of Asia to provide a measure of cultural or religious commonality to this vast region.

Making Buddhism Chinese

■ **Change**
What facilitated the rooting of Buddhism within China?

Buddhism initially entered China via the Silk Road trading network during the first and second centuries C.E. The stability and prosperity of the Han dynasty, then at its height, ensured that the new "barbarian" religion held little appeal for native

Chinese. Furthermore, the Indian culture from which Buddhism sprang was at odds with Chinese understandings of the world in many ways. Buddhism's commitment to a secluded and monastic life for monks and nuns seemed to dishonor Chinese family values, and its concern for individual salvation or enlightenment appeared selfish, contradicting the social orientation of Confucian thinking. Its abstract philosophy ran counter to the more concrete, "this-worldly" concerns of Chinese thinkers; and the Buddhist concept of infinite eons of time, endlessly repeating themselves, was quite a stretch for the Chinese, who normally thought in terms of finite family generations or dynastic cycles. No wonder that for the first several centuries C.E., Buddhism was largely the preserve of foreign merchants and monks living in China.

In the half millennium between roughly 300 and 800 C.E., however, Buddhism took solid root in China within both elite and popular culture, becoming a permanent, though fluctuating, presence in Chinese life. How did this remarkable transformation unfold? It began, arguably, with the collapse of the Han dynasty around 200 C.E. The chaotic, violent, and politically fragmented centuries that followed seriously discredited Confucianism and opened the door to alternative understandings of the world. Nomadic rulers, now governing much of northern China, found Buddhism useful in part because it was foreign. "We were born out of the marches," declared one of them, "and though we are unworthy, we have complied with our appointed destiny and govern the Chinese as their prince. . . . Buddha being a barbarian god is the very one we should worship."[30] Rulers and elite families provided money and land that enabled the building of many Buddhist monasteries, temples, and works of art. In southern China, where many northern aristocrats had fled following the disastrous decline of the Han dynasty, Buddhism provided some comfort in the face of a collapsing society. Its emphasis on ritual, morality, and contemplation represented an intellectually and esthetically satisfying response to times that were so clearly out of joint.

Meanwhile, Buddhist monasteries increasingly provided an array of social services for ordinary people. In them, travelers found accommodation; those fleeing from China's many upheavals discovered a place of refuge; desperate people received charity; farmers borrowed seed for the next planting; the sick were treated; children learned to read. And for many, Buddhism was associated with access to magical powers as reports of miracles abounded. Battles were won, rain descended on drought-ridden areas, diseases were cured, and guilt was relieved—all through the magical ministrations of charismatic monks.

Accompanying all of this was a serious effort by monks, scholars, and translators to present this Indian religion in terms that Chinese could relate to. Thus the Buddhist term *dharma*, referring to the Buddha's teaching, was translated as *dao*, or "the way," a notion long familiar in both Daoist and Confucian thinking (see Chapter 5). The Buddhist notion of "morality" was translated with the Confucian term that referred to "filial submission and obedience." Some Indian concepts were modified in the process of translation. For example, the idea that "husband supports wife," which reflected a considerable respect for women and mothers in early Indian Buddhism, became in translation "husband controls wife."[31]

As Buddhism took hold in China, it was primarily in its broader Mahayana form—complete with numerous deities, the veneration of relics, many heavens and hells, and bodhisattvas to aid the believer—rather than the more psychological and individualistic Theravada Buddhism (see Chapter 5). One of the most popular forms of Buddhism in China was the Pure Land School, in which faithfully repeating the name of an earlier Buddha, the Amitabha, was sufficient to ensure rebirth in a beautifully described heavenly realm, the Pure Land. In its emphasis on salvation by faith, without arduous study or intensive meditation, Pure Land Buddhism became a highly popular and authentically Chinese version of the Indian faith.

China's reunification under the Sui and early Tang dynasties witnessed growing state support for Buddhism. The Sui emperor Wendi (reigned 581–604 C.E.) had monasteries constructed at the base of China's five sacred mountains, further identifying the imported religion with traditional Chinese culture. He even used Buddhism to justify his military campaigns. "With a hundred victories in a hundred battles," he declared, "we promote the practice of the ten Buddhist virtues."[32] With state support and growing popular acceptance, monasteries became centers of great wealth, largely exempt from taxation, owning large estates; running businesses such as oil presses, water mills, and pawn shops; collecting gems, gold, and lavish works of art; and even employing slaves. But Buddhism, while solidly entrenched in Chinese life by the early Tang dynasty, never achieved the independence from state authorities that the Christian church acquired in Europe. The examinations for becoming a monk were supervised by the state, and education in the monasteries included the required study of the Confucian classics. And in the mid-ninth century, the state showed quite dramatically just how much control it could exercise over the Buddhist establishment.

Losing State Support: The Crisis of Chinese Buddhism

■ Change
What were the major sources of opposition to Buddhism within China?

The impressive growth of Chinese Buddhism was accompanied by a persistent undercurrent of resistance and criticism. Some saw the Buddhist establishment, at least potentially, as a "state within a state" and a challenge to imperial authority. More important was a deepening resentment of its enormous wealth. One fifth-century critic, referring to monks, put the issue squarely: "Why is it that their ideals are noble and far-reaching and their activities still are base and common? [They] become merchants and engage in barter, wrangling with the masses for profit."[33] When state treasuries were short of funds, government officials cast a covetous eye on wealthy and tax-exempt monasteries. Furthermore, Buddhism was clearly of foreign origin and offensive for that reason to some Confucian and Daoist thinkers. The celibacy of the monks and their withdrawal from society, the critics argued, undermined the Confucian-based family system of Chinese tradition.

Such criticisms took on new meaning in the changed environment of China after about 800 C.E. After centuries of considerable foreign influence in China, a growing resentment against foreign culture, particularly among the literate classes, increasingly took hold. The turning point may well have been the An Lushan rebellion (755–763), in which a general of foreign origin led a major revolt against the Tang dynasty. Whatever its origins, an increasingly xenophobic reaction set in among the upper classes, reflected in a desire to return to an imagined "purity" of earlier times.[34] In this setting, the old criticisms of Buddhism became more sharply focused. In 819, Han Yu, a leading figure in the Confucian counterattack on Buddhism, wrote a scathing memorial to the emperor, criticizing his willingness to honor a relic of the Buddha's finger.

> Now the Buddha was of barbarian origin. His language differed from Chinese speech; his clothes were of a different cut; his mouth did not pronounce the prescribed words of the Former Kings. . . . He did not recognize the relationship between prince and subject, nor the sentiments of father and son. . . . I pray that Your Majesty will turn this bone over to the officials that it may be cast into water or fire.[35]

Several decades later, the Chinese state took direct action against the Buddhist establishment as well as against other foreign religions. A series of imperial decrees between 841 and 845 ordered some 260,000 monks and nuns to return to normal life as tax-paying citizens. Thousands of monasteries, temples, and shrines were either destroyed or turned to public use, while the state confiscated the lands, money, metals, and serfs belonging to monasteries. Buddhists were now forbidden to use gold, silver, copper, iron, and gems in constructing their images. These actions dealt a serious blow to Chinese Buddhism. Its scholars and monks were scattered, its creativity diminished, and its institutions came even more firmly under state control.

Despite this persecution, Buddhism did not vanish from China. At the level of elite culture, its philosophical ideas played a role in the reformulation of Confucian thinking that took place during the Song dynasty. At the village level, Buddhism became one element of Chinese popular religion, which also included the veneration of ancestors, the honoring of Confucius, and Daoist shrines and rituals. Temples frequently included statues of Confucius, Laozi, and the Buddha, with little sense of any incompatibility among them. "Every black-haired son of Han," the Chinese have long said, "wears a Confucian thinking cap, a Daoist robe, and Buddhist sandals." Unlike Europe, where an immigrant religion triumphed over and excluded all other faiths, Buddhism in China became assimilated into Chinese culture alongside its other traditions.

Reflections: Why Do Things Change?

The rapidity of change in modern societies is among the most distinctive features of recent history, but change and transformation, though at various rates, have been constants in the human story since the very beginning. Explaining how and why human societies change is perhaps the central issue that historians confront, no matter which societies or periods of time they study. Those who specialize in the history of some particular culture or civilization often emphasize sources of change operating within those societies, although there is intense disagreement as to which are most significant. The ideas of great thinkers, the policies of leaders, struggles for power, the conflict of classes, the impact of new technologies, the growth or decline in population, variations in local climate or weather—all of these and more have their advocates as the primary motor of historical transformation.

Of course, it is not necessary to choose among them. The history of classical and postclassical China illustrates the range of internal factors that have driven change in that civilization. The political conflicts of the "era of warring states" provided the setting and the motivation for the emergence of Confucianism and Daoism, which in turn have certainly shaped the character and texture of Chinese civilization over many centuries. The personal qualities and brutal policies of Shihuangdi surely played a role in China's unification and in the brief duration of the Qin dynasty. The subsequent creation of a widespread network of canals and waterways as well as the country's technological achievements served to maintain that unity over very long periods of time. But the massive inequalities of Chinese society generated the peasant upheavals, which periodically shattered that unity and led to new ruling dynasties. Sometimes natural events, such as droughts and floods, triggered those rebellions.

World historians, more so than those who study particular civilizations or nations, have been inclined to find the primary source of change in contact with strangers, in external connections and interactions, whether direct or indirect. The histories of China and East Asia provide plenty of examples for this point of view as well. Conceptions of China as the "middle kingdom," infinitely superior to all surrounding societies, grew out of centuries of involvement with its neighbors. Some of those neighbors became Chinese as China's imperial reach grew, especially to the south. Even those that did not, such as Korea, Vietnam, and Japan, were decisively transformed by proximity to the "radiating civilization" of China. China's own cuisine, so distinctive in recent centuries, may well be a quite recent invention, drawing heavily on Indian and Southeast Asian cooking. Buddhism, of course, is an obvious borrowing from abroad, although its incorporation into Chinese civilization and its ups and downs within China owed much to internal cultural and political realities.

In the end, clear distinctions between internal and external sources of change in China's history—or that of any other society—are perhaps misleading. The boundary between "inside" and "outside" is itself a constantly changing line. Should the borderlands of northern China, where Chinese and Turkic peoples met and mingled, be regarded as internal or external to China itself? And, as the histories of Chinese Buddhism and of Japanese culture so clearly indicate, what comes from beyond is always transformed by what it encounters within.

Second Thoughts

What's the Significance?

Sui dynasty	tribute system	Shotoku Taishi
Tang dynasty	Xiongnu	*bushido*
Song dynasty economic	Khitan/Jurchen people	Chinese Buddhism
revolution	Silla dynasty (Korea)	Emperor Wendi
Hangzhou	*hangul/chu nom*	
foot binding	Trung sisters	

To assess your mastery of the material in this chapter, see the **Online Study Guide** at bedfordstmartins.com/strayer.

Big Picture Questions

1. In what ways did Tang and Song dynasty China resemble the classical Han dynasty period, and in what ways had China changed?
2. Based on this chapter, how would you respond to the idea that China was a self-contained or isolated civilization?
3. In what different ways did nearby peoples experience their giant Chinese neighbor, and how did they respond to it?
4. How can you explain the changing fortunes of Buddhism in China?
5. How did China influence the world beyond East Asia? How was China itself transformed by its encounters with a wider world?

Next Steps: For Further Study

Samuel Adshead, *Tang China: The Rise of the East in World History* (2004). Explores the role of China within the larger world.

Patricia Ebrey, *The Inner Quarters* (1993). A balanced account of the gains and losses experienced by Chinese women during the changes of the Song dynasty.

Mark Elvin, *The Pattern of the Chinese Past* (1973). A classic account of the Chinese economic revolution.

Edward Shaffer, *The Golden Peaches of Samarkand* (1985). Examines the interaction between China and Central Asia during the Tang dynasty.

Murasaki Shikibu, *The Tale of Genji,* translated by Royall Tyler (2002). Written around 1000, this saga of Japanese court life is sometimes called the world's first novel.

Arthur F. Wright, *Buddhism in Chinese History* (1959). An older account filled with wonderful stories and anecdotes.

Upper River during the Qing Ming Festival, http://www.ibiblio.org/ulysses/gec/painting/qingming/full.htm. A scrolling reproduction of a huge Chinese painting, showing in detail the Song dynasty city of Kaifeng.

For Web sites and documents related to this chapter, see **Make History** at bedfordstmartins.com/strayer.

CHAPTER TEN

The Worlds of European Christendom

Connected and Divided

500–1300

"We embraced each other once, then again and again. We were like brothers meeting after a long separation."[1] That is how the Eastern Orthodox patriarch Athenagoras described his historic meeting with Roman Catholic Pope Paul VI in early 1964 near the Mount of Olives in Jerusalem, the very site where Jesus had spent the night before his arrest. Not for more than 500 years had the heads of these two ancient branches of Christianity personally met. Now they held each other and exchanged gifts, including a representation of two of Christ's disciples embracing. Then they lifted mutual decrees of excommunication that representatives of their respective churches had imposed in 1054. It was a small step in a still very incomplete process of overcoming this deep rift within Christianity, which had been in the making for well over a thousand years. How had the world of Christendom come to be so sharply divided, both religiously and politically, as well as in terms of the larger historical trajectories of its eastern and western halves?

DURING THE POSTCLASSICAL ERA, CHRISTIANITY PROVIDED a measure of cultural commonality for the diverse societies of western Eurasia, much as Chinese civilization and Buddhism did for East Asia. By 1300, almost all of these societies—from Spain and England in the west to Russia in the east—had embraced in some form the teachings of the Middle Eastern Jewish carpenter called Jesus, but the world of European Christendom was deeply divided, both politically and

---

Charlemagne: This fifteenth-century manuscript painting depicts Charlemagne, King of the Franks, who was crowned Emperor by the pope in 800 C.E. His reign illustrates the close and sometimes conflicted relationship of political and religious authorities in postclassical Europe. It also represents the futile desire of many in Western Europe to revive the old Roman Empire, even as a substantially new civilization was taking shape in the aftermath of the Roman collapse several centuries earlier. (Victoria & Albert Museum, London, UK/The Bridgeman Art Library) religiously, in a way that the Chinese world was not. Its eastern half, known as the Byzantine Empire or Byzantium, continued the traditions of the Roman Empire, though on a smaller scale, until its conquest by the Muslim Turks in 1453. Centered on the magnificent city of Constantinople, Byzantium gradually evolved a distinctive civilization, all the while claiming to be Roman and seeking to preserve the heritage of the classical Mediterranean. With a particular form of Christianity known as Eastern Orthodoxy, the Byzantine Empire housed one of the major third-wave civilizations.

In Western or Latin Christendom, encompassing what we now know as Western Europe, political and religious leaders also tried to maintain links to the classical world, as illustrated by the spread of Christianity, the use of Latin in elite circles, and various efforts to revive or imitate the Roman Empire. The setting, however, was far different. In the West, the Roman imperial order had largely vanished by 500 C.E., accompanied by the weakening of many features of Roman civilization. Roads fell into disrepair, cities decayed, and long-distance trade shriveled. What replaced the old Roman order was a highly localized society — fragmented, decentralized, and competitive — in sharp contrast to the unified state of Byzantium. Like Byzantium, the Latin West ultimately became thoroughly Christian, but it was a gradual process lasting centuries, and its Roman Catholic Church, increasingly centered on the pope, had an independence from political authorities that the Eastern Orthodox Church did not. Moreover, the western church in particular and its society in general were far more rural than Byzantium and certainly had nothing to compare to the splendor of Constantinople. However, slowly at first and then with increasing speed after 1000, Western Europe emerged as an especially dynamic, expansive, and innovative third-wave civilization, combining elements of its classical past with the culture of Germanic and Celtic peoples to produce a hybrid civilization.

Europe eventually became the global center of Christianity, but that destiny was far from clear in 500 C.E. At that time, only about one-third of the world's Christians lived in Europe, while the rest found their homes in various parts of Africa, the Middle East, and Asia.[2] There they often followed distinct forms of Christianity, such as Nestorianism, which was regarded as heretical in Europe for its belief that Jesus had two quite distinct natures, one human and one divine. In Egypt, India, and Persia, remnants of earlier and larger Christian communities have survived as tolerated minorities into the present. By contrast, in early Armenia and Ethiopia (Axum), Christianity became the faith of the majority and has continued to express the national identity of peoples long cut off from contact with other Christian societies. Finally, the early Christian communities of North Africa, Nubia, Central Asia, and western China were largely eliminated as these regions subsequently embraced alternative religious traditions, such as Islam, Buddhism, or Confucianism. In this chapter, however, the historical spotlight falls on those regions that became the center of the Christian world — Byzantium and Western Europe.

Eastern Christendom: Building on the Past

Unlike most empires, Byzantium has no clear starting point. Its own leaders, as well as its neighbors and enemies, viewed it as simply a continuation of the Roman Empire. Some historians date its beginning to 330 C.E., when the Roman emperor Constantine, who became a Christian during his reign, established a new capital, Constantinople, on the site of an ancient Greek city called Byzantium. At the end of that century, the Roman Empire was formally divided into eastern and western halves, thus launching a division of Christendom that has lasted into the twenty-first century. Although the western Roman Empire collapsed during the fifth century, the eastern half persisted for another thousand years. Housing the ancient civilizations of Egypt, Greece, Syria, and Anatolia, the eastern Roman Empire (Byzantium) was far wealthier, more urbanized, and more cosmopolitan than its western counterpart; it possessed a much more defensible capital in the heavily walled city of Constantinople; and it had a shorter frontier to guard. Byzantium also enjoyed access to the Black Sea and command of the eastern Mediterranean. With a stronger army, navy, and merchant marine as well as clever diplomacy, its leaders were able to deflect the Germanic and Hun invaders who had overwhelmed the western Roman Empire.

Much that was late Roman—its roads, taxation system, military structures, centralized administration, imperial court, laws, Christian church—persisted in the east for many centuries. Like Tang dynasty China seeking to restore the glory of the Han era, Byzantium consciously sought to preserve the legacy of classical civilization and the Roman Empire. Constantinople was to be a "New Rome," and Byzantines referred to themselves as "Romans." Fearing contamination by "barbarian" customs, emperors forbade the residents of Constantinople from wearing boots, trousers, clothing made from animal skins, and long hairstyles, all of which were

■ Continuity and Change

In what respects did Byzantium continue the patterns of the classical Roman Empire? In what ways did it diverge from those patterns?

Snapshot **Key Moments in Byzantine History**

Founding of Constantinople	330
Final division of Roman Empire into eastern and western halves	ca. 395
Reign of Justinian; attempted reconquest of western empire	527–565
Loss of Syria/Palestine, Egypt, and North Africa to Arab forces	7th century
Iconoclastic controversy	726–843
Conversion of Vladimir, prince of Kiev, to Christianity	988
Mutual excommunication of pope and patriarch	1054
Crusaders sack Constantinople	1204
Ottomans seize Constantinople; end of Byzantine Empire	1453

associated with Germanic peoples, and insisted instead on Roman-style robes and sandals. But much changed as well over the centuries, marking the Byzantine Empire as the home of a distinctive civilization.

The Byzantine State

Perhaps the most obvious change was one of scale, as the Byzantine Empire never approximated the size of its Roman predecessor (see Map 10.1). The western Roman Empire was permanently lost to Byzantium, despite Emperor Justinian's (reigned 527–565) impressive but short-lived attempt to reconquer the Mediterranean basin. The rapid Arab/Islamic expansion in the seventh century resulted in the loss of Syria/Palestine, Egypt, and North Africa. Nonetheless, until roughly 1200, a more compact Byzantine Empire remained a major force in the eastern Mediterranean, controlling Greece, much of the Balkans (southeastern Europe), and Anatolia. A reformed administrative system gave appointed generals civil authority

Map 10.1   The Byzantine Empire
The Byzantine Empire reached its greatest extent under Emperor Justinian in the mid-sixth century C.E. It subsequently lost considerable territory to various Christian European powers as well as to Muslim Arab and Turkic invaders.

in the empire's provinces and allowed them to raise armies from the landowning peasants of the region. From that territorial base, the empire's naval and merchant vessels were active in both the Mediterranean and Black seas.

In its heyday, the Byzantine state was an impressive creation. Political authority remained tightly centralized in Constantinople, where the emperor claimed to govern all creation as God's worldly representative, styling himself the "peer of the Apostles" and the "sole ruler of the world." The imperial court tried to imitate the awesome grandeur of what they thought was God's heavenly court, which in fact resembled ancient Persian imperial splendor. Aristocrats trained in classical Greek rhetoric and literature took jobs in the administration in order to participate in court ceremonies that maintained their elite status. Parades of these silk-clad administrators added splendor to the imperial court, which also included mechanical lions that roared, birds that sang, and an immense throne that quickly elevated the emperor high above his presumably awestruck visitors. Nonetheless, this centralized state touched only lightly on the lives of most people, as it focused primarily on collecting taxes, maintaining order, and suppressing revolts. "Personal freedom in the provinces was constrained more by neighbors and rival households," concluded one historian, "than by the imperial government."[3]

After 1085, Byzantine territory shrank, owing to incursions by aggressive Christian European powers, by Catholic Crusaders, and later by Turkic Muslim invaders. The end came in 1453 when the Turkic Ottoman Empire, then known as the "sword of Islam," finally took Constantinople. One eyewitness to the event wrote a moving lament to his fallen city.

> And the entire city was to be seen in the tents of the [Turkish] camp, the city deserted, lying lifeless, naked, soundless, without either form or beauty. O city, head of all cities, center of the four corners of the world, pride of the Romans, civilizer of the barbarians.... Where is your beauty, O paradise...? Where are the bodies of the Apostle of my Lord...? Where are the relics of the saints, those of the martyrs? Where are the remains of Constantine the Great and the other emperors?... Oh, what a loss![4]

The Byzantine Church and Christian Divergence

■ Comparison
How did Eastern Orthodox Christianity differ from Roman Catholicism?

Intimately tied to the state was the Church, a relationship that became known as *caesaropapism*. Unlike Western Europe, where the Roman Catholic Church maintained some degree of independence from political authorities, in Byzantium the emperor assumed something of the role of both "Caesar," as head of state, and the pope, as head of the Church. Thus he appointed the patriarch, or leader, of the Orthodox Church; sometimes made decisions about doctrine; called church councils into session; and generally treated the Church as a government department. "The [Empire] and the church have a great unity and community," declared a twelfth-century patriarch. "Indeed they cannot be separated."[5] A dense network of bishops and priests brought the message of the Church to every corner of the empire, while numerous monasteries accommodated holy men, whose piety, self-denial, and good works made them highly influential among both elite and ordinary people.

Orthodox Christianity had a pervasive influence on every aspect of Byzantine life. It legitimated the supreme and absolute rule of the emperor, for he was a God-anointed ruler, a reflection of the glory of God on earth. It also provided a cultural identity for the empire's subjects. Even more than being "Roman," they were orthodox, or "right-thinking," Christians for whom the empire and the Church were equally essential to achieving eternal salvation. Constantinople was filled with churches and the relics of numerous saints. And the churches were filled with icons—religious paintings of Jesus, Mary, and the other saints—some of them artistic masterpieces, that many believed conveyed the divine presence to believers. Obscure theological issues about the Trinity and especially about the relationship of God and Jesus engaged the attention of ordinary people. One fourth-century bishop complained: "I wish to know the price of bread; one answers 'The Father is greater than the Son.' I inquire whether my bath is ready; one answers 'The Son has been made out of nothing.'"[6] Partisans of competing chariot-racing teams, known as the Greens and the Blues, vigorously debated theological issues as well as the merits of their favorite drivers.

St. Mark's Basilica
Consecrated in 1094, this ornate cathedral, although located in Venice, Italy, is a classic example of Byzantine architecture. Such churches represented perhaps the greatest achievement of Byzantine art and were certainly the most monumental expressions of Byzantine culture. (Erich Lessing/Art Resource, NY)

As Eastern Orthodoxy evolved, it came to define itself against an emerging Latin Christianity centered on papal Rome, as a deepening divide opened within the world of Christendom. Both had derived, of course, from the growth of Christianity in the Roman Empire and therefore had much in common—the teachings of Jesus; the Bible; the sacraments; a church hierarchy of patriarchs, bishops, and priests; a missionary impulse; and intolerance toward other religions. Despite these shared features, a general sense of a single widespread Christian community was increasingly replaced by an awareness of difference, competition, and outright hostility that even a common fear of Islam could not overcome. In part, this growing religious divergence reflected the political separation and rivalry between the Byzantine Empire and the emerging kingdoms of Western Europe. As the growth of Islam in the seventh century (described more fully in Chapter 11) submerged earlier centers of Christianity in the Middle East and North Africa,

Constantinople and Rome alone remained as alternative hubs of the Church. But they were now in different states that competed with each other for territory and for the right to claim the legacy of imperial Rome.

Beyond such political differences were those of language and culture. Although Latin remained the language of the Church and of elite communication in the West, it was abandoned in the Byzantine Empire in favor of Greek, which remained the basis for Byzantine education. More than in the West, Byzantine thinkers sought to formulate Christian doctrine in terms of Greek philosophical concepts.

Differences in theology and church practice likewise widened the gulf between Orthodoxy and Catholicism, despite agreement on fundamental doctrines. Disagreements about the nature of the Trinity or the relative importance of faith and reason gave rise to much controversy. One major issue involved the veneration of icons, popular paintings of saints and biblical scenes, usually painted on small wooden panels. Between 726 and 843, the Eastern Orthodox Church, on orders from Byzantine emperors, took the offensive against the use of icons in worship, arguing that they too easily became "idols," distracting believers from the adoration of God himself. Perhaps influenced by Islam's prohibition on the representation of the human form, this effort, known as *iconoclasm*, involved the actual destruction of much-loved icons and generated considerable opposition within Byzantium itself until it was ended in the mid-ninth century. But while it lasted, iconoclasm was highly offensive within Roman Catholic circles as well, for most of the Roman popes were fervent supporters of icon veneration.

Other more modest differences also occasioned mutual misunderstanding and disdain. Priests in the West shaved and, after 1050 or so, were supposed to remain celibate, while those in Byzantium allowed their beards to grow long and were permitted to marry. Orthodox ritual called for using bread leavened with yeast in the Mass, but Catholics used unleavened bread. More significant was the question of authority. Eastern Orthodox leaders sharply rejected the growing claims of Roman popes to be the sole and final authority for all Christians everywhere.

The rift in the world of Christendom grew gradually from the seventh century on, punctuated by various efforts to bridge the mounting divide between the western and eastern branches of the Church. A sign of this continuing deterioration occurred in 1054 when representatives of both churches mutually excommunicated each other, declaring in effect that those in the opposing tradition were not true Christians. The Crusades, launched in 1095 by the Catholic pope against the forces of Islam, made things worse. Western Crusaders, passing through the Byzantine Empire on their way to the Middle East, engaged in frequent conflict with local people and thus deepened the distrust between them. From the western viewpoint, Orthodox practices were "blasphemous, even heretical." One western observer of the Second Crusade noted that the Greeks "were judged not to be Christians and the Franks [French] considered killing them a matter of no importance."[7] During the Fourth Crusade in 1204, western forces seized and looted Constantinople and ruled Byzantium for the next half century. Their brutality only confirmed Byzantine views of their Roman Catholic despoilers as nothing more than barbarians. According to one Byzantine account, "they sacked the sacred places and trampled on divine things . . . they tore children from their mothers . . . and they defiled virgins in the holy chapels, fearing neither God's anger nor man's vengeance."[8] After this, the rupture in the world of Christendom proved irreparable.

Byzantium and the World

■ Connection

In what ways was the Byzantine Empire linked to a wider world?

Beyond its tense relationship with Western Europe, the Byzantine Empire, located astride Europe and Asia, also interacted intensively with its other neighbors. On a political and military level, Byzantium continued the long-term Roman struggle with the Persian Empire. That persisting conflict weakened both of them and was one factor in the remarkable success of Arab armies as they poured out of Arabia in the seventh century. Although Persia quickly became part of the Islamic world, Byzantium held out, even as it lost considerable territory to the Arabs. A Byzantine military innovation, known as "Greek fire"—a potent and flammable combination of oil, sulfur, and lime that was launched from bronze tubes—helped to hold off the Arabs. It operated something like a flamethrower and subsequently passed into Arab and Chinese arsenals as well. Byzantium's ability to defend its core regions delayed for many centuries the Islamic advance into southeastern Europe, which finally occurred at the hands of the Turkish Ottoman Empire in the fifteenth and sixteenth centuries.

Economically, the Byzantine Empire was a central player in the long-distance trade of Eurasia, with commercial links to Western Europe, Russia, Central Asia, the Islamic world, and China. Its gold coin, the bezant, was a widely used currency in the Mediterranean basin for more than 500 years, and wearing such coins as pendants was a high-status symbol in the less developed kingdoms of Western Europe.[9] The luxurious products of Byzantine craftspeople—jewelry, gemstones, silver and gold work, linen and woolen textiles, purple dyes—were much in demand. Its silk industry, based on Chinese technology, supplied much of the Mediterranean basin with this precious fabric.

The cultural influence of Byzantium was likewise significant. Preserving much of ancient Greek learning, the Byzantine Empire transmitted this classical heritage to the Islamic world as well as to the Christian West. In both places, it had an immensely stimulating impact among scientists, philosophers, theologians, and other intellectuals. Some saw it as an aid to faith and understanding of the world, while others feared it as impious and distracting (see the section on "Reason and Faith").

Byzantine religious culture also spread widely among Slavic-speaking peoples in the Balkans and Russia. As lands to the south and the east were overtaken by Islam, Byzantium looked to the north. By the early eleventh century, steady military pressure had brought many of the Balkan Slavic peoples, especially the Bulgars, under Byzantine control. Christianity and literacy accompanied this Byzantine offensive. Already in the ninth century, two Byzantine missionaries, Cyril and

Methodius, had developed an alphabet, based on Greek letters, with which Slavic languages could be written. This Cyrillic script made it possible to translate the Bible and other religious literature into these languages and greatly aided the process of conversion.

The Conversion of Russia

The most significant expansion of Orthodox Christianity occurred among the Slavic peoples of what is now Ukraine and western Russia. In this culturally diverse region, which also included Finnic and Baltic peoples as well as Viking traders, a modest state known as Kievan Rus—named after the most prominent city, Kiev—emerged in the ninth century C.E. Like many of the new third-wave civilizations, the development of Rus was stimulated by trade, in this case along the Dnieper River, linking Scandinavia and Byzantium. Loosely led by various princes, especially the prince of Kiev, Rus was a society of slaves and freemen, privileged people and commoners, dominant men and subordinate women. This stratification marked it as a third-wave civilization in the making (see Map 10.3 on page 283).

Religion reflected the region's cultural diversity, with the gods and practices of many peoples much in evidence. Small numbers of Christians, Muslims, and Jews were part of the mix. Then, in the late tenth century, a decisive turning point occurred. The growing interaction of Rus with the larger world prompted Prince Vladimir of Kiev to affiliate with one of the major religions of the area. He was searching for a faith that would unify the diverse peoples of his region, while linking Rus into wider networks of communication and exchange. According to ancient chronicles, he actively considered Judaism, Islam, Roman Catholicism, and Greek Orthodoxy before finally deciding on the religion of Byzantium. He rejected Islam, the chronicles tell us, because it prohibited alcoholic drink and "drinking is the joy of the Russes." The splendor of Constantinople's Orthodox churches apparently captured the imagination of Rus's envoys, for there they reported, "we knew not whether we were in heaven or on earth."[10] Political and commercial considerations no doubt also played a role in Vladimir's decision, and he acquired a sister of the Byzantine emperor as his bride, along with numerous Byzantine priests and advisers. Whatever the precise process, it was a freely made decision. Eastern Orthodox Christianity thus came to Rus without the pressure of foreign military defeat or occupation. Eventually, it took deep root among the Russian people.

It was a fateful choice with long-term implications for Russian history, for it brought this fledgling civilization firmly into the world of Orthodox Christianity, separating it from both the realm of Islam and the Roman Catholic West. Like many new civilizations, Rus borrowed extensively from its older and more sophisticated neighbor. Among these borrowings were Byzantine architectural styles, the Cyrillic alphabet, the extensive use of icons, a monastic tradition stressing prayer and service, and political ideals of imperial control of the Church, all of which became part of a

■ **Connection**

How did links to Byzantium transform the new civilization of Kievan Rus?

transformed Rus. Orthodoxy also provided a more unified identity for this emerging civilization and religious legitimacy for its rulers. Centuries later, when Byzantium had fallen to the Turks, a few Russian church leaders proclaimed the doctrine of a "third Rome." The original Rome had betrayed the faith, and the second Rome, Constantinople, had succumbed to Muslim infidels. Moscow was now the third Rome, the final protector and defender of true Orthodox Christianity. Though not widely proclaimed in Russia itself, such a notion reflected the "Russification" of Eastern Orthodoxy and its growing role as an element of Russian national identity. It was also a reminder of the enduring legacy of a thousand years of Byzantine history, long after the empire itself had vanished.

Western Christendom: Constructing a Hybrid Civilization

The western half of the Christian world followed a rather different path than that of the Byzantine Empire. For much of the postclassical millennium, it was distinctly on the margins of world history, partly because of its geographic location at the far western end of the Eurasian landmass. Thus it was far removed from the growing routes of world trade—by sea in the Indian Ocean and by land across the Silk Roads to China and the Sand Roads to West Africa. Not until the Eastern and Western hemispheres were joined after 1500 did Western Europe occupy a geographically central position in the global network. Internally, Europe's geography made political unity difficult. It was a region in which population centers were divided by mountain ranges and dense forests as well as by five major peninsulas

$\mathcal{S}napshot$ **Key Moments in the Evolution of Western Civilization**	
End of the western Roman Empire	476
Papacy of Gregory I	590–604
Muslim conquest of Spain	711
Charlemagne crowned as emperor	800
Otto I crowned as Holy Roman Emperor	962
Viking colony in Newfoundland	1000
Investiture conflict	1059–1152
Crusades begin	1095
Translations of Greek and Arab works available in Europe	12th–13th centuries
Thomas Aquinas	1225–1274
Marco Polo visits China	1271–1295

and two large islands (Britain and Ireland). However, its extensive coastlines and interior river systems facilitated exchange within Europe, while a moderate climate, plentiful rainfall, and fertile soils enabled a productive agriculture that could support a growing population.

In the Wake of Roman Collapse: Political Life in Western Europe, 500–1000

In the early centuries of the postclassical era, history must have seemed more significant than geography, for the Roman Empire, long a fixture of the western Mediterranean region, had collapsed. The traditional date marking the fall of Rome is 476, when the German general Odoacer overthrew the last Roman emperor in the West. In itself not very important, this event has come to symbolize a major turning point in the West, for much that had characterized Roman civilization also weakened, declined, or disappeared in the several centuries before and after 476. Any semblance of large-scale centralized rule vanished. Disease and warfare reduced Europe's population by more than 25 percent. Land under cultivation contracted, while forests, marshland, and wasteland expanded. Urban life too diminished sharply, as Europe reverted to a largely rural existence. Rome at its height was a city of 1 million people, but by the tenth century it numbered perhaps 10,000. Public buildings crumbled from lack of care. Outside Italy, long-distance trade dried up as Roman roads deteriorated, and money exchange gave way to barter in many places. Literacy lost ground as well. Germanic peoples, whom the Romans had viewed as barbarians—Goths, Visigoths, Franks, Lombards, Angles, Saxons—now emerged as the dominant peoples of Western Europe. In the process, Europe's center of gravity moved away from the Mediterranean toward the north and west.

■ **Comparison**
How did the historical development of the European West differ from that of Byzantium in the postclassical era?

Yet much that was classical or Roman persisted, even as a new order emerged in Europe. On the political front, a series of regional kingdoms—led by Visigoths in Spain, Franks in France, Lombards in Italy, and Angles and Saxons in England—arose to replace Roman authority, but many of these Germanic peoples, originally organized in small kinship-based tribes with strong warrior values, had already been substantially Romanized. Contact with the Roman Empire in the first several centuries C.E. generated more distinct ethnic identities among them, militarized their societies, and gave greater prominence to Woden, their god of war. As Germanic peoples migrated into or invaded Roman lands, many were deeply influenced by Roman culture, especially if they served in the Roman army. On the funeral monument of one such person was the telling inscription: "I am a Frank by nationality, but a Roman soldier under arms."[11]

■ **Change**
What replaced the Roman order in Western Europe?

The prestige of things Roman remained high, even after the empire itself had collapsed. Now as leaders of their own kingdoms, the Germanic rulers actively embraced written Roman law, using fines and penalties to provide order and justice in their new states in place of feuds and vendettas. One Visigoth ruler named

Athaulf (reigned 410–415), who had married a Roman noblewoman, gave voice to the continuing attraction of Roman culture and its empire.

> At first I wanted to erase the Roman name and convert all Roman territory into a Gothic empire. . . . But long experience has taught me that . . . without law a state is not a state. Therefore I have more prudently chosen the different glory of reviving the Roman name with Gothic vigour, and I hope to be acknowledged by posterity as the initiator of a Roman restoration.[12]

Several of the larger, though relatively short-lived, Germanic kingdoms also had aspirations to re-create something of the unity of the Roman Empire. Charlemagne (reigned 768–814), ruler of the Carolingian Empire, occupying what is now France, Belgium, the Netherlands, and parts of Germany and Italy, erected an embryonic imperial bureaucracy, standardized weights and measures, and began to act like an imperial ruler. On Christmas Day of the year 800, he was crowned as a new Roman emperor by the pope, although his realm splintered shortly after his death (see Map 10.2). Later Otto I of Saxony (reigned 936–973) gathered much of Germany under his control, saw himself as renewing Roman rule, and was likewise invested with the title of emperor by the pope. Otto's realm, subsequently known as the Holy Roman Empire, was largely limited to Germany and soon proved little more than a collection of quarreling principalities. Though unsuccessful in reviving anything approaching Roman authority, these efforts testify to the continuing appeal of the classical world, even as a new political system of rival kingdoms blended Roman and Germanic elements.

Map 10.2   Western Europe in the Ninth Century Charlemagne's Carolingian Empire brought a temporary unity to parts of Western Europe, but it was subsequently divided among his three sons, who waged war on one another.

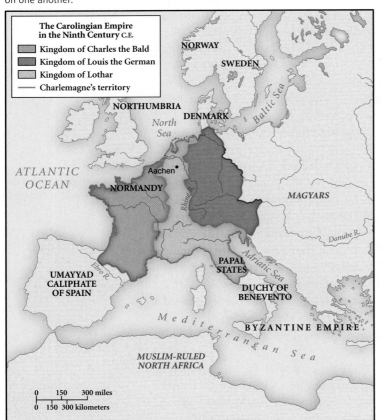

The Carolingian Empire
in the Ninth Century C.E.
- Kingdom of Charles the Bald
- Kingdom of Louis the German
- Kingdom of Lothar
- Charlemagne's territory

NORWAY
SWEDEN
NORTHUMBRIA
DENMARK
Baltic Sea
North Sea
ATLANTIC OCEAN
Aachen
NORMANDY
Rhine
MAGYARS
Danube R.
Ebro R.
PAPAL STATES
Adriatic Sea
DUCHY OF BENEVENTO
UMAYYAD CALIPHATE OF SPAIN
Mediterranean Sea
BYZANTINE EMPIRE
MUSLIM-RULED NORTH AFRICA

0   150   300 miles
0   150   300 kilometers

In the Wake of Roman Collapse: Society and the Church, 500–1000

Within these new kingdoms, a highly fragmented and decentralized society with great local variation emerged. In thousands of independent, self-sufficient, and largely isolated landed estates or manors, power—political, economic, and social—was exercised by a warrior elite of landowning lords. In the constant competition of these centuries, lesser lords and knights swore allegiance to greater lords or kings and thus became their vassals, frequently receiving lands and booty in return for military service.

Such reciprocal ties between superior and subordinate were also apparent at the bottom of the social hierarchy, as Roman-style slavery gradually gave way to serfdom. Unlike slaves, serfs were not the personal property of their masters, could not be arbitrarily thrown off their land, and were allowed to live in families. However, they were bound to their masters' estates as peasant laborers and owed various payments and services to the lord of the manor. One family on a manor near Paris in the ninth century owed four silver coins, wine, wood, three hens, and fifteen eggs per year. Women generally were required to weave cloth and make clothing for the lord, while men labored in the lord's fields. In return, the serf family received a small farm and such protection as the lord could provide. In a violent and insecure world adjusting to the absence of Roman authority, the only security available to many individuals or families lay in these communities, where the ties to kin, manor, and lord constituted the primary human loyalties. It was a world apart from the stability of life in imperial Rome or its continuation in Byzantium.

Also filling the vacuum left by the collapse of empire was the Roman Catholic Church, yet another link to the now defunct Roman world. Its hierarchical organization of popes, bishops, priests, and monasteries was modeled on that of the Roman Empire and took over some of its political, administrative, educational, and welfare functions. Like the Buddhist establishment in China, the Church later became extremely wealthy, with reformers often accusing it of forgetting its central spiritual mission. It also provided a springboard for the conversion of Europe's many "pagan" peoples. Numerous missionaries, commissioned by the pope, monasteries, or already converted rulers, fanned out across Europe, generally pursuing a "top-down" strategy. Frequently it worked, as local kings and warlords found status and legitimacy in association with a literate and "civilized" religion that still bore something of the grandeur of Rome. With "the wealth and protection of the powerful," ordinary people followed their rulers into the fold of the Church.[13] This process was similar to Buddhism's appeal for the nomadic rulers of northern and western China following the collapse of the Han dynasty. Christianity, like Buddhism, also bore the promise of superior supernatural powers, and its spread was frequently associated with reported miracles of healing, rainfall, fertility, and victory in battle.

But it was not an easy sell. Outright coercion was sometimes part of the process. For example, when Charlemagne conquered the Saxons of northern Germany, he converted them to Christianity through mass baptisms, under the threat of death for anyone who refused. More often, softer methods prevailed. The Church proved willing to accommodate a considerable range of earlier cultural practices, absorbing them into an emerging Christian tradition. Pope Gregory (reigned 590-604) famously instructed his missionaries in England

> that the temples of the idols in that nation ought not to be destroyed; but let the idols that are in them be destroyed; let holy water be made and sprinkled in

the said temples; let altars be erected and relics placed; . . . that the nation, see-ing that their temples are not destroyed . . . , may the more familiarly resort to the places to which they have been accustomed.[14]

Thus amulets and charms to ward off evil became medals with the image of Jesus or the Virgin Mary; traditionally sacred wells and springs became the sites of churches; festivals honoring ancient gods became Christian holy days. December 25 was selected as the birthday of Jesus, for it was associated with the winter solstice, the coming of more light, and the birth or rebirth of various deities in pre-Christian European traditions. By 1100, most of Europe had embraced Christianity. Even so, priests and bishops had to warn their congregations against the worship of rivers, trees, and mountains, and for many people, ancient gods, monsters, trolls, and spirits still inhabited the land. The spreading Christian faith, like the new political framework of European civilization, was a hybrid.

Church authorities and the nobles/warriors who exercised political influence reinforced each other. Rulers provided protection for the papacy and strong encour-agement for the faith. In return, the Church offered religious legitimacy for the powerful and the prosperous. "It is the will of the Creator," declared the teaching of the Church, "that the higher shall always rule over the lower. Each individual and class should stay in its place [and] perform its tasks."[15] But Church and nobility com-peted as well as cooperated, for they were rival centers of power in post-Roman Europe. Particularly controversial was the right to appoint bishops and the pope himself; this issue, known as the investiture conflict, was especially prominent in the eleventh and twelfth centuries. Was the right to make appointments the responsibil-ity of the Church alone, or did kings and emperors also have a role? In the compro-mise that ended the conflict, the Church won the right to appoint its own officials, while secular rulers retained an informal and symbolic role in the process.

Accelerating Change in the West, 1000–1300

The pace of change in this emerging civilization picked up considerably in the sev-eral centuries after 1000. For the preceding 300 years, Europe had been subject to repeated invasions from every direction. Muslim armies had conquered Spain and threatened Europe. Magyar (Hungarian) invasions from the east and Viking incur-sions from the north likewise disrupted and threatened post-Roman Europe. But by the year 1000, these invasions had been checked and the invaders absorbed into settled society. The greater security and stability that came with relative peace arguably opened the way to an accelerating tempo of change. The climate also seemed to cooperate. A generally warming trend after 750 reached its peak in the eleventh and twelfth centuries, enhancing agricultural production.

Whatever may have launched this new phase of European civilization, com-monly called the High Middle Ages, the signs of expansion and growth were widely evident. The population of Europe grew from perhaps 35 million in 1000 to about

■ Change
In what ways was European civilization changing after 1000?

Map 10.3   Europe in the High Middle Ages

By the eleventh century, the national monarchies—of France, Spain, England, Poland, and Germany—that would organize European political life had begun to take shape. The earlier external attacks on Europe from Vikings, Magyars, and Muslims had largely ceased, although it was clear that European civilization was developing in the shadow of the Islamic world.

80 million in 1340. With more people, many new lands had to be opened for cultivation in a process paralleling that of China at the same time. Great lords, bishops, and religious orders organized new villages on what had recently been forest or wasteland. Marshes were drained; land was reclaimed from the sea in the Netherlands; everywhere trees were felled. By 1300, the forest cover of Europe had

been reduced to about 20 percent of the land area. "I believe that the forest . . . covers the land to no purpose," declared a German abbot, "and hold this to be an unbearable harm."[16]

The increased production associated with this agricultural expansion stimulated a considerable growth in long-distance trade, much of which had dried up in the aftermath of the Roman collapse. One center of commercial activity lay in Northern Europe from England to the Baltic coast and involved the exchange of wood, beeswax, furs, rye, wheat, salt, cloth, and wine. The other major trading network centered on northern Italian towns such as Florence, Genoa, and Venice. Their trading partners were the more established civilizations of Islam and Byzantium, and the primary objects of trade included the silks, drugs, precious stones, and spices from Asia. At great trading fairs, particularly those in the Champagne area of France near Paris, merchants from Northern and Southern Europe met to exchange the products of their respective areas, such as northern woolens for Mediterranean spices. Thus the self-sufficient communities of earlier centuries increasingly forged commercial bonds among themselves and with more distant peoples.

The population of towns and cities likewise grew, on the sites of older Roman towns, at trading crossroads and fortifications, and around cathedrals all over Europe. Some had only a few hundred people, but others became much larger. In the early 1300s, London had about 40,000 people, Paris had approximately 80,000, and Venice by the end of the fourteenth century could boast perhaps 150,000. To keep these figures in perspective, Constantinople housed some 400,000 people in 1000, Córdoba in Muslim Spain about 500,000, the Song dynasty capital of Hangzhou more than 1 million in the thirteenth century, and the Aztec capital of Tenochtitlán perhaps 200,000 by 1500. Nonetheless, urbanization was proceeding apace in Europe. These towns gave rise to and attracted new groups of people, particularly merchants, bankers, artisans, and university-trained professionals such as lawyers, doctors, and scholars. Many of these groups, including university professors and students, organized themselves into guilds (associations of people pursuing the same line of work) in order to regulate their respective professions. In doing so, they introduced a new and more productive division of labor into European society.

Between the eleventh and thirteenth centuries, economic growth and urbanization offered European women substantial new opportunities. Women were active in a number of urban professions, such as weaving, brewing, milling grain, midwifery, small-scale retailing, laundering, spinning, and, of course, prostitution. In twelfth-century Paris, for example, a list of 100 occupations identified 86 as involving women workers, of which 6 were exclusively female. In England, women worked as silk weavers, hatmakers, tailors, brewers, and leather processors and were entitled to train female apprentices in some of these trades. In Frankfurt, about one-third of the crafts and trades were entirely female, another 40 percent were dominated by men, and the rest were open to both. Widows of great merchants sometimes continued their husbands' businesses, and one of them, Rose Burford, lent a large sum of money to the king of England to finance a war against Scotland in 1318.

European Women at Work This manuscript painting from the Middle Ages shows women and men cooperating in the baking of bread, long a staple of European diets. (Bibliothèque nationale de France)

By the fifteenth century, such opportunities were declining. Most women's guilds were gone, and women were restricted or banned from many others. Even brothels were run by men. Technological progress may have been one reason for this change. Water- and animal-powered grain mills replaced the hand-grinding previously done by women, and larger looms making heavier cloth replaced the lighter looms that women had worked. Men increasingly took over these professions and trained their sons as apprentices, making it more difficult for women to remain active in these fields.

If urban work roles were diminishing for women, religious life provided other possibilities. As in Buddhist lands, substantial numbers of women, particularly from aristocratic families, were attracted to the secluded life of poverty, chastity, and obedience within a nunnery for the relative freedom from male control that it offered. Here was one of the few places where some women could exercise authority and obtain a measure of education. Operating outside of monastic life, the Beguines were groups of laywomen, often from poorer families in Northern Europe, who lived together, practiced celibacy, and devoted themselves to weaving and to working with the sick, the old, and the poor. Another religious role was that of anchoress, a woman who withdrew to a locked cell, usually attached to a church, where she devoted herself wholly to prayer and fasting. Some of them gained reputations for great holiness and were much sought after for spiritual guidance. For a few women—the nun Hildegard of Bingen and the anchoress Julian of Norwich, for example—religious life brought considerable public prominence and spiritual influence.

A further sign of accelerating change in the West lay in the growth of territorial states with more effective institutions of government commanding the loyalty, or at least the obedience, of their subjects. Since the disintegration of the Roman Empire, Europeans' loyalties had focused on the family, the manor, or the religious community, but seldom on the state. Great lords may have been recognized as kings, but their authority was extremely limited and was exercised through a complex network of feudal relationships with earls, counts, barons, and knights, who often felt little obligation to do the king's bidding. But in the eleventh through the thirteenth century, the nominal monarchs of Europe gradually and painfully began to consolidate their authority, and the outlines of French, English, Spanish, Scandinavian, and other states began to appear, each with its own distinct language and culture (see Map 10.3). Royal courts and embryonic bureaucracies were established, and groups of professional administrators appeared. Territorial kingdoms were not universal, however. In Italy, city-states flourished as urban areas grew wealthy and powerful, whereas the Germans remained loyal to a large number of small principalities within the Holy Roman Empire.

Europe Outward Bound: The Crusading Tradition

■ Change
What was the impact of the Crusades in world history?

Accompanying the growth of European civilization after 1000 were efforts to engage more actively with both near and more distant neighbors. This "medieval expansion" of Western Christendom took place as the Byzantine world was contracting under pressure from the West, from Arab invasion, and later from Turkish conquest. The western half of Christendom was on the rise, while the eastern part was in decline. It was a sharp reversal of their earlier trajectories.

Expansion, of course, has been characteristic of virtually every civilization and has taken a variety of forms—territorial conquest, empire building, settlement of new lands, vigorous trading initiatives, and missionary activity. European civilization was no exception. As population mounted, settlers cleared new land, much of it on the eastern fringes of Europe. The Vikings of Scandinavia, having raided much of Europe, set off on a maritime transatlantic venture around 1000 that briefly established a colony in Newfoundland in North America, and more durably in Greenland and Iceland. As Western economies grew, merchants, travelers, diplomats, and missionaries brought European society into more intensive contact with more distant peoples and with Eurasian commercial networks. By the thirteenth and fourteenth centuries, Europeans had direct, though limited, contact with India, China, and Mongolia. Europe clearly was outward bound.

Nothing more dramatically revealed European expansiveness and the religious passions that informed it than the Crusades, a series of "holy wars" that captured the imagination of Western Christendom for more than four centuries, beginning in 1095. In European thinking and practice, the Crusades were wars undertaken at God's command and authorized by the pope as the Vicar of Christ on earth. They required participants to swear a vow and in return offered an indulgence, which removed the penalties for any confessed sins, as well as various material benefits, such as immunity from lawsuits and a moratorium on the repayment of debts. Any number of political, economic, and social motives underlay the Crusades, but at their core they were religious wars. Within Europe, the amazing support for the Crusades reflected an understanding of them "as providing security against mortal enemies threatening the spiritual health of all Christendom and all Christians."[17] Crusading drew upon both Christian piety and the warrior values of the elite, with little sense of contradiction between these impulses.

The most famous Crusades were those aimed at wresting Jerusalem and the holy places associated with the life of Jesus from Islamic control and returning them to Christendom (see Map 10.4). Beginning in 1095, wave after wave of Crusaders from all walks of life and many countries flocked to the eastern Mediterranean, where they temporarily carved out four small Christian states, the last of which was recaptured by Muslim forces in 1291. Led or supported by an assortment of kings, popes, bishops, monks, lords, nobles, and merchants, the Crusades demonstrated a growing European capacity for organization, finance, transportation, and recruitment, made all the more impressive by the absence of any centralized direction for the project. They also demonstrated an amazing cruelty. The seizure of Jerusalem in 1099 was

Map 10.4 The Crusades

Western Europe's crusading tradition reflected the expansive energy and religious impulses of an emerging civilization. It was directed against Muslims in the Middle East, Sicily, and Spain as well as the Eastern Orthodox Christians of the Byzantine Empire. The Crusades also involved attacks on Jewish communities, probably the first organized mass pogroms against Jews in Europe's history.

Christians and Muslims
This fourteenth-century painting illustrates the Christian seizure of Jerusalem during the First Crusade in 1099. The crowned figure in the center is Godefroi de Bouillon, a French knight and nobleman who played a prominent role in the attack and was briefly known as the king of Jerusalem. (Snark/Art Resource, NY)

accompanied by the slaughter of many Muslims and Jews as the Crusaders made their way, according to perhaps exaggerated reports, through streets littered with corpses and ankle deep in blood to the Sepulcher of Christ.

Crusading was not limited to targets in the Islamic Middle East, however. Those Christians, both Spanish and foreign, who waged war for centuries to reclaim the Iberian Peninsula from Muslim hands were likewise declared "crusaders," with a similar set of spiritual and material benefits. So too were Scandinavian and German warriors who took part in wars to conquer, settle, and convert lands along the Baltic Sea. The Byzantine Empire and Russia, both of which followed Eastern Orthodox Christianity, were also on the receiving end of Western crusading, as were Christian heretics and various enemies of the pope in Europe itself. Crusading, in short, was a pervasive feature of European expansion, which persisted as Europeans began their oceanic voyages in the fifteenth century and beyond.

Surprisingly perhaps, the Crusades had little lasting impact, either politically or religiously, in the Middle East. European power was not sufficiently strong or long-lasting to induce much conversion, and the small European footholds there had come under Muslim control by 1300. The penetration of Turkic-speaking peoples from Central Asia and the devastating Mongol invasions of the thirteenth century were far more significant in Islamic history than were the temporary incursions of European Christians. In fact, Muslims largely forgot about the Crusades until the late nineteenth and early twentieth centuries, when their memory was revived in the context of a growing struggle against European imperialism.

In Europe, however, interaction with the Islamic world had very significant long-term consequences. Spain, Sicily, and the Baltic region were brought permanently into the world of Western Christendom, while a declining Byzantium was further weakened by the Crusader sacking of Constantinople of 1204 and left even more vulnerable to Turkish conquest. In Europe itself, popes strengthened their position, at least for a time, in their continuing struggles with secular authorities. Tens of thousands of Europeans came into personal contact with the Islamic world, from which they picked up a taste for the many luxury goods available there, stimulating a demand for Asian goods. They also learned techniques for producing sugar on large plantations using slave labor, a process that had incalculable consequences in later centuries as Europeans transferred the plantation system to the Americas.

Muslim scholarship, together with the Greek learning that it incorporated, also flowed into Europe, largely through Spain and Sicily.

If the cross-cultural contacts born of crusading opened channels of trade, technology transfer, and intellectual exchange, they also hardened cultural barriers between peoples. The rift between Eastern Orthodoxy and Roman Catholicism deepened further and remains to this day a fundamental divide in the Christian world. Christian anti-Semitism was both expressed and exacerbated as Crusaders on their way to Jerusalem found time to massacre Jews in a number of European cities. European empire building, especially in the Americas, continued the crusading notion that "God wills it." Crusading's impact has been felt even in more recent times. In the past two centuries, as the worlds of Europe and Islam collided, both sides found many occasions in which images of the Crusades, however distorted, proved politically or ideologically useful.[18]

The West in Comparative Perspective

At one level, the making of Western civilization in the postclassical era was unremarkable. Civilizations had risen, fallen, renewed themselves, and evolved at many times and in many places. The European case has received extraordinary scrutiny, not so much because of its special significance at the time, but because of its later role as a globally dominant region. Historians have sometimes sought to account for Western Europe's global influence after 1500 in terms of some unique feature of its earlier history. However we might explain Europe's later rise to prominence on the world stage, its development in the several centuries after 1000 made only modest ripples beyond its own region. In some respects, Europe was surely distinctive, but it was not yet a major player in the global arena. Comparisons, particularly with China, help to place European developments in a world history context.

Catching Up

As the hybrid civilization of the West evolved, it was clearly less developed in comparison to Byzantium, China, India, and the Islamic world. Its cities were smaller, its political authorities weaker, its economy less commercialized, its technology inferior to the more established civilizations. Muslim observers who encountered Europeans saw them as barbarians. "Their bodies are large, their manners harsh, their understanding dull, and their tongues heavy. . . . Those of them who are farthest to the north are the most subject to stupidity, grossness and brutishness."[19] That was the opinion of a tenth-century Arab geographer. Muslim travelers over the next several centuries saw more to be praised in West African kingdoms, where Islam was practiced and gold was plentiful.

Furthermore, thoughtful Europeans who directly encountered other peoples often acknowledged their comparative backwardness. "In our time," wrote a twelfth-century European scholar, "it is in Toledo [a Spanish city long under

Muslim rule] that the teaching of the Arabs . . . is offered to the crowds. I hastened there to listen to the teaching of the wisest philosophers of this world."[20] The Italian traveler Marco Polo in the thirteenth century proclaimed Hangzhou in China "the finest and noblest [city] in the world." In the sixteenth century, Spanish invaders of Mexico were stunned at the size and wealth of the Aztec capital, especially its huge market, claiming that "we had never seen such a thing before."[21]

■ Change
In what ways did borrowing from abroad shape European civilization after 1000?

Curious about the rest of the world, Europeans proved quite willing to engage with and borrow from the more advanced civilizations to the east. Growing European economies, especially in the northwest, reconnected with the Eurasian trading system, with which they had lost contact after the fall of Rome. Now European elites eagerly sought spices, silks, porcelain, sugar, and much else that was available on the world market. Despite their belief in Christianity as the "one true religion," Europeans embraced scientific treatises and business practices from the Arabs, philosophical and artistic ideas from the pagan Greeks, and mathematical concepts from India. It was China, however, that was the most significant source of European borrowing, although often indirectly. From that East Asian civilization, Europeans learned about the compass, papermaking, gunpowder, nautical technology, iron casting, a public postal service, and more. When the road to China opened in the thirteenth and fourteenth centuries, many Europeans, including the merchant-traveler Marco Polo, were more than willing to make the long and difficult journey, returning with amazing tales of splendor and abundance far beyond what was available in Europe. When Europeans took to the oceans in the fifteenth and sixteenth centuries, they were seeking out the sources of African and Asian wealth. Thus the accelerating growth of European civilization was accompanied by its reintegration into the larger Afro-Eurasian networks of exchange and communication.

In this willingness to borrow, Europe resembled several other third-wave civilizations of the time. Japan, for example, took much from China; West Africa drew heavily on Islamic civilization; and Russia actively imitated Byzantium. All of them were then developing civilizations, in a position similar to the developing countries of the third world in the twentieth century. The whole process, of course, was then rather less deliberate and self-conscious than it became in the last century.

Technological borrowing required adaptation to the unique conditions of Europe and was accompanied by considerable independent invention as well. Together these processes generated a significant tradition of technological innovation that allowed Europe by 1500 to catch up with, and in some areas perhaps to surpass, China and the Islamic world. That achievement bears comparison with the economic revolution of Tang and Song dynasty China, although Europe began at a lower level and depended more on borrowing than did its Chinese counterpart. But in the several centuries surrounding 1000 at both ends of Eurasia, major processes of technological innovation were under way.

In Europe, technological breakthroughs first became apparent in agriculture as Europeans adapted to the very different environmental conditions north of the Alps in the several centuries following 500 C.E. They developed a heavy-wheeled plow, which could handle the dense soils of Northern Europe far better than the light or "scratch" plow used in Mediterranean agriculture. To pull the plow, Europeans began to rely increasingly on horses rather than oxen and to use iron horseshoes and a more efficient collar, which probably originated in China or Central Asia and could support much heavier loads. In addition, Europeans developed a new three-field system of crop rotation, which allowed considerably more land to be planted at any one time. These were the technological foundations for a more productive agriculture that could support the growing population of European civilization, and especially its urban centers, far more securely than before.

Beyond agriculture, Europeans began to tap nonanimal sources of energy in a major way, particularly after 1000. A new type of windmill, very different from an earlier Persian version, was widely used in Europe by the twelfth and thirteenth centuries. The water-driven mill was even more important. The Romans had used that type of mill largely to grind grain, but their development was limited, given that few streams flowed all year and many slaves were available to do the work. By the ninth century, however, water mills were rapidly becoming more evident in Europe. In the early fourteenth century, a concentration of sixty-eight mills dotted a one-mile stretch of the Seine River near Paris. In addition to grinding grain, these mills provided power for sieving flour, tanning hides, making beer, sawing wood, manufacturing iron, and making paper. Devices such as cranks, flywheels, camshafts, and complex gearing mechanisms, when combined with water or wind power, enabled Europeans of the High Middle Ages to revolutionize production in a number of industries and to break with the ancient tradition of depending almost wholly on animal or human muscle as sources of energy. So intense was the interest of European artisans and engineers in tapping mechanical sources of energy that a number of them experimented with perpetual-motion machines, an idea borrowed from Indian philosophers.

Technological borrowing also was evident in the arts of war. Gunpowder was invented in China, but Europeans were probably the first to use it in cannons, in the early fourteenth century, and by 1500 they had the most advanced arsenals in the world. In 1517, one Chinese official, upon first encountering European ships and weapons, remarked with surprise, "The westerns are extremely dangerous because of their artillery. No weapon ever made since memorable antiquity is superior to their cannon."[22] Advances in

European Technology Europeans' fascination with technology and their religious motivation for investigating the world are apparent in this thirteenth-century portrayal of God as a divine engineer, laying out the world with a huge compass. (Erich Lessing/Art Resource, NY)

shipbuilding and navigational techniques—including the magnetic compass and stern-post rudder from China and adaptations of the Arab lateen sail, which enabled vessels to sail against the wind—provided the foundation for European mastery of the seas.

Europe's passion for technology was reflected in its culture and ideas as well as in its machines. About 1260, the English scholar and Franciscan friar Roger Bacon wrote of the possibilities he foresaw, and in doing so, he expressed the confident spirit of the age.

> Machines of navigation can be constructed, without rowers…which are borne under the guidance of one man at a greater speed than if they were full of men. Also a chariot can be constructed, that will move with incalculable speed without any draught animal….Also flying machines may be constructed so that a man may sit in the midst of the machine turning a certain instrument by means of which wings artificially constructed would beat the air after the manner of a bird flying…and there are countless other things that can be constructed.[23]

Pluralism in Politics

■ Comparison
Why was Europe unable to achieve the kind of political unity that China experienced? What impact did this have on the subsequent history of Europe?

Unlike the large centralized states of Byzantium, the Islamic world, and China, post-Roman European civilization never regained the unity it had under Roman rule. Rather, political life gradually crystallized into a system of competing states (France, Spain, England, Sweden, Prussia, the Netherlands, and Poland, among others) that has persisted into the twenty-first century and that the European Union still confronts. Geographic barriers, ethnic and linguistic diversity, and the shifting balances of power among its many states prevented the emergence of a single European empire, despite periodic efforts to re-create something resembling the still-remembered unity of the Roman Empire.

This multicentered political system shaped the emerging civilization of the West in many ways. It gave rise to frequent wars, enhanced the role and status of military men, and drove the "gunpowder revolution." Thus European society and values were militarized far more than in China, which gave greater prominence to scholars and bureaucrats. Intense interstate rivalry, combined with a willingness to borrow, also greatly stimulated European technological development. By 1500, Europeans had gone a long way toward catching up with their more advanced Asian counterparts in agriculture, industry, war, and sailing.

But endemic warfare did not halt European economic growth. Capital, labor, and goods found their way around political barriers, while the common assumptions of Christian culture and the use of Latin and later French by the literate elite fostered communication across political borders. Europe's multistate system thus provided enough competition to be stimulating but also sufficient order and unity to allow economic endeavors to prosper.

The states within this emerging European civilization also differed from those to the east. Their rulers generally were weaker and had to contend with competing sources of power. Unlike the Orthodox Church in Byzantium, with its practice of caesaropapism, the Roman Catholic Church in the West maintained a degree of independence from state authority that served to check the power of kings and lords. European vassals had certain rights in return for loyalty to their lords and kings. By the thirteenth century, this meant that high-ranking nobles, acting through formal councils, had the right to advise their rulers and to approve new taxes.

This three-way struggle for power among kings, warrior aristocrats, and church leaders, all of them from the nobility, enabled urban-based merchants in Europe to achieve an unusual independence from political authority. Many cities, where wealthy merchants exercised local power, won the right to make and enforce their own laws and appoint their own officials. Some of them—Venice, Genoa, Pisa, and Milan, for example—became almost completely independent city-states. In the case of other cities, kings granted charters that allowed them to have their own courts, laws, and governments, while paying their own kind of taxes to the king instead of feudal dues. Powerful, independent cities were a distinctive feature of European life after 1100 or so. By contrast, Chinese cities, which were far larger than those of Europe, were simply part of the empire and enjoyed few special privileges. Although commerce was far more extensive in China than in a developing Europe, the powerful Chinese state favored the landowners over merchants, monopolized the salt and iron industries, and actively controlled and limited merchant activity far more than the new and weaker royal authorities of Europe were able to do.

The relative weakness of Europe's rulers allowed urban merchants more leeway and, according to some historians, paved the way to a more thorough development of capitalism in later centuries. It also led to the development of representative institutions or parliaments through which the views and interests of these contending forces could be expressed and accommodated. Intended to strengthen royal authority by consulting with major social groups, these embryonic parliaments did not represent the "people" or the "nation" but instead embodied the three great "estates of the realm"—the clergy (the first estate), the landowning nobility (the second estate), and urban merchants (the third estate).

Reason and Faith

A further feature of this emerging European civilization was a distinctive intellectual tension between the claims of human reason and those of faith. Christianity, of course, had developed in a classical world suffused with Greek rationalism. Some early Christian thinkers sought to maintain a clear separation between the new religion and the ideas of Plato and Aristotle. "What indeed has Athens to do with Jerusalem?" asked Tertullian (150–225 C.E.), an early church leader from North Africa. More common, however, was the notion that Greek philosophy could serve as a "handmaiden" to faith, more fully disclosing the truths of Christianity. In the reduced circumstances of Western Europe after the collapse of the Roman Empire,

■ **Comparison**

In what different ways did classical Greek philosophy and science have an impact in the West, in Byzantium, and in the Islamic world?

European University Life in the Middle Ages
This fourteenth-century manuscript painting shows a classroom scene from the University of Bologna in Italy. Note the sleeping and disruptive students.
(Bildarchiv Preussischer Kulturbesitz/Art Resource, NY)

the Church had little direct access to the writings of the Greeks, although some Latin translations and commentaries provided a continuing link to the world of classical thought.

But intellectual life in Europe changed dramatically in the several centuries after 1000, amid a rising population, a quickening commercial life, growing towns and cities, and the Church's growing independence from royal or noble authorities. Moreover, the West was developing a legal system that guaranteed a measure of independence for a variety of institutions—towns and cities, guilds, professional associations, and especially universities. An outgrowth of earlier cathedral schools, these European universities—in Paris, Bologna, Oxford, Cambridge, Salamanca—became "zones of intellectual autonomy" in which scholars could pursue their studies with some freedom from the dictates of religious or political authorities, although that freedom was never complete and was frequently contested.[24]

This was the setting in which European Christian thinkers, a small group of literate churchmen, began to emphasize, quite self-consciously, the ability of human reason to penetrate divine mysteries and to grasp the operation of the natural order. An early indication of this new emphasis occurred in the late eleventh century when students in a monastic school in France asked their teacher, Anselm, to provide them a proof for the existence of God based solely on reason, without using the Bible or other sources of divine revelation.

The new interest in rational thought was applied first and foremost to theology, the "queen of the sciences" to European thinkers. Here was an effort to provide a rational foundation for faith, not to replace faith or to rebel against it. Logic, philosophy, and rationality would operate in service to Christ. Of course, some people opposed this new emphasis on human reason. Bernard of Clairvaux, a twelfth-century French abbot, declared, "Faith believes. It does not dispute."[25] His contemporary and intellectual opponent, the French scholar William of Conches, lashed out: "You poor fools. God can make a cow out of a tree, but has he ever done so? Therefore show some reason why a thing is so or cease to hold that it is so."[26]

European intellectuals also applied their newly discovered confidence in human reason to law, medicine, and the world of nature, exploring optics, magnetism, astronomy, and alchemy. Slowly and never completely, the scientific study of nature, known as "natural philosophy," began to separate itself from theology. In

European universities, natural philosophy was studied in the faculty of arts, which was separate from the faculty of theology, although many scholars contributed to both fields.

This mounting enthusiasm for rational inquiry stimulated European scholars to seek out original Greek texts, particularly those of Aristotle. They found them in the Greek-speaking world of Byzantium and in the Arab world, where they had long ago been translated into Arabic. In the twelfth and thirteenth centuries, an explosion of translations from Greek and Arabic into Latin gave European scholars direct access to the works of ancient Greeks and to the remarkable results of Arab scholarship in astronomy, optics, medicine, pharmacology, and more. Much of this Arab science was now translated into Latin and provided a boost to Europe's changing intellectual life, centered in the new universities. One of these translators, Adelard of Bath (1080-1142), remarked that he had learned, "under the guidance of reason from Arabic teachers," not to trust established authority.[27]

It was the works of the prolific Aristotle, with his logical approach and "scientific temperament," that made the deepest impression. His writings became the basis for university education and largely dominated the thought of Western Europe in the five centuries after 1200. In the work of the thirteenth-century theologian Thomas Aquinas, Aristotle's ideas were thoroughly integrated into a logical and systematic presentation of Christian doctrine. In this growing emphasis on human rationality, at least partially separate from divine revelation, lay one of the foundations of the later Scientific Revolution and the secularization of European intellectual life (see Chapter 16).

Surprisingly, nothing comparable occurred in the Byzantine Empire, where knowledge of the Greek language was widespread and access to Greek texts was easy. Although Byzantine scholars kept the classical tradition alive, their primary interest lay in the humanities (literature, philosophy, history) and theology rather than in the natural sciences or medicine. Furthermore, both state and church had serious reservations about classical Greek learning. In 529, the emperor Justinian closed Plato's Academy in Athens, claiming that it was an outpost of paganism. Its scholars dispersed into lands that soon became Islamic, carrying Greek learning into the Islamic world. Church authorities as well were suspicious of classical Greek thought, sometimes persecuting scholars who were too enamored with the ancients. Even those who did study the Greek writers did so in a conservative spirit, concerned to preserve and transmit the classical heritage rather than using it as a springboard for creating new knowledge. "The great men of the past," declared the fourteenth-century Byzantine scholar and statesman Theodore Metochites, "have said everything so perfectly that they have left nothing for us to say."[28]

In the Islamic world, classical Greek thought was embraced "with far more enthusiasm and creativity" than in Byzantium.[29] A massive translation project in the ninth and tenth centuries made Aristotle and many other Greek writers available in Arabic. That work contributed to a flowering of Arab scholarship, especially in the sciences and natural philosophy, between roughly 800 and 1200 (see Chapter 11), but it also stimulated a debate about faith and reason among Muslim thinkers, many of whom greatly admired Greek philosophical, scientific, and medical texts. As in the Christian world, the issue was whether secular Greek thought was an aid or a threat to the faith. Western European church authorities after the thirteenth century had come to regard natural philosophy as a wholly legitimate enterprise and had thoroughly incorporated Aristotle into university education, but learned opinion in the Islamic world swung the other way. Though never completely disappearing from Islamic scholarship, the ideas of Plato and Aristotle receded after the thirteenth century in favor of teachings that drew more directly from the Quran or from mystical experience. Nor was natural philosophy a central concern of Islamic higher education as it was in the West. The integration of political and religious life in the Islamic world, as in Byzantium, contrasted with their separation in the West, where there was more space for the independent pursuit of scientific subjects.

Reflections: Remembering and Forgetting: Continuity and Surprise in the Worlds of Christendom

Many of the characteristic features of Christendom, which emerged during the era of third-wave civilizations, have had a long life, extending well into the modern era. The crusading element of European expansion was prominent among the motives of Spanish and Portuguese explorers. Europe's grudging freedom for merchant activity and its eagerness to borrow foreign technology arguably contributed to the growth of capitalism and industrialization in later centuries. The endemic military conflicts of European states, unable to recover the unity of the Roman Empire, found terrible expression in the world wars of the twentieth century. The controversy about reason and faith resonates still, at least in the United States, in debates about the authority of the Bible in secular and scientific matters. The rift between Eastern Orthodoxy and Roman Catholicism remains one of the major divides in the Christian world. Modern universities and the separation of religious and political authority likewise have their origins in the European Middle Ages. Such a perspective, linking the past with what came later, represents one of the great contributions that the study of history makes to human understanding.

Yet that very strength of historical study can be misleading, particularly if it suggests a kind of inevitability, in which the past determines the future. Some historians have argued, looking backward from the present, that Europe's industrial transformation and global domination in the nineteenth century grew inexorably out of its unique character as a changing civilization after 1000. This kind of thinking, however, misses the great surprise of Europe's more recent historical trajectory, and it minimizes the way people at the time understood their world.

Surely in 1000, few people would have predicted the startling reversal of roles between the Eastern and Western wings of Christendom, which the next several centuries witnessed. At that time, the many small, rural, unsophisticated, and endlessly quarreling warrior-based societies of Western Europe would hardly have borne comparison with the powerful Byzantine Empire and its magnificent capital of Constantinople. Even in 1500, when Europe had begun to catch up with China and the Islamic world in various ways, there was little to predict its remarkable transformation over the next several centuries and the dramatic change in the global balance of power that this transformation produced. To recapture the unexpectedness of the historical process and to allow ourselves to be surprised, it may be useful on occasion to forget the future and to see the world as contemporaries viewed it.

Second Thoughts

What's the Significance?

Byzantine Empire
Justinian
Constantinople
caesaropapism
Eastern Orthodox
  Christianity
iconoclasm
Kievan Rus

Vladimir, prince of Kiev
Roman Catholic
  Christianity
Charlemagne
Holy Roman Empire
the West as a "hybrid
  civilization"

system of competing
  states
Crusades
European cities
Aristotle and classical
  Greek learning

To assess your mastery of the material in this chapter, see the **Online Study Guide** at bedfordstmartins.com/strayer.

Big Picture Questions

1. How did the histories of the Byzantine Empire and Western Europe differ during the era of third-wave civilizations?
2. What accounts for the different historical trajectories of these two expressions of Christendom?
3. How did Byzantium and Western Europe interact with each other and with the larger world of the postclassical era?
4. Was the civilization of the Latin West distinctive and unique, or was it broadly comparable to other third-wave civilizations?
5. How does the history of the Christian world in the postclassical era compare with that of Tang and Song dynasty China?

Next Steps: For Further Study

Renate Bridenthal et al., eds., *Becoming Visible: Women in European History* (1998). A series of essays that reflects recent scholarship on women.

Edward Grant, *Science and Religion from Aristotle to Copernicus* (2004). Demonstrates the impact of Greek philosophy and science in Europe, with comparisons to Byzantium and the Islamic world.

Barbara A. Hanawalt, *The Middle Ages: An Illustrated History* (1999). A brief and beautifully illustrated introduction to the Middle Ages in European history.

Rowena Loverance, *Byzantium* (2004). A lavishly illustrated history of the Byzantine Empire, drawing on the rich collection of artifacts in the British Museum.

Christopher Tyerman, *Fighting for Christendom: Holy Wars and the Crusades* (2005). A very well-written, up-to-date history of the Crusades designed for nonspecialists.

Mark Whittow, *The Making of Byzantium, 600–1025* (1996). An engaging account of Byzantium at its height, with an emphasis on its external connections.

"Middle Ages," http://www.learner.org/exhibits/middleages. An interactive Web site with text and images relating to life in Europe after the collapse of the Roman Empire.

وَكَادَ يَنْزِعُ الجِمَالَ الشُّمُرَ وَاللَّشَدَ
مَا الحَجُّ سَيْرُكَ تَأْوِيباً وَإِدْلَاجاً وَلَا الْعِيَابُمْ أَجْمَالاً وَأَحْدَاجا

الحَجُّ أَنْ تَقْصِدَ البَيْتَ الحَرَامَ عَلَى تَجْرِيدٍ لِلْحَجِّ لَا تَبْغِي بِهِ حَاجا
وَتَنْطَوِي كَامِلَ الإِنْصَافِ مُتَّخِذاً رَدْعَ الهَوَى وَابْدِيَاً هَادِياً وَالحَقَّ مِنْهَاجا

CHAPTER ELEVEN

The Worlds of Islam

Afro-Eurasian Connections

600–1500

"There were tens of thousands of pilgrims, from all over the world. They were of all colors, from blue-eyed blondes to black-skinned Africans. But we were all participating in the same ritual, displaying a spirit of unity and brotherhood that my experiences in America had led me to believe never could exist between the white and non-white. . . . I have never before seen sincere and true brotherhood practiced by all colors together, irrespective of their color."[1] So said Malcolm X, the American black radical leader and convert to Islam, following his participation in 1964 in the *hajj*, or pilgrimage, to Mecca. That experience persuaded him to abandon his earlier commitment to militant black separatism, for he was now convinced that racial barriers could indeed be overcome within the context of Islam.

As the twenty-first century dawned, Islam had acquired a serious presence in the United States, with more than 1,200 mosques and an estimated 8 million Muslims, of whom some 2 million were African Americans. Here was but one sign of the growing international influence of the Islamic world. Independence from colonial rule, the Iranian Revolution of 1979, repeated wars between Israel and its Arab neighbors, the rising price of oil—all of this focused global attention on the Islamic world in the second half of the twentieth century. Osama bin Laden and the September 11, 2001, attacks on the United States, U.S. military action in Afghanistan and Iraq, and the increasing assertiveness of Muslims in Europe likewise signaled the growing role of Islam in world affairs in the first decade of the new millennium.

The Hajj: The pilgrimage to Mecca, known as the *hajj*, has long been a central religious ritual in Islamic practice. It also embodies the cosmopolitan character of Islam as pilgrims from all over the vast Islamic realm assemble in the city where the faith was born. This painting shows a group of joyful pilgrims, led by a band, on their way to Mecca. (Bibliothèque nationale de France)

PROMINENCE ON THE WORLD STAGE, OF COURSE, was nothing new for Muslim societies. For a thousand years (roughly 600–1600), peoples claiming allegiance to Islam represented a highly successful, prosperous, and expansive civilization, encompassing parts of Africa, Europe, the Middle East, and Asia. While Chinese culture and Buddhism provided the cultural anchor for East Asia during the postclassical millennium and Christianity did the same for western Eurasia, the realm of Islam touched on both of them and decisively shaped the history of the entire Afro-Eurasian world.

The significance of a burgeoning Islam was enormous. It thrust the previously marginal and largely nomadic Arabs into a central role in world history, for it was among them and in their language that the newest of the world's major religions was born. The sudden emergence and rapid spread of that religion in the seventh century C.E. was accompanied by the creation of a huge empire that stretched from Spain to India. Both within that empire and beyond it, a new and innovative civilization took shape, drawing on Arab, Persian, Turkish, Greco-Roman, South Asian, and African cultures. It was clearly the largest and most influential of the new third-wave civilizations. Finally, the broad reach of Islam generated many of the great cultural encounters of this age of accelerating connections, as that civilization challenged and provoked Christendom, penetrated and was transformed by African cultures, and also took root in India, Central Asia, and Southeast Asia. The spread of Islam continued in the modern era so that by the beginning of the twenty-first century, perhaps 1.2 billion people, or 22 percent of the world's population, identified as Muslims.

The Birth of a New Religion

Most of the major religious or cultural traditions of the classical era had emerged from the core of established civilizations—Confucianism and Daoism from China, Hinduism and Buddhism from India, Greek philosophy from the Mediterranean world, and Zoroastrianism from Persia. Christianity and Islam, by contrast, emerged more from the margins of Mediterranean and Middle Eastern civilizations. The former, of course, appeared among a small Middle Eastern people, the Jews, in a remote province of the Roman Empire, while Islam took hold in the cities and deserts of the Arabian Peninsula.

The Homeland of Islam

■ **Description**
In what ways did the early history of Islam reflect its Arabian origins?

The central region of the Arabian Peninsula had long been inhabited by nomadic Arabs, known as Bedouins, who herded their sheep and camels in seasonal migrations. These peoples lived in fiercely independent clans and tribes, which often engaged in bitter blood feuds with one another. They recognized a variety of gods, ancestors, and nature spirits; valued personal bravery, group loyalty, and hospitality; and greatly treasured their highly expressive oral poetry. But there was more to Arabia than camel-herding nomads. Scattered oases, the highlands of Yemen, and interior mountains supported sedentary village-based agriculture, and in the northern and southern regions of Arabia, small kingdoms had flourished in earlier times. Arabia also sat astride increasingly important trade routes, which connected the Indian Ocean world with that of the Mediterranean Sea and gave rise to more cosmopolitan commercial cities, whose values and practices were often in conflict with those of traditional Arab tribes.

Arabia at the Time of Muhammad

One of those cities, Mecca, came to occupy a distinctive role in Arabia. Though somewhat off the major long-distance trade routes, Mecca was the site of the Kaaba, the most prominent religious shrine in Arabia, which housed representations of some 360 deities and was the destination for many pilgrims. Mecca's dominant tribe, the Quraysh, had come to control access to the Kaaba and grew wealthy by taxing the local trade that accompanied the annual pilgrimage season. By the sixth century C.E., Mecca was home to people from various tribes and clans as well as an assortment of individual outlaws, exiles, refugees, and foreign merchants, but much of its growing wealth was concentrated in the hands of a few ruling Quraysh families.

Furthermore, Arabia was located on the periphery of two established and rival civilizations of that time—the Byzantine Empire, heir to the Roman world, and the Sassanid Empire, heir to the imperial traditions of old Persia. This location, coupled with long-distance trade, ensured some familiarity with the larger world, particularly in the cities and settled farming regions of the peninsula. Many Jews and Christians as well as some Zoroastrians lived among the Arabs, and their monotheistic ideas became widely known. By the time of Muhammad, most of the settled Arabs had acknowledged the preeminent position of Allah, the supreme god of the Arab pantheon, although they usually found the lesser gods, including the three daughters of Allah, far more accessible. Moreover, they increasingly identified Allah with Yahweh, the Jewish High God, and regarded themselves too as "children of Abraham." A few Arabs were beginning to explore the possibility that Allah/Yahweh was the only God and that the many others, residing in the Kaaba and in shrines across the peninsula, were nothing more than "helpless and harmless idols."[2]

To an outside observer around 600, it might well have seemed that Arabs were moving toward Judaism religiously or that Christianity, the most rapidly growing religion in western Asia, would encompass Arabia as well. Any such expectations, however, were thoroughly confounded by the dramatic events of the seventh century.

The Messenger and the Message

The catalyst for those events and for the birth of this new religion was a single individual, Muhammad Ibn Abdullah (570–632 C.E.), who was born in Mecca. Orphaned early in life, he was adopted by an uncle, became a widely traveled trader, and married a wealthy widow, Khadija, herself a prosperous merchant, who provided him with financial and emotional support. A highly reflective man deeply troubled by the religious corruption and social inequalities of Mecca, he often undertook

■ **Comparison**
How does the core message of Islam compare with that of Judaism and Christianity?

$\mathcal{S}$napshot   **Key Moments in the Early History of Islam**

Birth of Muhammad	570
Beginning of Muhammad's revelations	610
Hijra (the emigration from Mecca to Medina)	622
Muhammad returns to Mecca in triumph	630
Death of Muhammad	632
Rightly Guided Caliphs	632–661
Arab victories against Byzantine and Persian forces	636–637
Conquest of Egypt	640
Compilation of the Quran	650s
Umayyad caliphate	661–750
Conquest of Spain	711–718
Abbasid caliphate	750–1258
Battle of Talas River	751

periods of withdrawal and meditation in the arid mountains outside the city. There, like the Buddha and Jesus, Muhammad had a powerful, overwhelming religious experience that left him convinced, albeit reluctantly, that he was Allah's messenger to the Arabs, commissioned to bring to them a scripture in their own language.

According to Muslim tradition, the revelations began in 610 and continued periodically over the next twenty-two years. Those revelations, recorded in the Quran, became the sacred scriptures of Islam, which to this day Muslims everywhere regard as the very words of God and the core of their faith. Intended to be recited rather than simply read for information, the Quran, Muslims claim, when heard in its original Arabic, conveys nothing less than the very presence of the divine. One of the earliest converts testified to its power: "When I heard the Quran, my heart was softened and I wept and Islam entered into me."[3]

In its Arabian setting, the Quran's message, delivered through Muhammad, was revolutionary. Religiously, it was radically monotheistic, presenting Allah as the only God, the all-powerful Creator, good, just, and merciful; rejecting as utterly false and useless the many gods housed in the Kaaba; and scorning the Christian notion of the Trinity. Allah was the "Lord sustainer of the worlds, the Compassionate, the Caring, master of the day of reckoning."[4] Here was an exalted conception of the Deity that drew heavily on traditions of Jewish and Christian monotheism. As "the Messenger of God," Muhammad presented himself in the line of earlier prophets—Abraham, Moses, Jesus, and many others. He was the last, "the seal of the prophets," bearing God's final revelation to humankind. It was not so much a call to a new faith as an invitation to return to the old and pure religion of Abraham from which Arabs, Jews, and Christians alike had deviated.

Submission to Allah ("Muslim" means "one who submits") was the primary obligation of believers and the means of achieving a place in paradise after death. According to the Quran, however, submission was not merely an individual or spiritual act, for it involved the creation of a whole new society. Over and again, the Quran denounced the prevailing social practices of an increasingly prosperous Mecca: the hoarding of wealth, the exploitation of the poor, the charging of high rates of interest on loans, corrupt business deals, the abuse of women, and the neglect of the widows and orphans. Like the Jewish prophets of the Old Testament, the Quran demanded social justice and laid out a prescription for its implementation. It sought a return to the older values of Arab tribal life—solidarity, equality, concern for the poor—which had been undermined, particularly in Mecca, by growing wealth and commercialism.

The message of the Quran challenged not only the ancient polytheism of Arab religion and the social injustices of Mecca but also the entire tribal and clan structure of Arab society, which was so prone to war, feuding, and violence. The just and moral society of Islam was the *umma*, the community of all believers, replacing tribal, ethnic, or racial identities. Such a society would be a "witness over the nations," for according to the Quran, "You are the best community evolved for mankind, enjoining what is right and forbidding what is wrong."[5] In this community, women too had an honored and spiritually equal place. "The believers, men and women, are protectors of one another," declared the Quran.[6] The umma, then, was to be a new and just community, bound by a common belief, rather than by territory, language, or tribe.

The core message of the Quran—following the law of God—was effectively summarized as a set of five requirements for believers, known as the Pillars of Islam. The first pillar affirmed the central tenets of Islam—absolute monotheism and a final revelation—in a simple but fundamental profession of faith: "There is no god but Allah, and Muhammad is the messenger of God." The second pillar was prayer, preferably five times a day at prescribed times and performed while facing toward Mecca. The accompanying rituals, including cleansing, bowing, kneeling, and prostration, expressed believers' submission to Allah and provided a frequent reminder, amid the busyness of daily life, that they were living in the presence of the divine. The third pillar, requiring believers to generously give their wealth to maintain the community and to help the needy, reflected the Quran's repeated demands for

Muslims, Jews, and Christians
The close relationship of three Middle Eastern monotheistic traditions is illustrated in this fifteenth-century Persian painting, which portrays Muhammad leading Moses, Abraham, and Jesus in prayer. The fire surrounding the prophet's head represents his religious fervor. The painting reflects the Islamic belief that the revelations granted to Muhammad built upon and completed those given earlier to Jews and Christians. (Bibliothèque nationale de France)

social justice. The fourth pillar called for a month of fasting—no food, drink, or sexual relations—from the first light of dawn to sundown during Ramadan, the ninth lunar month of the Islamic calendar. It provided an occasion for self-purification and a reminder of the needs of the hungry. The fifth pillar urged a pilgrimage to Mecca, where believers from all over the Islamic world assembled once a year and put on identical simple white clothing as they performed rituals reminding them of key events in Islamic history. A moving display of religious devotion, the hajj or pilgrimage expressed in a compelling fashion the unity of the umma.

A further requirement for believers, sometimes called the sixth pillar, was "struggle," or *jihad* in Arabic. Its more general meaning, which Muhammad referred to as the "greater jihad," was the personal effort of each Muslim against greed and selfishness, a spiritual striving toward living a God-conscious life. In its "lesser" form, the "jihad of the sword," the Quran authorized armed struggle against the forces of unbelief and evil as a means of establishing Muslim rule and of defending the umma from the threats of infidel aggressors. The understanding and use of the jihad concept varied widely within the history of Islam and remains a matter of controversy in the twenty-first century.

The Transformation of Arabia

■ Change
In what ways was the rise of Islam revolutionary, both in theory and in practice?

As the revelations granted to Muhammad became known in Mecca, they attracted a small following of some close relatives, a few prominent Meccan leaders, and an assortment of lower-class dependents, freed slaves, and members of poorer clans. Those teachings also soon attracted the vociferous opposition of Mecca's elite families, particularly those of Muhammad's own tribe, the Quraysh. Muhammad's claim to be a "messenger of Allah," his rigid monotheism, his call for social reform, his condemnation of Mecca's business practices, and his apparent disloyalty to his own tribe enraged the wealthy and ruling families of Mecca. So great had this opposition become that in 622 Muhammad and his small band of followers emigrated to the more welcoming town of Yathrib, soon to be called Medina, the city of the Prophet. This agricultural settlement of mixed Arab and Jewish population had invited Muhammad to serve as an arbitrator of their intractable conflicts. The emigration to Yathrib, known in Arabic as the *hijra*, was a momentous turning point in the early history of Islam and thereafter marked the beginning of a new Islamic calendar.

The Islamic community, or umma, that took shape in Medina was a kind of "supertribe," but very different from the traditional tribes of Arab society. Membership was a matter of belief rather than birth, allowing it to expand rapidly. Furthermore, all authority, both political and religious, was concentrated in the hands of Muhammad, who proceeded to introduce radical changes. Usury was outlawed, tax-free marketplaces were established, and a mandatory payment to support the poor was imposed.

In Medina, Muhammad not only began to create a new society but also declared Islam's independence from its earlier affiliation with Judaism. In the early years, he had anticipated a warm response from Jews and Christians, based on a common monotheism and prophetic tradition, and had directed his followers to pray facing Jerusalem. But when some Jewish groups allied with his enemies, Muhammad acted harshly to suppress them, exiling some and enslaving or killing others. This was not, however, a general suppression of Jews, since others among them remained loyal to Muhammad's new state. But the prophet now redirected Muslims' prayer toward Mecca, essentially declaring Islam an Arab religion, though one open to all.

From its base in Medina, the Islamic community rapidly extended its reach throughout Arabia. Early military successes against Muhammad's Meccan opponents convinced other Arab tribes that the Muslims and their God were on the rise, and they sought to negotiate alliances with the new power. Growing numbers, though not all, converted. The religious appeal of the new faith, its promise of material gain, the end of incessant warfare among feuding tribes, periodic military actions skillfully led by Muhammad, and the Prophet's willingness to enter into marriage alliances with leading tribes—all of this contributed to the consolidation of Islamic control throughout Arabia. In 630, Mecca itself voluntarily surrendered, and Muhammad purged the Kaaba of its idols, declaring it a shrine to the one God, Allah. By the time Muhammad died in 632, most of Arabia had come under the control of this new Islamic state, and many had embraced the new faith.

Thus the birth of Islam differed sharply from that of Christianity. Jesus' teaching about "giving to Caesar what is Caesar's and to God what is God's" reflected the minority and subordinate status of the Jews within the Roman Empire. Early Christians found themselves periodically persecuted by Roman authorities for more than three centuries, requiring them to work out some means of dealing with an often hostile state. The answer lay in the development of a separate church hierarchy and the concept of two coexisting authorities, one religious and one political, an arrangement that persisted even after the state became Christian.

The young Islamic community, by contrast, found itself constituted as a state, and soon a huge empire, at the very beginning of its history. Muhammad was not only a religious figure but also, unlike Jesus or the Buddha, a political and military leader able to implement his vision of an ideal Islamic society. Nor did Islam give rise to a separate religious organization, although tension between religious and political goals frequently generated conflict. No professional clergy mediating between God and humankind emerged within Islam. Teachers, religious scholars, prayer leaders, and judges within an Islamic legal system did not have the religious role that priests held within Christianity. No distinction between religious law and civil law, so important in the Christian world, existed within the realm of Islam. One law, known as the *sharia*, regulated every aspect of life. The sharia (literally, a path to water, which is the source of life) evolved over the several centuries following the birth of this new religion and found expression in a number of separate schools of Islamic legal practice.

In little more than twenty years (610–632), a profound transformation had occurred in the Arabian Peninsula. A new religion had been born, though one that had roots in earlier Middle Eastern traditions. A new and vigorous state had emerged, bringing peace to the warring tribes of Arabia. Within that state, a distinctive society, which served ever after as a model for Islamic communities everywhere, had begun to take shape. In his farewell sermon, Muhammad described the outlines of this community.

> All mankind is from Adam and Eve, an Arab has no superiority over a non-Arab nor a non-Arab has any superiority over an Arab; also a white has no superiority over a black nor a black has any superiority over a white—except by piety and good action. Learn that every Muslim is a brother to every Muslim and that the Muslims constitute one brotherhood.[7]

The Making of an Arab Empire

It did not take long for the immense transformations occurring in Arabia to have an impact beyond the peninsula. In the centuries that followed, the energies born of those vast changes profoundly transformed much of the Afro-Eurasian world. The new Arab state became a huge empire, encompassing all or part of Egyptian, Roman/Byzantine, Persian, Mesopotamian, and Indian civilizations. The Islamic faith spread widely within and outside that empire. So too did the culture and language of Arabia, as many Arabs migrated far beyond their original homeland. From the mixing and blending of these many peoples emerged the new and distinctive third-wave civilization of Islam, bound by the ties of a common faith but divided by differences of culture, class, politics, gender, and religious understanding. These enormously consequential processes—the making of a new religion, a new empire, and a new civilization—were central to world history during the postclassical millennium.

War and Conquest

■ Change

Why were Arabs able to construct such a huge empire so quickly?

Within a few years of Muhammad's death in 632, Arab armies engaged the Byzantine and Persian Sassanid empires, the great powers of the region. It was the beginning of a process that rapidly gave rise to an Islamic/Arab empire that stretched from Spain to India, penetrating both Europe and China and governing most of the lands between them (see Map 11.1). In creating that empire, Arabs were continuing a long pattern of tribal raids into surrounding civilizations, but now the Arabs were newly organized in a state of their own with a central command able to mobilize the military potential of the entire Arab population. The Byzantine and Persian empires, weakened by decades of war with each other and by internal revolts, continued to view the Arabs as a mere nuisance rather than a serious threat. But the Sassanid Empire was defeated by Arab forces during the 650s, while Byzantium soon lost the southern half of its territories. Beyond these victories, Arab forces, operating on both land and sea, swept westward across North Africa, conquered Spain in the early 700s, and attacked southern France. To the east, Arab forces reached the Indus River and seized some of the major oases towns of Central

Map 11.1   The Arab Empire and the Initial Expansion of Islam, 622–900 C.E.
Far more so than with Buddhism or Christianity, the initial spread of Islam was both rapid and extensive. And unlike the other two world religions, Islam gave rise to a huge empire, ruled by Muslim Arabs, which encompassed many of the older civilizations of the region.

Asia. In 751, Arab armies inflicted a crushing defeat on Chinese forces in the Battle of Talas River, which had lasting consequences for the cultural evolution of Asia, for it checked the further expansion of China to the west and made possible the conversion of Central Asia's Turkic-speaking people to Islam.

The motives driving the creation of the Arab Empire were in many ways similar to those of other empires. The merchant leaders of the new Islamic community wanted to capture profitable trade routes and wealthy agricultural regions. Individual Arabs found in military expansion a route to wealth and social promotion. The need to harness the immense energies of the Arabian transformation was also important. The fragile unity of the umma threatened to come apart after Muhammad's death, and external expansion provided a common task for the community.

Also apparent in the making of the Arab Empire was a distinctly religious dimension. To the Arabs themselves, the only possible explanation for their amazing, indeed miraculous, success was that "God gave us the victory over them, allowing us to take their countries and to settle in their lands, their homes, and their property, we having no strength or force other than the truth."[8] Many viewed the mission of empire in terms of jihad, bringing righteous government to the peoples they conquered, but this did not mean imposing Islam on individuals at the point of a sword. Initially, Arabs regarded Islam as a revelation uniquely their own and discouraged conversion. By the middle of the eighth century, however, they had come to view it as a universal religion actively seeking converts, but even then they recognized Jews, Christians, and Zoroastrians as "people of the book," giving them the status of *dhimmis* (protected subjects). Such people were permitted to freely practice their own religion, so long as they paid a special tax known as the *jizya*. Theoretically the tax was a substitute for military service, supposedly forbidden to non-Muslims. In practice, many dhimmis served in the highest offices within Muslim kingdoms and in their armies as well.

In other ways too, the Arab rulers of an expanding empire sought to limit the disruptive impact of conquest. To prevent indiscriminate destruction and exploitation of conquered peoples, occupying Arab armies were restricted to garrison towns, segregated from the native population. Local elites and bureaucratic structures were incorporated into the new Arab Empire. Nonetheless, the empire worked many changes on its subjects, the most enduring of which was the mass conversion of Middle Eastern peoples to Islam.

Conversion to Islam

■ Explanation
What accounts for the widespread conversion to Islam?

Becoming a Muslim was for some people no doubt a profound spiritual or psychological transformation, but far more often it was "social conversion," defined as "movement from one religiously defined social community to another."[9] It happened at various rates and in different ways, but in the four centuries or so after the death of Muhammad, millions of individuals and many whole societies within the Arab Empire found their cultural identity bound up with a belief in Allah and the message of his prophet as they came to associate themselves with a community of people known as Muslims. How had this immense cultural change occurred?

In some ways, perhaps, the change was not so dramatic, as major elements of Islam—monotheism; ritual prayer and cleansing ceremonies; fasting; divine revelation; the ideas of heaven, hell, and final judgment—were quite familiar to Jews, Christians, and Zoroastrians. Furthermore, Islam was from the beginning associated with the sponsorship of a powerful state, quite unlike the experience of early Buddhism or Christianity. Conquest called into question the power of old gods, while the growing prestige of the Arab Empire attracted many to Allah. Although deliberately forced conversion was rare, living in an Islamic-governed state provided a variety of incentives for claiming Muslim identity.[10] Slaves and prisoners of war were among the early converts, particularly in Persia. Converts could also avoid the jizya, a tax imposed on non-Muslims. In Islam, merchants found a religion friendly to commerce, and in the Arab Empire they enjoyed a huge and secure arena for trade. People aspiring to official positions found conversion to Islam an aid to social mobility.

Conversion was not an automatic or easy process. Vigorous resistance delayed conversion for centuries among the Berbers of North Africa; a small group of zealous Spanish Christians in the ninth century provoked their own martyrdom by publicly insulting the Prophet; and some Persian Zoroastrians fled to avoid Muslim rule. More generally, though, a remarkable and lasting religious transformation occurred throughout the Arab Empire. In Persia, for example, between 750 and 900, about 80 percent of the population had made the transition to a Muslim religious identity, while retaining their own ancient language.[11] In places where large-scale Arab migration had occurred, such as Egypt, North Africa, and Iraq, Arabic culture and language, as well as the religion of Islam, took hold. Such areas are today both Muslim and Arab, while Iran, Turkey, and Pakistan, for example, have "Islamized" without "Arabizing."

Divisions in the Islamic World

The ideal of a unified Muslim community, so important to Muhammad, proved difficult to realize as conquest and conversion vastly enlarged the Islamic umma. A central problem was that of leadership and authority in the absence of Muhammad's towering presence. Who should hold the role of caliph, the successor to Muhammad as the political leader of the umma, the protector and defender of the faith? That issue crystallized a variety of emerging conflicts within the Islamic world—between early and later converts, among various Arab tribes and factions, between Arabs and non-Arabs, between privileged and wealthy rulers and their far less fortunate subjects. Many of these political and social conflicts found expression in religious terms as various understandings of the Quran and of Muhammad's life and teachings took shape within the growing Islamic community.

The first four caliphs, known among most Muslims as the Rightly Guided Caliphs (632–661), were close "companions of the Prophet," selected by the Muslim elders of Medina. Division surfaced almost immediately as a series of Arab tribal rebellions and new "prophets" persuaded the first caliph, Abu Bakr, to suppress them forcibly. The third and fourth caliphs, Uthman and Ali, were both assassinated, and by 656, less than twenty-five years after Muhammad's death, civil war pitted Muslim against Muslim.

Out of that conflict emerged one of the deepest and most enduring rifts within the Islamic world. On one side were the Sunni Muslims, who held that the caliphs were rightful political and military leaders, selected by the Islamic community. On the other side of this sharp divide was the Shia (an Arabic word meaning "party" or "faction") branch of Islam. Its adherents felt strongly that leadership in the Islamic world should derive from the line of Ali and his son Husayn, blood relatives of Muhammad, both of whom died at the hands of their political or religious enemies.

In the beginning, therefore, this divide was simply a political conflict without serious theological or religious meaning, but over time the Sunni/Shia split acquired deeper significance. For Sunni Muslims, religious authority in general

■ Comparison
What is the difference between Sunni and Shia Islam?

The Kaaba
Located in Mecca, this stone structure covered with a black cloth and known as the Kaaba, was originally home to the numerous deities of pre-Islamic Arabia. Cleansed by Muhammad, it became the sacred shrine of Islam and the destination of countless pilgrims undertaking the hajj. Part of that ritual involves circling the Kaaba seven times, as shown here in a photograph from 2004. (Dan Mohiuddin, photographer)

emerged from the larger community, particularly from the religious scholars known as *ulama*. Shia Muslims, on the other hand, invested their leaders, known as *imams*, with a religious authority that the caliphs lacked, allowing them alone to reveal the true meaning of the Quran and the wishes of Allah. For much of early Islamic history, Shia Muslims saw themselves as the minority opposition within Islam. They felt that history had taken a wrong turn and that they were "the defenders of the oppressed, the critics and opponents of privilege and power," while the Sunnis were the advocates of the established order.[12] Various armed revolts by Shias over the centuries, most of which failed, led to a distinctive conception of martyrdom and to the expectation that their defeated leaders were merely in hiding and not really dead and that they would return in the fullness of time. Thus a messianic element entered Shia Islam. The Sunni/Shia schism was a lasting division in the Islamic world, reflected in conflicts among various Islamic states, and was exacerbated by further splits among the Shia. Those divisions echo still in the twenty-first century.

As the Arab Empire grew, its caliphs were transformed from modest Arab chiefs into absolute monarchs of the Byzantine or Persian variety, complete with elaborate court rituals, a complex bureaucracy, a standing army, and centralized systems of taxation and coinage. They were also subject to the dynastic rivalries and succession disputes common to other empires. The first dynasty, following the era of the Rightly Guided Caliphs, came from the Umayyad family (ruled 661–750). Under its rule, the Arab Empire expanded greatly, caliphs became hereditary rulers, and the capital moved from Medina to the cosmopolitan Roman/Byzantine city of Damascus in Syria. Its ruling class was an Arab military aristocracy, drawn from various tribes. But Umayyad rule provoked growing criticism and unrest. The Shia viewed the Umayyad caliphs as illegitimate usurpers, and non-Arab Muslims resented their second-class citizenship in the empire. Many Arabs protested the luxurious living and impiety of their rulers. The Umayyads, they charged, "made God's servants slaves, God's property something to be taken by turns among the rich, and God's religion a cause of corruption."[13]

Such grievances lay behind the overthrow of the Umayyads in 750 and their replacement by a new Arab dynasty, the Abbasids. With a splendid new capital in Baghdad, the Abbasid caliphs presided over a flourishing and prosperous Islamic civilization in which non-Arabs, especially Persians, now played a prominent role.

Persian cultural influence was reflected in a new title for the caliph, "the shadow of God on earth." But the political unity of the Abbasid Empire did not last long. Beginning in the mid-ninth century, many local governors or military commanders effectively asserted the autonomy of their regions, while still giving formal allegiance to the caliph in Baghdad. Long before Mongol conquest put an official end to the Abbasid Empire in 1258, the Islamic world had fractured politically into a series of "sultanates," many ruled by Persian or Turkish military dynasties.

A further tension within the world of Islam, though seldom a violent conflict, lay in different answers to the central question: What does it mean to be a Muslim, to submit wholly to Allah? That question took on added urgency as the expanding Arab Empire incorporated various lifestyles, customs, and practices that had been unknown during Muhammad's lifetime. One answer lay in the development of an extensive body of Islamic law, known as the sharia. It was the work of religious scholars, the ulama, primarily in the eighth and ninth centuries.

■ Comparison
In what ways were Sufi Muslims critical of mainstream Islam?

Based on the Quran, the life and teachings of Muhammad, deductive reasoning, and the consensus of scholars, the emerging sharia addressed in great detail practically every aspect of religious and social life. While Christendom focused on correct belief, the sharia was far more concerned with correct behavior. It was a blueprint for an authentic Islamic society, providing detailed guidance for prayer and ritual cleansing; marriage, divorce, and inheritance; business and commercial relationships; the treatment of slaves; political life; and much more. Debates among the ulama led to the creation of four schools of law among Sunni Muslims and still others in the lands of Shia Islam. To the ulama and their followers, living as a Muslim meant following the sharia and thus participating in the creation of an Islamic society.

A second and quite different understanding of the faith emerged among those who saw the worldly success of Islamic civilization as a distraction and deviation from the purer spirituality of Muhammad's time. Known as *Sufis*, they represented Islam's mystical dimension, in that they sought a direct and personal experience of the divine. Through renunciation of the material world, meditation on the words of the Quran, the use of music and dance, the veneration of Muhammad and various "saints," Sufis pursued the obliteration of the ego and spiritual union with Allah. To describe that inexpressible experience, they often resorted to metaphors of drunkenness or the embrace of lovers. "Stain your prayer rug with wine," urged the famous Sufi poet Hafiz, referring to the intoxication of the believer with the divine presence. Rabia, an eighth-century woman and Sufi master, conveyed something of the fervor of early Sufi devotion in her much-repeated prayer:

> O my Lord, if I worship Thee from fear of Hell, burn me in Hell; and if I worship Thee from hope of Paradise, exclude me thence; but if I worship Thee for Thine own sake, then withhold not from me Thine Eternal Beauty.[14]

This mystical tendency in Islamic practice, which became widely popular by the ninth and tenth centuries, was sharply critical of the more scholarly and legalistic practitioners of the sharia. To Sufis, establishment teachings about the law and correct behavior, while useful for daily living, did little to bring the believer into the presence of God. For some, even the Quran had its limits. Why spend time reading a love letter (the Quran), asked one Sufi master, when one might be in the very presence of the Beloved who wrote it?[15] Furthermore, they felt that many of the ulama had been compromised by their association with worldly and corrupt governments. Sufis therefore often charted their own course to God, implicitly challenging the religious authority of the ulama. For these orthodox religious scholars, Sufi ideas and practice verged on heresy, as Sufis claimed to be one with God, to receive new revelations, or to incorporate religious practices from outside the Islamic world.

Despite their differences, the legalistic emphasis of the ulama and the Sufis' spirituality never became irreconcilable versions of Islam. A major Islamic thinker, al-Ghazali (1058–1111), himself both a legal scholar and a Sufi practitioner, in fact worked out an intellectual accommodation among different strands of Islamic thought. Rational philosophy alone could never enable believers to know Allah, he argued. Nor were revelation and the law sufficient, for Muslims must know God in their hearts, through direct personal encounter with Allah. Thus al-Ghazali incorporated Sufism into mainstream Islamic thinking. Nonetheless, differences in emphasis remained an element of tension and sometimes discord within the world of Islam.

Women and Men in Early Islam

■ Change
How did the rise of Islam change the lives of women?

What did the rise of Islam and the making of the Arab Empire mean for the daily lives of women and their relationship with men? Virtually every aspect of this question has been and remains highly controversial. The debates begin with the Quran itself. Did its teachings release women from earlier restrictions, or did they impose new limitations? At the level of spiritual life, the Quran was quite clear and explicit: men and women were equal.

> Those who surrender themselves to Allah and accept the true faith; who are devout, sincere, patient, humble, charitable, and chaste; who fast and are ever mindful of Allah—on these, both men and women, Allah will bestow forgiveness and rich reward.[16]

But in social terms, and especially within marriage, the Quran, like the written texts of almost all civilizations, viewed women as inferior and subordinate.

> Men have authority over women because Allah has made the one superior to the other, and because they spend their wealth to maintain them. Good women are obedient. They guard their unseen parts because Allah has guarded them. As for those from whom you fear disobedience, admonish them and send them to beds apart and beat them. Then if they obey you, take no further action against them.[17]

More specifically, the Quran provided a mix of rights, restrictions, and protections for women. The earlier Arab practice of female infanticide, for example, was forbidden. Women were given control over their own property, particularly their dowries, and were granted rights of inheritance, but at half the rate of their male counterparts. Marriage was considered a contract between consenting parties, thus making marriage by capture illegitimate. Within marriage, women were expected to enjoy sexual satisfaction and could sue for divorce if they had not had sexual relations for more than four months. Divorce was thus possible for both parties, although it was far more readily available for men. The practice of taking multiple husbands, which operated in some pre-Islamic Arab tribes, was prohibited, while polygyny (the practice of having multiple wives) was permitted, though more clearly regulated than before. Men were limited to four wives and required to treat each of them equally. The difficulty of doing so has been interpreted by some as virtually requiring monogamy. Men were, however, permitted to have sexual relations with consenting female slaves, but any children born of those unions were free, as was the mother once her owner died. Furthermore, men were strongly encouraged to marry orphans, widows, and slaves.

Men and Women at Worship This sixteenth-century Persian painting of a mosque service shows older men with beards toward the front, younger men behind them, and veiled women and children in a separate area. (Bodleian Library, University of Oxford, Ms. Ouseley. Add 24, fol. 55v)

Such Quranic prescriptions were but one factor shaping the lives of women and men. At least as important were the long-established practices of the societies into which Islam spread and the growing sophistication, prosperity, and urbanization of Islamic civilization. As had been the case in Athens and China during their "golden ages," women, particularly in the upper classes, experienced growing restrictions as Islamic civilization flourished culturally and economically in the Abbasid era. In early Islamic times, a number of women played visible public roles, particularly Muhammad's youngest wife, Aisha. Women prayed in the mosques, although separately, standing beside the men. Nor were women generally veiled or secluded. As the Arab empire grew in size and splendor, however, the position of women became more limited. The second caliph, Umar, asked women to offer prayers at home. Now veiling and the seclusion of women became standard practice among the upper and ruling classes, removing them from public life. Separate quarters within the homes of the wealthy were the domain of women, from which they could emerge only completely veiled. The caliph Mansur (ruled 754–775) carried this separation of the sexes even further when he ordered a separate bridge for women to be built over the Euphrates in the new capital of Baghdad. Such seclusion was less possible for lower-class women, who lacked the servants of the rich and had to leave the home for shopping or work.

Such practices derived far more from established traditions of Middle Eastern cultures than from the Quran itself, but they soon gained an Islamic rationale in the writings of Muslim thinkers. The famous philosopher and religious scholar al-Ghazali clearly saw a relationship between Muslim piety and the separation of the sexes.

> It is not permissible for a stranger to hear the sound of a pestle being pounded by a woman he does not know. If he knocks at the door, it is not proper for the woman to answer him softly and easily because men's hearts can be drawn to [women] for the most trifling [reason]. . . . However, if the woman has to answer the knock, she should stick her finger in her mouth so that her voice sounds like that of an old woman.[18]

Other signs of a tightening patriarchy—such as "honor killing" of women by their male relatives for violating sexual taboos and, in some places, clitorectomy (female circumcision)—likewise derived from local cultures, with no sanction in the Quran or Islamic law. Where they were practiced, such customs often came to be seen as Islamic, but they were certainly not limited to the Islamic world. In many cultures, concern with family honor, linked to women's sexuality, dictated harsh punishments for women who violated sexual taboos.

Negative views of women, presenting them variously as weak, deficient, and a sexually charged threat to men and social stability, emerged in the *hadiths*, traditions about the sayings or actions of Muhammad, which became an important source of Islamic law. A changing interpretation of the Adam and Eve story illustrates the point. In the Quran, equal blame attaches to both of them for yielding to the temptation of Satan, and both alike ask for and receive God's forgiveness. Nothing suggests that Eve tempted or seduced Adam into sin. In later centuries, however, several hadiths and other writings took up Judeo-Christian versions of the story that blamed Eve, and thus women in general, for Adam's sin and for the punishment that followed, including expulsion from the garden and pain in childbirth.[19]

Even as women faced growing restrictions in society generally, Islam, like Buddhism and Christianity, also offered new outlets for them in religious life. The Sufi practice of mystical union with Allah allowed a greater role for women than did mainstream Islam. Some Sufi orders had parallel groups for women, and a few welcomed women as equal members. Within the world of Shia Islam, women teachers of the faith were termed *mullahs*, the same as their male counterparts. Islamic education, either in the home or in Quranic schools, allowed some to become literate and a few to achieve higher levels of learning. Visits to the tombs of major Islamic figures as well as the ritual of the public bath provided some opportunity for women to interact with other women beyond their own family circle.

Islam and Cultural Encounter: A Four-Way Comparison

In its earliest centuries, the rapid spread of Islam had been accompanied by the creation of an immense Arab Empire, very much in the tradition of earlier Mediterranean and Middle Eastern empires. By the tenth century, however, little

Map 11.2 The Growing World of Islam (900–1500) Islam as a religion, a civilization, and an arena of commerce continued to grow even as the Arab Empire fragmented.

political unity remained, and in 1258 even the powerless symbol of that earlier unity vanished as Mongol forces sacked Baghdad and killed the last Abbasid caliph. But even as the empire disintegrated, the civilization that was born within it grew and flourished. Perhaps the most significant sign of a flourishing Islamic civilization was the continued spread of the religion both within and beyond the boundaries of a vanishing Arab Empire (see Map 11.2), although that process differed considerably from place to place. The examples of India, Anatolia, West Africa, and Spain illustrate the various ways that Islam penetrated these societies as well as the rather different outcomes of these epic cultural encounters.

The Case of India

In South Asia, Islam found a permanent place in a long-established civilization as invasions by Turkic-speaking warrior groups from Central Asia, recently converted to Islam, brought the faith to India. Thus the Turks became the third major carrier

■ **Comparison**

What similarities and differences can you identify in the spread of Islam to India, Anatolia, West Africa, and Spain?

The Sultanate of Delhi

of Islam, after the Arabs and Persians, as their conquests initiated an enduring encounter between Islam and a Hindu-based Indian civilization. Beginning around 1000, those conquests gave rise to a series of Turkic and Muslim regimes that governed much of India until the British takeover in the eighteenth and nineteenth centuries. The early centuries of this encounter were violent indeed, as the invaders smashed Hindu and Buddhist temples and carried off vast quantities of Indian treasure. With the establishment of the Sultanate of Delhi in 1206, Turkic rule became more systematic, although their small numbers and internal conflicts allowed only a very modest penetration of Indian society.

In the centuries that followed, substantial Muslim communities emerged in India, particularly in regions less tightly integrated into the dominant Hindu culture. Disillusioned Buddhists as well as low-caste Hindus and untouchables found the more egalitarian Islam attractive. So did peoples just beginning to make the transition to settled agriculture. Others benefited from converting to Islam by avoiding the tax imposed on non-Muslims. Sufis were particularly important in facilitating conversion, for India had always valued "god-filled men" who were detached from worldly affairs. Sufi missionaries, willing to accommodate local gods and religious festivals, helped to develop a "popular Islam" that was not always so sharply distinguished from Hinduism.

Unlike the earlier experience of Islam in the Middle East, North Africa, and Persia, where it rapidly became the dominant faith, in India it was never able to claim more than 20 to 25 percent of the total population. Furthermore, Muslim communities were especially concentrated in the Punjab and Sind regions of northwestern India and in Bengal to the east. The core regions of Hindu culture in the northern Indian plain were not seriously challenged by the new faith, despite centuries of Muslim rule. One reason perhaps lay in the sharpness of the cultural divide between Islam and Hinduism. Islam was the most radically monotheistic of the world's religions, forbidding any representation of Allah, while Hinduism was surely among the most prolifically polytheistic, generating endless statues and images of the divine in many forms. The Muslim notion of the equality of all believers contrasted sharply with the hierarchical assumptions of the caste system. The sexual modesty of Muslims was deeply offended by the open eroticism of some Hindu religious art.

Although such differences may have limited the appeal of Islam in India, they also may have prevented it from being absorbed into the tolerant and inclusive embrace of Hinduism as had so many other religious ideas, practices, and communities. The religious exclusivity of Islam, born of its firm monotheistic belief and the idea of a unique revelation, set a boundary that the great sponge of Hinduism could not completely absorb.

Certainly not all was conflict across that boundary. Many prominent Hindus willingly served in the political and military structures of a Muslim-ruled India. Mystical seekers after the divine blurred the distinction between Hindu and

Muslim, suggesting that God was to be found "neither in temple nor in mosque." "Look within your heart," wrote the great fifteenth-century mystic poet Kabir, "for there you will find both [Allah] and Ram [a famous Hindu deity]."[20] In fact, during the early sixteenth century, a new and distinct religious tradition emerged in India, known as Sikhism, which blended elements of Islam, such as devotion to one universal God, with Hindu concepts, such as karma and rebirth. "There is no Hindu and no Muslim. All are children of God," declared Guru Nanak (1469–1539), the founder of Sikhism.

Nonetheless, Muslims, usually living quite separately, remained a distinctive minority within an Indian civilization, which they now largely governed but which they proved unable to completely transform.

The Case of Anatolia

At the same time that India was being subjected to Turkic invasion, so too was Anatolia, where the largely Christian and Greek-speaking population was governed by the Byzantine Empire. Here, as in India, the invaders initially wreaked havoc as Byzantine authority melted away in the eleventh century. Sufi missionaries likewise played a major role in the process of conversion. The outcome, however, was a far more profound cultural transformation than in India. By 1500, the population was 90 percent Muslim and largely Turkic-speaking, and Anatolia was the heartland of the powerful Turkish Ottoman Empire that had overrun Christian Byzantium. Why did the Turkic intrusion into Anatolia generate a much more thorough Islamization than in India?

■ Comparison

Why was Anatolia so much more thoroughly Islamized than India?

One factor clearly lies in a very different demographic balance. The population of Anatolia—perhaps 8 million—was far smaller than India's roughly 48 million people, but far more Turkic-speaking peoples settled in Anatolia, giving them a much greater cultural weight than the smaller colonizing force in India. Furthermore, the disruption of Anatolian society was much more extensive. Massacres, enslavement, famine, and flight led to a sharp drop in the native population. The Byzantine state had been fatally weakened. Church properties were confiscated, and monasteries were destroyed or deserted. Priests and bishops were sometimes unable to serve their congregations. Christians, though seldom forced to convert, suffered many discriminations. They had to wear special clothing and pay special taxes, and they were forbidden to ride saddled horses or carry swords. Not a few Christians came to believe that these disasters represented proof that Islam was the true religion.[21] Thus Byzantine civilization in Anatolia, focused on the centralized institutions of church and state, was rendered leaderless and dispirited, whereas India's decentralized civilization, lacking a unified political or religious establishment, was better able to absorb the shock of external invasion while retaining its core values and identity.

The Turkish rulers of Anatolia built a new society that welcomed converts and granted them material rewards and opportunity for high office. Moreover, the

Map 11.3   The Ottoman Empire by the Mid-Fifteenth Century

As Turkic-speaking migrants bearing the religion of Islam penetrated Anatolia, the Ottoman Empire took shape, reaching into southeastern Europe and finally displacing the Christian Byzantine Empire. Subsequently, it came to control much of the Middle East and North Africa as well.

cultural barriers to conversion were arguably less severe than in India. The common monotheism of Islam and Christianity, and Muslim respect for Jesus and the Christian scriptures, made conversion easier than crossing the great gulf between Islam and Hinduism. Such similarities lent support to the suggestion of some Sufi teachers that the two religions were but different versions of the same faith. Sufis also established schools, mills, orchards, hospices, and rest places for travelers and thus replaced the destroyed or decaying institutions of Christian Anatolia.[22] All of this contributed to the thorough religious transformation of Anatolia and laid a foundation for the Ottoman Empire, which by 1500 became the most impressive and powerful state within the Islamic world (see Map 11.3).

Islamization did not completely eliminate the influence of Turkish culture. For example, their tradition of a freer, more gender-equal life for women, common among pastoral people, persisted well after conversion to Islam, much to the distress of the Moroccan visitor Ibn Battuta during his travels among them in the fourteenth century: "A remarkable thing that I saw . . . was the respect shown to women by the Turks, for they hold a more dignified position than the men. . . . The windows of the tent are open and her face is visible, for the Turkish women do not veil themselves."[23] He was not pleased.

The Case of West Africa

Still another pattern prevailed in West Africa. Here Islam accompanied Muslim traders across the Sahara rather than being brought by invading Arab or Turkic armies. Its acceptance in the emerging civilization of West African states in the centuries after 1000 was largely peaceful and voluntary, lacking the incentives associated elsewhere with foreign conquest. Introduced by Muslim merchants from an already Islamized North Africa, the new faith was accepted primarily in the urban centers of the West African empires—Ghana, Mali, Songhay, Kanem-Bornu, and others (see Map 11.4). For African merchant communities, Islam provided an important link to Muslim trading partners, much as Buddhism had done in Southeast Asia. For the monarchs and their courts, it offered a source of literate officials to assist in state administration as well as religious legitimacy, particularly for

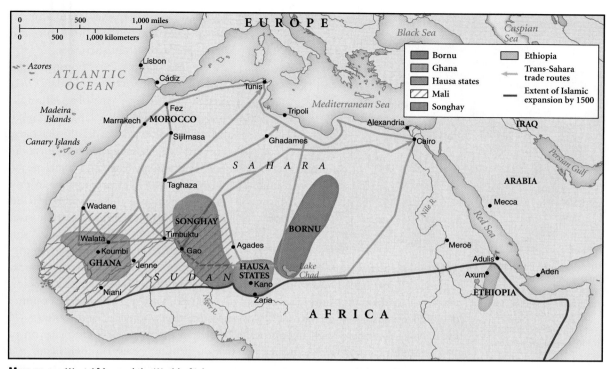

Map 11.4   West Africa and the World of Islam
Both trans-Saharan commerce and Islam linked the civilization of West Africa to the larger Muslim world.

those who gained the prestige conferred by a pilgrimage to Mecca. Islam was a world religion with a single Creator-God, able to comfort and protect people whose political and economic horizons had expanded well beyond the local realm where ancestral spirits and traditional deities might be effective. It had a religious appeal for societies that were now participating in a wider world.

By the sixteenth century, a number of West African cities had become major centers of Islamic religious and intellectual life, attracting scholars from throughout the Muslim world. Timbuktu boasted more than 150 lower-level Quranic schools and several major centers of higher education with thousands of students from all over West Africa and beyond. Libraries held tens of thousands of books and scholarly manuscripts. Monarchs subsidized the construction of mosques as West Africa became an integral part of a larger Islamic world. Arabic became an important language of religion, education, administration, and trade, but it did not become the dominant language of daily life. West Africa did not experience the massive migration of Arab peoples that had promoted the Arabization of North Africa and the Middle East. Moreover, in contrast to India and Anatolia, Sufi holy men played little role until at least the eighteenth century. Scholars, merchants, and rulers, rather than mystic preachers, initially established Islam in West Africa.

The Great Mosque at Jenne
This mosque in the city of Jenne, initially constructed in the thirteenth century, illustrates the assimilation of Islam into West African civilization. (Bildagentur/TIPS Images)

Islam remained the culture of an urban elite and spread little into the rural areas of West Africa until the nineteenth century. No thorough religious transformation occurred in West Africa as it had in Anatolia. Although many rulers adopted Islam, they governed people who steadfastly practiced African religions and whose sensibilities they had to respect if social peace were to prevail. Thus they made few efforts to impose the new religion on their rural subjects or to govern in strict accordance with Islamic law. Ibn Battuta, a fourteenth-century Arab visitor, was appalled that practicing Muslims in Mali permitted their women to appear in public almost naked and to mingle freely with unrelated men. "The association of women with men is agreeable to us," he was told, "and a part of good conduct to which no suspicion attaches. They are not like the women of your country."[24] Ibn Battuta also noted with disapproval a "dance of the masks" on the occasion of an Islamic festival and the traditional practice of sprinkling dust on their heads as a sign of respect for the king. Sonni Ali, a fifteenth-century ruler of Songhay, observed Ramadan and built mosques, but he also consulted traditional diviners and performed customary sacrifices. In such ways, Islam became Africanized even as parts of Africa became Islamized.

The Case of Spain

The chief site of Islamic encounter with Catholic Europe occurred in Spain (called al-Andalus by Muslims), which was conquered by Arab and Berber forces in the early eighth century during the first wave of Islamic expansion. But Islam did not overwhelm Christianity as it did later in Anatolia. In fact, Muslim Spain in the several centuries that followed conquest has often been portrayed as a vibrant civilization characterized by harmony and tolerance between its Muslim rulers and its Christian and Jewish subjects.

Certainly Spain's agricultural economy was the most prosperous in Europe during the ninth and tenth centuries, and at that time its capital of Córdoba was among the largest and most splendid cities in the world. Muslims, Christians, and Jews alike contributed to a brilliant high culture in which astronomy, medicine, the arts, architecture, and literature flourished. It was largely from Spain that the rich heritage of Islamic learning became available to Christian Europe.

Furthermore, social relationships among upper-class members of different faiths were easy and frequent. More than a few Christians converted to Islam, and many others, known as *Mozarabs* (would-be Arabs), learned Arabic, veiled their women, stopped eating pork, appreciated Arabic music and poetry, and sometimes married Muslims. One Christian bishop complained that Spanish Christians knew the rules of Arabic grammar better than those of Latin. During the reign of Abd al-Rahman III (912–961), freedom of worship was declared as well as the opportunity for all to rise in the bureaucracy of the state.

Even assimilated or Arabized Christians, however, remained infidels in the eyes of their Muslim counterparts, and by the late tenth century the era of toleration began to erode. Warfare with the remaining Christian states in northern Spain picked up in the tenth and eleventh centuries, and more puritanical and rigid forms of Islam entered Spain from North Africa. In these circumstances, the golden age of religious harmony faded. Under the rule of Abu Amir al-Mansur (981–1002), an official policy of tolerance turned to one of overt persecution against Christians, which now included the plundering of churches. Social life also changed. Devout Muslims avoided contact with Christians; Christian homes had to be built lower than those of Muslims; priests were forbidden to carry a cross or a Bible, lest they offend Muslim sensibilities; and Mozarabs were permitted to live only in particular places. Thus, writes one scholar, "the era of harmonious interaction between Muslim and Christian in Spain came to an end, replaced by intolerance, prejudice, and mutual suspicion."[25]

That intolerance was perpetuated as the Christian reconquest of Spain gained ground after 1200. Many Muslims were then forced out of Spain, while those who remained could no longer give the call to prayer, go on pilgrimage, or publicly practice their faith. When the reconquest was completed in 1492, all Jews, some 200,000 of them, were likewise expelled from the country. Thus, as Christianity was displaced by Islam in Anatolia, the opposite process was taking place in Spain.

The World of Islam as a New Civilization

As the religion spread and the Abbasid dynasty declined, the civilization of Islam, like Western Christendom and the Hindu world, operated without a single political center, bound more by a shared religious culture than by a shared state. Unlike the other civilizations, however, the Islamic world by 1500 embraced at least parts of virtually every other civilization in the Afro-Eurasian hemisphere. It was in that sense "history's first truly global civilization," although the Americas, of course, were not involved.[26] What held the Islamic world together? What enabled many people to feel themselves part of a single civilization despite its political fragmentation, religious controversies, and cultural and regional diversity?

Networks of Faith

At the core of that vast civilization was a common commitment to Islam. No group was more important in the transmission of those beliefs and practices than the ulama. These learned scholars were not "priests" in the Christian sense, for in Islam,

■ **Description**
What makes it possible to speak of the Islamic world as a distinct and coherent civilization?

at least theoretically, no person could stand between the believer and Allah. Rather they served as judges, interpreters, administrators, prayer leaders, and reciters of the Quran, but especially as preservers and teachers of the sharia. Supported mostly by their local communities, some also received the patronage of *sultans*, or rulers, and were therefore subject to criticism for corruption and undue submission to state authority. In their homes, mosques, shrines, and Quranic schools, the ulama passed on the core teachings of the faith. Beginning in the eleventh century, formal colleges called *madrassas* offered more advanced instruction in the Quran and the sayings of Muhammad; grammar and rhetoric; sometimes philosophy, theology, mathematics, and medicine; and, above all else, law. Teaching was informal, mostly oral, and involved much memorization of texts. It was also largely conservative, seeking to preserve an established body of Islamic learning.

The ulama were an "international elite," and the system of education they created served to bind together an immense and diverse civilization. Common texts were shared widely across the world of Islam. Students and teachers alike traveled great distances in search of the most learned scholars. From Indonesia to West Africa, educated Muslims inhabited a "shared world of debate and reference."[27]

Paralleling the educational network of the ulama were the emerging religious orders of the Sufis. By the tenth century, particular Sufi *shaykhs*, or teachers, began to attract groups of disciples who were eager to learn their unique devotional practices and ways of achieving union with Allah. The disciples usually swore eternal allegiance to their teacher and valued highly the chain of transmission by which those teachings and practices had come down from earlier masters. In the twelfth and thirteenth centuries, Sufis began to organize in a variety of larger associations, some limited to particular regions and others with chapters throughout the Islamic world. The Qadiriya order, for example, began in Baghdad but spread widely throughout the Arab world and into sub-Saharan Africa. Sufi orders were especially significant in the frontier regions of Islam because they followed conquering armies or traders into Central and Southeast Asia, India, Anatolia, West Africa, and elsewhere. Their passionate preaching, exemplary living, and reputation for supernatural powers gained a hearing for the new faith. Their emphasis on devotion rather than law allowed the Sufis to accommodate elements of local belief and practice and encouraged the growth of a popular or blended Islam. But that flexibility also often earned them the enmity of the ulama, who were sharply critical of such deviations from the sharia.

Like the madrassas and the sharia, Sufi religious ideas and institutions spanned the Islamic world and were yet another thread in the cosmopolitan web of Islamic civilization. Particular devotional teachings and practices spread widely, as did the writings of such famous Sufi poets as Hafiz and Rumi. Devotees made pilgrimages to the distant tombs of famous teachers, who, they often believed, might intercede with God on their behalf. Wandering Sufis, in search of the wisdom of renowned shaykhs, found fellow seekers and welcome shelter in the compounds of these religious orders.

In addition to the networks of the Sufis and the ulama, many thousands of people, from kings to peasants, made the grand pilgrimage to Mecca—the hajj—each year, no doubt gaining some sense of the umma. There men and women together, hailing from all over the Islamic world, joined as one people to rehearse the central elements of their faith. The claims of local identities based on family, clan, tribe, ethnicity, or state never disappeared, but now overarching them all was the inclusive unity of the Muslim community. For at least the few days of the hajj, the many worlds of Islam must surely have seemed a single realm.

Networks of Exchange

The world of Islamic civilization cohered not only as a network of faith but also as an immense arena of exchange in which goods, technologies, food products, and ideas circulated widely. It rapidly became a vast trading zone of hemispheric dimensions. In part, this was due to its central location in the Afro-Eurasian world and the breaking down of earlier political barriers between the Byzantine and Persian empires. Furthermore, commerce was valued positively within Islamic teaching: Muhammad himself had been a trader, and the pilgrimage to Mecca likewise fostered commerce. The extraordinary spurt of urbanization that accompanied the growth of Islamic civilization also promoted trade. Baghdad, established in 756 as the capital of the Abbasid Empire, soon grew into a magnificent city of half a million people. The appetite of urban elites for luxury goods stimulated both craft production and the desire for foreign goods.

■ **Connection**
In what ways was the world of Islam a "cosmopolitan civilization"?

Thus Muslim merchants, Arabs and Persians in particular, quickly became prominent and sometimes dominant players in all of the major Afro-Eurasian trade routes of the postclassical era—in the Mediterranean Sea, along the revived Silk Roads, across the Sahara, and throughout the Indian Ocean basin (see Chapter 8). By the eighth century, Arab and Persian traders had established a commercial colony in Canton in southern China, thus linking the Islamic heartland with Asia's other giant and flourishing economy. Various forms of banking, partnerships, business contracts, and instruments for granting credit facilitated these long-distance economic relationships and generated a prosperous, highly developed, "capitalist" economy that spanned the Old World.[28]

The vast expanses of Islamic civilization also facilitated a substantial exchange of agricultural products and practices from one region to another, the largest such transfer in world history prior to Europe's encounter with the Americas. The Muslim conquest of northwestern India opened the Middle East to a veritable treasure trove of crops that had been domesticated long before in South and Southeast Asia, including rice, sugarcane, new strains of sorghum, hard wheat, bananas, lemons, limes, watermelons, coconut palms, spinach, artichokes, and cotton. Some of these subsequently found their way into the Middle East and Africa and by the thirteenth century to Europe as well.[29] Both cotton and sugarcane, associated with complex production processes and slave labor, came to play central roles in the formation of the modern global system after 1500. These new crops and the development of the intensified agricultural techniques that often accompanied them contributed to increased food production, population growth, urbanization, and industrial development characteristic of the Muslim Middle East in early Abbasid times.

Technology too diffused widely within the Islamic world. Ancient Persian techniques for obtaining water by drilling into the sides of hills now spread across North Africa as far west as Morocco. Muslim technicians made improvements on rockets, first developed in China, by developing one that carried a small warhead and another used to attack ships.[30] Papermaking techniques entered the Abbasid Empire from China in the eighth century, with paper mills soon operating in Persia, Iraq, and Egypt. This revolutionary technology, which everywhere served to strengthen bureaucratic governments, spread from the Middle East into India and Europe over the following centuries.

Ideas likewise circulated across the Islamic world. The religion itself drew heavily and quite openly on Jewish and Christian precedents. Persia also contributed much in the way of bureaucratic practice, court ritual, and poetry, with Persian becoming the primary literary language of elite circles. Scientific, medical, and philosophical texts, especially from ancient Greece, the Hellenistic world, and India,

A Muslim Astronomical Observatory
Drawing initially on Greek, Indian, and Persian astronomy, the Islamic world after 1000 developed its own distinctive tradition of astronomical observation and prediction, reflected in this Turkish observatory constructed in 1557. Muslim astronomy subsequently exercised considerable influence in both China and Europe. (University Library, Istanbul, Turkey/The Bridgeman Art Library)

were systematically translated into Arabic, for several centuries providing an enormous boost to Islamic scholarship and science. In 830, the Abbasid caliph al-Mamun, himself a poet and scholar with a passion for foreign learning, established the House of Wisdom in Baghdad as an academic center for this research and translation. Stimulated by Greek texts, a school of Islamic thinkers, known as Mutazalites ("those who stand apart"), argued that reason, rather than revelation, was the "surest way to truth."[31] In the long run, however, the philosophers' emphasis on logic, rationality, and the laws of nature was subject to increasing criticism by those who held that only the Quran, the sayings of the Prophet, or mystical experience represented a genuine path to God.

But the realm of Islam was much more than a museum of ancient achievements from the civilizations that it encompassed. Those traditions mixed and blended to generate a distinctive Islamic civilization with many new contributions to the world of learning.[32] (See the Snapshot.) Using Indian numerical notation, for example, Arab scholars developed algebra as a novel mathematical discipline. They also undertook much original work in astronomy and optics. They built upon earlier Greek and Indian practice to create a remarkable tradition in medicine and pharmacology. Arab physicians

Snapshot   Key Achievements in Islamic Science and Scholarship

Person/Dates	Achievement
al-Khwarazim (790–840)	Mathematician; spread use of Arabic numerals in Islamic world; wrote first book on algebra
al-Razi (865–925)	Discovered sulfuric acid; wrote a vast encyclopedia of medicine drawing on Greek, Syrian, Indian, and Persian work and his own clinical observation
al-Biruni (973–1048)	Mathematician, astronomer, cartographer; calculated the radius of the earth with great accuracy; worked out numerous mathematical innovations; developed a technique for displaying a hemisphere on a plane
Ibn Sina (Avicenna) (980–1037)	Prolific writer in almost all fields of science and philosophy; especially known for *Canon of Medicine*, a fourteen-volume work that set standards for medical practice in Islamic and Christian worlds for centuries
Omar Khayyam (1048–1131)	Mathematician; critic of Euclid's geometry; measured the solar year with great accuracy; Sufi poet; author of *The Rubaiyat*
Ibn Rushd (Averroës) (1126–1198)	Translated and commented widely on Aristotle; rationalist philosopher; made major contributions in law, mathematics, and medicine
Nasir al-Din Tusi (1201–1274)	Founder of the famous Maragha observatory in Persia (data from Maragha probably influenced Copernicus); mapped the motion of stars and planets
Ibn Khaldun (1332–1406)	Greatest Arab historian; identified trends and structures in world history over long periods of time

such as al-Razi and Ibn Sina accurately diagnosed many diseases, such as hay fever, measles, smallpox, diphtheria, rabies, diabetes, and more. In addition, treatments such as using a mercury ointment for scabies, cataract and hernia operations, and filling teeth with gold emerged from Arab doctors. The first hospitals, traveling clinics, and examinations for physicians and pharmacologists also were developed within the Islamic world. In the eleventh and twelfth centuries, this enormous body of Arab medical scholarship entered Europe via Spain, and it remained at the core of European medical practice for many centuries.[33]

Reflections: Learning from Outsiders: A Tale of Two Travelers

Historians generally prefer to rely on "insiders" for understanding the societies and cultures they study. Documents, artifacts, and images created by people actually living in those times and places have an authenticity that accounts from foreigners may lack. Nonetheless, scholars often find it necessary, and helpful, to make use of records written by outsiders as well. In describing the interacting worlds of Afro-Eurasia in the postclassical millennium, historians frequently draw on the experience and observations of those travelers who traversed that vast space. Their writings reveal much about themselves and their home cultures as well as about the distant peoples and places they visited. Among these travelers, none have been more useful to historians than Ibn Battuta, a Moroccan Muslim, and Marco Polo, an Italian Christian.

Nothing more effectively conveys the extent and the unity of the Islamic world than the travels of Ibn Battuta (1304–1368). Born in Morocco, he traversed nearly 75,000 miles during his extraordinary journeys, which took him to Spain and Anatolia; West and East Africa; Arabia, Iraq, and Persia; Central and Southeast Asia; India and China. He traveled at various times as a pilgrim, making the hajj twice; as a Sufi devotee; as a legal scholar who served for a time as a judge in India; and frequently in the company of Muslim merchants.

Remarkably, almost all of his extensive travels occurred within the "house of Islam," where he moved among people who shared his faith and often his language, and where the sharia provided, at least in theory, the basis of social life. As a visitor from a more established Islamic society, he was often highly critical of the quality of Islamic observance. In West Africa, in Turkish lands, and in the Maldive Islands of the Indian Ocean, Ibn Battuta was appalled at the freedom of women and the scanty clothing they wore. In India, he ordered eighty lashes for Muslims found drinking wine. Still, they were Muslims. Only China seemed wholly foreign, for there he could not explain the country's prosperity and security in terms of Islam.

> China was beautiful, but it did not please me.... I was greatly troubled thinking about the way paganism dominated this country.... That disturbed me so much that I stayed indoors most of the time and only went out when necessary. During my stay in China, whenever I saw any Muslims I always felt as though I were meeting my own family and close kinsmen.[34]

Ibn Battuta has frequently been compared with the European traveler Marco Polo (1254–1324), who had made his way a few decades earlier from Italy to China, where he served at the court of Khubilai Khan for seventeen years. Returning to Italy in 1295, Marco Polo wrote an account of his travels and the lands he visited, which became widely popular in Europe as a source of information about the mysterious East. Christopher Columbus carried a marked-up copy of the book on his transatlantic journeys, believing that he was seeking by sea the places Marco Polo had visited by land.

Marco Polo's travels were but the best-known example of a European civilization newly reaching out to reconnect with a wider world. Unlike Ibn Battuta, Polo felt himself constantly an outsider, "a stranger in a strange land," for he was traveling almost everywhere beyond the borders of Christendom. Perhaps because he was an outsider, Polo did not register the kind of disapproval or culture shock that Ibn Battuta experienced in the face of deviations from heartland Islamic practice. He reported prolifically on the strange ways and peoples he encountered, but without the disdain that often characterized Ibn Battuta's commentaries.

The respective journeys of these two travelers reveal much about the world of the thirteenth and fourteenth centuries. Most important, they show that Islamic civilization was then the central fact of the Afro-Eurasian world, while Europe was still on the margins. Memories of that earlier prominence and achievement both sustained and frustrated Muslims when, in the centuries after 1700, Europeans increasingly assumed the central role in world affairs. Those memories also inspired resistance to Western dominance in the twentieth century and beyond.

Second Thoughts

What's the Significance?

Quran	Umayyad caliphate	Timbuktu
umma	Abbasid caliphate	al-Andalus
Pillars of Islam	sharia	madrassas
hijra	al-Ghazali	House of Wisdom
jizya	Sikhism	Ibn Sina
ulama	Anatolia	Ibn Battuta

To assess your mastery of the material in this chapter, see the **Online Study Guide** at bedfordstmartins.com/strayer.

Big Picture Questions

1. What distinguished the first centuries of Islamic history from the early history of Christianity and Buddhism? What similarities and differences characterized their religious outlooks?
2. How might you account for the immense religious and political/military success of Islam in its early centuries?
3. In what ways can Islamic civilization be described as "cosmopolitan"?
4. "Islam was simultaneously both a single world of shared meaning and interaction and a series of separate and distinct communities, often in conflict with one another." What evidence could you provide to support both sides of this argument?
5. What changes did Islamic expansion generate in those societies that encountered it, and how was Islam itself transformed by those encounters?

Next Steps: For Further Study

For Web sites and documents related to this chapter, see **Make History** at bedfordstmartins.com/strayer.

Reza Aslan, *No God but God* (2005). A well-written and popular history of Islam by an Iranian immigrant to the United States.

Richard Bulliet, *Conversion to Islam in the Medieval Period* (1979). A scholarly study of the meaning and process of conversion in the early history of Islam and in several distinct places.

Richard Eaton, *Islamic History as Global History* (1990). A short account by a major scholar that examines Islam in a global framework.

John Esposito, ed., *The Oxford History of Islam* (1999). Up-to-date essays on various periods and themes in Islamic history. Beautifully illustrated.

Francis Robinson, ed., *Cambridge Illustrated History of the Islamic World* (1996). A series of essays by major scholars, with lovely pictures and maps.

Judith Tucker, *Gender and Islamic History* (1994). A brief overview of the changing lives of Islamic women.

"The Travels of Ibn Battuta: A Virtual Tour with the Fourteenth Century Traveler," http://www.sfusd.k12.ca.us/schwww/sch618/Ibn_Battuta/Battuta's_Trip_Twelve.html. A beautifully illustrated journey across the Islamic world in the early 1300s.

CHAPTER TWELVE

Pastoral Peoples on the Global Stage

The Mongol Moment

1200–1500

In 1937, the great Mongol warrior Chinggis Khan lost his soul, some seven centuries after his death. According to Mongol tradition, a warrior's soul was contained in his spirit banner, consisting of strands of hair from his best horses attached to a spear. For many centuries, Chinggis Khan's spirit banner had been housed in a Buddhist monastery in central Mongolia, where lamas (religious teachers) had tended it.[1] But in the 1930s, Mongolia, then under Communist control and heavily dominated by Stalin's Soviet Union, launched a brutal antireligious campaign that destroyed many monasteries, executed some 2,000 monks, and led to the vanishing of Chinggis Khan's spirit banner and thus his soul.

By the end of the twentieth century, as communism faded away, the memory of Chinggis Khan, if not his spirit banner, made a remarkable comeback in the land of his birth. Vodka, cigarettes, a chocolate bar, two brands of beer, the country's best rock band, and the central square of the capital city all bore his name, while his picture appeared on Mongolia's stamps and money. Rural young people on horseback sang songs in his honor, and their counterparts in urban Internet cafés constructed Web sites to celebrate his achievements. The country organized elaborate celebrations in 2006 to mark the 800th anniversary of his founding of the Mongol Empire.

ALL OF THIS IS A REMINDER OF THE ENORMOUS AND SURPRISING ROLE that the Mongols played in the Eurasian world of the thirteenth and fourteenth centuries and of the continuing echoes of that long-vanished empire. More generally, the story of the Mongols serves as a useful

Chinggis Khan at Prayer: This sixteenth-century Indian painting shows Chinggis Khan at prayer in the midst of battle. He is perhaps praying to Tengri, the great sky god, on whom the Mongol conqueror based his power. (Werner Forman/Art Resource, NY)

corrective to the almost exclusive focus that historians often devote to agricultural peoples and their civilizations, for the Mongols, and many other such peoples, were pastoral nomads who disdained farming while centering their economic lives around their herds of animals. Normally they did not construct elaborate cities, enduring empires, or monumental works of art, architecture, and written literature. Nonetheless, they left an indelible mark on the historical development of the entire Afro-Eurasian hemisphere, and particularly on the agricultural civilizations with which they so often interacted.

Looking Back and Looking Around: The Long History of Pastoral Nomads

The "revolution of domestication," beginning around 11,500 years ago, involved both plants and animals. People living in more favored environments were able to combine farming with animal husbandry and on this economic foundation generated powerful and impressive civilizations with substantial populations. But on the arid margins of agricultural lands, where productive farming was difficult or impossible, an alternative kind of food-producing economy emerged around 4000 B.C.E., focused on the raising of livestock. Peoples practicing such an economy learned to use the milk, blood, wool, hides, and meat of their animals to occupy lands that could not support agricultural societies. Some of those animals also provided new baggage and transportation possibilities. Horses, camels, goats, sheep, cattle, yaks, and reindeer were the primary animals that separately, or in some combination, enabled the construction of pastoral or herding societies. Such societies took shape in the vast grasslands of inner Eurasia and sub-Saharan Africa, in the Arabian and Saharan deserts, in the subarctic regions of the Northern Hemisphere, and in the high plateau of Tibet. Pastoralism emerged only in the Afro-Eurasian world, for in the Americas the absence of large animals that could be domesticated precluded a herding economy. But where such animals existed, their domestication shaped unique societies adapted to diverse environments.

The World of Pastoral Societies

■ **Comparison**

In what ways did pastoral societies differ from their agricultural counterparts?

Despite many differences among pastoral societies, they shared several important features that distinguished them from settled agricultural communities and civilizations. Pastoral societies' generally less productive economies and their need for large grazing areas meant that they supported far smaller populations than did agricultural societies. People generally lived in small and widely scattered encampments of related kinfolk rather than in the villages, towns, and cities characteristic of agrarian civilizations. Beyond the family unit, pastoral peoples organized themselves in kinship-based groups or clans that claimed a common ancestry, usually through the male line. Related clans might on occasion come together as a tribe, which could also absorb unrelated people into the community. Although values stressing equality

$\mathcal{S}$napshot   **Varieties of Pastoral Societies[2]**

Region and Peoples	Primary Animals	Features
Inner Eurasian steppes (Xiongnu, Yuezhi, Turks, Uighurs, Mongols, Huns, Kipchaks)	Horses; also sheep, goats, cattle, Bactrian (two-humped) camel	Domestication of horse by 4000 B.C.E.; horseback riding by 1000 B.C.E.; site of largest nomadic empires
Southwestern and Central Asia (Seljuks, Ghaznavids, Mongol Il-khans, Uzbeks, Ottomans)	Sheep and goats; used horses, camels, and donkeys for transport	Close economic relationship with neighboring towns; provided meat, wool, milk products, and hides in exchange for grain and manufactured goods
Arabian and Saharan deserts (Bedouin Arabs, Berbers, Tuareg)	Dromedary (one-humped) camel; sometimes sheep	Camel caravans made possible long-distance trade; camel-mounted warriors central to early Arab/Islamic expansion
Grasslands of sub-Saharan Africa (Fulbe, Nuer, Turkana, Masai)	Cattle; also sheep and goats	Cattle were a chief form of wealth and central to ritual life; little interaction with wider world until nineteenth century
Subarctic Eurasia (Lapps)	Reindeer	Reindeer domesticated only since 1500 C.E.; little impact on world history
Tibetan plateau (Tibetans)	Yaks; also sheep, cashmere goats, some cattle	Tibetans supplied yaks as baggage animal for overland caravan trade; exchanged wool, skins, and milk with valley villagers and received barley in return

and individual achievement were strong, in some pastoral societies clans were ranked as noble or commoner, and considerable differences emerged between wealthy aristocrats owning large flocks of animals and poor herders.

Furthermore, nomadic societies generally offered women a higher status, fewer restrictions, and a greater role in public life than their sisters in agricultural civilizations enjoyed. Everywhere they were involved in productive labor as well as having domestic responsibility for food and children. The care of smaller animals such as sheep and goats usually fell to women, although only rarely did women own or control their own livestock. Among the Mongols, the remarriage of widows carried none of the negative connotations that it did among the Chinese, and women could initiate divorce. Mongol women frequently served as political advisers and were active in military affairs as well. A thirteenth-century European visitor, the Franciscan friar Giovanni DiPlano Carpini, recorded his impressions of Mongol women:

> Girls and women ride and gallop as skillfully as men. We even saw them carrying quivers and bows, and the women can ride horses for as long as the men; they have shorter stirrups, handle horses very well, and mind all the property. [Mongol] women make everything: skin clothes, shoes, leggings, and everything made of leather. They drive carts and repair them, they load camels, and are quick and vigorous in all their tasks. They all wear trousers, and some of them shoot just like men.[3]

Certainly literate observers from adjacent civilizations noticed and clearly disapproved of the freedom granted to pastoral women. Ancient Greek writers thought that the pastoralists with whom they were familiar were "women governed." To Han Kuan, a Chinese Confucian scholar in the first century B.C.E., China's northern nomadic neighbors "[made] no distinction between men and women."[4]

The most characteristic feature of pastoral societies was their mobility. As people frequently on the move, they are often referred to as nomads because they shifted their herds in regular patterns. These movements were far from aimless wanderings, as popular images often portray them, but rather sought to systematically follow the seasonal changes in vegetation and water supply. It was a life largely dictated by local environmental conditions and based on turning grass, which people cannot eat, into usable food and energy. Nor were nomads homeless; they took their homes, often elaborate felt tents, with them. According to a prominent scholar of pastoral life, "They know where they are going and why."[5]

Even though nomadic pastoralists represented an alternative to the agricultural way of life that they disdained, they were almost always deeply connected to, and often dependent on, their agricultural neighbors. Few nomadic peoples could live solely from the products of their animals, and most of them actively sought access to the foodstuffs, manufactured goods, and luxury items available from the urban workshops and farming communities of adjacent civilizations. Particularly among the nomadic peoples of inner Eurasia, this desire for the fruits of civilization periodically stimulated the creation of tribal confederations or nomadic states that could more effectively deal with the powerful agricultural societies on their

■ **Connection**
In what ways did pastoral societies interact with their agricultural neighbors?

The Scythians
An ancient horse-riding nomadic people during the classical era, the Scythians occupied a region in present-day Kazakhstan and southern Russia. Their pastoral way of life is apparent in this detail from an exquisite gold necklace from the fourth century B.C.E. (Private Collection/Photo Boltin Picture Library/The Bridgeman Art Library)

borders. The Mongol Empire of the thirteenth century was but the most recent and largest in a long line of such efforts, dating back to the first millennium B.C.E.

Constructing a large state among nomadic pastoralists was no easy task. Such societies generally lacked the wealth needed to buy the professional armies and bureaucracies that everywhere sustained the states and empires of agricultural civilizations. And the fierce independence of widely dispersed pastoral clans and tribes as well as their internal rivalries made any enduring political unity difficult to achieve. Nonetheless, charismatic leaders, such as Chinggis Khan, were periodically able to weld together a series of tribal alliances that for a time became powerful states. In doing so, they often employed the device of "fictive kinship," designating allies as blood relatives and treating them with a corresponding respect.

Despite their limited populations, such states had certain military advantages in confronting larger and more densely populated civilizations. They could draw upon the horseback-riding and hunting skills of virtually the entire male population and some women as well. Easily transferred to the role of warrior, these skills, which were practiced from early childhood, were an integral part of pastoral life. But what sustained nomadic states was their ability to extract wealth, through raiding, trading, or extortion, from agricultural civilizations such as China, Persia, and Byzantium. As long as that wealth flowed into pastoral states, rulers could maintain the fragile alliances among fractious clans and tribes. When it was interrupted, however, those states often fragmented.

Pastoral nomads interacted with their agricultural neighbors not only economically and militarily but also culturally as they "became acquainted with and tried on for size all the world and universal religions."[6] At one time or another, Judaism, Buddhism, several forms of Christianity, and Islam all found a home somewhere among the nomadic peoples of inner Eurasia. So did Manichaeism, a religious tradition born in third-century Persia and combining elements of Zoroastrian, Christian, and Buddhist practice. Usually conversion was a top-down process as nomadic elites and rulers adopted a foreign religion for political purposes, sometimes changing religious allegiance as circumstances altered. Nomadic peoples, in short, did not inhabit a world totally apart from their agricultural and civilized neighbors.

Surely the most fundamental contribution of pastoralists to the larger human story was their mastery of environments unsuitable for agriculture. Through the creative use of their animals, they brought a version of the food-producing revolution and a substantial human presence to the arid grasslands and desert fringes of Afro-Eurasia. As the pastoral peoples of the Inner Asian steppes learned the art of horseback riding, by roughly 1000 B.C.E., their societies changed dramatically. Now they could accumulate and tend larger herds of horses, sheep, and goats and move more rapidly over a much wider territory. New technologies, invented or adapted by pastoral societies, added to the mastery of their environment and spread widely across the Eurasian steppes, creating something of a common culture in this vast region. These innovations included complex horse harnesses, saddles with iron stirrups,

The Xiongnu Confederacy

■ Significance
In what ways did the Xiongnu, Arabs, and Turks make an impact on world history?

a small compound bow that could be fired from horseback, various forms of armor, and new kinds of swords. Agricultural peoples were amazed at the centrality of the horse in pastoral life. As one observer noted, "From their horses, by day and night every one of that [nomadic] nation buys and sells, eats and drinks, and bowed over the narrow neck of the animal relaxes in a sleep so deep as to be accompanied by many dreams."[7]

The Xiongnu: An Early Nomadic Empire

What enabled pastoral peoples to make their most visible entry onto the stage of world history was the military potential of horseback riding, and of camel riding somewhat later. Their mastery of mounted warfare made possible a long but intermittent series of nomadic empires across the steppes of inner Eurasia and elsewhere. For 2,000 years, those states played a major role in Eurasian history and represented a standing challenge to and influence upon the agrarian civilizations on their borders.

During the classical era, one such large-scale nomadic empire was associated with the people known as the Xiongnu, who lived in the Mongolian steppes north of China (see Chapter 9). Provoked by Chinese penetration of their territory, the Xiongnu in the third and second centuries B.C.E. created a huge military confederacy that stretched from Manchuria deep into Central Asia. Under the charismatic leadership of Modun (reigned 210–174 B.C.E.), the Xiongnu Empire effected a revolution in nomadic life. Earlier fragmented and egalitarian societies were now transformed into a far more centralized and hierarchical political system in which power was concentrated in a divinely sanctioned ruler and differences between "junior" and "senior" clans became more prominent. "All the people who draw the bow have now become one family," declared Modun. Tribute, exacted from other nomadic peoples and from China itself, sustained the Xiongnu Empire and forced the Han dynasty emperor Wen to acknowledge, unhappily, the equality of people he regarded as barbarians. "Our two great nations," he declared, no doubt reluctantly, "the Han and the Xiongnu, stand side by side."[8]

Although it subsequently disintegrated under sustained Chinese counterattacks, the Xiongnu Empire created a model that later Turkic and Mongol empires emulated. Even without a powerful state, various nomadic or seminomadic peoples played a role in the collapse of already weakened classical Chinese and Roman empires and the subsequent rebuilding of those civilizations (see Chapter 4).

The Arabs and the Turks

It was during the era of third-wave civilizations (500–1500 C.E.) that nomadic peoples made their most significant mark on the larger canvas of world history. Arabs,

Berbers, Turks, and Mongols—all of them of nomadic origin—created the largest and most influential empires of that postclassical millennium. The most expansive religious tradition of the era, Islam, derived from a largely nomadic people, the Arabs, and was carried to new regions by another nomadic people, the Turks. In that millennium, most of the great civilizations of outer Eurasia—Byzantium, Persia, India, and China—had come under the control of previously nomadic people, at least for a time. But as pastoral nomads entered and shaped the arena of world history, they too were transformed by the experience.

The first and most dramatic of these nomadic incursions came from Arabs. In the Arabian Peninsula, the development of a reliable camel saddle somewhere between 500 and 100 B.C.E. enabled nomadic Bedouin (desert-dwelling) Arabs to fight effectively from atop their enormous beasts. With this new military advantage, they came to control the rich trade routes in incense running through Arabia. Even more important, these camel nomads served as the shock troops of Islamic expansion, providing many of the new religion's earliest followers and much of the military force that carved out the Arab Empire. Although intellectual and political leadership came from urban merchants and settled farming communities, the Arab Empire was in some respects a nomadic creation that subsequently became the foundation of a new and distinctive civilization.

Even as the pastoral Arabs encroached on the world of Eurasian civilizations from the south, Turkic-speaking nomads were making inroads from the north. Never a single people, various Turkic-speaking clans and tribes migrated from their homeland in Mongolia and southern Siberia generally westward and entered the historical record as creators of a series of nomadic empires between 552 and 965 C.E., most of them lasting little more than a century. Like the Xiongnu Empire, they were fragile alliances of various tribes headed by a supreme ruler known as a *kaghan*, who was supported by a faithful corps of soldiers called "wolves." From their base in the steppes, these Turkic states confronted the great civilizations to their south—China, Persia, Byzantium—alternately raiding them, allying with them against common enemies, trading with them, and extorting tribute payments from them. Turkic language and culture spread widely over much of Inner Asia, and elements of that culture entered the agrarian civilizations. In the courts of northern China, for example, yogurt thinned with water, a drink derived from the Turks, replaced for a time the traditional beverage of tea, and at least one Chinese poet wrote joyfully about the delights of snowy evenings in a felt tent.[9]

A major turning point in the history of the Turks occurred with their conversion to Islam between the tenth and fourteenth centuries. This extended process represented a major expansion of the faith and launched the Turks into a new role as the third major carrier of Islam, following the Arabs and the Persians. It also brought the Turks into an increasingly important position within the heartland of an established Islamic civilization as they migrated southward into the Middle East. There they served first as slave soldiers within the Abbasid caliphate, and then, as the caliphate declined, they increasingly took political and military power themselves.

In the Seljuk Turkic Empire of the eleventh and twelfth centuries, centered in Persia and present-day Iraq, Turkic rulers began to claim the Muslim title of *sultan* rather than kaghan. Although the Abbasid caliph remained the formal ruler, real power was exercised by Turkic sultans.

Not only did Turkic peoples become Muslims themselves, but they carried Islam to new areas as well. Their invasions of northern India solidly planted Islam in that ancient civilization. In Anatolia, formerly ruled by Christian Byzantium, they brought both Islam and a massive infusion of Turkic culture, language, and people, even as they created the Ottoman Empire, which by 1500 became one of the great powers of Eurasia. In both places, Turkic dynasties governed and would continue to do so well into the modern era. Thus Turkic people, many of them at least, had transformed themselves from pastoral nomads to sedentary farmers, from creators of steppe empires to rulers of agrarian civilizations, and from polytheistic worshippers of their ancestors and various gods to followers and carriers of a monotheistic Islam.

The Masai of East Africa

■ Comparison
Did the history and society of the East African Masai people parallel that of Asian nomads?

In East African history as well, the relationship between nomads and settled farmers worked itself out over many centuries, although solid historical information in this case largely dates to after 1500. Unlike Inner Asia, no large states or chiefdoms developed among either agricultural or pastoral peoples in present-day Kenya and Tanzania. Instead the nomadic cattle-keeping Masai and their settled agricultural neighbors found another way to bind their people together beyond the ties of village and clan. Adolescent boys from a variety of villages or lineages were initiated together in a ritual that often included circumcision, an experience that produced a profound bond among them. This ceremony created an "age-set," which then moved through a series of "age-grades" or ranks, from warrior through elder, during their lives. Such a system provided an alternative to the state as a means of mobilizing young men for military purposes, for integrating outsiders into the community, and for establishing a larger social identity.

Sharp distinctions and strong views separated people practicing different economies. From the viewpoint of the Masai, who composed songs and poems in honor of their cattle, pastoralism was a vastly superior way of life, whereas farming was seen as demeaning and as destroying land that could be much better used for grazing. Farmers were fit only to provide beer, wives, and occasionally food for herding peoples. Conversely, agricultural peoples often saw the Masai as arrogant, aggressive, and lazy, stubbornly unwilling to engage in the hard work of cultivation or even to eat the products of the land.[10]

But ways of life were hardly static in East Africa. Earlier in their history, the proudly pastoral Masai had in fact raised sorghum and millet, fully

The Masai of East Africa

abandoning cultivation only in the eighteenth and nineteenth centuries as they migrated southward from the upper Nile Valley into the more arid regions of central Kenya. Later several Masai groups returned to agriculture after bitter conflicts in the mid-nineteenth century drove them to the periphery of Masai territory. Furthermore, the Masai, while trumpeting the superiority of their culture, were altogether willing to admit others into its charmed circle, much like the Chinese in relation to surrounding barbarians. Outsiders could become Masai, and many did so by obtaining a herd of cattle, by joining a Masai age-set, by learning the language, or by giving a woman in marriage to a Masai man and receiving "bride-wealth" in cattle in return.

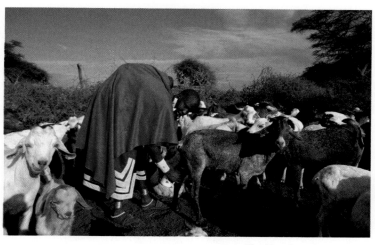

The Masai
This contemporary Masai woman from Tanzania is milking goats while carrying a child on her back, in much the same fashion as her ancestors have done for centuries. (The Africa Image Library, photographersdirect .com. Photographer: Ariadne Van Zandbergen)

The Masai were also dependent on those practicing other ways of life. Although they despised hunters as "poor people without cattle," the Masai relied on them for animal skins, bows and arrows, shields, and, most of all, honey, which was required in their ritual ceremonies. They were even more involved with neighboring agricultural peoples. Despite a great deal of mutual raiding and warfare, that relationship also involved substantial economic exchange as women conducted frequent trade to supplement the diet of milk, meat, and blood derived from their cattle. Elaborate peace negotiations after periods of conflict, frequent intermarriage, and occasional military alliances against a common enemy also brought the Masai into close contact with nearby farmers, such as the Gikuyu. And in times of desperation owing to drought or disease, the Masai might find refuge with hunters or farmers with whom they had long-established relationships.[11]

The prestige and the military success of the Masai encouraged those agricultural societies to borrow elements of Masai culture, such as hairstyles, shield decorations, terms referring to cattle, and the name for their High God. Farming societies also adopted elements of Masai military organization, the long Masai spear, and the practice of drinking cow's milk before battle.[12] Peaceful interaction and mutual dependence as well as conflict and hostility characterized the relationship of nomadic herders and settled farmers in East Africa, much as it did in Eurasia.

Breakout: The Mongol Empire

Of all the pastoral peoples who took a turn on the stage of world history, the Mongols made the most stunning entry. Their thirteenth-century breakout from Mongolia gave rise to the largest land-based empire in all of human history, stretching

Map 12.1   The Mongol Empire
Encompassing much of Eurasia, the Mongol Empire was divided into four khanates after the death of Chinggis Khan.

from the Pacific coast of Asia to Eastern Europe (see Map 12.1). This empire joined the nomadic peoples of the inner Eurasian steppes with the settled agricultural civilizations of outer Eurasia more extensively and more intimately than ever before. It also brought the major civilizations of Eurasia—Europe, China, and the Islamic world—into far more direct contact than in earlier times. Both the enormous destructiveness of the process and the networks of exchange and communication that it spawned were the work of the Mongols, numbering only about 700,000 people. It was another of history's unlikely twists.

For all of its size and fearsome reputation, the Mongol Empire left a surprisingly modest cultural imprint on the world it had briefly governed. Unlike the Arabs, the Mongols bequeathed to the world no new religion or civilization. Whereas the Islamic community offered a common religious home for all converts—conquerors and conquered alike—the Mongols never tried to spread their own faith among subject peoples. At the level of family life, that religion centered on rituals invoking the ancestors, which were performed around the hearth. Rulers sometimes consulted religious specialists, known as *shamans*, who might predict the future, offer sacrifices, and communicate with the spirit world, and particularly with Tengri, the supreme sky god of the Mongols. There was little in this tradition to attract outsiders, and in any event the Mongols proved uninterested in religious imperialism.

The Mongols offered the majority of those they conquered little more than the status of defeated, subordinate, and exploited people, although people with skills were put to work in ways useful to Mongol authorities. Unlike the Turks, whose languages and culture flourish today in many places far from the Turkic homeland, Mongol culture remains confined largely to Mongolia. Furthermore, the Mongol Empire, following in the tradition of Xiongnu and Turkic state building, proved to be "the last, spectacular bloom of pastoral power in Inner Eurasia."[13] Some Mongols themselves became absorbed into the settled societies they conquered. After the decline and disintegration of the Mongol Empire, the tide turned against the pastoralists of inner Eurasia, who were increasingly swallowed up in the expanding Russian or Chinese empires. Nonetheless, while it lasted and for a few centuries thereafter, the Mongol Empire exercised an enormous impact throughout the entire Eurasian world.

Snapshot   Key Moments in Mongol History

Birth of Temujin	1162
Temujin gains title of Chinggis Khan ("universal ruler")	1206
Reign of Chinggis Khan	1206–1227
Beginning of Mongol conquests	1209
Conquest of China	1209–1279
Initial assault on Persia	1219–1221
Conquest of Russia	1237–1240
Attacks in Eastern Europe; then withdrawal	1241–1242
Mongol seizure of Baghdad	1258
Khubilai Khan as ruler of China	1271–1294
Failed Mongol attacks on Japan	1274, 1281
Conversion of Il-khan Ghazan to Islam	1295
High point of plague in Europe	1348–1350
Ming dynasty established; end of Mongol rule in China	1368
End of "Mongol yoke" in Russia; Moscow emerges as center of Russian state	1480

From Temujin to Chinggis Khan: The Rise of the Mongol Empire

■ **Description**

Identify the major steps in the rise of the Mongol Empire.

World historians are prone to focus attention on large-scale and long-term processes of change in explaining "what happened in history," but in understanding the rise of the Mongol Empire, most scholars have found themselves forced to look closely at the role of a single individual—Temujin (1162–1227), later known as Chinggis Khan ("universal ruler"). The twelfth-century world into which he was born found the Mongols an unstable and fractious collection of tribes and clans, much reduced from a somewhat earlier and more powerful position in the shifting nomadic alliances in what is now Mongolia. "Everyone was feuding," declared a leading Mongol shaman. "Rather than sleep, they robbed each other of their possessions. . . . There was no respite, only battle. There was no affection, only mutual slaughter."[14]

The early life of Temujin showed few signs of a prominent future. The boy's father had been a minor chieftain of a noble clan, but he was murdered by tribal rivals before Temujin turned ten, and the family was soon deserted by other members of the clan. As social outcasts, Temujin's small family, headed by his resourceful mother, was forced to live by hunting, fishing, and gathering wild foods. Without livestock, they had fallen to the lowest level of nomadic life. In these desperate circumstances, Temujin's remarkable character came into play. His personal magnetism and courage and his inclination to rely on trusted friends rather than ties of kinship allowed him to build up a small following and to ally with a more powerful tribal leader. This alliance received a boost from Chinese patrons, who were always eager to keep the nomads divided. Military victory over a rival tribe resulted in Temujin's recognition as a chief in his own right with a growing band of followers.

Temujin's rise to power amid the complex tribal politics of Mongolia was never a sure thing. What contributed to his growing power were shifting alliances and betrayals, a mounting string of military victories, the indecisiveness of his enemies, a reputation as a leader generous to friends and ruthless to enemies, and the incorporation of warriors from defeated tribes into his own forces. In 1206, a Mongol tribal assembly recognized Temujin as Chinggis Khan, supreme leader of a now unified Great Mongol Nation. It was a remarkable achievement, but one little noticed beyond the highland steppes of Mongolia. That would soon change.

The unification of the Mongol tribes raised an obvious question: What was Chinggis Khan to do with the powerful army he had assembled? Without a common task, the new and fragile unity of the Mongols would surely dissolve into quarrels and chaos; and without external resources to reward his followers, Chinggis Khan would be hard pressed to maintain his supreme position. Both considerations pointed in a single direction—expansion, particularly toward China, long a source of great wealth for nomadic peoples.[15]

In 1209, the first major attack on the settled agricultural societies south of Mongolia set in motion half a century of a Mongol world war, a series of military campaigns, massive killing, and empire building without precedent in world history. In the process, Chinggis Khan, followed by his sons and grandsons (Ogodei, Mongke, and Khubilai), constructed an empire that contained China, Korea, Central Asia, Russia, much of the Islamic Middle East, and parts of Eastern Europe (see Map 12.1). "In a flash," wrote a recent scholar, "the Mongol warriors would defeat every army, capture every fort, and bring down the walls of every city they encountered. Christians, Muslims, Buddhists, and Hindus would soon kneel before the dusty boots of illiterate young Mongol horsemen."[16]

Various setbacks—the Mongols' withdrawal from Eastern Europe (1242), their defeat in Egypt (1260), the failure of their invasion of Japan owing to violent typhoons (1274, 1281), and the difficulty of penetrating the tropical jungles of Southeast Asia—marked the outer limits of the Mongol Empire. But what an empire it was! How could a Mongol confederation, with a total population of less than 1 million people and few resources beyond their livestock, assemble an imperial structure of such staggering transcontinental dimensions?

Explaining the Mongol Moment

Like the Roman Empire but far more rapidly, the Mongol Empire grew of its own momentum without any grand scheme or blueprint for world conquest. Each fresh victory brought new resources for making war and new threats or insecurities that seemed to require further expansion. As the empire took shape and certainly by the end of his life, Chinggis Khan came to see his career in terms of a universal mission. "I have accomplished a great work," he declared, "uniting the whole world in one empire."[17] Thus the Mongol Empire acquired an ideology in the course of its construction.

What made this "great work" possible? The odds seemed overwhelming, for China alone, after all, outnumbered the Mongols 100 to 1 and possessed incomparably greater resources. Nor did the Mongols enjoy any technological superiority over their many adversaries. Clearly the key to the Mongols' success lay in their army. According to one scholar, "Mongol armies were simply better led, organized, and disciplined than those of their opponents."[18] In an effort to diminish a divisive tribalism, Chinggis Khan reorganized the entire social structure of the Mongols into military units of 10, 100, 1,000, and 10,000 warriors, an arrangement that allowed for effective command and control. Conquered tribes especially were broken up and their members scattered among these new units, which enrolled virtually all nomadic men and supplied the cavalry forces of Mongol armies. A highly prestigious imperial guard, also recruited across tribal lines, marked the further decline of the old tribalism as a social revolution, imposed from above by Chinggis Khan, reshaped Mongol society.

An impressive discipline and loyalty to their leaders characterized Mongol military forces, and discpline was reinforced by the provision that should one or two members of a unit desert in battle, all were subject to the death penalty. More

■ **Explanation**
What accounts for the political and military success of the Mongols?

positively, loyalty was cemented by the leaders' willingness to share the hardships of their men. "I eat the same food and am dressed in the same rags as my humble herdsmen," wrote Chinggis Khan. "I am always in the forefront, and in battle I am never at the rear."[19] Such discipline and loyalty made possible the elaborate tactics of encirclement, retreat, and deception that proved decisive in many a battle. Furthermore, the enormous flow of wealth from conquered civilizations benefited all Mongols, though not equally. Even ordinary Mongols could now dress in linens and silks rather than hides and felt, could own slaves derived from the many prisoners of war, and had far greater opportunities to improve their social position in a constantly expanding empire.

To compensate for their own small population, the Mongols incorporated huge numbers of conquered peoples into their military forces. "People who lived in felt tents"—mostly Mongol and Turkic nomads—were conscripted en masse into the cavalry units of the Mongol army, while settled agricultural peoples supplied the infantry and artillery forces. As the Mongols penetrated major civilizations, with their walled cities and elaborate fortifications, they quickly acquired Chinese techniques and technology of siege warfare. Some 1,000 Chinese artillery crews, for example, took part in the Mongol invasion of distant Persia. Beyond military recruitment, Mongols demanded that their conquered people serve as laborers, building roads and bridges and ferrying supplies over long distances. Artisans, craftsmen, and skilled people generally were carefully identified, spared from massacre, and often sent to distant regions of the empire where their services were required.

A Mongol Warrior
Horseback-riding skills, honed in herding animals and adapted to military purposes, were central to Mongol conquests, as illustrated in this Ming-dynasty Chinese painting of a mounted Mongol archer. (Victoria and Albert Museum, London/V & A Picture Library)

A French goldsmith, captured by Mongol forces in Hungary, wound up as a slave in the Mongol capital of Karakorum, where he constructed an elaborate silver fountain that dispensed wine and other intoxicating drinks.

A further element in the military effectiveness of Mongol forces lay in a growing reputation for a ruthless brutality and utter destructiveness. Chinggis Khan's policy was clear: "whoever submits shall be spared, but those who resist, they shall be destroyed with their wives, children and dependents . . . so that the others who hear and see should fear and not act the same."[20] The Central Asian kingdom of Khwarizm, whose ruler had greatly offended Chinggis Khan by murdering and mutilating Mongol envoys and merchants, was among the first, but by no means the last, to feel the full effects of Mongol terror. City after city was utterly destroyed, and their soldiers were passed out in lots to Mongol troops for execution, while women and skilled craftsmen were enslaved. Unskilled civilians served as human shields for attacks on the next city or were used as human fill in the moats surrounding those cities.

One scholar explained such policies in this way: "Extremely conscious of their small numbers and fearful of rebellion, Chinggis often chose to annihilate a region's entire population, if it appeared too troublesome to govern."[21] These policies also served as a form of psychological warfare, a practical inducement to surrender for those who knew of the Mongol terror. Historians continue to debate the extent and uniqueness of Mongol brutality, but their reputation for unwavering harshness proved a military asset.

Underlying the purely military dimensions of the Mongols' success was an impressive ability to mobilize both the human and material resources of their growing empire. Elaborate census taking allowed Mongol leaders to know what was available to them and made possible the systematic taxation of conquered people. An effective system of relay stations, about a day's ride apart, provided rapid communication across the empire and fostered trade as well. Marco Polo, the Italian trader who traveled through Mongol domains in the thirteenth century, claimed that the Mongols maintained some 10,000 such stations, together with 200,000 horses available to authorized users. The beginnings of a centralized bureaucracy with various specialized offices took shape in the new capital of Karakorum. There scribes translated official decrees into the various languages of the empire, such as Persian, Uighur, Chinese, and Tibetan.

Other policies appealed to various groups among the conquered peoples of the empire. Interested in fostering commerce, Mongol rulers often offered merchants 10 percent or more above their asking price and allowed them the free use of the relay stations for transporting their goods. In administering the conquered regions, Mongols held the highest decision-making posts, but Chinese and Muslim officials held many advisory and lower-level positions in China and Persia respectively. In religious matters, the Mongols welcomed and supported many religious traditions—Buddhist, Christian, Muslim, Daoist—as long as they did not become the focus of political opposition. This policy of religious toleration allowed Muslims to seek converts among Mongol troops and afforded Christians much greater freedom than they had enjoyed under Muslim rule.[22] Toward the end of his life and apparently feeling his approaching death, Chinggis Khan himself summoned a famous Daoist master from China and begged him to "communicate to me the means of preserving life." One of his successors, Mongke, arranged a debate among representatives of several religious faiths, after which he concluded: "Just as God gave different fingers to the hand, so has He given different ways to men."[23] Such economic, administrative, and religious policies provided some benefits and a place within the empire—albeit subordinate—for many of its conquered peoples.

Encountering the Mongols: Comparing Three Cases

The Mongol moment in world history represented an enormous cultural encounter between nomadic pastoralists and the settled civilizations of Eurasia. Differences among those civilizations—Confucian China, Muslim Persia, Christian Russia—ensured considerable diversity as this encounter unfolded across a vast realm. The process of conquest, the length and nature of Mongol rule, the impact on local people, and the extent of Mongol assimilation into the cultures of the conquered—all this and more varied considerably across the Eurasian domains of the empire. The experiences of China, Persia, and Russia provide brief glimpses into several expressions of this massive clash of cultures.

China and the Mongols

■ Change
How did Mongol rule change China? In what ways were the Mongols changed by China?

Long the primary target for nomadic steppe-dwellers in search of agrarian wealth, China proved the most difficult and extended of the Mongols' many conquests, lasting some seventy years, from 1209 to 1279. The invasion began in northern China, which had been ruled for several centuries by various dynasties of nomadic origin, and was characterized by destruction and plunder on a massive scale. Southern China, under the control of the native Song dynasty, was a different story, for there the Mongols were far less violent and more concerned to accommodate the local population. Landowners, for example, were guaranteed their estates in exchange for their support or at least their neutrality. By whatever methods, the outcome was the unification of a divided China, a treasured ideal among educated Chinese. This achievement persuaded many of them that the Mongols had indeed been granted the Mandate of Heaven and, despite their foreign origins, were legitimate rulers.

Having acquired China, what were the Mongols to do with it? One possibility, apparently considered by the Great Khan Ogodei in the 1230s, was to exterminate everyone in northern China and turn the country into pastureland for Mongol herds. That suggestion, fortunately, was rejected in favor of extracting as much wealth as possible from the country's advanced civilization. Doing so meant some accommodation to Chinese culture and ways of governing, for the Mongols had no experience with the operation of a complex agrarian society.

That accommodation took many forms. The Mongols made use of Chinese administrative practices, techniques of taxation, and their postal system. They gave themselves a Chinese dynastic title, the Yuan, meaning "great beginnings." They transferred their capital from Karakorum in Mongolia to what is now Beijing, building a wholly new capital city there known as Khanbalik, the "city of the khan." Thus the Mongols were now rooting themselves solidly on the soil of the world's most sophisticated civilization, well removed from their homeland on the steppes. Khubilai Khan, the grandson of Chinggis Khan and China's Mongol ruler from

Marco Polo and Khubilai Khan
In ruling China, the Mongols employed in high positions a number of Muslims and a few Europeans, such as Marco Polo, shown here kneeling before Khubilai Khan in a painting from the fifteenth century. (Ms 2810 f.5. Nicolo and Marco Polo before the Great Khan [vellum], Boucicaut Master, [fl. 1390–1430, and workshop]/Bibliothèque nationale de France, Paris, France/The Bridgeman Art Library)

1271 to 1294, ordered a set of Chinese-style ancestral tablets to honor his ancestors and posthumously awarded them Chinese names. Many of his policies evoked the values of a benevolent Chinese emperor as he improved roads, built canals, lowered some taxes, patronized scholars and artists, limited the death penalty and torture, supported peasant agriculture, and prohibited Mongols from grazing their animals on peasants' farmland. Mongol khans also made use of traditional Confucian rituals, supported the building of some Daoist temples, and were particularly attracted to a Tibetan form of Buddhism, which returned the favor with strong political support for the invaders.

Despite these accommodations, Mongol rule was still harsh, exploitative, and foreign. Marco Polo, who lived in China during the time of Khubilai Khan, observed the hostility between the Mongols and their Chinese subjects.

> The Cathayans [Chinese] detest the Grand Kaan's rule because he set over them governors who were Tartars [Mongols], or still more frequently Saracens [Muslims], and these they would not endure, for they were treated by them just like slaves.[24]

The Mongols did not become Chinese, nor did they accommodate every aspect of Chinese culture. Deep inside the new capital they established the so-called Forbidden City, where the royal family and court could continue to experience something of steppe life. Animals roamed freely in large open areas, planted with steppe grass. Many of the Mongol elite much preferred to live, eat, sleep, and give birth in the traditional tents that sprouted everywhere. In administering the country, the Mongols largely ignored the traditional Chinese examination system and relied heavily on foreigners, particularly Muslims from Central Asia and the Middle East, to serve as officials, as Marco Polo observed, while keeping the top decision-making posts for themselves. Few Mongols learned Chinese, and Mongol law discriminated against the Chinese, reserving for them the most severe punishments. In social life, the Mongols forbade intermarriage and prohibited Chinese scholars from learning the Mongol script. Mongol women never adopted foot binding and scandalized the Chinese by mixing freely with men at official gatherings and riding to the hunt with their husbands. Furthermore, the Mongols honored and supported merchants and artisans far more than Confucian bureaucrats had been inclined to do.

However one assesses Mongol rule in China, it was brief, lasting little more than a century. By the mid-fourteenth century, intense factionalism among the Mongols, rapidly rising prices, furious epidemics of the plague, and growing peasant rebellions combined to force the Mongols out of China. By 1368, rebel forces had triumphed, and thousands of Mongols returned to their homeland in the steppes. For several centuries, they remained a periodic threat to China, but during the Ming dynasty that followed, the memory of their often brutal and alien rule stimulated a renewed commitment to Confucian values and practices and an effort to wipe out all traces of the Mongols' impact.

Persia and the Mongols

■ Comparison

How was Mongol rule in Persia different from that in China?

A second great civilization conquered by the Mongols was that of an Islamic Persia. There the Mongol takeover was far more abrupt than the extended process of conquest in China. A first invasion (1219–1221), led by Chinggis Khan himself, was followed thirty years later by a second assault (1251–1258) under his grandson Hulegu, who became the first il-khan (subordinate khan) of Persia. More destructive than the conquest of Song dynasty China, the Mongol offensive against Persia and Iraq had no precedent in their history, although Persia had been repeatedly attacked, from the invasion of Alexander the Great to that of the Arabs. The most recent incursion had featured Turkic peoples, but they had been Muslims, recently converted, small in number, and seeking only acceptance within the Islamic world. The Mongols, however, were infidels in Muslim eyes, and their stunning victory was a profound shock to people accustomed to viewing history as the progressive expansion of Islamic rule. Furthermore, Mongol military victory brought in its train a degree of ferocity and slaughter that simply had no parallel in Persian experience. The Persian historian Juwayni described it in fearful terms:

> Every town and every village has been several times subjected to pillage and massacre and has suffered this confusion for years so that even though there be generation and increase until the Resurrection the population will not attain to a tenth part of what it was before.[25]

The sacking of Baghdad in 1258, which put an end to the Abbasid caliphate, was accompanied by the massacre of more than 200,000 people, according to Hulegu himself.

Beyond this human catastrophe lay the damage to Persian and Iraqi agriculture and their peasant farmers. Heavy taxes, sometimes collected twenty or thirty times a year and often under torture or whipping, pushed large numbers of peasants off their land. Furthermore, the in-migration of nomadic Mongols, together with their immense herds of sheep and goats, turned much agricultural land into pasture and sometimes into desert. In both cases, a fragile system of underground water channels that provided irrigation to the fields was neglected, and much good agricultural land was reduced to waste. Some sectors of the Persian economy gained, however. Wine production increased because the Mongols were fond of alcohol, and the Persian silk industry benefited from close contact with a Mongol-ruled China. In general, though, even more so than in China, Mongol rule in Persia represented "disaster on a grand and unparalleled scale."[26]

Nonetheless, the Mongols in Persia were themselves transformed far more than their counterparts in China. They made extensive use of the sophisticated Persian bureaucracy, leaving the greater part of government operations in Persian hands. During the reign of Ghazan (1295–1304), they made some efforts to repair the damage caused by earlier policies of ruthless exploitation, by rebuilding damaged cities and repairing neglected irrigation works. Most important, the Mongols who conquered Persia became Muslims, following the lead of Ghazan, who converted to Islam in 1295. No such widespread conversion to the culture of the conquered occurred in China or in Christian Russia. Members of the court and Mongol elites learned at least some Persian, unlike most of their counterparts in China. A number of Mongols also turned to farming, abandoning their nomadic ways, while some married local people. When the Mongol dynasty of Hulegu's descendants collapsed in the 1330s for lack of a suitable heir, the Mongols were not driven out of Persia as they had been from China. Rather they and their Turkic allies simply disappeared, through assimilation into Persian society. From a Persian point of view, the barbarians had been civilized.

Russia and the Mongols

When the Mongol military machine rolled over Russia between 1237 and 1240, it encountered a relatively new third-wave civilization, located on the far eastern fringe of Christendom (see Chapter 10). Whatever political unity this new civilization of Kievan Rus had earlier enjoyed was now gone, and various independent princes proved unable to unite even in the face of the Mongol onslaught. Although they had interacted extensively with nomadic people of the steppes north of the Black Sea, nothing had prepared them for the Mongols.

The devastation wrought by the Mongol assault matched or exceeded anything experienced by the Persians or the Chinese. City after city fell to Mongol forces,

■ **Comparison**

How was the Russian experience of Mongol domination different from that of Persia or China?

Mongol Russia
This sixteenth-century painting depicts the Mongol burning of the Russian city of Ryazan in 1237. Similar destruction awaited many Russian towns that resisted the invaders. (Sovfoto/Eastfoto)

which were now armed with the catapults and battering rams adopted from Chinese or Muslim sources. The slaughter that sometimes followed was described by Russian chroniclers, although twentieth-century historians often regard such accounts as exaggerated.

> They likewise killed the Prince and Princess, and men, women, and children, monks, nuns, and priests, some by fire, some by the sword, and violated nuns, priests' wives, good women and girls in the presence of their mothers and sisters.[27]

From the survivors and the cities that surrendered early, laborers and skilled craftsmen were deported to other Mongol lands or sold into slavery. A number of Russian crafts were so depleted of their workers that they did not recover for a century or more.

If the ferocity of initial conquest bore similarities to the experiences of Persia and China, Russia's incorporation into the Mongol Empire was very different. To the Mongols, it was the Kipchak Khanate, named after the Kipchak Turkic-speaking peoples north of the Caspian and Black seas, among whom the Mongols had settled. To the Russians, it was the "Khanate of the Golden Horde." By whatever name, the Mongols had conquered Russia, but they did not occupy it as they had China and Persia. Because there were no garrisoned cities, permanently stationed administrators, or Mongol settlement, the Russian experience of Mongol rule was quite different than elsewhere. From the Mongol point of view, Russia had little to offer. Its economy was not nearly as developed as that of more established civilizations; nor was it located on major international trade routes. It was simply not worth the expense of occupying. Furthermore, the availability of extensive steppe lands for pasturing their flocks north of the Black and Caspian seas meant that the Mongols could maintain their preferred nomadic way of life, while remaining in easy reach of Russian cities when the need arose to send further military expeditions. They could dominate and exploit Russia from the steppes.

And exploit they certainly did. Russian princes received appointment from the khan and were required to send substantial tribute to the Mongol capital at Sarai, located on the lower Volga River. A variety of additional taxes created a heavy burden, especially on the peasantry, while continuing border raids sent tens of thousands of Russians into slavery. The Mongol impact was highly uneven, however. Some Russian princes benefited considerably because they were able to manipulate their role as tribute collectors to grow wealthy. The Russian Orthodox Church likewise flourished under the Mongol policy of religious toleration, for it received exemption from many taxes. Nobles who participated in Mongol raids earned a share of the loot. Some cities, such as Kiev, resisted the Mongols and were devastated, while others collaborated and were left undamaged. Moscow in particular emerged as the primary collector of tribute for the Mongols, and its princes parlayed this position into a leading role as the nucleus of a renewed Russian state when Mongol domination receded in the fifteenth century.

The absence of direct Mongol rule had implications for the Mongols themselves, for they were far less influenced by or assimilated within Russian cultures than their counterparts in China and Persia had been. The Mongols in China had turned themselves into a Chinese dynasty, with the khan as a Chinese emperor. Some learned calligraphy, and a few came to appreciate Chinese poetry. In Persia, the Mongols had converted to Islam, with some becoming farmers. Not so in Russia. There "the Mongols of the Golden Horde were still spending their days in the saddle and their nights in tents."[28] They could dominate Russia from the adjacent steppes without in any way adopting Russian culture. Even though they remained culturally separate from Russia, eventually the Mongols assimilated to the culture and the Islamic faith of the Kipchak people of the steppes, and in the process they lost their distinct identity and became Kipchaks.

Despite this domination from a distance, "the impact of the Mongols on Russia was, if anything, greater than on China and Iran [Persia]," according to a leading scholar.[29] Russian princes, who were more or less left alone if they paid the required tribute and taxes, found it useful to adopt the Mongols' weapons, diplomatic rituals, court practices, taxation system, and military draft. Mongol policies facilitated, although not intentionally, the rise of Moscow as the core of a new Russian state, and that state made good use of the famous Mongol mounted courier service, which Marco Polo had praised so highly. Mongol policies also strengthened the hold of the Russian Orthodox Church and enabled it to penetrate the rural areas more fully than before. Some Russians, seeking to explain their country's economic backwardness and political autocracy in modern times, have held the Mongols responsible for both conditions, though most historians consider such views vastly exaggerated.

Divisions among the Mongols and the growing strength of the Russian state, centered now on the city of Moscow, enabled the Russians to break the Mongols' hold by the end of the fifteenth century. With the earlier demise of Mongol rule in China and Persia, and now in Russia, the Mongols had retreated from their brief but spectacular incursion into the civilizations of outer Eurasia. Nonetheless, they continued to periodically threaten these civilizations for several centuries, until their homelands were absorbed into the expanding Russian and Chinese empires. But the Mongol moment in world history was over.

The Mongol Empire as a Eurasian Network

During the postclassical millennium, Chinese culture and Buddhism provided a measure of integration among the peoples of East Asia; Christianity did the same for Europe, while the realm of Islam connected most of the lands in between. But it was the Mongol Empire, during the thirteenth and fourteenth centuries, that brought all of these regions into a single interacting network. It was a unique moment in world history and an important step toward the global integration of the modern era.

Toward a World Economy

■ **Connection**

In what ways did the Mongol Empire contribute to the globalization of the Eurasian world?

The Mongols themselves produced little of value for distant markets, nor were they active traders. Nonetheless, they consistently promoted international commerce, largely so that they could tax it and thus extract wealth from more developed civilizations. The Great Khan Ogodei, for example, often paid well over the asking price in order to attract merchants to his capital of Karakorum. The Mongols also provided financial backing for caravans, introduced standardized weights and measures, and gave tax breaks to merchants.

In providing a relatively secure environment for merchants making the long and arduous journey across Central Asia between Europe and China, the Mongol Empire brought the two ends of the Eurasian world into closer contact than ever before and launched a new phase in the history of the Silk Roads. Marco Polo was only the most famous of many European merchants, mostly Italians, who made their way to China through the Mongol Empire. So many traders attempted the journey that guidebooks were published with much useful advice about the trip. Merchants returned with tales of rich lands and prosperous commercial opportunities, but what they described were long-established trading networks of which Europeans had been largely ignorant.

The Mongol trading circuit was a central element in an even larger commercial network that linked much of the Afro-Eurasian world in the thirteenth century (see Map 12.2). Mongol-ruled China was the fulcrum of this vast system, connecting the overland route through the Mongol Empire with the oceanic routes through the South China Sea and Indian Ocean. Here, some historians have argued, lay the beginnings of those international economic relationships that have played such a major role in the making of the modern world.

Diplomacy on a Eurasian Scale

Not only did the Mongol Empire facilitate long-distance commerce, but it also prompted diplomatic relationships from one end of Eurasia to the other. As their invasion of Russia spilled over into Eastern Europe, Mongol armies destroyed Polish, German, and Hungarian forces in 1241–1242 and seemed poised to march

Map 12.2   Trade and Disease in the Fourteenth Century
The Mongol Empire played a major role in the commercial integration of the Eurasian world as well as in the spread of the plague across this vast area.

on Western Europe. But the death of the Great Khan Ogodei required Mongol leaders to return to Mongolia, and Western Europe lacked adequate pasture for Mongol herds. Thus Europe was spared the trauma of conquest, but fearing the possible return of the Mongols, both the pope and European rulers dispatched delegations to the Mongol capital, mostly led by Franciscan friars. They hoped to learn something about Mongol intentions, to secure Mongol aid in the Christian crusade against Islam, and, if possible, to convert Mongols to Christianity.

These efforts were largely in vain, for no alliance or widespread conversion occurred. In fact, one of these missions came back with a letter for the pope from the Great Khan Guyuk, demanding that Europeans submit to him. "But if you should not believe our letters and the command of God nor hearken to our counsel," he warned, "then we shall know for certain that you wish to have war. After that we do not know what will happen."[30] Perhaps the most important outcome of these diplomatic probings was the useful information about lands to the east that European missions brought back. Those reports contributed to a dawning European awareness of a wider world.

Somewhat later, in 1287, the Il-khanate of Persia sought an alliance with European powers to take Jerusalem and crush the forces of Islam, but the Persian Mongols' conversion to Islam soon put an end to any such anti-Muslim coalition. Within the Mongol Empire itself, close relationships developed between the courts of Persia and China. They regularly exchanged ambassadors, shared intelligence information, fostered trade between their regions, and sent skilled workers back and forth. Thus political authorities all across Eurasia engaged in diplomatic relationships with one another to an unprecedented degree.

Cultural Exchange in the Mongol Realm

Accompanying these transcontinental economic and diplomatic relationships was a substantial exchange of peoples and cultures. Mongol policy forcibly transferred many thousands of skilled craftsmen and educated people from their homelands to distant parts of the empire, while the Mongols' religious tolerance and support of merchants drew missionaries and traders from afar. The Mongol capital at Karakorum was a cosmopolitan city with places of worship for Buddhists, Daoists, Muslims, and Christians. Actors and musicians from China, wrestlers from Persia, and a jester from Byzantium provided entertainment for the Mongol court. Persian and Arab doctors and administrators were sent to China, while Chinese physicians and engineers found their skills in demand in the Islamic world.

This movement of people facilitated the exchange of ideas and techniques, a process actively encouraged by Mongol authorities. A great deal of Chinese technology and artistic conventions—such as painting, printing, gunpowder weapons, compass navigation, high-temperature furnaces, and medical techniques—flowed westward. Acupuncture, for example, was poorly received in the Middle East because it required too much bodily contact for Muslim taste, but Chinese techniques for diagnosing illness by taking the pulse of patients proved quite popular, as they involved minimal body contact. Muslim astronomers brought their skills and knowledge to China because Mongol authorities wanted "second opinions on the reading of heavenly signs and portents" and assistance in constructing accurate calendars, so necessary for ritual purposes.[31] Plants and crops likewise circulated within the Mongol domain. Lemons and carrots from the Middle East found a welcome reception in China, while the Persian Il-khan Ghazan sent envoys to India, China, and elsewhere to seek "seeds of things which are unique in that land."[32]

Europeans arguably gained more than most from these exchanges, for they had long been cut off from the fruitful interchange with Asia, and in comparison to the Islamic and Chinese worlds, they were less technologically developed. Now they could reap the benefits of much new technology, new crops, and new knowledge of a wider world. And almost alone among the peoples of Eurasia, they could do so without having suffered the devastating consequences of Mongol conquest. In these circumstances, some historians have argued, lay the roots of Europe's remarkable rise to global prominence in the centuries that followed.

The Plague: A Eurasian Pandemic

Any benefits derived from participation in Mongol networks of communication and exchange must be measured alongside the Eurasian catastrophe known as the "plague" or the "pestilence" and later called the Black Death. Originating most likely in Central Asia, the bacteria responsible for the disease spread across the trade routes of the vast Mongol Empire in the early fourteenth century (see Map 12.2). Carried by rodents and transmitted by fleas to humans, the plague erupted initially in 1331 in northeastern China and by 1347 had reached Western Europe. Its introduction to Europe is often attributed to a Mongol siege in 1346 of the Genoese city of Caffa in the Crimea, in which the Mongols, using catapults, hurled corpses infected with the plague into the city. It was perhaps the first recorded instance of biological warfare.

The disease itself was associated with swelling of the lymph nodes, most often in the groin; terrible headaches; high fever; and internal bleeding just below the skin. Infected people generally died within a few days. In the densely populated civilizations of China, the Islamic world, and Europe as well as in the steppe lands of the nomads, the plague claimed enormous numbers of human victims, causing a sharp contraction in Eurasian population for a century or more. Chroniclers reported rates of death that ranged from 50 to 90 percent of the affected population, depending on the time and place. Estimates for Europe suggest that between one-third and two-thirds of the population died within a few years. This intense first wave of the plague was followed by periodic visitations over the next several centuries. The plague, however, was not universal, for India and sub-Saharan Africa were much less affected than other regions of Eurasia.

Although the plague in the fourteenth century represented a crisis all across Eurasia, our best information about its impact comes from Western

■ **Change**
Disease changes societies. How might this argument apply to the plague?

The Plague
In this English painting from the fifteenth century, a priest offers last rites to a man dying of the plague, while a smiling death figure wounds him with a spear and God looks down from above. What message does this picture convey? (British Library/HIP/Art Resource, NY)

Europe.[33] In some places, such as city governments in Italy, authorities learned practical ways of dealing with the disease by establishing quarantines, hiring doctors, and organizing burials, but the response of most people, no doubt, was couched in religious terms. So great was the initial shock of this massive mortality that chroniclers described it in apocalyptic language. "So many have died," wrote an Italian observer in 1348, "that everyone believes it is the end of the world." Viewing the plague as God's judgment on a sinful world, many took part in the flagellant movement, in which people flogged themselves, sometimes almost to death, to atone for the sins that must have caused the pestilence. Attacks on Jews, who were sometimes held responsible for spreading the disease, sent many of them fleeing to Poland, where authorities welcomed their urban and commercial skills, leading to a flourishing of Jewish culture in the several centuries that followed. Still others fled into hedonism because life was so uncertain, while many joined mystical movements aimed at escaping from the world in an intense personal relationship with God. A clergyman in England expressed the dismay many must have felt.

> For God is deaf nowadays and will not hear us
> And for our guilt, he grinds good men to dust.[34]

Beyond its immediate devastation, the plague worked longer-term changes in European society. Labor shortages following the initial outburst provoked sharp conflict between scarce workers, who sought higher wages or better conditions, and the rich, who resisted such demands. A series of peasant revolts in the fourteenth century reflected this tension, which also undermined the practice of serfdom. That labor shortage also may have fostered a greater interest in technological innovation and created, at least for a time, more employment opportunities for women. Thus a resilient European civilization survived a cataclysm that had the power to destroy it. In a strange way, that catastrophe may have actually fostered its future growth.

Whatever its impact in particular places, the plague also had larger consequences. Ironically, that human disaster, born of the Mongol network, was a primary reason for the demise of that network in the fourteenth and fifteenth centuries. Population contracted, cities declined, and the volume of trade diminished all across the Mongol world. By 1350, the Mongol Empire itself was in disarray, and within a century the Mongols had lost control of Chinese, Persian, and Russian civilizations. The Central Asian trade route, so critical to the entire Afro-Eurasian world economy, largely closed.

This disruption of the Mongol-based land routes to the east, coupled with a desire to avoid Muslim intermediaries, provided incentives for Europeans to take to the sea in their continuing efforts to reach the riches of Asia. Their naval technology gave them military advantages on the seas, much as the Mongols' skill with the bow and their mobility on horseback gave these nomads a decisive edge in land battles. As Europeans penetrated Asian waters in the sixteenth century, they took on, in some ways, the role of the Mongols in organizing and fostering world trade and in creating a network of communication and exchange over an even larger area. Like the Mongols, Europeans were people on the periphery of the major established civilizations; they too were economically less developed in comparison to Chinese and Islamic civilizations; and both were prone to forcibly plundering the wealthier civilizations they encountered.[35] Europeans, of course, brought far more of their own culture and many more of their own people to the societies they conquered, as Christianity, European languages, settler societies, and their science and technology took root within their empires. Although their imperial presence lasted far longer and operated on a much larger scale, European actions at the beginning of their global expansion bore a striking resemblance to those of their Mongol predecessors. They were, as one historian put it, "the Mongols of the seas."[36]

Reflections: Changing Images of Nomadic Peoples

Until recently, nomads generally received "bad press" in history books. Normally they entered the story only when they were threatening or destroying established civilizations. In presenting a largely negative image of pastoral peoples, historians were reflecting the long-held attitudes of literate elites in the civilizations of Eurasia. Fearing and usually despising nomadic peoples, educated observers in China, the Middle East, and Europe often described them as bloodthirsty savages or barbarians, bringing only chaos and destruction in their wake. Han Kuan, a Chinese scholar of the first century B.C.E., described the Xiongnu people as "abandoned by Heaven ... in foodless desert wastes, without proper houses, clothed in animal hides, eating their meat uncooked and drinking blood."[37] To the Christian Saint Jerome (340–420 C.E.), the nomadic Huns "filled the whole earth with slaughter and panic alike as they flitted hither and thither on their swift horses."[38] Almost a thousand years later, the famous Arab historian Ibn Khaldun described nomads in a very similar fashion: "It is their nature to plunder whatever other people possess."[39]

Because nomadic peoples generally did not have written languages, the sources available to historians came from less-than-unbiased observers in adjacent agricultural civilizations. Furthermore, in the long-running conflict across the farming/pastoral frontier, agricultural civilizations ultimately triumphed. Over the centuries, some nomadic or barbarian peoples, such as the Germanic tribes of Europe and the Arabs, created new civilizations. Others, such as the Turkic and Mongol peoples, took over existing civilizations or were encompassed within established agrarian empires. By the early twentieth century, and in most places much earlier, nomadic peoples everywhere had lost their former independence and had often shed their nomadic life as well. Since "winners" usually write history, the negative views of nomads held by agrarian civilizations normally prevailed.

Reflecting more inclusive contemporary values, historians in recent decades have sought to present a more balanced picture of nomads' role in world history, emphasizing what they created as well as what they destroyed. These historians have highlighted the achievements of nomadic peoples, such as their adaptation to inhospitable environments; their technological innovations; their development of horse-, camel-, or cattle-based cultures; their role in fostering cross-cultural exchange; and their state-building efforts.

A less critical or judgmental posture toward the Mongols may also owe something to the "total wars" and genocides of the twentieth century, in which the mass slaughter of civilians became a strategy to induce enemy surrender. During the cold war, the United States and the Soviet Union were prepared, apparently, to obliterate each other's entire population with nuclear weapons in response to an attack. In light of this recent history, Mongol massacres may appear a little less unique. Historians living in the glass houses of contemporary societies are perhaps more reluctant to cast stones at the Mongols. In understanding the Mongols, as in so much else, historians are shaped by the times and circumstances of their own lives as much as by "what really happened" in the past.

Second Thoughts

What's the Significance?

To assess your mastery of the material in this chapter, see the **Online Study Guide** at bedfordstmartins.com/strayer.

pastoralism	Temujin/Chinggis Khan	Kipchak Khanate/Golden
Xiongnu	the Mongol world war	Horde
Modun	Yuan dynasty China	Black Death/plague
Turks	Khubilai Khan	
Masai	Hulegu	

Big Picture Questions

1. Prior to the rise of the Mongols, in what ways had pastoral peoples been significant in world history?
2. What accounts for the often negative attitudes of settled societies toward the pastoral peoples living on their borders? Why have historians often neglected pastoral peoples' role in world history?
3. In what ways did the Mongol Empire resemble other empires, and in what ways did it differ from them? Why did it last a relatively short time?
4. In what different ways did Mongol rule affect the Islamic world, Russia, China, and Europe?
5. How would you define both the immediate and the long-term significance of the Mongols in world history?
6. How would you assess the perspective of this chapter toward the Mongols? Does it strike you as negative and critical of the Mongols, as "bending over backward" to portray them in a positive light, or as a balanced presentation?

Next Steps: For Further Study

John Aberth, *The First Horseman: Disease in Human History* (2007). A global study of the history of disease, with a fine chapter on the Black Death.

Thomas Allsen, *Culture and Conquest in Mongol Eurasia* (2001). A history of cultural exchange within the Mongol realm, particularly between China and the Islamic world.

Thomas J. Barfield, *The Nomadic Alternative* (1993). An anthropological and historical survey of pastoral peoples on a global basis.

Carter Finley, *The Turks in World History* (2005). The evolution of Turkic-speaking people, from their nomadic origins to the twentieth century.

Jack Weatherford, *Genghis Khan and the Making of the Modern World* (2004). A lively, well-written, and balanced account of the world the Mongols made and the legacy they left for the future.

"The Mongols in World History," http://afe.easia.columbia.edu/mongols. A wonderful resource on the Mongols generally, with a particular focus on their impact in China.

For Web sites and documents related to this chapter, see **Make History** at bedfordstmartins.com/strayer.

CHAPTER THIRTEEN

The Worlds of the Fifteenth Century

During 2005, Chinese authorities marked the 600th anniversary of the initial launching of their country's massive maritime expeditions in 1405. Some eighty-seven years before Columbus sailed across the Atlantic with three small ships and a crew of about ninety men, the Chinese admiral Zheng He had captained a fleet of more than 300 ships and a crew numbering some 27,000 people, which brought a Chinese naval presence into the South China Sea and the Indian Ocean as far as the East African coast. Now in 2005, China was celebrating. Public ceremonies, books, magazine articles, two television documentaries, an international symposium, a stamp in honor of Zheng He—all of this and more was part of a yearlong remembrance of these remarkable voyages.

Given China's recent engagement with the larger world, Chinese authorities sought to use Zheng He as a symbol of their country's expanding, but peaceful, role on the international stage. Until recently, however, his achievement was barely noticed in China's collective memory, and for six centuries Zheng He had been largely forgotten or ignored. Columbus, on the other hand, had long been highly visible in the West, celebrated as a cultural hero and more recently harshly criticized as an imperialist, but certainly remembered. The voyages of both of these fifteenth-century mariners were pregnant with meaning for world history. Why were they remembered so differently in the countries of their origin?

THE FIFTEENTH CENTURY, DURING WHICH BOTH ZHENG HE AND COLUMBUS undertook their momentous expeditions, proved in retrospect to mark a major turning point in the human story. At the time, of course,

The Meeting of Two Worlds: This famous sixteenth-century engraving by the Flemish artist Theodore de Bry shows Columbus landing in Hispaniola (Haiti), where the Taino people bring him presents, while the Europeans claim the island for God and queen. In light of its long-range consequences, this voyage was arguably the most important single event of the fifteenth century. (Bildarchiv Preussischer Kulturbesitz/Art Resource, NY)

Snapshot   **Major Developments around the World in the Fifteenth Century**

Region	Major Developments
Central, East, and Southeast Asia	Ming dynasty China, 1368–1644 Conquests of Timur, 1370–1406 Zheng He's maritime voyages, 1405–1433 Spread of Islam into Southeast Asia Rise of Malacca Civil war among competing warlords in Japan
South Asia/India	Timur's invasion of India, 1398 Various Muslim sultanates in northern India Rise of Hindu state of Vijayanagar in southern India Founding of Mughal Empire, 1526
Middle East	Expansion of Ottoman Empire Ottoman seizure of Constantinople, 1453 Founding of Safavid Empire in Persia, 1501 Ottoman siege of Vienna, 1529
Christendom/Europe	European Renaissance Portuguese voyages of exploration along West African coast Completion of reconquest of Spain, ending Muslim control End of the Byzantine Empire, 1453 End of Mongol rule in Russia; reign of Ivan the Great, 1462–1505
Africa	Songhay Empire in West Africa, 1464–1591 Kingdom of the Kongo in West Central Africa Expansion of Ethiopian state in East Africa Kingdom of Zimbabwe/Mwene Mutapa in southern Africa
The Americas/Western Hemisphere	Aztec Empire in Mesoamerica, 1345–1521 Inca Empire along the Andes, 1438–1533 Iroquois confederacy (New York State) "Complex" Paleolithic societies along west coast of North America
Pacific Oceania	Paleolithic persistence in Australia Chiefdoms and stratified societies on Pacific islands Yap as center of oceanic trading network with Guam and Palau

no one was aware of it. No one knew in 1405 that the huge armada under Zheng He's command would be recalled in 1433, never to sail again. And no one knew in 1492 that Columbus's minuscule fleet of three ships would utterly transform the world, bringing the people of two "old worlds" and two hemispheres permanently together, with enduring consequences for them all. The outcome of the processes set in motion by those three small ships included the Atlantic slave trade, the decimation of the native population of the Americas, the massive growth of world population, the Industrial Revolution, and the growing prominence of Europeans on the world stage. But none of these developments were even remotely foreseeable in 1492.

Thus the fifteenth century, as a hinge of major historical change, provides an occasion for a bird's-eye view of the world through a kind of global tour. This excursion around the world will serve to briefly review the human saga thus far and to establish a baseline from which the transformations of the modern era might be measured. How then might we describe the world, and the worlds, of the fifteenth century?

The Shapes of Human Communities

One way to describe the world of the fifteenth century is to identify the various types of societies that it contained. Bands of hunters and gatherers, villages of agricultural peoples, newly emerging chiefdoms or small states, nomadic/pastoral communities, established civilizations and empires—all of these social or political forms would have been apparent to a widely traveled visitor in the fifteenth century. They represented alternative ways of organizing human communities and responded to differences in the environment, in the historical development of various regions, and in the choices made by particular peoples. The balance among these distinctive kinds of societies at the end of the postclassical millennium (1500) was quite different than it had been at the beginning (500).

Paleolithic Persistence

Despite millennia of agricultural advance, substantial areas of the world still hosted gathering and hunting societies, known to scholars as Paleolithic ("old stone-age") peoples. All of Australia, much of Siberia, the arctic coastlands, and parts of Africa and the Americas fell into this category. These peoples were not simply relics of a bygone age, however. They too had changed over time, though more slowly than their agricultural counterparts, and they too interacted with their neighbors. In short, they had a history, although most history books largely ignore them after the age of agriculture arrived. Nonetheless, this most ancient way of life still had a sizable and variable presence in the world of the fifteenth century.

Consider, for example, Australia. That continent's many separate groups, some 250 of them, still practiced a gathering and hunting way of life in the fifteenth century, a pattern that continued well after Europeans arrived in the late eighteenth century.

■ Comparison

In what ways did the gathering and hunting people of Australia differ from those of the northwest coast of North America?

Over many thousands of years, these people had assimilated various material items or cultural practices from outsiders—outrigger canoes, fish hooks, complex netting techniques, artistic styles, rituals, and mythological ideas—but despite the presence of farmers in nearby New Guinea, no agricultural practices penetrated the Australian mainland. Was it because large areas of Australia were unsuited for the kind of agriculture practiced in New Guinea? Or did the peoples of Australia, enjoying an environment of sufficient resources, simply see no need to change their way of life?

Despite the absence of agriculture, Australia's peoples had mastered and manipulated their environment, in part through the practice of "firestick farming," a pattern of deliberately set fires, which they described as "cleaning up the country." These controlled burns served to clear the underbrush, thus making hunting easier and encouraging the growth of certain plant and animal species. In addition, native Australians exchanged goods among themselves over distances of hundreds of miles, created elaborate mythologies and ritual practices, and developed sophisticated traditions of sculpture and rock painting. They accomplished all of this on the basis of an economy and technology rooted in the distant Paleolithic past.

A very different kind of gathering and hunting society flourished in the fifteenth century along the northwest coast of North America among the Chinookan, Tulalip, Skagit, and other peoples. With some 300 edible animal species and an abundance of salmon and other fish, this extraordinarily bounteous environment provided the foundation for what scholars sometimes call "complex" or "affluent" gathering and hunting cultures. What distinguished the northwest coast peoples from those of Australia were permanent village settlements with large and sturdy houses, considerable economic specialization, ranked societies that sometimes included slavery, chiefdoms dominated by powerful clan leaders or "big men," and extensive storage of food.

Although these and other gathering and hunting peoples persisted still in the fifteenth century, both their numbers and the area they inhabited had contracted greatly as the Agricultural Revolution unfolded across the planet. That relentless advance of the farming frontier continued in the centuries ahead as the Russian, Chinese, and European empires encompassed the lands of the remaining Paleolithic peoples. By the early twenty-first century, what was once the only human way of life had been reduced to minuscule pockets of people whose cultures seemed doomed to a final extinction.

Agricultural Village Societies

■ **Change**
What kinds of changes were transforming West African agricultural village societies and those of the Iroquois as the fifteenth century dawned?

Far more numerous than hunters and gatherers were those many peoples who, though fully agricultural, had avoided incorporation into larger empires or civilizations and had not developed their own city- or state-based societies. Living usually in small village-based communities and organized in terms of kinship relations, such people predominated during the fifteenth century in much of North America, in Africa south of the equator, and in parts of the Amazon River basin and

Southeast Asia. They had created societies largely without the oppressive political authority, class inequalities, and seclusion of women that were so common in civilizations. Historians have largely relegated such societies to the periphery of world history, marginal to their overwhelming focus on large-scale civilizations. Viewed from within their own circles, though, these societies were of course at the center of things, each with its own history of migration, cultural change, social conflict, incorporation of new people, political rise and fall, and interaction with strangers.

In the forested region of what is now southern Nigeria in West Africa, for example, three quite different patterns of political development emerged in the centuries between 1000 and 1500 (see Map 13.3, p. 376). Each of them began from a base of farming village societies whose productivity was generating larger populations.

Among the Yoruba people, a series of city-states emerged, each within a walled town and ruled by an *oba*, or king (many of whom were women), who performed both religious and political functions. As in ancient Mesopotamia or classical Greece, no single state or empire encompassed all of Yorubaland. Nearby lay the kingdom of Benin, a small, highly centralized territorial state that emerged by the fifteenth century and was ruled by a warrior king named Ewuare, said to have conquered 201 towns and villages in the process of founding the new state. His administrative chiefs replaced the heads of kinship groups as major political authorities, while the ruler sponsored extensive trading missions and patronized artists who created the remarkable brass sculptures for which Benin is so famous.

East of the Niger River lay the lands of the Igbo peoples, where dense population and extensive trading networks might well have given rise to states, but the deliberate Igbo preference was to reject the kingship and state-building efforts of their neighbors, boasting on occasion that "the Igbo have no kings." Instead they relied on other institutions—title societies in which wealthy men received a series of prestigious ranks, women's associations, hereditary ritual experts serving as mediators, a balance of power among kinship groups—to maintain social cohesion beyond the level of the village. It was a "stateless society," famously described in Chinua Achebe's *Things Fall Apart*, the most widely read novel to emerge from twentieth-century Africa.

The Yoruba, Bini, and Igbo peoples did not live in isolated, self-contained societies, however. They traded actively among themselves and with more distant peoples, such as the large African kingdom of Songhay far to the north. Cotton cloth, fish, copper and iron goods, decorative objects, and more drew neighboring peoples into networks of exchange. Common artistic traditions reflected a measure of cultural unity in a politically fragmented region, and all of these peoples seem to have changed from a matrilineal to a patrilineal system of tracing their descent. Little of this registered in the larger civilizations of the Afro-Eurasian world, but to the peoples of the West African forest during the fifteenth century, these processes were central to their history and their daily lives. Soon, however, all of them would be caught up in the transatlantic slave trade and would be changed substantially in the process.

Benin Bronzes
British colonial forces in 1897 looted the palace of the king of Benin and seized more than 1,000 exquisite brass figures, most of which were associated with court ceremonies. Here is a sixteenth-century representation of the Queen Mother of Benin. (National Museum, Lagos, Nigeria/The Bridgeman Art Library)

Across the Atlantic in what is now central New York State, other agricultural village societies were also in the process of substantial change during the several centuries preceding their incorporation into European trading networks and empires. The Iroquois-speaking peoples of that region had only recently become fully agricultural, adopting maize- and bean-farming techniques that had originated long ago in Mesoamerica. As this productive agriculture took hold by 1300 or so, the population grew, the size of settlements increased, and distinct peoples emerged, such as the Onondaga, Seneca, Cayuga, Oneida, and Mohawk. Frequent warfare also erupted among them. Some scholars have speculated that as agriculture, largely seen as women's work, became the primary economic activity, "warfare replaced successful food getting as the avenue to male prestige."[1]

Whatever caused it, this increased level of conflict among Iroquois peoples triggered a remarkable political innovation—a loose alliance or confederation among five Iroquois peoples based on an agreement known as the Great Law of Peace (see Map 13.5, p. 383). It was an agreement to settle their differences peacefully through a confederation council of clan leaders, some fifty of them altogether, who had the authority to adjudicate disputes and set reparation payments. Operating by consensus, the Iroquois League of Five Nations effectively suppressed the blood feuds and tribal conflicts that had only recently been so widespread. It also coordinated their peoples' relationship with outsiders, including the Europeans, who arrived in growing numbers in the centuries after 1500.

The Iroquois League also gave expression to values of limited government, social equality, and personal freedom, concepts that some European colonists found highly attractive. One British colonial administrator declared in 1749 that the Iroquois had "such absolute Notions of Liberty that they allow no Kind of Superiority of one over another, and banish all Servitude from their Territories."[2] Such equality extended to gender relationships, for among the Iroquois, descent was matrilineal (reckoned through the woman's line), married couples lived with the wife's family, and women controlled agriculture. While men were hunters, warriors, and the primary political officeholders, women selected and could depose those leaders.

Wherever they lived in 1500, over the next several centuries independent agricultural peoples such as the Iroquois, Yoruba, and Igbo were increasingly encompassed in expanding economic networks and conquest empires based in Western Europe or in Russia. In this respect, they repeated the experience of many other village-based farming communities that had much earlier found themselves forcibly included in the powerful embrace of Egyptian, Mesopotamian, Roman, Indian, Chinese, and other civilizations.

■ Significance

What role did Central Asian and West African pastoralists play in their respective regions?

Herding Peoples

Nomadic pastoral peoples impinged more directly and dramatically on civilizations than did hunting and gathering or agricultural village societies. The Mongol incursion, and the enormous empire to which it gave rise, was one in a long series of challenges from the steppes, but it was not the last. As the Mongol Empire disinte-grated, a brief attempt to restore it occurred in the late fourteenth and early fif-teenth centuries under the leadership of a Turkic warrior named Timur, known in the West as Tamerlane (see Map 13.1, p. 370).

With a ferocity that matched or exceeded that of his model, Chinggis Khan, Timur's army of nomads brought immense devastation yet again to Russia, Persia, and India. Timur himself died in 1405, while preparing for an invasion of China. Conflicts among his successors prevented any lasting empire, although his descen-dants retained control of the area between Persia and Afghanistan for the rest of the fifteenth century. That state hosted a sophisticated elite culture, particularly at its splendid capital of Samarkand, as its rulers patronized artists, poets, traders, and craftsmen. Timur's conquest proved to be the last great military success of nomadic peoples from Central Asia. In the centuries that followed, their homelands were swallowed up in the expanding Russian and Chinese empires, as the balance of power between steppe nomads of inner Eurasia and the civilizations of outer Eurasia turned decisively in favor of the latter.

In Africa, pastoral peoples stayed independent of established empires several centuries longer than the nomads of Inner Asia, for not until the late nineteenth century were they incorporated into European colonial states. The experience of the Fulbe, West Africa's largest pastoral society, provides a useful example of an African herding people with a highly significant role in the fifteenth century and beyond. From their homeland in the western fringe of the Sahara along the upper Senegal River, the Fulbe migrated gradually eastward in the centuries after 1000 C.E. (see Map 13.3, p. 376). Unlike the pastoral peoples of Inner Asia, they generally lived in small communities among agricultural peoples and paid various grazing fees and taxes for the privilege of pasturing their cattle. Relations with their farming hosts often were tense because the Fulbe resented their subordination to agricultural peoples, whose way of life they despised. That sense of cultural superiority became even more pronounced as the Fulbe, in the course of their eastward movement, slowly adopted Islam. Some of them in fact dropped out of a pastoral life and set-tled in towns, where they became highly respected religious leaders. In the eigh-teenth and nineteenth centuries, the Fulbe were at the center of a wave of reli-giously based uprisings, or jihads, that greatly expanded the practice of Islam and gave rise to a series of new states, ruled by the Fulbe themselves.

Civilizations of the Fifteenth Century: Comparing China and Europe

Beyond the foraging, farming, and herding societies of the fifteenth-century world were its civilizations, those city-centered and state-based societies that were far larger and more densely populated, more powerful and innovative, and much more unequal in terms of class and gender than other forms of human commu-nity. Since the First Civilizations had emerged between 3500 and 1000 B.C.E., both the geographic space they encompassed and the number of people they embraced had grown substantially. By the fifteenth century, a considerable majority of the world's population lived within one or another of these civilizations, although most of these people no doubt identified more with local communities than with a larger civilization. What might an imaginary global traveler notice about the world's major civilizations in the fifteenth century?

Ming Dynasty China

■ **Description**
How would you define the major achievements of Ming dynasty China?

Such a traveler might well begin his or her journey in China, heir to a long tradition of effective governance, Confucian and Daoist philosophy, a major Buddhist presence, sophisticated artistic achievements, and a highly productive economy. That civilization, however, had been greatly disrupted by a century of Mongol rule, and its population had been sharply reduced by the plague. During the Ming dynasty (1368–1644), however, China recovered (see Map 13.1). The early decades of that dynasty witnessed an effort to eliminate all signs of foreign rule, discouraging

Map 13.1   Asia in the Fifteenth Century
The fifteenth century witnessed the massive Ming dynasty voyages into the Indian Ocean as well as the last major eruption of nomadic power in Timur's empire.

Map legend:
- Ming dynasty China
- Timur's empire about 1405
- Delhi Sultanate
- Vijayanagara
- ← Routes of Ming dynasty voyages

0   500   1,000 miles
0   500   1,000 kilometers

the use of Mongol names and dress, while promoting Confucian learning based on earlier models from the Han, Tang, and Song dynasties. Emperor Yongle (reigned 1402–1422) sponsored an enormous *Encyclopedia* of some 11,000 volumes. With contributions from more than 2,000 scholars, this work sought to summarize or compile all previous writing on history, geography, ethics, government, and more. Culturally speaking, China was looking to its past.

Politically, the Ming dynasty reestablished the civil service examination system that had been neglected under Mongol rule and went on to create a highly centralized government. Power was concentrated in the hands of the emperor himself, while a cadre of eunuchs (castrated men) personally loyal to the emperor exercised great authority, much to the dismay of the official bureaucrats. The state acted vigorously to repair the damage of the Mongol years by restoring millions of acres to cultivation; rebuilding canals, reservoirs, and irrigation works; and planting, according to some estimates, a billion trees in an effort to reforest China. As a result, the economy rebounded, both international and domestic trade flourished, and the population grew. During the fifteenth century, China had recovered and was perhaps the best-governed and most prosperous of the world's major civilizations.

China also undertook the largest and most impressive maritime expeditions the world had ever seen. Since the eleventh century, Chinese sailors and traders had been a major presence in the South China Sea and in Southeast Asian port cities, with much of this activity in private hands. But now, after decades of preparation, an enormous fleet, commissioned by Emperor Yongle himself, was launched in 1405, followed over the next twenty-eight years by six more such expeditions. On board more than 300 ships of the first voyage was a crew of some 27,000, including 180 physicians, hundreds of government officials, 5 astrologers, 7 high-ranking or grand eunuchs, carpenters, tailors, accountants, merchants, translators, cooks, and thousands of soldiers and sailors. Visiting many ports in Southeast Asia, Indonesia, India, Arabia, and East Africa, these fleets, captained by the Muslim eunuch Zheng He, sought to enroll distant peoples and states in the Chinese tribute system (see Map 13.1). Dozens of rulers accompanied the fleets back to China, where they presented tribute, performed the required rituals of submission, and received in return abundant gifts, titles, and trading opportunities. Chinese officials were amused by some of the exotic products to be found abroad—ostriches, zebras, and giraffes, for example. Officially described as "bringing order to the world," Zheng He's expeditions served to establish Chinese power and prestige in the Indian Ocean and to exert Chinese control over foreign trade in the

Comparing Chinese and European Ships
Among the largest vessels in Zheng He's early-fifteenth-century fleet was this "treasure ship," measuring more than 400 feet long and carrying a crew of perhaps 1,000 men. The figure at the bottom right represents one of Columbus's ships. (© Dugald Stermer)

region. The Chinese, however, did not seek to conquer new territories, establish Chinese settlements, or spread their culture. On one of the voyages, Zheng He erected on the island of Ceylon (Sri Lanka) a tablet honoring alike the Buddha, Allah, and a Hindu deity.

The most surprising feature of these voyages was how abruptly and deliberately they were ended. After 1433, Chinese authorities simply stopped such expeditions and allowed this enormous and expensive fleet to deteriorate in port. "In less than a hundred years," wrote a recent historian of these voyages, "the greatest navy the world had ever known had ordered itself into extinction."[3] Part of the reason involved the death of the emperor Yongle, who had been the chief patron of the enterprise. Many high-ranking officials had long seen the expeditions as a waste of resources because China, they believed, was the self-sufficient "middle kingdom," requiring little from the outside world. In their eyes, the real danger to China came from the north, where nomadic barbarians constantly threatened. Finally, they viewed the voyages as the project of the court eunuchs, whom these officials despised. Even as these voices of Chinese officialdom prevailed, private Chinese merchants and craftsmen continued to settle and trade in Japan, the Philippines, Taiwan, and Southeast Asia, but they did so without the support of their government. The Chinese state quite deliberately turned its back on what was surely within its reach—a large-scale maritime empire in the Indian Ocean basin.

European Comparisons: State Building and Cultural Renewal

■ **Comparison**
What political and cultural differences stand out in the histories of fifteenth-century China and Western Europe? What similarities are apparent?

At the other end of the Eurasian continent, similar processes of demographic recovery, political consolidation, cultural flowering, and overseas expansion were under way. Western Europe, having escaped Mongol conquest but devastated by the plague, began to regrow its population during the second half of the fifteenth century. As in China, the infrastructure of civilization proved a durable foundation for demographic and economic revival.

Politically, too, Europe joined China in continuing earlier patterns of state building. In China, however, this meant a unitary and centralized government that encompassed almost the whole of its civilization, while in Europe a decidedly fragmented system of many separate, independent, and highly competitive states made for a sharply divided Christendom (see Map 13.2). Many of these states—Spain, Portugal, France, England, the city-states of Italy (Milan, Venice, and Florence), various German principalities—learned to tax their citizens more efficiently, to create more effective administrative structures, and to raise standing armies. A small Russian state centered on the city of Moscow also emerged in the fifteenth century as Mongol rule faded away. Much of this state building was driven by the needs of war, a frequent occurrence in such a fragmented and competitive political environment. England and France, for example, fought intermittently for more than a century in the Hundred Years' War (1337–1453) over rival claims to territory in France. Nothing remotely similar disturbed the internal life of Ming dynasty China.

Map 13.2   Europe in 1500
By the end of the fifteenth century, Christian Europe had assumed its early modern political shape as a system of competing states threatened by an expanding Muslim Ottoman Empire.

A renewed cultural blossoming, known in European history as the Renaissance, likewise paralleled the revival of all things Confucian in Ming dynasty China. In Europe, however, that blossoming celebrated and reclaimed a classical Greek tradition that earlier had been obscured or viewed through the lens of Arabic or Latin translations. Beginning in the vibrant commercial cities of Italy between roughly 1350 and 1500, the Renaissance reflected the belief of the wealthy elite that they were living in a wholly new era, far removed from the confined religious world of feudal Europe. Educated citizens of these cities sought inspiration in the art and literature of ancient Greece and Rome—they were "returning to the sources," as they put it. Their purpose was not so much to reconcile these works with the ideas of Christianity, as the twelfth- and thirteenth-century university scholars had done, but to use them as a cultural standard to imitate and then to surpass. The elite patronized great Renaissance artists such as Leonardo da Vinci, Michelangelo, and Raphael, whose paintings and sculptures were far more naturalistic, particularly in portraying the human body, than those of their medieval counterparts.

Although religious themes remained prominent, Renaissance artists now included portraits and busts of well-known contemporary figures and scenes from ancient mythology. In the work of scholars, known as "humanists," reflections on secular topics such as grammar, history, politics, poetry, rhetoric, and ethics complemented more religious matters. For example, Niccolò Machiavelli's (1469–1527) famous work *The Prince* was a prescription for political success based on the way politics actually operated in a highly competitive Italy of rival city-states rather than on idealistic and religiously based principles. To the question of whether a prince should be feared or loved, Machiavelli replied:

> One ought to be both feared and loved, but as it is difficult for the two to go together, it is much safer to be feared than loved. . . . For it may be said of men in general that they are ungrateful, voluble, dissemblers, anxious to avoid danger, and covetous of gain. . . . Fear is maintained by dread of punishment which never fails. . . . In the actions of men, and especially of princes, from which there is no appeal, the end justifies the means.[4]

Heavily influenced by classical models, Renaissance figures were more interested in capturing the unique qualities of particular individuals and in describing the world as it was than in portraying or exploring eternal religious truths. In its focus on the affairs of this world, Renaissance culture reflected the urban bustle and commercial preoccupations of the Italian cities. Its secular elements challenged the otherworldliness of Christian culture, and its individualism signaled the dawning of a more capitalist economy of private entrepreneurs. A new Europe was in the making, rather more different from its own recent past than Ming dynasty China was from its pre-Mongol glory.

European Comparisons: Maritime Voyaging

■ **Comparison**

In what ways did European maritime voyaging in the fifteenth century differ from that of China? What accounts for these differences?

A global traveler during the fifteenth century might be surprised to find that Europeans, like the Chinese, were also launching outward-bound maritime expeditions. Initiated in 1415 by the small country of Portugal, those voyages sailed ever farther down the west coast of Africa, supported by the state and blessed by the pope (see Map 13.3). As the century ended, two expeditions marked major breakthroughs, although few suspected it at the time. In 1492, Christopher Columbus, funded by Spain, Portugal's neighbor and rival, made his way west across the Atlantic hoping to arrive in the East and, in one of history's most consequential mistakes, ran into the Americas. Five years later, in 1497, Vasco da Gama launched a voyage that took him around the tip of South Africa, along the East African coast, and, with the help of a Muslim pilot, across the Indian Ocean to Calicut in southern India.

Snapshot   **Key Moments in European Maritime Voyaging**

Portuguese seize Ceuta in Morocco	1415
Prince Henry the Navigator launches Portuguese exploration of the West African coast	1420
Portuguese settle the Azores	1430s
Chinese fleets withdrawn from Indian Ocean	1433
Portuguese reach the Senegal River; beginning of Atlantic slave trade	1440s
Portuguese contact with Kongo; royal family converts to Christianity	1480s
Sugar production begins in Atlantic islands (Canaries, São Tomé)	1480s
Establishment of trading station at Elmina (in present-day Ghana)	1480s
First transatlantic voyage of Columbus	1492
John Cabot sails across North Atlantic to North America	1496
Vasco da Gama enters Indian Ocean and reaches India	1497–1498
Portuguese attacks on various Swahili cities; establishment of Fort Jesus at Mombasa; Portuguese contacts with Christian Ethiopia	1497–1520s
Magellan's voyage to Asia via the Americas; first circumnavigation of the globe	1520–1523

The differences between the Chinese and European oceangoing ventures were striking, most notably perhaps in terms of size. Columbus captained three ships and a crew of about 90, while da Gama had four ships, manned by perhaps 170 sailors. These were minuscule fleets compared to Zheng He's hundreds of ships and crew in the many thousands. "All the ships of Columbus and da Gama combined," according to a recent account, "could have been stored on a single deck of a single vessel in the fleet that set sail under Zheng He."[5]

Motivation as well as size differentiated the two ventures. Europeans were seeking the wealth of Africa and Asia—gold, spices, silk, and more. They also were in search of Christian converts and of possible Christian allies with whom to continue their long crusading struggle against threatening Muslim powers. China, by contrast, faced no equivalent power, needed no military allies in the Indian Ocean basin, and required little that these regions produced. Nor did China possess an impulse to convert foreigners to Chinese culture or religion as the Europeans surely did. Furthermore, the confident and overwhelmingly powerful Chinese fleet sought neither conquests nor colonies, while the Europeans soon tried to monopolize by force the commerce of the Indian Ocean and violently carved out huge empires in the Americas.

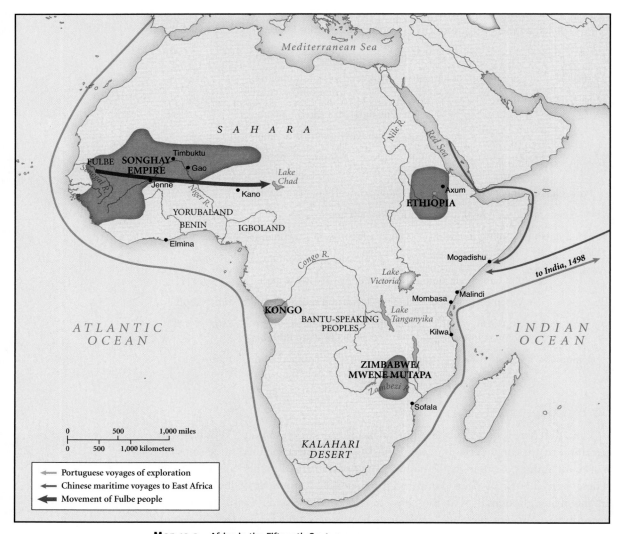

Map 13.3   Africa in the Fifteenth Century
By the 1400s, Africa was a virtual museum of political and cultural diversity, encompassing large empires, such as Songhay; smaller kingdoms, such as Kongo; city-states among the Yoruba, Hausa, and Swahili peoples; village-based societies without states at all, as among the Igbo; and nomadic pastoral peoples, such as the Fulbe. Both European and Chinese maritime expeditions touched on Africa during that century, even as Islam continued to find acceptance in the northern half of the continent.

The most striking difference in these two cases lay in the sharp contrast between China's decisive ending of its voyages and the continuing, indeed escalating, European effort, which soon brought the world's oceans and growing numbers of the world's people under its control. This is the reason that Zheng He's voyages were so long neglected in China's historical memory. They led nowhere, whereas the initial European expeditions, so much smaller and less promising, were but the initial steps on a journey to world power. But why did the Europeans continue a process that the Chinese had deliberately abandoned?

In the first place, of course, Europe had no unified political authority with the power to order an end to its maritime outreach. Its system of competing states, so unlike China's single unified empire, ensured that once begun, rivalry alone would drive the Europeans to the ends of the earth. Beyond this, much of Europe's elite had an interest in overseas expansion. Its budding merchant communities saw opportunity for profit; its competing monarchs eyed the revenue that could come from taxing overseas trade or from seizing overseas resources; the Church foresaw the possibility of widespread conversion; impoverished nobles might imagine fame and fortune abroad. In China, by contrast, support for Zheng He's voyages was very shallow in official circles, and when the emperor Yongle passed from the scene, those opposed to the voyages prevailed within the politics of the court.

Finally, the Chinese were very much aware of their own antiquity, believed strongly in the absolute superiority of their culture, and felt with good reason that, should they need something from abroad, others would bring it to them. Europeans too believed themselves unique, particularly in religious terms as the possessors of Christianity, the "one true religion." In material terms, though, they were seeking out the greater riches of the East, and they were highly conscious that Muslim power blocked easy access to these treasures and posed a military and religious threat to Europe itself. All of this propelled continuing European expansion in the centuries that followed.

The Waldseemüller Map of 1507
Just fifteen years after Columbus landed in the Western Hemisphere, this map, which was created by the German cartographer Martin Waldseemüller, reflected a dawning European awareness of the planet's global dimensions and location of the world's major landmasses. (Bildarchiv Preussischer Kulturbesitz/Art Resource, NY)

The Chinese withdrawal from the Indian Ocean actually facilitated the European entry. It cleared the way for the Portuguese to enter the region, where they faced only the eventual naval power of the Ottomans. Had Vasco da Gama encountered Zheng He's massive fleet as his four small ships sailed into Asian waters in 1498, world history may well have taken quite a different turn. As it was, however, China's abandonment of oceanic voyaging and Europe's embrace of the seas marked different responses to a common problem that both civilizations shared—growing populations and land shortage. In the centuries that followed, China's rice-based agriculture was able to expand production internally by more intensive use of the land, while the country's territorial expansion was inland toward Central Asia. By contrast, Europe's agriculture, based on wheat and livestock, expanded primarily by acquiring new lands in overseas possessions, which were gained as a consequence of a commitment to oceanic expansion.

Civilizations of the Fifteenth Century: The Islamic World

■ Comparison
What differences can you identify among the four major empires in the Islamic world of the fifteenth and sixteenth centuries?

Beyond the domains of Chinese and European civilization, our fifteenth-century global traveler would surely have been impressed with the transformations of the Islamic world. Stretching across much of Afro-Eurasia, the enormous realm of Islam experienced a set of remarkable changes during the fifteenth and early sixteenth centuries, as well as the continuation of earlier patterns. The most notable change lay in the political realm, for an Islamic civilization that had been severely fragmented since at least 900 now crystallized into four major states or empires (see Map 13.4). At the same time, a long-term process of conversion to Islam continued the cultural transformation in Afro-Eurasian societies both within and beyond these new states.

In the Islamic Heartland: The Ottoman and Safavid Empires

The most impressive and enduring of these new states was the Ottoman Empire, which lasted in one form or another from the fourteenth to the early twentieth century. It was the creation of one of the many Turkic warrior groups that had earlier migrated into Anatolia. By the mid-fifteenth century, these Ottoman Turks had already carved out a state that encompassed much of the Anatolian peninsula and had pushed deep into southeastern Europe (the Balkans), acquiring in the process a substantial Christian population. In the two centuries that followed, the Ottoman Empire extended its control to much of the Middle East, coastal North Africa, the lands surrounding the Black Sea, and even farther into Eastern Europe.

The Ottoman Empire was a state of enormous significance in the world of the fifteenth century and beyond. In its huge territory, long duration, incorporation of many diverse peoples, and economic and cultural sophistication, it was

Map 13.4 Empires of the Islamic World
The most prominent political features of the vast Islamic world in the fifteenth and sixteenth centuries were four large states: the Songhay, Ottoman, Safavid, and Mughal empires.

one of the great empires of world history. In the fifteenth century, only Ming dynasty China and the Incas matched it in terms of wealth, power, and splendor. The empire represented the emergence of the Turks as the dominant people of the Islamic world, ruling now over many Arabs, who had initiated this new faith more than 800 years before. In adding "caliph" (successor to the Prophet) to their other titles, Ottoman sultans claimed the legacy of the earlier Abbasid Empire. They sought to bring a renewed unity to the Islamic world, while also serving as protector of the faith, the "strong sword of Islam."

The Ottoman Empire represented a new phase in the long encounter between Christendom and the world of Islam. In the Crusades, Europeans had taken the aggressive initiative in that encounter, but now the rise of the Ottoman Empire reversed their roles. The seizure of Constantinople in 1453 marked the final demise of Christian Byzantium and allowed Ottoman rulers to see themselves as successors to the Roman Empire. In 1529, a rapidly expanding Ottoman Empire laid siege to Vienna in the heart of Central Europe. The political and military expansion of Islam, at the expense of Christendom, seemed clearly under way. Many Europeans spoke fearfully of the "terror of the Turk."

Des obrilien hamerling Vnd Trüchses

In the neighboring Persian lands to the east of the Ottoman Empire, another Islamic state was also taking shape in the late fifteenth and early sixteenth centuries—the Safavid Empire. Its leadership was also Turkic, but in this case it had emerged from a Sufi religious order founded several centuries earlier by Safi al-Din (1252–1334). The long-term significance of the Safavid Empire, which was established in the decade following 1500, was its decision to forcibly impose a Shia version of Islam as the official religion of the state. Over time, this form of Islam gained popular support and came to define the unique identity of Persian (Iranian) culture.

This Shia empire also introduced a sharp divide into the political and religious life of heartland Islam, for almost all of Persia's neighbors practiced a Sunni form of the faith. For a century (1534–1639), periodic military conflict erupted between the Ottoman and Safavid empires, reflecting both territorial rivalry and sharp religious differences. In 1514, the Ottoman sultan wrote to the Safavid ruler in the most bitter of terms:

Ottoman Janissaries Originating in the fourteenth century, the Janissaries became the elite infantry force of the Ottoman Empire. Complete with uniforms, cash salaries, and marching music, they were the first standing army in the region since the days of the Roman Empire. When gunpowder technology became available, Janissary forces soon were armed with muskets, grenades, and handheld cannon. This image dates from the seventeenth century. (Austrian National Library, picture archive, Vienna: Cod. 8626, fol. 15r)

You have denied the sanctity of divine law...you have deserted the path of salvation and the sacred commandments...you have opened to Muslims the gates of tyranny and oppression...you have raised the standard of irreligion and heresy.... [Therefore] the *ulama* and our doctors have pronounced a sentence of death against you, perjurer and blasphemer.[6]

This Sunni/Shia hostility has continued to divide the Islamic world into the twenty-first century.

On the Frontiers of Islam: The Songhay and Mughal Empires

While the Ottoman and Safavid empires brought both a new political unity and a sharp division to the heartland of Islam, two other states performed a similar role on the expanding African and Asian frontiers of the faith. In the West African savannas, the Songhay Empire rose in the second half of the fifteenth century. It was the most recent and the largest in a series of impressive states that operated at a crucial intersection of the trans-Saharan trade routes and that derived much of their revenue from taxing that commerce. Islam was a growing faith in Songhay but was limited largely to urban elites. This cultural divide within Songhay largely accounts for the religious behavior of its fifteenth-century monarch Sonni Ali (reigned 1465–1492), who gave alms and fasted during Ramadan in proper Islamic style but also enjoyed a reputation as a magician and possessed a charm thought to render his soldiers invisible to their enemies. Nonetheless, Songhay had become a major center of Islamic learning and commerce by the early sixteenth century. A North African traveler, known as Leo Africanus, remarked on the city of Timbuktu:

> Here are great numbers of [Muslim] religious teachers, judges, scholars, and other learned persons who are bountifully maintained at the king's expense. Here too are brought various manuscripts or written books from Barbary [North Africa] which are sold for more money than any other merchandise....Here are very rich merchants and to here journey continually large numbers of negroes who purchase here cloth from Barbary and Europe....It is a wonder to see the quality of merchandise that is daily brought here and how costly and sumptuous everything is.[7]

Sonni Ali's successor made the pilgrimage to Mecca and asked to be given the title "Caliph of the Land of the Blacks." Songhay then represented a substantial Islamic state on the African frontier of a still-expanding Muslim world.

The Mughal Empire in India bore similarities to Songhay, for both governed largely non-Muslim populations. Much as the Ottoman Empire initiated a new phase in the interaction of Islam and Christendom, so too did the Mughal Empire continue an ongoing encounter between Islamic and Hindu civilizations. Established in the early sixteenth century, the Mughal Empire was the creation of yet another Islamized Turkic group, which invaded India in 1526. Over the next century, the Mughals (a Persian term for Mongols) established unified control over most of the Indian peninsula, giving it a rare period of political unity and laying the foundation for subsequent British colonial rule. During its first several centuries, the Mughal Empire, a land of great wealth and imperial splendor, was the location of a remarkable effort to blend many Hindu groups and a variety of foreign Muslims into an effective partnership. The inclusive policies of the early Mughal emperors showed that Muslim rulers could accommodate their overwhelmingly Hindu subjects in somewhat the same fashion as Ottoman authorities provided religious autonomy for their Christian peoples. In southernmost India, however, the distinctly Hindu kingdom of Vijayanagara flourished in the fifteenth century, even as it borrowed architectural styles from the Muslim states of northern India and sometimes employed Muslim mercenaries in its military forces.

Together these four Muslim empires—Ottoman, Safavid, Songhay, and Mughal— brought to the Islamic world a greater measure of political coherence, military power, economic prosperity, and cultural brilliance than it had known since the early centuries of Islam. This new energy, sometimes called a "second flowering of Islam," impelled the continuing spread of the faith to yet new regions. The most prominent of these was oceanic Southeast Asia, which for centuries had been intimately bound up in the world of Indian Ocean commerce. By the fifteenth century, that trading network was largely in Muslim hands, and the demand for Southeast Asian spices was mounting as the Eurasian world recovered from the devastation of Mongol conquest and the plague. Growing numbers of Muslim traders, many of them from India, settled in Java and Sumatra, bringing their faith with them. Thus, unlike the Middle East and India, where Islam was established in the wake of Arab or Turkic conquest, in Southeast Asia, as in West Africa, it was introduced by traveling merchants and solidified through the activities of Sufi holy men.

The rise of Malacca, strategically located on the waterway between Sumatra and Malaya, was a sign of the times (see Map 13.1, p. 370). During the fifteenth century, it was transformed from a small fishing village to a major Muslim port city and became a springboard for the spread of Islam throughout the region. The Islam of Malacca, however, demonstrated much blending with local and Hindu/Buddhist traditions, while the city itself, like many port towns, had a reputation for "rough behavior." An Arab Muslim pilot in the 1480s commented critically:

> They have no culture at all.... You do not know whether they are Muslim or not.... They are thieves, for theft is rife among them and they do not mind.... They appear liars and deceivers in trade and labor.[8]

Nonetheless, Malacca, like Timbuktu, became a center for Islamic learning, and students from elsewhere in Southeast Asia were studying there in the fifteenth century. As the more central regions of Islam were consolidating politically, the frontier of the faith continued to move steadily outward.

Civilizations of the Fifteenth Century: The Americas

■ Comparison
What distinguished the Aztec and Inca empires from each other?

Across the Atlantic, centers of civilization had long flourished in Mesoamerica and in the Andes. The fifteenth century witnessed new, larger, and more politically unified expressions of those civilizations in the Aztec and Inca empires. Both were the work of previously marginal peoples who had forcibly taken over and absorbed older cultures, giving them new energy, and both were decimated in the sixteenth century at the hands of Spanish conquistadores and their diseases. To conclude this global tour of world civilizations, we will send our weary traveler to the Western Hemisphere for a brief look at these American civilizations (see Map 13.5).

The Aztec Empire

The empire known to history as the Aztec state was largely the work of the Mexica people, a seminomadic group from northern Mexico who had migrated southward and by 1325 had established themselves on a small island in Lake Texcoco. Over the next century, the Mexica developed their military capacity, served as mercenaries

Map 13.5   The Americas in the Fifteenth Century

The Americas before Columbus represented a world almost completely separate from Afro-Eurasia. It featured similar kinds of societies, though with a different balance among them, but it completely lacked the pastoral economies that were so important in the Eastern Hemisphere.

Map labels:

Inuit seal hunters
Forest hunter-gatherers
West coast foraging, hunting and fishing peoples
Plateau fishers and hunter-gatherers
Plains bison hunters
Plains farmers
Iroquois Confederation
Desert hunter-gatherers
Mississippian Mound Builders
Gulf of Mexico
Chichén Itzá
Maya
Tenochtitlán
Aztec Empire
MESO-AMERICAN CIVILIZATION
Caribbean Sea
ATLANTIC OCEAN
North Andean chiefdoms
Amazon R.
Amazonian chiefdoms
Rainforest farmers
PACIFIC OCEAN
ANDEAN CIVILIZATION
Inca Empire
Machu Picchu
Cuzco
Savanna and highland farmers
Savanna hunter-gatherers
Pampas hunter-gatherers
Shellfish gatherers and seal hunters

0   500   1,000 miles
0   500   1,000 kilometers

Legend:
- Hunting/gathering peoples
- Village farming peoples
- Chiefdoms
- State-based civilizations

for more powerful people, negotiated elite marriage alliances with them, and built up their own capital city of Tenochtitlán. In 1428, a Triple Alliance between the Mexica and two other nearby city-states launched a highly aggressive program of military conquest, which in less than 100 years brought more of Mesoamerica within a single political framework than ever before. Aztec authorities, eager to shed their rather undistinguished past, now claimed descent from earlier Mesoamerican peoples such as the Toltecs and Teotihuacán.

With a core population recently estimated at 5 to 6 million people, the Aztec Empire was a loosely structured and unstable conquest state, which witnessed frequent rebellions by its subject peoples. Conquered peoples and cities were required to regularly deliver to their Aztec rulers impressive quantities of textiles and clothing, military supplies, jewelry and other luxuries, various foodstuffs, animal products, building materials, rubber balls, paper, and more. The process was overseen by local imperial tribute collectors, who sent the required goods on to Tenochtitlán, a metropolis of 150,000 to 200,000 people, where they were meticulously recorded.

That city featured numerous canals, dikes, causeways, and bridges. A central walled area of palaces and temples included a pyramid almost 200 feet high. Surrounding the city were "floating gardens," artificial islands created from swamplands that supported a highly productive agriculture. Vast marketplaces reflected the commercialization of the economy. A young Spanish soldier who beheld the city in 1519 described his reaction:

> Gazing on such wonderful sights, we did not know what to say, or whether what appeared before us was real, for on one side, on the land there were great cities, and in the lake ever so many more, and the lake was crowded with canoes, and in the causeway were many bridges at intervals, and in front of us stood the great city of Mexico.[9]

Beyond tribute from conquered peoples, ordinary trade, both local and long-distance, permeated Aztec domains. The extent of empire and rapid population growth stimulated the development of markets and the production of craft goods, particularly in the fifteenth century. Virtually every settlement, from the capital city to the smallest village, had a marketplace that hummed with activity during weekly market days. The largest was that of Tlatelolco, near the capital city, which stunned the Spanish with its huge size, its good order, and the immense range of goods available. Hernán Cortés, the Spanish conquistador who defeated the Aztecs, wrote that "every kind of merchandise such as can be met with in every land is for sale there, whether of food and victuals, or ornaments of gold and silver, or lead, brass, copper, tin, precious stones, bones, shells, snails and feathers."[10] Professional merchants, known as *pochteca*, were legally commoners, but their wealth, often exceeding that of the nobility, allowed them to rise in society and become "magnates of the land."

Among the "goods" that the pochteca obtained were slaves, many of whom were destined for sacrifice in the bloody rituals so central to Aztec religious life. Long a part of Mesoamerican and many other world cultures, human sacrifice

■ Description
How did Aztec religious thinking support the empire?

assumed an unusually prominent role in Aztec public life and thought during the fifteenth century. Tlacaelel (1398–1480), who was for more than half a century a prominent official of the Aztec Empire, is often credited with crystallizing the ideology of state that gave human sacrifice such great importance.

In the Aztecs' cyclical understanding of the world, the sun, central to all of life and identified with the their patron deity Huitzilopochtli, tended to lose its energy in a constant battle against encroaching darkness. Thus the Aztec world hovered always on the edge of catastrophe. To replenish its energy and thus postpone the descent into endless darkness, the sun required the life-giving force found in human blood. Because the gods had shed their blood ages ago in creating humankind, it was wholly proper for people to offer their own blood to nourish the gods in the present. The high calling of the Aztec state was to supply this blood, largely through its wars of expansion and from prisoners of war, who were destined for sacrifice. The victims were "those who have died for the god." The growth of the Aztec Empire therefore became the means for maintaining

Aztec Women
Within the home, Aztec women cooked, cleaned, spun and wove cloth, raised their children, and undertook ritual activities. Outside the home, they served as officials in palaces, priestesses in temples, traders in markets, teachers in schools, and members of craft workers' organizations. This domestic image comes from the sixteenth-century Florentine Codex, which was compiled by the Spanish but illustrated by Aztec artists. (Templo Mayor Library Mexico/Gianni Dagli Orti/The Art Archive)

cosmic order and avoiding utter catastrophe. This ideology also shaped the techniques of Aztec warfare, which put a premium on capturing prisoners rather than on killing the enemy. As the empire grew, priests and rulers became mutually dependent, and "human sacrifices were carried out in the service of politics."[11] Massive sacrificial rituals, together with a display of great wealth, served to impress enemies, allies, and subjects alike with the immense power of the Aztecs and their gods.

Alongside these sacrificial rituals was a philosophical and poetic tradition of great beauty, much of which mused on the fragility and brevity of human life. Here are a few lines from the fifteenth-century work of Nezahualcoyotl (1402–1472), a poet and king of the city-state of Texcoco, which was part of the Aztec Empire:

Truly do we live on Earth?
Not forever on earth; only a little while here.
Be it jade, it shatters.

Be it gold, it breaks.
Be it a quetzal feather, it tears apart.
Not forever on earth; only a little while here

Like a painting, we will be erased.
Like a flower, we will dry up here on earth.
Like plumed vestments of the precious bird,
That precious bird with an agile neck,
We will come to an end.[12]

The Inca Empire

While the Mexica were constructing an empire in Mesoamerica, a relatively small community of Quechua-speaking people, known to us as the Inca, was building the Western Hemisphere's largest imperial state along the spine of the Andes Mountains, which run almost the entire length of the west coast of South America. Much as the Aztecs drew upon the traditions of the Toltecs and Teotihuacán, the Incas incorporated the lands and cultures of earlier Andean civilizations: the Chavín, Moche, Nazca, and Chimu. The Inca Empire, however, was much larger than the Aztec state; it stretched some 2,500 miles along the Andes and contained perhaps 10 million subjects. Although the Aztec Empire controlled only part of the Mesoamerican cultural region, the Inca state encompassed practically the whole of Andean civilization during its short life in the fifteenth and early sixteenth centuries.

Both the Aztec and Inca empires represent rags-to-riches stories in which quite modest and remotely located people very quickly created by military conquest the largest states ever witnessed in their respective regions, but the empires themselves were quite different. In the Aztec realm, the Mexica rulers largely left their conquered people alone, if the required tribute was forthcoming. No elaborate administrative system arose to integrate the conquered territories or to assimilate their people to Aztec culture.

■ **Description**
In what ways did Inca authorities seek to integrate their vast domains?

The Incas, on the other hand, erected a rather more bureaucratic empire, though with many accommodations for local circumstances. At the top reigned the emperor, an absolute ruler regarded as divine, a descendant of the creator god Viracocha and the son of the sun god Inti. In theory, the state owned all land and resources, and each of the some eighty provinces in the empire had an Inca governor. At least in the central regions of the empire, subjects were grouped into hierarchical units of 10, 50, 100, 500, 1,000, 5,000, and 10,000 people, each headed by local officials, who were appointed and supervised by an Inca governor or the emperor. A separate set of "inspectors" provided the imperial center with an independent check on provincial officials. Births, deaths, marriages, and other population data were carefully recorded on *quipus*, the knotted cords that served as an accounting device. A resettlement program moved one-quarter or more of the population to new locations, in part to disperse conquered and no doubt resentful people.

Efforts at cultural integration required the leaders of conquered peoples to learn Quechua. Their sons were removed to the capital of Cuzco for instruction in Inca culture and language. Even now, millions of people from Ecuador to Chile still speak Quechua, and it is the official second language of Peru after Spanish. While the Incas required their subject peoples to acknowledge major Inca deities, these subject peoples were then largely free to carry on their own religious traditions. Human sacrifice took place on great public occasions or at times of special difficulty, but nothing remotely on the scale of the Aztec practice.

Like the Aztec Empire, the Inca state represented an especially dense and extended network of economic relationships within the "American web," but these relationships took shape in quite a different fashion. Inca demands on their conquered people were expressed, not so much in terms of tribute, but as labor service, known as *mita*, which was required periodically of every household.[13] What people produced at home usually stayed at home, but almost everyone also had to work for the state. Some labored on large state farms or on "sun farms," which supported temples and religious institutions; others herded, mined, served in the military, or toiled on state-directed construction projects. Those with particular skills were put to work manufacturing textiles, metal goods, ceramics, and stonework. The most well known of these specialists were the "chosen women," who were removed from their homes as young girls, trained in Inca ideology, and set to producing corn beer and cloth at state centers. Later they were given as wives to men of distinction or sent to serve as priestesses in various temples, where they were known as "wives of the Sun." In return for such labor services, Inca ideology, expressed in terms of family relationships, required the state to provide elaborate feasts at which large quantities of food and drink were consumed.

The Inca state played a major role in the distribution of goods as well as their production. A sixteenth-century Spanish observer wrote that "in each of the many provinces there were many storehouses filled with supplies and other needful things.... When there was no war, this stock of supplies and food was divided up among the poor and widows.... If there came a lean year, the storehouses were opened and the provinces were lent what they needed."[14] Thus the authority of the state penetrated and directed the Incas' society and economy far more than did that of the Aztecs.

If the Inca and Aztec civilizations differed sharply in their political and economic arrangements, they resembled each other more closely in their

Machu Picchu
Machu Picchu, high in the Andes Mountains, was constructed by the Incas in the 1400s on a spot long held sacred by local people. Its 200 buildings stand at some 8,000 feet above sea level, making it truly a "city in the sky." According to scholars, it was probably a royal retreat or religious center, rather than serving administrative, commercial, or military purposes. The outside world became aware of Machu Picchu only in 1911, when it was discovered by a Yale University archeologist. (Crispin Rodwell/Alamy)

gender systems. Both societies practiced what scholars call "gender parallelism," in which "women and men operate in two separate but equivalent spheres, each gender enjoying autonomy in its own sphere."[15]

In both Mesoamerican and Andean societies, such systems had emerged long before their incorporation into the Aztec and Inca empires. In the Andes, men reckoned their descent from their fathers and women from their mothers, while Mesoamericans had long viewed children as belonging equally to their mothers and fathers. Parallel religious cults for women and men likewise flourished in both societies. Inca men venerated the sun, while women worshipped the moon, with matching religious officials. In Aztec temples, both male and female priests presided over rituals dedicated to deities of both sexes. Particularly among the Incas, parallel hierarchies of male and female political officials governed the empire, while in Aztec society, women officials exercised local authority under a title that meant "female person in charge of people." Social roles were clearly defined and different for men and women, but the domestic concerns of women—childbirth, cooking, weaving, cleaning—were not regarded as inferior to the activities of men. Among the Aztec, for example, sweeping was a powerful and sacred act with symbolic significance as "an act of purification and a preventative against evil elements penetrating the center of the Aztec universe, the home."[16] In the Andes, men broke the ground, women sowed, and both took part in the harvest.

None of this meant gender equality. Men occupied the top positions in both political and religious life, and male infidelity was treated more lightly than was women's unfaithfulness. As the Inca and Aztec empires expanded, military life, limited to men, grew in prestige, perhaps skewing an earlier gender parallelism. In other ways, the new Aztec and Inca rulers adapted to the gender systems of the people they had conquered. Among the Aztecs, the tools of women's work, the broom and the weaving spindle, were ritualized as weapons; sweeping the home was believed to assist men at war; and childbirth for women was regarded as "our kind of war."[17] Inca rulers did not challenge the gender parallelism of their subjects but instead replicated it at a higher level, as the *sapay Inca* (the Inca ruler) and the *coya* (his female consort) governed jointly, claiming descent respectively from the sun and the moon.

Webs of Connection

■ **Connection**
In what different ways did the peoples of the fifteenth century interact with one another?

Few people in the fifteenth century lived in entirely separate and self-contained communities. Almost all were caught up, to one degree or another, in various and overlapping webs of influence, communication, and exchange. Such interactions represent, of course, one of the major concerns of world history. What kinds of webs or networks linked the various societies and civilizations of the fifteenth century?[18]

Perhaps most obvious were the webs of empire, large-scale political systems that brought together a variety of culturally different people. Christians and Muslims encountered each other directly in the Ottoman Empire, as did Hindus and Muslims in the Mughal Empire. No empire tried more diligently to integrate its diverse peoples than the fifteenth-century Incas.

Religion too linked far-flung peoples, and divided them as well. Christianity provided a common religious culture for peoples from England to Russia, although the great divide between Roman Catholicism and Eastern Orthodoxy endured, and in the sixteenth century the Protestant Reformation would shatter permanently the Christian unity of the Latin West. Although Buddhism had largely vanished from its South Asian homeland, it remained a link among China, Korea, Tibet, Japan, and parts of Southeast Asia, even as it splintered into a variety of sects and practices. More than either of these, Islam actively brought together its many peoples. In the hajj, the pilgrimage to Mecca, Africans, Arabs, Persians, Turks, Indians, and many others joined as one people as they rehearsed together the events that gave birth to their common faith. And yet the divisions and conflicts within the umma persisted, as the violent hostility between the Sunni Ottoman Empire and the Shia Safavid Empire so vividly illustrates.

Long-established patterns of trade among peoples occupying different environments and producing different goods were certainly much in evidence during the fifteenth century, as they had been for millennia. Hunting societies of Siberia funneled furs and other products of the forest into the Silk Road trading network traversing the civilizations of Eurasia. In the fifteenth century, some of the agricultural peoples in southern Nigeria were receiving horses brought overland from the drier regions to the north, where those animals flourished better. The Mississippi River in North America and the Orinoco and Amazon rivers in South America facilitated a canoe-borne commerce along those waterways. Coastal shipping in large seagoing canoes operated in the Caribbean and along the Pacific coast between Mexico and Peru. In the Pacific, the Micronesian island of Yap by the fifteenth century was the center of an oceanic trading network, which included the distant islands of Guam and Palau and used large stone disks as money. Likewise the people of Tonga, Samoa, and Fiji intermarried and exchanged a range of goods, including mats and canoes.

The great long-distance trading patterns of the Afro-Eurasian world, in operation for a thousand years or more, likewise continued in the fifteenth century, although the balance among them was changing (see Map 13.6). The Silk Road overland network, which had flourished under Mongol control in the thirteenth and fourteenth centuries, contracted in the fifteenth century as the Mongol Empire broke up and the devastation of the plague reduced demand for its products. The rise of the Ottoman Empire also blocked direct commercial contact between Europe and China, but oceanic trade from Japan, Korea, and China through the islands of Southeast Asia and across the Indian Ocean picked up considerably. Larger ships made it possible to trade in bulk goods such as grain as well as luxury products, while more sophisticated partnerships and credit mechanisms greased the wheels of commerce. A common Islamic culture over much of this vast region likewise smoothed the passage of goods among very different peoples, as it also did for the trans-Saharan trade.

Map 13.6   Religion and Commerce in the Afro-Eurasian World
By the fifteenth century, the many distinct peoples and societies of the Eastern Hemisphere were linked to one another by ties of religion and commerce. Of course, not everyone was involved in long-distance trade, and many people in areas shown as Buddhist or Islamic on the map practiced other religions.

A Preview of Coming Attractions: Looking Ahead to the Modern Era, 1500–2000

Connections born of empire, culture, and commerce linked many of the peoples in the world of the fifteenth century, but none of them operated on a genuinely global scale. Although the densest webs of connection had been woven within the Afro-Eurasian zone of interaction, this huge region had no sustained ties with the Americas, and neither of them had meaningful contact with the peoples of Pacific Oceania. That situation was about to change as Europeans in the sixteenth century and beyond forged a set of genuinely global relationships that linked all of these regions. That enormous process and the many consequences that flowed from it marked the beginning of what historians commonly call the modern age—the more than five centuries that followed the voyages of Columbus starting in 1492.

Over those five centuries, the previously separate worlds of Afro-Eurasia, the Americas, and Pacific Oceania became inextricably linked, with enormous consequences for everyone involved. Global empires, a global economy, global cultural exchanges, global migrations, global disease, global wars, and global environmental changes have made the past 500 years a unique phase in the human journey. Those webs of communication and exchange have progressively deepened, so much so that by the end of the twentieth century few people in the world lived beyond the cultural influences, economic ties, or political relationships of a globalized world.

A second distinctive feature of the past five centuries involves the emergence of a radically new kind of human society, also called "modern," which took shape first in Europe during the nineteenth century and then in various forms elsewhere in the world. The core feature of such societies was industrialization, rooted in a sustained growth of technological innovation. The human ability to create wealth made an enormous leap forward in a very short period of time, at least by world history standards. Accompanying this economic or industrial revolution was an equally distinctive and unprecedented jump in human numbers, a phenomenon that has affected not only human beings but also many other living species and the earth itself (see the Snapshot).

Modern societies were far more urbanized and much more commercialized than ever before, as more and more people began to work for wages, to produce for the market, and to buy the requirements of daily life rather than growing or making those products for their own use. These societies gave prominence and power to holders of

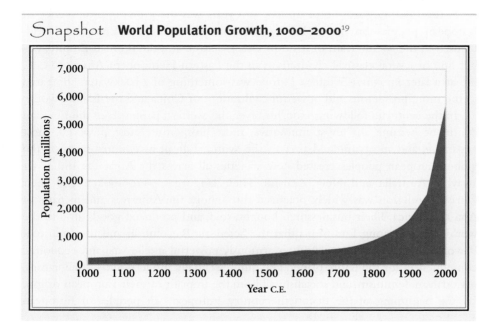

Snapshot   **World Population Growth, 1000–2000**[19]

urban wealth—merchants, bankers, industrialists, educated professionals—at the expense of rural landowning elites, while simultaneously generating a substantial factory working class and diminishing the role of peasants and handicraft artisans.

Modern societies were generally governed by states that were more powerful and intrusive than earlier states and empires had been, and they offered more of their people an opportunity to play an active role in public and political life. Literacy in modern societies was far more widespread than ever before, while new national identities became increasingly prominent, competing with more local loyalties. To the mix of established religious ideas and folk traditions were now added the challenging outlook and values of modern science, with its secular emphasis on the ability of human rationality to know and manipulate the world. Modernity has usually meant a self-conscious awareness of living and thinking in new ways that deliberately departed from tradition.

This revolution of modernity, comparable in its pervasive consequences only to the Agricultural Revolution of some 10,000 years ago, introduced new divisions and new conflicts into the experience of humankind. The ancient tensions between rich and poor within particular societies were now paralleled by new economic inequalities among entire regions and civilizations and a much-altered global balance of power. The first societies to experience the modern transformation—those in Western Europe and North America—became both a threat and a source of envy to much of the rest of the world. As modern societies emerged and spread, they were enormously destructive of older patterns of human life, even as they gave rise to many new ways of living. Sorting out what was gained and what was lost during the modern transformation has been a persistent and highly controversial thread of human thought over the past several centuries.

A third defining feature of the last 500 years was the growing prominence of European peoples on the global stage. In ancient times, the European world, focused in the Mediterranean basin of Greek culture and the Roman Empire, was but one of several classical civilizations in the Eastern Hemisphere. After 500 C.E., the area later known as Western Europe was something of a backwater, compared to the more prosperous and powerful civilizations of China and the Islamic world.

In the centuries following 1500, however, this western peninsula of the Eurasian continent became the most innovative, most prosperous, most powerful, most expansive, and most imitated part of the world. European empires spanned the globe. European peoples created new societies all across the Americas and as far away as Australia and New Zealand. Their languages were spoken and their Christian religion was widely practiced throughout the Americas and in parts of Asia and Africa. Their businessmen bought, sold, and produced goods around the world. It was among Europeans that the Scientific Revolution and the Industrial Revolution first took shape, with enormously powerful intellectual and economic consequences for the entire planet. The quintessentially modern ideas of liberalism, nationalism, feminism, and socialism all bore the imprint of their European origin. By the beginning of the twentieth century, Europeans or peoples of European descent exercised unprecedented influence and control over the earth's many other peoples, a wholly novel experience in human history.

For the rest of the world, growing European dominance posed a common task. Despite their many differences, the peoples of Asia, Africa, the Middle East, the Americas, and Pacific Oceania all found themselves confronted by powerful and intrusive Europeans. The impact of this intrusion and how various peoples responded to it—resistance, submission, acceptance, imitation, adaptation—represent critically important threads in the world history of the past five centuries.

Reflections: What If? Chance and Contingency in World History

Seeking meaning in the stories they tell, historians are inclined to look for deeply rooted or underlying causes for the events they recount. And yet, is it possible that, at least on occasion, history turns less on profound and long-term causes than on coincidence, chance, or the decisions of a few that might well have gone another way?

Consider, for example, the problem of explaining the rise of Europe to a position of global power in the modern era. What if the Great Khan Ogodei had not died in 1241, requiring the forces then poised for an assault on Germany to return to Mongolia? It is surely possible that Central and Western Europe might have been overrun by Mongol armies as so many other civilizations had been, a prospect that could have drastically altered the trajectory of European history. Or what if the Chinese had decided in 1433 to continue their huge maritime expeditions, creating an empire in the Indian Ocean basin and perhaps moving on to "discover" the Americas and Europe? Such a scenario suggests a wholly different future for world history than the one that in fact occurred. Or what if the forces of the Ottoman Empire had taken the besieged city of Vienna in 1529? Might they then have incorporated even larger parts of Europe into their expanding domain, calling a halt to Europe's overseas empire-building enterprise?

None of this necessarily means that the rise of Europe was merely a fluke or an accident of history, but it does raise the issue of "contingency," the role of unforeseen or small events in the unfolding of the human story. An occasional "what if" approach to history reminds us that alternative possibilities existed in the past and that the only certainty about the future is that we will be surprised.

Second Thoughts

What's the Significance?

Paleolithic persistence	Iroquois	Ming dynasty China
Benin	Timur	Zheng He
Igbo	Fulbe	European Renaissance

To assess your mastery of the material in this chapter, see the **Online Study Guide** at bedfordstmartins.com/strayer

Ottoman Empire	Songhay Empire	Aztec Empire
seizure of Constantinople (1453)	Timbuktu	Inca Empire
Safavid Empire	Mughal Empire	
	Malacca	

Big Picture Questions

1. Assume for the moment that the Chinese had *not* ended their maritime voyages in 1433. How might the subsequent development of world history have been different? Is there value in asking this kind of "what if" or counterfactual question? Or is it an irrelevant waste of time?
2. How does this chapter distinguish among the various kinds of societies that comprised the world of the fifteenth century? Are there other ways of categorizing the world's peoples that might work as well or better?
3. What would surprise a knowledgeable observer from 500 C.E., were he or she to make a global tour in the fifteenth century? What features of that earlier world might still be recognizable?
4. What predictions about the future might a global traveler of the fifteenth century reasonably have made? Would it depend on precisely when those predictions were made?

Next Steps: For Further Study

For Web sites and documents related to this chapter, see **Make History** at bedfordstmartins.com/strayer.

Terence N. D'Altroy, *The Incas* (2002). A history of the Inca Empire that draws on recent archeological and historical research.

Edward L. Dreyer, *Zheng He: China and the Oceans in the Early Ming Dynasty* (2006). The most recent scholarly account of the Ming dynasty voyages.

Halil Inalcik and Donald Quataert, *An Economic and Social History of the Ottoman Empire, 1300–1914* (1994). A classic study of the Ottoman Empire.

Robin Kirkpatrick, *The European Renaissance, 1400–1600* (2002). A beautifully illustrated history of Renaissance culture as well as the social and economic life of the period.

Charles Mann, *1491: New Revelations of the Americas before Columbus* (2005). A review of Western Hemisphere societies and academic debates about their pre-Columbian history.

J. R. McNeill and William H. McNeill, *The Human Web* (2003). A succinct account of the evolving webs or relationships among human societies in world history.

Michael Smith, *The Aztecs* (2003). A history of the Aztec Empire, with an emphasis on the lives of ordinary people.

"Ming Dynasty," http://www.metmuseum.org/toah/hd/ming/hd_ming.htm. A sample of Chinese art from the Ming dynasty from the collection of the Metropolitan Museum of Art.

"Renaissance Art in Italy," http://witcombe.sbc.edu/ARTHrenaissanceitaly.html. An extensive collection of painting and sculpture from the Italian Renaissance.

Notes

Prologue

1. Adapted from Carl Sagan, *The Dragons of Eden* (New York: Random House, 1977), 13–17.
2. See David Christian, *Maps of Time* (Berkeley: University of California Press, 2004).
3. Voltaire, *Treatise on Toleration,* chap. 22.
4. See David Christian, "World History in Context," *Journal of World History* 14, no. 4 (December 2003), 437–58.

Part One

Chapter 1

1. Richard Rainsford, "What Chance, the Survival Prospects of East Africa's Last Hunting and Gathering Tribe," 1997, http://www.ntz.info/gen/n00757.html.
2. What follows comes from Sally McBreatry and Alison S. Brooks, "The Revolution That Wasn't: A New Interpretation of the Origin of Modern Human Behavior," *Journal of Human Evolution* 39 (2000), 453–563.
3. Peter Bogucki, *The Origins of Human Society* (Oxford: Blackwell, 1999), 94–95.
4. Paul G. Bahn and Jean Vertut, *Images of the Ice Age* (New York: Facts on File, 1988), chap. 7.
5. John Mulvaney and Johan Kaminga, *Prehistory of Australia* (Washington, D.C.: Smithsonian Institution Press, 1999), 93–102.
6. For a recent summary of this debate, see Charles C. Mann, *1491: New Revelations of the Americas before Columbus* (New York: Alfred Knopf, 2005), chap. 5.
7. Brian M. Fagan, *Ancient North America* (London: Thames and Hudson, 1995), 77–87.
8. Ben Finney, "The Other One-Third of the Globe," *Journal of World History* 5, no. 2 (Fall 1994): 273–85.
9. David Christian, *Maps of Time* (Berkeley: University of California Press, 2004), 143.
10. Richard B. Lee, *The Dobe Ju/'hoansi* (New York: Harcourt Brace, 1993), 58.
11. J. C. Beaglehole, *The Journals of Captain James Cook* (Cambridge: Hakluyt Society, 1968), 1:399.
12. Inga Clendinnen, *Dancing with Strangers* (Cambridge: Cambridge University Press, 2005), 159–67.
13. Marshall Sahlins, "The Original Affluent Society," in *Stone Age Economics* (London: Tavistock, 1972), 1–39.
14. Christopher Ehret, *The Civilizations of Africa* (Charlottesville: University of Virginia Press, 2002), chap. 2.
15. Marija Gimbutas, *The Language of the Goddess* (San Francisco: HarperCollins, 1989), 316–18.
16. D. Bruce Dickson, *The Dawn of Belief* (Tucson: University of Arizona Press, 1990), 210.
17. Derived from Christian, *Maps of Time*, 208.
18. Brian Fagan, *People of the Earth* (New York: HarperCollins, 1992), 200–201.
19. Jan Platvoet, "At War with God: Ju/'hoan Curing Dances," *Journal of Religion in Africa* 29, no. 1 (1999): 5.
20. J. David Lewis-Williams, *Believing and Seeing: Symbolic Meaning in Southern San Rock Paintings* (London: Academic Press, 1981).
21. Lee, *The Dobe Ju/'hoansi*. Unless otherwise noted, all information and quotes about the Ju/'hoansi come from this book.
22. Elizabeth Marshall Thomas, *The Harmless People* (New York: Vintage Books, 1989), 180.
23. For a contemporary account of a curing dance, see Bradford Keeney, "Ropes to God: Experiencing the Bushman Spiritual Universe," *Parabola* 27, no. 3 (2002), S1–S16.
24. Platvoet, "At War with God."
25. Brian Fagan, *Before California* (New York: Rowman and Littlefield, 2003), 153–55, 341–44.
26. Jeanne E. Arnold, *The Origins of a Pacific Coast Chiefdom* (Salt Lake City: University of Utah Press, 2001), 14.
27. Chester King, "Chumash Inter-Village Economic Exchange," in *Native Californians*, edited by Lowell John Bean and Thomas C. Blackburn (Menlo Park: Ballena Press, 1976), 289–318. The quote is on p. 297.

Chapter 2

1. "Population 1: The Town That's Been Reclaimed by the Prairie," *International Observer*, November 20, 2005, http://observer.guardian.co.uk/international/story/0,690 3,1646659,00.html?gusrc=rss.
2. Peter Bellwood, *First Farmers* (London: Blackwood, 2005), 7.

3. Mark Nathan Cohen, *The Food Crisis in Prehistory* (New Haven: Yale University Press, 1977).

4. Bruce Smith, *The Emergence of Agriculture* (New York: Scientific American Library, 1995), 206–14.

5. Jared Diamond, *Guns, Germs, and Steel* (New York: Vintage, 1997), 132, 157–75.

6. Bellwood, *First Farmers*, 54–55.

7. Steven Mithen, *After the Ice* (Cambridge, Mass.: Harvard University Press, 2004), 87.

8. Neil Roberts, *The Holocene: An Environmental History* (Oxford: Blackwell, 1998), 116.

9. Nina V. Federoff, "Prehistoric GM Corn," *Science* 302 (November 2003): 1158.

10. Diamond, *Gun, Germs, and Steel*, 367.

11. The most recent summary of an immense literature on the spread of languages is found in Bellwood, *First Farmers*.

12. Many of these dates are much debated. See John Staller et al., *Histories of Maize* (Boston: Academic Press, 2006).

13. John A. Mears, "Agricultural Origins in Global Perspective," in *Agricultural and Pastoral Societies in Ancient and Classical History*, edited by Michael Adas (Philadelphia: Temple University Press, 2001), 63–64.

14. Elizabeth Wayland Barber, *Women's Work: The First 20,000 Years* (New York: W. W. Norton, 1994), chap. 3.

15. Andrew Sherrat, "The Secondary Exploitation of Animals in the Old World," *World Archeology* 15, no. 1 (June 1983): 90–104.

16. Clive Ponting, *A Green History of the World* (New York: St. Martin's Press, 1991), 69.

17. Anatoly M. Khazanov, *Nomads and the Outside World* (Madison: University of Wisconsin Press, 1994), 15.

18. Ian Hodder, "Women and Men at Catalhoyuk," *Scientific American* 15, no. 1 (2005): 35–41.

19. Allen W. Johnson and Timothy Earle, *The Evolution of Human Societies* (Stanford, Calif.: Stanford University Press, 2000), 281–94.

Chapter 3

1. http://www.utahoutventures.com/multiactivity/raftoffroadtours.htm.

2. Charles C. Mann, *1491: New Revelations of the Americas before Columbus* (New York: Alfred A. Knopf, 2005), 174–91; Proyecto Arqueológico Norte Chico, Project Description, 2005, http://www.fieldmuseum.org/research_collections/anthropology/anthro_sites/PANC/proj_desc.htm.

3. Jonathan Mark Kenoyer, *Ancient Cities of the Indus Valley Civilization* (Oxford: Oxford University Press, 1998), 83–84.

4. For a summary of many theories, see Stephen K. Sanderson, *Social Transformations* (Oxford: Blackwell, 1995), chap. 3.

5. Robert Carneiro, "A Theory of the Origin of the State," *Science* 169 (1970): 733–38.

6. Susan Pollock, *Ancient Mesopotamia* (Cambridge: Cambridge University Press, 1999), 48.

7. *The Epic of Gilgamesh*, translated and edited by Benjamin R. Foster (New York: W. W. Norton, 2001), 10, Tablet I:226–32.

8. Miriam Lichtheim, *Ancient Egyptian Literature* (Berkeley: University of California Press, 1975), 2:168–75.

9. Samuel Noah Kramer, *History Begins at Sumer* (Philadelphia: University of Pennsylvania Press, 1981), 3–4.

10. James Legge, trans., *The Chinese Classics* (London: Henry Frowde, 1893), 4:171–72.

11. Marija Gimbutas, *The Living Goddess* (Berkeley: University of California Press, 1999).

12. Margaret Ehrenberg, *Women in Prehistory* (London: British Museum Publications, 1989), 107.

13. David Christian, *Maps of Time* (Berkeley: University of California Press, 2004), 256–57, 263–64.

14. Sherry Ortner, "Is Female to Male as Nature Is to Culture?" in *Women, Culture, and Society,* edited by Michelle Rosaldo and Louise Lamphere (Stanford, Calif.: Stanford University Press, 1974), 67–88.

15. Gerda Lerner, *The Creation of Patriarchy* (New York: Oxford University Press, 1986), 70.

16. Lichtheim, *Ancient Egyptian Literature*, 2:184–85.

17. Lichtheim, *Ancient Egyptian Literature*, 2:168–75.

18. Prologue to *The Code of Hammurabi*, http://www.wsu.edu/~dee/MESO/CODE.HTM.

19. Gary Urton, "From Knots to Narratives: Reconstructing the Art of Historical Record-Keeping in the Andes from Spanish Transcriptions of Inka Khipus," *Ethnohistory* 45, no. 3 (1998): 409–38.

20. Adolf Erman, *The Literature of the Ancient Egyptians,* translated by Aylward M. Blackman (London: Methuen, 1927), 136–37.

21. H. and H. A. Frankfort, *Before Philosophy* (Baltimore: Penguin Books, 1963), 39, 138.

22. Quoted in Peter Stearns et al., *World Civilizations* (New York: Longman, 1996), 1:30.

23. *The Epic of Gilgamesh*, translated by N. K. Sandars (New York: Penguin Classics, 1972).

24. For both Egyptian quotes, see Lichtheim, *Ancient Egyptian Literature*, 1:41–42; 2:124–26.

25. See Clive Ponting, *A Green History of the World* (New York: St. Martin's Press, 1991), chap. 5.

26. Samuel Kramer, *The Sumerians* (Chicago: University of Chicago Press, 1963), 142.

27. Cyril Aldred, *The Egyptians* (London: Thames and Hudson, 1998), 138.

28. For a recent summary of a long debate about the relationship of Egypt and Africa, see David O'Connor and Andrew Reid, eds., *Ancient Egypt in Africa* (London: UCL Press, 2003).

29. James B. Pritchard, ed., *Ancient Near Eastern Texts Relating to the Old Testament* (Princeton: Princeton University Press, 1969), 647–48.

30. Lichtheim, *Ancient Egyptian Literature,* 1:25–27.

31. Joan Oates, *Babylon* (London: Thames and Hudson, 1986), 91.

32. Marvin Harris, ed., *Cannibals and Kings* (New York: Vintage, 1978), 102.

Part Two

1. Stephen K. Sanderson, *Social Transformation* (Oxford: Blackwell, 1995), chap. 4.

2. From Sanderson, *Social Transformation*, 103.

3. Colin Ronan and Joseph Needham, *The Shorter Science and Civilization in China* (Cambridge: Cambridge University Press, 1978), 58.

4. Sidney W. Mintz, *Sweetness and Power* (New York: Penguin Books, 1985), chap. 2.

5. William H. McNeill, *Plagues and Peoples* (New York: Doubleday, 1977), 94.

6. See world population estimates by region in Paul Adams et al., *Experiencing World History* (New York: New York University Press, 2000), 334.

Chapter 4

1. Cullen Murphy, *Are We Rome? The Fall of an Empire and the Fate of America* (Boston: Houghton Mifflin, 2007).

2. J. M. Cook, *The Persian Empire* (London: J. M. Dent & Sons, 1983), 76.

3. George Rawlinson, trans., *The Histories of Herodotus* (London: Dent, 1910), 1:131–40.

4. Erich F. Schmidt, *Persepolis I: Structures, Reliefs, Inscriptions*, OIP 68 (Chicago: University of Chicago Press, 1953), 63.

5. Quoted in Lynn Hunt et al., *The Making of the West* (Boston: Bedford/St. Martin's, 2005), 75.

6. Christian Meier, *Athens* (New York: Metropolitan Books, 1993), 93.

7. B. Jowett, trans., *Thucydides Translated into English* (Oxford: Oxford University Press, 1881) 1:115–29.

8. Arrian, *The Campaigns of Alexander,* translated by Aubrey de Selincourt, revised by J. R. Hamilton (London: Penguin, 1971), 395–96.

9. Stanley Burstein, *The Hellenistic Period in World History* (Washington, D.C.: American Historical Association, 1996), 12.

10. Norman F. Cantor, *Antiquity* (New York: HarperCollins, 2003), 25.

11. Greg Woolf, "Inventing Empire in Ancient Rome," in *Empires: Perspectives from Archeology and History*, edited by Susan Alcock et al. (Cambridge: Cambridge University Press, 2001), 314.

12. S. A. M. Adshead, *China in World History* (London: McMillan Press, 1988), 4–21.

13. See Padma Manian, "Harappans and Aryans: Old and New Perspectives on Ancient Indian History," *The History Teacher* 32, no. 1 (November 1998): 17–32.

14. Stanley Wolpert, *A New History of India* (New York: Oxford University Press, 1993), chap. 5.

15. Zhengyuan Fu, *Autocratic Tradition and Chinese Politics* (New York: Cambridge University Press, 1993), 188.

Chapter 5

1. S. N. Eisenstadt, ed., *The Origins and Diversity of Axial Age Civilizations* (Albany: SUNY Press, 1986), 1–4; Karen Armstrong, *The Great Transformation* (New York: Alfred A. Knopf, 2006).

2. Arthur Waley, *Three Ways of Thought in Ancient China* (Garden City, N.Y.: Doubleday, 1956), 159–60.

3. Nancy Lee Swann, trans., *Pan Chao: Foremost Woman Scholar of China* (New York: Century, 1932), 111–14.

4. Quoted in Huston Smith, *The Illustrated World's Religions* (San Francisco: HarperCollins, 1994), 123.

5. Lao Tsu, *Tao Te Ching*, translated by Gia-Fu Feng and Jane English (New York: Vintage Books, 1972), 80.

6. *Laws of Manu*, V, 146–48. Quoted in Swarna de Silva, "The Place of Women in Buddhism," 1994, http://www.enabling .org/ia/vipassana/Archive/D/DeSilva/WomenInBuddhism/ womenInBuddhismSwarnaDeSilva.html.

7. Quoted in Karen Andrews, "Women in Theravada Buddhism," http://www.enabling.org/ia/vipassana/ Archive/A/Andrews/womenTheraBudAndrews.html.

8. A. L. Basham, *The Wonder That Was India* (London: Sidgwick and Jackson, 1967), 309.

9. S. A. Nigosian, *The Zoroastrian Faith: Tradition and Modern Research* (Montreal: McGill–Queen's University Press, 1993), 95–97.

10. Isaiah 1:11–17.

11. Plato, *Apologia*.

12. Hippocrates, *On the Sacred Disease*, in *The Human Record*, edited by Alfred Andrea and James Overfield (Boston: Houghton Mifflin, 2005), 1:104–5.

13. Thanissaro Bhikkhu, trans., Karaniya Metta Sutta, 2004, http://www.accesstoinsight.org/tipitaka/kn/snp/snp.1.08 .than.html.

14. Matthew 5:43–44.

15. See Marcus Borg, ed., *Jesus and Buddha: The Parallel Sayings* (Berkeley, Calif.: Ulysses Press, 1997).

16. For a popular summary of the voluminous scholarship on Jesus, see Stephen Patterson et al., *The Search for Jesus: Modern Scholarship Looks at the Gospels* (Washington, D.C.: Biblical Archeological Society, 1994).

17. Galatians 3:28.

18. Ephesians 5:22; 1 Corinthians 14:35.

19. Ekkehard W. Stegemann and Wolfgang Stegemann, *The Jesus Movement: A History of Its First Century* (Minneapolis: Fortress Press, 1999), 291–96.

20. Ramsay MacMullen, *Christianizing the Roman Empire* (New Haven: Yale University Press, 1984), chap. 4.

21. Peter Brown, *The Rise of Western Christendom* (London: Blackwell, 2003), 69–71.

22. Mary Ann Rossi, "Priesthood, Precedent, and Prejudice: On Recovering the Women Priests of Early Christianity," *Journal of Feminist Studies* 7, no. 1 (1991): 73–94.

23. Chai-Shin Yu, *Early Buddhism and Christianity* (Delhi: Motilal Banarsidass, 1981), 211.

Chapter 6

1. Po Chu-I, "After Passing the Examination," in Alfred Waley, *More Translations from the Chinese* (New York: Alfred A. Knopf, 1919), 37.

2. Quoted in Michael Lowe, *Everyday Life in Early Imperial China* (New York: Dorset Press, 1968), 38.

3. Selected Poems from the Tang Dynasty, http://www.lingshidao.net/hanshi/tang1.htm.

4. A. L. Basham, *The Wonder That Was India* (London: Sidgwick and Jackson, 1967), 138.

5. Karl Jacoby, "Slaves by Nature: Animals and Human Slaves," *Slavery and Abolition* 15 (1994): 89–97.

6. Orlando Patterson, *Slavery and Social Death* (Cambridge, Mass.: Harvard University Press, 1982).

7. Basham, *The Wonder That Was India*, 152.

8. Sarah Pomeroy et al., *Ancient Greece* (New York: Oxford University Press, 1999), 63, 239.

9. R. Zelnick-Abramovitz, *Not Wholly Free* (Leiden: Brill, 2005), 337, 343.

10. Keith Bradley, *Slavery and Society at Rome* (Cambridge: Cambridge University Press, 1994), 30.

11. 1 Peter 2:18.

12. Milton Meltzer, *Slavery: A World History* (New York: Da Capo Press, 1993), 189.

13. Quoted in Bret Hinsch, *Women in Early Imperial China* (Oxford: Rowman and Littlefield, 2002), 155.

14. Nancy Lee Swann, trans., *Pan Chao: Foremost Woman Scholar of China* (New York: Century Co., 1932), 111–14.

15. Lisa Raphals, *Sharing the Light: Representations of Women and Virtue in Early China* (Albany: SUNY Press, 1998).

16. Valerie Hansen, *The Open Empire* (New York: Norton, 2000), 183–84; Thomas Barfield, *The Perilous Frontier* (Cambridge: Blackwell Publishing, 1989), 140.

17. Vivian-Lee Nyitray, "Confucian Complexities," in Teresa A. Meade and Merry E. Weisner-Hanks, *A Companion to Gender History* (Oxford: Blackwell Publishing, 2004), 278.

18. Aristotle, *Politica*, ed. Loeb Classical Library, 1254b10–14.

19. Quoted in Pomeroy et al., *Ancient Greece*, 146.

Chapter 7

1. *Rethinking Schools on Line,* Fall 1999, http://www.rethinkingschools.org/archive/14_01/poor141.shtml.

2. Thomas Benjamin, "A Time of Reconquest: History, the Maya Revival, and the Zapatista Rebellion in Chiapas," *American Historical Review* 105, no. 2 (April 2000): 417.

3. Population figures are taken from Paul Adams et al., *Experiencing World History* (New York: New York University Press, 2000), 334.

4. Roderick J. McIntosh, *Ancient Middle Niger* (Cambridge: Cambridge University Press, 2005), 10.

5. Roderick J. McIntosh, *The Peoples of the Middle Niger* (Oxford: Blackwell, 1998), 177.

6. Kairn A. Klieman, *"The Pygmies Were Our Compass"* (Portsmouth, N.H.: Heinemann, 2003), chaps. 4, 5.

7. Christopher Ehret, *The Civilizations of Africa* (Charlottesville: University of Virginia Press, 2000), 175.

8. See Jan Vansina, *Paths in the Rainforest* (Madison: University of Wisconsin Press, 1990), 95–99.

9. Richard E. W. Adams, *Prehistoric Mesoamerica* (Norman: University of Oklahoma Press, 2005), 16.

10. Richard E. W. Adams, *Ancient Civilizations of the New World* (Boulder, Colo.: Westview Press, 1997), 53–56; T. Patrick Culbert, "The New Maya," *Archeology* 51, no. 5 (September–October 1998): 47–51.

11. William Haviland, "State and Power in Classic Maya Society," *American Anthropologist* 94, no. 4 (1992): 937.

12. Jared Diamond, *Collapse* (New York: Viking, 2005), chap. 5.

13. Esther Pasztory, *Teotihuacan: An Experiment in Living* (Norman: University of Oklahoma Press, 1997), 193.

14. George L. Cowgill, "The Central Mexican Highlands . . . ," in *The Cambridge History of the Native Peoples of the Americas*, vol. 2, part 1, *Mesoamerica*, edited by Richard E. W. Adams and Murdo J. MacLeod (Cambridge: Cambridge University Press, 2000), 289.

15. Karen Olsen Bruhns, *Ancient South America* (Cambridge: Cambridge University Press, 1994), 126–41; Sylvia R. Kembel and John W. Rick, "Building Authority at Chavin de Huantar," in *Andean Archeology*, edited by Helaine Silverman (Oxford: Blackwell, 2004), 59–76.

16. Garth Bawden, *The Moche* (Oxford: Blackwell, 1996), chaps. 9, 10.

17. John E. Kicza, *The Peoples and Civilizations of the Americas before Contact* (Washington, D.C.: American Historical Association, 1998), 43–44.

18. Much of this section draws on Brian Fagan, *Ancient North America* (London: Thames and Hudson, 2005), chaps. 14, 15. The quote is on p. 345.

19. George R. Milner, *The Moundbuilders* (London: Thames and Hudson, 2004).

20. David Hurst Thomas, *Exploring Ancient Native America* (New York: Routledge, 1999), 137–42.

21. Stephen H. Lekson and Peter N. Peregrine, "A Continental Perspective for North American Archeology," *The SAA Archeological Record* 4, no. 1 (January 2004): 15–19.

22. Fagan, *Ancient North America*, 475.

23. Quoted in Lynda Norene Shaffer, *Native Americans before 1492* (Armonk, N.Y.: M. E. Sharpe, 1992), 70.

Part Three

1. Marshall G. S. Hodgson, *The Venture of Islam* (Chicago: University of Chicago Press, 1974), 1:71.

2. Lynda Shaffer, "Southernization," *Journal of World History* 5, no. 1 (Spring 1994): 7.

Chapter 8

1. Somini Sengupta, "Sahara Journal," *New York Times*, November 25, 2003.

2. Seneca the Younger, *Declamations*, vol. 1.

3. Liu Xinru, "Silks and Religion in Eurasia, A.D. 600–1200," *Journal of World History* 6, no. 1 (Spring 1995): 25–48.

4. Jerry Bentley, "Hemispheric Integration, 500–1500 C.E.," *Journal of World History* 9, no. 2 (Fall 1998): 241–44.

5. See Jerry Bentley, *Old World Encounters* (New York: Oxford University Press, 1993), 42–53, 69–84.

6. Liu Xinru, *The Silk Road* (Washington, D.C.: American Historical Association, 1998), 10.

7. See William H. McNeill, *Plagues and Peoples* (New York: Doubleday, 1977), chaps. 3, 4.

8. Boccaccio, *The Decameron*, translated by M. Rigg (London: David Campbell, 1921), 1:5–11.

9. Kenneth McPherson, *The Indian Ocean* (Oxford: Oxford University Press, 1993), 15.

10. Janet L. Abu-Lughod, *Before European Hegemony* (Oxford: Oxford University Press, 1989), 269.

11. Nigel D. Furlonge, "Revisiting the Zanj and Revisioning Revolt," *Negro History Bulletin,* vol. 62 (December 1999).

12. Patricia Risso, *Merchants and Faith: Muslim Commerce and Culture in the Indian Ocean* (Boulder, Colo.: Westview, 1995), 54.

13. McPherson, *The Indian Ocean*, 97.

14. Kenneth R. Hall, *Maritime Trade and State Development in Early Southeast Asia* (Honolulu: University of Hawaii Press, 1985), 101.

15. Lynda Norene Shaffer, *Maritime Southeast Asia to 1500* (Armonk, N.Y.: M. E. Sharpe, 1996), 37, 46.

16. M. C. Horton and T. R. Burton, "Indian Metalwork in East Africa: The Bronze Lion Statuette from Shanga," *Antiquities* 62 (1988): 22.

17. Ross Dunn, *The Adventures of Ibn Battuta* (Berkeley: University of California Press, 1986), 124.

18. Christopher Ehret, *The Civilizations of Africa* (Charlottesville: University of Virginia Press, 2002), 255.

19. Ehret, *The Civilizations of Africa*, 227–32.

20. Nehemia Levtzion and Jay Spaulding, eds., *Medieval West Africa: Views from Arab Scholars and Merchants* (Princeton, N.J.: Marcus Wiener, 2003), 5.

21. Quoted in John Iliffe, *Africans: The History of a Continent* (Cambridge: Cambridge University Press, 1995), 75–76.

22. See Martin Raish and John L. Sorenson, *Pre-Columbian Contact with the Americas across the Oceans: An Annotated Bibliography* (Provo, Utah: Research Press, 1996).

23. J. R. McNeill and William McNeill, *The Human Web* (New York: W. W. Norton, 2003), 160.

24. Lauren Ristvet, *In the Beginning* (New York: McGraw-Hill, 2007), 165.

25. Maria Rostworowski de Diez Canseco, *History of the Inca Realm* (Cambridge: Cambridge University Press, 1999), 209–12.

26. Anthony Andrews, "America's Ancient Mariners," *Natural History*, October 1991, 72–75.

27. Richard Blanton and Gary Feinman, "The Mesoamerican World System," *American Anthropologist* 86, no. 3 (September 1984): 677.

Chapter 9

1. *The Guardian*, June 15, 2006.

2. John K. Fairbank, ed., *The Chinese World Order* (Cambridge, Mass.: Harvard University Press, 1968).

3. Mark Elvin, *The Retreat of the Elephants* (New Haven: Yale University Press, 2004), chap. 1. The quote is on p. 19.

4. Mark Elvin, *The Pattern of the Chinese Past* (London: Eyre Methuen, 1973), 55.

5. Samuel Adshead, *T'ang China: The Rise of the East in World History* (New York: Palgrave, 2004), 30.

6. Elvin, *The Pattern of the Chinese Past*, part 2; William McNeill, *The Pursuit of Power* (Chicago: University of Chicago Press, 1984), 50.

7. See "The Attractions of the Capital," in Patricia B. Ebrey, *Chinese Civilization: A Sourcebook* (New York: Free Press, 1993), 178–85.

8. Marco Polo, "The Glories of Kinsay," *Medieval Sourcebook*, http://www.fordham.edu/halsall/source/polo-kinsay.html.

9. John K. Fairbank, *China: A New History* (Cambridge, Mass.: Harvard University Press, 1992), 89.

10. J. R. McNeill and William H. McNeill, *The Human Web* (New York: W. W. Norton, 2003), 123.

11. Francesca Bray, *Technology and Gender: Fabrics of Power in Late Imperial China* (Berkeley: University of California Press, 1997), 116.

12. Patricia Ebrey, *The Inner Quarters* (Berkeley: University of California Press, 1993), 207.

13. Ebrey, *The Inner Quarters*, 37–43.

14. Ebrey, *The Inner Quarters*, 6.

15. See Nicolas DiCosmo, *Ancient China and Its Enemies* (Cambridge: Cambridge University Press, 2002), chap. 6.

16. DiCosmo, *Ancient China and Its Enemies*, 94.

17. Quoted in Thomas J. Barfield, "Steppe Empires, China, and the Silk Route," in *Nomads in the Sedentary World*, edited by Anatoly M. Khazanov and Andre Wink (Richmond: Kurzon Press, 2001), 237.

18. Quoted in Edward H. Shafer, *The Golden Peaches of Samarkand* (Berkeley: University of California Press, 1963), 28.

19. Susan Mann, "Women in East Asia," in *Women's History in Global Perspective,* edited by Bonnie Smith (Urbana: University of Illinois Press, 2005), 2:53–56.

20. Joseph Buttinger, *A Dragon Defiant: A Short History of Vietnam* (New York: Praeger, 1972), 32–34; Jerry Bentley, *Old World Encounters* (New York: Oxford University Press, 1993), 85–86.

21. Cited in "Trung Trac and Trung Nhi," http://www.viettouch.com/trungsis.

22. Liam C. Kelley, *Beyond the Bronze Pillars: Envoy Poetry and the Sino-Vietnamese Relationship* (Honolulu: University of Hawai'i Press, 2005).

23. "Chronicles of Japan," in *Nibongi*, translated by W. G. Aston (London: Kegan Paul, 1896), 2:128–33.

24. H. Paul Varley, "Japan, 550–838," in *Asia in Western and World History*, edited by Ainslee T. Embrey and Carol Gluck (Armonk, N.Y.: M. E. Sharpe, 1997), 353.

25. Quoted in McNeill, *The Pursuit of Power*, 40.

26. John Fairbank et al., *East Asia: Tradition and Transformation* (Boston: Houghton Mifflin, 1978), 353.

27. Arnold Pacey, *Technology in World Civilization* (Cambridge, Mass.: MIT Press, 1991), 50–53.

28. McNeill, *The Pursuit of Power*, 24–25.

29. Hugh Clark, "Muslims and Hindus in the Culture and Morphology of Quanzhou from the Tenth to the Thirteenth Century," *Journal of World History* 6, no. 1 (Spring 1995): 49–74.

30. Quoted in Arthur F. Wright, *Studies in Chinese Buddhism* (New Haven: Yale University Press, 1990), 16.

31. Arthur F. Wright, *Buddhism in Chinese History* (Stanford, Calif.: Stanford University Press, 1959), 36–39.

32. Quoted in Wright, *Buddhism in Chinese History*, 67.

33. Quoted in Eric Zurcher, *The Buddhist Conquest of China* (Leiden: E. J. Brill, 1959), 1:262.

34. Jacquet Gernet, *A History of Chinese Civilization* (Cambridge: Cambridge University Press, 1996), 291–96.

35. Edwin O. Reischauer, *Ennin's Travels in China* (New York: Ronald Press, 1955), 221–24.

Chapter 10

1. "East and West Churches Reconcile," http://chi.gospelcom.net/DAILYF/2002/12/daily-12-07-2002.shtml.

2. Paul R. Spickard and Kevin M. Cragg, *A Global History of Christians* (Grand Rapids, Mich.: Baker Academic, 1994), chap. 6.

3. Leonora Neville, *Authority in Byzantine Provincial Society, 950–1100* (Cambridge: Cambridge University Press, 2004), 2.

4. Deno John Geanakoplos, *Byzantium: Church, Society, and Civilization Seen through Contemporary Eyes* (Chicago: University of Chicago Press, 1984), 389.

5. Geanakoplos, *Byzantium*, 143.

6. Quoted in A. A. Vasiliev, *History of the Byzantine Empire* (Madison: University of Wisconsin Press, 1978), 79–80.

7. Geanakoplos, *Byzantium*, 362.

8. Geanakoplos, *Byzantium*, 369.

9. Rowena Loverance, *Byzantium* (Cambridge, Mass.: Harvard University Press, 2004), 43.

10. Daniel H. Kaiser and Gary Marker, *Reinterpreting Russian History* (Oxford: Oxford University Press, 1994), 63–67.

11. Quoted in Patrick J. Geary, *Before France and Germany* (New York: Oxford University Press, 1988), 79.

12. Quoted in Stephen Williams, *Diocletian and the Roman Recovery* (London: Routledge, 1996), 218.

13. Peter Brown, *The Rise of Western Christendom* (London: Blackwell, 1996), 305.

14. Karen Louise Jolly, *Tradition and Diversity: Christianity in a World Context to 1500* (Armonk, N.Y.: M. E. Sharpe, 1997), 195.

15. Quoted in John M. Hobson, *The Eastern Origins of Western Civilization* (New York: Cambridge University Press, 2004), 113.

16. Clive Ponting, *A Green History of the World* (New York: St. Martin's, 1991), 121–23.

17. Christopher Tyerman, *Fighting for Christendom: Holy Wars and the Crusades* (Oxford: Oxford University Press, 2004), 16.

18. Edward Peters, "The Firanj Are Coming—Again," *Orbis* 48, no. 1 (Winter 2004), 3–17.

19. See Peter Stearns, *Western Civilization in World History* (New York: Routledge, 2003), 52.

20. Quoted in Jean Gimple, *The Medieval Machine* (New York: Holt, 1976), 178.

21. Stuart B. Schwartz, ed., *Victors and Vanquished* (Boston: Bedford/St. Martin's, 2000), 147.

22. Quoted in Carlo Cipolla, *Before the Industrial Revolution* (New York: Norton, 1976), 207.

23. Quoted in S. Lilley, *Men, Machines, and History* (New York: International, 1965), 62.

24. See Toby Huff, *The Rise of Early Modern Science* (Cambridge: Cambridge University Press, 1993).

25. Quoted in Edward Grant, *Science and Religion from Aristotle to Copernicus* (Westport, Conn.: Greenwood Press, 2004), 158.

26. Quoted in L. Thorndike, *A History of Magic and Experimental Science* (New York: Columbia University Press, 1923), 2:58.

27. Quoted in Edward Grant, *God and Reason in the Middle Ages* (Cambridge: Cambridge University Press, 2001), 70.

28. Grant, *Science and Religion*, 228–29.

29. Marcia L. Colish, *Medieval Foundations of the Western Intellectual Tradition* (New Haven: Yale University Press, 1997), 128.

Chapter 11

1. Al-Hajj Malik El-Shabazz (Malcolm X), "The Pilgrimage to Mecca," Islam on Line, http://www.islamonline.net/English/hajj/2002/01/Exper-ience/article2.shtml.

2. Reza Aslan, *No God but God* (New York: Random House, 2005), 14

3. Quoted in Karen Armstrong, *A History of God* (New York: Ballantine Books, 1993), 146.

4. Quran 1:5.

5. Quran 3:110.

6. Quran 9:71.

7. "The Prophet's Farewell Sermon," Islam on Line, http://www.islamonline.net/English/In_Depth/mohamed/1424/kharitah/article02.shtml.

8. Quoted in Patricia Crone, "The Rise of Islam in the World," in the *Cambridge Illustrated History of the Islamic World*, edited by Francis Robinson (Cambridge: Cambridge University Press, 1996), 11.

9. Richard Bulliet, *Conversion to Islam in the Medieval Period* (Cambridge, Mass.: Harvard University Press, 1979), 33.

10. Nehemiah Levtzion, ed., *Conversion to Islam* (New York: Holmes and Meier, 1979), chap. 1.

11. Jerry Bentley, *Old World Encounters* (New York: Oxford University Press, 1993), 93.

12. Bernard Lewis, *Islam and the West* (New York: Oxford University Press, 1993), 157.

13. Quoted in Crone, "The Rise of Islam in the World," 14.

14. Quoted in Margaret Smith, *Readings from the Mystics of Islam* (London: Luzac, 1972), 11.

15. Aslan, *No God but God*, 201.

16. Quran 33:35.

17. Quran 4:34.

18. Quoted in Judith Tucker, "Gender and Islamic History," in *Islamic and European Expansion*, edited by Michael Adas (Philadelphia: Temple University Press, 1993), 46.

19. Nikki R. Keddie, "Women in the Middle East since the Rise of Islam," in *Women's History in Global Perspective*, edited by Bonnie G. Smith (Urbana: University of Illinois Press, 2005), 74–75.

20. William T. deBary, ed., *Sources of Indian Tradition* (New York: Columbia University Press, 1958), 2:355–57.

21. V. L. Menage, "The Islamization of Anatolia," in *Conversion to Islam*, edited by Nehemia Levtzion (New York: Holmes and Meier, 1979), chap. 4.

22. Ira M. Lapidus, *A History of Islamic Societies* (Cambridge: Cambridge University Press, 1988), 304–6.

23. Quoted in Keddie, "Women in the Middle East," 81.

24. Ross Dunn, *The Adventures of Ibn Battuta* (Berkeley: University of California Press, 1986), 300.

25. Jane I. Smith, "Islam and Christendom," in *The Oxford History of Islam*, edited by John L. Esposito (Oxford: Oxford University Press, 1999), 317–21.

26. Richard Eaton, "Islamic History as Global History," in *Islamic and European Expansion*, edited by Michael Adas (Philadelphia: Temple University Press, 1993), 12.

27. Francis Robinson, "Knowledge, Its Transmission and the Making of Muslim Societies," in the *Cambridge Illustrated History of the Islamic World*, edited by Francis Robinson (Cambridge: Cambridge University Press, 1996), 230.

28. Janet L. Abu-Lughod, *Before European Hegemony* (Oxford: Oxford University Press, 1989), 216–24.

29. Andrew Watson, *Agricultural Innovation in the Early Islamic World* (Cambridge: Cambridge University Press, 1983).

30. Arnold Pacey, *Technology in World History* (Cambridge, Mass.: MIT Press, 1991), 8, 74.

31. Robinson, "Knowledge, Its Transmission," 215.

32. Ahmad Dallal, "Science, Medicine, and Technology: The Making of a Scientific Culture," in *The Oxford History of Islam*, edited by John L. Esposito (Oxford: Oxford University Press, 1999), chap. 4.

33. David W. Tschanz, "The Arab Roots of European Medicine," *Aramco World*, May–June 1997, 20–31.

34. Dunn, *The Adventures of Ibn Battuta*, 258.

Chapter 12

1. Jack Weatherford, *Genghis Khan and the Making of the Modern World* (New York: Crown, 2004), xv.

2. Data derived from Thomas J. Barfield, "Pastoral Nomadic Societies," in *Berkshire Encyclopedia of World History* (Great Barrington: Berkshire, 2005), 4:1432–37.

3. Giovanni Carpini, *The Story of the Mongols,* translated by Erik Hildinger (Boston: Braden, 1996), 54.

4. Quoted in Peter B. Golden, "Nomads and Sedentary Societies in Eurasia," in *Agricultural and Pastoral Societies in Ancient and Classical History,* edited by Michael Adas (Philadelphia: Temple University Press, 2001), 73.

5. Thomas J. Barfield, *The Nomadic Alternative* (Englewood Cliffs, N.J.: Prentice Hall, 1993), 12.

6. Anatoly Khazanov, "The Spread of World Religions in Medieval Nomadic Societies of the Eurasian Steppes," in *Nomadic Diplomacy, Destruction and Religion from the Pacific to the Adriatic,* edited by Michael Gervers and Wayne Schlepp (Toronto: Joint Center for Asia Pacific Studies, 1994), 11.

7. Quoted in Gregory Guzman, "Were the Barbarians a Negative or Positive Factor in Ancient and Medieval History?" *The Historian* 50 (August 1988): 558–72.

8. Carter Finley, *The Turks in World History* (Oxford: Oxford University Press, 2005), 28–37.

9. Finley, *The Turks in World History,* 40.

10. Thomas Spear and Richard Waller, eds., *Being Maasai* (London: James Curry, 1993), 6, 12.

11. Richard Waller, "Ecology, Migration, and Expansion in East Africa," *African Affairs* 84 (1985): 347–70; Thomas Spear, *Kenya's Past* (London: Longman, 1981), 107.

12. Godfrey Muriuki, *A History of the Kikuyu* (Nairobi: Oxford University Press, 1974), chap. 4.

13. David Christian, *A History of Russia, Central Asia, and Mongolia* (London: Blackwell, 1998), 1:385.

14. Quoted in Christian, *A History of Russia,* 389.

15. David Morgan, *The Mongols* (Oxford: Blackwell, 1986), 63–67.

16. Weatherford, *Genghis Khan*, 86.

17. Chinggis Khan, "Letter to Changchun," in *The Human Record,* edited by Alfred J. Andrea and James Overfield (Boston: Houghton Mifflin, 2005), 1:431.

18. Thomas T. Allsen, *Mongol Imperialism* (Berkeley: University of California Press, 1987), 6.

19. Chinggis Khan, "Letter to Changchun."

20. Quoted in Weatherford, *Genghis Khan*, 111.

21. Barfield, *The Nomadic Alternative*, 166.

22. Peter Jackson, "The Mongols and the Faith of the Conquered," in *Mongols, Turks, and Others,* edited by Reuven Amitai and Michael Biran (Leiden: Brill, 2005), 262.

23. Quoted in Christian, *A History of Russia*, 425.

24. Quoted in Jerry Bentley, *Old World Encounters* (Oxford: Oxford University Press, 1993), 143.

25. Quoted in David Morgan, *Medieval Persia* (London: Longman, 1988), 79.

26. Morgan, *Medieval Persia,* 82.

27. Daniel H. Kaiser and Gary Marker, *Reinterpreting Russian History* (Oxford: Oxford University Press, 1994), 100.

28. Charles J. Halperin, *Russia and the Golden Horde* (Bloomington: Indiana University Press, 1985), 126.

29. Charles H. Halperin, "Russia in the Mongol Empire in Comparative Perspective," *Harvard Journal of Asiatic Studies* 43, no. 1 (June 1983): 261.

30. Quoted in Kevin Reilly, ed., *Worlds of History* (Boston: Bedford, 2004), 1:420.

31. Thomas Allsen, *Culture and Conquest in Mongol Eurasia* (Cambridge: Cambridge University Press, 2001), 211.

32. Quoted in Allsen, *Culture and Conquest*, 121.

33. See John Aberth, *The First Horseman: Disease in Human History* (Upper Saddle River, N.J.: Pearson Prentice Hall, 2007), chap. 1.

34. Quoted in Norman Cantor, *In the Wake of the Plague* (New York: Free Press, 2001), 6.

35. Andre Gunder Frank, *ReOrient* (Berkeley: University of California Press, 1998), 256.

36. Arnold Pacey, *Technology in World Civilization* (Cambridge, Mass.: MIT Press, 1990), 62.

37. Quoted in Golden, "Nomads and Sedentary Societies," 72–73.

38. Quoted in Guzman, "Were the Barbarians a Negative or Positive Factor?" 558–72.

39. Quoted in Barfield, *The Nomadic Alternative*, 3.

Chapter 13

1. Brian Fagan, *Ancient North America* (London: Thames and Hudson, 2005), 503.

2. Quoted in Charles C. Mann, *1491: New Revelations of the Americas before Columbus* (New York: Alfred A. Knopf, 2005), 334.

3. Louise Levanthes, *When China Ruled the Seas* (New York: Simon and Schuster, 1994), 175.

4. Niccolò Machiavelli, *The Prince* (New York: New American Library, 1952), 90, 94.

5. Frank Viviano, "China's Great Armada," *National Geographic*, July 2005, 34.

6. John J. Saunders, ed., *The Muslim World on the Eve of Europe's Expansion* (Englewood Cliffs, N.J.: Prentice Hall, 1966), 41–43.

7. Leo Africanus, *History and Description of Africa* (London: Hakluyt Society, 1896), 824–25.

8. Quoted in Patricia Risso, *Merchants and Faith* (Boulder, Colo.: Westview Press, 1995), 49.

9. Quoted in Stuart B. Schwartz, ed., *Victors and Vanquished* (Boston: Bedford/St. Martin's, 2000), 8.

10. Quoted in Michael E. Smith, *The Aztecs* (London: Blackwell, 2003), 108.

11. Smith, *The Aztecs*, 220.

12. Miguel León-Portilla, *Aztec Thought and Culture*, translated by Jack Emory Davis (Norman: University of Oklahoma Press, 1963), 7; Miguel León-Portilla, *Fifteen Poets of the Aztec World* (Norman: University of Oklahoma Press, 1992), 80–81.

13. Terence N. D'Altroy, *The Incas* (London: Blackwell, 2002), chaps. 11, 12.

14. Pedro de Cieza de León, *The Incas*, translated by Harriet de Onis (Norman: University of Oklahoma Press, 1959), 177–78.

15. For a summary of this practice among the Aztecs and Incas, see Karen Vieira Powers, *Women in the Crucible of Conquest* (Albuquerque: University of New Mexico Press, 2005), chap. 1.

16. Powers, *Women in the Crucible of Conquest*, 25.

17. Louise Burkhart, "Mexica Women on the Home Front," in *Indian Women of Early Mexico*, edited by Susan Schroeder et al. (Norman: University of Oklahoma Press, 1997), 25–54.

18. The "web" metaphor is derived from J. R. McNeill and William H. McNeill, *The Human Web* (New York: W. W. Norton, 2003).

19. Graph from David Christian, *Maps of Time* (Berkeley: University of California Press, 2004), 343.

Acknowledgments

Chapter 3

Benjamin R. Foster. "Come then, Enkidu, to ramparted Uruk." Excerpt (7 lines) from *The Epic of Gilgamesh*, translated by Benjamin R. Foster, p. 10. Tablet 1: 226–232. Copyright © 2001 by W.W. Norton & Company. Used by permission of W.W. Norton & Company, Inc.

Miriam Lichtheim. "Seven days to yesterday, I have not seen the 'sister.'" As appears in *Ancient Egyptian Literature*, volume 2, pp. 184–185 by Miriam Lichtheim, translator. Copyright © 1976 by University of California Press. Reproduced with permission of University of California Press, in the format Textbook via Copyright Clearance Center.

Miriam Lichtheim. "Now the scribe lands on the shore." From *Ancient Egyptian Literature*, volume 2, translated by Miriam Lichtheim, pp. 168–175. As appears in *A Book of Readings: the New Kingdom* by Miriam Lichtheim, translator. Copyright © 1976 by University of California Press. Reproduced with permission of University of California Press, in the format textbook via Copyright Clearance Center.

N. K. Sandars. "You will never find that life for which you are looking. . . ." Excerpts from *The Epic of Gilgamesh*, translated with an introduction by N. K. Sandars (Penguin Classics 1960, Third Edition 1972). Copyright © N.K. Sandars, 1960, 1964, 1972. Reproduced by permission of Penguin Books, Ltd.

Miriam Lichtheim. "The gatekeeper comes out to you." From *Ancient Egyptian Literature*, volume 2, translated by Miriam Lichtheim, pp. 124–126. As appears in *A Book of Readings: the New Kingdom* by Miriam Lichtheim, translator. Copyright © 1976 by University of California Press. Reproduced with permission of University of California Press, in the format textbook via Copyright Clearance Center.

Samuel Kramer. "After your city had been destroyed, how now can you exist!" From *The Sumerians*, translated by Samuel Kramer, p. 142. Copyright © 1963 by University of Chicago Press. Used by permission of University of Chicago Press.

Samuel Kramer. "In those days the dwellings of Agade were filled with gold." Translated by Samuel Kramer. As appears in *Ancient Near Eastern Texts Relating to the Old Testament* by James Pritchard, ed., pp. 647–648. Copyright © 1969 Princeton University Press. Used by permission of Princeton University Press.

Chapter 5

Lao Tsu. "A small country has few people." From *Tao Te Ching* by Lau Tsu, translated by Gia-Fu Feng and Jane English, p. 80. Copyright © 1972 by Gia-Fu Feng and Jane English. Translation copyright © 1997 by Jane English. Used by permission of Alfred A. Knopf, a division of Random House, Inc.

Sappho. "If you will come, I shall put out new pillows for you to rest on." From *Sappho: A New Translation* by Mary Bernard, translator. Copyright © 1958 by University of California Press. Reproduced with permission of University of California Press, in the format Textbook via Copyright Clearance Center.

Ovid. "Add gifts of mind to bodily language. . . ." From *The Art of Love and Other Poems*, translated by H. H. Mozley. Published by William Heinemann, 1929, pp. 73, 75.

Chapter 9

Yuan Chen. "Ever since the Western horsemen began raising smut and dust." Quoted in *The Golden Peaches of Samarkand: A Study of T'ang Exotics*, by Edward H. Shafer, translator. Copyright © 1963 by University of California Press. Reproduced by permission of University of California Press in the format Textbook via Copyright Clearance Center.

Chapter 13

Miguel Leon-Portilla. "Like a painting, we will be erased." From *Fifteen Poets of the Aztec World* by Miguel Leon-Portilla, editor and translator. Copyright © 1992 by the University of Oklahoma Press, Norman. Reprinted by permission.

Maps

Map 1.2 is adapted from Peter Bellwood, *First Farmers: The Origins of Agricultural Societies* (Blackwood, 2005). Spot Maps 2.1 and 12.1 are adapted from Jerry H. Bentley and Herbert F. Ziegler, *Traditions and Encounters,* Third Edition (McGraw-Hill, 2006). Maps 3.3 and 5.1 are adapted from Jerry H. Bentley and Herbert F. Ziegler, *Traditions and Encounters,* Second Edition (McGraw-Hill, 2003). Map 7.1 is adapted from Craig Lockard, *Societies, Networks, and Transitions: A Global History* (Houghton, 2008).

Index

Names of individuals in **boldface**
 (f) figures, including charts and graphs
 (i) illustrations, including photographs and artifacts
 (m) maps
 (t) tables